Illuminati

FORMULA FOR TOTAL MIND CONTROL

By: Dr. Alfred Adams

Illuminati Formula For Total mind Control

© 2011 by Dr. Alfred Adams All rights reserved. Published 2011

Published by Nearing Midnight L.L.C.

Cover Art and Editing By Whyte Lady Designs L.L.C.

www.nearingmidnight.com
www.thenearingmidnightshow.com

ISBN 13: 978-0-615-49117-2
ISBN: 0-615-49117-2

Printed in the USA.

About The Author

With the death of his fiancé to suicide, after she lost both of her parents and a brother in a quick series of events, Dr. Adams began a study of biblical prophecy that has reshaped his life in an irreversible way. He knew that faith, hope, peace, and most of all love were essential to the Bible.

In the wake of his father's death in 2004, Dr. Adams wrote Nearing Midnight. He started The Nearing Midnight Show hosted by Dr. Adams, in 2006. He also co-hosted the Nearing Midnight TV show, which illuminated world events with the light of biblical prophecy. The show aired in the Lafayette, Louisiana area to 500,000 households. The Nearing Midnight TV show was a great stepping stone for Dr. Adams to be able to become the supporting host for the television show Keys to the Word, which aired in the Greater New Orleans area to one million households on UPN/WB.

Adams received an Honorary Degree of Doctor of Ministry from Cornerstone Christian College based in Lafayette, Louisiana. He was made an Honorary Louisiana State Representative by Robert Faucheux, Jr. in September 2006. In November 2006, Dr. Adams was also made an Honorary Louisiana State Senator by Louisiana State Senator, Nick Gautreaux. He was made an Honorary Military Police Officer of the Directorate of Emergency Services, Ft. Benning, Georgia in May 2007. These rare awards of honorariums from both houses and from Ft. Benning are testament of Dr. Adams' works.

Dr. Adams has written several books, and has produced several documentaries.

TABLE OF CONTENTS

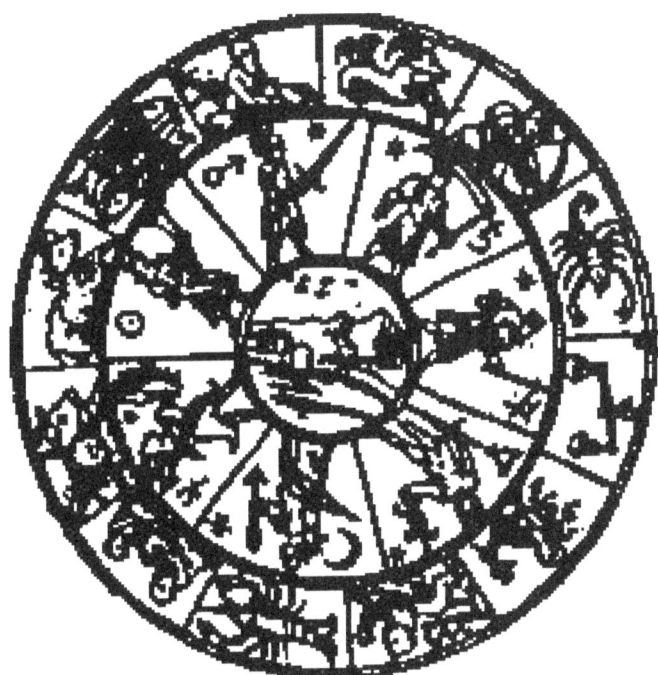

CHAPTER ONE:

THE SELECTION AND PREPARATION OF THE VICTIM

One of the primary reasons that the Monarch mind-control programming was named Monarch programming was because of the Monarch butterfly. The Monarch butterfly learns where it was born (its roots) and it passes this knowledge via genetics on to its offspring (from generation to generation). This was one of the key animals that tipped scientists off, that knowledge can be passed genetically. The Monarch program is based upon Illuminati and Nazi goals to create a Master race in part through genetics. If knowledge can be passed genetically (which it is), then it is important that parents be found that can pass the correct knowledge onto those victims selected for the Monarch mind-control. The primary important factor for the trauma-based mind-control is the ability to disassociate. It was discovered that this ability is passed genetically from generation to generation. American Indian tribes (who had traumatic ritual dances and who would wait motionless for hours when hunting), children of Fakirs in India (who would sleep on a bed of nails or walk on hot coals), children of Yogis (those skilled in Yoga, who would have total control over their body in trance), Tibetan Buddhists, Children of Vodoun, Bizango and other groups have a good ability to disassociate.

The children of multigenerational abuse are also good at dissociation. The Illuminati families and European occultists went to   India, and Tibet to study occultism and eastern philosophy. These Europeans learned yoga, tantric yoga, meditations, and trances and other methods to disassociate. These skills are passed on to their children via genetics. A test is run when the children are about 18 months old to determine if they can dissociate enough to be selected for programming or not. Mind-controlled slaves are created for different purposes, hierarchy or non-hierarchy purposes. The Illuminati create mind-controlled slaves who are to function within the Illuminati hierarchy. These slaves will usually have their genealogies hidden, and will be created to have excellent cover lives to insure that they are not detected. They will be given multifunctional programming, and will usually be used to help program other slaves. The abuse will not be as physically visible as it will be on the bodies of slaves who are not born to be part of the Illuminati elite. Members of Moriah's Luciferian elite will have undergone as much trauma as other slaves (Moriah = the Illuminati). However, the torture scars and the control are better concealed.

These children will often receive lavish experiences as well as talks to convince them that they are part of the elite. (By the way, body scars will show up better under black light. That is the same black light as used in clubs.) The Illuminati and other organizations have also programmed individuals who are simply expendable. These are sex slaves who are used up and killed very early in life, one-time use saboteurs, breeders, soldiers, drug couriers and so forth. The bodies of these people will often show visible torture scars. The expendable are the children of parents who were blackmailed into turning their children over to the CIA. This is all hidden by the power of the National Security Act. These are children, who have been sold by pedophile fathers, or pornographic parents. The programmers/masters program them with the expectation that they will be "thrown from the freedom train" when they get to age 30. (Freedom Train is the code word for the Monarch trauma-based mind-control. To be thrown from the Freedom Train means to be killed.) The CIA and the Illuminati are skilled at blackmailing parents to give up their children. They would watch the mail for porn. Pedophile and murderers who abuse their children are warned that they will go to prison for long lengths of time if they do not cooperate by selling their children into mind-controlled slavery. In return for the parent's cooperation, they provide rich financial rewards to the parent(s). It's clearly a case of "if you don't cooperate you lose in life big time, if you do cooperate you win big time."

Ministers are often set up with Betas (a sexual model) who then blackmail them. The ministers do not want to lose their status and profession via scandals, so they agree to turn their children over when young to the CIA to work with. The Illuminati like to blackmail these ministers when they are finished with their Seminary schooling and committed to the ministry at about 33 years of age. The idea of having nothing to fall back on after they have committed their entire life to one profession is too much for these weak willed men, and they buckle under the threats. If they don't buckle under, the resulting consequences will remove them from ministry. The type of father who is most preferred by the Programmers to offer up their children for programming is the pedophile. If a father will abuse his own little baby girl, then the Programmers know that the man has no conscience. This father's involvement in criminal activity, and thereby his vulnerability, can be continually increased. They want men who they believe will not develop any qualms later on in life about what they have done. A man, who waits until his daughter is a teenager to molest her, is usually esteemed to have too much conscience for the programmers. A big distinction must be made between hierarchy Monarch slaves, and non-hierarchy Monarch slaves. The reason there is such a big distinction is that they are not programmed the same way.

Since this book is giving the recipe for how to create a Monarch slave, we will have to cover the distinction between slaves within the Illuminati and those slaves who function outside of the Illuminati hierarchy. It is important to stress that the label "Monarch" is used in this book in a generic sense for the modern trauma-based total mind-control that is taking place. Whether an Illuminati mind-controlled slave is technically in the Monarch records or out of the actual Monarch Program data files kept on computer is merely a technicality. If you would like to know more about how the Illuminati created the CIA, please reference some of Fritz Spring meier's writings. I know that some of its directors were members of the Illuminati and I strongly suspect that the other CIA directors were probably full-fledged members too. The two organizations need each other. If the CIA didn't have the international backing of the movers and shakers of the world, it would have been exposed and done away with. Likewise, the Illuminati, because it is so secret, needs organizations through which it can work.

The CIA is a front for the Illuminati, and the CIA in turn sets up fronts. Some of those fronts, are elaborate well-staffed, well-equipped programming sites, (such as many of the state mental hospitals, McGill Psychiatric Training Network consisting of 8 Montreal hospitals esp. St. Mary's, NASA in Huntsville, AL; The Presidio in CA; and NOTS at China Lake, CA, to name a few. For a more complete list see Appendix A.) The Illuminati couldn't do it alone without its fronts. Satanists within the Network & the CIA took over Boy's Town, NE in the early 1950s, & used that famous orphanage for a constant supply of boys for programming. Boy's Town is perhaps the most famous, but there are whole long lists of others. When the Monarch Programming started, the top men were Illuminati. Originally, Joseph Mengele was the lead programmer. He had already achieved the rank of Grand Master (later Ipssimus) within the Illuminati. He had become skilled in music, in Kabalistic Magic, in dancing, in abortions, and in torture (by the way, Mengele had a sadistic mother) and programming children. Many of the concentration camp children that Mengele programmed still survive and still love him to this day as "Daddy". Mengele disappeared from Auschwitz in Jan. 1945, several months before the final chaos began in the Third Reich. He disappeared so the Illuminati could smuggle him to the U.S., so that his exceptional knowledge of programming, honed and fined tuned on thousands of concentration camp child victims, could be put to use on a grand scale in the U.S.

He travelled worldwide but especially in western U.S. doing his programming accompanied by his pair of two black servants. American Monarch survivors remember his spotless German uniform, his shiny boots which he wore during programming, his thick German accent, his handsome features, his cleft chin, the space in his front teeth, the way he would jab with his thumb while programming, as if he were still saying "links, rechts" to lines of Jewish coming into the concentration camps. The reason Mengele was so excited to do the selection process of inmates coming into Auschwitz was that he was choosing inmates for his numerous mind-control trauma experiments. He was especially anxious to get identical twins, because his genetic research related to mind control needed persons of identical genetic makeup. Traditionally, the Illuminati had been having their children inspected by a woman with the rank of Grande Mother. She would determine the fitness of the children and then present them for a formal acceptance ceremony at age 3 to the Grande Druid Council. This procedure didn't change when Mengele came over. The programming just jumped from being an occult science to one that had full access to the Medical, Psychiatric, Judicial, Scientific and Governmental sectors via the power of the National Security Act and the Intelligence agencies. The Illuminati's programming of multiples prior to Mengele's arrival were simplistic compared to the sophisticated techniques engineered by the Nazi Germans, whose Mind Control research included some non-German nationals such as some Italians.

Just as a victim who is killed by an 18th century musket is just as much victimized as someone killed by an M-16, so a victim of the pre -1946 programming was just as victimized as those programmed with more sophisticated techniques. For the Illuminati, the child's programming is planned by the Circle (another name for their organization) before it is born. From the Illuminati's perspective their plans involve generational spirits and positions within the hierarchy. The child is conceived according to their rituals, and the steps that that child will go through follows a well-thought out detailed regimen for programming it. In contrast, the children from foster homes, or pedophiles do not receive the same regimen. Hierarchy slaves will in turn be used to program and train other hierarchy children, while CIA slaves and Mafia slaves and KKK slaves etc. will be discarded.

This is why a Presidential Model is "thrown from the Freedom Train [the name of the Monarch Program in the Underworld]". Women and men in the Illuminati will continue to help with the programming their entire lives. The Illuminati is programming such vast numbers of children, they need every one of their able members to help. Moriah's total membership worldwide numbers in the millions. The

Illuminati regimen for their children is far more controlling than the CIA's programming. Not everyone in the Illuminati gets their mind-split and becomes a programmed multiple. However, everyone does get some type of mind-control. Those who have been spared multiplicity still must participate in a two-week intense mind-control session that might be compared to the Army's Ranger school. Those who participate in this have learned obedience. Those who haven't learned obedience are forced into ritual gladiator type duels or other punishments to eliminate them. Finally, a traitor's death as pictured on one of the Tarot cards is waiting. Sharon Tate was left hanging in the No. 12 Tarot Card's "hangman" position from the house rafters.

The best therapists will quietly admit that traditional therapy is inadequate. Unless God intervenes, people who are born into the Illuminati don't escape it while alive. This book isn't a mere exercise of academic thinking, but is written with the assurance that freedom is possible, there are viable answers. Some children live in foster homes, or with adopted parents, or in orphanages, or with caretakers and guardians. Because these children are at the mercy of the non-related adults, these types of children frequently are sold to become mind-controlled slaves of the intelligence agencies. In review, remember that because many of these organizations are controlled by the Illuminati; an Illuminati slave may often work for one of these front groups, while the Illuminati maintain control over the base-program. The intelligence networks were started by and run by the Illuminati. They are Illuminati fronts. The use of slaves crosses many organizational boundaries within the overall Network. If a slave is to be used as a Delta model (assassination), they may be selected for strength and dexterity. The Delta Force is the army's elite unit made up of Monarch slaves. If they are to operate as a Beta model, sexual slave, they will be chosen for mastering technique.

Occasionally they might in some circumstances be selected for how pretty the programmers expect the child to become. Some parents have produced good looking children and are actually sought-after to bear children to sell into the Mind Controlled Slavery "Freedom Train" System. However, vastly more important for Beta Sex Slaves is their ability to be programmed to have charm, seductive skills, charisma, and creativity. Beauty is in the eye of the beholder, and the programmers can put almost any kind of body to use as a sex slave. Almost any sex slave can fit somewhere into the script of the Illuminati/New World Order/crime syndicate "porn" movies. I place porn in quotation marks because what they call porn doesn't resemble what the public thinks of porn. We're not talking Playboy type porn, we're talking ghastly horrible atrocities that are as sick as anything done in the Nazi concentration camps. For instance, it takes little acting ability or beauty to have one's head chopped off while having sex. There are different types of sexual slaves, but the Illuminati wants to get Beta alters which are sharp, talented, skilled, and resourceful. They will use these Beta alters, such as the Black Widow alters, for espionage and blackmail.

To make sure that the child's mind develops properly, the baby will be interacted with so that those areas of the brain that are important to develop will develop to the maximum. It is a well-known fact, that areas of the brain grow according to how much stimulation and use that area of the brain receives. For this reason, Grande Dames, who are involved in programming, will spend time drawing and showing faces to the child and seeing if the child can recognize identical faces. Almost any other item will be used, candy canes with stripes (match the candy canes with the same no. of stripes), trees, or pencils. The child must learn to match identical items very early, even before they can speak. This is so they will be able to build mirror images into their mind. All the senses are trained for building the mirror images; for instance such as silks and cottons can be used for the sense of touch. The child will have to match textures.

The Programmer, the Grande Dame, and Grande Mothers will teach the child to have good abilities in copying, reflecting, repeating, echoing, or re-echoing, and mirroring. They will be taught for hours how to re-echo something verbatim. Some of these teaching methods are almost like games. For instance, 20 pins will be in a box and the small child is given a short time to decide how many pins are in the box.

A certain level of intelligence and creativity is needed for time to be spent on programming. You cannot program a mind which is weak. Most of the people programmed are very intelligent. One study of multiples said that multiples were 130 or above in IQ and then mistakenly blamed their multiplicity on their IQ. Attempts to program people with low intelligence or no creativity were discovered to be a waste of time. Methods are used to greatly enhance the victim's intelligence and creativity. The Illuminati will also work on enhancing their psychic abilities such as telepathy and clairvoyance.

The head programmers have their own little mottos about building solid structures which they like to express to new trainees. These include, *"An unstructured house [mind of the slave] is like unto a house without walls"*, *"A house undisciplined is like unto a house without walls, it will crumble within itself"*, and "A house divided against its self will not stand."

Much of the structuring will be discussed in chapter 7, but the structuring begins at birth for the victim, so this chapter will discuss the first steps. In order to build a solid good house, one needs to have a solid foundation. In order to build a solid foundation, one needs to know how the land lays and what the weaknesses of the land are. One needs to design one's house to take advantage of the natural lay of the land, if it is sand or rock or clay, etc. Will storms come from this or that direction? Where will the house need extra protection? The very same principles pertain to programming, a structure is being built.

Many evil geniuses within the Illuminati added their contributions to the Monarch programming. One of the most important was John Gittinger of Oklahoma, because he was the genius who could understand how a little child's mind worked in early infancy. In order to work with something, you must know what you are working with. John Gittinger, who is no longer alive, worked at programming for years. His contribution was in the mental assessment area. John Gittinger (b. 1909) was the director of psychological services at the state hospital in Norman, Oklahoma. He got a master's degree at age 30, and joined the CIA's MK Ultra Mind Control in 1950. He was a high school guidance counselor and a Navy lieutenant commander during W.W.II. In the late 1970s, he moved back to Oklahoma. He was heavy set and goateed. It's been said he looked like the actor Walter Slezak. He had an insatiable curiosity about understanding human personality.

When the Illuminati looked around for men skilled in personality assessment to assist the Monarch Programming, John W. Gittinger was one of their men who they selected. Gittinger was not the only researcher into personality that the CIA hired, but he was their top man in terms of the programming of children. From the end of W.W. II until he began with the CIA in 1950, Gittinger was studying how to assess personality. At the Oklahoma State Hospital, he had large numbers of adults who could be studied. Most of Gittinger's work became highly classified after he started doing personality assessment for the CIA. The Rolling Stone article of July 18, 1974 asked why years of research into personality assessment should be so secret. In fact it was so secret, that Gittinger was not allowed to talk to journalists, even though it was public knowledge that Gittinger did personality assessment work/research. The reason that such an apparently benign science was kept secret is that it plays a major part in the success of the Monarch Programming. John Gittinger designed the PAS (Personality Assessment System). This is an extraordinary method to evaluate human behavior and predict their future behavior.

As far as we know, most of the PAS is still classified SECRET. The PAS is based on the ability to differentiate different types of people. There are 3 major differentiations (or dimensions). They are called the E-I dimension, the R-F dimension, and the A-U dimension. People are born with their original placement within each of these three spectrums. In other words there are 3 axes that can be graphed to describe a baby's personality. The baby might be graphed-- I (Internalizer), F (Flexible), and A (Role Adaptive). If the baby was graphed this way (i.e. I-F-A), then the Programmers would automatically know this child's mind will become a social or religious reformer. The child's programming charts would then be labeled some suitable occupation such as "Environmental Activist", "Pentecostal Church Reformer", "Consumer Advocate", or "Activist Against Narcotics". The programming for that child then would follow 6 month goals to develop that mind-controlled slave into one of the best in that occupation.

In fact, one of my sources for this book is indeed I-F-A. Which helps explain why he is trying to reform society and religion with his own books. While it took my source many years to find his correct nitch in life, programmed multiples are steered in the correct direction very early in life with all the breaks and all the money needed from the Network to open opportunities.

There are three possibilities for the child in regards to his original personality components. He can express the component, or suppress or repress it. As the child goes through life, he has two periods within which he can change (suppress or repress) his behavior/personality. In the PAS, the first period is called "compensation" and the second is called "modification". The amount of punishment for a personality trait and pressure to change from others will determine the amount of change which the child's mind will perform on its original personality.

The activity level of a person at each point in their life is also measured. The intensity of each of the scores is also rated. The actual PAS system is far more detailed than the example above, but it serves to give a simplified idea of how it works. The essential dynamics of an entire personality can be written in a short code which might be written for example 12(E-uc Fcu + A+u+u)H+. However, even that code is shortened E-uc can be written simply i'.

The basic 3 dimensions to personality provide 8 basic types. However, the PAS allows for 6 basic positions in each of these 8 basic types which yields 216 discrete basic types. Next, the person can change their predisposed primitive personality initially 5 different ways, and this then gives $(30)^3$ or 27,000 different types. The second change can be done on 4 types of modification which makes for 1,728,000 types. Then the programmers can factor in activity level, their "Normal" level (intelligence base), age, gender, education, and life experiences. In other words, what appears to be simple has a high degree of calibration to it.

The person who was best with the PAS was its creator Gittinger himself. His intuition along with his PAS system, gave him an uncanny idea of how a person's s mind works now, and how it would work in the future. He sadistically reveled in putting his skill to use programming children.

The actual assessment codes that have appeared on programming assessment charts which the Monarch child assessment teams have used to evaluate, describe, & assess a child to be programmed follow the standard symbols created for PAS. Some about Gittinger's work has escaped the secrecy of the intelligence agencies. Concerning the Gittinger Personality Assessment System see "An Introduction to the Personality Assessment System" by John Winne and John Gittinger, Journal of Community Psychology Monograph Supplement No. 38. Rutland, Vermont: Clinical Psychology Publishing Co., Inc. 1973. See also the Rolling Stone magazine article, July 18, 1974, "The CIA Won't Go Public".

Because so little is known about the PAS test, it needs to be explained some. Observations in relation to the Wechsler Intelligence Test provided the initial ideas behind the PAS. The digit-span subtest of the Wechsler Intelligence Test, which rates the ability to remember numbers forms the basic test used for the E-I dimension. What Gittinger discovered was that short order cooks had good number-memory which = Internalizer personality or "I". A high digit span in any person tells much about them. People who don't separate themselves well from their environment are Externalizers = E. The "I" personality was a good baby. The "E" type who prefers doing to thinking is a "too-curious" baby, who will make demands. I's would often be pressured to become more outgoing, and E's are often pressured by parents to be more self-sufficient, and to progress from crawling (which they like) to learn to walk. Pure Internalizers become more withdrawn after several drinks, and uncompensated E's are more likely to become sloppy drunks, garrulous. Based on the E-I dimension, predictions can also be made for how LSD will affect a person. This is the E-I dimension.

The block design subtest shows whether a person is a Regulated (R) or a Flexible (F) person. This is the R-F dimension. The regulated person had no trouble learning by rote but didn't understand what he learned. The Flexible person on the other hand had to understand something before he learned it. R children could learn to play the piano easily, but the great concert piano players were F children who had persevered to master what they considered drudgery. The third dimension is the Role Adaptive (A) or a Role Uniform (U) person. A could be defined as Charisma, while people tend to ignore the U. The CIA has 40 patterns that a skilled observer looks for, and these then are related to the PAS and Wechsler subtests.

Illuminati Mothers-of-Darkness alters, trained in observation, chart what they see a child do. A child's behavior with certain toys, certain hand responses, and certain social responses can be observed and used to assess how this child would score on the PAS test. EEG (Electroencephalogram) patterns co-relate to the PAS digit-span test. This allowed them to use the EEG patterns to overcome cultural bias in the test. It also gave the Monarch programmers the perfect tool to assess small children before they have verbal skills.

David R. Saunders, at the Univ. of Colorado, working with the CIA, wrote a paper in 1961 showing the connection between alpha waves and digit span. In 1960, Mundy-Castle wrote about the connections between EEG printouts and Wechsler-Bellevue Test variables. This is just the tip of the iceberg for EEG use in determining pre-verbal personality in children. Salvatore et al wrote at the Massachusetts Mental Health Center, Boston, Mass, clear back in 1954 about the "predictive potential of Gittinger's theory" in an unpublished research paper (The Massachusetts Mental Health Center was an early participant in all this).

The child's guardians must teach the small victim obedience. They must teach the child to keep its eyes open and to hold still. These skills are important, because the child will be subjected to the EEGs in vast amounts. The hospital equipment would be something like an 11-channel Grass EEG machine where 11 electrodes are placed on the child's head, and brain wave patterns are printed out charting such things as background, variability, discharges, background suppressions, sharp waves, etc. The electrodes will have designations

(B) Suggests the quality of the compensations and modifications he has achieved in response to social and environmental pressures;

(C) Provides an understanding of personality development in terms of the interaction of primary structure, environmental pressures, and adaptive tendencies;

(D) Offers a procedure for evaluating the surface or contact personality developed over time;

(E) Makes possible the assessment of the fundamental discrepancies between the surface personality and the underlying personality structure--discrepancies that typically produce tension, conflict and anxiety.

Winne, John F. and John W. Gittinger. "Journal of Community Psychology Monograph Supplement No. 38. Rutland, Vermont: Clinical Psychology Publishing Co., Inc. 1973, p. 99."

Wow! Gittinger's description of PAS is specifically the needs & goals that the programmers had when they initiate programming the personality splits in tiny 18-month old children!

People associated with a list of organizations called "The Network" may assent to use their child for trauma-based programming. Children from families where one or both parents belong to these organizations are often routinely sent off in early childhood for trauma-based mind control. We are now in 3rd and 4th generations of people who are programmed multiples, even deeper generations in some Illuminati bloodlines. What can't be covered here is the enormous secret drama involved in Moriah finding and implementing control over parents via prescribed or illegal drugs, fear, blackmail etc. so that they will assist them in getting the children programmed. If the motherly instinct is too strong, the mom may be prescribed tranquilizers, so that there is a stable house for the child's front alters to grow up in. Unreliable non-multiple fathers are "debriefed" by Ilium, multiples which debrief & then erase their memories of what is happening to the children. Parents may have only a limited view.

If the Illuminati's preferred plan is followed, it has 4 beginning foundational stages to prepare the victim for programming. Let's list these, and then afterwards explain in detail these first 4 stages. One programmer named the stages 2, 3, 4 as stages 1, 2, 3, but the In Utero preparations and preliminary ceremonies actually form an initial first stage. The first stage is the initial ceremonies & the In Utero traumatization. The second stage is to have a premature birth, the third stage is to provide intense love for the child for the first 18 months by 2-3 selected Illuminati caregivers, and the fourth stage is to pull that love away and split the mind of the child permanently. Not every Illuminati child is born premature, but many are, because that is the preferred method for programming.

FOUNDATION STEP 1: PREPARATION OF THE CHILDREN BY SPIRITUAL PREPARATIONS AND IN UTERO TRAUMATIZATION – "THE MOON CHILDREN"

The preparation for someone to be programmed also concerns the ability of a person to be demonized. Generational satanic families are sold out to Satan, and their children belong to Satan in a way that non-generational children do not. Because of the generational curses and the genetic bent toward the occult, the Illuminati children are very good candidates for Monarch programming. Part of the programming includes the layering in of demonic forces and the participation in blood rituals in order to draw in the most powerful of demons. An in-depth review about this important but controversial subject is in chapter 10. The Moonchild rituals are the rituals to demonize a fetus and the demons that are invoked are not the small ones but very powerful ones. In working with victims of this programming, it is clear that high level demons were placed within these people at very early ages, many of them it is believed were demonized before they were born by rituals like the Moonchild rituals.

Blood sacrifices and human sacrifices are always required for this level of magic. Aleister Crowley (1875-1947) was a Satanist who was a 33rd degree Scottish Rite Freemason. He also was a leader in a number of other Masonic rites as well as an OTO leader, a chief in such as T3, T4 etc. In special programming sites, a machine with electrodes will be hooked up to the child's head for repeated tests. The newer machines accommodate up to 30 1/2 diameter pads (electrodes) which are attached with electrode adhesive tape or small needled ends to the child's scalp. The child's hair will be parted in an area, and the electrodes will be hooked to the skull. The attendant will tell the child, "Don't move. Keep your eyes open. Look at this point. Don't blink. Don't move your body." Then this procedure will be repeated for 45 minutes to an hour. Eventually hundreds of read-out from electrodes clipped to the skull of the child will chart the brain waves of the child. From these brain waves, the programmers can determine what type of personality the child has.

This personality assessment criteria and ability is one of the guarded secrets of the programming. Should unexpected behavior crop up, the slave may be hauled in for more EEGs. The PAS tests would reveal to Gittinger what a person's weaknesses were. The PAS shows what a person wants. And these are called the soft spots of a person's personality. Also the PAS shows mental weaknesses, where a person will be unstable and can be broken down. Certain types of stresses will have a cumulative effect of hurting a person. A stress-producing campaign is run against CIA targets, and by doing this they can neutralize a potential enemy. This information collected from children who are potential victims for the Monarch programming, is essential for knowing how to structure that child's programming. For instance IFU children often are autistic, IRU are schizophrenic children, and IR or IF are fantasy prone. It will be further explained shortly how this aids programming. An Internalizer personality would be important deep inside an alter system, while an Externalizer would be useful for a front personality. Internalizers are predisposed to the production of mental fantasy.

By knowing what the child was, the programmers know what they already have, and what they must add or build into the thinking of the alters they will create. Likewise, some alters need to be R and some F. And some need to be A and some U. Regulated (R) personalities like to have narrow limitations on their activity. This makes them suitable for programming. The R's readily accept authority, and will not try to step out of the range of their habits. The R has a marked ability to learn without understanding. They easily learn material by rote, because they do not need to understand it before they will learn it. This is another asset they have that the programmers like. The programmers may or may not want an A, Role Adaptive personality. A future country singer needs charisma, a future computer programmer does not. Without being able to finely determine what is there, the programming could not be fine tuned. If the child is good in math it will have its programming scripts steered in that direction. If it has artistic brainwaves, then the programmer will use art work in programming. The art work of the European artist M.C. Escher is exceptionally well suited for programming purposes.

For instance, in his 1947 drawing "Another World", the rear plane in the center serves as a wall in relation to the horizon, a floor in connection with the view through the top opening and a ceiling in regards to the view up towards the starry sky. Reversals, mirror images, illusion, and many other qualities appear in Escher's art work which makes all 76 or more of his major works excellent for programming. The use of these kinds of elements will be explained later. Five children each given the same "Alice in Wonderland" script will each use the script differently during programming. The programmer takes the child's own creativity and works with that unique creativity. The child must create the images itself if the programming is to hold. It won't work if the images are someone else's. The child organizes its internal world to suit his/her own experiences such as castles, boxes, rooms, and dollhouses. The PAS type testing will continue during the early years of the slave's life to make sure the programming has not driven the child crazy or psycho. The child will move down the script decided for it for its whole life, based on these early tests.

More about how this works later. The EEG tests run frequently on children to be programmed also show brain tumors, and medical problems beside just the brain wave patterns. The PAS tests can show how easy a person can be hypnotized. If the testing by the EEG's doesn't reveal a child who can be easily hypnotized, they will be rejected for programming, even though modern drugs and extreme torture in some cases will be applied to "salvage" children they really think they need to program but are clearly not easily hypnotizable. EEG's can also be used to see what state of consciousness the brain is in. The Monarch Programming is based on structuring MPD alter systems which is covered in Chapter 7. The success of this structuring (its excellent fine tuning) comes from the initial testing, which means programs are properly built on whatever foundation the mind has. The CIA front Human Ecology Society tested the PAS. In 1962, the CIA moved Gittinger's base of operations to another CIA front on Connecticut Ave., Washington, D.C. called Psychological Assessment Associates.

Because Gittinger believed genetic-based differences exist in people, which is one of the bases for the Monarch Programming, his work was not accepted by main stream psychology. In 1974, Gittinger described the PAS system, *"...the Personality Assessment System (PAS):*

(A) Indicates the kinds of internal and external cues to which the individual is most likely to respond;

(B) Suggests the types of stimuli that are most likely to produce behavioral change;

(C) Provides an understanding of the inter-, intra-, and impersonal environments in which a person is most likely to function efficiently; and

(D) Offers insight into what constitutes stress and predicts probable behavioral response to such stress, including maladjustments, should they occur.

"In the area of experience, the PAS offers a method for obtaining specific clues to personality structure and functioning. Thus, the PAS:

(A) Allows for direct inferences concerning an individual's primary response style;

Stella Matutina, and an MI-6 (British overseas intelligence) agent. His writings have been important within 20th century Satanism and with black magicians. He wrote Moonchild which was first published in 1917. The idea of the Moonchild is that via black magic a perfect soul can be captured. The belief in reincarnation, which is prevalent among the Illuminati and Satanic groups, lends itself to the belief that souls compete for a particular embryo. On page 107- 108 of Moonchild the idea is expressed,

"To produce a man who should not be bound up in his heredity, and should have the environment which they desired for him."

This perfect soul in a proper person is called Homunculus. The magical work upon which this is based is said to be derived from Bacon, Albertus Magnus and Paracelsus who were all reported in occult circles to have captured souls and placed them into brass statues.

The Hittites, the people of Asia Minor and Syria have long sought the ability to create a superman and a superwoman. The Illuminati's inside occult history places the Hittites in their ancestry. Clear back in 1917, long before Superman appeared in comics and movies, Aleister Crowley was writing about a superman. The magical idea is to capture a soul from the 4th dimension. In the book Moonchild, the villa used to produce a Moonchild was called "The Butterfly Net". The Monarch Project then which is named after the Monarch butterfly is also an allusion to the Moonchild project where butterflies are an allusion to souls, what Christians call demonic spirits. The actual rituals carried out to create a Moonchild are described in detail in three of Crowley's writings. A vague description of the rituals can be seen by reading the book Moonchild.

The villa was really an occult temple laid out in sacred geometrics. It had figures of satyrs, fauns, and nymphs. It had statues of Artemis. Lots of silver objects and crescents and 9-pointed stars were at the villa, because these objects all relate to the Moon in magic. The woman who was pregnant was surrounded by objects related to the moon. The moon's influence was repeatedly invoked. A small triangular silver altar to Artemis was used. There was a sacred spring where the woman was washed. The number 9 which is sacred to the moon was used along with its square 81. Prayers were made to Artemis, and there was the reenactment of the capture of Diana by Pan. The woman was coached to identify herself with what is known as Grandmother Moon, in the book she simply is called the Moon or Diana, by identifying her thoughts and actions with the deities one is wanting to invoke. The creation of the Moonchildren within the Monarch Project involves high level magic by the circle of Illuminati black magicians involved with a particular individual's programming. It should be noted that Grande Master and Grande Dame alters will understand demonology, but the sections, or levels, of alter above them are not informed.

One of the biggest secrets kept from most of the slave's alters is that their System was demonized while a fetus. First, this would give religious front alters the information they need to get them on the right track towards healing, and it could also adversely affect the programming lies of some of the front alters who don't realize how premeditated the trauma and torture is. The front alters of victims themselves remember the cover story that the moon children were produced via torture in the cages as little children.

The Illuminati have also planned that every one of the ten commandments of God will be violated in their favor with the child. They prefer the child to be born out of wedlock so that it is a bastard. This breaks God's commandment on adultery, and also gives them more leverage to destroy the child's self-esteem. This entire plan involves generational curses which are spoken and unspoken. During Illuminati ceremonies, Ceremonial pacts which concern having the child out of wedlock to mock God are made.

While the Illuminati destroy any godly spiritual foundation, they are creating a solid rock hard foundation of "love" (adoration or idolatry) within the newborn upon which they will build the programming. The second commandment is "Do not take the Lord's name in vain". In the Black Mass, the names of God are invoked to get spirits with blasphemous names such as Yahweh Elohim. Most parts of the little child will never even hear the Lord's name. He will only hear the name of his master, who will someday be presented to him as "God". The hand that rocks the cradle rules the world. The child is being bonded to his future programmers. Much later, great attention will be given to set up staged events to insure that the victim being programmed hates God.

The formal Monarch Mind-Control project was developed from observations of high level satanic families. These families had no qualms about the concept of traumatizing the fetus.

Italian generational witchcraft is called the Ways of the Strega. These generational occult bloodlines, especially in Tuscany and Naples, are very much into generational ancestor spirits. These were the ones that Aleister Crowley went to learn how to create, Moon Children. Remember, that Italian and German generational Illuminati families were studied by the Italian fascists and the German Nazis to develop a scientific understanding of mind control. The Illuminati families in Germany were secretly and scientifically studied in the 1920s to determine what exactly was happening and how to systematically improve the Illuminati's control over the people they were already programming.

Discipline and training has been lavished for centuries upon the children of these elite bloodlines. The contribution of the 20th century was the systematic collection and scientific study of all the various methodologies into one cohesive programming package. This research was begun on a large scale in 1940s, and has been systematically added to since then.

Families who wanted dissociative children learned that dissociative babies could be born if the child in the womb is tortured. Thin needles are inserted through the mother into the fetus to prick the pre-born child. Mothers, who are pregnant with children to be programmed, are also severely traumatized during their pregnancy with a whole assortment of traumas, which simultaneously traumatizes the babies which they carry. For instance, the father may purposely abandon the pregnant mother in the middle of a forest, or blast the mother with loud frightening music, and then follow this up with love.

FOUNDATION STEP 2: THE TRAUMA OF A PREMATURE BIRTH

A premature birth is important because the naturally occurring events around a premature birth insure that the child is naturally traumatized. Studies, such as Fenaroff, 1972, have found that only 7-8% of the live births were premature, but 25 to 40%, about a third, of all battered children were born premature. It appears that the satanic cult involvement with causing premature births may be reflected in this type of statistic. Some of the Illuminati-induced premature births have made the newspapers, because the preemies set records for being born so small. Premature labor is induced, it is not natural, but the traumas that occur to the preemie are.

Specialized drugs, not just the exogenous oxytocins normally used to induce labor, are used on a mother to place her in a deeper trance than a twilight sleep. Remember, that the underdeveloped liver & kidneys of the preemie make it difficult to naturally purge meds from the preemie's body.

The mother will begin the process of delivery at this time. However, the mother must be brought out of this deep sleep in order to push the baby through the birth canal. The baby is too weak to help with the birthing process. This is the hardest type of birth that there is, because the baby is not able to help the mother in the small ways that a full term baby would. The strain on the heart of the mother is extreme. The Illuminati have learned that a mother can usually give 2 or 3 preemie births like this before she risks death to try it again.

If this type of birth is repeated too often the woman's heart will fail. This is why the Illuminati will have their breeders give 2 or 3 preemies for programming, and then have their breeders switch to full term babies which are used for sacrifice. If we describe how breeders and babies are used we must speak in general terms, because each bloodline, each baby, each mother is a separate case. However, there are some patterns that should be pointed out.

A bloodline will often want a female's first born male to be sacrificed

ILLUMINATI: FORMULA FOR TOTAL MIND CONTROL

to their belief system and the Lilith programming which is given the alters who function within the Kabalistic Tree of Life which is built in during Mengele's programming for the deeper sections, or levels, of alters which are trained in Illuminati black magic. This subject will be dealt with later. The Illuminati breeders may be women who were preemies themselves. Sometimes they skip a generation with the trauma of a premature birth to get a mother with a good sound heart. Some of these breeders have excellent bloodlines, but during their own preemie birth their brains were damaged and they don't have the super-intelligence the Illuminati wants for programming. However, they still need to have had enough creativity to have allowed themselves to become a programmed multiple.

When breeders are used by the Illuminati to obtain babies for programming, the Illuminati selects women who are themselves programmed multiples. They are used for breeders, because genetically they have genes for intelligence, even though they aren't brilliant. These women of lesser intelligence will only make the beginning Priestess level of the women and might obtain a rank in that level of High Priestess. All these women, no matter their circumstances have been made to believe that offering their babies to Satan is the highest honor, so many of them do not have normal qualms about their job. It is important to interject that the Illuminati are Luciferians, but worship Lucifer/Satan. Satanists are organizationally a separate set up, with a separate history, but both groups have many common practices, including child sacrifice.

There is a science in how the Illuminati hides bloodlines, sometimes families are used as brooders for other important bloodlines. It will only be mentioned in passing here, because it is relevant to the selection process of how children are slated to be programmed. The Illuminati is fully aware of rare blood types and other genetic properties that run in bloodlines, and breed individuals to get certain traits, and they also take into consideration that certain weaknesses such as weak hearts or AB-negative blood with no RH factor will call for special attention.

The criteria for non-Illuminati cults for their breeders are much lower. Often these are the cults' leftovers. That is the difference between the good breeding of the Illuminati, and the degenerate thinking of the openly satanic groups. The Satanic groups which are organized into hubs and some of the lesser occult groups like the KKK, have women which are kept under lock and key to serve as breeders. Breeders are kept from having outside talents that would help them function in the outside world. Some are not allowed to have driver's licenses and other basics. How does the occult world manage to work things out within a hospital setting? The independent satanic cults may not use hospitals. I have worked with enough first hand information to be familiar with some of the cults which have home births attended by their own midwives.

An example is the Satanic cult in Seminole & Garvin counties of Oklahoma where their section houses in the countryside have had unrecorded home births for years. First hand information also confirms that hospitals in Tacoma, Vancouver, Portland, and San Francisco are used by the Illuminati for premature births. By extension, it can be understood that many hospitals across the United States are now staffed with a large number of nurses and doctors who are loyal to the occult world, called by insiders the "Network", headed by the Illuminati. The preemies are attended to by satanic witches who are nurses, many of them multiples themselves. Further on in this book, we will cover how the Illuminati are turning out a great number of pediatricians via programming to insure control over the preliminary programming stages. If the occult world wants a mother to see her preemie, the occult nurses on night shifts will quietly let cult mothers in to bond with their preemies.

There is a lot of corruption that goes on unnoticed too. These doctors and nurses have taken lots of preemies for the Network to use for programming experiments. If the mother is a low income mother, the Freemasons will let them use their network of hospitals for free. Some of these premature children are described as dead and taken with the excuse that "they can't breathe". They then are used for programming experimentation. The Illuminati, working in conjunction with other occult groups, schemes up methods by which they can get other people's babies. This gives them additional children to work on.

By giving low income mothers free births at Masonic hospitals, the occult world can later contrive some reason for stripping a low income mother who is on drugs of her guardianship of her baby. They take these children, some of them drug babies, for programming uses.

The mothers of different animals are examples of how important touch is to any baby. A mother cow, or dog will nudge its offspring soon after it is born. They will also begin to teach the baby immediately after it is born. Studies have learned that most mammals lick their newborn, which has been observed to be critical for the healthy physical development of the baby animal. The Illuminati want the same development for their offspring. Research showed that rocking and stroking preemies helps them develop motor skills and respiratory functions. It takes the place of the licking animals give their offspring. The stroking even helps cardiac (heart) functions during the preemies sleep. Giving stimulus to a part of the brain will cause that part of the brain to grow.

Although the premature child cannot speak, it still craves attention. Even if it hurts, the child wants, even needs, to be held. The child can be touched, and it will crave that touching even if it hurts. Already the mixing of love and pain is beginning. Their skin will be thin and sensitive to touch. It will hurt to be touched and preemies can even have their skin bruised by a sheet.

A premature birth will create a fighter spirit within the child. If the child does not have a strong instinct for survival, and does not fight to survive the premature birth, then it will not fight to survive during the tortures of the programming. By having a premature birth, the selection process has already started. Which child will be a fighter? The preemie will be emotionally deprived of getting to suck on a real mother's breast, but will be fed with an eye-dropper or bottle.

Often a transdisciplinary team will be created at the hospital to take charge of the preemie. They will run one of the various standard assessments, perhaps the Neonatal Behavioral Assessment Scale (NBAS) or the Bayley Scale of Infant Development. Objectives will then be developed for the short and the long term based on each infant's identified needs. The NBAS will look at:

a) The ability to shut out disturbing stimuli
b) Responsiveness to auditory & visual stimuli
c) Muscle tone & motor skills
d) Irritability
e) Capacity to cuddle
f) Skin color
g) Reflexes.

Every part of the preemie's body will be violated. A Catheter will likely be put in the little baby's bladder, because preemies' urinary tracts tend to close up, and bed sores must be avoided too. They will also usually be given I.V.s. This will give them more fluid to eliminate. This is healthy for the Preemie to keep their kidneys well. However, it also serves as part of the natural traumatic process. Some will be given oxygen. The preemie will be adjusting to the light, temperature, sound, humidity and gravity of the new world it has been thrust into. Their hearts will have problems. Some of these, like Mitro-valve prolapsed, may stay with the child for a life-time. They often have difficulties with their lungs.

Studies on preemies have shown that they tend to have a sober affect with few smiles, and then the smiles come only if their eyes are averted from who is in front of them. They are less social and they depend upon the primary person, usually a caretaker at the hospital, to give them assistance and encouragement to interact socially (Als & Brazelton, 1981).

When the child is born, the Illuminati make sure that its first view is of one of the people who will help program it. Often this is a Grande Dame within the hierarchy, but it might also be a male programmer. Over the following months the programmer figure will repeatedly talk to the child in loving cooing tones. The most loving soothing words are all that is permitted at this stage. The child is being naturally bonded to the programmer. Mengele was the best of experts at this type of bonding. The programmers talk to each other in terms like, "this child is a piece of clay." They view themselves as the potters to that clay. When the Preemie is born it copes with the pain by being dissociative.

The soothing voice of the programmer is said and heard in hypnotic tones. The hypnotic voice of the programmer is taking advantage of the dissociative trance-like state of the child in pain. The hypnotic voice is grooming the child from the womb. Hypnotic cues are placed into the child's mind even at this young age. Hypnotic cues use all the senses. In reality, the programmers are hypnotizing the little babies.

Soon the preemie's eyes will open when the preemie senses the presence of the programmer in the room. The preemie's eyes will follow the programmer around as he or she walks around the child's room. The child's eyes are following the voice of the programmer. Ronald Shor, a respected researcher into hypnotism, wrote in the Amer. Journal of Psychotherapy, Vol. 13, 1959, pp. 582-602,

"Only in the fetus can one conceive of an ideally pure trance state, that is, a state in which there is a total absence of a functioning reality-orientation. In the developing organism in utero the first momentary experiences exist concretely, independent of any structured background of experience. The only organization that can take place at first is that which is genetically given. But except for this natural, ontogenetically undeveloped state there is always some degree of structuring."

In other words, if you want to hypnotize someone, the ideal is when they are a fetus, because the baby soon begins to get a grasp of reality. That reality gives the child something to compare with what the hypnotist is wanting to program in. Notice, also the awareness on Shor's part, that there is some structuring of the mind done naturally via genetics.

This again underscores the importance of why the programmers like multi-generational victims--because they pass via genetics some of the mental structuring needed for the smooth programming of the next generation.

By looking into the preemie's eyes and talking, the programmer begins to teach the baby. The preemie learns that its primary caretaker is its controller. The controller controls its access to its bottle and everything else in its life. The Illuminati are teaching the child to view its controller as God from the first second it is born. They want the child to worship the programmer. The programmer is literally saving the preemie's life. By talking & cooing to the child the programmer's voice becomes more real to the child than itself.

The controllers begin stretching the mind of the child as soon as it is born. The two or three people who control the early baby's life begin teaching it with hypnotic voices as soon as it is born. Subliminal tapes are used to teach the baby immediately. The goal is to teach the child to read and speak much earlier than other children. In the Monarch Program's controlled setting, children who can read at six months, can still be programmed for social skills. In an uncontrolled setting, children taught this earlier tend to have their intellectual skills outstrip their social skills, and they develop serious problems with their peers and schools.

Children can be hypnotized easier than adults, but it has to be done differently, especially if the child is preverbal. Rubbing the child, stroking its head, and patting the child help soothe the child into relaxing. The hypnotist must not make rapid tonal changes in their voice. These are reasons why gentle Illuminati women programmers are such an asset at this stage. The newborn child is taught obedience. It is allowed to cry to develop its lungs, but at some early point it is taught not to cry. Tape is placed over the child's mouth, and it is told over and over "no" with the index finger gesturing. They get approval if they don't cry. This type of programming is called behavior modification, and will be further covered in a later chapter.

The baby is rigidly taught total obedience. In review of step 3, one tried and often used technique is to have the baby born premature. The baby must undergo lots of trauma, and must learn to be a fighter to survive. Babies have been taken by induced labor or C-Section at premature ages intentionally to insure that the baby will suffer trauma. When the premature baby leaves the comfort of the womb it experiences trauma. By taking the baby prematurely, it also gives the programmers an advanced start on the programming.

FOUNDATION STEP 3: LOVE BOMBING THE CHILD UNTIL ABOUT 18 MONTHS

The third stage is smothering the child in love. The love is given so that it can be taken away in the fourth stage. Unless love is given so that it can be taken away, there is no trauma. Illuminati children are never spanked in the first year and a half. They are very lovingly controlled. This pattern of smothering new converts in love called "love bombing" in preparation for removing that love and acceptance to get obedience is done by some cults to new members too.

The Illuminati child learns about their body. Their bowels are allowed to function properly and they are kept meticulously clean. They must be taught to appreciate their body, before the trauma of stripping them of everything they value. Dissociation does not have to be taught to the child, because they have a genetic leaning toward it, and the premature birth has taught them to dissociate. All in all, the child has been allowed only to build a relationship with its programmer. The child has learned to trust, obey and adore the programmer during the first 18 months of its life. Its mind is lining up with hypnotic suggestions, cues, and is being obedient.

FOUNDATION STEP 4: FRACTURING THE MIND

The fourth stage is built upon the foundation of dissociation created in the first & second stages, and the love created in the third stage. The demonology of the first step also helps pull in demons associated with programming, tunneling in the mind, and multiplicity, which are used in the fourth foundational step. Often in the fourth step, the child's mind will fracture along the same dissociation fracture lines that the trauma of the premature birth created.

If the child is not a premature baby, it will need some additional help to want to dissociate. The child can have its senses overwhelmed repeatedly to the point that it learns to react to its surroundings by what appears on the outside as numbness, and mentally is simply dissociation. Everything imaginable can be used to overwhelm the caged little child's senses and create dissociation. Rotten foul odors of the child's excrement, of ammonia, and rotten food while it huddles in its cage will overwhelm the child's sense of smell. Being fed blood over-whelms the sense of taste. The chanting of the Programmers dressed in Satanic garb, banging noises, rock music and the electric hum, and ultrasonic stimulation overwhelms the child's sense of hearing. The child's natural developing sense of shapes is taken advantage of by spinning the child and making it feel like it is going to fall. The child will also be deprived of sleep and drugged. Together all this will pro-vide the dissociative base for splitting the core.

The fourth stage is to strip the child of everything nice and lovely in the world. The child is caged and tormented by electric shock. The child's senses will be overloaded and they will become numb. Eye-witnesses have described these hundreds of numbed children as "zombies". This stage and the programming put in after the founda-tional dissociation is created will form the next chapter.

In the fourth step, the child is starved, cold and naked. When they finally see their beloved master or beloved adult caretaker appear af-ter suffering from 42 to 72 hours, they are excited and they dissociate the pain of the previous hours of deprivation. Help appears to be on the scene. At that point the programmer/beloved adult shows his/her most vicious side, and the child in order to deal with how this loving caretaker has not only rejected them but is now hurting them dissoci-ates along the same fractures of dissociation created by the trauma of the premature birth. The details of how the mind is split will be dealt with further in the next chapter.

In review of steps 3 and 4, part of the programming is to have the pri-mary initial abuser bond with the child. A close loving bond is needed between a child and the initial abuser so that a clean split is created when the initial mind-splitting trauma is carried out. The clean split occurs when the child is confronted with two irreconcil-able opposing viewpoints of someone who is important to them. The child can't reconcile the two extremely opposite views of the same person, one being a loving caretaker, and the other being the worst kind of abuser. The person the child trusted the most is the person the child fears the most. Some professional therapists have come to realize that this is how the core is split.

Jody Lienhart, a multiple herself, in her PhD dissertation correctly identifies the double bind of having two extremely opposite views of the most important person in the child's life as the fundamental splitting mechanism. She writes in her 1983 dissertation on p. 6-7,

"Implicit in each of the studies of childhood trauma is the pervasive nature of paradoxical communication. Frequently, this double bind communication style appears during the formative, preverbal stages of childhood in which the interpretation of these messages is confused. This results in insufficient experimental learning which would allow translation of the confused appropriate messages... "

This study presents the theoretical assumption that multiple personality is developed through early childhood state-dependent learning. Which means that learning is linked to a state of mind.). Furthermore, it is hypothesized that this learning occurs as a result of the hypnoidal effects of childhood trauma such as abuse and sexual molestation. The child, unable to translate the paradoxical nature of the messages he receives, fragments into a trance state. Furthermore, it is suggested that memories incorporated during each of these hypnoidal experiences are similar to knowledge acquired during state-dependent learning. Lienhart used her own memories as the basis for the type of trauma that suggests in her dissertation could create MPD. That trauma for her was her uncle forcing his penis into her mouth and almost choking her. The child is not in a position to flee, so the mind dissociates. She happened to have experienced a common trauma used to split a core. In order to split the core, the mind has to be trained to dissociate.

The ability to dissociate is obtained by being genetically bred from dissociative parents, by having a premature birth/traumatic birth if possible, and by the conditioning done at the original programming center (between 18 mo. & 3 years) where intermittent electric shock along with all the senses being overwhelmed, along with sleep deprivation and drugs create a dissociative base to split the core.

The initial sadistic abuse to split the mind is called "severing the core." Each person's original mind is like an open computer. The original computer-like mind, in order to continue working when confronted with overwhelming trauma, splits a part of the mind off and walls it up with amnesia barriers. From this area further splits can be made. One of the major technical feats to make computers useable was to figure out how to be able to wall off and protect memory in the computer from being accessed and used. When they succeeded in engineering isolated memory the other problems were minor.

When someone has been traumatized from the fetus on up there is no single cores such as therapists usually look for. The Core for the programmers is the un-split essence of the mind which drives or provides energy for the System. This Core is not an alter, but is an essence that the programmers hide. The programmers do not touch the core in the fashion they do alters. They hide the core. Part of the drama that is carried out during the entire victim's life is their mind trying to protect this untouched core essence from being touched. If they think anyone, the therapist or the abuser, is going to tamper with it, the mind and its parts will protect that core. As strange as it may seem, when a therapist talks about integration, they often scare the victim's mind that the integrity of the core and its innocence will be violated, and the victim's mind does everything it can to avoid contaminating the integrity of their core (i.e. they sabotage therapy and return to their programmer who understands their safety issue). Initially, in the 1940s, the Illuminati researched what would happen if the Core was allowed to meet up with the alters., They discovered that the brain's essence or energy will work to pull the mind back together.

Therefore, the Core is separated and hidden from all the alters. In Illuminati systems, it is usually placed in the middle of its first splits, which are also sources of energy and which are well hidden. They are dehumanized parts which function as gems, which are programmed as in the Alice In Wonderland story to change shape and color if they are approached, which rarely happens. These parts will be discussed in other chapters including how a system is structured. A dissociative carousel is also attached around the core. After the core is hidden, the rest of the alters will be programmed not to look for the energy/ synthesizing part of the system. The real "core" or primal part of the unconscious will have an adult representative of it in a Monarch System. This primal part has a toddler switch upon which all the programming is built. An event in the child's life is used to build the programming upon. The Illuminati know about the various base programs and the foundational traumas, and some of this is kept secret from programmers who come from front organizations of the Illuminati.

There are a number of parts which will be called "cores"--simply because they were early parts, but there is no intact single person who represents all of the mind. All that is left are fragments of the mind, each segment walled off with amnesia. The alters who perceive themselves to be "cores" are alters who have been programmed to think they are the core alter. The mind has a way of knowing the truth, and these alters may realize that their programmed story line is suspicious, but they won't know what is "fishy" about it, so they tend to be in denial about their identity. These substitute or mock cores will often be in denial that they are even MPD. In some cases, where scripture was used to program with, the core was told that it would be "blessed by multiplying as the seeds in the stars of heaven and the sands of the sea" if "thou hast obeyed my voice", which is misuse of Gen. 22:17-18. Alters which represent the "sands of the sea" pop up if an alter tries to get to the core, see chapter 10 about scriptures used in programming.

THE INITIAL SPLITS

The initial part of a person's mind before splitting occurs is called the core. Theoretically, the core makes parts to protect itself. The initial splitting is called "splitting the core" and there is an art or science in knowing how to split a core. However, I disagree with the standard core model". I believe it is more accurate to say that the initial splits are stronger because they somehow are integrated closer to the mind. Later splits made from later splits, are in a sense less connected to the full mind. During a torture session, the initial splits are always the strongest. So when they torture someone and get 20 personality splits, they will use perhaps the first 13 and discard the rest or use them for single task jobs. Discard areas are created in the mind---these are variously called concentration camps, garbage dumps, or whatever. The victim's mind is trained to create these dumping grounds for the splits that the programmers don't want to use. As the programming got refined, so did the methods for discarding unwanted splits.

In children, who receive programming at a very early age, the initial splits may be done in the womb. If the fourth step is carried out in a timely fashion at 18 months after the in utero trauma and a premature birth, then during the first 18 months the mind will never have a chance to pull itself together. If however, the fourth step is not done at around 18 months and no further trauma is maintained, the child's mind will pull back together by the age of two and a half. The initial splits are the most energetic and the easiest to manipulate. In Illuminati systems these early parts are dehumanized into thinking they are gems and crystals. These gems and crystals then "power" the entire mind-control system that is programmed over the following years into the child's mind. The gems are not perceived as alters, so the proxy core wouldn't integrate with what is perceived as an inanimate object. The proxy core is allowed to want to move toward health with a therapist, it is programmed to move toward healing, but to lead the therapist away from the true core.

She or he is programmed to believe it is the true core. The real core & its first splits, which are the gems, are placed hypnotically at the mind's deepest level in an area of the mind few therapists ever search. As outlined above, other initial splits are led to believe they are cores. Part of the reason there is a illusive search on the part of therapists for a core, is that people have not accepted the reality that there is no one person (personality) in charge of a Monarch System who can simply decide to quit coping with life by stopping their MPD. Many therapists want to believe that some person is the "real" person and the rest are simply subordinate alters created to handle the core's trauma. I believe this is an inadequate understanding of what is happening.

The elements that make up who a person is, such as memories, are fractured. The fragments have in turn often been built up into full-blown personalities with all the elements of full-blown personalities.

There is no "real" person, just as if you smash a mirror into a thousand pieces, there is no single piece that is the "real" mirror but rather simply fragments that can in turn operate as mirrors. However, there is still a primal self. Early splits are led to believe they are the core. The cult will hide the initial splits beyond recognition.

Some of the third wave of splits will be created into what are named Silence alters. They are trained never to talk. (At least some Illuminati alter systems call these early splits "Silences".) These early splits are then hidden and used to blackmail other alters who were created later. The other alters, who are formed after the Silences (who are pre-language alters) are convinced that if they don't behave the Silences will have something drastic happen to them.

Some of the pre-talking Silence alters are then placed in places such as Moloch's Temple to keep as hostages. Alters are created down the road to guard the Silences. They guard in the full sense, controlling the Silences, and any access to the Silences. Since the Silences are early splits they are more important for the full integration of the mind, which the programmers want to insure doesn't happen.

Probes are pushed into the brain at the base of the skull, in a very precise and methodical way during the initial core trauma. This is done to create guards for the carousel. For more about the early primal splits see the section on the Carousel in Chapter 7 on structuring, and the next chapter on how the trauma is done. Because the Programmers will tamper with the alters so much to get the satanic alters and the special purpose alters which they want, they need to use some of the first splits as front alters. They need strong front alters who have a sense of who they are. If they waited until later to get front alters, the alters wouldn't be as strong and would have already lost their identity. The 3rd wave of alters created often will in turn be split to provide alters to build the front section of a System. The front "cores" which are decoys will be set up with opposites, one alter will love the programmer the other will hate him.

One alter will trust the programmer, the other will fear the programmer. Therapists spend all their time trying to reconcile this conflict which is placed out front as a decoy to keep them busy. Meanwhile, the gems along with the rest of the loyal cult alters will have the ability to create whatever is needed within the System. The entire system of alters is always shifting and many of the true alters are in hiding. The person is made to feel like he or she has been sliced like meat, much as a bologna slicer makes slices of bologna. This layering program is very dangerous and severe. Overlays of all kinds, demonic, hypnotic illusion, etc. are layered over real alters so that even the identity of what is a real alter is hidden. The point is that decoys which keep therapists busy are created, while the entire structure shifts and rearranges and restructures itself to keep itself hidden.

Often the Illuminati encourage early front splits to learn about Christ and legitimately accept Him at a very early age. This acceptance will be used as the basis of the trauma to create strong satanic alters. Just as the handler will bond with the child to split it, the handler will allow some early parts of the System to bond with Christ in order to enhance the trauma that "God" will do to the System. This also allows the handlers to have a balancing point. Without the full range of capabilities within a Slave alter system a dangerous imbalance toward evil could propel the slave into situations where they don't have the ability to succeed. In many ways, the slave's world becomes a microcosm of the real world, having a mixture of adult and child alters, Christian, secular, and Satanic alters. Another thing which happens with the first splits is the creation of mirror images.

Some of the time, in the early splitting procedures, the child creates extra splits. In the early stages, these strong extra splits are made into mirror images of regular alters. Some of these mirror images are known to be placed into the mind before any splitting occurs.

As long as the victim's dissociation exists, the potential for mischief exists for the programmers. This is why integration can be a positive goal for a Monarch multiple if the deprogrammer knows what he is doing. After suffering decades of the most horrible traumas imaginable and the most severe abuse as slaves, most slaves have minds which are habitually dissociative. These older minds of slaves require a miracle to cease remaining permanently dissociative. It does take a great deal of brain energy to maintain the amnesic walls, and the minds of people in their 70's and 80's will stop maintaining those walls and these elderly will begin to remember. But by that time, they are considered senile, and their memories are discounted.

FURTHER SELECTION CONSIDERATIONS

The Illuminati have their own criteria as to who they select. The preference is that they be blue-eyed blond Caucasians and not to have obvious physical defects or visible scars. The Freemasons also reject physically defective candidates. After they test the child for its intelligence, creativity, and dissociative skills, they will bring the children before the Grande Druid Council.

Formal approval of girls and boys into the Illuminati is done at a presentation by the Queen Mother and the Grand Druid Council at age three. However, the children have already been inspected by the Queen Mother before a formal physical inspection. Sexuality is an important issue for the physical part of the Illuminati inspection of little boys and girls. This is part of the physical criteria, as well as the physical health of the child. Creativity, strength, bloodlines, and intelligence will also be taken into consideration.

The standard trauma-based mind control which produces programmed multiple personalities is started on children before the age of 6. After the age of 6, it is difficult to follow this type of MPD/DID programming. However, this does not mean people aren't programmed after age 6. Trauma-based personality splits remain isolated in the mind better than hypnotic-based personality splits, but most people can be hypnotized to create alter personalities. Some SRA survivors have programming but don't have alter systems. A rare few do not have systems, but only a few dissociative states, such as a night self, and a day self.

A wide variety of approaches have been experimented with and operationally carried out. This book will concentrate more on the Monarch Systems which are created by programming infants. This is usually the most devastating, traumatic, controlling, and effective approach.

The Catholic Church has long said give me a child by the age of 5 and they will be Catholic. The Catholic Church is one of the largest parts of the network that carries out Monarch Mind Control. It is a fact, that if the Jesuits can place in their programming, what they call the "Keys to the Kingdom" Monarch Mind Control within a child, they will control his destiny. One Jesuit priest is on record as stating that there is nothing he can't make anyone do with torture. The Jesuits developed torture to a fine art in the inquisition. Imagine the expertise they have brought to the Monarch Program which begins torturing children at 18 months onward with every sophisticated torture device invented. If the Jesuits brag that they can convince adults to do anything via torture, what about baby children?

While the Monarch programming is done with children, one variety of it is done on adults. Adults who are selected are also chosen on the basis of the ability to disassociate and their availability. There are certain tests given by the branches of the military which identify people who disassociate well. Their "Cumes", that is their accumulated school records, are also examined. This type of person may be singled out and sent to get programming. Some of these persons end up in the various intelligence agencies, where they are trapped for their entire lifetimes. Some of the victims of the programming are war vets, Americans who were POWs, people in mental hospitals, people who just happened to work for Illuminati connected companies, and people going into acting. The intelligence agencies often begin mind-control on adult individuals when an individual joins their organization. If an intelligence or military group can exercise a high level of external control over an individual, they may not need the level of programming that some of the occult cults and the Illuminati need.

The Illuminati place their membership among the world at large, and with the requirement that centuries of secrecy be maintained. This secrecy can only be maintained by insuring that strong early programming is done to create fail safe systems with large number of dark alters and heavy layers of demonic forces. Many will scoff at the concept of demons being layered in, but whatever name one wants to call these forces, they are being layered in, and exert a powerful force behind the programming. The programming will break down if memories are recovered, so demonic imps are layered in to protect the memories from coming out. The entire phenomena will be gone into great detail and explained in rational terms in the course of this book. No matter how a therapist explains these demonic imps, they need to be dealt with if the memories are not to be protected. There are various methods for controlled memory retrieval, (journaling, hypnosis, safe rooms with screens, deliverance etc.) which we will not go into at this point, because we are providing the recipe, not the solution.

While most Illuminati victims are in-house from their own occult bloodlines, a certain renegade group of Illuminati programmers have proven to the Illuminati that they can adequately program non-Illuminati children. I am familiar with some of the people involved in this, but will not mention names. What we have covered in this chapter is how premeditated, deliberate, and precise the plans are by the programmers for the lives of these mind-controlled slaves. The programming places their lives on very rigid scripts. There are different uses for mind-controlled slaves. What applies to one slave may not apply to another one. Not everyone is a good candidate for programming. Sometimes only part of a family will be programmed. Whatever the particulars about the programming, it will be sufficient to place the individual's mind totally under the control of the handler. We have also given the details of how the candidates are selected, tested, prepared and the programming initiated.

CHAPTER 2

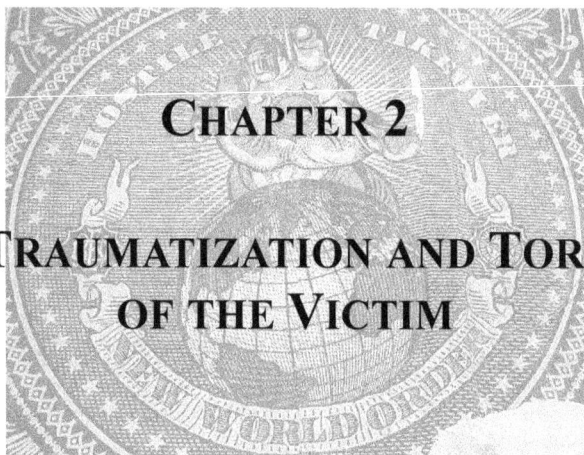

THE TRAUMATIZATION AND TORTURE OF THE VICTIM

The basis for the success of the Monarch mind-control programming is that different personalities or personality parts called alters can be created who do not know each other, but who can take the body at different times. The amnesia walls that are built by traumas, form a protective shield of secrecy that protects the abusers from being found out, and prevents the front personalities who hold the body much of the time to know how their System of alters is being used. The shield of secrecy allows cult members to live and work around other people and remain totally undetected. The front alters can be wonderful Christians, and the deeper alters can be the worst type of Satanic monster imaginable--a Dr. Jekyll/Mr. Hyde effect. A great deal is at stake in maintaining the secrecy of the intelligence agency or the occult group which is controlling the slave.

The success rate of this type of programming is high but when it fails, the failures are discarded through death. Each trauma and torture serves a purpose. A great deal of experimentation and research went into finding out what can and can't be done. Charts were made show-ing how much torture a given body weight at a given age can handle without death. Now this is why the Nazis did all those strange con-centration camp experiments, where they tested how quickly people would freeze or die from various traumas. It was for mind control!

The abusers are very specific and scientific in their torture. A lab technician with a clip board walks around monitoring the children when they receive their initial traumas. Heart monitors are closely watched. Still many children died from the programming. The programmers learned that when a child rolled up in a fetal position it had given up the will to live. They learned to time how fast this would occur to get an idea how far to push the child. Parents in eastern United States were taken to Harvard University for training to teach them how much trauma they could give their children at home before they would die. After the children got back from their initial programming they were to receive daily traumas to keep them dissociative.

THE INITIAL SPLITS AND PROGRAMMING DONE AT CHINA LAKE, CA

The primary or initial torture for many children in western U.S. was done at China Lake which officially has gone under the designations Naval Ordinance Test Station (pronounced in short as NOTS), Naval Weapons Center, NWC, Ridgecrest (the town nearby), and Inyo-kern (the area). the address of Nimitz Hospital is the code "232 Naval Air Weapons Station". The base was set up to test "new weapons". Evidently, the Navy decided that mind controlled people were an important weapon to test. Most of the "new weapons" created at China Lake were for the most part human robots turned out in large numbers. The Monarch Mind Control was carried out in large airplane hangers on the base which have been able to house thousands of tiny cages just large enough for human babies. Lots of 1,000 babies was a small batch. According to people who worked in the hangers helping program, many batches were 2,000 or 3,000 babies. Many survivors remember the thousands of cages housing little children from ceiling to floor.

The cages were hot wired (electrified on the ceiling, bottom and sides) so that the children who are locked inside can receive horrific electric shocks to their bodies to groom their minds to split into multiple personalities. These cages are called Woodpecker Grids. The victim sees a flash of light when high D.C. voltage is applied. Later, this flash of light is used with hypnotic induction to make the person think they are going into another dimension when they are blasted with high voltage. In the Peter Pan programming, the Programmers tell the slaves that this is "riding the light." One of the popular traumas after the small child has endured the Woodpecker Grid cages for days is to rape it. The rape is intentionally brutal so that it will be as traumatic as possible. Many of the technical people on the base are civilians. This is in part because part of the research involves mind-control, and Illuminati civilian mind-control experts have come and gone from the base.

The California Institute of Technology at Pasadena is intimately connected to China Lake's research (and by the way to the Illuminati). Also much of the work at the facility is for the intelligence agencies and not the military. Intelligence assets are often civilians. One of the things developed in the California Universities and then implemented at China Lake was color programming, which will be covered later in this book. Red and green were discovered to be the most visible colors for programming. Various colored flashing lights were used in programming at NOTS. Survivors of the programming all remember flashing lights. The use of flashing lights has been introduced into American culture by the CIA. If a person goes into bars and places where bands play, you will notice multi-colored lights flashing. The flashing lights create disassociation, especially in people who are programmed.

HOW CHILDREN ARE TRANSPORTED TO A MAJOR PROGRAMMING SITE

An example of just one of the bases used for early programming is the large and very secret China Lake facility in California near Death Valley. The children are brought into the China Lake NWC, aka NOTS, base by trains, planes and cars. A number of the small airfields which fly these children into China Lake have been identified. One, which is no longer in use for moving children, was a private air strip at Sheridan, OR which was beside a large lumber mill. The lumber mill had an agreement to secretly house the children who had their mouths taped. Neighbors in the area were bought off, and warned that if they talked they would be in trouble for breaching national security. The area has lots of mills joined by train tracks, which were used to shuttle the children around. Tied into this network was a

Catholic Monastery which lies between Sheridan and McMinnville, close to the rail network.

The Union Train Station in Portland, OR has underground tunnels where children were temporarily warehoused in cages before continuing on their journey. The Jesuits were active in this part of the child procurement. Catholic adoption agencies (which are many), nuns who get pregnant, third world parents, and parents who will sell their children were all sources of children for programming. When one thinks about how many corrupt people there are and how many towns and cities are on the West Coast, and how many children are produced by Satanic breeders, illegal aliens and other parents who'd rather have the money than children and the reader begins to realize how procuring batches of 1,000 or 2,000 children was no problem for the Illuminati working through intelligence agencies such as the CIA, NIS, DIA, FBI, and FEMA. The Finders, a joint CIA/FBI group procured children for the Network for years. Some of the children needed for programming are to be used for sacrifices to traumatize those being programmed.

The secret FEMA airstrip at Santa Rosa has planes landing and leaving all night. Some of these flights go east and then land at the secret 1800-square-mile China Lake Naval Research Base, and are believed to carry children for programming. This airstrip is called the SANTA ROSA AIR CENTER. When I tried to get FAA information on this airstrip they played stupid as if it didn't exist, yet it is in operation.

Near Santa Rosa is the Bohemian Grove. Southwest of Santa Rosa is this air center which is not used by the public. This airport was recently used by private pilots as a F.B.O. It was built during W.W. II as a training base for P-32 pilots, and deactivated in 1952. After the war, it was leased to private companies (such as the CIA). The paved areas are 4' of concrete and can land the heaviest planes in use. There are no buildings over two stories in the entire area, and no control tower. The FBI have a contingent in the Federal building downtown Santa Rosa, and "FEMA" has a radio station at the airport. The Army reserve also has some buildings in the area.

However, there is some highly secret activity going on underground at the airport. 6-7 small planes sneak out of the closed base a day, and for a base of its description that is closed, that is very interesting. The planes take off in the evening and do not turn their lights on until hundreds of feet into the air. The Press Democrat of Santa Rosa ran an article on Thurs., Apr. 22, 1993 about the Federal government selling 70 acres of property just to the east of the airport. However, when one reads closely, the land is going to be offered to a host of Federal agencies. The property was "being used by FEMA" (707-542-4534). If one thinks about it, it is unlikely that the radio station is a FEMA transmitter station. The close vicinity of this secret activity to the elite's Bohemian Grove makes this an interesting site for study.

The airport used for the Bohemian Grove visitors is north of Santa Rosa on Hwy 101, the Sonoma County Airport. United Express and American Eagle, which flies to and from San Jose, fly into this airport, which has a control tower. In 1964, the airport was reported to have also carried about 600 military operations, either a takeoff or landing, per year. It was around this time that the Federal government made an agreement with Sonoma County Airport to help pay for the runway to be extended & strengthened and the airport to be upgraded in numerous ways.

The elite from around the world fly into here to go to the Bohemian Grove, which is in the Monte Rio area. Monarch slaves are regularly abused at the Grove for the entertainment of Bohemian Grove members in kinky sex theme rooms, such as the dark room and the necrophilia room. Secret NWO business is conducted in the small, dark lounge with a wooden sign naming it UNDERGROUND.

Slaves are hunted in the woods for sport, and occult rituals, including infant sacrifice, are held outdoors in the Grove. These airfields are described in detail so that the reader can begin to catch on to the network of small planes and airfields the Monarch system uses to transport children. The children are trickled in from various collection points to China Lake. Monarch slaves, many of them children themselves are used in this extensive child procurement system. Children are also used to entice and kidnap other children. Teenage slaves are used to escort and transport little children on trains, buses, and planes. The triangular-shaped airfield at China Lake (see image in Appendix C) has traditionally begun very early in the morning with lots of activity. The night flights from FEMA's Santa Rosa airfield being an example of incoming flights. The airfield connects to the main base area via Sandquist Road. Children are landed at this field, while others are driven through the gates guarded by marines, and others come through via the east-west rail line. The fact that children are driving through the gates is not alarming because inside the military perimeter is a high school, a junior high school and 3 other schools. Some of the adults of the children being programmed stay in military barracks (Quonset huts and one story buildings) while they wait.

A male Monarch victim remembers a large hanger building at China Lake with a concrete floor and row after row of cages suspended from the ceiling filling the large building. One of the Programmers was dressed similar to a Catholic Priest. The electric current that ran to the cages made a hum, like an electric fence. There was a marble slab that served as an altar where black-hooded robed people would take a bone handled knife and sacrifice little children in front of the other children in the cages. (Memories from other survivors about the place will be mentioned later.)

MORE ABOUT THE SECRET CHINA LAKE BASE

Charles Manson, a programmed Monarch slave who received initial programming at China Lake, lived with his cult only 45 miles northwest of China Lake at the remote Myers and Barker ranches. Scotty's Castle in Death Valley, Bakersfield, Edwards AFB, and Papa Ludo's Store & Tavern (with its secret underground programming center) are all in the vicinity of China Lake and all have been programming sites too. Old route 66 went by China Lake, which now is just off U.S. 395. The area's tavern has been named the Hideaway. The building was low, away from the highway, with a large unlit parking lot. Only people who knew how to enter it by the obscure entrance on the side could get in. The Hideaway Tavern has been a local hangout for the CIA men in China Lake. It has served them excellent steaks. The base headquarters is known as the White House, and it looks somewhat like a yacht clubhouse. Northwest of the airfield, at 39-64 & 4-33 E on the quad maps, the government has built a large magical seal of Solomon (hexagram) with each leg 1/4 mile long on the ground. What was it like for a victim in the early 1950's in a NOTS area programming center?

One of the buildings in the area used for programming was described as having a flat roof and a tan exterior. A fence ran around the building. Inside the front door was an old oak reception type desk. A series of 3 doors connected by tunnels were gone through. One entered into a hallway, and then took a left into the programming room. Tunnels connected the different hallways. The programming room was painted a good dissociative color white. In the middle of the room, cages were suspended with chimps. The examining table was metal, which was cold for the victim, but easy to wash for the attendants. The victim was placed in cages and could observe white dots light up in different dot patterns over the door on a panel of lights. The low level shocks to the victim were coordinated with the dot patterns. (Some of this relates to domino programming.)

An attendant monitored the entire scenario on charts, while the child was repeatedly traumatized with low-voltage shocks. Needles were poked in the child, the room was made dark and then lit. Voices said, "Love me, love me not." This was part of the love me, don't love me part of programming. "Good girls ride the silvery wings." This was to build the ability to condition trancing by the victim upon electro-shock.

German & British scientists/mind control programmers came to NOTS after W.W. II, including Joseph Mengele (known as Dr. Green, or Greenbaum, and other pseudonyms). The Illuminati's Dr. Black worked out of China Lake also. Dr. White (Dr. Ewin Cameron) worked on the east coast, although he did fly in every so often to the west coast to meet with the other top programmers. Dr. Blue was another of the important leading Illuminati programmers.

These top programmers supervised other lesser programmers. If something went wrong, they might fly a child from a programming location to a specialist to get it special help for its programming. The men and women of the Illuminati helped the top programmers out. The Grande Mothers, and the Grande Masters of the Illuminati participated in helping with the programming.

As a child of the Illuminati progressed through its programming, three people had oversight over its programming: its Grande Mother, its Grande Dame, and the Programmer. The Illuminati functions off a chain of command similar to the military. In fact a big secret is that Satan's realm actually served as the model for military and political structures. As a child begins its programming, it is monitored in a fashion similar to hospitals where charts are filled and then these charts are filed. Tests and evaluations are done regularly. Goals are set which are six month programming goals. These will say in effect, we need to accomplish this by doing a, b, c, d in the next six months. This is somewhat similar to an I.E.P. (individual education plan) which the special education teachers in Oregon set up for each student. At some point, the strong points and the weaknesses of the child will be identified, and then a decision will be made as to what occupation the Illuminati want to program the person to become. If the young boy is aggressive and has sadistic tendencies, the Illuminati call it "a war monger" and label its chart "This child will be a general."

Then they proceed to program it to become a general. Nurses, teachers, and child physicians must be programmed with a gentleness to their System. Other occupations, such as lawyers can be allowed to be ruthless. Many of the children have religious fronts labeled for their programming, and a very popular occupation for Illuminati men is to become clergymen. Religious leaders make up the majority of fathers of Monarch survivors that have sought help. Most Illuminati victims have parents who are important religious leaders, many of them top clergymen in the established churches.

WHAT TRAUMA DOES

In recent times, the military and the science of psychology is paying attention to what they call PTSD (post-traumatic stress disorder). PTSD are the psychopathic debilitating effects of trauma and chronic nature of reactions to trauma. Intrusive flashbacks of the trauma will occur if the mind doesn't protect itself from reminders of the trauma. The mind creates avoidance patterns to protect itself from thinking about the trauma. Panic symptoms occur when the person undergoes physiological arousal to traumatic cues. A trauma will create a certain "shatteredness" within the victim. The victim will develop life assumptions about being vulnerable, about having little personal worth, and that life is not fair. They may develop phobias to constantly check their environment for safety and constantly monitor others to make sure they are not mistreated.

For centuries warfare has taken place, and military men have experienced PTSD. However, a full description and investigation into the disorder has been done only in recent history. The U.S. military has prevented any serious counseling for their troops suffering from this. Peer "counselors" and rap groups were allowed, and misled by the army to believe that they would be adequate.

PTSD will often lead to outbursts of rage, chronic depression, or borderline dysfunctions. The PTSD in Monarch victims is masked by the MPD/DID and the programming. Then in turn, the programming masks the MPD. When the programming is complete, front alters have been created which can function with smiles and cheerful attitudes, while underneath, the mind is full of shattered hurting alters, who the slave is unaware of.

Self-punishment and social withdrawal are natural symptoms of PTSD, and the programmers have no trouble enhancing and programming these functions into their alter systems. Certain alters end up holding the anger, the fear, the social withdrawal, the guilt, and the desire for self-punishment. These are held in check by the programming, and take the body when the slave steps outside of the programmed path. The bad memories in the minds of men who suffer from PSTD have been noted to re-cycle and self-perpetuate themselves as they lie unresolved in the memory cells. Bad memories for the victims of Monarch programming are used to hold the MPD, the programming in place and also to keep the victim in compliance. In 1954, Maslow published his hierarchy of needs, which when applied to Monarchs and PSTD victims means that they can not progress in therapy until their survival and safety needs are met.

However, the Programmers/abusers know that it is important to keep the slave away from safety. To this end, the Programmers employ people externally to monitor slaves, and internal alters in the victim's mind to be monitoring alters and reporting alters. Reporting alters can always reach the Network of abusers via 1-800 telephone numbers which change every 2 weeks. They can also call their handler. Reporting alters are very unemotional and serve as tape recorders which mechanically report any developments that might threaten the programming to their handler.

Alters programmed to commit suicide are also built into the Systems. For instance, for a system hacker--an outsider-- to work with the alters of an internal Grand Druid Council, aka Executive committee alters, or judge alters, a System almost insures 99% of the time suicide of the Monarch slave.

In at least 99% of the cases where Monarchs who have come in for therapy, they still lack safety, which is a higher need than trying to go against their programming. This is why so few people have really gotten free. To undo the programming, the victim needs safety. The programmers know this, and have set up almost fail safe methods where the victim is not even safe from their own system of alters, let alone Big Brother.

Therapists call their Monarch victims "survivors" a misnomer, because in reality they are still in the middle of ongoing abuse. Some therapists may mistakenly think that it is helpful to tell the victim, "These fears you are having are from the past." Deliverance ministries may also try to stop the victim's fears, without understanding the reasons behind the ongoing fear. Other chapters will deal with the extensive back up methodologies. At this point, it is mentioned in the context of this chapter to establish to the reader that the abuse and torture continue non-stop. Some of this would naturally occur any-way, but the Programmers enhance this naturally occurring phenom-ena many-fold to insure that the slave will continually abuse them-selves.

This means as time progresses, some Monarch systems are timed to shatter certain levels & to create new levels. If the Programmers want, they can shatter a front Christian alter level and create a new level of New Age believing alters to replace the original front. The abuse can be done by the victim themselves to themselves, because programming alters are given the ability to pull up horrific memories via codes. Those traumatic memories, which shattered the mind the first time, are still capable of doing it again when they are abreacted, that is relived by the body & mind. More and more people are experi-encing working with someone with multiple personalities. However, very few multiples ever discover more than the front parts of their systems.

Very few people, outside of the programmers, have much idea of what an entire system of alters is like, therefore some of the things that this book will describe will seem foreign to those people who have learned a little about multiplicity. There are several models to describe what happens inside a multiple's brain as it develops multi-ple personalities. The brain is very complex. Recent brain research confirms that the brain was far more complex than imagined. In an average brain there are 10,000,000,000 individual neuron (nerve cells). Each of these has 10 with 100 zeros following it worth of in-terconnections. In other words, an average brain has vastly more in-terconnections than the total number of atoms in the universe! Often about 1/2 million different chemical reactions take place every min-ute in the average brain, and the number can be several times that during intense activity. A Monarch's brain has been worked on to be even more active than a normal person's brain. The left & the right side of the Monarch's brain both work simultaneously, and the vari-ous personalities are all busy working simultaneously on different tracks.

To describe the complexity of what is happening with someone's mind which has been messed with so dramatically for years, means that at times only an approximate model is presentable.

There are several terms which are used in speaking about multiples, which have developed several meanings. Unless these terms are correctly defined, misconceptions about them can cloud an understanding of what happens during Monarch programming. First, researchers have discovered that deep within a person, the brain truly understands in a pure awareness all about itself. This is true for everyone. This pure awareness has been named various names, including Hidden Observer. If a man is obnoxious and seems to have a total lack of awareness that he irritates people; just know that deep down an awareness realizes exactly what he is and what he does. The multiple's brain at some deep awareness knows what has happened to it.

The term Hidden Observer is fraught with danger though. A demonic entity called the Hidden Observer works hand in glove with the programmer to program the individual. The Hidden Observer is able to see everything the System does. The people who control the slave frequently call up the Hidden Observer to ask questions. In this case, it is a demonic entity, and yet it is this Hidden Observer, which each System has, that some therapists are trying to access to understand the System. This Hidden Observer only tells the truth to its Master, because it is demonic.

The next term which is misunderstood is the term "the core". The programmers set up various alters to pretend to be the core, and the core's protector. The real core is quite hidden, and not placed within the regular grid of the alter system's chart. It will take some explaining to convey what happens to the mind, and what the real core is.

THE TYPES OF TRAUMA

One thing discovered by research into the genetic transmission of learned knowledge by humans to their children was that people are born with certain fears. Snakes, blood, seeing internal body parts, and spiders are all things that people are born fearing. The phobias toward these things are passed down genetically from one generation to another. In searching for traumas to apply to little children, the Programmers found that these natural phobias which occur in most people from birth will work "wonderful" to split the mind. Along this line, the following are samples of traumas done to program slaves:

A) being locked in a small confined spot, a pit or cage with spiders and snakes.
B) being forced to kill, and cut up and eat innocent victims,
C) immersion into feces, urine and containers of blood.

Then being made to eat these things. These are standard traumas. Often a slave will experience not only all of the above but many others before they reach 4 or 5 years of age. It is important to traumatize the child early before it has a chance to develop its ego states. By the way, when the child is placed into a small box with spiders or snakes, they will often be told that if they play dead the snake will not bite them. This carries out two things for the programmers, it lays the basis for suicide programs (i.e. "if-you-are-dead, then you-are-safe" thinking) and it teaches the child to dissociate. Traumas to split the mind are not just high voltage, or natural phobias, but encompass the full range of the emotional and spiritual being of the victim.

The victim is eventually stripped of every spiritual or emotional resource by a variety of traumas, such as "blood orgies" where male and female genitals are cut, torture sessions on all types of medieval torture machines, staged events where actors imitating God, Jesus Christ, police, and therapists curse the victim, reject the victim, and even "kill" the victim in simulated drug deaths. Children are placed in hospitals in captive abusive conditions. Children are tied to innocent children which are systematically and brutally killed while the children are made to believe that they are guilty for the child's punishment. Near death experiences such as drowning have become an art with these abusers. Trained dogs, monkeys and other animals are used to further traumatize the victims.

An Illuminati slave will most likely have experienced all of the last few paragraphs above, plus much more. Toby, was one of the trained NOTS chimpanzees. He was trained to be sadistic. The other trained chimpanzees at China Lake included "Gabie" or Gabriel, who tickled the victim while they were tied up; Rastice, who had a toy chest with diamonds, bracelets, & a scepter which electro-shocked; Zoro, who could do anything mean; Elmore, who cuddled as a mother but ate raw flesh; plus others. An example of something said during programming with the chimps is, "THREE LITTLE MONKEYS IN A CAGE, DO, RE, ME, FA, SO, LA, TE, DO". Joseph Mengele, aka Dr. Green, was skilled at using German shepherds to attack people.

Mengele got a reputation in the Nazi concentration camps for using German shepherds, before he was brought over to America. He used dogs to help program American children. (The Process Church often uses German Shepherds too.) He was also skilled in abortions, and was involved in weird traumas involved with babies being born, or the simulated births of dead rats (or other gross things) from the vaginas of girls being programmed. When the Satanic cults tie their victims with wire for rituals, some of these people will lose their toes or fingers from the wire. At times little fingers and the top part of ring fingers are lost in Satanic cult rituals too.

Many of the traumas and tortures are carried out by alters or persons who are sadistic. How does the Network get sadistic men to torture little children? Three different respectable studies (Harrower, 1976/ Milgram, 1974/ & Gibson 1990) show that essentially all human males can be taught to engage in sadistic behavior. There may be a few exceptions, but the point is that sadistic people are not in short supply for programming. Some of the alter systems have extremely brutal sadistic alters. In fact, the Mothers of Darkness alters are an important balancing point to prevent the sadistic male programmers from killing more of the children they are working on.

These sadists get a laugh at hurting little children. The more pain, the more charge and excitement they get out of it. Sadists enjoy gaining total control over a person. In order to do this, they take charge over the little child's basic body functions, such as sleeping, eating, and pooping. They enjoy terrorizing the little child, so Monarch slaves end up watching hours of sadistic behavior done to others before they are even 5 years old. The worse the trauma, the more the sadistic programmers enjoy it. Sensory deprivation, forced labor, poisoning, and rape of every orifice of the child are popular tortures by the programmers. The child soon learns that he is at the mercy of crazy people who can only be satisfied by total submission, and the willingness to allow someone else to think for you. The child will be made to eat faces, blood, other disgusting things, while the programmer eats good meals.

Some of this sadistic behavior is toward a goal. Cutting a person's tongue and putting salt on it reinforces the no-talk programming. Making someone throw up to cause eating disorder programming. Dislocating shoulders to cause dissociation. When the child victim's crying is heard, they immediately apply torture so the child thinks it will suffocate. This is behavior modification, and is covered later in chapter 9. This trains the child not to cry.

Around age 3, a Black Mass, a sick evil communion, is performed which is so ugly, that the child hides in dissociation by creating a "locked-up"/or "obscure" child. This early flip provides a base for dark side programming. This locked up child can have a powerful healing (with system wide effects) by being part of a positive love-filled communion.

There are many traumas which can be carried out, which leave no physical scars, but do leave the child with the deepest emotional and spiritual scars. This is often necessary when programming young children who the outside world will see soon after their programming session. Holding one's arms out is a simple torture. Tickling and sensory deprivation are two tortures that leave no marks. Burial caskets, some outside and some at inside locations are often used on slaves. That is why many slaves fear being buried alive. The Programmers place all types of creepy insects in the caskets when they bury the person alive.

Another type of sensory deprivation is done by placing the victim in salt water (for buoyancy and weightlessness). Then the victim is fitted with sensitive sensors that shock the person if the victim moves. The shock puts the person back into unconsciousness. The brain is trained to stop all external body movement from the conscious mind.

This type of sensory deprivation is used to place in the posthypnotic commands to do something at some future date far into the future. The program is placed into the mind at the same primal level that the mind uses to tell the heart to beat.

One of the "appropriate" tortures is to place a bar between a little girl's legs which spreads the girl's loins for rape. Then the bent spread legs are flapped, while the victim is specifically told she is a "Monarch butterfly". Many victims have created butterflies in their minds while being raped. The programmers may tell some of their victims that out of caterpillar-worms come beautiful butterflies. While raping the child, the Programmers will describe their sperm fluid as "honey comb", and will cry out "hallelujah" when they come. It doesn't take long for the child to realize it has no ability to resist what is being done to it.

The will of the child victim is destroyed, and in its place remains a pliable slave. If the slave doesn't learn correctly they receive more pain. A fish hook in the vagina is a popular one. Older males have their genitals hurt during additional or reprogramming sessions. They may have to eat the skin taken from their genitals. The mind of the victim is not only divided from itself, but the very process of torture, makes the victim distrustful of humans in general. On top of this distrust, the programmers will layer in programming to isolate the person from healthy relationships, which in turn increases the victim's feeling of helplessness. They are divided from their own parts (their own self) and the world in general. For instance, the water, cave and sand tortures make the survivor fearful of oceans.

The victim may be traumatized by being lowered on ropes or a cage on ropes into the water from a cliff, or may end up being buried alive in sand and watching the tide come in, or simply being totally buried alive in sand and abandoned. For a while, the Illuminati was big on water torture because they had built into their systems a weakness that water would destroy the clone armies that protected programming, and they needed their slave systems to be fearful of water. Slaves are frequently lowered into black holes, or pits containing the most scariest things possible. This is a frequent trauma, because the victim when left in a dark hole for hours or days without any contact with the world or water & food will develop deep emotional scars & dissociation rather than tale-telling signs of physical abuse. This torture is used essentially on all Monarch slaves.

Some of the traumas are done for specific medical reasons. For instance, the person is starved by only allowing 300 calories per day for say a small woman of 125 lbs. Sugar & proteins are severely limited, so that the brain is starved into submission. Water deprivation, which is taught to parents who raise Monarch slaves, is used from time to time on slaves to raise the brain's temperature which happens when the brain swells from lack of water. When the brain gets woozy & overheated it hallucinates and has a hard time remembering events. If water deprivation is combined with electroshock it makes it harder yet for the victim to remember anything. Heavy exercise along with long periods of little sleep (2-3 hours/day) causes an overproduction of endorphins in the brain and victims begin to robotically respond to commands. This was done to one of my sources under the pretense of military "training".

One of my other sources experienced it as part of her mind-control. The brain under such stress may flip its functions from right to left & vice-versa. Hypnosis is easier when a brain is tired. Most victims remember being suspended upside down. This was honed to a fine art by Mengele with concentration camp victims, while records were made of how fast blood drained from a child or adult's stomach when they were dunked upside down into a tank of ice cold water. The cold water tests supplied the data on temperature levels as consciousness faded. This information then was used later on in America to help the survival rate of children given the same trauma. Simply hanging a person upside down for one or two hours will begin to play tricks on the mind. The mind will begin to dissociate, and will begin to reverse the primordial brain functions such as pain is pleasure. The person's mind rearranges.

This is often done with Beta alters or Beta models to get them to think that the pain of sadistic rape is a pleasure. After this reversal in the mind that "PAIN IS LOVE", the S&M kitten alters will beg their handler to slap them, tie them up, hurt them, etc. They will tease their handler, and tell him he is not a real man if he shows any mercy in how the pain is inflicted.

Fire/burning torture is used in the porcelain face programming. The charismatic branch of the satanic Network (such as the Assembly of God churches) uses porcelain face programming. This is done by using wax masks upon the victim, and giving them fire torture. The person actually thinks that their face has melted. At that point, the programmer pretends to be a god & a hero, and tells the person he will give them a new face, a porcelain mask.

These new faces by the way, look like the ones sold in so many stores. The memories of abuse are then hypnotically hid behind the masks. To take off the masks is to abreact & burn again. If anyone touches the faces of alters with porcelain face programming, the alters will feel a burning sensation because their masks are not to be tampered with. This means that these alters have via torture & hypnosis lost their own faces! This is part of the dehumanization process which chapter 10 talks about. As long as these alters stay in denial of what has happened to them, they do not have to face the burn torture memories.

Some alters are tortured in a fashion that the eye area is traumatized and they squint the left eye. They look like Baron Guy de Rothschild of France's left eye looks. Guy de Rothschild is a major handler/programmer, but the reason for his drooping eye is not known. Perhaps it was torture.

The ritual aspect of trauma needs to be covered. By traumatizing someone on a specific day--say, repeatedly traumatizing them on their birthday--is far more damaging than just simply traumatizing them. The reason is that every time that person's birth date recycles they are put back into their memories of abuse. Sexual abuse of a child is more powerful when it is put into the context of demonic magic. The abuser's semen is magic and seals the programming. The ritual aspect of it, and the repetitive nature of the abuse creates several dynamics that accompany the abuse that wouldn't occur in non-ritual abuse. The lie that accompanies such abuse is that this institu-tionalized abuse is an obligation for both the abuser and the victim. For instance, the mind-control of the Beast Barracks experience at West Point, USMA is an institutionalized abuse that allows the abuser to side step responsibility for sadistic behavior, and sets the stage for the abuse to be continued under the disguise of tradition.

Finally, there is one more category of trauma, those to produce cos-metic looks. For instance, breast implants or electro-shock to create moles at certain locations for either as a sign telling other handlers the extent of the programming or for a Marilyn Monroe look. A "stage trick" is to use a multi-needle device to scar the tissue. The scar which is made in a pattern, a popular one is the satanic Goat's head of Mendes, can be made visible by hypnotic command. This allows the handler to look powerful to uninformed viewers and is fur-ther discussed in chapter 8. This stage trick has been done by the oc-cult world for centuries.

WHAT OCCURS WHEN THE MIND SPLITS

During battles soldiers have been known to wall off horrible events with amnesia walls. Just like the soldier who walls off a traumatic battle scene where he sees his buddy disemboweled by a grenade, so the child walls off trauma. However, the soldier must only endure a relatively small amount of trauma compared to the children who are programmed under the Monarch trauma-based mind control. A sol-dier may remember his trauma, by being triggered by something that reminds him of the trauma. Likewise, the child victim will have things that trigger it too. One way of describing the split, is to say that the child's mind is saying, "This isn't happening to me, its happening to some one else" and a split in the personality occurs. The new split will have the characteristics of what it split from. The programmer will ask the alter being tortured to create something in the mind when the split is created--such as "I want 12 white fluffy kittens."

The programmer, demons, and the child's creativity work together with the dissociation to create alters. Those 12 white fluffy kittens will have the characteristics and memories of what they were made from. However, they are separated from each other by dissociation, and they will be given their own script and own separate identity by the programmer. The dissociation between some alters who are co-conscious is not full blown amnesia. After the Programmer has instructed the child what alters he wants made when he tortures the child, the Programmer will inject a truth serum to determine whether the correct alters were made and the correct amount.

The child's creativity is being guided by torture. The Programmer will often also call up the Hidden Observer and ask it what has happened internally in the mind of the victim. Another better way of looking at what happens is to understand that the part of the brain that records personal memory--that is the personal history memory section, is divided up into little pieces by amnesia walls built to protect itself from the repeated traumas. Each section is walled off from another section by amnesia. Each trauma has an amnesia wall built around it. Each trauma memory is sectioned off. That walled off section is a piece of memory that will be identified, and a hypnotic cue attached by the programmers that will pull it up to the conscious mind. And further, if the programmers so desire, it can be given a history, a name, a job, and developed into a full-blown personality. It's important to grasp that the entire mind is not sectioned off into parts.

Some areas of the mind, such as the area that holds skills & talents, is available to all the alters who want to access that talent. The talent doesn't belong to that alter but to the System. Autobiographical memory is remembered differently than simple facts & skills involving primitive parts of the brain. A sense of time & a sense of self are attached to autobiographical memories--these things are stripped of an alter as it functions within the programming. Memory storage is also linked to the brain's state of mind at the time. Hormones released at the time of an experience will modulate the strength of the memory of that experience.

The limbic-hypothalamic system of the brain, which consists of the amygdala, hippocampus, cingulate gyrus, fornix, septum, certain nuclei of the thalamus, and the Papez circuit, has a central modulating part which interacts with peripheral hormones. Peripheral epinephrine will be released if the amygdala is electrically stimulated. The adrenal medulla releases epinephrine that is vital for memory storage. In other words, there are hormones which help the brain remember or not. A particular talent is not used by every alter. A non-sexual alter, an alter with an asexual identity, is not going to access talents involved in sexual foreplay. This is because memories are both occurrent states & also dispositions, and when a disposition is dissociated the alter must maintain a different set of dispositions. A three year child alter is not going to access abilities to write. To do so for these alters would mean attacking the amnesia walls which hold horrible memories. That would mean going against the programming with its penalties, and their own understanding of "reality" which is the programmed story line that the alter has been convinced of under penalty of losing its life.

To dissociate a memory and to take on a particular role and identity involves a constant re-interpretation of past events. It may also mean that the alter must contrive an interpretation of present events. The 3 year old may, for instance, see breasts but decide they belong to someone else in the system who they share the body with. This is in part dictated by the necessity of obscuring the pain of the trauma that separates the alter from the rest. Each day that the alter confronts reality, they will face the threat that old memories will not agree with the story line created. For instance, the handler's sexual advances carried out in front of that asexual/nonsexual alter must be misconstrued so that the illusion of not having been raped is continued. This is why normal life has a way of breaking down the multitude of lies and programming of the deeper alters, which live in a fantasy world created during the programming. The deeper alters have never had the chance to experience life outside of their programming, since they hold the body only at infrequent specialized moments which are disjointed in time.

The alters created to be fronts to normally hold the body will be given lots of programming to help them hold onto certain denials, so that they will find it necessary to ignore or reinterpret dreaded associations linked with dissociated memories. For instance, a Christian front alter is sincerely very righteous and holy. The thought that this person, technically the alter's System of persons, could have done the most horrible savage demonic activities is inconceivable. The memories of ritual are safely ignored, because the reality would undermine everything the person is.

This phenomena is not just seen in memory dissociation, but also under hypnosis when a person accepts a suggestion which flies in the face of the reality they can see. If a person accepts the suggestion that there is no dog in the room, they will struggle internally to maintain that illusion. If asked to walk on a collision course with the dog, they will unconsciously move around it, and if asked why they stumbled around the dog, they will construct an artificial excuse, which is accepted even though it is transparently implausible. One of the Monarch Programmers Orne called this "trance logic." Trance logic is the ploys and strategies to maintain a dissociative or hypnotic hallucination.

The frontal lobes of the cerebral cortex which are called the Brodmann areas no. 9-12 are responsible for a person's own responses to circumstance, i.e. what some call "personality". When the mind is split, this natural personality is not erased but rather is a collected pool upon which various responses from it are attached to various personalities". Damage to these Brodmann areas tends to give an overall effect of making the person passive. The programming is not designed to damage these areas, only to control what emotions they contain are linked in memory to the various memory fragments that will be made into personalities. The reticular formation is the location of the brain's mechanism which determines the state of consciousness all the way from alert, to hypnotic trance, to sleep, to coma. It interacts with the frontal lobes and the rest of the brain. Each memory is a function of several parts of the brain working together.

Memory is a function of alertness/state of consciousness (reticular formation), the emotions (Brodmann Areas 9-12), the Thalami (priorities given to memories), and several complicated processes where the brain categorizes and interfiles the info with other remembered data. By building in amnesia walls between Event memories, and by producing altered states of consciousness, the memories of a slave can be "nested" as the Programmers call it. "Nested" means that it is hidden behind several "locked doors" when the mind files the memory. Sometimes the person must go back to the altered state to recover a memory. The electro-shock also scrambles the brain's filing of a memory, so that it is filed in bits and pieces.

Because of the use of electro-shock, if memories do start surfacing they surface in pieces. Sometimes a complete memory will be held by thousands of parts who the mind must bring together to recover the full memory. It has been discovered that memory retrieval is best when the environment is identical to when the memory took place. If we memorize numbers underwater, we will recall them better under-water. Another thing discovered about trauma memories is that they are stored in the sensory motor processes, rather than just in the nor-mal memory sites of the brain. These memories are called body memories, and they do not lie. The False Memory Spindrome is way off base on their attacks, but then all of us who know the real story realize that they are just a cover-up damage control scheme of the CIA.

THE CORE

Let's return to describing the "core" or that part of the brain which is intact at the beginning. If we pause to consider that a non-multiple person will experience struggles in their mind when simultaneous, overlapping but conflicting desires meet in conflict--i.e. "should I lay in bed, go to work, or go fishing today?" A particular part of the brain (a Synthesizing Self) is capable of ordering such a conflict--it tran-scends all these conflicting ego states.

A single Synthesizing Self in the brain is likewise responsible for the de-synthesizing of the ego states. The victim in order to appease the programmers sets up different and opposite alters relative to a single System's needs. The formation of alters is systematically and intelli-gently guided by the programmers, especially in the early stages. The alters are created to meet the needs of the System that the program-mers impose upon it, and not to adapt to an abusive parent.

Some therapists have failed to see that alter formation is not natural, but a maladaptive practice that is guided by the victim's desire to please, and its fear of the programmers. The pool of abilities will be shared in different combinations among the various alters. An alter may have a unique ability that consists of subsidiary traits which may not be unique but are shared by other alters. As a child develops if certain areas of the brain are stimulated, then those areas grow. If they are not stimulated, then the brain will not grow brain cells in the area. In other words, experience shapes the way parts of our brains develop. The way brain cells grow, that is how they make their connections, is believed by researchers to be the actual place that memory is held. The growth in connections, in their meaningful ways, creates meaningful patterns that make up memory. When memory storage occurs, changes in terminals of axons ending on the dendrites occurs.

Dendrite spines (which look like trees) develop. One tree (dendrite spine) might look like an oak in winter -- another might look like a mass of seaweed. For various reasons, as the brain of a multiple grows--it physically grows different than a normal person's brain. The brain can get around what has been done to it in some ways, but it needs to be borne in mind that we are not dealing with just bad memories--but brains which have had their physical makeup & functioning altered. It is interesting to see how each different alter has a different EEG profile. One of the primary brain areas affected by the torture and programming are the areas which store event (personal history) memory. These areas are the hippocampus and the cortex of the frontal brain lobes which work with the two thalamus. General knowledge is stored in the neocortex (the grey area of the brain or the outer thin layer. The brain has practically no limit to memory. However, it will select what it wants to remember, and it will decide how it will file what it remembers.

Hypnotic suggestions to "forget" something often simply means the person remembers the event--but labels the file "forgotten". Slaves are always under hypnotic suggestions to forget what they have experienced--however, usually the brain in actuality only appears to comply and then secretly records the event. Hypnosis will be dealt with in chapter 4.

HOW PROGRAMMING IS ANCHORED

All the programming of each & every slave is anchored upon some type of trauma. One of the first fundamental traumas will be watched, filmed, coded & used as an anchor. For instance, the most brutal rape of a girl by her father will be used as an anchor upon which to build the Beta programming.

In chapter 1 it was discussed how the primary severing of the core was incest. Extreme psychosis is created within a child trying to deal with the issues created by the incest from the child's most important figure--their father figure. In Moriah's slaves, this is the standard method to sever the core, & create an anchoring trauma. When Mayer Amschel Rothschild (orig. named Bauer) was on his deathbed, he demanded from his sons, that they protect the power of the House of Rothschild through incest. Electroshock can cause pain, but this is nothing compared to the confusion in the mind caused by incest issues.

Entire worlds of loyal alters whose only function is loyalty to the biological incestual father are created in the slave. This world of loyal alters may be the Daisy world. The hardest bonding to break within Illuminati slaves is this bond to their incestual father. Non-Illuminati mind-controlled slaves are bonded to other people--the cult leader or programmer. Whatever fundamental trauma is decided upon, all the rest of the programming will be built upon that anchor in the victim's mind. (See chapters. 7 to 9 for further information on how the programming is layered in.) This fundamental trauma is not the bottom BEAST computer which sets at the bottom of the subconscious mind. Internal computers are complex. This is simply an anchoring memory that the programmers begin with. In large systems, the programmers will choose an experience that all of the alters are familiar with.

When large programmed alter systems come in for a major overhaul, the Programmers will call up section by section with the correct code words until they are all at the front of the mind. When this is done, thousands of alters are pulled up co-conscious & worked on all to-gether. When this occurs it is an exceptionally big surprise for most alters who have lived their entire existence in dissociated isolation from other alters in their system. Why would the programmers do this? For several reasons, speed and the desire to have common an-choring experiences, & common programming imagery.

HOW THE OLFACTORY NERVES ARE TRAUMATIZED

Blood and perfume have been linked together in magic for thousands of years. The magical writings are full of the different concoctions created for ritual smells. Some of these over the centuries were smells which were discovered to cause people to go into a trance or dissoci-ate. A common wretched smell at Satanic/Illuminati rituals is the smell of human flesh, as it is heated to make candles in wooden ritual cups. It is reported that the stench of human flesh burning can cause dissociation. The power of scents was noticed in ancient China by Li Po. The alchemists studied scents very carefully.

The case at Loudon, Fr. (written about in Chapter 10, pp. 295-296), had nuns going into different dissociative states at the smell of differ-ent flowers. Cinnamon is a widespread scent used in programming deeper parts in a system. The smell of feces & urine is a trauma to a small caged child. Interestingly, urine also contains An-alpha which is the scent element which triggers the human mind sexually. Moriah knows how to use the various scents, incenses etc. Astral magic uses various perfumes.

WHEN MOONCHILD TRAUMAS MISCARRY

According to someone who has helped with the programming and Moon Child ceremonies, occasionally the child while in the womb when traumatized by the Moonchild rituals, retreats into its mind like a cocoon, and develops autism. Autism is an emotional problem where the child withdraws from reality and goes into its own private world of altered states. The programmers for many years did not know why some children developed autism from the trauma rather than MPD (DID), but in some cases it seems related to high 1.0. and genetics. The programmers are not able to reach such children, and essentially all were discarded into mental hospitals or used in rituals, until about 20 years ago when more and more of them were allowed to survive in public. An article "Altered States", based on the Donna William's autobiographical book Somebody Somewhere seems to buttress that autism can be mind-control duds. Williams is both autistic & MPD.

Her book reveals that autistic children have acute sensory perception (intelligence) rather than retardation. There are different types of autism, and the authors do not understand the topic well enough to write much more than this. It is quite possible autism may have several causes, some which do not relate to the failure to become MPD (DID), but may be the result of some other cause. However, the increase in autistic children is believed by the authors to be the result of increased trauma-based mind control. MS (multiple sclerosis) is another side effect, which can stem from brain stem scarring.

RITUAL TORTURE DEVICE

Several victims of Illuminati trauma, remember a special ritual torture device that is put inside a person and causes excruciating pain. It is made from only one kind of wood, a special wood, possibly myrtle. It has a painted spider on it, between two satanic symbols.

REVIEW

In review, the elements that make up a single whole personality-- family history, personal history and memories of abilities, talents and one's self-image have all been stripped from the child when the mind divides itself up into sections walled off by amnesia walls. When the programmers work with each memory part, they have the option to give it all the elements of whatever personality they want it to have. They can even make it into an animal or an inanimate object, because that little fragment has no chance to contradict what it is being programmed to believe. Although the memory part of the brain (which provides a person's personality, is) divided, other parts of the brain function intact. Much of the elements of Monarch Mind Control are based on things that are observed in normal life--dissociation, mental & chemical dependence, denial, charisma, discipline, personality and torture which have been refined into skilled methodologies for controlling a person and then combined into a GROUP PACKAGE.

UNDERSTANDING THE RITUALS AND TRAUMA

Illuminati rituals are based upon the most ancient Mystery religions. The Rothschild's, like the ancient Canaanite Mystery rituals, and use Acadian-Hittite-Canaanite-Babylonian rituals. The rituals from ancient Egypt are also heavily used by the Illuminati. The Collins-Sinclair's type Illuminati bloodlines and some of the other Illuminati families with a northern European/Celtic background, are very much into Druid rituals. Understand that historically, the Druids gave up paganism for the truth of Christ, but that now neo-paganism would have people return to what the Celtic leadership gave up about two thousand years ago. The one participant of high level satanic ritual drew several pictures of hearts which her coven placed into jars.

Some illustrations from the Egyptian Book of the Dead are included to show that the rituals of keeping hearts in a jar is straight from the Egyptian Book of the Dead. The heart was placed in a jar for weighing it for judgment. The twin (mirror-image) goddess Maat at times stands beside the scales, and at the same time Maat is also placed onto one side of the scale. This is similar to Christ judging a person, while also being the standard against which a person is judged. In the Papyrus of Qenna the head of Anubis is on the beam and the ape, wearing disk and crescent, is seated upon a pylon-shaped pedestal beside the balance. Another picture shows Horus holding Maat in his hand, weighing the heart in the presence of the Maat goddesses, and Anubis, who is holding the deceased by the hand, is presenting the heart to Osiris while Isis and Nephthys in the forms of apes sit nearby. The drawing of the ritual stick shows what one type of stick used in Satanic rituals looks like.

CHAPTER 3

THE USE OF DRUGS

The science of Pharmacology (drugs) has given the Programmers a vast array of mind-altering and body-altering drugs. Some of the drugs are not used to directly alter the mind, but to change the body (make the skin burn), or make the person vomit, or some other reaction that can be harnessed to further their nefarious programming goals. If they want a little girl to develop breasts they might give her hormones. Neuroscientists are now familiar with chemicals which cause personality traits.

If one wants to create raving paranoia, simply provide the brain with too much dopamine in the emotional centers of the brain and too little dopamine in the seat of reasoning area of the brain. Reduce serotonin in the person and the person will be unable to connect disagreeable consequences with what provoked them. In other words, they can't protect themselves from danger.

Thorazine was used regularly at the CIA's Jonestown, Guyana group control experiment. Survivors of Jonestown have testified as to its effectiveness. After this gruesome experiment in mind control came to its end with a massacre, large amounts of drugs were discovered. Just one footlocker at Jonestown alone contained 11,000 doses. The authorities prevented chemical autopsies of the bodies to insure secrecy of this sophisticated concentration camp which was used for medical and psychiatric experimentation by the CIA.

An examination of the drugs that are used in mental hospitals to alter the minds of patients offers a clear indication of what is being used in the Monarch Mind Control programming.

DRUGS USED FOR MIND CONTROL

The CIA/Illuminati programming centers have more than 600-700 different drugs at their disposal.

They can make a person feel like he is in heaven, or burning in hell. The drugs are at times used with elaborate light, sound and motion shows that produce whatever effect the programmer wants to produce.

They can make a person believe he is shrinking, or that he is double with mirrors, or that he is dying. Many of the new synthetic drugs are known only to the Illuminati/Intelligence community.

A partial list of the drugs available for their mind control, aka MK Ultra Programming, is found in Appendix B. This list comes from CIA documents obtained from the Freedom of Information Act and from what Multiples used as Programmers remember.

HERBS

When the victim's body is saturated with all the drugs they can assimilate, they will receive herbs, which often have a drug effect.

- Ayahuasca - a vine of Brazil whose alkaloids such as Telapatin are said to produce a telepathic state where the recipient can see through people like glass and read their minds.
- Bayberry - hemorrhaging
- Calamas - part of a cerebral tonic
- Cayenne Pepper - stimulant
- Charcoal - absorbent cleanser
- Caladium Sequinum - injected into body parts to cause excruciating pain
- Clove Oil - placed in nose for relief from the pain of dental tortures
- Hemlock - a poison, used more to kill than for programming
- Hops - sleep aid aka Beerflower

- Lady's Slipper - relaxant
- Kava Kava - sedative

- Mistletoe - for dizziness, and lower blood pressure
- Narcissus - an aphrodisiac for males
- Opium - enchanting trip
- Potions - made from roots, powders, dried blood and animal parts are given
- Rosemary - mild heart tonic
- Saffron - sedative
- Sage - part of a cerebral tonic
- Sandalwood & Henbane - when burned the fumes cause convulsions & temp. insanity
- Skullcap - relaxant
- Sunflower Seed Oil - this may be used to help with brain stem scarring
- Valarium Root - works just like Valarium, also helps cramps
- Witch Hazel - hemorrhaging
- Yerba Mate - part of a cerebral tonic

A BRIEF HISTORY OF THE USE

Religious groups, shamans, medicine men, witches and cults have been using mind altering drugs throughout history. The medieval witches used potions of hemlock and aconite for their flying ointments. These are herbs, natural drugs, which will create delirium. Contemporary witnesses reported that covens during the medieval ages would apply the potion of hemlock and aconite to cause their new witch to go delirious, and then would transport the person to the Sabbat, where they would be told they flew there.

The Haitian satanic Vodoun cult, which has been manipulated by the CIA/Illuminati, has sorcerers called bokors. The Vodoun cult in Haiti is being used for trauma-based mind control. One of the items of the cult is to take the plant Datura stramonium and add this plant with other things. The plant is the active ingredient of a potent psychoactive drug, the "zombie cucumber" which produces amnesia and a pseudo-death of the victim. The brain doesn't die, but the mind is shut off.
The victim is brought back to life as a zombie--a slave of the bokor. The powder to create a zombi is called zombificant in French-Creole.

The ceremonies to kill and resurrect the zombie are full of magic and demonology also.

Magic, drugs and demonology have always gone hand in hand. Drugs remove the part of the will that prevents demonic possession. Drugs are considered powerful demonizing substances by the those skilled in demonology. If demonic possession is seen as part of mind-control, then cocaine, hashish, crack, and some of the other drugs are part of the effort to enslave people. The power of magic to kill, just as the power of faith can heal, will be discussed in chapter 10.

In Basutoland in Drakersbergs, the Zulu witchdoctors use drugs and trauma to create tokoloshes (mind-controlled zombie slaves). It is said that in recent years, they are using less children and more baboons and monkeys to get tokoloshes. The point is that drugs have been and continue to be used by the occult world for controlling people.

The intelligence agencies working through the U.S. government financed drug research. An example is that Dr. Beecher of Harvard University was given via the U.S. Army Surgeon General's Office $150,000 to investigate "the development and application of drugs which will aid in the establishment of psychological control."

Research into drugs for mind-control began in 1947 at Bethesda Naval Hospital in Maryland. A CIA report described this research as *"to isolate and synthesize pure drugs for use in effecting psychological entry and control of the individual."* At the California Medical Facility at Vacaville, Dr. Arthur Nugent, conducted research into drugs for mind control under the auspices of the CIA.

The Bureau of Narcotics worked with the CIA to establish "safe houses" where drugs which were seized were given to victims. Some other hospitals which began working with the intelligence agencies with dispensing drugs for mind control include Mount Sinai Hospital, Boston Psychopathic Hospital, University of Illinois, University of Michigan, University of Minnesota, Valley Forge General Hospital, Detroit Psychopathic Clinic, Mayo Clinic, the National Institute of

Health, and Letterman Hospital in the Presidio, CA.

The military did drug research/programming at the Army Chemical School in Ft. McClellan, AL and at the Edgewood Chemical Center. In 1958, Dr. Louis Gottschalk, working for the CIA suggested that addictive drugs be used to control people. Some GIs who became addicted to pain killing drugs were subsequently blackmailed by withholding the painkillers until they complied with the demands asked of them.

Cocaine has been frequently given to Monarch slaves to get them addicted and give their handlers more control over them. There is spray cocaine, and powdered cocaine, etc. Because the Monarch slaves are used to haul drugs and to launder the drug money, they are right in the middle of large supplies of drugs. If you hear the expression "The snow is falling" it is the Network's lingo for cocaine.

Cocaine is reported to give people a feeling of power and to act as an aphrodisiac.

APPLICATIONS FOR DRUGS IN PROGRAMMING

Drugs are used during programming. Although drugs used to assist programming mean nothing to the common person, they each have a specific purpose within a certain type of programming.

Some specific uses for drugs during programming include:

- Putting People Into A Trance
- Teaching Alters To Go Deeper Into A Trance To Escape Drug Effects And Pain
- Enhancing The Trauma
- Inducing Out of Body Experiences
- Creating Pain
- Creating Blood Vessels That Hurt
- Controlling Histamine Production
- Helping Create Illusions (No Hands, No Feet, No Face, etc.)
- Teaching Alters To Stay In Position

- To Assist Other Programming Modalities, Such As High Tech Harmonic Machines Which Implant Thoughts
- Hormones (Speeding Up Sexual Growth Or Other Body Developments)
- To Enhance Or Reduce Memory
- To Build The Image Of The Programmer's Power

At this point, it is appropriate to point out that the personalities of a multiple do not respond uniformly to the same dose of the same drug. Understanding how a drug will effect particular alters is a science in itself. If an alter is holding the body, it will receive more of the effect of a drug.

Let's say Paraldehyde is given to a multiple. A possible reaction would be that some alters will feel no effect, some will be sedated to a drunken stupor, and child alters may be unconscious or hyperactive. Chloral hydrate might put some alters to sleep while others remain wide awake. Sometimes the personality holding the body may fight the influence of a drug to keep the body.

Prochlorperazine is sometimes given by therapists to help alters cope with nausea and vomiting. Most alters will be programmed not to accept drugs except from their master. Lithium suppresses alter switching in some systems. An alter to "protect" the system from the therapist's helpful medications may develop "allergic" responses. Alcohol is a drug. The reaction of an alter System to it will again be varied. Child alters may become unconscious, while the adult alters don't even become inebriated by large quantities of hard liquor.

Within males, dangerous violent personalities may take the body. In the medical world, often an approximate correct dosage will work. However, with the programming the doses must be extremely fine tuned. Some of the best skilled medical doctors and assistants help with the programming. The Illuminati will initially give the small child a small dose of a drug. They will chart its effect, give it a urinalysis to see how long it stays in the body etc. This is just the testing stage, they are not doing any programming. A number of drugs will be tested, but only one at a time. They clear a child's body of a drug before they give it another one. They prefer not to mix meds. They will start small to insure they don't overdose and then increase the dosage until they notice the correct behavior pattern. This will be charted in detail on the slave's chart.

Each child's body chemistry is different, so the suggested dosages are only ball park figures which are not precise enough. If too much of a drug is given, the programmers can easily turn a child into a psychotic basket case.

One of the secrets of the Illuminati/Intelligence agencies is that they have secret antidotes for most medications, which, if they have to give them to a child, then they will. They will use an antidote, for instance, to keep a child from going into heart failure. The Programmers will have some helpful drugs and herbs on stock too. It is reported that Glutamic Acid (1000 mg. 3 times/day) will take care of the intense headaches that alters get from lots of switching. Witch hazel leaves and comfrey root will help internal bleeding.

PUTTING PEOPLE INTO A TRANCE

About 90% of the population can be placed into the somnambulistic hypnotic trance, the deepest possible, simply by giving them hypnotic drugs. The list in Appendix B gives over 2 dozen drugs that can be used to assist taking someone in hypnotic trance. Special drugs have been designed which will place someone into a deep trance very quickly.

If an alter is not being cooperative when they are accessed, they can be locked in place mentally and given a quick shot of a fast-acting hypnotic-inducing drug. One drug which was popular for programming was Demerol, which would be administered intravenously (by IV). It takes about 5-7 minutes to take full effect after administration via an I.V.

The dosage can be administered so that the effect remains until the programming session is over. It may be administered about every half hour if appropriate. Children will receive 1 to 2.2 mg/kg dose.

Another drug, a truth serum, also consistently works on people making them totally compliant to any directive. Under Baradanga people will give their bank account numbers and anything else a person might want.

These type of drugs are almost sufficient in themselves to get compliance out of a person. If one realizes that these drugs are used in conjunction to torture, elaborate systems of lies and deception, traumabonds, and all the rest of the sciences of mind-control used in the programming, it is easy to see how they are producing totally compliant human robots.

TEACHING ALTERS TO GO DEEPER INTO A TRANCE TO ESCAPE DRUG EFFECTS AND PAIN

Much of the training in this area is based upon the child's horror and fear toward the all powerful master programmer. When the programmer wants the child's alters to learn to trance deeper, he will give a drug that the alter doesn't like. The child's alter will then be told to go deeper into the mind if they want to escape the effect of the drug.

This enforces the dissociative state being trained for the alter. The suggestion or story line that is given to the alter is frequently the picture of a train. The child is told that the conductor is at the front of the train, but he must move to the back of the train through the train cars. The child is taught to count cars when they go by as if they were steps in the mind.

This is training the child to descend into deeper levels of the subconscious. The train illustration has been used by programmers when they want the child to remember the drug experience. The programmer wants this experience remembered, at least for a while, because it helps increase the child's fear.

If the programmer wants the child to forget the drug experience while learning trance depths, then the imagery of a plane taking off and disappearing in the clouds works.

ENHANCING THE TRAUMA

Drugs will be used to enhance the spinning effect when the mind is being programmed to have vortexes and to set up traps within the slave's mind. One particular drug enhances the trauma by 100 times.

Drugs can be useful for instance, to enhance a child's terror of the experience of this child being placed in a small box in the fetal position for 24 hours. This helps shorten the programming time, and it also makes the programming more intense. The programmers know what antidotes to give to pull the child out of the enhancement. Marijuana enhances perception of color and noise, but it is not used to enhance trauma.

The mind does not program well under marijuana. That is why there has been such a big campaign to keep it illegal, even though many studies show it to be safer than alcohol.

PRODUCING OUT OF BODY EXPERIENCES

Various hallucinogenic drugs, LSD included, will produce an out of body experience for the victim, if the drugs are administered correctly. The Programmer will prepare the victim with various information and story lines during the administration of the drug.

When Monarch slaves are being deprogrammed, they may have a memory where their skin feels inflamed and itchy, like a bad mosquito bite.

The experience may also have the sensation of floating in an unreal world. This may well be an LSD trip given the slave during experimentation and programming. The CIA was using LSD beginning in the very early part of the 1950s. Several victims report that some type of potion causes a person to dream while they are awake.
PCP which is "angel dust" is one way to disconnect the cortex from the limbic system and go into an altered state.

CREATING PAIN

This is done with a long list of drugs. Drops of salt water and pepper water are applied to the eyes of victims to make their eyes sting. Another pain in the eye takes place when lights are flashed signaling, "I love you, I love you not." The child is pulled two ways by this message.

Dr. Green (Mengele) enjoyed pulling daisy petals while saying these words. If the last petal was "I love you not," the child would be put to death. Surviving children were left traumatized.

CREATING BLOOD VESSELS THAT HURT

Blood pressure is raised by drugs and then certain drugs are added which make the veins burn. The alter is taught to cut the burning veins. This is programming which is laid in to control the slave from straying from the script he or she is given. If they stray, then a cutting program is activated which was laid in via a combination of drugs in the method just stated.

CONTROLLING HISTAMINE PRODUCTION

The control of histamine production is an important secret ingredient to the Monarch Mind Control. The breast implants placed into women help stimulate histamine production, which is used in conjunction with drug-assisted programming (See Chapter 8.)

HELPING CREATE ILLUSIONS (NO HANDS, NO FEET, NO FACE, ETC.)

A programmer working with a hallucinogenic drug can make an alter believe that it has lost a particular body part. Because most of these alters have little memory or no memory and little frame of reference, what they are told while under the influence of drugs seems very real to them.
Teaching Alters To Stay In Position

Some alters don't like to stay in position. But through the use of drugs, and the side effect of drugs, they soon learn the importance of staying in position. If they are disobedient, the memory of the bad side effects from not staying in position in the mind can be pulled up by a code and the alter can relive the pain from having disobediently moved from position.

This is very effective in teaching alters to stay in their little position that is assigned them in the mind.

TO ASSIST OTHER PROGRAMMING MODALITIES, SUCH AS HIGH TECH HARMONIC MACHINES WHICH IMPLANT THOUGHTS

The machines are used in conjunction with designer drugs. An example of how drugs can be important is as follows:

The neurons in the hippocampus which is part of the memory process use acetylcholine. Drugs that block acetylcholine interfere with memory. The neurons and the chemical neural transmitters are understood much better today. Where and how a thought is created in the brain is understood by the programmers in detail. No one is in a position to physically prevent the Illuminati and others from taking their children and others to labs where chemicals and harmonics can be used in sophisticated computer guided ways to implant thoughts into the children's minds. As the child's brain is shaped according to its environment, the level of everyday brain chemicals and the shape of the various areas of the brain can be determined by the programmers.

This is why a recent article on Prozac (Newsweek, Feb. 7, 1994) uses a quote from Alice In Wonderland for its title, "One pill makes you larger, and one pill makes you small".

This article (on page 38) quotes brain researcher Restak, "For the first time, we will be in a position to design our own brain." On the previous page in big letters it reads, "Scientific insights into the brain are raising the prospect of made-to-order, off-the-shelf personalities."
Another programming modality assisted by drugs is behavior modification. Aversion therapy using a vomit-inducing drug is used on chil-

dren.

Another example of drugs helping assist programming is to give someone LSD and then interview the child while it is hallucinating. The hallucinations are then used as programming building blocks by using hypnotic techniques. One way to build on a LSD trip is to tell the child if they ever do a particular thing (such as touch programming, remember programming, and integrate parts, etc.) the victim is to go crazy and hallucinate like they are presently doing. This means that they will be locked up in a crazy house for the rest of their life.

Rather than be put in straight-jackets with other crazy people it would be better for the person to commit suicide. By constantly reinforcing this message, some alters will adopt the script "that they are doing the body good to kill it if any alter personality touches the programming," because otherwise the body will be locked up in a crazy house.

Drugs are used in programming to establish a pattern or a script. There must be a pattern of dissociation. Parts can't just dissociate into nothing, otherwise there would be nothing to build on. Drugs will play a major role in the structuring of the alter system, which is covered in Chapter 7.

The child doesn't know where the effect of the drug is coming from. The programmer will take credit for the power of the drug. Whoever administers the drug has power in the child's mind. The mind wants to be safe.

I am familiar with a recent example here in Oregon of someone who escaped from being sacrificed at a Satanic Ritual. The legal system told the woman she was crazy when she reported to the police that she had escaped from a Satanic Ritual where they were going to sacrifice her. To control her, the judge ordered 3 types of antipsychotics, twice the normal dose of two kinds of lithium carbonate to put her into a lethargic stupor, Paxil as an antidepressant, and Benztropine Mesylate as an anti-Parkinson agent. The antipsychotics were Thiothixene, Thioridazine Hydrochloride, and Perphenazine which are all addictive.

This woman may or may not be a multiple. But this clearly shows the type of mental control via drugs that could be slapped onto someone who dares report Satanic activity to an establishment which has been sadly corrupted from top to bottom. One victim of government mind control tried to get free. The first psychiatrist the person tried to go to was cooperating with U.S. Intelligence and gave her Stelazine, which aggravated the victim's situation. When the victim spied a general's uniform in the closet of this psychiatrist, she got another psychiatrist, who unfortunately turned out to be an ex-DoD employee. He placed her on Haldol Decanoate, Klonopin, and Benzatropine. The combined effect of these drugs is to erase memory, and create a dissociative disorder.

All of the drugs were highly addicted. Another fleeing victim was given Trazodone by a physician who was cooperating with the Intelligence agencies. This almost gave the victim a heart attack because it aggravated her heart condition. And yet another escaping victim apparently also fell prey to dirty CIA doctors who were practicing in public without warning people of their intelligence connections. This victim was given a combination of Compazine and Xanax, in dosages that the Physicians Desk Reference warns against. The doctor, who prescribed this, worked out of an office named after an MK Ultra programmer. There are other important things to mention about when drugs are used in Monarch programming.

Some of the cautions that the programmers are alert to include:

A) Watching the heart so that it doesn't stop. Many of the children who have been programmed have died from heart failure. The programmers are very careful to have heart monitors on the victim, and to have paddles ready to revive the body. Because so much of their drugging affects the heart, they accept that they will lose a few to heart failure.

B) Making sure that drugs aren't given to children who are allergic to them. The programmers take the time to insure that they have the family histories of allergies to drugs, and they will test the children too, before proceeding with drugs. They not only learn the family & individual responses to drugs, but they can test during programming to determine a drug's blood level in a child. For instance, pentobarbital at a blood level of 5 mcg/ml aids hypnosis, at 15 makes the victim comatose with reflexes, and at 30 makes the person comatose w/ extreme difficulty in breathing. In everyday life, 30 mcg/ml would kill the child. Pentobarbital blood levels can be tested by an enzyme multiplied immunoassay technique. For longer-acting Phenobarbital gas chromatography is used. TCA's are tested by radioimmunoassay, high-perf. liquid chromatography & thin layer chromatography. Some hypnotics are tested by colorimetry, photometry, & spectrophotometry.

C) Switching to herbs when the body is saturated with drugs. When the child's body has had all the manufactured drugs it can absorb, the programmers switch to a vast collection of natural herbs.

D) Providing the antidote for AIDS. Monarch slaves are routinely given the antidote for AIDS and have been since the 1960s-1970s.

E) Knowing how much of a drug each part can take, small young alters can't take as much. Multiples within a single system have varying levels of tolerance toward drugs. A small child alter may be killed by an adult dosage, even though the age of the body is that of an adult. The programmers are acutely aware of how to deal with multiple personalities.

F) Providing salt to balance the electrolytes in the mind of a programmed multiple personality. An electrolyte imbalance can cause a multiple personality's mind to go wacky and start spinning. The Multiple could possibly go into shock and die. The programmers are very experienced in understanding the unique requirements of a multiple personality.

G) An important plant extract for watching brain wave activity is the large plant enzyme horseradish peroxidase (HRP).

Perhaps it would be worthwhile to briefly mention that all the major chemical and drug companies are run by the Illuminati.

It would take another book to explain who controls what and how they connect in, and this author could write it. Instead, we will try to give a quick over view. Rather than cover 2 dozen large drug companies, three major drug companies have been randomly selected to show a quick view of how all the drug companies are deeply involved with Monarch mind-control programming.

Since the purpose of this book is to show how the mind control is done, this sample of names is given only to convey to the reader that the drugs that the Illuminati/Intelligence agencies need are never in short supply, **and** the labs to develop designer drugs for mind-control are not in short supply either.

ELI LILLY CO. -- Trustee of Eli Lilly Endowment Walter William Wilson - Illuminati, married to Helen Scudder (of the wealthy powerful Scudder family), prominent partner of Morgan, Stanley & Co. controlled by Henry Morgan also a member of the Illuminati. Executive Vice-pres. of Eli Lilly Landrum Bolling, represented Eli Lilly at the secret annual Dartmouth conferences, overseen by the Illuminati. Chairman of Eli Lilly Richard D. Wood, dir, of the Rockefeller's Standard Oil, Chemical Bank of NY, and the American Enterprise Institute for Public Policy Research. Dir. Eli Lilly C. William Verity, Jr., director. Chase Manhattan Bank and assoc. with U.S. intelligence, and works with Mrs. Rockefeller as a member of USTEC. Dan Quayle and George Bush (CIA director and Monarch handler) have been part of Eli Lilly management too.

MONSANTO CHEMICAL COMPANY -- President Earle H. Harbison, Jr.-CIA. and director of Bethesda General Hospital where they program Monarch slaves. He is also the president of the Mental Health Association.

STERLING DRUG CO. (an I.G. Farben spinoff) -- connected to the Krupp Illuminati family. Chairman W. Clark Wescoe, dir of the super secret Tinker Foundation which is a CIA foundation. Dir. Gordon T. Wallis, Illuminati, dir, of the Fed. Reserve Bank of NY, CFR, Director Martha T. Muse, CIA, pres. of the Tinker Foundation, dir. of the Order of St. John of Jerusalem (Knights of Malta), and dir. of

Georgetown Center for Strategic Studies.

SUMMARY

As the reader can see, the use of drugs in the Monarch Trauma-based Mind Control is extensive and requires skilled technicians, nurses, and doctors. Because of the long-held control by the Illuminati families over narcotics and drug manufacture/sales, there is no difficulty for the programmers to get large quantities of secret designer drugs. The minor occult cults have to get by with a more limited supply of mind altering drugs, unless they directly connect in with the bigger picture. The power of drugs to control a person's life is not absolute , although someone who lives with a cocaine addict or alcoholic might disagree, but when coupled with all the other methods in a sophisticated system of mind-control, drugs just further reinforce the absolute power of the Illuminati over an individual.

CHAPTER 4

UNDERSTANDING THE BASICS OF HYPNOSIS

Dissociation is used as a defense to protect a person from overwhelming pain and trauma. It is a natural ability of the brain. Hypnosis or hypnotic trance is a form of dissociation. There are a number of types of dissociation: amnesia, somnambulistic states, localized paralyses, anesthesia's, and hallucinations. Hypnosis can reproduce all of these dissociative states. The mind naturally hypnotizes itself under various conditions. Perhaps the reader has been driving along a familiar road and the next thing you knew you were arriving home, having driven in a trance. Now let's suppose you are driving to a movie and you are discussing next week's plans with your wife. The complex thinking required to drive just happens. You are awake talking to your wife, and yet on another level you were in trance driving the car. You as a subject were both in hypnotic trance (driving) and awake (talking about plans). There are 5 levels to the subconscious that the mind will naturally dissociate to. The other deeper levels require help to access. People naturally can think on two levels.

Because people's minds function on multiple levels and there is a continua on a spectrum that runs from conscious to unconscious, it is often difficult to pinpoint just exactly what state of mind the brain is in at a certain point, because there is no single answer. A light trance is where a person is daydreaming about his girlfriend. A moderate trance is where he imagines he is in bed. A deep trance is where he physically feels he is in bed with his girlfriend. Sleep is where one dreams of being in bed. Behavior modification is carried out in the light to deep trances. The deep trance is a very creative level. Hypnosis appears to affect several areas of the brain. The brain stem is modified into the hypnotic state, and the midbrain centers are inhibited so that other areas--the motor, sensory and memory areas can be manipulated. Further not all hypnosis works the same way.

Hypnosis can be used on the intellectual part of the mind, the social-spiritual part of the mind, and the primitive reproductive part of the mind. The skilled hypnotist will decide which area he wants and how to work with that area. Both Christians and Illuminati members who are skilled in understanding demonology, believe that there is a demonic side to hypnosis also. It should come as no shock to people that in the World Book Encyclopedia hypnosis is listed under Magic as a related article, but not under Medicine.

Some Christians class hypnosis as a form of divination and enchantment. It certainly can be a form of control. In occultist William Bernard Crow's book Witchcraft, Magic & Occultism, it lists hypnotism as an occult science. There is open debate whether hypnotism is simply part of the brain's natural abilities or if supernatural elements are part of the process. There is no debate that historically, hypnosis for centuries has been the guarded secret of the occult world.

During shock or stress, the body's limbic-hypothalamic-pituitary-adrenal system, releases substances which encode all the internal and external pieces of information being sensed into a deep level of consciousness. These memories often become dissociated from normal states of consciousness. In other words, when the mind-body returns to this state (where it was in during shock/stress) the mind can re-access those memories. However, until the mind returns to this shocked state, it doesn't pick up the information it has embedded. The Monarch programmers are acutely aware of how the mind functions, and how information and memories can be trapped in the mind. There are different neurophysiologic states. Also there are said to be 12 levels to the subconscious mind. Then on top of this the mind has the ability to create amnesia barriers.

Hypnosis is a valuable tool to move the mind to different neurophysiologic states and to get the mind to different levels of the subconscious mind. Hypnosis can also play a role in working around amnesia, since both are types of dissociation. Hyperventilation helps a person induct into a hypnotic trance. Torture, depersonalization, fear and acute anxiety stimulate the body to hyperventilate. So the fear, torture and depersonalization are aids for the hypnotist to help induct a person into a hypnotic trance. Hypnotic cues can be given to cause the body to go into various dissociative states. This could be a post-hypnotic suggestion that causes hyperventilation and an accompanying trance state. Hypnotic cues that are tied to every day objects enhance the programming. Everything in life becomes a cue to reinforce the programming. That may seem on the surface to be an exaggeration, but it is only slightly enlarged from the truth.

The programmers do in fact examine a person's life, and then tailor their cues to what the person will be around. For instance, the programmer may force the child to smoke and then tell it that every time they blow out smoke they will think about their master. The programmed alters don't dare not to smoke on fear that they will be punished. The smoking in turn reinforces the power of the hypnotist/ master. Much of the good that therapy can do is in effect to de-trance or dehypnotize clients. Most of the alters of a Monarch system go their entire lives in trance. Common objects in a person's life that can be hypnotically given a programming meaning include music, tones, colors, the sight of a book or Bible, the pyramid on the back of a dollar bill, pictures of God, silk scarves, jewelry, lights, sounds, TV programs, and countless other things. The limit to this is simply the programmer's creativity. The power of hypnosis is often underrated because the power of the mind is underrated.

The mind can decide to control its breathing, heart beat, blood pressure and other things that were once thought to be involuntary. The brain produces a substance which is a tiny peptide molecule called encephalin which acts just like morphine and reduces pain. The brain can be hypnotically trained to release encephalin so that the brain doesn't perceive pain. A common hypnotic device for washing away pain is running water. The victim is hypnotically told to go to a waterfall and wash their pain away. According to a programmer the average healing rate is 3 times quicker under hypnosis than without. The fantastic abilities of the mind to control what happens to it are very remarkable (such as its natural healing abilities), but most of this is being kept a National Secret so that it can be used against humanity to enslave us to demonic-empowered power hungry monsters, rather than to benefit humanity. Several people in intelligence agencies quietly bemoan the fact that secret research could be helping humanity instead of controlling it.

The human mind has been found to be like an immense symphony orchestra, each part doing what it does best under the guidance of a director part similar to the conductor of an orchestra. A non-multiple's brain delegates responsibility to parts of his brain yet retains control over the process. His mind will shift from one ego state to another, & still retain its identity. In contrast, the multiple's brain also delegates responsibility and shifts from one ego state to another, BUT doesn't retain a "cohesive selfhood" or self-identity. The mental mechanisms are similar, but the experience is vastly different. Rather than an orchestra playing together, the multiple's brain is full of competing isolated parts, instruments so to speak, that are playing in isolation. Out of the chaos of all these independent amnesic parts, the programmer through hypnosis & fear then becomes the conductor to help bring order out of chaos. If the multiple is to regain a chance to orchestrate their own life again, they must re-establish communication between the different parts of what should have been their own orchestra, and get internal people to harmonize their music of life.

Good programmers do not need to formally induct their victim into hypnosis. However, if they need to, the Monarch slaves are well conditioned to respond to numbers being counted and fingers being snapped. Hypnosis was a well developed art by the early 20th century. And testing and refining continued all along. For instance, the. U.S. military was conducting extensive tests of subjects under hypnosis during W.W. II. In spite of all this, the CIA was still seeking better rapid induction techniques for their slaves during the 1950s. MK Ultra Subproject 128 dealt with rapid induction techniques, especially Subproject 128-1.

Some of their drug testing was done at Lexington, KT Detention Hospital. The ability to distinguish between magic and hypnotism may not exist for the child in situations where they are witnesses to the power of hypnotism exercised by a programmer. This makes the adult programmer, who is a big person look all powerful. Another danger inherent in hypnosis are complications, side effects, that hit a percentage of those who are subjected to it. Hilgard (1974) discovered 31% of the 120 university students participating in a study of hypnosis had complications that lasted from 5 min. to 3 hours after trance, which included headaches, dizziness, nausea and stiff necks.

One of my sources is aware of one woman who, after the one & only hypnotic session she was the subject of, developed the complication of having nightmares of snakes crawling all over her. For further study the reader may want to read MacHovec, Frank. "Hypnosis Complications, Risk Factors, and Prevention" American Journal of Clinical Hypnosis. Vol. 31, No.1, July, '88, p. 40.

Regular gentle electrical stimulation in many parts of the brain including the lower part of the reticular formation can change the state of consciousness from alert to sleepy. An electrical band attached to a box is sometimes placed on the victim to produce a hypnotic state. There are several ways to alter a person's state of consciousness, but the most popular one by Monarch handlers is to use a combination of drugs and hypnosis. Drugs are used to facilitate hypnosis. Modern drugs do almost all the work for the hypnotist. They place the person in an altered state and make them willing to take any order. Often survivors remember orange or grape drinks, or something else which they were given, which were used to give the child drugs. One Monarch slave (Cathy O'Brien) wrote about having been given hypnotic drugs via a Grasshopper ice cream drink.

Occasionally, hypnosis must be carried out by the programmers on unwilling subjects. They have 3 major ways to get around this. They can induce hypnosis by disguising what the hypnotist is doing, they can wait until the person is asleep and talk to him while asleep, or they can administer drugs. The Network also has some high-tech equipment which stimulates the orgiastic state, sexual ecstasy, part of the brain. By moving the body into this state, the mind opens up all the unconscious states. Then sophisticated brain wave machines program thoughts into the person. A computer disk is put into the electric shock machine and it runs a program that sends electric jolts down six nodes. The brain's reticular formation serves as the brain's mechanism involved in regulating alertness and awareness.

Various kinds of stimuli will enter the brain through its various methods of sensing and learning. With total sensory deprivation (done by placing the victim in a salt water tank with electrodes that shock the body until it stops all movement) the reticular formation will place the mind into a primitive state of consciousness where the programmers can place in post-hypnotic commands to do something on a certain date. The end time programming, that has Monarch slaves doing something at a specific date to create anarchy or to help the Anti-Christ come to power has been put in at this level. As previously mentioned, this level achieved by total sensory deprivation of the Monarch slave is the same primitive level as the brain's commands to keep the heart beating. Depending on what type of signals are coming in to it from the various sensing agents of the brain, the reticular formation will then make a decision what state of consciousness to place the mind in. If the reticular formation does not send out "alert" signals, then the brain will get sleepy. Damage to the reticular formation can cause a coma.

The two thalamus lie just above the brain stem. The right and left thalamus are the brain's selective attention mechanism. That is to say, they decide what it is important for the brain to focus its attention on. The right thalamus is connected to attention to visual shapes and the left to our attention to things describable in words. Ten to fifteen repetitions at one second intervals are enough to cause the brain to lose interest in something. At this point the neuron's in the reticular formation quit paying attention to whatever it is. For instance, your brain will listen to a clock tick for only 15 intervals before it quits listening to a clock in the room. But the brain's alertness can be reactivated by a strong and sudden stimulus like a loud sound or a flash of light. This is why 3 gunshots or 3 flashes of light are used as standard access triggers for Monarch slaves. Three was also found to be the best number to get the job done.

THE HISTORY OF HYPNOSIS FOR PROGRAMMING

A Masonic magazine for higher Masonic rites where sex magic is performed entitled Freemasonry Universal, Vol. 5, 1929, p. 58 states,

"Certain Forces are sent through the candidate's body during the ceremony, especially at the moment when he is created, received and constituted an Entered Apprentice Freemason. Certain parts of the Lodge have been heavily charged with magnetic force especially in order that the Candidate may absorb as much as possible of this force. The first object of this curious method of preparation is to expose to this influence those various parts of the body which are especially used in the ceremony. In ancient Egypt, there was another reason for these preparations, for a weak current of physical electricity was sent through the candidate by means of a rod or sword with which he was touched at certain points. It is partly on this account that at this first initiation the candidate is deprived of all metals since they may very easily interfere with the flow of currents."

Long story short, the Masonic lodges have been using hypnotism and electric shock in their initiation rituals for a long time. The combination of fear and hypnotism combine to help seal the lips of an initiate from telling what in some lodges are secrets of criminal activity. The Brahmin caste in India practice yoga, and other meditations where they regularly go into altered states of consciousness. Centuries ago, the Brahmin fakirs learned about drugs, tortures, and magical methodologies to produce hallucinations and altered states of consciousness. The worship of Bacchus in the west and Shiva in the east were similar, as were the bloodthirsty rites of Kali and Moloch. Occultists in India have also gone to cemeteries for centuries, like the Illuminati to draw spiritual power from graves. When eastern and western occultists linked up they realized they had a great deal in common.

The ancient Egyptian writings many centuries B.C. talk about the third eye and temple trances. Hypnosis appears to have been practiced in these ancient temples. All over the world, altered states of consciousness have been used. The feared Scandinavian warriors called Berserkers were in a mildly-programmed altered state of consciousness which made them fearless.

HOW TO PROGRAM WITH HYPNOSI

George Estabrooks was the first major hypnotist to publicly recognize the potential for hypnosis. He contacted MI-6 and other military and intelligence groups in hopes he could interest them in the military and intelligence potentials of hypnosis. What was George Estabrooks connection to the Illuminati? George Estabrooks was a Rhodes Scholar, which is an entry-level group for the Illuminati. For those who haven't studied this, it would be appropriate to give a brief explanation of these things. The Illuminati in 1919 created the Royal Institute of International Affairs (RIIA). The Astor Illuminati family were major financial backers of the RIIA.

Waldorf Astor was appointed to the RIIA. The American equivalent to the RIIA is the CFR. The RIIA and CFR set up Round Table Groups (based on the King Arthur myths) which were initially named by Cecil Rhodes "Association of Helpers". High ranking Mason/ Illuminatus Cecil Rhodes also created the Rhodes Scholarship to bring select men from the English speaking world and Germany to learn how to bring in the One World Government that the Illuminati has long had planned. The Cliveden Estate of the Cliveden Astors (of the Illuminati) has played an important role in the preparation of Rhodes Scholars. Bill Clinton and Fred Franz, the late president of the Watchtower Society, are two examples of men selected for Rhodes Scholarships. Bill Clinton went through the program.

However, Franz decided not to go to London in order to help lead C.T. Russell's cult as "oracle" after Watchtower Pres. C.T. Russell was ritually killed on Halloween, 1916 and his remains buried under a pyramid. He later served as President himself from 1977-1994. The Watchtower Society leadership is a front for a part of the Illuminati which practices Enochian Magic. The power of Enochian magic is the Watchtowers. A powerful part of Bethel headquarter workers are Multiple Personalities, and have cult alters who speak in Enochian. Some multiples work in the art department and have been secretly placing hidden occult symbolism into Watchtower & Awake! magazines. Now back to Estabrooks, who was also himself part of the Illuminati. In his book "Hypnotism", which came out in 1946, he wrote in his chapter Hypnotism in Warfare (again bear in mind that Estabrooks writes this in 1946 and has been advocating what he writes for perhaps the 15 previous years!)

"This chapter is not taken from a mystery novel. The facts and the ideas presented are, so to speak, too true to be good, but no psychologist of standing would deny the validity of the basic ideas involved. He might, of course, be somewhat startled at our proposed use of these basic ideas and techniques, for he has never given this matter much thought.... The use of hypnotism in warfare represents the cloak and dagger idea at its best--or worst. Even if we did know the answers to some of the weird proposals in this chapter, those answers could never be given for obvious reasons. The reader must use his imagination for specific outcomes in specific cases which have not been made public, probably never will be made public. Any topflight physicist is familiar with the basic laws of atomic fission and he is quite free to discuss those laws. But he may or may not know what is happening on some government research project in this field. If he does know, he is not shouting it from the housetops, probably not even whispering it to his best friend. The same applies to hypnotism in the field of warfare. Our interest here lies in some of the more unfamiliar sides of hypnotism which may make it of use in warfare. Again, no psychologist would deny the existence of such phenomena...."

"The only possible way of determining whether or not a subject will commit a murder in hypnotism is literally to have him commit one.. "

But warfare...undoubtedly will, answer many of these questions. A nation fighting with its back to the wall is not worried over the niceties of ethics [like Nazi Germany]. If hypnotism can be used to advantage, we may rest assured that it will be so employed. Any "accidents" which may occur during the experiments will simply be charged to profit and loss, a very trifling portion of that enormous wastage in human life which is part and parcel of war....

One in every five adult humans can be thrown into the hypnotic trance, somnambulism, of which they will have no memory whatsoever when they awaken.

From the military viewpoint there are a few facts which are of great interest. Can this prospective subject, this 'one-in-five" individual, be hypnotized against his will? Obviously, no prisoner of war will be cooperative if he knows that the hypnotist is looking for military information, nor will any ordinary citizen if he suspects that the operator will use him to blow up a munitions plant. The answer to this very vital question is "yes", though we prefer to say "without his consent" instead of "against his will." We do not need the subject's consent when we wish to hypnotize him, for we use a 'disguised" technique. The standard way to produce hypnotism in the laboratory is with the so-called sleep technique. The operator "talks sleep" to the subject, who eventually relaxes and goes into a trance, talking in his sleep and answering questions.

Now suppose... we attach a blood pressure gauge to the subject's right arm and the psycho galvanic reflex to the palm of his hand, just to make everything look shipshape. These devices are for measuring his ability to relax. We also point out that, of course, the very highest state of relaxation will be his ability actually to fall into a deep sleep while we are talking to him. We also stress the great importance of the ability to relax in this modern world of rush and worry, promising to show him how to get results as one end of these experiments. All this is by way of buildup. Probably not one of our readers, if exposed to this procedure, would realize that this was preparation for hypnotism, but would co-operate willingly in this very interesting psychological experiment.

We then proceed to "talk sleep," much the same as in ordinary hypnosis, carefully avoiding any reference to a trance or making any tests with which the subject might be familiar, all the while checking on blood pressure and psycho galvanic reflex to keep up the front. Finally we make the test of somnambulism, or deep hypnotism. We see if the subject will talk to us in his sleep without awakening. If this does not succeed, the subject wakes up completely, and in this case we simply repeat the experiment, hoping for better luck next time. But if we do succeed, if the individual belongs to the "one-in-five" club, the subject is just as truly hypnotized as by any other method, and from now on everything is plain sailing. By use of the posthypnotic suggestion...we simply say, "Listen carefully. After you wake up I will tap three times on the table with my pencil. You will then have an irresistible impulse to go sound asleep."

The next trance is just that easy to get, and the subject has no idea that it is the pencil which has sent him off. ... But we must go even further than this. Once a person has become accustomed to hypnotism, has been repeatedly hypnotized, it becomes very easy for any operator to throw him into the trance. Obviously this will not do if we are to use hypnotism in warfare. So we plug this gap again by suggestion in the somnambulistic state. We assure the subject that in the future no one will be able to hypnotize him except with the special consent of the operator. This takes care of things very nicely....We sit down with the subject...We are talking about the latest boxing match when the operator taps three times on the table with his pencil. Instantly--and we mean instantly--the subject's eyes close and he's sound "asleep."

While in trance he sees a black dog come into the room, feels the dog, goes to the telephone and tells its owner to come get it. The dog is of course purely imaginary. We give him electric shock which would be torture to a normal person, but he does not even notice it. We straighten him out between two chairs and sit on his chest while he recites poetry. Then we wake him up. He immediately starts talking about that boxing match! A visitor to the laboratory interrupts him.

"What do you know of hypnotism?"

The subject looks surprised, "Why, nothing."

"When were you hypnotized last?"

"I have never been hypnotized."
"Do you realize that you were in a trance just ten minutes ago?"

"Don't be silly! No one has hypnotized me and no one ever can."

"Do you mind if I try?"

"Not at all. If you want to waste your time it's all right with me."

So the visitor, a good hypnotist, tries, but at every test the subject simply opens his eyes with a bored grin. Finally he gives up the attempt and everyone is seated as before. Then the original operator taps on the table with his pencil. Immediately the subject is in deep hypnotism. We now add another concept. We can coach the subject so that in the trance he will behave exactly as in the waking state. Under these circumstances we could defy anyone, even a skilled psychologist, to tell whether the subject was "asleep" or "awake."

There are tests which will tell the story but in warfare we cannot run around sticking pins into everyone we meet just to see if he is normal. So rapid can this shift be from normal to trance state [the programming state], and so "normal" will the subject appear in trance, that the writer has used such a subject as a bridge partner. He plays one hand in trance and one hand "awake" with no one any the wiser. [This happens with Monarch slaves all the time. Few people ever catch on that alters are under trance.]

Suppose we deliberately set up that condition of multiple personality to further the ends of military intelligence. Let us start with a very simple illustration. For example, we can hypnotize a man in a hotel in, say, Rochester. We then explain to him in hypnotism that we wish the numbers and state names of all out-of-state cars parked in the block surrounding the hotel. He is to note these very carefully in his unconscious mind but will have no conscious memory of having done so. Then we awaken him and ask him, in the waking state to go out and get us a tube of toothpaste. He leaves the hotel and wanders around the block in search of that tube.

Finally, he returns, apologizing for his delay, saying that it was necessary for him to go entirely around the block before he noticed a drugstore in the very building itself. This, he says, was very stupid of him but apparently men are made that way. Did he notice anything of interest as he made his walk? "Nothing! Oh, yes, there was a dog fight down at the corner." And he described the battle in detail. We now hypnotize him. He knows what we are seeking and at once proceeds to give us numbers and states of strange cars, very pleased with the fact that he can recall thirteen. He evidently enjoys the game immensely and is quite proud of his memory. Then we awaken him and see what he knows in the conscious state.

"How many cars are there around the building?"

"I don't know."

"What are the numbers of the out-of-state licenses around the building?"

"Good heavens, I have no idea. I think there is a California car near the front entrance, but I have no idea as to its number."

A friend tries his hand. "Now look here. You were hypnotized half an hour ago and you left this room under posthypnotic suggestion." The subject gets irritated. "Look here yourself. I'm getting tired of that silly joke. This is the third time today you've pulled it. All right. I was hypnotized and saw pink elephants all over the lobby. Have it your way." And the subject sits down to a magazine, obviously angry that this man cannot find something more amusing to say. Often the hypnotic subject will react in this manner. Push him just a little too far and he becomes irritated, obviously a trick of the unconscious to end the argument and avoid any danger of being found out.... The reader's very natural reaction is, "Why all this rigmarole?"... There are certain safeguards if we use hypnotism.

First, there is no danger of the agent's selling out. More important would be the conviction of innocence which the man himself had, and this is a great aid in many situations. He would never "act guilty" and if ever accused of seeking information would be quite honestly indignant. This conviction of innocence on the part of a criminal is perhaps his greatest safeguard under questioning by the authorities.

Finally, it would be impossible to "third degree" him and so pick up the links of a chain. This is very important, for the most hardened culprit is always liable to "talk" if the questioners are ruthless enough.

In the instance we are about to outline, we may or may not be dealing with multiple personality.... The little experiment I have just cited could be successful with any good somnambulist and would require about ten hours preparation. The example I now cite would work only with a certain number of the very best somnambulists and instead of ten hours preparation, we had better allow ten months....

Perhaps we had better start by defending our position. Is it unethical? Perhaps, but science merely states the facts.... Now let us return to our presentation. We start with an excellent subject, and he must be just that, one of those rare individuals who accepts and who carries through every suggestion without hesitation. In addition, we need a man or a woman who is highly intelligent and physically tough.

Then we start to develop a case of multiple personality through the use of hypnotism. In his normal waking state, which we will call Personality A, or PA, this individual will become a rapid communist. He will join the party, follow the party line and make himself as objectionable as possible to the authorities. Note that he will be acting in good faith. He is a communist, or rather his PA is a communist and will behave as such. Then we develop Personality B (PB), the secondary personality, the unconscious personality, if you wish, although this is somewhat of a contradiction in terms.

This personality is rabidly American and anti-communist. It has all the information possessed by PA, the normal personality, whereas PA does not have this advantage.... The proper training of a person for this role would be long and tedious, but once he was trained, you would have a super spy compared to which any creation in a mystery story is just plain weak. [This is what the Illuminati have done. They create good Christian fronts, with Illuminati dark alters who can see what the Christians are doing.] *My super spy plays his role as a communist in his waking state, aggressively, consistently, fearlessly. But his PB is a loyal American, and PB has all the memories of PA.*

As a loyal American, he will not hesitate to divulge those memories, and needless to say we will make sure he has the opportunity to do so when occasion demands. Here is how this technique would work .... [skipping this story and several others, we come to:] *We choose a good subject and then let him in on the plot. We disclose to him that he is an excellent hypnotic subject and we wish to use him for counterespionage. We suspect that in the near future someone is going to try hypnosis on him. He is to bluff, to co-operate to the very best of his ability, fake every test that is made and stay wide awake all the time. The test we fear most is that of an analgesia insensitivity to pain.*

So we coach him carefully with posthypnotic suggestions to the effect that even when wide awake and bluffing he will be able to meet every test which may be made here, be it with ammonia under the nose, a needle, or worst of all, the use of electricity, which can be made extremely painful and is easy to use. Under these circumstances it will be virtually impossible to tell whether this man is bluffing or really in trance. [The story continues that the master hypnotist thinks he has got a good subject and has hypnotized him deep. Then the subject tells him that he was only bluffing. The whole affair provides a nightmare for any counterintelligence group using hypnotism. They can be totally bluffed, unless they turn to high tech equipment to see what is really happening.]

Estabrooks also explains how a man can be hypnotized and told he is only testing the preparedness of security. He is told he has a fake bomb, but is really given a real bomb. The subject is sent to a location, and blows up with the real bomb. The subject blows up with the bomb so the evidence of the hypnotic lie is lost.

Hypnosis changes the threshold of the how the senses perceive. Sensitivity can be increased or decreased, hallucinations can be perceived even though there is the absence of any appropriate stimuli, and things that exist can go unperceived by the mind. For instance, alters who are used for porn are hypnotized not to see the camera. Alters used for any type of sexual service are hypnotized repeatedly to not see faces. The slave will actually see blurs where people's faces are.

The Programmers like to manipulate. Children are set in front of circus mirrors that make them taller or smaller for programming. They are set in front of mirrors which duplicate their image. Here in Oregon, there is a site with a magnetic anomaly which bends light. It is called the Oregon Vortex. The Programmers take small children there for programming. Anything that creates an illusion, seems to be noticed by the Programmers and is put to use somehow. The CIA has employed magicians like John Mulholland to help them create illusions. Magician John Mulholland wrote a manual for the CIA on how to deceive unwitting subjects.

Under drugs and hypnosis, when a small child is set in front of a mirror that elongates its body and or then shortens, the reality of the programming script seems real. The programmer can hypnotically call upon the child's mind to totally hallucinate seeing something, or he can support the illusion by handing the child a doll and telling it that it is a child, or handing the child a pencil and telling the child it is a flower. A great deal of acting and props are used during the programming. What child can tell fool's gold from real gold? The bottom line is that generally, no matter which way the Programmers do it, whether by an illusion or an outright hypnotic-suggested hallucination, the event for the child is real. The majority of traumas are real events, but the scripts that are given are after the trauma are fictional.

HYPNOSIS CAN BOOST THE CREATICITY OF THE VICTIM TO ADOPT SCRIPTS

Creativity is a function of attentiveness, playfulness, anxiety, limitations, relaxation, the trance state, responsiveness and absorption. A good programmer can assist or boost the creativity of the child. The programmer can tell stories and programming scripts in a vivid way, so that the sensory pictures are bold and strong. The child can taste and feel and touch in their minds the script being given them. Besides the language of the programmer other aids such as fear and drugs can enhance a victim's attentiveness. Playfulness comes naturally to children.

They naturally pretend and use fantasy in their play. Because children are innately creative they are far easier to program. Researchers have also discovered that creativity needs an element of anxiety and chaos in the person's life. If everything is orderly and in perfect harmony, the creative juices will not flow. The conscious mind and the subconscious mind need to grapple. For creativity to be productive it must occur within limits. For instance, the concerto is created within the limits of a piano keyboard. The programmer, and the Grande Dame and the Grande Mother of the Illuminati victim carefully guide the child's creativity and set limits. The spark of creativity occurs when there is an alternation of intense concentration and relaxation.

The programmers must work back and forth between torture and kindness. A light trance will allow the mind to surface -creative ideas. That is why writers and composers get ideas when they are in a light trance driving, in a light sleep, or shaving or some other place where a light trance occurs. Receptivity is the willingness to accept a creative idea when it comes. The final part of creativity is one's absorption into the process of creativity. The artist may get so immersed into the portrait that he is painting that the portrait seems alive and real, the actual person. This immersion, where things imagined become real, is important to keep the creative juices flowing.

The hypnotist/programmer can enhance the creative process by giving the child positive encouragement to reduce their fears and inhibitions to creativity. The programmer could say to the older child (a younger child might be told something else),

"You take all of your fear of not being creative and put them into a sack. The sack now becomes a bundle of energy. Now imagine you are opening the sack and out of the sack comes a rainbow of energy. It is powerful, it is positive. You are now full of new ideas. You can feel this power surge through your body. Your mind is now clear and focused, focused, you feel confident, sure of your talent and eager to set your new ideas into motion, and you control the energy in your life, you are very successful in controlling the energy in your life...you take a few breaths and relax.

You notice the neighborhood around you, there is a beautiful park, you begin to notice how beautiful the day is, and you begin to feel a fresh new energy flowing through your body... the more calm you become the more enthusiastic and creative you become...you will feel free to create, to enjoy your creative talent, to invent, to shape, and form new and wonderful ideas."

This is not to say that the Illuminati programmer or Mother of Darkness assistant will use this type of hypnotic suggestions, but sometimes it does become necessary to teach some children how to dissociate, and how to become creative. If they do not develop these abilities, they may lose their life to the torture.

THE VITAL ROLE OF MOVIES FOR HYPNOTIZING SMALL CHILDREN

As mentioned before, the hypnotist will find children easier to hypnotize if they know how to do it with small children. One method that is effective is to say to the small children, "Imagine you are watching a favorite television show." This is why the Disney movies and the other shows are so important to the programmers. They are the perfect hypnotic tool to get the child's mind to dissociate in the right direction. The programmers have been using movies since almost day one to help children learn the hypnotic scripts.

For children they need to be part of the hypnotic process. If the hypnotist allows the child to make up his own imagery, the hypnotic suggestions will be stronger. Rather than telling the child the color of a dog, the programmer can ask the child. This is where the books and films shown the child assist in steering its mind in the right direction. If the hypnotist talks to a child, he must take extra precaution not to change the tone of his voice and to have smooth transitions. Most of the Disney films are used for programming purposes. Some of them are specifically designed for mind-control.

SPINNING TOPS

One method for inducting children into a dissociative state is to have them look at a large spinning top, as the colors whirl around. Carousel rides have also been popular to induce trances. A good sampling of optical illusions can be found in Katherine Joyce's book Astounding Optical Illusions. NY: Sterling Pub. Co., 1994. The illusion The Temple makes one feel they are in a passageway leading to a small door.

The Escalator makes one feel they are going up and down, and could be used for building in an internal elevator. We know that optical illusions have been used, but we are not saying that these particular ones have been. For a programmer to use an optical illusion, he would first submerge the victim into a drugged state with the appropriate mind altering music and sounds and then flash the illusion onto the wall that the victim was facing. With virtual reality the child can really be immersed into a weird head trip.

THE HYPNOTIC VOICE OF THE PROGRAMMER

Programmers will adopt either an authoritarian voice, which is commanding and direct or a permissive soft tone. Bear in mind the slave who has the authoritarian voice used on it, sees the programmer as God with the authority of life or death over its (his or her) body and soul. The heightened expectation from the commanding tone, will increase the suggestions chance for success. However a softer tone, will relax the victim, and the hypnotist and the programming victim become partners in the hypnotic process. The advantage of the softer tone, is that the creativity of the victim is enhanced and participates more in the process. The hypnotic induction become more real when the victim participates more in the process.

The Monarch programmer will either use a monotone voice or a rhythmic voice. Remember, the professor who could lull his students to sleep. He had a hypnotic voice, without knowing it. A singsong or rhythmic voice is comforting. It can also be used by the Programmer. One continuous thread of words strung together are used to close out distractions. After a suggestion or command is given, a pause is made by the programmer in talking so that the suggestion is taken into the mind. Otherwise anxiety is experienced by the victim's mind, and the suggestion will not be accepted as well. Cisco, the co-author provides an example of how a hypnotic script can go with music,

"Close your eyes for your eyes will only tell the truth. And the truth isn't what you want to see. In the dark it is easy to pretend that the truth is what it ought to be. "Softly, deftly, music shall caress you. Hear it, feel it secretly possess you. Open up your mind, let your fantasies unwind in this darkness which you know you cannot fight. The darkness of the music of the night. "Close your eyes, start a journey through a strange new world. Leave all thoughts of the world you knew before. Close your eyes and let music set you free. Only then can you belong to me. "Floating, falling, sweet intoxication. Touch me, trust me, savor each sensation. Let the dream begin, let your darker side give in to the power of the music I write. You alone can make my song take flight. Help me make the music of the night. "Helpless to resist the notes I write, For I compose the music of the night. Hearing is believing, music is deceiving. Hot as lightening, soft as candle light. Dare you trust the music of the night?"

When the authors have bumped into men who are programmers and handlers for the CIA, they have noticed that many of these men have warm personalities and have a certain trained hypnotic voice which they use even when not programming. During rituals, the various magical languages used in witchcraft employ repetition, alliteration, nonsense syllables, newly coined words, and ancient words that are chanted or sung in a limited-range that makes the sounds become hypnotic. Sounds like the mantra "a-u-u-in-in" are chanted.

Gestures during rituals are also made which intensify the effects. Rituals can not be classified as having nothing to do with programming. There is such a great attempt to secularize and make clinical what the victim experiences, and the idea that witchcraft is part of the programming is an unpopular notion with some. Combining witchcraft with hypnotic language can be powerful with group dynamics. Repetitive sounds, such as a drum beating influences the locus coeruleus part of the brain. Drums can help induce trance.

KEEPING THE MIND DISSOCIATIVE

Illuminati parents (as well as other adults who care for a Monarch child) are given special instructions on how to raise the child to be dissociative. The parents are admonished that their child will have a successful future and so will they if they follow the instructions. If they don't follow the instructions, they are minded their child's life could be forfeited. These are some of the types of instructions that are given:

A) Spend 15 minutes/day teaching the child to write backwards to develop the brain in a particular fashion.

B) Giving daily doses of prolonged isolation, such as dark closets, dark cellars, the corners of dark rooms. During the prolonged iso-lation, the child cannot turn on the lights, go to the bathroom, make a noise or anything else. The child will learn to dissociate. The child is also trauma bonded to the abuser because each time the child is let out, it is grateful to the abuser. The child can be drowned in a pool and then resuscitated, and the exact amount of time to keep the child under will be given. The child can be placed in a freezer, and again the exact amount of time can be given to the parent. The child is not to roam about the house freely. The adults' area is off-limits. The child must move with permission.

C) Systematic punishment without provocation with the message "keep secrets". Hear no evil, see no evil, do no evil. This needs to be done several times a week to reinforce the codes of silence and the programming for silence.

D) A needle which is gripped halfway up is stuck into the child a quarter inch deep on the child's muscles, buttocks or thigh to help continue dissociative behavior. On special occasions (birthdays, holidays) the hands and feet which are most sensitive to pain are stuck. When the feet or hands are stuck, they will often stick the needles under the nails. The ears are also on occasion stuck with needles. It also conditions the child to obey the commands of her handlers, who will use needles to access the minds various personalities. Various spots on the body when stuck with needles along with certain codes become access points for certain alters.

E) Anytime a child argues, has a temper tantrum, or gets angry the child is to be slapped in the face. This is a quick trauma. It is to be followed with a lighted cigarette applied to the child to burn the skin the second the child gets submissive from the slap. If a cigarette can't be found, a stove top or some other hot item is to be found. At four years of age, the child begins programming to burn itself. If there are any bruises showing, the child can be kept home for a day or two.

F) Anytime the child becomes willful it is to have its mouth washed out with soap. The child should be made to chew off a piece and swallow the foam.

G) The child should be raped daily and then tortured. This helps with the sexual programming later, and begins a reversal in the mind that pain is love, and pain is pleasure.

Some of the first memories that female Monarchs recover are their memories of their fathers raping them. This is because the programmers allow these memories to be less dissociated than the later ones where the slave may be sexually servicing an important Monarch slave handler like the Rev. Billy Graham. (Graham is covered in full in Chapter 5.) In later situations like that, the kitten alters which do the sexual servicing will be electro-shocked to block their memory as well as given hypnotic cues. The fathers or step-fathers are often not the person who will be their master when they grow up. The abuse of this person will serve as a cover for the programming. If the person's front alters discover they are MPD, the will initially blame their multiplicity on the first abuser they remember, which then serves as a cover.

KEEPING THE MIND IN ALPHA STATE

The entire alter system of a Monarch slave has their sleep patterns controlled. Many alters are programmed not to sleep. They stay awake 24 hours a day internally. Someone has to take the body and sleep--but whichever alters are set up to do it, they are hypnotically commanded to only sleep three hours, to insure that the mind stays in an alpha state easy to program. Because alters which do not hold the body "rest" mentally in a sense--when they take the body they are fresh. In this way, a multiple can function without as much sleep as a normal person, but the price they pay is that their mind stays in an easy-to-program easy-to-hypnotize state. REM sleep allows the person to harmonize the mind's inner world with its outer environment. The periods of REM sleep lengthen as the hours of sleep progress. By preventing long periods of sleep, long periods of REM sleep are prevented from occurring, and the victim remains in a more controllable state of mind.

HYPNOTIC CODES, CUES AND TRIGGERS

When a Programmer creates something, it will be a reflection of himself to some degree. Just like handwriting and art are a reflection of the person who makes them. Understanding the connections between a Programmer and his creation could take a book in itself. The following is extracted from the history of an ancient occult sect, still functioning today. It is the type of thing, that the programmers feed their minds on, which in turn provides them the patterns which show up in programming. Here it is: *In the ancient occult world, at the gates of palaces the doorkeeper had to be shown "the seals"--the secret names of God or pictures with magical power, and the words "R Akiva". When the person passed this entrance, he comes to the palace of pure marble stones, do not say, "water, water." Then the person will enter into the world or the celestial Garden of Eden or the Realm of the Heavenly Palaces.*

The Story of Sinbad, the golden lamp and genie would be another example of an occult story that could be used.

Within the Illuminati, Gematria (which is the cabalistic teachings about numbers) is very important for knowing the codes of the deep darker alters. There are several reasons for why Monarch slaves have lots of codes and structures which come from witchcraft:
A) Their programmers are witches and witchcraft is the world view

on the mind of the programmer;

B) The slaves are reminded of their entrapment to Satan and their cult whenever they hear their codes;

C) The alters internally will work magic, even while they don't hold the body, and placing magical structures inside facilitates this internal magic;

D) Using magical words makes the programming look like magic;

E) The internal alters are being inculcated into occult underworld life and doctrine.

A rather remarkable book is Aleister Crowley's book "777 and Other Qabalistic Writings of Aleister Crowley". It is remarkable for the deprogrammer to understand many of the programming code links that the programmers may have used. In 777's forward,. Aleister Crowley wrote,

"777 is a cabalistic dictionary of ceremonial magic, oriental mysticism, comparative religion and symbology. It is also a handbook for ceremonial invocation and for checking the validity of dreams and visions. It is indispensable to those who wish to correlate these apparently diverse studies." (Crowley, 777, p. vii)

Later he writes, *"The book 777 has for its primary object the construction of a magical alphabet."* (p. xvii)

For instance, Crowley gives the Officers in the Masonic Lodges the Hebrew passwords of their grades. In another example of the book, Crowley gives a list of the Hindu chakra points with the Buddhist names, and their ancient Egyptian names. This is the type of occult knowledge that is hard to come by. Crowley's List of Correspondences are perhaps the best one will find printed in the occult world. They show the correspondences that occultists make between things. For instance, if we want to know what corresponds to the Hebrew letter Dalath.

The letter means door. Door corresponds to the number 14, the Cabalistic Tree of Life pathway between the two top circles on each side of "the crown", sky blue on the Queen scale of color, Aphrodite, Venus and Freya, and the gems Emerald and Turquoise, and the perfume sandalwood. All these things correspond within Cabalistic magic. For someone trying to understand why a particular color, and name is given to a deep dark side alter Crowley's book is helpful in some Monarch systems. The Mother-of-Darkness alters (and Supreme Master alters in males) of the Illuminati must do pathworking rituals when they hold the body and participate in Illuminati activities.

These Mother-of-Darkness alters are placed internally in the Cabalistic Tree of Life. Crowley's book provides the mystic number that goes to each part (plane, or circle) of the Tree of Life and its Snake positional number. The mystic number of the Sephiroth that corresponds to the number to each of the 22 paths that must be worked is also given. The occult concept is that to achieve divinity one must go on the Tree of Life from being Malkuth to become Kether. Although it is not the intent to propagate occult doctrine, for those who want to know how Illuminati Monarch slaves get to where they are as adults, and what the codes are in their System, then we need to cover briefly the Cabbalistic Tree of Life. (More will be written about this in Chapter 10 on spiritual control.) Let the reader picture 3 circles in a line. These three circles sit at the top of the Cabalistic Tree of Life. They are the top 3 circles of ten circles which all have names within an Illuminati Monarch slave. The center circle is "the crown" and holds the honored alter who actually is the Bride of the Anti-Christ.

The Anti-Christ is also known as Black Saturn, and other names. Satan himself is known within a Monarch system often by the name Bilair, Bilar, or Bilid which are his cabalistic names. The honored alter who is married to him sits on a pedestal revolving with 2 other alters. In the occult world, goddesses are triune: maiden, mother and crone. The one to the left of center is Midnight (the Mother figure), and the other is Morning Star (the maiden). Morning Star (Stella Matutina) may be a very young alter, rather than a teenager. On top of the Cabalistic Tree of Life will sit a pyramid. Each of the ten circles (rooms for the alters who live in them) of the Tree of Life is created with a different Illuminati ceremony. Before a Mother-of-Darkness Monarch slave is 16, they will have gone through all the ceremonies involved in the creation of the alters which correspond to the 10 rooms of the Tree of Life. At age 16, the system's demons will then guide the system on a personalized pathway and a baby (the firstborn) will be sacrificed by the System.

The blood of this first born is spiritually placed in a box under the Tree of Life. This is in accord with the Lilith story. The spirit Lilith (sometimes with an alter Lilith) will work with the spirits of Zerodieth and Lucifer. There are several trees which can be placed within a Monarch slave, including the ash, the oak, the ygdrassil, the willow, and the Tree of Evil, which is an evil counterpart to the Tree of Life. These will be dealt with under the chapter on structures. This chapter will provide the hypnotic codes, cues, triggers or whatever one wants to call these words, noises, and sensory inputs that manipulate these poor victims turned into Monarch robots. Other chapters will explain about the structures these codes go to, and also the spiritual dimensions of these codes and structures.

Another way to see things is to recognize that the programmers have created "power words" to which they have attached memory and programming. If a de-programmer observes closely the word usage of the victim, you will begin to spot power words of the abuser, for instance, "white rabbit". A cipher is when symbols are used to represent letters. One can used letter frequencies to break ciphers. Likewise, there are frequencies to code words. The Illuminati's intelligence agencies have programmed thousands upon thousands of slaves. There are only so many code words to pick from and some of these code words are favorites. From source's experience, the following are favorite code words that have been used to program slaves with:

CHARLOTTE, CHECKMATE, CHRISTMAS, CLARA, CLOVERLEAF, COURIER, CRAYON, CRYSTAL, DAISY, DAVY, DELLA, DELTA, DEMON, DIANA, DINAH, DIRTY, DIME, DOT, DOVE, DRAGON, DUCK, DUMBO, EAGLE, EASY, ECHO, ELAINE, ELEPHANT, ELLEN, EMERALD, EMPIRE, ESTER, EUREKA, EVERGREEN, FAITH, FALCON, FARMER,

FELIX, FIREFLY, FIVE BROTHERS, FIVE SISTERS, FLASH-LIGHT, FLOSSY, FLYING + [other word], FOX, FREEZE, FRIENDSHIP, FULL HOUSE, GALAHAD, GAMMA, GARGOYLE, GEMINI, GEORGE, GIPSY, GOLEM, GOLDEN + [other word], GOOSE, GRACE, GRANNY, GREEN DIAMOND, GULL, GWEN, HADES, HALF-MOON, HAMMER, HARRIET, HAWK, HAZEL, HELENE, HELIOS, HEN, HERMES, HIGH BALL, HIGH CARD, HOLE-IN-THE-WALL, HOPE, HOPI, HOUNDDOG, HOURGLASS, HUSTHER, HYDRA, ICEBERG, IDA, IMP, INCUBUS, INSECT, IRIS, IROQUOIS, ITEM, JACKASS, JAGUAR, JANET, JANICE, JASON, JASPER, JAVELIN, JENNY, JEZEBEL, JIG, JULIET, JOAN, JOSHUA, JUDY, JUPITER, KANGAROO, KANSAS, KATY, KING, KILO, KITTY, KOMET, LACE, LADY + [other word], LAMP, LAURA, LEAP FROG, LEOPARD, LIGHT-NING, LILY, LION, LITTLE + [other word], LOVE, LUCKY + [other word], MAE WEST, MAGIC, MAJESTIC, MAMIE, MANDREL, MARIE, MARK, MARTHA, MAX, MEADOWS, MER-CURY, MIGHTY MOUSE, MILLION DOLLAR, MINNIE MOUSE, MONA LISA, MONTE CARLO, MOTHER, MUMMY, NANCY, NAOMI, NAVAJO, NIMROD, NOAH, NORA, NUT-CRACKER, OBOE, OCTOPUS, OLD FAITHFUL, OLIVE, OPAL, OPHELIA, ORION, OSCAR, OWL, OZMA, PACKAGE, PAM-ELA, PANDORA, PANTHER, PAPERCLIP, PAPA, PAT, PATSY, PEGASUS, PENTHOUSE, PHANTOM, PHOENIX, PINECONE, PISTOL PETE, PLATO, PLUTO, POLLY, PYTHON, QUAIL, QUEBEC, QUEEN, QUEEN BEE, QUEENIE, QUEST, QUICK SILVER, RACHEL, RAINBOW, RAM, RANGER, RASCAL, RAT, RAVEN, REBECCA, RED DIAMOND, RED HILL, RENO, REX, RHUBARB, RITA, ROBOT, ROMEO, ROOSTER, ROSIE, ROVER, RUBY, RUTH, SABRE, SAINT, SAINT + [another word], SALLY, SAN ANTONIO, SAPPHIRE, SARAH, SATURN, SCAM-PER, SCOUT, SEA GULL, SEAL, SERGEANT, SERGEANT-DELTA, SHADOW, SHARK, SHENANDOAH, SHO, SICKLE, SIGMA, SILVER, SNOW + (other word), ZEBRA, ZENITH, ZERO, ZYPPER, ZOMBIE, ZULU, ZUNI."

The word FOX is an example of a significant occult code word. F-o-x consists of the 6th, 15th (1+5), & the 24th (2+ 4) letters of the alphabet, which yield 666. The reader needs to bear several things in mind. First, the programmers generally have intelligent, well sounding codes, that do form patterns. For instance, a woman's name from the Bible will be used as a code, with subparts or subcodes having other female names from the Bible. Deeper Illuminati parts will have goddess and god names, and king and queen names for cult alters. These are the names the handler or cult uses--NOT their access codes. The codes for slaves follow patterns.

There are standard and unique codes. The internal programming alters have the power to change codes if they need to protect the programming. They will have to hypnotically work with alters when they trance out at night. In other words, most of their programming of front alters will be done when a System lies down for "sleep"--more accurately described as "for trance." If the internal alters change many codes, in their efforts to protect the system, they will even make it difficult for the handler/programmer to get into the system. Ciphers developed rotors that require lines to line up. Some simple schemes using this principle appear in some Monarch systems.

This is part of the science of structuring. Intelligence codes often come from the Bible or popular fiction books. The deeper codes are occult words, often in foreign languages such as Arabic, which is an important language in the upper occult world. Slaves will be given COVER NAMES for ops, and often males receive female names and vice versa. Very shortly, we will provide the Monarch hypnotic cues (codes) for the multitude of functions that a Monarch's mind must carry out. The type of programming which is placed in a slave varies. For intelligence operations the slave will have to have BONA FIDES, which are codes to allow two people to meet. All slaves are given CONTROL SIGNS which allow them to indicate via a code that they are in trouble. A RECOGNITION signal allows two people to make contact. For instance, the handler might fly his distinctive sounding plane over a slave's house in a pre-arranged signal. It might also be a particular colored scarf, and a particular set of phrases. A GO-AWAY code is a prearranged signal that means it is unwise to make contact. The go-away signal may be simply placing one's hands in one's pocket or turning the porch lights off. A "GO TO GROUND" signal means to go into hiding. A MAYDAY BOOK exists for Illuminati and Intelligence slaves which allows them to call if they are about to be arrested. A telephone number is left open for just this purpose. Also common universal Illuminati codes can be used by the slave to get set free from police and judges.

Within the Jehovah's Witnesses, especially their headquarters, the Illuminati uses Enochian language to program with. With Druidic branches Druidic symbols are used. With the Jewish groups, Hebrew is used. Other languages are also used. An Illuminati System can easily have 6 different languages used as programming codes. The foreign language codes will be for small parts of the System only. Special artificial languages are also employed, as well as sign language. See Appendix D for a list of Monarch Mind-Control Codes.

HYPNOSIS IN PROGRAMS AND OTHER USES

The programmers will begin their programming by extreme torture. After a certain amount of torture the victim is willing to say or believe anything to stop the torture. At this point a thought will be planted into the victim's mind. This thought will be linked to a false memory put in via hypnosis or movies, or other method, and it will be linked to a command put in by hypnosis etc. and the original thought, the command, the false memory will be linked by a single emotion which will link them all together. The result will be something like this: *It is two weeks before Halloween (thought), I must get ready for Halloween rituals (command) because I have always had a habit of going to Halloween rituals (false memory). If I don't I will have a heart attack and die (memory of torture linked to thoughts).*

Programming is layered in. Layer after layer of programming is put in. Each alter (personality) of the victim is used as if it is a component of a large system. The result is that no alter (personality) is the whole, but only a cog in a great machine. Can a single cog rebel against the whole machine? It is very difficult for a single component of thousands of components to rebel against the abusers.

ALICE IN WONDERLAND PROGRAMMING AS IT PETAINS TO AN AL-

TER GOING DOWN IN TRANCE FOR INTERNAL PROGRAMMING (Going down the tree; Going through the mirror; Going underneath something; Growing tall)

The internal programmers (and some other alters) have the ability to send other alters into deep trances. One of the programs for doing this is based on the Alice In Wonderland Theme and it was experienced like this for a level 2 alter who managed to stay in communication with her deprogrammer:

When the alter went down in her mind she went down on the inside of the trunk of a tree, like Alice In Wonderland. At the bottom she saw a keyhole, a table, and on the table was love potion #9. She automatically drank the love potion which shrinks her to a dot and then she goes through the keyhole. So normally this process means she goes through the keyhole. She managed to stay in contact with her deprogrammer during this deep trance. After the key hole she saw thousands of looking glass mirrors. A tree comes and wraps itself around her and loves her. As she ascends (comes up in trance) she stretches up and enlarges. In coming up out of trance she gets stuck at level 8 due to some interference from deeper alters. She, in accord with her programming, senses her Master's love. Normally she would have simply tranced out, and another alter would have taken her place and she would have no recollection of the entire process. The alter has been programmed to have backup amnesia. Backup amnesia means that one doesn't remember that one lost time, one doesn't remember that one forgot, etc. In short it means you don't remember that you don't remember.

This is an example of hypnosis used internally by the programming and the Programming alters to control other alters. The deepening of the trance was given the imagery of Alice falling down the tree. In the various stories used in programming, there is some part of the story that can be used as the story line for trance induction, these include:

- Wizard of Oz - going into the poppies,

- Star Wars - time warp, riding the light
- Star Trek - being beamed, replicators etc.

Hypnosis is used to anchor suggestions about sleep patterns, panic programs, phobias, health healing programs and health problems programs, pain control and pain programs, motivation programs, a suicide program called "hypnosleep", an insanity program, and countless other uses. Hypnosis is used to steer a person's mind in the direction that they have been labeled. For instance, if they have been selected to become a doctor, they will be programmed for success as a doctor. New patterns of thought, feeling and behavior are inserted to build confidence in the goals of the Illuminati. Positive experiences are used to help boost the person's feelings, and then the new messages are anchored "Imagine these messages taking root. Your new messages are growing stronger and stronger." The Alice In Wonderland programming theme is used in air-water programs and mirror programs which the Illuminati, the CIA, NASA, the Jesuits and others like so well. The idea is that there exists a mirror world which is a reversal. Along with it is attached the idea that the slave can enter into a timeless dimension, or as some refer to it "interdimensional time travel." Later, the victim will be further brought under the spell of this mirror programming by going to locations around the nation, like the Magic Time Machine restaurants in San Antonio and Dallas, TX where mirrors are placed on doors, ceilings, walls, and restrooms of the establishment and programming themes are part of the everything at these restaurants. The handler may tell the slave, "LOSE YOURSELF IN THE INFINITY MIRRORS." When hypnotically programming in programs, the Programmers place in many types of images and programs.

Some examples would be having the concept of obedience equal the fountain of youth. The fountain of youth flows in the victim's mind unless they step out side of their orders. This can be linked to the Shangri-la story, where a woman ages as soon as she leaves her place in Shangri-la. Another example, is the hypnotic imagery involving the formation of an island from a volcano. The story is turned into a programming script to allow the System to be radically restructured. This Volcano programming is a System's turning program. A volcano erupts from deep down, and lava pours into the sea. Mountains are pushing up from deep in the mind. To survive people must cross from the old to the new island on a bridge that naturally forms. Fire births the new territory and destroys the old. The new mountains develop trees which become safe places for the alters to roost upon.

HYPNOTICALLY BUILDING IN STRUCTURES

Later in the book, the art of building structures internally in the mind of the victim will be covered. However, since the process involves hypnotism it would be appropriate to discuss briefly how hypnosis can begin to work a tree structure into the mind of the child. First, the programmer hypnotically suggests that his penis is a growing tree. Later, the programmer might begin, "You know those big trees in the park that look so big and straight and stretch way up toward the sky? Stand up and be one of those trees. Stand up really straight and tall as tall as you can be, and stretch your arms out toward the sky like branches on that big oak tree. Now those big trees have long, deep roots that keep them from falling over. Feel your feet go down, down through the floor, just like roots on the big strong oak tree."

Final note: there is no way that this book could give every last song or story that has been used for programming, nor was it the intention to do so. We have wanted to point out the popular story lines used, although we have missed some such as the Chronicles of Narnia and Little Red Riding Hood (which is used in several ways along the lines of you think you're going to Papa's, or Grandma's house & you end up with a wolf).

Our list left out many programming songs--all the Rolling Stone's songs, Alabama's Old Flame, etc.

CHAPTER FIVE:

THE SKILL OF LYING; THE ART OF DECEIT

The rule of thumb that the programmers/handlers go by is that they will say anything to get the job done. A CIA handler will tell his agent in the field whatever will work to get the field agent's coopera-tion on a mission. There is no height nor breadth nor length to these people's deception. They have successfully kept some deceptions ac-tive for decades, if not for centuries.

THE USE OF FICTION

The history behind the Wizard of Oz programming is interesting. It suggests that the Wizard of Oz has had an important part in the occult world all along. One of the secrets of the Mystery Religions, espe-cially the Egyptian Isis mystery religion, was the ability to use drugs and torture to create multiple personalities. The word Oz is known to have been used by its author as an abbreviation for Osirus. Monarch victims have the "golden penis of Osirus" placed into them. The Grimm brothers, who were cabalistic Jews, gathered the folk occult stories together. Their stories are full of spells, trances, and drugs. Sleeping Beauty is put to sleep, and the trigger to wake her is a kiss on the lips. These are serious hints that the occult world didn't stop programming people with dissociative states and triggers when the ancient Egyptian empires fell. Instead of using modern lingo such as "hypnotize", they would say "cast a spell." Later in Freemasonry, the Right Worshipful Master would "charge" (meaning hypnotize) an initiate.

The occultist Baum, a member of the Theosophical Society, was in-spired by some spirit who gave him the "magic key" to write the

Wizard of Oz book, which came out in 1900. The book's story is full of satanic activity and satanic thinking. The story was chosen in the late 1940s to be the basis for the Illuminati/Intelligence community's trauma-based total mind control programming. As a way of enhancing the effect of the programming, Monarch slaves are conditioned to place trigger items into their lives. When the movie was made, Judy Garland, who had lived a life touched by the occult world's abuse, was chosen to act as Dorothy. Judy's later husband, Mickey De Vinko was a Satanist and the chief assistant to Roy Radin, a rich Satanist who worked with the Illuminati, and who controlled the "Process Church" covens which had as members mass murderers Berkowitz and Monarch slave Charlie Manson. There are several members of the Carr family, who are also tied into both De Vinko and Radin's Process Church and the Illuminati.

With the numerous long term connections between the Wizard of Oz books, and movie to the highest levels of the occult world, it is not without reason that one can theorize that the original series of 14 Oz books had an ulterior motive behind them. The 14 books of the Oz series are:

1) The Wizard of Oz,

2) The Land of Oz,

3) Ozma of Oz,

4) Dorothy and the Wizard in Oz,

5) The Road to Oz,

6) The Emerald City of Oz,

7) The Patchwork Girl of Oz,

8) Tik-tok of Oz,

9) The Scarecrow of Oz,

10) Rinkitink in Oz,

11) The Lost Princess of Oz,

12) 12) The Tinman Woodsman of Oz,

13) 13) The Magic of Oz,

14) 14) Glinda of Oz.

These books are still being sold, and are being read to children who are being programmed with trauma-based total mind control. The 14 books came out in various editions. The originals came out in 1900 and shortly thereafter. In the 1930s, the 1940's, and the 1950's the words were retype set and given different pages. (When working with a survivor it might help to identify what decade the edition the slave was programmed with, because the pictures and the page numbers varied from edition to edition.)

Of course, having good pictures is an asset in programming, because the child will visualize off of the pictures when building its internal world. In addition to this, large Wizard of Oz theme parks are being built by the Illuminati to provide places to carry out programming and to reinforce the programming which traps the minds of Monarch slaves. The best example of this, is the audacious MGM Grand complex in Las Vegas, although other theme parks around America also use a Wizard of Oz theme. If you have read Fritz Springmeier's "Be Wise As Serpents" you will know how the Theosophical Society ties in with Freemasonry, Satanism, and Lucis Trust. Several famous members of the Theosophical Society include:

- Adolf Hitler - a Satanist who practiced human sacrifice, & who had HPB's book at his side.
- Mahatma Gandhi - a Hindu guru considered a god by some of his followers. Gandhi was successful with the British in part because of the Theosophical Society.
- H.P. Blavatsky - The founder of the Theosophical Society. She referred to herself as HPB. She was initiated by Illuminatus Mazzini into Carbonarism , a form of Freemasonry, illumined by the Great White Lodge in 1856, was part of the Hermetic Brotherhood of Luxor, and spent lots of time with the Eddy Illuminati family in Vermont, who were well known mediums. She also was a member of the occult fraternities the Order of the Druses, the Adoptive Branch of the Ancient & Primitive Rite of Freema-

sonry, & the hermetic Masonic rites of Memphis and Mizoram. She was trained to handle live snakes by Sheik Yusuf benMakerzi, the chief of the Serpent Handlers, and she was hypnotized by occultist Victor Michal and to some degree from 1866 was under his influence.

- Alice Bailey - Head of Lucis Trust.
- Henry Steel Olcott - An important occultist.
- Elvis Presley - A Monarch slave.
- Manly P. Hall - An Illuminati Theta Programmer, and at least a Grand Master within the Illuminati who sat on the Grand Druid Council.
- Frank Baum - The man who wrote the book The Wizard of Oz was a member of the Theosophical Society. L. Frank Baum lived in South Dakota and created The Wizard of Oz book as a theosophical fairy tale incorporating the "ancient wisdom" of the Mystery Religions. The books have so much material from inside the secret world of the Illuminati, that the few who understand the Illuminati wonder if Baum wasn't an insider. The moral of the book is that we must rely upon ourselves, for we alone have the power to save ourselves. This was part of the original lie of Satan in the garden. Satan has simply dressed up the same original lie into different packaging and is distributing it worldwide as the most popular American fairy tale. L. Frank Baum explained how he came to write the book,

"It was pure inspiration.... It came to me right out of the blue. I think that sometimes the Great Author has a message to get across and He has to use the instrument at hand. I happened to be that medium, and I believe the magic key was given me to open the doors to sympathy and understanding, joy, peace and happiness." (Hearn, Michael P. ed., The Annotated Wizard of Oz. NY: Clarkson N. Potter, 1973, p. 73.)

In Baum's time, the head of the Theosophical Society, H.P. Blavatsky had been putting out her journal called "Lucifer". In other words, I highly suspect Baum knew what the Theosophical Society was all about, and that he himself was deeply into the occult. The book "The Wizard of Oz" came out in 1900. It wasn't until 1939 that the movie was made. This next section will cover the numerous parallels between the Wizard of Oz material and the occult world and the occult world's programming. This is broken up into 3 sections:

PARALLELS BETWEEN:

I.   THE WIZARD OF OZ BOOK & OCCULTISM
II. THE WIZARD OF OZ MOVIE & ILLUMINATION RITUALS
III. THE WIZRD OF OZ BOOK SERIES & MONARCH PROGRAMMING

For those readers who are unfamiliar with the occult world, some of these parallels at first may seem stretched. When one sees how many parallels there are, then occult nature of the books begins to sink in. The authors could provide the reader with more parallels between Satanism and The Wizard of Oz book, but we believe the following will suffice. Some parallels may also apply to the movie.

I. THE WIZARD OF OZ BOOK & OCCULTISM

- Auntie Em represents HP Blavatsky's "Mulaprakriti" and Uncle Henry represents HPB's "Unmanifested Logos".
- The carnival huckster (later seen as the Wizard) is advertised as being connected to the royal families of Europe. The Royal families of Europe are secret Satanists, from powerful occult bloodlines.
- Dorothy is brought to Oz by a cyclone. The word cyclone originally was the Greek word cyclone which means both a circle or the coil of a snake. In other words, the snake takes Dorothy to Oz.
- Dorothy's three companions represent the mental, emotional, and physical bodies that HPB wrote about. Dorothy acquired these three companions just as Theosophy says we will when we come into incarnation. To quote HPB "There is no danger that dauntless courage cannot conquer; there is not trial that spotless purity cannot pass through; there is no difficulty that strong intellect cannot surmount." (Algeo, John. "The Wizard of Oz: The Perilous Journey", The Quest, Summer 1993. Wheaton, Il.: Theosophical Society in America p.53.)
- In the book, the Tin Woodsman was an ordinary being of flesh,

but a wicked witch casts a spell on him. He kept chopping off parts of his body, which were then replaced by a tinsmith, until he became the first bionic man, with a completely mechanic body. Boy, hasn't the Illuminati been trying to do this one!?
- In step with Wizard of Oz mind-control programming, the wicked witch & naughty children cannot stand water but dissolve. Robotic clones are created in the minds of Monarch slaves which can only be mentally dissolved by mentally placing water on them.
- Dorothy goes questing in Oz. Theosophists (New Agers, Satanists, etc.) go on quests.
- Oz is shaped like a Mandala with Emerald City in the center, an impassable barrier, four-sidedness, 4 symbolic colors, the circle and the center. The colors and directions given in Oz may also have other symbolic meanings in the occult. For instance, Emerald City is green and green is the fourth point of the Eastern Star (women's Freemasonry) & Satan's color. A The route that Dorothy follows in Oz has the shape of a T with its 3 points defining an inverted triangle.
- The Yellow Brick Road suggests gold, the perfect metal. Gold is considered to be divine & the source of wisdom by the Illuminati. HPB had written "There is a Road, steep and thorny, beset with perils of every kind, but yet a Road, and it leads to the very heart of the universe." This was the yellow brick road that Baum the Theosophist sought to portray in his fairy tale. The book contains a great deal more perils and adventures on the road than the movie.
- The article shows that the great teacher is a humbug but Dorothy and her own companions have the abilities to help themselves if they only will realize their own powers through the help of the good witch of the south. This is in line with the Theosophical Society's, the Church of Satan's, and other occult groups teachings which teach that the individual has the capabilities within themselves to achieve anything. One of the Theosophical Society's publications states, "Prepare thyself, for thou wilt have to travel on alone. The teacher can but point the way." ("The Voice of Silence" as quoted in "The Wizard of Oz" article, Quest, Summer, 1993 p. 54.) Part of the mind set of Satanism is that reality and

fantasy become blurred. This blurring has been part of the brainwashing that is being systematically given to American children.

Monarch slaves they have an incredibly difficult time trying to differentiate between reality and fantasy within because of all the mind programming they have been subjected too. There are several techniques which will determine for Monarch survivors if their memories are real. In the board game called Illuminati!, put out by people connected to the Illuminati, the game states, *"Don't believe any of this, it is all true."* These are the type of double-bind self contradictory statements that Satanists love to spew out. Monarch slaves are programmed full of double-binds. With the Satanist's penchant for blurring reality in mind, read the following quote where the President of the Theosophical Society admiringly describes the Wizard of Oz,

"Part of Baum's joke is that things are never what they seem. Dorothy seems to be a simple and harmless little girl, but it is she who kills the wicked witches of both East and West. The Scarecrow seems to lack brains, but he has all the ideas in the company. The Tin Woodman seems to lack a heart, but he is so full of sentiment that he is always weeping. The Cowardly Lion seems to be a coward, but he takes brave action whenever it is called for. The Wizard seems to be great and powerful, but he is actually a humbug. Oz seems to be a glorious and delightful land and Kansas to be dry, gray, and dull--but Oz is a world of illusion and Kansas is really home. Things are not what they seem, in Oz or Kansas."

II. THE WIZARD OF OZ MOVIE & ILLUMINATION RITUALS

- The close relationship between Dorothy and her dog is a very subtle connection between the satanic cults use of animals as familiars. Those who read Volume 1, may remember the example written about on how Illuminati Kingpin Alfred I. du Pont's dog Mummy served as Alfred's familiar spirit. Animals are very often used in ritual. This connection is very subtle, perhaps too subtle for it to be worthy of mention, except that those in Satanism will see the significance, even though others won't. What is trivial to one person may not be to the next. A Monarch slave as a child will be allowed to bond with a pet. The child will want to bond with a pet anyway because people are terrifying by this point. Then the pet is killed in porn to traumatize the child. This happens quite frequently.

- The Rainbow--with its seven colors have long had an occult significance of being a great spiritual hypnotic device. Constance Cumbey, in her book "The Hidden Dangers of the Rainbow", which exposes the New Age Occult Movement, correctly writes, *"The Rainbow (also called the Antahkarana or Rainbow Bridge) is used as a hypnotic device.,,* (p.261) The Supreme Council of the 33rd0 of Freemasonry has used the rainbow on the cover of their magazine. In a book teaching Druidism (as in Illuminati Druidism), The 21 Lessons of Merlyn, the Rainbow is described as *"A true sign of Magic...it exists in both worlds at once!"*
- Elvira Gulch is a woman who owns 1/2 of the county where Dorothy lives in Kansas. She is shown later in the Land of Oz transformed as a witch. Many of the Illuminati elite are rich and lead double lives. People who meet them at a ritual will see the dark side of these rich people. At the rituals, people are tranced from drugs, chanting, and mind control; they are "over the rainbow."
- Professor Marvel uses a crystal ball which he claims was used by the Priests of Isis. Isis and Osirus are both part of the Ancient Egyptian Mystery religion and modern Satanism.
- Kansas is black & white, Oz is in color. Reality is downplayed in witchcraft and Satanism. Make believe is considered more colorful than reality. Also as an escape from this world, Satanists use drugs to enhance their perception of colors. Some of the famous writers took drugs which put them into altered states of consciousness in order to release their creativity.
- Both good and bad witches in Oz carry staffs. In Satanism & the Illuminati, Priestesses also carry similar staffs. Also the idea that there are good and evil witches -- white and black magic is straight from the occult, and follows the Illuminati's Gnostic beliefs.
- Several scenes involve transference of power via transference of slippers from a witch. In Illuminati ritual, to transfer power, a Matriarch, or Mother of Darkness will kill the person in a position

of authority with a strike on the forehead with a special mace like staff, and then put on their slippers. Ruby colored slippers are actually used as a symbol of authority at the Matriarch level in the Illuminati. The shoes are said to be golden at the Mothers of Darkness level in the Illuminati.

- The bad witch uses poison, poisoned apples and poisoned brew. Satanic covens in real life do this same thing.
- The wizard is portrayed as someone who rules and is benevolent. In witchcraft, wizards do rule, even though in some groups wizards are simply called witches.
- Winged monkeys in the haunted forest, harkens back to the pagan cultures which placed wings on various animal idols.
- The trees are alive like animals in the film. The Illuminati believe that the trees have spirits. In one of the Oz films, even the stones have personality and talk. This comes straight out of Druidism.
- The Tin Man is a person which has been part of Illuminati ceremonies. The first initial ceremony that children of the Illuminati may remember is where a Tin Man with an ax watches over their presentation to the coven.
- If the parent presents the child, nothing is done, but if the parent refuses to present the children, then the Tin Man in the ritual will use his axe to sever the child's head on a chopping block. The Tin Man will also appear in Tin Man programming, and a Tin Man's Castle may well be built in the Monarch slave's head, but the point here is that the Tin Man is also part of ritual.
- Dorothy kills the wicked witch of the west by a sharp blow to the forehead with the witch's staff. This is what is done in the Illuminati, when an elderly witch is being replaced. In both cases, whether in the movie or in real life in the Illuminati, when a witch is killed the people have a ceremony. In real life in the secret world of the Illuminati, a scroll is used to certify that the witch is dead both physically and spiritually. The movie had this in it. Just one example of the thousands of Illuminati Grande Dames killed in ritual like this is the recent billionaires Dorris Duke, who was ritually killed in 1993 on Halloween, also called All Hallows Eve, in the Beverly Hills, CA area. The Illuminati method for killing a Grande Dame and passing her spiritual power on is done with reverence. No blood is to be spilt out of respect for the elderly

woman who gives up her life willingly. At death, the last breath is inhaled by the replacement to transfer the power. There may be as many as 2,197 Grande Dames at such a coronation. The Grande Mothers (whose Systems are mistresses for Satan and hierarchy leaders) and the next rank, the Grande Dames, are often veiled in ritual and would wear robes with different colored lining. The different colors of linings show the different grades. A typical Grande Mother vestment or robe is a black satin & velvet dress with a draped neckline, and ritual symbols down the center of the robe. After someone like Dorris Duke willingly gives her (their) life, her head is served on a silver platter at a banquet. For the deeper alters of a high level slave, this is part of their way of life; they are told it is their birthright and heritage. Such alters will not be able to identify with the culture at large. To give up their programming, means giving up their magical powers and their culture, which they have had to work hard for. To leave they would need to see something that they perceive as better. They are locked into their slavery due do to their exposure to only a secret Illuminati culture and value system. Because of their dissociation with the rest of their own System of alters, they don't perceive a need to change their lifestyle anymore than a Bushman would be able to feel a need to wear shoes. Why should the Bushman want shoes, if he has gotten along without them? Why should a high level slave want change, when they have gotten along without it? Experience shows that during deprogramming most of the lower level alters will want to escape their abuse, but the higher level ritual alters are so separated from the abuse they don't want to give up their status and culture.

- Throughout the movie, scrolls are used. As stated, Moriah continues to use scrolls for their official ritual functions.
- The wicked witch of the west says that her question was not "to kill or not to kill" Dorothy?, but rather HOW to kill Dorothy for "these things must be done delicately." This is exactly the attitude displayed within the Illuminati.
- The film has occult items such as crystal balls in several scenes, haunted castles, magic and a benevolent wizard.
- At one point the Lion says, "I do believe in spooks [ghosts], I do, I do, I do, I do." Today, intelligence agents are also called spooks.

- The Lion, Tinman, Dorothy and the Scarecrow must prove themselves worthy to receive the benevolence from Oz. The occult is full of rituals where the participant must prove himself worthy.
- The phrase "seeds of learning" is used in Illuminati ceremonies. Staffs like the movie has are used by various occult groups. These staffs often serve as stun guns, so that shocks can be applied during ceremonies. The shocks may be applied so that the victim doesn't remember the ceremony.

III. THE WIZRD OF OZ BOOK SERIES & MONARCH PROGRAMMING

The following are parts of the Wizard of Oz Monarch Programming, which is a base programming put in when the child is very young. Some of the slaves know portions of the Wizard of Oz script word-for-word.

- Dorothy is told she doesn't have a brain if she has gotten into trouble.
- Dorothy is looking for a place where there is no trouble which is a place "over the rainbow." To escape pain, alters go over the rainbow. (This is a.k.a. in Alice In Wonderland Programming as "going through the looking glass".)
- Dorothy becomes unconscious, the world begins spinning, and then she sees disjointed pictures. This also happens to Monarch slaves. Later in the film, Dorothy states, "My! people come and go so quickly." This is exactly what happens to the Monarch slave whose multiple personalities come and go. When the multiple personalities switch in and out very fast a spinning process can start which can be dangerous if it doesn't stop. Just like most hiccuping stops on its own, the rapid uncontrolled switching, which can be triggered by stress, usually stops on its own. Systems which subconsciously know they are going to be tortured and used may out of a subconscious fear begin this revolving switching. It is said that the Monarch victim will become comatose if the rapid spinning goes on too long. Personalities are switched in what are called "tornado spins" or "tornado spinning" and personalities called "spin off" personalities come up according to the number of revolutions the slave is commanded to spin.

By spinning the slave, the master can choose what sexual perversion he wants as each "spin off" personality has been trained to carry out a different perversion.

- Over the rainbow in Oz is for the Monarch slave to be in a trance, and into a certain area of the programming. To be fluctuating at both ends as an observer and not a participant or to go to the other extreme and become a participant. The theme song of the movie goes, *"Somewhere over the Rainbow... there's a land where the dreams that you dare to dream really come true."* These lyrics are a method to hypnotically confuse the brain to perceive that the "over the Rainbow experience", which is usually horrible abuse, is a "dream". The dissociative mind is only too happy to call the trauma a dream, which is lived as a reality for a moment, but is nevertheless recorded by the mind as a fantasy. The term for this is crypto-amnesia, which means the process where the proper functioning of memory is hypnotically messed up. The slave's internal world becomes "reality" and the external real world becomes the Land of Oz which is perceived as make-believe.

- Dwarfs are used in the internal programming. (Hollywood hired a large number of them for the movie's cast. They are called Munchkins in the movie.) Mengele, known as the programmer Dr. Green, was especially interested in experimenting traumas on dwarfs.

- For bona-fides & recognition signals, the Monarch slaves wear diamonds to signify they are presidential models, rubies to signify their Oz programming for prostitution, and emeralds to signify their programming to do drug business. Rings are also used to signify what activity the slave is doing, and what rank or level they are in the occult.

- Monarch slaves are taught to "follow the yellow brick road." No matter what fearful things lie ahead, the Monarch slave must follow the Yellow Brick Road which is set out before them by their master. For some slaves used as track stars, their Yellow Brick Road was the track they had to run. The Yellow Brick Road is the runway in which alters were trained to fly off from to exit their internal world and take the body. The Yellow Brick Road also pertains to the assignment that an alter is given. To follow the Yellow Brick Road is to go down the road that has been assigned by command. The Yellow Brick Road programming is placed into the child's mind via the Yellow Brick Road of the Wizard of Oz story. Remember the key words, "Follow the Yellow Brick Road." To get someone onto the Yellow Brick Road you must know the access code to get them through the poppy field. The color codes are important to get an alter through the field of poppies. "Fiddler" is important word to get to the yellow brick road (it signifies the programmer in the context of "the programmer is here, go over the rainbow") and then the alters eat what is variously called MUSIC or a SCRIPT or A LETTER which are words meaning "instructions." In the 1900 edition of the book on page 31-32 says (programming cues are in caps), "She closed the door, locked it, and put the KEY carefully in the pocket of her dress. And so, with Toto trotting along soberly behind her, SHE STARTED ON HER JOURNEY. THERE WERE SEVERAL ROADS NEAR BY, BUT IT DID NOT TAKE HER LONG TO FIND THE ONE PAVED WITH YELLOW BRICK. Within a short time she was walking briskly toward the EMERALD CITY, HER SILVER SHOES tinkling merrily on the hard, YELLOW ROAD BED. The sun shone BRIGHT AND THE BIRDS SANG SWEET and Dorothy did not feel nearly as bad as you might think a little girl would who had been SUDDENLY WHISKED AWAY FROM HER OWN COUNTRY AND SET DOWN IN THE MIDST OF A STRANGE LAND....The houses of the Munchkins were odd-looking dwellings,...ALL WERE PAINTED BLUE, for in this country of the EAST BLUE WAS THE FAVORITE COLOR.. .FIVE LITTLE FIDDLERS PLAYED AS LOUDLY AS POSSIBLE AND THE PEOPLE WERE LAUGHING AND SINGING, while a big table nearby was loaded with DELICIOUS FRUITS [the programs] and NUTS, PIES, and cakes, and many OTHER GOOD THINGS TO EAT [scripts to ingest]."

- Monarch slaves are threatened with fire, like the Scarecrow. They also see people dismembered like the Scarecrow was dismembered. For them it is not an idle threat. The front alters also have hearts full of pain like Scarecrow.

- Certain alters are not given courage and most have their hearts taken from them. The alters who are programmed not to have hearts are hypnotically told the same thing the Tin Man says, "I could be human if I only had a heart." (See Chapter 4, where it discusses hypnosurgery.)

- Some alters are taught they are stupid and have no brain. Scarecrow is asked the question, "How can you talk without a brain? Scarecrow answers, "Some people without a brain can do a lot of talking."

- Emerald City is used in programming. Emerald City in the programming will be well guarded and hard to reach. Several important things will be placed inside the Emerald City, including the deeper Illuminati alters.

- Castles are used in the programming. Lots of castles, either in the mind's imagery or purely demoniac are placed into the slave's mind.

- Winged monkeys are able to watch in the movies somewhat as spy satellites. Winged monkeys are used in the programming to create a fear of always being watched.

- The flowers used in the movie and books, are also used in the programming. The witch uses poppy flowers to put the lion and Dorothy to sleep. Opium and cocaine are used to tranquilize Monarch slaves. An alter of a slave will get trancy when they enter the poppy field. (Heroin and cocaine come from poppies.) In the film, Dorothy says, "What is happening? I'm so sleepy." She and the lion get sleepy for no apparent reason very quickly. Monarch slaves do the same thing. Waking up with snow in the movie is nothing less than an allusion to cocaine which is a common substance given to Monarch slaves to help make them dependent.

- Dorothy states at one point in the movie that she "doesn't remember". She then follows this up with "I guess it doesn't matter."

- Hourglasses appear in the movie in several spots, and they also occur in various contexts in people who have been programmed by the Monarch programming. Some victims of the programming have hour glass configurations each created around a separate axis. The hour glasses have the ability to be rotated which causes certain alters to be brought forward. Monarch slave masters have also used hour glasses to indicate to their slaves that death was imminent and that time was running out. This is the way the wicked witch used the hour glass on Dorothy, who happens to be saved just as the hour glass runs out. Some Monarch slave masters actually have large hour glasses (sometimes 3' high) like in the movie. In Cathy O'Brien's autobiography of her life as a Monarch slave "Transformation of America" she has a photograph of Secretary of Defense Cheney's hour glass on his desk with him seated. This hour glass was used to threaten her as a slave. When a Monarch slave sees an hour glass they may switch, but basically it is a reminder that the slave masters have the power to run a person's time out. One slave was told, "The sand that sifts through the hourglass is a measure of your worthiness to live or die." The hour glass shape is basically two triangles which touch at their peaks, or an X configuration with the tops of the X having lines. The child's mind is to visualize this configuration as a compass, as the four points N, S, E, W, they are to see the X configuration also as an x, y axis upon which a city is structured. The hour glass then is tied to several other concepts which integrate themselves well with the basic X shape of the hour glass. Circles with X's are stacked on top of each other to form the different worlds which contain the alters. The two pie shaped pieces of the hour glass will hold one world, while the hour glass configuration made by the other two adjacent pieces hold the looking glass mirror images of each alter. Each hour glass is called 2 quadrants. To remove 4 quadrants would of course take both alters and mirror images with it. In mathematics, it could be stated that regular alters are in quadrant x,y and -x, -y. And that the looking glass people--the mirror images, early splits made from each alter as a copy, are in quadrants -x, y and x, -y. (See Chapter on how to structure a System)

- "Click your heels together and be there in a snap" is both in the movie and in the programming cues. Military Monarch slave models are especially taught to click their heels together. (Joseph Mengele, Dr. Black, Michael Aquino and others also liked to click their Nazi boots together while they programmed children.)
- "SILENCE!" is both in the movie and a command of the Oz Programming. This word SILENCE stands for a code of "no talk" which runs deep in the mind of the slave.
- As in the movie, certain slave alters will talk to their masters as

Dorothy did, "If you please, Sir..."

- The keys (and triggers) to control the switching of personalities and to give orders are frequently based on Wizard of Oz material. A Monarch slave owner might use cues based on the Wizard of Oz such as "THERE'S A PAIR OF MAGIC SHOES TO WEAR WITH YOUR DRESS...SOMETHING IN LIGHTENING...TO TRANSPORT YOU FASTER THAN THE OL' RUBY SLIPPERS." Quote from O'Brien, Cathy. "Operation Carrier Pigeon", Monograph, pg. 2. A cryptic death threat given to Cathy as a slave by handler Secretary of Defense Cheney to kill her daughter by taking off her daughter's ears was then backed up by the hypnotic command based on Wizard of Oz programming, "I'LL GET HER, MY PRETTY. . .YOUR LITTLE GIRL."
- The programming that is related to the Tin Man produces a monarch slave which is described as "A WELL OILED MACHINE" by the handlers. U.S. Senator Allen Simpson, one of the perpetrators of the Monarch Program, referred to the Tin Man programming when he told a slave "THESE ARE BUT EMPTY SHELLS OF THE LIFE THEY WERE ONCE POSSESSED. LIKE YOU ARE--EMPTY AND VOID OF LIFE."
- Phrases like "troubles melt" can be found in both the movie and in the programming.

Let's now cover what programming is based on the Oz books, that isn't found in the movie. A great deal of the Oz programming comes from the books, of which only the first book was used for the movie. The public is familiar with the movie which is based on the first one, but in general doesn't know the other books exist. We will not go through the scripts of all 14 books--there isn't room for that, but by going through a few of the books, the reader will begin to see the massive amount of material which was used for programming scripts in the Oz books. It is one thing to say, the Wizard of Oz was used as a mind-control programming script, but that doesn't convey the extent of it. Large sections of the 14 books are almost perfect for mind-control. If you take the trouble to read these quotes, you may find yourself startled at what you thought at first glance was a nice child story!

- pg. 38 Book 1 The Wizard of Oz, "That is true," said the Scarecrow. "You see," he continued, confidently, "I DON'T MIND MY LEGS AND ARMS AND BODY BEING STUFFED, BE-CAUSE I CANNOT GET HURT. IF ANYONE TREADS ON MY TOES OR STICKS A PIN INTO ME, IT DOESN'T MAT-TER, FOR I CAN'T FEEL IT." This is teaching dissociation. The slaves actually do have pins & needles stuck into them, or tooth-picks under their fingernails, etc. If anyone asks the slave a ques-tion they can say according to the script, "I don't know anything." The infant slave will be taught words like this "STICKS & STONES MAY BREAK MY BACK, BUT WORDS WILL NEVER HURT ME, BECAUSE I'M NOT HERE."

- pg. 41 Book 1 The Wizard of Oz, "It never hurt him, however, and Dorothy would pick him up and set him upon his feet again, while he joined her in laughing merrily at his own mishap." This is teaching the programming "IT'S O.K., IT DOESN'T MAT-TER, NOTHING WRONG HERE" that the slave is taught to tell the world.
- pg. 40 Book 1 The Wizard of Oz, "nest of rats in the straw, ...at the scarecrow." The mice in a Monarch System which control the turning of the quadrant's clock, hide from the scarecrow.
- pg. 42 Book 1 The Wizard of Oz, "fewer fruit trees..." If the slave eats the fruit [code for programs] without permission, the dwarf munchkins will beat the alter with their clubs. Also on this page HOME is called KANSAS, and it is described as "how gray eve-rything was there." In other words, reality isn't as great and color-ful as the make believe internal world you can build in your mind to escape this hell we're giving you.
- pg. 43 Book 1 The Wizard of Oz, The Scarecrow looked at her reproachfully, and answered, "My life has been so short that I really know nothing whatever. I was only made day before yester-day. What happened in the world before that time is all unknown to me. Luckily, when the farmer made my head, one of the first things he did was to paint my ears, so that I heard what was going on." This is the script read to new alters, to help them have a clean slate before programming them with another new script. This is coupled with the Wizard of Oz theme that the Wizard gives brains (what to think) to the Scarecrow. The alters are hyp-notically programmed that if they think on their own--then they

are empty headed like the Scarecrow. They can only have some-thing in their head if they let the Wizard give them what to think.

- pg. 45 Book 1 The Wizard of Oz, "It was a lonely life to lead, for I had nothing to think of, having been made such a little while before." This is part of the script read a new alter.
- pg. 48 Book 1 The Wizard of Oz, "So the Scarecrow led her through the trees until they reached the cottage, and Dorothy en-tered and found a bed of dried leaves in one corner. She lay down at once, and with Toto beside her, soon fell into a sound sleep. the Scarecrow who was never tired, stood up in another corner and waited..." This was used to program part of a script for an Illumi-nati ceremony.
- pg. 57 Book 1 The Wizard of Oz, "So the old woman went to the wicked Witch of the East, and promised her two sheep and a cow if she would prevent the marriage. Therefore, upon the wicked Witch enchanted my axe, and when I was chopping away...the axe slipped all at once and cut off my left leg. "This at first seemed a great misfortune, for I knew a one-legged man could not do very well as a woodchopper. So I went to a tinsmith and had him make me a new leg out of tin. The leg worked very well, once I was used to it; but my action angered the wicked Witch of the East, for she had promised the old woman I should not marry the pretty Munchkin girl. When I began chopping again my axe slipped and cut off my right leg. Again I went to the tinner, and again he made me a leg out of tin. After this the enchanted axe cut off my arms, one after the other; but, nothing daunted, I had them replaced with tin ones. The wicked Witch then made the axe slip and cut off my head, and at first I thought that was the end of me. But the tinner happened to come along, and he made me a new head out of tin." This is an Illuminati ceremony script done by Dr. Mengele with children at a very young age. It was a blood oath to "Green" that if they let anyone touch the programming they would cut themselves.
- pg. 58 Book 1 The Wizard of Oz, "...splitting me into two halves. Once more the tinner came to my help and made me a body of tin, fastening my tin arms...But alas! I had now no heart, so that I lost all my love for the Munchkin girl... I had known was the loss of my heart. While I was in love I was the happiest man on earth;

but no one can love who has not a heart, and so I am resolved to ask Oz to give me one."

- pg. 66 Book 1 The Wizard of Oz, The Scarecrow, the Tin Woodsman and Dorothy expect that the Wizard of Oz can give a brain, a heart, and send Dorothy back to Kansas. Under programming the Master as the Wizard can give alters what he wants including sending them back to Kansas (their internal reality).

- pg. 77 Book 1 The Wizard of Oz, "...they could see the road of yellow brick running through a beautiful country, with green meadows dotted with bright flowers and all the road bordered with trees hanging full of delicious fruits." This is used for the imagery of the yellow brick road.

- pg. 87 Book 1 The Wizard of Oz, "Scarlet poppies...their odor is so powerful that anyone who breathes it falls asleep, and if the sleeper is not carried away from the scent of the flowers he sleeps on and on forever. But Dorothy did not know this, nor could she get away from the bright red flowers that were everywhere about; so presently her eyes grew heavy and she felt she must sit down to rest and to sleep." This is an important part of the programming. This is the story line for trancing deep.

- pg. 112 Book 1 The Wizard of Oz, "Then the Guardian of the Gates put on his own glasses and told them he was ready to show them to the palace. Taking a big golden key from a peg on the wall he opened another gate, and they all followed him through the portal into the streets of the Emerald City." This is helpful imagery in setting up the internal Emerald City and its guards.

- **BOOK 3. OZMA OF OZ**

- pg. 20 Book 3 Ozma of Oz, "But the wind, as if satisfied at last with its mischievous pranks, stopped blowing this ocean and hurried away to another part of the world to blow something else; so that the waves, not being joggled any more, began to quiet down and behave themselves." Used to create protective programming, notice how the wind is personified.

- pg. 23 Book 3 Ozma of Oz, "So she sat down in a corner of the coop, leaned her back against the slats, nodded at the friendly stars before she closed her eyes, and was asleep in half a minute."

Alters may be trained to trance when placed in a corner.

- pg. 27 Book 3 Ozma of Oz, "No, indeed; I never care to hatch eggs unless I've a nice snug nest, in some quiet place, with a baker's dozen of eggs under me. That's thirteen, you know, and it's a lucky number for hens. So you may as well eat this egg." This has been used often to get 13 splits when torturing. Many Illuminati Systems were set up on 13 grids.

- pg. 30 Book 3 Ozma of Oz, "Next to the water [programming cue to build Atlantis] was a broad beach of white sand and gravel [programming cue to build Troy], and farther back were several rocky hills, while beyond these appeared a strip of green trees [programming cue to build a green forest] that marked the edge of a forest. But there were no houses to be seen, nor any sign of people [programming cue for alters to be invisible] who might inhabit this unknown land." This page along with others near it, have been used to build the structures in the internal world of Illuminati slaves. In brackets are a sample of how it could be used when building an internal world.

- pg. 34 Book 3 Ozma of Oz, "Why eating live things....You ought to be ashamed of yourself!" "Goodness me!" returned the hen, in a puzzled tone; how queer you are, Dorothy! Live things are much fresher and more wholesome than dead ones, and you humans eat all sorts of dead creatures." This is used to encourage cannibalism.

- pg. 35 Book 3 Ozma of Oz, "...a large sized golden key." To encourage the imagery of golden keys, which are used frequently in the internal system. The next chapter "Letter in the Sand" has singing trees in it, which have been popular items for the Illuminati due to their druid beliefs.

- pg. 39 Book 3 Ozma of Oz, "Bye, bye, and bye, when she was almost in despair, the little girl came upon two trees that promised to furnish her with plenty of food. One was quite full of square paper boxes, which grew in clusters on all the limbs, and upon the biggest and ripest boxes the word 'Lunch' could be read, in neat letters. The tree seemed to bear all the year around, for there were lunch-box blossoms on some of the branches, and on others tiny little lunch-boxes that were as yet quite green, and evidently not fit to eat." Boxes are built internally in the slave's mind and a box will contain a program. The food is the programming that the slave is to eat and digest. The programming in the box might be songs, nursery rhymes, or a poem or anything. (On page 41, there is a full page picture of a girl picking a lunch-pail from a tree limb to eat it.)

- pg. 40 Book 3 Ozma of Oz, "The little girl stood on tip-toe and picked one of the nicest and biggest lunch-boxes, and then she sat down upon the ground and eagerly opened it. Inside she found, nicely wrapped in white papers, a ham sandwich, a piece of sponge-cake, a pickle, a slice of new cheese and an apple. Each thing had a separate stem,..." The lunch-boxes on the tree are the programs which the programmers put in. The stems are what link the programming stories together in the child's mind.

- pg. 42 Book 3 Ozma of Oz, "I had a pair of silver shoes, that carried me through the air. ..said Dorothy." In the programming silver shoes are used as cues to go into altered states (i.e. through the air.)

- pg. 44 Book 3 Ozma of Oz, "embroidered garments of many colors" Color programming for the ribbons.

- pg. 47 Book 3 Ozma of Oz, "We'll get you in time, never fear! And when we do get you, we'll tear you into little bits." "Why are you so cruel to me? asked Dorothy. "I'm a stranger in your country, and have done you no harm." "No harm!" cried one who seemed to be their leader. "Did you not pick our lunch-boxes and dinner pails? Have you not a stolen dinner-pail still in your hand?...it is the law here that whoever picks a dinner-pail without our permission must die immediately." The programming message to all of this is that no one had better touch the dinner-pails which represent the programs or they are to die immediately. Armies like in the story guard the internal programming of the slave.

- pg. 51 Book 3 Ozma of Oz, these pages describe a crack in rocks that is a door. This is used for Petra programming.

- pg. 52 Book 3 Ozma of Oz, "golden key"..."within the narrow chamber of rock was the form of a man--or, at least, it seemed like a man...his head and limbs were copper. Also his head and limbs were copper, and these were jointed or hinged to his body in a peculiar way, with metal caps over the joints, like the armor worn by knights in days of old." These are a System's robots which are said by the programmers to be friends, and which are invisible. You can see other people's robots but not one's own internal robots.

- pg. 53 Book 3 Ozma of Oz, "This copper man is not alive at all." The clone robots are made to think they are not alive, but just robots. In reality they are little child alters suited up to think they are robots.

- pg. 55 Book 3 Ozma of Oz, "...back view of the copper man, and in this way discovered a printed card that hung between his shoulders, it being suspended from a small copper peg at the back of his neck." The robots are put in by a combination of several stories. The deep sea divers of 20,000 Leagues Under the Sea, and the Wizard of Oz's Copper Man reinforce each other. "Extra Responsive Mechanical man fitted with our special clock-work attachment. Thinks, Speaks, Acts, and Does Everything but Live. Manufactured only at our Works at Evna, Land of Ev. All infringements will be promptly Prosecuted according to Law." This huge sign is part of the robotic programming the clone robots receive. Notice that they are drilled into total obedience--all infringements will be promptly Prosecuted. Obey the law that your Master gives you.

- pg. 56 Book 3 Ozma of Oz, "DIRECTIONS FOR USING
  For THINKING: --Wind the Clock-work Man under his left arm, (marked No. 1)
  For SPEAKING: --Wind the Clock-work Man under his right arm, (marked No. 2)
  For WALKING: --Wind Clock-work in the -middle of his back, (marked No. 3)
  N.B.--This Mechanism is guaranteed to work perfectly for a thousand years." These instructions were used to build Dr. Green's (Mengele's) boxes and the robots.

- pg. 58 Book 3 Ozma of Oz, "The words sounded a little hoarse and creaky, and they were uttered all in the same tone, without any change of expression whatever; but both Dorothy and Billina understood them perfectly." This was used to program the internal robots to speak in unison and to repeat themselves.

- pg. 60 Book 3 Ozma of Oz, "Af-ter that I re-mem-ber noth-ing until you wound me up a-gain." The internal robots forget and then are prepared again for war.

- pg. 62 Book 3 Ozma of Oz, "From this time forth I am your o-be-di-ent servant. What-ev-er you com-mand, that I will do will-ing-ly--if you keep me wound up." This is used to teach the internal robots obedience to their programming.

- pg. 67 Book 3 Ozma of Oz, "Within the pail were three slice of turkey, two slices of cold tongue, some lobster salad, four slices of bread and butter, a small custard pie, an orange and nine large strawberries and some nuts and raisins. Singularly enough, the nuts in this dinner-pail grew already cracked, so that Dorothy had no trouble in picking out their meats to eat." This is given to front alters as the front programming so that they see the programs as only "fruit".

- pg. 68 Book 3 Ozma of Oz, "Do the lunch-box trees and the din-ner-pail trees belong to the Wheelers? the child asked Tiktok, while engaged in eating her meal. 'Of course not,' he answered. 'They belong to the roy-al fam-il-y of Ev, on-ly of course there is no roy-al fam-il-y just now be-cause King Ev-ol-do jumped in-to the sea and his wife and ten children have been trans-formed by the Nome King...you will find the roy-al 'E' stamped up-on the bottom of ev-er-y din-ner pail." The Nome King in the program-ming became the ruler of the demons/system within the Monarch system. Several story lines from a number of sources are over-lapped to reinforce the programming scripts. The programmers will use other stories to introduce themselves into the system too. In case readers don't know, a Monarch system will have hidden powerful alters that are made in the image of their programmers, that serve as personal representatives of the programmers.

- pg. 79 Book 3 Ozma of Oz, "I am only a ma-chine, and can-not feel sor-row or joy, no mat-ter what hap-pens." This is teaching mechanical dissociation, and coincides with Tin Man program-ming.

- pg. 83 Book 3 Ozma of Oz, "For the Princess Langwidere is a different person every time I see her, and the only way her sub-jects can recognize her at all is by means of a beautiful ruby key which she always wears on a chain attached to her left wrist. When we see the key we know we are beholding the Princess."

"That is strange," said Dorothy, in astonishment. "Do you mean to say that so many different princesses are one and the same person?" "Not exactly," answered the Wheeler. "There is, of course, but one princess; but she appears to us in many forms, which are all more or less beautiful." Doesn't this sound like MPD! Did Frank Baum know about MPD?

- pg. 90 Book 3 Ozma of Oz, "Princess Langwidere's sitting-room was paneled with great mirrors, which reached from the ceiling to the floor; also the ceiling was composed of mirrors, and the floor was of polished silver that reflected every object upon it. So when Langwidere sat in her easy chair and played soft melodies upon her mandolin, her form was mirrored hundreds of times, in walls, and ceilings and floor, and whichever way..." This is the mirror programming that has been done to so many victims!

- pg. 91 Book 3 Ozma of Oz, "Now I must explain to you that the Princess Langwidere had thirty heads." Isn't this story line convenient for programming?

- pg. 94 Book 3 Ozma of Oz, ...Langwidere to a position in front of cupboard No. 17, the Princess unlocked the door with her ruby key and after handing head No.9, which she had been wearing, to the maid, she took No. 17 from its shelf and fitted it to her neck....There was one trouble with No. 17; the temper that went with it (and which was hidden...)was fiery, harsh and haughty in the extreme, and it often led the Princess to do unpleasant things which she regretted when she came to wear her other heads." Does the reader see how this is programming to switch personalities. And personality No. 17 is locked up--which is a common programming methodology. The fiery, harsh anger--those are the demonic imps that the victim is coached to accept as normal which are layered in. (See chapter 10).

- pg. 98 Book 3 Ozma of Oz, "'To hear is to obey,' answered the big red colonel, and caught the child by the arm."

- pg. 99 Book 3 Ozma of Oz, "...the colonel had by this time managed to get upon his feet again, so he grabbed fast hold of the girl and she was helpless to escape."

- pg. 102 Book 3 Ozma of Oz, "Once a cyclone had carried her across it, and a magical pair of silver shoes had carried her back again."

- pg. 103 Book 3 Ozma of Oz, "Fist came a magnificent golden chariot, drawn by a great Lion and an immense Tiger, who stood shoulder to shoulder and trotted along as gracefully as a well-matched team of thoroughbred horses. And standing upright within the chariot was a beautiful girl clothed in flowing robes of silver gauze and wearing a jeweled diadem upon her dainty head. She held in one hand the satin ribbons that guided her astonishing team, and in the other an ivory wand that separated at the top into two prongs, the prongs being tipped by the letters '0' and 'Z', made of glistening diamonds set closely together." The way this was used for programming is that guard alters are made out of kittens, who believe they are fierce tigers and lions and other wild cats. Ozma, represents the Illuminati Queen Mother with her crown and scepter.
- pg. 104 Book 3 Ozma of Oz, On this page we see Ozma of Oz, the Scarecrow, the Saw-Horse, the Tin Woodman, and soldiers. These characters were used in the programming. Toward the bottom of the page is something that was built into the Systems so that alters would stay in place in their internal world, "...the green carpet rolled itself up again...In order that their feet might not come in contact with the deadly, life-destroying sands of the desert."
- pg. 117 Book 3 Ozma of Oz, "Dorothy took the key to Tiktok from her pocket and wound up the machine man's action, so that he could bow properly when introduced to the rest of the company."
- pg. 119-120 Book 3 Ozma of Oz," 'Let me introduce to you a new friend of mine, the Hungry Tiger."...he displayed two rows of terrible teeth and a mouth big enough to startle anyone.' 'Dreadfully hungry," answered the Tiger, snapping his jaws together with a fierce click.'" This is programming for deeper cats in an alter system. The next page tells how this is used to teach the child alter cannibalism. "...the tiger. "For my part, I'm a savage beast, and have an appetite for all sorts of poor living creatures, from a chipmonk to fat babies.' 'How dreadful!' said Dorothy. 'Isn't it, though?' returned the Hungry Tiger licking his lips with his long red tongue. 'Fat babies! Don't they sound delicious? ...If I had no conscience I would probably eat the babies

and then get hungry again, which would mean that I had sacrificed the poor babies for nothing....For it is the nature of tigers to be cruel and ferocious, and in refusing to eat harmless living creatures I am acting as no good tiger has ever before acted." This part of the book is used to help teach the child alters which think they are tigers to be cannibalistic and actually participate in eating babies. This is all filmed to be used against the mind-controlled slave.

- pg. 130-3 1 Book 3 Ozma of Oz, " 'No one knows, exactly,' replied the Princess. 'For the King, whose name is Roquat of the Rocks, owns a splendid palace underneath the great mountain which is at the north end of this kingdom, and he has transformed the queen and her children into ornaments and bric-a-brac with which to decorate his rooms.'" 'I'd like to know," said Dorothy, 'Who this Nome King is?'

- 'I will tell you, replied Ozma. 'He is said to be the Ruler of the Underground World, and commands the rocks and all that the rocks contain. Under his rule are many thousands of the Nomes, who are queerly shaped but powerful sprites that labor at the furnaces and forges of their king, making gold and silver and other metals which they conceal in the crevices of the rocks, so that those living upon the earth's surface can only find them with great difficulty. Also they make diamonds and rubies and emeralds, which they hide in the ground; so that the kingdom of Nomes is wonderfully rich, and all we have of precious stones and silver and gold is what we take from the earth and rocks where the Nome King has hidden them....the Ruler of the Underground World is not fond of those who live upon the earth's surface, and never appears among us. If we wish to see King Roquat of the Rocks, we must visit his won country, where he is all powerful, and therefore it will be a dangerous undertaking....the furnaces of the Nome King....a single spark of fire might destroy me entirely.' 'The furnaces may also melt my tin,' said the Tin Woodman; but I am going.'" 'I can't bear heat,' remarked the Princess... This is used to program in the dwarfs who mine the jewels (programs). The dwarfs are often demonic imps or gnomes, rather than being real alters. Notice that the story line fits in beautifully with the Hell Pit that the Programmers so often put at the basement of people's minds. The Hell Pit would have pro-gramming to make someone burn. If someone approaches where the Dwarfs live (which is deep underground--deep in the mind) they will burn. Notice again the words diamonds, rubies, emer-alds, silver and gold which are all parts of programming codes.

- pg. 139 Book 3 Ozma of Oz, " 'But I know enough to obey my masters, and to gid-dup, or whoa, when I'm told to." This is teaching obedience. "Lower down the table were the twenty-seven warriors of Oz." This was used to create alters within the internal world.
- pg. 147-148 Book 3 Ozma of Oz, The form was that of a gigantic man built out of plates of cast iron, and it stood with one foot on either side of the narrow road and swung over its right shoulder an immense iron mallet, with which it constantly pounded the earth. These resounding blows explained the thumping sounds they had heard, for the mallet was much bigger than a barrel, and where it struck the path between the rocky sides of the mountain it filled all the space through which our travelers would be obliged to pass.

- Of course they at once halted, a safe distance away from the terri-ble iron mallet. The magic carpet would do them no good in this case, for it was only meant to protect them from any dangers upon the ground beneath their feet, and not from dangers that appeared in the air above them. "Wow!" said the Cowardly Lion, with a shudder. "It makes me dreadfully nervous to see that big hammer pounding so near my head. One blow would crush me into a door -mat.""The ir-on gi-ant is a fine fellow," said Tiktok, "and works as stead-i-ly as a clock. He was made for the Nome King by Smith & Tin-ker, who made me, and his du-ty is to keep folks from find-ing the un-der-ground pal-ace. Is he not a great work of art?"... "No," replied the machine; "he is only made to pound the road, and has no think-ing or speak-ing at-tach-ment. But he pounds ve-ry well, I think.". "Is there no way to stop his machin-ery?" "On-ly the Nome King, who has the key, can do that," an-swered Tiktok....Meanwhile the giant continued to raise his iron mallet high in the air and to strike the path terrific blows that ech-oed through the mountains like the roar of cannon." This was used as the script to place in Thor, a giant who protects the programming. Very severe split brain headaches are programmed to occur to the victim, whenever the internal Thor pounds his hammer. If the programming is threatened, Thor and the imps (demons) appear, to protect it. There are an entire series of events using programming and obedient alters that takes place to protect the programming, if it is ever threatened.

- pg. 159 Book 3 Ozma of Oz, "There was no reply, except that the shifting Nomes upon the mountain laughed in derision. 'You must not command the Nome King.' said Tiktok, 'for you do not rule him, as you do your own people.' The purpose of this part is to prepare the child's alters to accept that internal Queens and other leading alters do not rule the demons that are placed into their system, and are not to order them around.
- pg. 163 Book 3 Ozma of Oz, "In the center of this room was a throne carved out of a solid boulder of rock, rude and rugged in shape but glittering with great rubies and diamonds and emeralds on every part of its surface. And upon the throne sat the Nome King.
- pg. 167 Book 3 Ozma of Oz, on this page is a picture of the Nome King telling Dorothy and Ozma that, "They belong to me and I shall keep them." In other words, the imps and their jewells belong to the king of the demons. Around his throne are steps with gems, and this imagery was used to build the internal gems in a system, with Satan/the Anti-Christ's throne at the top of the stairs.
- pg. 170 Book 3 Ozma of Oz, "Although this army consisted of rock-colored Nomes, all squat and fat, they were clothed in glittering armor of polished steel, inlaid with beautiful gems. Upon his brow each wore a brilliant electric light, and they bore sharp spears and swords and battle-axes of solid bronze. It was evident they were perfectly trained, for they stood in straight rows, rank after rank, with their weapons held erect and true, as if awaiting but the word of command to level them upon their foes." 'This,' said the Nome King, 'is but a small part of my army. No ruler upon Earth has ever dared to fight me, and no ruler ever will, for I am too powerful to oppose.' This was to help build acceptance within the child of the layering of armies of demons.

- pg. 180, Book 3 Ozma of Oz, "For upon the edge of the table rested a pretty grasshopper, that seemed to have been formed from a single emerald." The next page has a picture of a grass-hopper wearing a hat and many shoes. This was used to help the victim take the hypnotic suggestion that their programmer was a grasshopper, a cricket. Mengele used a clicker which helped with this hypnotic suggestion too.

- pg. 182-183 Book 3 Ozma of Oz, "...the King returned to his throne.... they were greatly disheartened by...the knowledge that she was now an ornament in the Nome King's palace -- a dread-ful, creepy place in spite of all its magnificence. Without their little leader they did not know what to do next, and each one, down to the trembling private of the army, began to fear he would soon be more ornamental than useful....'Never mind,' said the jolly monarch. 'If he doesn't care to enter the palace...I'll throw him into one of my fiery furnaces.'

- pg. 184 Book 3 Ozma of Oz, "...twenty-six officers filed into the palace and made their guesses---and became ornaments." Story line used to program parts to become useful ornaments. "...he wore a heavy gold chain around his neck to show that he was the Chief Steward of the Nome King..." Many of the abusers signify their power to the slaves, by wearing a gold chain around their neck.

- pg. 186 Book 3 Ozma of Oz, on this page it states that some magical power gave the King the ability to know all that took place in his palace. By crediting their abilities to an occult magi-cal dimension, the programmers enhanced their appearance of power to the child victim. pg. 192 Book 3 Ozma of Oz, on this page and the surrounding pages, the people who have become or-naments are also assigned colors. The Queen of Ev "are all orna-ments of a royal purple color." and "all those people from Oz into green ornaments."

- pg. 194 Book 3 Ozma of Oz, 'If I wore the magic belt which en-ables you to work all your transformations, and gives you so much other power....What color will you make the Kansas girl? asked the Steward. 'Gray, I think,' said his Majesty. 'And the Scarecrow and the machine man?' 'Oh, they shall be of solid gold, because they are so ugly in real life.' This was the script to bring in the color programming. Color programming is discussed in Chapter 7 (Structuring), Chapter 11 (Internal Controls) , and in Chapter 4 where the hypnoidal codes are given.

- pg. 192 Book 3 Ozma of Oz, 'What more do you want?' demanded the King. 'A fat baby. I want a fat baby,' said the Hungry Tiger. 'A nice, plump, juicy, tender, fat baby.' When the alters are forced to accept that they are tigers and other cats, then they are encouraged (forced) into cannibalism.
- pg. 200 Book 3 Ozma of Oz, "So Tiktok touched a yellow glass vase that had daisies painted on one side, and he spoke at the same time the word 'Ev.' .... In a flash the machine man had disappeared,..." This was part of the programming to introduce daisies and switching.
- pg. 201 Book 3 Ozma of Oz, "Next she touched the image of a purple kitten that stood on the corner of a mantel, and as she pronounced the word 'Ev' the kitten disappeared, and a pretty, fair-haired boy stood beside her." This is teaching the switching of alters and their color programming.

We will stop our coverage of the Ozma of Oz book here. We have only partially covered only two of the 14 Oz books, all of which were used as programming scripts. There are many more sections in this series of 14 books that served as programming scripts, but you, the reader, have got the basic idea. It is still important to go over how some of the other books were used in programming, so that the reader begins to see how the story lines assist in programming, and how the story lines are so frequently tied together from perhaps 12 different stories to reinforce one alter's programming.

Alice Through the Looking Glass

- 'I can't believe that!' said Alice. 'Can't you?' the Queen said in a pitying tone. 'Try again: draw a long breath, and shut your eyes.' Alice laughed. 'There's no use trying,' she said. 'One can't believe impossible things.' 'I dare say you haven't had much practice,' said the Queen. 'When I was your age, I always did it for half an hour a day. Why, sometimes I've believed as many as six impossible things before breakfast." The chapter "Which

Dreamed It" in Alice Through the Looking Glass has sexual programming, the Red Queen is purring. The story where Walruses make believe it is oysters is used for programming. Other sexual programming occurs in the chapter "It's my own invention" where the Knight In Crimson (& White) Armor are prisoners which dual for her.

- Tweedle Dee & Tweedle Dum is used for S&M programming, which has a hand signal involving rotating the thumbs of a clasp hand. Alters go through the looking glass, and fall down an oak tree by falling into a deeper and deeper trance. Monarch programming is a reflection of how Satan's mind works. Lewis Carroll's book with its inversion themes fits in with this type of thinking. Lewis Carroll loved the humor of logical contradictions. In the book, Alice wonders if cats eat bats or bats eat cats, and she is told that to say what she means is not the same as meaning what she says. When she eats the left side of the mushroom, she grows large; the right side has the reverse effect. These changes in size are in themselves reversals.

- A large girl and small puppy end up to be a large puppy and a small girl. In Sylvia and Bruno, we are presented with an anti-gravity wool that can be placed into a parcel to make it weigh less than nothing, a watch that reverses time, a black light, and a projective plane with outside inside and inside outside. The slave learns that E-V-I-L is simply L-I-V-E backwards. In the looking glass world, the Red Queen knows of a hill so large that compared to it the hill in question is a valley. Also she knows of dry biscuits which quench thirst, a messenger who whispers by shouting, and Alice who runs as fast as she can to stay in one place. (Sometimes it seems we really do have to run fast to stay in place.) The King of Hearts thinks its not unusual to write letters to nobody, and the White King compliments Alice on having keen enough eyesight to see nobody at a great distance down the road. Can you see why this book was so good to program us?

In the book Through the Looking Glass all asymmetrical objects (that means all objects which can't be superimposed on their mirrored image) "go the other way." There are left-right reversals. Tweedledee and Tweedledum are mirror image twins. The White Knight sings about squeezing his right foot into a left shoe, and there are several mentions of corkscrews. A Helix (a corkscrew) is an asymmetric structure with distinct left and right forms. The book's type of thinking was extended beyond asymmetrical objects to asymmetrical relations of all types. For example, Alice walks backward, in the railway carriage the guard tells her she is traveling the wrong way. The king has two messengers, "one to come and one to go." The White Queen explains the advantages of living backward in time, the looking glass cake is handed around first, then sliced. Odd and even numbers, which are equivalent to left and right or on and off are worked into the story at several points.

For instance, the White Queen requests jam every other day. Going through the looking glass takes us to a world where the ordinary world is turned upside down and backward. Things go every which way except the way they are supposed to go. Anti-matter is a mirror image. Anti-matter milk will explode Alice, but an Anti-matter Alice on the other side of the looking glass can drink the anti-matter milk. In Chapter 11 Alice captures the Red Queen. It results in a legitimate checkmate of the Red King, who has slept through the entire live size chess game without moving. The checkmate ends the dream, but leaves open in the story the question of whether the dream was Alice's or the Red King's. The programming has so often been only a dream to us.

The outside world was so often just an unreal dream to us. What was real and what was not real? The real world (for other people) was full of contradictions, and the unreal world (our internal world) was consistent. Everything was upside down, forwards and backwards. In the Looking Glass book, one shuttles back and forth mysteriously between real and dream worlds. "So, either I've been dreaming about life or I only dream that life is but a dream." As a slave breaks away from the programming, life becomes a bewildering confusion as the slave is pulled between two worlds. The internal world has everything the alter needs, the external world is a harsh cold reality that doesn't have much to offer. People in the external world can help make it real for a slave. The handlers will never do this.

Alters will need a reason to want to come out of the internal reality which they are programmed to. believe in. For so long much of life was seen as a dream. It will be hard to get a grasp on what was real and what was the lie. Many of the lies are more real than the truth. Life was sometimes like the parallel dreams of the Red King and Alice, like two mirrors facing each other.

THE TALL BOOK OF MAKE BELIEVE

This book was published by Harper & Row in 1950 and was indeed tall, the pages being 4" x 9 1/2". All of the stories in The Tall Book of Make Believe were used one way or the other in programming. We will just touch on some notable points.

On page 14, the programmer would read the first paragraph of the poem and then say "sleep, sleep, sleep." "Have you ever heard of the Sugar-Plum Tree? 'Tis a marvel of great renown! It blooms on the shore of the Lollypop Sea in the garden of Shut-Eye Town; The fruit that it bears is so wondrously sweet (As those who have tasted it say) That good little children have only to eat of that fruit to be happy next day. Sleep, Sleep, Sleep."

On page 16-17, there is a story about how a child is dragged under the kitchen door and becomes flat. There is a picture of a child being pulled under a door and coming out flat on page 17. This was used as part of the script to make the ribbons for the slaves. The ribbons in a system can go under doors and through the entire system.

On page 23, Rosa the flat person (pancake person) is shown again. This is ribbon. The top of the page has a large cricket like creature that was said to the child to be the programmer (Dr. Mengele).

On page 38 is a poem about a Mr. Nobody. The programmers like to have alters identify themselves as "nobody".

On page 39 is a poem/story about "someone" who comes tapping...but it is "only the cricket whistling". This was used to help program in that the 3 taps were the cricket (the cover image for the programmer.)

On page 50, is the story of a girl who when she lays down becomes a different person Mrs. Brown.

On page 67 is a poem Foreign Lands, where the child sees "the sky's blue looking glass" and then ends up "to where the roads on either hand lead onward into fairyland.. .and all the playthings come alive." In other words, what is in effect being communicated is: take the hypnotic image of flying into the sky in Papa's silver plane (as the plane goes up the trance goes higher -deeper) and then go into a fantasy land where all your wishes can come true--so that you can escape the hell us programmers are giving you.

On page 79 is the story of a ghost named Georgie who would run home and warn people at home when things were broken. This was part of the "fix me" programming--so that ghost-like alters, known as reporting alters, call "HOME" to "PAPA" if the programming is touched.

On page 84 is the story "How they bring back The Village of Cream Puffs When the Wind Blows it away." This story has several programming words in it, these words and their meanings are as follows: In programming the "Village of Liver-and-Onions" is a code word for "the coven. "Prairie" means "ceremony site", and in another story "picnic" means "ritual". It's doubtful that most alters would remember these meanings, but they helped the abusers confuse the child. Imagine the victim trying to describe a ritual and telling someone that a village of liver & onions had a picnic.

ALIEN PROGRAMMING SCRIPTS

There are numerous scripts for the Alien programming. Recent novels and Hollywood movies provide a non-ending pool of programming resources for the Programmers. Visual reality headgear and other high-tech methods can easily be incorporated into an alien abduction theme. The following are samples of some of the people who my sources and I have spent time with, who on one level knew they needed help, but didn't know just what they felt uneasy about.

PERSON 1. Had been abducted by aliens since she was a small child. Different types of aliens took her. Her mother worked for the CIA at Area 51. Her mother was abusive to her. One of her best friends is a Monarch slave. When the aliens come a bright light appears and then they abduct her. The aliens she works with the most look exactly like people, and in their handwriting show severe abuse. These benevolent aliens have taken her fetuses several times. She has time-travelled to their planet. She is dissociative. The government authorities are constantly monitoring and tracking her, and have made an effort to be smudge her record, so that it appears like she is loony tunes. This is the type of case that this book's co-author has spent time working with. Doesn't this sound more like human mind-control than real aliens?

PERSON 2. This person hears aliens within his head (which when described sounds like a case of MPD (DID)). The aliens would take him and force him to have homosexual activities even though he didn't want to participate. But that was O.K. to him, because they were a superior race and if these benevolent aliens which are so far advanced beyond us, want to have sex with him, that is their prerogative. This person has a lot of depression. This person wonders why the authorities seem to keep track of him.

PERSON 3. This person worked at Area 51. Has a photographic memory throughout his entire MPD system. He realizes that he is MPD. His best friend claims to be an alien, a god of sorts, and is known by both myself and one of my sources to be part of Naval Intelligence. This best friend acts more like a handler than an alien, and this Area 51 worker gives his best friend total allegiance. This man has all kinds of alien type stories, which sound in many cases like programming. This person admits that his family is Illuminati, and the front alters say he has watched Illuminati rituals as an adult, but hasn't participated. He shows signs of severe abuse. He is afraid to talk about trauma-based mind-control, but loves to talk about aliens.

In fact, all three of the persons discussed shied away from talking about Monarch mind-control, as if it were something not important, but they all love to talk about aliens.

And the list of interesting people like this could go on. When Mind-controlled slaves who have alien programming are being abducted by the intelligence agencies for their use and for programming here are some of the details of how and what occurs: A bright light is shined into their house. They have been hypnotically conditioned to view this light as a Flying Saucer, whether it is a helicopter or something else. As the NWO does have Flying Saucers, sometimes the real thing is used. Men in Black, just like in SRA cases, are often associated with the abductions. And the slaves frequently speak about "shadows in the mind." The slaves are taken to rooms where examining tables with white sheets and X-ray machines, Headgear and medical equipment is in place.

The alien equipment has gotten more high-tech over the last 40 years. The aliens wear suits that are full of occult symbolism. The people are restrained with clamps and electrical shock and energy is used on them. They are told that they are receiving information. They are given tracking implants and other implants. All of the 3 above persons, receive information from the aliens regularly. Almost all of the elements of Monarch trauma-based mind-control appear in these abduction accounts, especially in the psychological features of the victim. The victims of alien abduction programming feel suicidal after they talk too much. They have headaches, sleep difficulties, nightmares, obsessive thoughts, a fear of hypnosis, trapped feelings, and paranoia. During their abductions the aliens use drugs, thought transfers, and painful medical procedures.

The aliens use language that parallels the messages given to SRA victims, just change the language from Satan is in charge to the Aliens are in charge . Cattle mutilations where the blood has been drained are associated with abductions. There are documented accounts where cattle mutilations have been connected to Satanic cults using helicopters. The victims of aliens are forced to be impregnated and then the fetus is repeatedly taken. The aliens are repeatedly telling these victims that a holocaust is soon to come. Another strange phenomena, that others and this author have noticed is that these victims of alien abduction seem to know each other, much in the same way that victims of Illuminati mind-control seem to know each other., and the aliens seem to know everything about the victims. The victims have amnesia of their abductions.

The memories of their abductions are hidden in altered states of consciousness, that hypnosis sometimes can pull up. Most victims are afraid of hypnosis or can't be hypnotized (they have been hypnotized not to allow anyone else to hypnotize them.)

To give credit where due, Bowart's Operation Mind Control Researcher's edition, (1994) has an excellent appendix with charts which compare SRA mind-control victims and alien abduction victims. The charts reveal how similar the two groups are. In preparing these paragraphs, we have used his charts as a basis for how we wrote these last two paragraphs up. However, the co-authors` experiences in working with abduction victims match the findings of Bowart. Do aliens from another planet exist? They may or may not. It is not a real issue. We have to face what is already on this planet. One source has several tapes of aliens of different types talking (which were obtained from abduction survivors) and their voices sound demonic and they are saying that they have been alive on this planet for many years.

One said something like he's been here on earth 500,000 years. If an alien has lived on this planet for 1/2 million years, when does he get residence status. My! If that is true, he is no alien--we are! But one thing is certain, this planet contains some very slimy evil creatures who are either real non-humans or very deceptive dark humans. The Bible calls them demons and reprobate men. The four most popular origins of supposed aliens on earth are all star groups relatively close to our solar system.

They are: the Pleiades, known as the 7 or 9 sisters, because there are 9 stars of which 7 are visible; Sirius, the dog constellation; the Orion constellation; and the twin stars of Zeta Reticulli, which twin stars were amazingly charted by Chinese astrologers in 3,000 B.C.! Myself and my sources, have kept an open mind on the issue, could there be any benevolent aliens? Some abductees believed that their aliens were benevolent, but when they are debriefed they admit that mind-control and sexual molestation is carried out by the aliens. Fritz, has concluded with other investigators on this question, there are no benevolent aliens, in fact the only aliens that may be around are what have been known as demons. People who have participated in high level Illuminati ceremonies report the presence of creatures that look like the various aliens. Some points might be briefly brought out. Other sources have amassed a great deal of evidence that the elite have human-built Flying Saucers.

Notice how the controlled media always link aliens with Flying Saucers and UFOs? This is an entire book in itself, however, the bottom line is that at least most (if not all) of the alien abductions are simply part of the NWO's mind-control. It is obvious that for various reasons (including the goals set down in the secret Iron Mountain government report), the government (including cooperating agencies like NASA) decided to use an alien abduction theme rather than a Satanic Ritual Abuse theme to their mind-control programming. The major differences in the programming methodology is that the blood rituals of the SRA are no longer used.

The reason why blood rituals are no longer needed is that the high-tech harmonic machines (which implant thoughts-see chap. 6) and other high-tech methods eliminate the need for the blood traumas. The victims of alien abductions are taken at random, where the Illuminati victims are abducted more frequently around ritual dates. The person who believes in UFOs and aliens is going to receive the same type of treatment as those who believe in Satanic Ritual Abuse. The legal system and society at large are conditioned to treat them as nuts. This protects their abusers. An Illuminati hierarchy member described their magic goal of pursuing a spiritual path through the finer frequencies of outer time. The alien programming is one way to experience this.

ISLAND OF THE BLUE DOLPHINS

This is a child's book by Scott O'Dell. The people of an island have both an everyday name and a magical name. When the chief gives his magical name to a Russian captain named Orlov, he and his warriors end up being killed in battle. The alters of Monarch slaves have names they can give outsiders and then their access code names which must be kept secret. Part of the story is to stay in line with what one's ancestors have done. Other items in the book, such as the four winds from the four directions fit in with programming too. The book is just one of many that the programmers want the children to hear so that they naturally adopt the correct programming scripts.

THE LORD OF THE RINGS

Some Illuminati survivors are always looking for a ring. Rings play a significant part in the lives and programming of slaves. One section that is coding/programming found in J.R.R. Tolkien's Lord of the Rings is One Ring to rule them all, One Ring to find them, One Ring to bring them all and in the darkness bind them.

THE MOST IMPORTANT PROGRAMMING SCRIPT - THE LESSER KEY

One of the most important scripts for the Illuminati Mind-control Programmers is the Lesser Key of Solomon Goetia, The Book of Evil Spirits. The Illuminati Doctors Green, Black, White and Blue (that is Mengele, Wheeler, Cameron, and Mueller) were fully knowledgeable about The Lesser Key of Solomon Goetia. In fact, all those who go beyond the initial levels in the Illuminati are required to study the entire book. It's an important ritual book.

It is very out of fashion to believe in demons. It is in fashion to believe in aliens, in ghosts, in the internal psychological wizard that guides you , and other things which to those high in demonology secretly know are simply covers for what used to be called demons. Both the high level Illuminati and the alert Christians are saying many of the same things concerning demons. Is "magical" phenomena real? Do the programmers really believe in it? In the Lesser Key of Solomon Goetia it answers,

"I am not concerned to deny the objective reality of all 'magical' phenomena; if they are illusions, they are at least as real as many unquestioned facts of daily life; and... they are at least evidence of some cause." (p.10)

The author of the Lesser Key of Solomon Goetia (L.W. De Laurence) then points out that all our sense impressions of the universe are dependent upon changes in the brain. Reality is a perception of the mind. So the author states,

"...we must include illusions, which are after all sense impressions as much as realities' are, in the class of 'phenomena dependent on brain changes.' Magical phenomena, however, come under a special sub-class, since they are willed, and their cause is the series of 'real' phenomena called the operations of ceremonial magic."

In other words, when the Illuminati practice ceremonial magic, their magic to them is as real as life, but they do not feel a need to defend its reality. People in the occult encourage children to fantasize. Fantasy is looked at with favor. Whether the power and healing and mind -control of demonology stems from illusion or Jung's autonomous power of the human psyche to attract & manifest archetypes through the human soul or some other source is not an issue for Satanists.

They are seeing results, power, healings and the destruction of their enemies by demonology. Within the Illuminati illusion, myth, and perception are all esteemed. Are they alone? Are they alone? No, they are not alone. The myth that the United States is a democracy is probably a far stronger "reality" in the minds of Americans than the actual reality that it is a tightly controlled secret oligarchy with a republican front. But in this case, which is the greater real reality? The American believes his myth enough that he dies for it. He fights the "war to end all wars" and then the "war to save the world FOR DEMOCRACY" (to quote some popular world war slogans). In the American mind, he achieves victory even though he has fought and died for a myth.

And even when the mythical goals he fought for aren't even achieved, he believes he has achieved a victory. The first world war never brought everlasting peace and the war to save the world for democracy ended after "victory" with more of the world under stronger totalitarian rule than before the war began.

The bottom line is that myths and illusions make up a large part of the reality of most people's lives.

Movie actors have repeatedly found out that they incur their fan's wrath if they try to reveal their real selves to the public. The point also is that the person practicing ceremonial magic will not be impressed by the average person, even if he be a minister, who has structured his life on myths and illusions, who will tell him that his ceremonial magic is not real.

The magician will naturally ask, "Who IS living in a world of reality?" Ceremonial magic is a very strong "reality" to the Illuminati's mind-controlled slaves, because the programmers make great efforts to develop the five "impressions" listed on page 11 of The Lesser Key, which are:

1) *Sight. The circle, square, triangle, vessels, lamps, robes, implements, etc.*

2) *Sound. The invocations.*

3) *Smell. The perfumes.*

4) *Taste. The Sacraments.*

5) *Touch. As under (1).*

These are reflected upon by the person, and these 5 produce unusual brain-changes. Later two more senses are also highly developed. Programmed multiple-slaves have visual and auditory acuity far beyond the normal person. The Lesser Keys of Solomon Goetia goes on to say, "The Spirits of the Goetia are portions of the human brain. Their seals therefore represent methods of stimulating or regulating those particular spots (through the eye)."

"The names of God are vibrations calculated to establish:

a) *General control of the brain....*
b) *Control over the brain in detail. (Rank or type of the Spirit)*
c) *Control of one special portion. (Name of Spirit.)*

The perfumes aid this through smell. Usually the perfume will only tend to control a large area; but there is an attribution of perfumes to letters of the alphabet enabling one, by a Kabalistic formula, to spell out the Spirit's name." (p. 12)

Did the reader grasp that? The most important script for the programmers is to use ceremonial magic which uses the names of God to establish GENERAL, & SPECIFIC CONTROL (via a hierarchical arrangement of demons) over a person's mind. More will be covered about this in Chapter 10. But while we are on the subject let's go just a little bit farther. "If, then, I say, with Solomon: 'The Spirit Cimieries teaches logic,' what I mean is: Those portions of my brain which are subservient the logical faculty may be stimulated and developed by following out the processes called 'The Invocation of Cimieries.'

And this is exactly what the programmers do. They invoke via many rituals all types of specific demons (or demonic energy) to enhance the particular mental functions they want. For instance, Typhon and Choronzon (also Horonzon) are demons who are essential in building the structure of a programmed multiple. They must be invoked before the early start of dividing the mind. Michael Bertieaux heads up the Horonzon Club, an unofficial part of Kenneth Grant's OTO.

The demon Horonzon (or Choronzon) looks like a grey alien, and was conjured up by Sir John Dee, who was Queen Elizabeth I's genius advisor and court sorcerer. Transyuggothian magic is carried out in order to reach Transyuggothian Space (also known as Trans-Plutonian Space and Universe B). The existence of these dimensions is kept very secret. The ancient cult of the Star Sirius, from which supposedly we are now getting aliens, had rituals to get one into the celebrated Universe B. Sirius B (the binary twin star that exists with the actual Sirius A star) represented the god Ra Hoor Khuit. Sirius A represented the Egyptian devil. Let's reflect on all this demonic "illusion". As stated, an American will die for the myth that America is saving the world for democracy.

This made sense to psychologists at the time. However, if a slave dies for what he sees as the reality of voodoo magic, the psychologist dismisses it as unimportant--a mere coincidence. Since voodoo magic doesn't exist in the psychologist's mind, the psychologist believes that magic carries no threat to its intended victim. Likewise, because the psychologist doesn't believe in demons, demons supposedly pose no threat to the mind-controlled slave.

The psychologist is really projecting his perception of reality upon someone else, and it doesn't work. The Illuminati programmers are counting on the therapists ignoring demonology. In Bowart's in-most -respects excellent book Operation Mind Control, (Researcher Edition, Ft. Bragg, CA: Flatland, 1994, p. 249.) asks the reader to self-hypnotize himself by several times "looking into your mind's eye". To Bowart, he sees the trance state as merely looking into your mind's eye. He does not attribute any demonic activity to be involved with such things.

No wonder, Bowart writes very disparagingly and critically about Christians who are trying to do demonic deliverances to slaves. But then as far as I know Bowart hasn't freed anyone of their mind-control either, he is just a reporter. Both ministers and psychologists have contempt for each other's excesses. We must bear in mind that the victims of this total mind-control have their bodies, minds, and spirits enslaved. The body, mind and spirit need to be simultaneously liberated. A great deal of the success of the Programmers is that ministers have rejected the study of the mind (psychology) and therapists have rejected spiritual things.

The victim is left without a way to heal both spirit and mind. Partial freedom is still slavery. And not only that but both therapists and ministers seem to feel the actual physical threats to the slave's body to be outside of their jurisdiction, and by default it is left up to the victim to provide. Which again without the body safe and healed, the mind and spirit are not fully free. There are therapists and others who pontificate about how evil Christian ministers are for trying to deliver mind-controlled slaves from their demonic possession. This is not the problem.

The problem is that the Illuminati have skillfully separated the various therapeutic elements both functionally and legally. The answer to the enslavement of body, soul, mind and spirit is a team of people who will address all the issues together. Both the psychologists and ministers see the excesses of each other, but a little humility would go a long way, for both sides to recognize each other's value. God works through all people, even those who resist Him. That is why he can rightly be called Almighty God.

EXTERNAL DECEPTIONS

There seems to be no end to the lies that are involved with the Monarch programming. The old adage that nothing is as it appears, is generally the rule. However, once one catches on to the common tactics of deceptions, the tactics themselves become red flags which can alert a thinking person to what is hidden. This is similar to those Russians who could read between the lines when reading communist propaganda and figure Out the truth. The deception begins with covering up the identity of the slave. Within the Illuminati, the art of hiding genealogies is a fine art. Children are swapped and placed with foster parents. Mothers all of a sudden have babies, when no one has noticed them being pregnant. Other researchers have been investigating court house records and other primary documents have seen court house records altered overnight, to cover up genealogical and financial information.

COVERS FOR INDIVIDUAL SLAVES

The individual slave is usually given a good cover. A good cover will be one that cannot be seen through, and still allows the person the freedom to get their job done. When building a cover, the following questions will be asked: how much will this cover allow this person to spend? what kind of people can this person associate with? where can this person go? and what kind of hobby can he or she have? By now, the Illuminati have their secret slaves in so many places that they have their bases covered in all fields. True life examples include: a Monarch programmer who appears to be simply a middle class housewife.

A Monarch computer programmer who appears to be a deaf and dumb mute when in the presence of the public, but the deeper brilliant alters work secretly at programming computers during the day. An international spy, who is a programmed multiple, who has a totally different set of I.D. and wigs, so that when they switch to certain alters used for the intelligence agencies--they not only act different, they look different, and have different valid I.D. An apparently dumb blond may be a very intelligent highly trained Monarch slave. Within the intelligence world Monarch slaves will function as Agent Provocateurs, which are people who join groups with the purpose of leading the group to do things that will cause it harm. The neo-Nazis are full of Agent Provocateurs as are some of the Patriot groups. Some Monarch slaves are what is called "clean agents" -- that is they have never been used in intelligence work, so they have no record of use.

Monarchs are great for being used by this or that group on a limited basis without anyone suspecting any connection. The Intelligence term for the elaborate cover histories they give one of their Monarch slaves to operate as an agent is called a "legend". Supporting documents will be placed into the appropriate government files to support the legend. The intelligence agencies may have several intact "legends" for different personalities of a slave. The intelligence term is NOTIONAL. It roughly means "a fictional entity for the sake of an intelligence operation." Notional organizations are created to steal strength away from sincere organizations. If a church (or non-CIA KKK group etc.) gets too sincere and powerful, a well-financed notional rival will start up, and then later fold under scandal. The net effect is to destroy the entire cause. At least half of the therapists helping Monarch slaves in the authors' area are programmed multiples themselves! The therapeutic community is heavily infiltrated. The help lines for women in crisis are all dirty. Some of the Christian groups that claim to help SRA victims are really fronts.
One recovering Monarch slave tells about how her father was the mayor of an important city in Pennsylvania. He was part of the Illu-

minati and he introduced drugs into his area, and had a monopoly on illegal drugs in the area. As mayor he established the first drug hot line, so that people could inform authorities about drug trafficking. He staffed the drug hot line with his own people and this allowed him to get tips to eliminate his competition. The intelligence agencies which are using mind-control are hiding their drug trafficking and criminal activities. One of the ways they do this is the so-called War on Drugs. The situation is so bad and widespread that even the controlled media has had news where they reported CIA agents smuggling drugs seized in South America into the U.S. using government channels.

When a slave is being programmed, the abusers will use schools, churches, Big Brothers, Boy Scouts and other activities to carry out the abuse and programming. Children pulled from classes will be given back-up amnesia so that they forget that they forgot. In other words, they are totally unaware that they have lost time when they were pulled out of the classroom. The teacher gives them a test score, and they are told they took a test during the missing time. How can the front alters deny it, when they have been hypnotized to believe it and they can see the test scores? Alter boys and boys at catholic orphanages have a record of being used by dirty priests.

Recently, numerous priests have been discovered molesting children, and hundreds of lawsuits are underway, but it is still not coming out that this abuse is connected to trauma-based mind-control. In the past, if the parents who were part of the Illuminati elite, but were not religious wanted their boy programmed, they could send him off to a military school run under the cooperation of the Catholic church and units such as the 6th U.S. Army, which became one of the primary infiltrated units. The 6th army uses the magical hexagram as its logo. This would provide the programmed child with a religious front. He could say, "I went to catholic school." The programming could be disguised as discipline, etc.

The establishment media have worked propaganda wonders for the abusers of the Monarch Mind-control. Britain is extremely repressive in their information control. If any news medium tries to leak the most simplest of information a secret document called a "notice" will be sent at any time of day to them from a D-notice committee, and the media will have to stop whatever reference is deemed a secret. In the U.S. it in effect works as tight, it just is not officially as tight. The abusers know that they also have an Incredulous Factor that can assist them.

Who would believe that a sweet child drinks blood and is cannibalistic? The more that they can do that is far fetched, the less credibility the child has if they do talk. Some children do try to talk. One Monarch slave talked at age five, and her entire family came down hard on her and blamed the child's talking for the death of one of the abusers. What kind of proof can a child bring that adults will accept? In the McMartin Preschool case about 800 children were witnesses whose stories corroborated the SRA and programming that was done, but the media, and the judicial system were able to cover up the abuse and make it look on television that the abusers were the victims! It wasn't until after the case was over and the property sold, that the tangible proof (the secret tunnels with paraphernalia) were found, and then the news media has covered that up too. The abusers will often wear masks and costumes.

Let's say a programmer wears a Mickey Mouse outfit, and the child would remember and tell, "Mickey Mouse hurt me." Now who is going to believe the child? The child has told the truth, but will be reprimanded for telling the truth. It doesn't take long for a severely abused child, who has been programmed to keep silent, to learn that no one wants to hear the truth anyway.

THE USE OF RELIGIOUS FRONTS

A great deal of Monarch programming and slave abuse, (as well as the drug trade) is done under three major covers or fronts:

Religious Fronts; the Front of National Security and the Military; and the Entertainment fields, especially the Country Western Industry, the Rock Music Industry and Hollywood.

The religious fronts were popular for centuries, especially when groups like the Jesuits, the Assassins, and other groups held immense power

Religious fronts are still being used such as J.Z. Knight, Elizabeth Claire Prophet's CUT church, the Church of Scientology, the Charismatic movement, Jim Jones & Jonestown, and David Koresh's group etc. Billy Ray Moore's Lord's Chapel is entirely a mind-control operation There is a nondenominational Pentecostal church in southern Washington whose entire membership is Satanists under mind-control. Various overseas "missionary" groups are covers for the CIA & mind-control

It would take a book to explain how these religious fronts are part of the total trauma-based mind-control and how they operate to protect mind-control, however there are publications which go into some of the CIA connections to these groups. It is suggested that interested persons read these publications. Some of the deceptions such as the lone assassin idea have been used for centuries as a cover for assassinations planned by the occult hierarchy. If we are going to really reveal how the Monarch Mind-control is done, we will have to explain how the deception is done. If one describes a chameleon only by saying "it is like a lizard", without mentioning the camouflage, then the most important part has been overlooked.

Religious fronts are an important part of the Illuminati program for making slaves. In fact, due to their Gnostic philosophy of balancing their good deeds with their bad deeds, it is almost essential to have a religious front through which one can do good deeds. Even though adding this section to the book will spur some to blindly lash out at the book, still the whole story needs to come out. When we, the authors of this book, write that the Monarch-type total mind-control threatens everything this nation stands for, we are not exaggerating. The Monarch Mind-control program has not been used just to program slaves--but it has been part of a much bigger deception.
When this deception is realized by this nation, it will shatter the very fabric of trust that Americans have in their institutions. If Americans

will begin to understand the power structure behind their institutions, and who controls this structure, they will begin to see the lies in the scripts that they have been fed since infancy. And YOU, the reader of this next section in this book, if you love the truth, can help begin the healing process to overcome some of the devastation that is going to rock this nation when the truth comes out.

This next section will help both Christian and non-Christian readers. The therapist can learn about what is happening so that they can better deal with what the SRA survivors are beginning to reveal. The grooming of the American people to believe massive amounts of lies did work, UNTIL a few loving therapists, ministers, and doctors began to liberate victims of the Monarch trauma-based mind-control. These programmed multiples began revealing a horror story of deception unparalleled in history. For the reader to deal with the next section means courage. It means that the reader will have to muster up some of the same type of love of truth that the mind-control survivors must muster to free themselves of the lies of their satanic programming. What we see and hear can be programming, in the same way SRA victims are deceived.

Everyone in the Illuminati of any significance has participated in grooming the public to believe that Billy Graham is a great man of God. Graham has stood beside each of the Presidents and the Pope. The Illuminati don't just program individuals, they program whole nations. The public has been led to believe in a television image. But what if the secular media's image of Billy Graham is not real? For Christians it means that they can quit trusting in a man, and place their trust fully on God. For secular readers, they can begin to see the extent of how America's institutions have been corrupted by the horrible trauma-based mind-control. The heart-beat of the Body of Christ is crying out that something is terribly wrong. We will address that.

All of us, whether Christian or not, must step out of the lies and look clearly out into the darkness and see every facet of this evil mind-control. When men who worship the god of this world place "In God We Trust" on the Federal Reserve bank notes, we who know the truth must step out of our dream world and realize that they mean Lucifer.

{ 165 }

By the way, the Federal Reserve is not a government agency, but a private banking institution of the Illuminati. This has been documented in a number of writings.) The issue at hand in this next section is to show how the institution called "the Christian church", and the world in general has been deceived by a programmed multiple and this trauma-based mind-control.

Secular readers will be shown that the doctrines that Christians want to believe in, have been subtly destroyed under the disguise of building them up. This is no different than the destruction of the positive values which hold any group together. (After the repeated collaboration by essentially all the Christian churches worldwide in many activities as the NCC, the Billy Graham Crusades, the Promise Keepers and other programs, the Christian churches, Orthodox, Catholic, Protestant & non-denominational can be considered one institution.) The infiltration and control of the Christian religion has been one of the easiest tasks of the Illuminati. The Christian churches are what the intelligence agencies called "SOFT TARGETS."

THE DECEPTION OF BILLY GRAHAM; A MIND-CONTROL FRONT
In 1992, Billy Graham broadcast all over the U.S. his radio show called Embrace America 2000. In the Louisiana area, it came over the KJAM Lafayette Station. During the show, Billy Graham told the American people we need to embrace the New World Order. Billy Graham is also on record stating that people can have salvation through paganism (another name for witchcraft). For instance, in McCall Magazine (Jan. 1987) Graham stated,

"I used to believe that pagans in far-off countries were lost--were going to hell. I no longer believe that. I believe that there are other ways of recognizing the existence of God--through nature, for instance."

Pagans believe that salvation can be obtained through nature. This is not a pleasant story. Billy Graham has been built up to be the most respected popular person in America. Who wants to find out they have been deceived? We will try to give you the facts, or evidence, and may God grant you wisdom as you read this. This section is not propaganda for my own personal views. Years ago, when one source set out on his search, he had no final outcome in mind. He wasn't concerned with concealing facts one way or the other. There is no desire to stampede our readers anywhere. We do want to clarify many issues. We do want to help the truth seeker. But my self and my sources personally have no battle to win, except that truth be brought forth. The issues at stake are not trivial. Historically, Billy Graham's deception is one of the "greatest" deceptions that has ever been perpetrated.

Some might argue the greatest, making Benedict Arnold, Quisling, and the Trojan Horse pale into insignificance. Allow us to introduce you just briefly into the world of the Illuminati, All top hierarchy Satanists are required to have covers, The Illuminatus will have multiple personalities, and he or she will have one personality that is particularly shown to the outside world. They (the Programmers, handlers and the Illuminati councils) try to get the best covers that they can. They like to be clergymen, but they are also mayors of big cities, lawyers, doctors, etc.

A Christian psychiatrist who has worked with numerous victims of Satanism and Multiple Personality Disorder wrote this observation after having worked with a large number of ex-multi-generational programmed Satanic multiples, *"Some Satanists have invaded the church as it is the perfect cover for them. They masquerade as angels of light and gravitate towards positions of leadership in order to have more influence. Because much of what they say is sound doctrinally, they are rarely detected. Most survivors whom I have worked with had Satanist parents who were in high positions in churches; many were pastors."* (Dr. Fox, Loreda. The Spiritual and Clinical Dimensions of Multiple Personality Disorder. Salida, CO: Books of Sangre de Cristo, p. 196.)

Let us repeat what Dr. Loreda Fox said,

"Most survivors whom I have worked with had Satanist parents who were in high positions in churches; many were pastors."
She didn't say "some," she said MOST. Independently, we have dis-

covered the very same thing. People don't grasp that just because a preacher can sincerely preach what seems a "perfect sermon," doesn't mean that he can't also be part of the Satanic hierarchy. What is happening with the Illuminati's ability to create programmed multiples is that we are getting perfect preachers who are secret hierarchy members.

Some of their "perfect sermons" are full of slides, such as "the Christian people need to get involved in the voting process. Christians love to hear such things, it tickles their ears, but the truth is that the entire voting process has been captured and corrupted. Voting machines have repeatedly been exposed to have been rigged, and the controlled media and public denial have prevented Americans from giving up their myth that the common man's votes run this nation.

In Fritz's Be Wise As Serpents book (which exposed Billy Graham as a Luciferian in 1991), it is explained that high level Satanism is Gnosticism which requires that "the Force" of these great satanic magicians be balanced. In other words, in high level Satanism your good deeds must balance your evil deeds. People do not realize that unless someone does "good" deeds they cannot be a high level Satanist. That is why some of the greatest philanthropists are also our leading national Satanists, To see Billy Graham do something commendable does not disqualify him from Satanism. In fact, it is a requirement if he's been part of the Illuminati, such as ex-insiders/witnesses say he was. In fact, it wasn't until working on this book that an eyewitness to the mind-control abuse of at the hands of Billy Graham offered to help contribute to this section of the book. In other words, an eyewitness helped write this.

This eyewitness account by the Co-author matches what the list of eyewitnesses that Fritz assembled in 1993 have said, But the eyewitness went further and exposed Billy Graham Crusades' skillful use of Monarch slaves to launder drug money. Several police officers have stated that today, there is for all practical purposes no police training helping police to understand Satanism. They are highly trained in many areas, but Satanism is avoided. When an SRA case involving multiplicity in Olympia, WA recently happened, the police who investigated the case found that they were treated as international experts in Satanism by other policemen.

They themselves knew that they knew very little. Where are the experts to teach us about how the Illuminati functions? Where are the experts who know who are in the Illuminati? There is no college open to the public that teaches Advanced Illuminati Studies 401, and gives degrees in Satanism. The expert witnesses are those who have managed to leave the Illuminati and Satanism, and stay alive long enough to talk. But the other side will argue, how can we verify the testimony of your witnesses Fritz? Remember what happened to over 100 people who had some type of knowledge about the Kennedy assassination? Jim Marrs in his book Crossfire on the Kennedy Assassination lists 103 people who were key figures in knowing about the assassination who have died, many in circumstances that indicate assassination.

The story we are dealing with here is just as sensitive to the elite as Kennedy's assassination, because it involves their preparations for the creation of a false Christ, called by Christians the Anti-Christ, who will be the master handler/programmer.

THE LIST OF KNOWN AND CREDIBLE WITNESSES

If the authors were to call my list of witnesses up to the witness stand, which I can't for it would be a death sentence to many of them, the list would include:

- 1 Council of Foreign Relations member, who is secretly against the New World Order
- 1 National Security Agency person, who is against the New World Order
- 1 CIA high level administrator
- 2 Satanists, still in covens, but unhappy enough with the situation to talk
- 4 ex-Satanists, 3 of which are eyewitnesses, all Christians now
- 2 ex-New Age leaders who worked with the Conspiracy, both became Christians

- 1 ex-33° Mason, now a Christian
- Various Christians who have worked with Billy Graham, Pastors, etc.
- Various therapists working with SRA victims The man who ran Security at the Sacramento Crusade
- Alice Braemer, a woman who worked as a secretary for Jeanne Dixon

None, with few exceptions, <u>none</u> of these people knew anything about what the other witnesses (sources) had said. The high degree of validation and collaboration that separate testimony by witnesses who have never seen each other and live in different parts of the country is very powerful. There are several questions that pop up into people's minds who are not familiar with who Fritz is, and are not familiar with these witnesses.

The type of worries some readers could be naturally having might be: But how are we, the readers, to know how accurate these people are? Are they trustworthy? Do they have a reputation for honesty? Could they possibly be giving false information to discredit a great man of God? These kind of questions can be natural questions for people unfamiliar with how this information was obtained. But we assure you, that what we pass on from these eyewitnesses can be relied upon. None of these worries have any substance to them, because the manner in which Fritz came to find out about Billy Graham has generally been while he was researching other things related to the Illuminati. The author has not been out to build a case, the case has built itself from numerous detached witnesses who have nothing to gain by telling what they know.

These witnesses have not come to Fritz to feed him bogus information. Just the paper trail on Billy Graham is very revealing in itself. Generally the information of these witnesses has been confided by these witnesses to their trusted friends. Initially, these witness have had no idea that the information they confided in their trusted close associates would go beyond their most trusted friends. These trusted friends then have had permission to let me contact them or find out their information. The reason why these people are believable is that the information they reveal could get them killed, and second, the manner and circumstances of how the information has originally un-folded has never been in any fashion or method that could be con-strued as an attempt to give false information.

CLARIFYING WHAT IS LOOKED FOR IN PROOF?

Too many people are considered guilty unless proven innocent--which means that a legitimate search for truth has NOT taken place. On the flip side, we must bear in mind that hidden information which has laid dormant for years may totally reverse our understanding of something. Exceptional circumstances may surprise us, If some item does not lend itself to totally irrefutable, totally unqualified claims, then knowing this, the proper investigator uses words like "almost certainly" and „most likely". If the investigator feels strongly that everything is totally clear, he may declare that something is correct "without qualification." This is the nature of proof. We need to under-stand the qualifications and reservations that often are attached to evi-dence or conclusions.

But we certainly do want to press our investigations as far as possible to get as many "unqualified" conclusions as possible. Of course, by the time we write this, we have already done our investigating, and have one conclusion without any qualification: Billy Graham is working for the Satanic Hierarchy. We want to try to introduce the material in such a way that you will get some sense of the search, so that you will not simply accept our conclusion but will make rational spirit-led critically-thought-out decisions about Billy Graham. So for the sake of the reader's investigation, please, let us unshackle our-selves from our prejudices and preconceived labels. Let us suspend our judgment about Billy Graham one way or the other, until we have thoroughly studied, prayed and gained discernment about this. It might be interesting to get some of the Masons who casually, without realizing what they were saying, have talked about Billy Graham's membership, or other aspects of his Masonic involvement.

It's doubtful that such men would be of any value on the witness stand. Their numerous Masonic oaths to lie and conceal Freemasonry under penalties of gruesome death would tend to have more influence on them than swearing on a Bible. (See Duncan's Masonic Ritual book, p. 30 for the 1st Degree oath.) This type of witness, because they talked accidentally and casually are very valuable witnesses to whoever accidentally hears them, but unfortunately they must be assumed to be still loyal to the Masonic Lodge and would be hostile witnesses that will not cooperate. If this were an actual court of law, depositions of Billy Graham's staff could be taken, so that it could be revealed to the court how many times they have lied. By showing their lies, their testimony would be impeached and Christians would realize that Billy Graham's staff have played a major role in the deception.

This article will put forth evidence that impeaches the testimony of Billy Graham's staff. We must refer readers to the Be Wise As Serpents book and other writings of Fritz for more information. Also some other books will be named too. Because these leaders are corrupt, they have been participating in the mass deception of the world about what Billy Graham does and who he is. In fact, if this were a court of law all types of people could be subpoenaed to take depositions, and we might find out many more things than we already know.

TH MOTIVATION OF THE CO-AUTHORS

Many people, who like Billy Graham, have imputed evil motives to anyone exposing Billy Graham. As the Scripture say at one point, "Am I to become your enemy because I tell you the truth?" The story about Billy Graham and his life-long career for the Illuminati is not an easy thing for us to write. We do not enjoy speaking negative things against people. We do enjoy speaking positive things about people. And yet no man, no servant of God is above reproach. We can personally have an inner peace that what we have done was what we should have done. Something needs to be done to wake mankind up before its too late.

CLARIFYING WHAT IS ACCEPTABLE TESTIMONY

In some subjects, going to the encyclopedia or almanac will settle questions. In dealing with the Illuminati and high levels of the occult world, unless the investigator is willing to listen to eye-witness testimony, he or she will get nowhere. There is rarely any written record of their secret activities. But how much stock can be put in eye-witnesses? Many people up to now have criticized Fritz for using eye -witnesses. But remember that if we did manage to get some paper trail or books on the subject, that book paper trail would not be acceptable in court, or even if allowed would not be as important as our eyewitnesses. In court, the written records can be introduced along with the person who recorded them. In other words, the personal witness is still important even with written documents.

The testimony of our eyewitnesses expose Billy Graham's mind-control activities. Still, we want to bear in mind that witnesses have varying degrees of credibility and knowledge. The qualifications of witness in relation to what they are testifying is important. But to simply dismiss all these witnesses because they are not paper is simply to cut ourselves off from many valuable sources of information. In accumulating evidence, the researcher will come upon two types of information. One is prearranged evidence and the other is called casual evidence.

Casual evidence is evidence that has just happened to appear by accident. An actual example is when friends of mine met a total stranger who happens to be a Mason and he offhandedly talks about Billy Graham being a Freemason. Casual evidence is simply evidence that happens without the interested party having anything to do with it surfacing. Finding casual evidence is generally "luck"', In this case, Fritz has bumped into a great deal of casual evidence, simply because he had his eyes open and has been investigating this area for several years. Because of the situation today in this nation, there is little chance to get a proper hearing of this information. In terms of the future, indeed, the backlash from this book may silence us. The truth will still remain, even if we and the other witnesses don't.

We can draw conclusions about ducks from studying various types of ducks. I can not draw conclusions about radios from studying ducks,

I can generalize about American made cars, but I can't include in my generalization about American cars an ox-cart in India. This may sound basic, and it is, yet people try to generalize by lumping the generational Satanists in with everybody else, and it just doesn't work. They also try to draw conclusions about the Freemasons on the basis of what the Rotary Club they belong to is like and it just doesn't work. In terms of trying to get a proper hearing today, one of the barriers is that people use their own experiences to draw conclusions. People have nothing in their experience to allow them to draw conclusions about the Illuminati programmers/handlers who are moral degenerates and programmed multiples, who will do anything, in spite of their nice fronts.

THE POLICIES OF DECEPTION BY THE BILLY GRAHAM CRUSADE STAFF

In 1992, a Christian named Richard Bennett, a friend of Fritz's confronted the Billy Graham Crusade staff. What he was concerned about was the Billy Graham crusade policy , hat has been in place since the 50's, of sending Catholics that come forward back to Catholic churches. Documentation shows that the deception is worse than that, new believers that have never gone to any church are sometimes referred by the Billy Graham counselors to the Catholic Church. Now, why would Richard and Fritz be concerned about the Catholic Church?

Richard Bennett was a priest from Ireland who worked at the Vatican, before giving his life to Christ. He knows how the Catholic hierarchy prevents people from realizing what they have in Christ. For those who have read Fritz's Be Wise As Serpents book chapter 2.2 you know that Fritz is very concerned when anyone gives their allegiance to a power structure that is part of the NWO and part of its Monarch trauma-based total mind control. Not everything about the Catholic church is wrong. Yet, the Billy Graham Crusade could never get the support it gets from conservative Christians if Billy Graham's staff didn't lie about where Crusade converts are sent.

What Richard and Fritz were concerned about was that new Christians would be sent to Catholic churches, which now are teaching Zen

Buddhism, New Age things, not the salvation by grace that these new Christians need. Granted the enthusiasm of these new Christians might infuse some life into the Catholic church, but a babe in Christ is defenseless. He needs nurture, and the chance to grow. It isn't meant for new Christians to be thrown to the wolves. Anyway, last Spring and Summer, the Billy Graham Crusade Executive committee was confronted face to face with the evidence of what the Billy Graham Crusade in Sept. '93 was going to do. Actually, more people than Richard did confront them, but Richard is one of the most knowledgeable ministries to the Catholics in this area.

What the Billy Graham Crusade Executive Committee told Richard Bennett was that he had nothing to worry about. That the crusade would never send anyone to a Catholic church, but that if new converts wanted to go there on their own, that was their own choice. Four Catholic leaders sat on the Executive Committee for the '92 Portland Crusade, Chancellor Mary Joe Telly, a deacon and two priests. On the Catholic radio station, (and we have it recorded,) Mary Joe Telly of the Billy Graham Executive Committee along with another Bishop Wall Schmidt told the Catholic listeners not to worry that if they came forward they would be guaranteed that they would be referred back to a Catholic church. They gave the assurance four times in that talk show. They said that the decision to send people who came forward to Catholic churches was firm because it had come right from the very top. This was 6 p.m KVDM Portland station.

Our recording of this is a record of just one of thousands of lies that the Billy Graham Crusade people have told Christians over the years. In fact, from the evidence it appears the Billy Graham Crusade people say whatever they have to, regardless of the truth. In the North Star Baptist, Nov. 1964 there was an article by Japheth Perez, who as a convert in the NY 1957 Billy Graham Crusade and a brand-new Christian, was sent to a Catholic church by the Billy Graham Crusade. Ian Paisley wrote this comment about Billy Graham's staff: *"Dr. Graham did not reply. He never does reply to letters like this. He states he never defends himself. He does have a staff, however, who are paid to defend him and who are never hampered by facts or bothered by ethics or logic in carrying out their duties. One of the group, George L. Edstrom, replied. The Jesuits themselves could not give a finer example of casuistry than his. It is thoroughly dishonest and deceitful,.....However, since this technique of deceit by misdirection, this failure to face up to the issues, this disregard of fact, and this blasphemous attempt to identify Dr. Graham's official connection with infidels and his flattery and endorsement of them with our Lord's ministry to publicans and sinners is so typical of the Graham organization..."* In Fritz's June '93 Newsletter From A Christian Ministry, a letter from Graham' s staff was reproduced with a point by point exposure of its lies. Christians are really not well aware of what the Billy Graham Crusade does. We quote a paragraph from a letter sent to Billy Graham clear back in the 1950s by a Pastor who, grieved by what Billy Graham was doing to the harvest field, said: *"Some people say that if you have just one convert in an evangelistic campaign, it is worth the meeting. That is not true.*

The evangelist, as the pastor and teacher, is given to the Body of Christ. The real test of an evangelistic campaign is not how many people are converted but what kind of a spiritual condition does it leave in a community. Billy Graham is not only failing in the number of people he leads to the Lord Jesus Christ in this day when hearts are hungry and most people are afraid of what may happen in the world and when it is easier to get people converted than it ever has been in my lifetime, but Billy Graham is pulling the limbs off of the evangelistic trees and the orchard is being left in bad condition. As we have often said, the real test of an evangelist is not just how many converts he has but does he leave the orchard in condition so it will keep bearing fruit."

BILLY GRAHAM'S ACTIVE ROLE IN SATANIC RITUAL ABUSE

Before we get into the details, we'll take an overview. Satanists thrive on power. Satan loves to give his followers power. Satan took Christ to the mountaintop and told Christ that he'd have a "crusade" and bring every one to follow Christ, if Christ would just bow down and worship him. Christ refused. Billy Graham accepted it. We know a great deal how the Satanists took Billy Graham, the brush salesman and made him into the famous evangelist that he has become. Additionally, we also know from victims of Satanism, that have come out of it, that Billy Graham has been a Satanist himself. How can this be? and how can we know this? One of the best witnesses is a Monarch program survivor, who has escaped from being a high-level Pentagon slave.

This survivor witnessed Billy Graham working for the Illuminati. This survivor also carried messages for the Satanic hierarchy and personally knows that Billy Graham has been carrying messages from the top secret Illuminati to Presidents and heads of state. This person's information has been backed up by independent witnesses. A second ex-Satanist also remembers Billy Graham as a Satanist. Still another person, an ex-Illuminati person, who has MPD stood in front of Billy Graham and watched his eyes. This person said that it was very clear that Billy Graham has MPD and that he switches personalities. By happenchance or God's will, Fritz received a report from one of the women who went to church with Billy Graham's wife Ruth.

The woman was told by Ruth in conversation that her husband Billy Graham is strange in that he always sleeps with his eyes open. It is characteristic of people who have MPD to sleep with their eyes open. People who have MPD may have a devout Christian personality and a devout Satanic personality all within a single body. This is not uncommon. In Billy Graham's case, he is fully aware of what he is doing for the enemy in all his personalities, although his Christian personality may not be ecstatic about it all. Billy Graham's Decision magazine has on its front page caption "'Changed From the Inside Out," and displays an infinity loop on the cover. Many Monarch slaves have had lots of programming around the infinity loop. This is an important trigger to remind them how they are captured by the unending repeating rebuilding programming.

There are countless little things like this, which are evidence that Billy Graham is playing a role in the satanic mind-control of the Illuminati. Dr. Schefflin, a mind-control expert, told me that he saw internal documents from the 1950s teaching Billy Graham's people on how to have a successful revival. These documents instructed crusade counselors on things which were elements of mind-control, such as delaying people from coming forward to confess Christ until the "right" time. If you've ever wondered how much Billy Graham knows--if the Illuminati haven't told him, a concerned Christian named David Hill, who was an ex-Mafia/ex-New Ager/ex-Mason did.

The concerned Christian was a friend of Franklin Graham, Billy's son, and he had lived for two years at Billy Graham's house. He didn't realize that Graham had been sucked into the New World Order until he had confronted Billy Graham. David Hill, who was a ex-Mason turned Christian, who had worked with many of the world's elite, spent 18 hours in a hotel room warning Billy Graham about the New World Order. Billy Graham told David Hill at the end of their two days of talking in this eastern U.S. hotel room that he was "a captive of that [NWO] organization." In other words, after placing himself under the Illuminati's sponsorship in the late '40s, Billy Graham has had the choice of continuing to do his job for them, or being destroyed.

Since they created who he is, they can destroy him. And he knows it. David Hill went on to try to expose the New World Order and lost his life (was murdered) just as he finished a manuscript exposing it. Even a well-informed Christian like David Hill, who tried to warn Billy Graham about the NWO, was unaware of the extent of the deception of the Illuminati's mind control. David didn't know about programmed multiples. David Hill, who was a high ranking Scottish Rite Freemason and an important Mafia figure before he came to Christ, had even been the go between for Billy Graham and Joe Banana, a Mafia kingpin. It was David Hill, who innocently believing in Billy Graham, arranged the meeting for the two men.

David Hill knew that William Randolph Hearst was part of the Illuminati, He was part of the branch Illuminati at what could be termed the 6th degree. William Randolph Hearst was totally into paganism. That is very obvious by a tour of his mansion in California which has been turned into a museum. It was William Randolph Hearst who financed the first three years of Billy Graham's Crusades. Stu PAK is associated with the Stewart Title Company. Stu Pak provides funds for Billy Graham and others. The head of Stu Pak is friends with Billy Graham and George Bush. The company has a lot of relatives running it. The Morris family is also tied to it. The people of Stewart Title Company are ruthless. The Van Duyn Illuminati family in California also helped Billy Graham's ministry get started.

One of the ways the Illuminati funneled money to Billy Graham was through a monthly check delivered to Jeanne Dixon's office, which was picked up every month by Billy Graham's staff. After Dixon's secretary came to Christ she tried to expose Billy Graham's connection to Jeanne Dixon. Jeanne Dixon sells crystal balls with snakes. She is part of the Illuminati. Billy Graham wrote her a letter calling her "a woman of God." Dixon's secretary had a copy of this letter with Billy Graham's signature on it, after she became a Christian.

In 1952, in Paris, Billy Graham and another evangelist had dinner with two prostitutes and each one took one of them home. Billy Graham had a wife and children at home, so the whole affair was totally improper for an evangelist even if Billy Graham didn't have sex with the woman. He told his friend only that the prostitute had taken off her clothes and he'd gotten scared and come back to their hotel room. See Frady, Marshall. Billy Graham, A Parable of American Righteousness. Boston: Little, Brown & Co., p.169-170.

In 1954, the man who ran security for the Sacramento Crusade saw a high-priced hooker sneak into Billy Graham's room prior to him going out for the Crusade. Billy Graham and this high priced hooker were alone together in the room, It is this type of thing that has opened Billy Graham up to blackmail. Should Graham ever try to stray from the proper course set for him by the Illuminati, they have plenty of ammunition to blackmail him. You may ask why would the Satanists from generational satanic families want to intimidate Billy Graham with fear? Why, isn't he from a generational satanic family? The answer is that the whole Satanic system operates off of fear. Intimidation & fear are standard everyday parts of their makeup and actions. Sort of the counterpart to the saying there is no honor among thieves. The Satanic hierarchy are in constant intimidation and power struggles.

When Billy Graham wanted to, he could call up Henry Kissinger and say, "Tell him to call me the minute he comes in." (Frady, p. 451) Henry Kissinger is right in the middle of what the Illuminati are doing. Another Illuminatus that Graham had a working relationship with is Henry Luce, friend of the Baruchs. Luce and Billy Graham spent several nights staying up talking late into the night. Knowing how the Illuminati work, it is very safe to assume that they have pushed Billy Graham into further degenerate acts.

They have probably done everything they can to pervert Billy Graham, so there is no telling what sexual sins remain hidden. Kissinger is a member of P2 Freemasonry. If we were to assume that Billy Graham were not involved (and that is a big IF since we know that he is), then if one studies P2 Masonic recruiting tactics given in the book In God's Name, p. 116, then the reader will grasp that anyone of Billy Graham's stature who associates so freely with P2 Freemasons will be targeted and blackmailed and forced to join. Once they join, new members are forced to compromise other possible targets. Billy Graham is part of the people who implement the Monarch program.

We know that he is serviced by Monarch sexual slaves (their kitten alters). It is very easy for the network to keep these poor victims (Monarch slaves) from talking, and so the full extent of much of what has gone on may not come out in our lifetimes. Another possible clue about Billy Graham's hidden life comes from Billy Graham himself. Do the readers remember how Jimmy Swaggert would disguise himself with sun glasses, etc. and his staff helped him carry out what he in part confessed? In Hollywood, Florida (yes, Florida!) Billy Graham said that he "often attends loveins and rock festivals incognito by putting on a false mustache and beard."

He also said he found the experience in doing that kind of thing "refreshing." This story was in the Chicago Daily News, Dec. 29, 1969. The article's purpose appears to have been to make Billy Graham look hip to today's rock and roll crowds of teenagers. Billy Graham described his friendship with Alan Dulles, I make every effort not to let it appear that I favor one party over another. I count Secretary Dulles a friend, but Senator Humphrey is also a good friend of mine, [who he met] ... when we were both swimming nude at the YMCA pool in Minneapolis where he was running for mayor." A friendship with Alan Dulles? Alan Dulles, director of the CIA, was one of the biggest perpetrators of the trauma-based mind-control that this book is about.

Humphrey also received orders from the Satanic hierarchy. And what is this swimming in nude? When Billy Graham had his 1954 Crusade, large sums of the money came directly from people in the Illuminati, the Whitneys, the Vanderbilts, the Rockefellers, and Chase Manhattan. Billy Graham has numerous times attended Hollywood cocktail parties. Just two examples of which are: one given by Debbie Reynolds, and another one which was a cocktail party for Hollywood stars put on by Nixon at his San Clemente, CA home on a Sunday evening. Billy Graham's schedule is filled with activities such as playing golf with people who are in the Illuminati, or are Hollywood types. The full impact of this constant fellowshipping with darkness is hard for people to grasp, because they picture that Graham is an evangelist and so therefore he must go where the sinners are.

There is an expression, show me a man' s friends and I'll tell you about him. It's one thing to spend time with evil to give it a chance to repent and come to the light, It is another to fellowship with evil and allow it to remain in darkness. Let us quote from a neutral source, a group who had been investigating the role of church and state. They were trying to determine for their study whether Billy Graham has had an impact on all the Presidents from Eisenhower to Clinton, This study was not pro or anti Graham, It was simply trying to determine what impact this religious leader is having on political leaders. Billy Graham has spent a lot of time with all the Presidents, so their question was "has Billy Graham had some type of impact?" Their conclusion printed in the Journal of Church and State concludes,"... .*could Graham speak the word of truth - especially when that word may be critical or slashing -to the man in the White House when he is on such friendly terms with him? On the basis of the evidence now available, the answer must be no.*"

What a person does on his free time is said to be revealing. Christ did spend his time with sinners, but he called them to repentance. In all my study of Billy Graham, I haven't seen any of the Hollywood movie stars or politicians change their lifestyles by their association with Billy Graham. A number of "conversions" have been artificially created, and given widespread publicity by the press. Pat Boone is the type of close friend of Billy Graham that perhaps typifies Billy Graham. He is someone well-received by the public. Billy Graham has enjoyed using him in Crusades.

Pat Boone continued playing in Playboy type night clubs while he was singing at Billy Graham Crusades. Pat Boone who is pro-Jewish, may be Jewish, because the State of Israel has given him some special positions. There is nothing wrong with having "Jewish blood", it just explains some of his connections. The Nugen Hand Bank was a CIA operation that laundered money, and did many illegal activities. Pat Boone was part of the Nugen Hand Bank scandal. Exactly how deep he was involved with the CIA's dirty dealing is unclear.

Pat Boone's daughter Debbie Boone made a hit out of the song "You Light Up My Life", the words of the song were written by a woman who worshipped Lucifer and wrote the song to Lucifer. Billy Graham has placed the emphasis in his Crusades on putting liberals, even Catholic priests, up on the platform with himself. When does Billy Graham ever spend time with solid devout Christians? Every time Billy Graham went to Moscow he tried to avoid the devout Christians of the unregistered churches who unwittingly tried unsuccessfully to meet with Graham. Instead, he would meet with the heads of the Orthodox Church, which, since all the changes in Russia, are now proven to have been KGB agents, although most of us had suspected that all along from the type of things they said and did.

How naive can Christians get? Do they really think that the Illuminati are going to let a legitimately powerful anointed Christian evangelist have regular access to their people? Don't Christians realize that if he was a real threat--someone who might really bring one of the top elite to Christ that they would be assassinating him, not wining and dining him.

--"BEWARE OF FALSE PROPHETS, WHICH COME TO YOU IN SHEEP CLOTHING, BUT INWARDLY THEY ARE RAVENING WOLVES." Mt. 7:15

"BEHOLD, I AM SENDING YOU FORTH AS LAMBS AMONG WOLVES." Lk. 10:3

The Apostle Paul warned Christian leaders, "Take heed therefore unto yourselves, and to all the flock, over the which the Holy Spirit hath made you overseers, to feed the church of God, which he hath purchased with his own blood. For I know this, that after my departing shall grievous wolves enter in among you, not sparing the flock." Acts 20:28-29

Bill Clinton, some senators, and Billy Graham's son Ned E. Graham invited the leaders of the Chinese house churches to a prayer breakfast in Washington D.C. Three delegates from the Three Self Patriotic Movement (TSPM) and 3 others from house churches were invited, Lin Xian-Gao, Li Tian-En, and Yuan Xiang-Chen.

Rev. Ned Graham visited these Chinese in person to extend the U.S. government's invitation. Graham told the Chinese Christians that the government would pick up the entire tab for the breakfast. In return the U.S. government wanted the Christians to promise not to speak to the American press or to any Americans comments that might hurt the image of the Red Chinese government. The Chinese government had promised the American government that they would guarantee safe entry and departure for these house church Christian leaders.

Then after the meeting, they were invited to Billy Graham's house. The Chinese Christians declined the invitation by Graham. Chinese pastor Lin said, *"If I went to the United States, I would tell the truth, not lies. To tell the truth would definitely be considered an act of damaging the image of the Chinese government which would create a pretext for the government to refuse my re-entry into China. But my commission from God is to serve Him faithfully in China only. There-*

fore, I choose to remain in China rather than to go abroad." Ned Graham (Billy's son) tried to talk the Chinese into coming, "I know that you surely do love your enemies, why then can you not compromise..."

The pastor answered, "Yes, we can forgive our enemies for persecuting or opposing us in their ignorance, but we can never love the false prophets or their heresy."' Ned also said, "It is a glorious and dignified thing to be invited by President Clinton. Many people seek it, but cannot obtain it. Fortunately, the Chinese did not buy it. (From China The Untold Story by The Voice of the Martyrs, Inc., 1995. pp. 25-31)

BUILDING AN IMAGE

There is another area of Billy Graham that we will only touch on. In one of Fritz's '92 newsletter, Billy Graham is quoted stating that he thought UFOs were angels of God. On either Jan. 28 or 29th (See Smyma, Feb. '93, p.3), Billy Graham was interviewed on television by David Frost. Billy Graham said he believed people in heaven are sent by God to other worlds to help them in redemption of life, This is edging somewhat close to what the Mormons believe, that "Christians" (that is Mormons) will each receive their own planet to be god of. In another show, Graham said he wanted to evangelize other planets. Fritz has repeatedly tried to warn Christians of the many demonic dangers associated with the entire UFO phenomena, and the Satanic Hierarchy's connection to UFOs. Billy Graham's idea that UFOs are good angels is a dangerous idea.

Billy Graham was given the contrived artificial image of being a great anti-Satanist. At the Chicago Crusade, 200 Satanists stood up in the crowds. Mayor Daily of Chicago then said from the stand, Billy we have 200 Satanists that want to disrupt your meeting shall I arrest them? What shall I do? And Billy said, No let's sing a song. The crowd sang a song and the Satanists left the stadium on their own. The whole affair was clearly staged and hokey, but Christians are very naive about Satanism and Billy Graham. This further confirmed to them that Billy Graham was a great anointed man of God. First, hard core Satanists don't show their faces in public. Second, the

Mayor of Chicago is not against the Satanists, he works with them, and there are reasons to suspect he is one. Third, Satanists, who do show themselves in public like Anton LaVey, want good publicity and would not carry out something like pretending to want to disrupt a Billy Graham crusade. Fourth, if a real threat had existed, Mayor Daily and the police wouldn't be asking Billy Graham what to do, they would be taking care of the problem. The police don't need to ask for permission to take care of troublemakers at the Crusade. Christians accepted this episode at its face value. Those who did clearly show the common church goers' poor understanding of those who seek to control and destroy the church. How Billy Graham plays a key role in reprogramming Monarch slaves. Two different talkative Satanists told sources of mine about 2 different coven meetings here in Portland in the Summer of 1993 where the covens discussed the benefits that the Satanists were going to get from the Billy Graham Crusade.

I know one of the benefits for the Satanists was that Monarch pro-gramees who had become Christians and had deactivated the effect of their mind-control programming were to be reprogrammed with Billy Graham' s help. When Billy Graham arrived in town, someone on his Crusade staff had managed to find and send out invitations to many of the survivors of Satanic ritual abuse (SRA) in Portland to come to a special meeting to personally meet with Billy Graham. At this special meeting with SRA victims, Billy Graham personally be-gan saying the buzz words to reactivate these people's programming, especially the Monarch survivors. (This comes from several wit-nesses.) For a number of years now, the Billy Graham Crusade has been putting messages across the bottom of television screens that has activation codes for Monarch survivors.

Those Monarch survivors who have become devote Christians to es-cape the nightmare of the Monarch mind-control are often not aware of the danger of watching the Billy Graham Crusade on television. When people are activated, special people are in the area and they take the Monarch survivors to what are called Near Death Trauma Centers. These centers are used then to reprogram these poor people. There were five in this area, of which we located 2 and forced them to move their sites. Religious fronts, denominations, individual churches and certain ministers, are used to hide criminal activity. Billy Graham, who is a programmed multiple himself, is exceptionally adept at managing his Monarch kittens.

The drug money laundered through his crusades is carefully handled by many Monarch slaves working in shifts and teams, so that the whole scheme can not be uncovered by catching one person. Billy Graham runs big operations all over the world under the disguise of evangelism. Another of the countless religious covers, that works with the Network's/Illuminati's drug activities involves the Mormon Bishop warehouses, which are used to store cocaine. Monarch slaves are involved with this. Different religious labels hide the same criminal Network. By the way, when giving the Patriarchal Blessing, the Mormon Patriarch if he has a Monarch slave will use hypnosis and triggers to convince the person what their future will be like.

One can't say this is happening in every case, but it is very widespread for the Patriarch's who give these blessings to be part of the Trauma-based mind-control operations. Billy Graham also personally delivers messages to the Presidents for the Illuminati, such as when he arrived just prior to Bush's decision to launch Desert Storm. Sometimes the papers even spell out that Billy Graham serves as a message boy, for instance, when he delivered a message in April, 92 from the Pope to North Korea's dictator Kim.

REFERENCES

The following three books were very helpful to me in terms of documenting Billy Graham's activities. All three authors were interested in documenting what Billy Graham is really all about. It may sound strange that I say that, but sadly most of the books that touch on Billy Graham like America's Hour of Decision Including a Life Story of Billy Graham are simply part of the deception process of the enemy. However, if anyone wants to know more about Billy Graham the following three books are very helpful in documenting Billy Graham's activities.

"Billy Graham:, A Parable of American Righteousness" by Marshall
Frady

Marshall Frady was a writer for Life and Newsweek. He has done an
incredible amount of research into Billy Graham's life. He doesn't
touch on the sinister side of Billy Graham, but by giving an honest
report about Billy Graham he tears off the "Hollywood-type mask" so
to speak that everyone has seen and believed. Marshall Frady simply
wanted to tell the whole story of Billy Graham, good, bad or otherwise. He spent many hours interviewing Billy Graham and many
other people involved in Billy Graham's life. When this book was
read by a devout Christian, it totally devastated this person's media-
built image of Billy Graham. For instance, items like Billy Graham
going to dinner with a prostitute and taking her home; Billy Graham
walking past his wife and not recognizing her; & Billy Graham's
New York Crusade refusing to allow street people into the crusade
because they were dirty.

However, another Christian borrowed my copy of it, and said after
looking at the book he didn't see anything wrong with Billy Graham
in the book. But then he just read portions of the book. Still, unless
one has spiritual discernment the book is probably not going to "blast
a person out of the water," because it is a biography not an exposé.
Until recently, this was the only really good biography that was available for Christians.

Many months before the Billy Graham 1993 Portland Crusade, the
advertisements for the crusade and the crusade activity here in Portland began. Pilgrim Discount, which is one of the best Christian
bookstores in the Portland area sells both used and new Christian
books. They had a used copy of Billy Graham a Parable of American
Righteousness. I watched for months to see if any Christians would
buy the book. Tens of thousands of Christians got involved in the
Billy Graham Crusade in the Portland area, but none had the interest
to read the only biography of Billy Graham available. Finally, just
shortly before the Crusade, a teenage Christian from Washington who
had been warned about Billy Graham and who was trying to keep
from being forced to attend, bought the book on a trip from Washing-

ton. This incident shows what Americans know--and what they want to know about Billy Graham is shallow media-hype. A Christian radio show here had the author of Billy Graham A Prophet with Honor on to promote his book, which was done just when the Crusade was days away.

"A Startling Exposure- Billy Graham and the Church of Rome" by Ian R. K. Paisley.

This is perhaps the best book as far as actual documentation. The book is probably rare, and not available. Ian R.K. Paisley has made it one of his projects of his life to expose Catholicism. Because Billy Graham works more with Catholics than Protestants Paisley as a concerned Christian obviously found himself learning about Billy Graham. Ian R.K. Paisley knows first hand how powerful Billy Graham and his establishment backers are. They have a colossal publication strength to discredit any critic of Billy Graham in whatever manner it takes -- even if it means outright lies and slander.

"Billy Graham Reformer? Politician? Preacher? Prophet? A Chronological Record Compiled from Public Sources" By The Church League of America 195 1-1982.

This book is from Edgar Bundy Ministries, It is a collection of articles that have appeared in the public media on Billy Graham over a period of 31 years. Billy Graham is condemned by his own words and his own actions. If people only took a look at what Billy Graham is on public record saying it would startle them.

Who is Billy Graham working for? Is he trying to build the Christian churches up, or is he trying to lay the foundation for a one-world religion? While some people may on first thought think that it is a great idea to have every one belong to the same religious structure, they need to reflect on the dangers inherent in one single religious body with all-encompassing power. The groundwork for such a dictatorial global religious body is already partially constructed, and is revealed in other writings of Fritz Springmeier. How many people know that in 1955 and 1956 Billy Graham announced that he had a policy of sending people who come forward at his crusades to the church of their choice whether that church or synagogue is Catholic, Protestant or Jewish.

For instance, the Protestant Church Life quotes Billy Graham in its 29 Sept 1956 issue, "Referring to the Billy Graham New York Crusade scheduled for May, 1957, Dr. Graham said: 'We're coming to New York not to clean it up, but to get people to dedicate themselves to God and to send them on to their own churches--Catholic, Protestant or Jewish."

There is one other book worth pointing out at this point, It was not a source book for my investigation, but I know the author, and the book came out recently, so it is likely still available. The book is *"The Assimilation of Evangelist Billy Graham into the Roman Catholic Church"* by Erwin Wilson.

The address is Quebec Baptist Missions, Box 113, Compton, Quebec, Canada, JOB iLO. It's s nice that men like Erwin Wilson are noticing Billy Graham's love affair with the Catholic Church. He picked up on Billy Graham's statement about the Pope, "Pope John Paul II has emerged as the greatest religious leader of the modern world and one of the greatest moral...leaders of this century." (The Saturday Evening Post, Feb, 1980.) However, several of these anti-Catholic ministries are rejecting the bigger picture. They have strongly resisted learning about mind-control and the exposure of the conspiracy in Be Wise As Serpents.

Because of this, several of these Christian ministries to Catholics have lots of information about Billy Graham and his close workings with the Catholic Church, but little comprehension of how the Catholic Church fits into the bigger picture, and how the New World Order is actually coming about. There has been widespread concern about Billy Graham among Christians. Because the controlled media doesn't report these concerns, people are not realizing the extent of the concerns which have been voiced. Even before the co-authors got involved in exposing the Illuminati and their control over religion and their plans for a New World Order, there has been a long history of concern by devout Christians over Billy Graham. There has been a growing dissatisfaction among conservative Christians towards Billy Graham. The introduction to Erwin Wilson's book which is written by Dr. Bob Jones (Chancellor of Bob Jones University) provides an introduction to the concerns Christians have about the man who has been set up by the media and the money elite to be their greatest leader.

We quote only a paragraph of what Dr. Bob Jones said, *"Some of us who grieved over Graham's first downward steps toward compromise with apostasy and biblical unbelief knew that he was pursuing a direction from which there would be no turning back. While we grieved over him and prayed for him, we had to warn men against his ministry as we had warned Billy against his direction."* The first area is doctrinal concerns by devout Christians, who have been deceived that Billy Graham thinks as they do. Christians usually take for granted that Billy Graham is sound doctrinally. The following paragraph of beliefs of Billy Graham were documented in 1993 by Fritz Springmeier in his June '1993 newsletter, with its large document packet.

"Main line Christians would be shocked to find out what Billy Graham really believes and is on public record as supporting. This will help show non-Christians, who read this, that Billy Graham is not really the Christian he pretends to be. This is not to preach at non-Christian readers, for some of the non-Christian readers will agree with Billy Graham's stands. These views are written to show how a major Christian leader can have a false public image that has survived mainly because the full public record of Billy Graham's stands are keep low key. If we are big enough to look at the deceptions of our politicians and statesmen, we must be big enough to face the deceptions of our ministers. Some of the areas that Billy Graham deviates from Scripture are as follows."

He is on public record supporting homosexuality, abortion, his disbelief in a literal hell, his support and practice of infant baptism to save children, his support for the Catholic church's worship of Mary (yet he calls himself a Protestant). He has repeatedly praised infidels and apostates as great Christians. He actively supported the American government policy to fight the Vietnam War. He would not challenge the idea that the Bible is mythology, when directly questioned. The deception doesn't stop with the Protestants, Catholic supporters have been kept in the dark about his abortion views. The deception goes way beyond Protestant, Catholic beliefs. As a programmed multiple who participates in Satanic Ritual, Billy Graham has deceived everyone.

The second area is concerns about his support for a One-World Church and a One-World-Government. This stems from:

1. *Billy Graham 's public endorsements of the World Council of Churches and the National Council of Churches.*

2. *Billy Graham's consistent attendance at the World Council of Churches' meetings.*

3. *that Billy Graham has done more than anyone in the world to bring about the One-World-Harlot church, and he has done more than anyone to unite all the Christian groups into one organization.*

4. *Billy Graham's support of the Pope and the Catholic church which is the largest Christian religion and one of the pillars of the New Age One-World religious body being set up.*

5. *The support that the NCC and WCC gives him.*

6. *The support that the internationalists and globalists give Billy Graham. Billy Graham was first asked to do his Portland Crusade in 1993 by the WCC/NCC representative in this area who is a homosexual, a new ager, and leader of the ecumenical movement.*

A third area is concern over the lack of depth that conversions at Billy Graham's crusades have, Some of the details on this are:

1. *Only 2% of the people coming forward at a Crusade have never been Christians and are actually giving their life to Christ for the first time, and of these 80% fall away.*

2. *A great majority of people that come forward are sent to Catholic and extremely liberal Churches, extremely few are sent to solid Bible believing churches., In the Catholic Standard and Times, Thursday, July 16, 1992, p. 10, this Catholic paper reported that 1,900 Catholics responded to Billy Graham's call to make decisions for Christ in the Philadelphia Crusade and were referred to about 250 parishes.*

3. *People that come forward are sent even to Jewish synagogues and New Age churches.*

4. *Converts are given the impression that Christ wants decisions for him, rather than that Christ wants disciples.*

5. *The people attending the crusades are almost all Christians, due to the high numbers of Christian counselors and the high number of church people which are always intentionally bussed in,* (Frady exposes this, and in 1992 a writer of the Williamette Week did a major story for the magazine detailing how she had searched the entire week at the Billy Graham Crusade for an unsaved person and failed to find a single non-Christian. There were a few, but so few she didn't find any. Williamette Week, Oct. 1,1992).

6. *Most decisions at the crusades are for trivial things such as to stop smoking.*

Interestingly, Christians with discernment spoke about how hurting the churches were after the Billy Graham Crusade here in Portland. They had been made wild promises of success, they were fleeced of their money, and then given a lukewarm spiritual boost. Their comments reminded me of this warning to Billy Graham clear back in the 1950s as to how he was ruining the harvest field. Part of Satan's Planetary control is through religious leaders. Christians have been conditioned to believe that Billy Graham is a great prophet of God by the establishment media, who have told us for years that Billy Graham was the most respected man in America, The percentages that the controlled Media have reported for Billy Graham's popularity may have been inflated.

There are several studies that show how the establishment uses polls dishonestly to manipulate thinking. The establishment media is able to create ideas so firmly within the mind of the public that it becomes almost impossible to deprogram people. What people see on T.V. becomes what you believe, The T.V. image becomes real. What actually happens at a crusade is far different from the media image. In Scotland for instance, a poll was taken of church membership one month before the Billy Graham Scotland Crusade, and two months after the Crusade. Church membership had actually declined substantially. So after spending millions of the Christians' dollars, Billy Graham had not even helped the church attendance of the Scottish churches.

When Billy Graham holds his crusades, the churches in the area sponsor the crusade. In Poland, in a nation 95% catholic, the churches that sponsored his crusade in Warsaw were Catholic churches and when people went forward they were sent to Catholic churches. Yet, when the mass media report on Crusades, it is made to sound like thousands of people became new Christians. Many of the devout Christians that have supported Billy Graham haven't thought through what is really going on at the crusades. They have been so caught up with the media image that they are not able to critically comprehend that the crusades are really major spiritual disasters. The book for counselors at the Billy Graham Crusade here in Portland specifically stated that only Billy Graham was allowed to proselytize, that the crusade counselors were forbidden to proselytize anyone at any time during the crusade, or else they would lose their Crusade badge as a counselor. (See these instructions in The Billy Graham Christian Life & Witness Course, Minneapolis, MN: Billy Graham Evangelistic Association, p. 47, Instructions A.6.)

But thousands of the Christians in Portland who became counselors for the '92 Crusade never gave it a second thought that only Billy Graham was allowed to proselytize, because they trusted Billy Graham. Money that could have gone to helping victims of mind-control went toward superficial decisions for Christ. Money that could have gone to doing some serious damage to the evil, has gone for Madison avenue hype and for big shows, On top of this, the large sums that are spent on the Billy Graham Crusades serve as a cover for the Networks money laundering that they do through Graham's Crusade using a series of Monarch slaves in a complex series of money drop offs.

A fourth area is concern over his methodology. A body language expert says that Billy Graham's talks are simply canned. They are well-rehearsed canned body movements and not coming from the heart. His crusade uses Madison-Avenue sales techniques instead of traditional scriptural methods to get converts. Billy Graham Crusades always spend great sums of money for bill boards promoting Billy Graham and bumper stickers promoting Billy Graham, the end result is that Billy Graham's name is usually promoted millions of times more often than Jesus Christ. Christianity is consistently watered down and identified with the world and its ways. And a great deal of boasting is done about numbers of decisions instead of real meaningful discipleship.

A fifth area is concern over Billy Graham acceptance of Communism. Although many people feel communism is dead, this area is still relevant. If you think communism is dead go live in North Korea, where Billy Graham went in 1992 full of praise for North Korea. See Christianity Today, May 18, 1992, p.55. (By the way, Billy Graham & family have sat on the board of Christianity Today, and still control it, so it wouldn't misquote him.)

1. *Billy Graham has repeatedly over international mass media claimed that there was no religious persecution under the communists,*

2. *Billy Graham has praised Mao-Tse-Tung's principles,*

3. *Graham has praised communist leaders on numerous occasions,*

4. *Dyed-in-the-wool communists who have been the ones giving orders to torture Christians for some reason feel comfortable spending time talking to Billy Graham.*

Even in the actual heritage and name of Billy Graham there is a connection between Marxism and a group of Satanists called Frankists.

One of the strongest satanic cults to take control over the Jewish population was called Sabbatianism. Jakob Frank assumed the role of leader of this group, and afterward this brand of Satanism was called Frankism. Freud's sexually-obsessed theories came from Frankism. Frank taught his followers to convert to another religion and hide behind that religion to practice their Satanism. One of several book on the subject of Frankism is *"The Contemporary Faces of Satan"* by Ratibor-Ray M. Jurjevich. Billy Graham's family when they originally came over to this nation were of the Frank family which is related to Jakob Frank. After coming over to this nation, they changed their name to Graham which is a Scottish name. Two groups of people who are over represented in the power structure over the last 200 years are Scots and cabalistic satanic "Jews." Obviously, not all Scotsmen nor Jews are involved in the NWO. Several other researchers independently discovered that Billy Graham's heritage was the Jewish Frank family.

However, Fritz was beginning to suspect that there must be some kind of Jewish blood in Billy Graham's heritage, because of the all the things he would stumble upon. For instance, the intimate connections Graham had with Jewish leaders and Jewish Christian ministries. His assurances to them that they are God's chosen people, a special group. Graham privately told them, that because they are a special chosen group they don't need to come to Christ. Fritz discovered all this by accident reading Jewish literature. Further, the paper called *"The C-9 Report For Internal Use Only"* states on page 11 that Billy Graham's daughters have lived in Israel, and that Billy Graham's son fought with the Israeli army in the Six-Day War.

In the Be Wise As Serpents book, chapter 2.1, "The Jewish author Gerald S. Strober in his book American Jews Community in Crisis, p. 110 states that after a resolution in Feb. 1973 at Pittsburgh by the NCC failed to declare the NCC against converting the Jews, that Billy Graham announced the following day a statement that God had a special place for the Jews and rejected coercive evangelistic efforts." Privately, Graham has assured Jewish leaders he is against converting the Jews to Christianity. Strober also informs his readers (p. 111) that many Christian organizations that are "Jewish Missions" take their marching orders from Billy Graham, This confirms numerous reports..." So Strober in effect is saying don't worry Graham is with us, and he controls most of the Christian organizations that are supposedly missions to evangelize us.

Messianic Jewish groups are strongly pro-Billy Graham, Some of these groups have gained in size and then strangely gone back into Judaism. That kind of thing has been happening here in Portland, not to mention other localities. Now it is clearer why Jews coming forward at Crusades have often been and are being referred by the Crusade people to Reformed Jewish synagogues.

How Billy Graham is a 33° Mason. This is an important issue, however, even if Billy Graham were not a 33° Mason, there are many things that he is doing that should warn Christians not to support him. There have been a number of people in casual conversation who have mentioned Billy Graham being a 33° Mason, for instance a CIA leader, a NSA person who is against the NWO, and various Masons. These accidental revelations are what can be considered casual evidence, in that it is accidentally heard.

Some of the people who have read Fritz's Be Wise As Serpents book have been experiencing validation of what was written on Billy Graham by their own casual contacts with people. These types of encounters are very meaningful to the people who experience them, but their significance is hard to communicate to others. Hopefully, readers of this, who are truth seekers, will have their own casual-evidence validation experience.

One piece of casual evidence came from a Shriner Clown. It turns out the only clowns who were chosen to perform for the Billy Graham 1993 Portland Crusade were Shriner Clowns. There were non-Masonic clowns available, even some Christian clowns, but the masons were the only ones Graham allowed to perform for him. Various people, who have worked in the system for the Illuminati, such as an ex-witch who is now a Christian, an ex-33° Mason now a Christian, and a CFR's person also now a Christian, all testify that Billy Graham is a 33* Freemason. A woman and a man who are ex-Satanists and now Christians also have mentioned about Billy Graham's Masonic membership. One has to understand that there is a close working relationship between the Lodge and the Illuminati.

To progress up the ranks in Satanism, they will require you to go through Freemasonry. Freemasonry then teaches people about the symbolism of the mystery religions. The lodges bring in female Monarch slaves for some of their Egyptian sexual magic rituals. If the reader were to get up in the morning and your mother, sister, and brother were in the kitchen and said that your mother had just drank a cup of coffee, you would be able to tell from their faces if they were telling the truth, and you would know that your mother had drank a cup of coffee. This is the way it is for us. We know these witnesses know the truth, and we know they are not making it up. But if people don't believe that, then they need to go scrounge up their own witnesses, and risk their own hide in doing the contacting. The material we present here is not frivolous work.

As pearls of value, we hope that this research is not taken and allowed to become pearls given to swine, because Billy Graham is such a key person for the Illuminati and the Satanic plan to bring in the Anti-Christ and the One-World-Religion, key parts of Graham's life have been intentionally shrouded, When he joined the Masonic lodge c. 1948, they intentionally kept his membership more secret than others. Why? They are secret about their membership in general, but even more so if the person is a key Illuminatus and a big key to their religious control, This is why they have kept the membership of Charles T. Russell, founder of the Watchtower Society quiet. This is why they keep the memberships of the Mormon prophets secret, It has been a consistent pattern by the Masonic Lodge to keep these key people's membership very quiet. It would be much easier if we had a membership certificate, but for people who don't want to believe no amount of evidence would suffice. In terms of a paper trail we have the following:

- Billy Graham's books consistently refer only to Masons.
- Billy Graham endorsed the Masonic DeMolay program for youth as God's work. This endorsement by Billy Graham is in a Ma-

sonic book that is used to educate people about "the craft", that means Freemasonry. That book is "The Clergy and The Craft" and it says that the people who are quoted in it are Masons. See Haggard, Forrest D. Transactions Missouri Lodge of Research, Vol. No. 27, The Clergy and the Craft, p. 127. where Graham endorses the Masonic youth program. In terms of witnesses who have put what they have witnessed in writing we have the following:

- Jim Shaw, ex-33° Mason the highest ranking Freemason to defect to Christianity, writes about Billy Graham being at his 33° initiation ceremony. Huntington House refused to print his book co-authored with Tom McKenney unless they took out Billy Graham's name on pg. 104, and substituted a general description. See *"The Deadly Deception"*, p. 104-105. Only Freemasons are allowed to attend these initiations. See *"The New Age, The Official Organ of The Supreme Council 33°"*. Wash., D.C., October 1961, p. 30.)

Some Christians have tried every thing in their mind to get around Jim Shaw's testimony. And the Masonic Lodge are now claiming that he wasn't a 33° Freemason. There is no doubt that he was a 33° Mason. What we are seeing is how important it is to the Illuminati to keep Billy Graham's membership secret. Originally, Dr. Morey who wrote a book on Freemasonry told me over the phone that Billy Graham was a 33° Freemason and that he had held his membership file in his hand in the library of the House of the Temple, which is where the Supreme Council of the 33° has their headquarters.

However, now he denies it and says that he only was told by the librarians that the file existed, but that he didn't examine the membership file. He wrote a letter to Christian News to the editor which was printed. At least, his letter to the editor of Christian News says that the Scottish Rite have a Billy Graham file. Fritz stands by his original statements about what Dr. Morey said, even though he has gone back on his original story and is getting people to think Fritz somehow invented what he told me. There are a great many things that are suspicious about Dr. Morey.

- His book on Freemasonry claims that Freemasonry started out a Christian organization.
- His book was printed by a company that uses the Knights Templar logo as their company logo, and whose company head is most likely a Freemason.

If it looks like a duck, quacks like a duck, and walks like a duck-- what do you think it is?

Long before I actually knew Billy Graham was a 33° Freemason, I felt that was the "most likely" explanation for what I was learning of him. What caused me to think that way? Everything about the man, just shouted Freemason. The way he talks, who he has as friends, etc. etc.

This article is not capable of going into depth about small nuances and details, but suffice it to say that the Masons know how to broadcast to other Masons that they are a Mason. It should be pointed out some of the key people for Billy Graham's staff have been Freemasons. Let's look at a few of the key people helping Billy Graham:

- William M. Watson -- DIRECTOR OF THE BILLY GRAHAM EVANGELISTIC ASSOCIATION, he is a Freemason, and he is also President of Occidental Petroleum Corporation. Chairman of Occidental was Armand Hammer. Watson is also a member of the development council of the Masonic run Baylor University. Baylor University has participated in the mind-control, (See also the expose of Baylor University in Be Wise As Serpents.) He also was a member of the advisory council to the Southwestern Baptist Theological Seminary in Ft. Worth which had at least three Freemasons on its board of trustees, and likely more.
- David M. McConnell -- DIRECTOR OF THE BILLY GRAHAM EVANGELISTIC ASSOCIATION, he is a Freemason, He was also U.S. ambassador to the United Nations (1968-69), business associate with Illuminatus Charles Gambrell, in Belk Stores of Charlotte, North Carolina.
- Arthur Lee Malory -- CO-CHAIRMAN of the BILLY GRAHAM CRUSADE Advisory Committee for the 1973 St. Louis Crusade -

- 32° Freemason, deacon in the So. Bapt. Church.

Who are some of the primary ministers that had worked with 33° Freemason Billy Graham over the years? Billy Graham has helped set up other 33° Masons in ministry. Billy Graham has placed his stamp of approval on almost every well-known apostate Christian out there. When Billy Graham had a crusade in Japan, the Japanese minister that he had up on the platform was a well-known extremely liberal Christian. A conservative Japanese was shocked. Billy Graham is also endorsing many of the books, and ministries of these apostates. Some of the three biggest ministers in the protestant world, Robert Schuller, Norman Vincent Peale, and Oral Roberts are all 33° Masonic brothers of 33° Freemason Billy Graham. See Roberts, Oral. *"Miracle of Seed Faith"*, p.9.)

Billy Graham has helped each of these brothers with their ministries. Robert Schuller taught principles of church growth to Unity School in Kansas City. A Christian, who used to be on staff there, said that Robert Schuller was fully aware that Luciferian Initiations were going on at the school and that he didn't care. Robert Schuller, 33° Freemason, was helped into ministry by Billy Graham. Schuller also participates in the Monarch program and is also sexually serviced by Monarch slaves.

Norman Vincent Peale's form of Christianity called "positive thinking" is actually only white witchcraft with different names. Peale simply is a "Christian" witch. Norman Vincent Peale, 33° Freemason, his church receives the bulk of people who came forward at the NY Crusade. Norman Vincent Peale is a 6° Illuminatus (Pilgrim Society), and a 33° Freemason. In the magazine Psychic Magazine of San Francisco Peale says of occultist Kreskin, All he's doing is dramatizing what I've been preaching in my writing for years. Norman Vincent Peale controls the approx. $200 million Presbyterian Minister's Fund. He celebrated the 25th anniversary of the United Nations. He was the keynote speaker at the birthday of the late Mormon prophet Spencer W. Kimball (a secret Mason).
Peale praised Kimball as a true prophet of God, and a great man of God. Peale practices witchcraft, and palms it off on unsuspecting

Christians under different terminology. The false unity movement which is so strong today, wants to unite the devout Christian with the likes of Norman Vincent Peale. Peale is a good friend of Billy Graham, and Billy Graham referred the largest number of new converts of the NY Billy Graham Crusade to Peale's church.

Oral Roberts, 33° Freemason, helped into ministry by his Masonic brother Billy Graham. Oral Roberts has been seen by witnesses participating in SRA and Mind-control. Oral Roberts University and the charismatic movement is another important religious front. The Charismatic movement has been infiltrated by multiples since day-one. The history of the infiltration is extensive. Oral Roberts has Cherokee blood. According to some things that Oral Roberts has said, some Christians think that he received his healing powers from an old Indian who healed him through Indian shamanism when Oral was young. At times, Oral does use the same methods that spirit mediums use to heal with. According to slaves who have been deprogrammed, they were in satanic rituals with Oral Roberts. Christian ministers, who have participated in his ministry are saying that they have seen massive swindling in his healing ministry. His university is being used as a programming center. His basketball team at one time had Monarch slaves playing on it. We do not know if they still do. Under the prayer tower is one of the programming sites. Billy Graham, a handler himself, helped launch Oral Roberts University, and is a friend of Oral Roberts.

From the Illuminati's point of view Tulsa is the Guardian City of Apollo. The City of Faith is to be the center for healing from Aesculapius, a demon related to Apollo. While portraying themselves as Christians, infiltrators within the charismatic movement are carrying out satanic rituals to get demonic healing powers. Tulsa is one of the, if not THE, main center for the campaign to infiltrate Christianity via the Charismatic/Pentecostal movement with programmed multiples.

G. Bromiey Oxnam, 33° Freemason, was head of the FCC churches, supportive friend of Billy Graham. G. Bromley Oxnam has a long history to him of working for the elite, interested readers can pick up his story in Be Wise As Serpents in the chapter that goes into the details about how the Christian churches were organized by the FCC and WCC for the Illuminati.

The NWO is infiltrating the churches via the Earth Stewardship Movement. An attempt was made at Rio de Janeiro to get an Earth Charter but there wasn't enough time, their were lots of N.O.G. delegates and just in general lots of people to coordinate (4,000 attended). Another Earth Summit was promised, but instead they decided at the end of Sept/Oct of '95 to have a State of the World Forum to be held by/sponsored by the Gorbachev Foundation at the Presidio, CA. The ex-head of the KGB, Gorbachev, is now headquartered in the Presidio, a major mind-control programming site. Christian basher Ted Turner was the chairman of the conference. The cost was $5,000 per person and the invitations went out to only select people. There were 100 handpicked politicians who received invitations, along with Billy Graham and Mother Teresa. This was coordinated with the 50th anniversary of the UN which was being celebrated all over the world.

FLEECING THE SHEEP

The charismatic movement claims to have the Holy Spirit in a special way, however, some seem to be lacking in all discernment that the Holy Spirit would give. There are several books exposing the big name Charismatic ministers. One is written by an ex-charismatic Assembly of God minister. He shows a picture in his book of an Assembly of God flier promoting the "Testimony of J. Edgar Hoover." Yes, the Assembly of God promoted the "testimony" of J. Edgar Hoover., while he was known to be a power hungry individual who practiced homosexuality. It was this type of hype that caused this minister to grow disillusioned with the charismatic movement's so called spirituality.

Recently, the spiritual discernment of Billy Graham and many other big time ministries was exposed when these big Christian ministries were conned out of $550 million dollars. Billy Graham introduced John G. Bennett to thousands of people at a recent Billy Graham Crusade in Philadelphia in 1992. John Bennett gave his testimony at the crusade. Because Billy Graham, John Templeton, and Laurance

Rockefeller were apparently supportive of John G. Bennett, big time Christian ministries "trusted" him. John told many of the big Christian ministries that if they gave him millions of dollars, for every million he received he would give them two million back.

Many of the big Christian ministries gave Bennett money. In fact, he collected $550 million, which he ran off with, from ministries such as Pat Robertson's, Bill Bright's, Chuck Colson's, Luis Palau's, Westminster Theological Seminary, Wheaton College, the Salvation Army and many others. The reader may have heard of this New Era Foundation scam. That's what it was. Bennett told these "Christian" leaders "Give New Era one million dollars and we'll give you back two million." The donations of hard earned money by many innocent Christian believers were lost, However, the Christian believers are partially responsible because the church has refused to clean house of wolves that set in their pulpits.

For instance, when Billy Graham came to the Portland area all the various denominations from the most liberal to the most conservative supported him. Only about a dozen churches did not get involved and only one church actively tried to expose Billy Graham. <u>EVEN THOUGH THERE HAS BEEN A MASS OF DOCUMENTATION EXPOSING BILLY GRAHAM AS A WOLF FOR 30 YEARS!</u> When the church refuses to follow God's Word and supports these men then they must take some of the blame when these men give their millions of hard earned dollars away to a con artist.

INADEQUATE REACTIONS

When people have been warned about Billy Graham, one of the common responses is to for people to call up the Billy Graham Crusade staff, If I ask a biologist a question about biology I can expect to get a credible answer, If I ask a mother about her son I can expect to get a credible answer. But how in the world can someone call up the Billy Graham Crusade staff and expect to get a credible answer to the question "Is Billy Graham a Mason?" The person that answers the phone is likely a secretary, someone who knows Billy Graham no more than the janitor. What does that person know about the Freemasons?

Because the Freemasons are a secret society, in general, there are only two basic categories of people

a) People Involved With Freemasonry - They certainly know what's going on in it, but they have taken blood oaths on penalty of death not to talk about it.
b) Those Who Aren't Involved With Freemasonry - They don't know anything about it.

There are only a few people who are not masons, who are informed about the Masons. The answer of some secretary over the phone to the question, Is Billy Graham a Freemason?" is of little value, because the secretary or other staff member has not had the opportunity to get reliable information. This is from the standpoint of getting a reliable witness, calling some secretary or staff member is simply not a credible response to all the documentation. No court would view a secretary of a large organization as an expert witness qualified to settle such a dispute. The second catch is that such witnesses are not reasonably unbiased. It is expected that Billy Graham's staff would front for him any questions that could expose him to bad publicity.

This last comment is not speculation. There is proof that Billy Graham's staff has consistently lied over the years to prevent negative publicity about Billy Graham. When Richard Nixon met with his political buddies to decide who to have run with him, the person he asked first in the smoke-filled room was Billy Graham. I have read the account of this in more than one place, but I will quote Marshall Frady's description of when Billy Graham was asked who he thought should run with Nixon as Nixon's vice-presidential running mate. Billy Graham chose 33° Masonic brother (then only 32°) Mark Hatfield. Here is Frady's description. *"His assimilation into the Nixon presidency had already been well underway, in fact, at that convention in Miami when, after Nixon's nomination, Graham wound up sitting in Nixon's penthouse suite among the smoggy late-night deliberations over Nixon's vice-presidential selection: Graham himself, whatever initial uncertainty he might have felt to find himself in such a political locker-room session, soon pitched into the proceedings with his own effusive recommendation of Mark Hatfield: "He's a great Christian leader. He's almost a clergyman. He's been an educator, and he's taken a more liberal stand on most issues than you, and I think the ticket needs that kind of balance."*

In 1992, Mark Hatfield, along with Prince Hall Freemason Jessie Jackson both were on television in July defending Billy Graham's actions. Mark Hatfield, according to a deprogrammed slave has been a user of Monarch sexual slaves. NY's Union Seminary is controlled and funded by the Rockefellers. President of Union Seminary was Dr. Henry Van Dusen. Billy Graham made him a prominent person in his crusade and said he was a "classic example" of a mass evangelism conversion, If that is a good example of Graham's conversions, we Christians should shudder.

It is no coincidence that the Southern Baptists of which Billy Graham is a member, is controlled by the Freemasons. Brook Hays, President of the Southern Baptist Convention was a high ranking Freemason as well as part of the CFR. None of the So. Bapt. Convention's Presidents have opposed Freemasonry. Pres. Bill Clinton, a slave handler, is a member of the Emmanuel Baptist Church which is a Southern Baptist Church in Little Rock, Ark. The late Bill Moyers who promoted the Mystery Religions was a Southern Baptist. Moyers went to the SW Baptist Theological Seminary, the same school run by one of Billy Graham's staff directors. John Buchanan is another Southern Baptist. John Buchanan went to a So. Bapt. Seminary, and then worked as a front man for People for the American Way started by Jewish Norman Lear, an anti-Christian. People might be shocked to learn of some of the New Age teachings and New Age teachers that have been allowed into the Southern Baptist churches. The Southern Baptist youth program is based on Masonic ideas and is very Masonic in its ritual.

SUMMARY

The reader is thanked for wading through a lot of difficult material and can now see why Billy Graham may well be the greatest deception that has ever been successfully pulled off. But as Abraham Lincoln said, "You can fool some of the people all of the time, and all of the people some of the time, but not all of the people all of the time." Ever since the early 1950s, there have been Christians exposing Billy Graham, But the control of the Christian media and the Christian seminaries is far more extensive than most people realize.

The Be Wise As Serpents book diagrams out how the Christian religious denominations are being controlled, and how the Masons and Illuminati-connected administrators and trustees have control of most of the Seminaries. Billy Graham without a doubt works directly for the Satanic hierarchy. But a rational and fair appraisal of what the man is, and what damage he has done to Christianity will probably not be given much of a chance. Nobody, no matter who they are is going to fool Christ. There will be a real evaluation done on judgment day and when that day comes Christ said,

"Many will say to me in that day, "LORD LORD, have we not prophesied in your name, cast out demons in your name, and done many wonders in your name? And then I will declare to them, I never knew you; depart from Me, you who practice lawlessness!" Mt 7:22-23

THE TOP SECRET AMISH FRONT (& HUTTERITES)

It will probably assist the reader to know that both of the authors have first hand experience with the following information about the Amish. Fritz was Amish for several years, as a Amish church member in church districts in Kansas, Missouri, and Illinois. He has also visited numerous Amish settlements in the U.S. & Canada, and lived/ worked with the horse and buggy Old Order Mennonites (not to be confused with the Old Order Amish Mennonites) in Ontario Canada for half a year. He has a manuscript of a book that he wrote about the Old Order Amish Mennonites, and has gone so far as to inquire with publishers like National Geographic if they would like some of his material. He has also attended a variety of Mennonite churches, including Church of God in Christ, Menn. (Holdeman's), Charismatic Mennonite, Conserv. Menn. and Beachy Amish churches across the U.S. He also knows first-hand that Illuminati slaves, some of who are programmers, have been infiltrated by the Illuminati into Mennonite churches.

Perhaps what may come across as the strangest religious front, and it is certainly one of the biggest secrets of the intelligence agencies is their use of the Old Order Amish Mennonites as a front. The Amish are the most pacifistic people, so the Illuminati/intelligence agencies have placed some of their best programmed assassins behind the front of being Amish. The front is real they are Amish,. Well, many of them are, some were Illuminati children switched at birth to give the programmers better bloodlines to work from. Some Amish women in cult families have let the Illuminati impregnate them with stronger bloodlines. Many Nazi bloodlines were hidden after WW II under the Mennonite/Amish cover. The Mennonites and some of the more progressive Amish adopt many children.

The Amish in Missouri (Jamestown), Kansas (south of Hutchison), and Oklahoma (Guthrie, OK), Kentucky, Ohio (Holmes Co., OH), and Pennsylvania (Lancaster, PA) have been involved in selling their children to the Illuminati. When the Illuminati would buy a child they would send in one of their own midwives to help with the birth and retrieve the child. Generally, the Amish would sell their children when they realized they were going to have twins. One would be given to the cult, and one would be kept by the Amish parents. Because these children are born outside of the system, and have no birth certificates, they made excellent children to use in porn.

They were often blond haired and blue eyed. The Amish women were not allowed to use birth control, it was forbidden by the church, and they were not allowed to have an abortion, and it was their duty to have sex with their husbands. It is possible that some parents sold their children just to get out of the responsibility of having another child. The Amish farms in Kansas and Oklahoma and in the border states like Missouri and Kentucky are mechanized with tractors, and they don't need the large families that the Amish in other places need.

Due to the strong legalism that pervades their church, some have tried to get around the tight spot that the rules place them in by selling a few unnoticed children. However, there is an active witchcraft practicing occult group within the Amish which is like a box within a box within a box. It is very secret. There are many ways of describing what is going on with the Amish. Let's describe quickly in half a page (it could be a book in itself) what a deep look at the spiritual dynamics of what is going on with their communities.

The rise of Satanism within their ranks is simply a natural outgrowth of the spiritual dynamics. There were two trees in the Garden of Eden, one was the Tree of Life and one was the Tree of the Knowledge of Good and Evil. The first meant being transformed by the Creator who made them into the image of the Spirit of God and receiving spiritual life, but the other tree was performance. The Tree of the Knowledge of Good and Evil (religion) includes both Law (good) and license (evil). As soon as a group gets legalistic, they fall from grace. They then separate themselves by their performance and say in effect "look at what we're doing" which is a form of pride. God resists the proud, so they through a number of spiritual dynamics lose fellowship with God.

This means they must cling to their legalistic traditions even more, because a live relationship with God is gone. Bible Studies are forbidden by most Amish church districts, and they don't get new revelation from God, they still are working off of the revelations of the 1600s, when they were traumatized and quit growing. When they split from the rest of the Mennonites, they were like a child alter split which never grows up. When a group gets legalism, they also get license, because the two grow from the same tree. Every Amish community has two large groups the legalistic ones and the license ones. The young people are even split this way. In Lancaster County, the Groffies" is the nickname of the large license group of young people who fornicate and drink. There is a smaller group of legalistic conservative young people too, who are at the other end of the spectrum. There is one group, gang might be a more appropriate name, called Jamborees who are an unruly and destructive collection of angry wild young people.

The Bishops in Lancaster Co. meet twice yearly to keep this large settlement of opposites together. A lot of compromise and looking the other way is done for the sake of peace. "Peace" at any price is the name of the game. Even before a prayer is said in church the minister calls out, "Wenn mer eenich sin, wella mer bete." This translates, "If we are in one accord, then let us pray." Because peace is so important, they are out of balance in getting it. They place peace far above truth. In order to have the appearance that everything is well, secrecy pervades everything like the air one breathes. Because their whole culture is secret, children raised in it aren't aware of how strong it is, it is simply a way of life, like it is for the Illuminati. Legalism values conformity.

Conformity prefers robotic obedience over understanding. In fact, one Bishop told Fritz, co-author of this book, "We don't want our young folks to understand why they do what they do, we only want obedience. Understanding is dangerous." Does the reader begin to see how the Amish make both the perfect setting for Monarch Mind-Control, and the perfect cover. The Amish are a very secret group. During their early history they suffered severe persecution. Their culture teaches them to suffer in silence, which today helps their Satanic abusers infiltrate their culture. In the past in Europe, when the Catholic or Protestant church caught them they were tortured to death.

They were hunted as animals and treated worse than animals when caught. This was the trauma, that Satan did to them, and the lie that was then handed them was that if they would cloister themselves secretly in the New World away from everyone else, they would be safe. The Amish have shut out from outsiders the true flavor of their culture and beliefs. They are silent about their problems. They tell themselves that outsiders couldn't possibly be interested in their affairs. The Amish themselves are very divided from each other. The divisions between Amish groups is called Zwietract. Zwietract can cover anything from a mild aloofness to a full fledged shunning (called the Meidung). The Amish aren't in general qualified to tell outsiders much in detail about their own heritage, or religion because they are so isolated from the other Amish settlements and have been raised in such an anti-intellectual culture.

Most Amish are content to know that the way they do things "was always done this way" and that their elders and forefathers were gifted men who examined things very closely. Their social norms are not intellectually questioned by most Amish, but then American society has been very isolationist in the world and few Americans question their society & norms. Americans even rebel in the prescribed fashion, whatever the elite tell society is the "in" "cool" "hot" stylish way to do things. The Amish are similar to the Mid-east culture in that they have a very indirect approach to saying things. They do not consider it proper to speak with a negative connotation about anybody. They also instinctively give pat answers to outsiders to blunt questions.

These pat answers border on being rigid, prejudiced, and simple. They serve the purpose to deter curiosity. The early Amish leaders were ex-Catholic priests, but most of the people were peasants who had little formal schooling, had little Bible knowledge, and came from southern Germany and the Rheinland where witchcraft was practiced by the common people. The Spirit of Witchcraft never left the Amish. It has always been with them. The folk witchcraft is called Brauche, and the craft is kept secret by old men who pass the incantations down in secret. When the Amish moved to Pennsylvania, they moved in next door to Rosicrucians.

When the Rosicrucian settlements fell apart they joined the Mennonites, thus bringing their hermetic magic along with them. Somewhere within the Amish were some families that were under cover for the Jesuits, and were sent in as spies long ago because they were corrupt. These families have been generational Satanists, which practice pedophilia and other crimes in the safety of their isolation. They were placed within the Amish to help the Catholic church destroy the Amish. In Europe that happened under Hitler, when all the Old Order Amish were arrested in 1938 and wiped out of Germany. Prior to WW II, the Nazi's part of the Illuminati sent over a number of programmed multiples which set up an unnamed cult in upstate New York. This cult was to help Hitler take power in the U.S. when the Nazi's won the war.

They did not win the war, but 60 years later this Satanic cult still operates. Now 2nd and 3rd generation programmed multiples are now part of this cult. Somehow this Illuminati mission coordinates with the Illuminati project to get Hitler's bloodline hidden among the Amish, although the authors are aware of Hitler's descendants being in Oregon, and Washington as well as Pennsylvania. One of them in Portland, Oregon works for the Federal government. Lancaster County is sometimes referred to as the mother church. This was one of the original counties which the Amish settled in when they first came over to the New World. William Penn invited Rosicrucians, Amish, and other dissident religious groups to Pennsylvania. The Satanic covens in Lancaster County, PA consist of members from Amish, Mennonite and Brethren churches. They are not simply all Amish.

Lancaster County's Amish will fellowship with all the approximately 200 other settlements of Amish around the country. What is a peculiar phenomena, is that many churches that do not fellowship with one another, will still maintain "communion" with Lancaster out of respect for it's place in Amish history. However, Lancaster County has some of the most immoral reprobate Amish that there could be. All this is hidden very well from the thousands of tourists, due to the secrecy of the Amish. The Amish do not often pay taxes, do not pay social security because they are exempt from the Social Security program, and send many of their children to Amish schools.

They are truly a separate society which maintains rigid secrecy. If you were the New World Order or the Illuminati where would you want to hide your assassins? The safest place is inside of the most pacifist group in the world, the Amish. Monarch mind-controlled slaves are being created out of Amish children. During W.W. II, Amish conscientious objectors were forced by the government to do alternate public service in lieu of military service. This was known as Civilian Public Service. Amish & Mennonite conscientious objectors were placed into Mental Hospitals to help.
They served at Allentown State Hosp., Allentown, PA; Cantonsville State Hosp., Cantonsville, MD; Cleveland State Hosp., Cleveland,

OH; Delaware State Hosp., Parnhurst, DL; Denver State Hosp., Denver, CO; Greystone Park State Hosp., Greystone Park, NJ; Harrisburg State Hosp., Harrisburg, PA; Hudson River State Hosp., Poughkeepsie, NY; Kalamazoo State Hosp., Kalamazoo, MI; Lima State Hosp., Lima, OH; Livermore State VA Hosp., Livermore, CA; Macedonia State Hosp., Macedonia, OH; Marlboro State Hosp., Marlboro, NJ; Mt. Pleasant State Hosp., Mt. Pleasant, 10; Norristown State Hosp., Norristown, PA; Provo State Hosp., Provo, UT; Rhode Is. State Hosp., Howard, RI; Roseburg VA State Hosp., Roseburg, OR; Staunton State Hosp., Staunton, VA; Tiffin State Hosp., Tiffin, OH; Wernersville State Hosp., Wernersville, PA; Ypsilanti State Hosp., Ypsilanti, MI.

The author, Fritz, believes that the complete story of how the Illuminati got a secret foothold into the Amish community lies in what happened to the anxious-to-please, compliant, innocent Amish boys, who were assigned to these mental hospitals. Many people do not realize that during W.W. I, several Mennonite/Hutterite conscientious objectors were tortured to death by our government. Not a pretty picture when you find out how sadistic our government was willing to be toward its own citizens.

Not only did the Amish boys go to lots of mental hospitals during W.W. II, but all of the religious groups that participated in the conscientious objector service (called Civilian Public Service) contributed boys to the Office of Scientific Research & Development, part of the Army, which was still using these boys for experiments until Dec. 31, 1946. What kinds of "experiments" were the Amish boys, who were offered up as guinea pigs, subjected to by the OSRD? We now know that some of these experiments were very dangerous to their human guinea pigs. 1-0 classification was the Selective Service Board's Conscientious Objector classification. During the Vietnam War, Amish young men went into I-W service, conscientious objector service, at mental and regular hospitals.

Their I-W service was for two years. Some of these young men were programmed at these hospitals. One Amish boy after he got home from I-W service committed suicide. The secret satanic families within various Amish settlements also offered up their children. This started a large scale super secret operation by the CIA/Intelligence agencies to set up Delta teams within the Amish. Who would ever suspect an Amishman? They have been expendable assassins for the CIA for years. These young men are strong farmboys. They have no connection between themselves and the outside world where they secretly carry out their missions, and if they die, there is no birth record, and perhaps a dozen other siblings for their family to continue on with.

During the Vietnam War, the Military's Selective Service did things differently than in W.W.II. Any hospital or mental hospital which applied for approval could get I-W, conscientious objector, boys. The Amish put together a Steering Committee to work with the government and the I-W service. In the I-W Steering Committee meetings ,and the author Fritz attended one, it was stated by Committee members "The boys do not come back the same [from the hospitals]" and that the I-W service in the mental hospitals was "proving unsatisfactory and harmful." Some of the mental hospitals which received Amish boys include Columbia Missouri's State Mental Hospital & Hospital complex, Colorado Psychopathic Hospital in Denver, all of the hospitals that got W.W. II I-Ws (as listed above), Central State Hospital, Indianpolis, IND, New Jersey State Hospital, Greystone Park, NJ, Philadelphia State Hospital, Philadelphia, PA, plus numerous others. At any one time, there were hundreds of Amish boys in I-W service.

It is suspected that many of these hospitals were involved in mind-control, and it is known that the Columbia, MO complex of hospitals and Mid-Missouri State Mental Hospital, 803 Stadium Dr., Columbia, Missouri and the Veteran's Hospital across the street were involved in mind-control for the CIA. A mental hospital had to apply to the Selective Service Board for approval to get I-W workers. Then their personnel departments would hire the I-W boys for positions such as nursing attendants. One State Mental Hospital administrator told Fritz that the whole I-W thing was "pretty confidential." The Amish Steering Committee worked with the Mennonite Central Committee (MCC) which in turn worked for some quasi-religious group which is privately funded called The National Service Board of Religious Objectors (NSBRO) still active in Washington, D.C.

The Amish were slow to act, but by the end of the Vietnam War, they had managed to get some of their farms approved for I-W service and in 1971, the Steering Committee was able to announce that 70 Amish I-W boys were working on Amish farms in 8 states, rather than in hospitals. However, this late change was too late to protect their settlements from infiltration from sophisticated Illuminati mind-control.

How It Is Done

A programmed Amish boy will likely be contacted by what is called a "CUT-OUT". This is the secret contact person who maintains contact between the Handler and the Amish Delta. CUT-OUT's can either be given several slaves (a BLOCK CUT-OUT) or in other cases only know the up-line handler and down-line person (a CHAIN CUT-OUT). If further secrecy is needed by the handler, he can use ''sterile telephones'' which the Illuminati/CIA have which cannot be traced, even by the telephone companies. When an Amish boy is activated and sent out on an assassination mission for the Illuminati/Intelligence agencies he is a professional at what he has been trained and programmed to do. Amish boys, programmed to be assassins, are used in what their handlers call "wet ops". This intelligence lingo means that human blood will run.

Wet ops, also called black ops are debriefed by a briefing team. The Amish multiple will have to give a detailed account of the finished operation, once under hypnosis, once with a polygraph, and once under the drug scopolamine (a truth serum). When the debriefing team, which includes a Mind-control Programmer, is satisfied that all of the inconsistencies between the different accounts have been ironed out, then the Programmer will block out all memory and guilt of the operation. The handler may write a "blind memorandum" which has no file no. or letterhead or name. Then Amish boy's assassination alters will be praised for having done a great service to humanity and to his country. The Amish boy can now be sent home to milk cows and work on his labor-intensive tobacco farm without any nagging guilt or horrible memories surfacing to trouble him (at least in theory).

Trained assassins do have memory flashes, as all Monarch slaves have, but they are only bits and pieces. People also do not realize that the Amish live in many more states than Pennsylvania. They move all over the United States. If an Amish man was travelling on a CIA mission there are numerous of excuses that could be made for why he could be on the move. There are far more Amish young people away from the Amish settlements than people realize because they dress like the world. Many young people leave with the knowledge that they can go back years later and be accepted back into their community. What are some of the mitigating factors in all of this? The Amish do their own butchering. They are down-to-earth people who are not afraid of blood. Essentially all Amish children grow up helping with butchering, and seeing life and death played out everyday on their farms.

The Amish do not embalm their dead, and have their own cemeteries. The Satanic cult within the Amish can reopen the graves and carry out satanic ceremonies afterward. Their cemeteries are small almost hidden sites with markers hidden in grass. Some of these graveyards blend in with their rural settings. Elmo, Joseph, and Victor Stoll are some prominent Amish men. Joseph and Elmo have travelled a great deal esp. to Central America. Joseph wrote a book on Child Training which teaches parents how to break a child's will. This author is supportive of discipline and respect. The book is pointed out, only because it is a paper trail to show that the Amish discipline and the Illuminati's discipline at times can be similar.

The only person who might see an Amish boy being disciplined, since they are a rural people, would be the immediate family or an occasional Amish guest. An Amish man seeing a father carrying out the Monarch steps to build dissociation would likely not see anything wrong. If the guest did see something wrong (i.e. too strict or mean), the objections would be kept very low key. For sure, no non-Amish would ever hear about it. The Illuminati families like the Dukes and Reynolds control tobacco production and cigarette manufacturing. In order to keep their lifestyle in Pennsylvania, the Amish have had to grow tobacco for the Illuminati controlled companies. This author can only speculate what economic leverage that has given the Illuminati over the Pennsylvania Amish.

HIDING A MAJOR PROGRAMMING CENTER

The blue prints of the Portland Mormon Temple at Lake Oswego, OR which sets over a secret underground programming site, were changed overnight after they were looked at. The original blueprints showed that Lake Oswego had allowed a building code to be broken. The blueprint was changed, showing that Lake Oswego's city employees were working along with the Mormon church and the CIA to keep everything running smooth with their high tech secret underground programming center, which has the front of being sacred temple grounds.

Three separate Monarch slaves independently described this underground installation, and there are other evidences of it too. In order to gain access to the underground programming tunnels, a person has to place their palm on the wall, where a disguised instrument identifies a person's hand. The entrances are disguised using the most sophisticated techniques. One is from the Temple Laundry Building south of the temple and another is from the hotel south of the temple. This hotel has a strange hard-to-find entrance to its parking lot, almost as if they haven't wanted uninvited guests. Tunnels are widely used at the other various programming sites.

EXTERNAL & INTERNAL DECEPTIONS

There are some stock tools of deception that are used both externally on the world and internally on the slave when their system is programmed and structured. Later in the book we will cover the structuring. Since this chapter covers deceptions, we will discuss them here, but the reader needs to bear in mind, they will be employed in the structuring/programming phases of the slave's life. They are deflection, blinds, slides, Hegelian dialectics, and deniability.

- a. Deflection is taking something good and deflecting its purpose. This is a stock tool. For instance, loyalty and obedience can be good virtuous things if given to the correct authority. But deflected to the false sadistic authority, they are disastrous. They use Deflection to redirect the power of truth which is opposed to them. Healthy foods, benevolence, ecology, love, acceptance, etc. are all part of the Creator's Christian walk. These truths and other are deflected from their original purpose of glorifying the Creator to glorifying their own programs. Rather than publicly opposing Christianity, they rename their own movements Christian, and then proceed to do very little for Christ, and everything for Lucifer. They are even deflecting worship of Jesus Christ onto worship of a demon named Jesus.

- b. The next externally and internally used stock tool is called "Blinds"- these are deliberate deceptions placed within their own writings to confuse the uninitiated. H.P.B. gives a good description of the use of these, so do Masonic writers like Albert Pike. H.P.B. writing describes the use of Blinds in The Secret Doctrine, Vol. 5 Adyar edition, p. 435. Blinds are used in CIA documents, they are incorporated into the scripts that the alters receive. For instance, the in utero Moon Child ceremonies are not revealed to the non-hierarchy alters, but they are told that the Moon Children have to do with the cage tortures.
- c. Slides are truth that has been warped just slightly to take an investigative person into a dead end. An example of a slide, is that the New World Order is satanic, but that only Nazis and stupid people think that Jews are involved. This is a slide, because then the Rothschild's who hide behind their Jewish-ness, can not be mentioned as suspects without people yelling "Anti-Semitism." In reality exposing these abusers has nothing to do with Anti-Semitism, it's simply that all abusers no matter what good front they have, need to be correctly identified as dangerous. Another example, an alter who pretends to be helpful is placed in the system who says that the door to get to a castle internally is the fifth door on the right in such and such hall. The answer is correct, but the door must be opened using the left side, rather than the right side where the door knob is located. Because the answer doesn't pan out then the idea that the door is the correct door is discarded, and the alter's knowledge is suspect. Lots of psychiatrists are writing papers about MPD with slides. They give some truth, and

then they give people a path to go down that will dead end them from ever finding the truth.

- d. They use Hegelian Dialectics. This dialectic process doesn't happen on its own so it often has to be forced into happening. The idea is that each idea ("ism") called a "thesis", like say Capitalism, naturally by definition has an opposite, an "antithesis". In Capitalism the antithesis is Communism. The conflict between the two produces a synthesis. By controlling both ends of the conflict, one controls the end product, the synthesis. More than not, the One-World-Power can be seen working behind both sides of many conflicts. Indeed, the Secret Societies have been historically shown to be behind all the revolutions and wars in Modern Europe since the American Revolution. In religious conflict, both sides are often being manipulated. Some of the various groups openly admit their strategy is designed to create a synthesis. You will find Hegelian Dialectics has been introduced into the U.S. educational system by the Skull & Bones Order, an Illuminati group. It was adopted in Russia by the Slavophiles in the 19th century. Communism, Nazism, Fabians, most New Age groups, Liberation Theology, and other parts of the Power use Hegelian Dialectics. Hegel in turn based his system on the ancient Greek atomists especially Democritus. Hegalian dialectics is built into the conflicting scripts that alters are given. Slaves who are twinned to another slave will find Hegelian dialectics employed in their twinning programming. The Hegelian dialectics can be worked in with the double-binds that the programmers love to use.
- e. esoteric language.
- f. Indirect interference with truthful information getting out. This is done by stealing the impact of the truth, by printing a parallel story with disinformation at the same time, or "leaking" an opposite story with disinformation at the same approximate time. Disinformation leaks can be done through the mass media, or an individual alter.
- g. deniability. When orders are given and language is used, it is on purpose vague so that the guilty can deny their guilt.

At this point, it might be appropriate to cover some standard CIA tactics. They use some Monarch slaves as "Live Letter Drops". An LLD is a person who will re-mail spy letters. They will use "dead drop boxes" which are simply places that an item or message is concealed to be retrieved by some other criminal in the Network. They may give the slave a gift which then has to be passed on. They may protect a written message by writing it on edible paper. Safe houses are used, indicated by things such as 2 lion statues along with prearranged O.K. signals, such as the position of a flower pot.

INTERNAL DECEPTIONS

When building an internal world, the programmers use every trick in the book to hide things. First the abuse has to be hidden in silence, and then the MPD has to be hidden. Next, the real core needs to be hidden. Then, the purpose of a Monarch slave needs to be hidden. All the time that this is going on, the programmers must constantly work at keeping the programmers' identities hidden, and their programming sites hidden. Programmers usually have cover names when programming, and then hypnotically have the victim see them as something else. For instance, Dr. Green had victims see him as a cricket. He even used a cricket noise maker while programming, that clicked. In recent times, the Programmers and handlers are programming their slaves to believe that they are aliens. The slave will generally be lied to that they have a "twin" somewhere.

Internally, the Programmer will begin making the System with the core related alters and then the front alters. The front alters will be rearranged in a fashion that the structure of the System is confused. The front alters will be given heavy programming, to convince them that nothing ever happened to them, they had a wonderful life. They will be given fictitious stories about the programming, so that almost every item in a System has a cover story to mislead an alter about what is going on.

Many things are placed in boxes. Clowns programmed to cut, are Jack-in-box clowns that pop up when an alter even thinks unapproved thoughts. Some of the important things in a System may be hidden out front. An alter on the front may think it is stupid, and yet they have access to internal maps of the entire system which they can remember only on code. If a person, such as a therapist or nosey alter, goes to look deep in the System for the material he might be frustrated. Under a fanatically un-sexual, asexual, alter, will be a sexual alter. Under a stupid alter, may be an alter gifted in a language or art. Alters are very often hidden behind opposite types of alters.

Important things in the System, and many unimportant things, are all well guarded. Sometimes particular alters have to serve as the guards. Some of these guards are called Gatekeepers. Gatekeeper alters will appear near the surface of a system, and then again deep in the System about level 10, and 12. Gatekeeper alters are alters that the programmer must go through to get to deeper levels. The Gatekeeper alters are very heavily programmed to keep them in place. They will receive intensive lies. Some of the access triggers which must accompany the verbal codes are kept secret, by virtue of the fact that no person in their right mind would use them, such as needles, electroshocks, or slaps to certain parts of the body to trigger deep alters to take the body. Items in a System will be disguised, such as the clockmaker alter. Demons will make clocks to appear in the system like anything they want.

The only way these can be adequately identified is that these clocks are always disguised as gold items. As the Programmers work, they like to find word games, plays on words and double-binds. They will also put in scrambling programs, deaf alters and foreign language codes to help protect their secrets. The alters who look the least to have programming may have the most.

Duplicate alters of most alters are created, so that even the alters themselves don't know if it is themselves or another alter. These duplicates are called mirrored images & looking glass people (LGPs). Some of the mirrored images may turn out to be demonic entities that have been placed using high level demonology. Suicide alters, who are trained to have a big smile and be clowns, mask their intention to kill the body when they take the body of a slave. A popular method for hiding things within the occult world, has been boxes within boxes.

A Masonic organization will have a rite, within a secret rite, with a secret group, with an insider clique. Common everyday items that surround the slave will be given special meanings. The songs the slave hears on the radio, will for instance have code words. The Programmers, due to the corruption of the music industry, know what hit songs are coming out, and they will haul their slaves in and program them according to the lyrics of the soon-to-be hits. The lyrics will be written so that programmed meanings can be attached to certain words and lines. Something as innocent as watching T.V., listening to the T.V. or to a sermon may actually be programming a special message into the victim.

Hand signals will even be done over the news or other shows. For instance, Bill Clinton at his inauguration made a satanic signal during the inauguration ceremony. This sign of Satan is a standard hypnotic induction hand signal for slaves. although some might interpret this as "I love you" which is handed by the right hand of a deaf person, this left handed signal will induct slaves no matter what some people think the meaning is.

No wise person would knowingly choose to fight their opponent blind and deaf, yet that seems to be the choice which many nominal Christians are choosing. They would like to live in denial and to characterize this book as doomsday stuff and then dismiss and ignore this material. They want to eat, drink and be happy. If people think that by putting their heads in the sand they can escape the future, or even the present difficulties, they may be in for a rude surprise.

THE USE OF ESTORIC LANGUAGE

One method of deception is the use of Esoteric language. Esoteric terms are understood by those deep in the occult, but are misunderstood by the common people. The best example is the term "Saturn."

SATURN - The word Saturn consistently turns up as an important word for the Illuminati and upper levels of the occult. Because Saturn is such an important concept, it should be covered in this part of the book. Therapists may encounter something to do with Saturn in a programmed multiple. Before Fritz began researching the elite of the occult world, Saturn was merely meant an enormous planet 95 times the size of the earth's mass, the 6th of the solar system in an orbit of 29.5 years around the sun. This means that the co-authors of this book are less than three Saturnian years old. Fritz was also aware that Saturn was the father of all Gods in the mythology of the ancient world.

David M. Talbot in his book "The Saturn Myth" documents how all over the world Saturn has been worshipped even more than the sun god. Saturn has been the secret god of the occult world.

When we read in Deut. 18:9-10, "When thou art come into the land which the Lord thy God giveth thee, thou shalt not learn to do after the abominations of those nations. There shall not be found among you any one that maketh his son or daughter to pass through the fire, or that useth divination, or an observer of times, or an enchanter, or a witch." All of these practices are abominations done by Satanists to-day and are becoming commoner among Americans. Note that the first item mentioned by Moses in this passage was passing (putting) children into the fire (of Moloch).

A commentary on Deut. 18:9-10 is:
"Moses groups together all the words which the language contained for different modes of exploring the future and discovering the will of God, for the purpose of forbidding every description of soothsaying, and places the prohibition of Moloch-worship at the head, to show the inward connection between soothsaying and idolatry, possibly because februation, or passing children through the fire in the wor-ship of Moloch, was more intimately connected with soothsaying and magic than any other description of idolatry." (Keil, Carl F. and Franz Delitzch. "Commentary on The Pentateuch", III, reprint, Grand Rapids, MI: Eerdmans Publishing Co., 1949, p.393.)

The worship of Moloch was the worship of Saturn. There are perhaps various routes one can take to learn this.
One route is a very close examination of the Scripture, especially the old Septuagint. Scriptures actually write of this fact in Amos 5:25-26

and Acts 7:41-43. Amos wrote,

"Did ye bring unto me sacrifices and offerings in the wilderness forty years, 0 House of Israel? Yea, ye have borne the tabernacle of your king ("siccuth malkecem", or in the Septuagint it reads "skenen tou Moloch"!), and the shrine (kiyyun) of your images, the star of your God, which ye made to yourselves"

The Christian Stephen quotes these passages of Amos and connects it with the worship of the golden calf (bull or Taurus). His words on this are recorded in Acts 7:4 1. He further connects it in the next verse with the worship of "the host of heaven". In line with translations like the Septuagint, he states in verse 43 that Amos 5 refers to the cult "of Moloch and the star of the god Rephan". Hebrew writing consists of only the consonants. The vowels can be added with what are termed vocalizations, which are dots. The Jewish scribes in their contempt for heathen gods placed vocalizations (vowel indicators) on the word Molech (M-L-CH) from a Hebrew word for "shame". Because the incorrect vocalization was added out of contempt for the heathen names of abominable gods, the word Molech (Saturn worship) has been mistranslated by some translators. AMOS 5:25-26

Further, the word Chiun (Kaimanu in Assyria) has been represented by the word Rephan in Acts 7:43. Rephan is Kaivan (Chiun) which is the Arabian and Syrian way of saying Saturn. Rephan apparently was a very limited or localized way of saying Saturn. The adoration of the calf (bull) in the wilderness was an important act of defiance by the Israelites-- while Moses went up on the mountain to speak to God face to face. This worship of the bull was actually worship of Saturn! Some call this star worship, and the bull was worshipped because at that time the constellation Taurus (the Bull) marked the position of the sun at the time of the spring equinox.

The fact that the calf was gold was no accident, gold has many Satanic connotations. For a modern occult reference connecting the

Bull, astrology and gold together see Esoteric Astrology by Alice Bailey (Lucis Trust, 1951), pp 378-79. Various scholars on ancient religion have written that the worship of Moloch was Saturn worship. For instance, Siculus Diodorus wrote, *". ..there was a brazen statue of Saturn putting forth the palms of his hands, bending in such a manner toward the earth, as that the boy who was laid upon them, in order to be sacrificed, should slip off, and so fall down headlong into a deep burning furnace...''*

The ancient Roman circus, like so many public activities in America, was based upon the occult. The circus had 7 circuits, and had a pyramid in the center with 3 alters, one to Saturn, one to Jove, and one to Mars.

This is an example of what the common people knew about Saturn. Moloch, then was the Sun God, during the Zodiac period from Taurus to Serpents and Scorpio which is when the sun is hottest. The Babylonians referred to Saturn as the "star of the sun". In the Mithraic Mysteries, Saturn was the Sun God. (See Hall, Manly P. The Lost Teachings of All Ages. p. facing 21.) In fact, Saturn was the Sun God of many of the Pagan religions, and was the foundation of the Solar Temple. (ibid. Hall tells us on pg. 97, Lower Left, that Saturn is the foundation of the Solar Temple.) The Ten tribes of the Israelites fell into the ritual sacrifices of Moloch (Saturn worship and sacrifice) which brought them their judgment of Assyrian captivity. (2 KGS 17:16- 17) Astrology, witchcraft, and ritual sacrifice were also associated with Saturn worship. Isaiah the prophet tells those who worship Saturn, *"Let now the astrologers, the star-gazers, the monthly prognosticators, stand up, and save thee."* ISA 47:13

Saturn did not save the Israelites from captivity. Ex-Illuminati members have revealed that Saturn is Satan. Yes, Saturn is Satan.

The Satanic Illuminati hierarchy teach the high level students that "those who serve Saturn promote the return of the lost son Saturn." The religion of Saturn is Saturnian Gnosis--which turns out to simply be a rehash of the Gnosticism that the high level Satanists believe in. Saturn is severe. Jupiter is mild. The merging of Saturn (severity) with Jupiter (mildness) is the creation of the new Golden Age--according to high level Satanic hierarchy teachings. The earth has been caught in a battle between a bi-polar world--the inner Solar Logos and the outer Saturnian sphere. The trans-Saturnian planets actually belong to Alcyone(!) which eventually gets its planets returned. This may be the reason, that the Satanic hierarchy has treated us to "good aliens from the Pleiades." Alcyone is a star in the Pleiades.

Saturnian Gnostic teachings are that darkness contains the light. What this means is that darkness is necessary for light to exist. And light appears within the matrix of darkness only by the Demiurge Sauternes--the Logos. This is what they teach. According to Albert Pike in the Masonic Text Book Morals and Dogma given to 320 Masons, the work of the Sun is the perfecting, also known as the deification of, man. Christians view that it is Satan's work to teach men that they can be deified, which is rebellion to the one and only true God.

SECRET HIGH LEVEL TEACHINGS

In secret Satanic rituals, the Grande Master has a scepter which represents his authority to wield power through the Lord of this world who is known as Saturn. New Age leaders are calling "Saturn" "Sanat Kumara". A devil by any name is still a devil. In the dialogue below a Mother of Darkness alter provides some interesting information.

Mother of Darkness: "Saturn is the gateway that must be opened. For a season God has winked that man might be illuminated. But excessive light destroys. Man must not forget his destiny is concerned with loving regeneration of the earth [Mother Gaia worship] and balance. Soon the other eye of God must open. Those who are illuminated have kept the balance point. The majority of mankind has not. Few seek the ancient seed of wisdom that springs from the brow of Lucifer. Man becomes... forgetful of His spiritual ancestry and destiny....They are Ellyllon. Keepers of nothing. They fill the earth with their passing and crowd the planes with nothingness. They are a waste of the energies. And so the other eye must open. Each man shall receive abundance in what he seeks. Some call it Karma..."
Interviewer: "What do you mean by the other eye?"

Mother of Darkness: "The other eye of God as some would say. Chemosh. Cleansing Fire. The outstreched arms of Molech."

Interviewer: "What has that got to do with Saturn?"

Mother of Darkness: "Everything. This is a most secret thing. Saturn is the gateway. The point at which all thought is fixed. The point at which all feeling shall be projected as the eye opens. Much ritual and preparation has gone into the issuance through the gateway of the ancient ones. There has been a gathering of the elemental essence to clothe them. A strengthened invisible quintessence to hold them in this plane at the time of advent."

Interviewer: "And what will be the result of this advent? What will it mean?"

Mother of Darkness: "A restoring of balance. Those who do not seek wisdom shall cease. Those who are so bound to the earth that they forget the light shall cease....When the other eye opens the dawn shall come. The Golden Dawn shall be upon us and the sun of righteousness shall rise with healing in His wings....The urge to sacrifice others is a gift. It is a liberation from the awful rigidity for at least it permits an awareness of other humans. However badly.. .treated as a result of that awareness they have served an important purpose. The balance is kept and the light dwells upon the illuminated. The energy is released into the circle and is converted into something powerful and useful....In this way you can see they do not truly die. Light increases. Wisdom grows....Death begets life. The sacred cycle of the ancients. The earth shall regenerate herself when the eye of Molech opens."

There the reader has it, secret teachings from a Mother of Darkness on Saturn. Gnosticism believes that there is a force, not Almighty God, that can be used for evil or good. Within the hierarchy of the Satanists (Moriah), their thinking has no problem understanding that Lucifer is the same person as Satan. Satan is what happens when the evil side of the Force is being used, and Lucifer is that person when the good side of the Force is being used. As in all of the Mystery Religions and in the occult world in general, people are told different things at different levels. Most people don't want to serve evil. They want to think they are good--their pride motivates them to want to be thought of as good and great. They will easily follow Lucifer, but are not going to admit to themselves or anyone that they are following Satan. NO problem--they are allowed to think they are Luciferians. OR if being a follower of Lucifer is too strong a statement, they can be a worshipper of almost thing. Satan in his pride has provided esoteric teachings on the worship of just about everything.

There are esoteric teachings about worshipping rock, mountains, trees, the stars, animal spirits, mother earth etc. If one probes deep enough into the layers of hidden meanings all these worships go back to Satan. The five primary interlocked concepts of Satan, are all represented by the Serpent, which are Lucifer (aka Light-bearer or godhood); Search for light or wisdom; sun worship, the Sun god, or energy; fire also called Kundalini force; and the regenerative principle which is phallic and sex worship. These 5 interconnected concepts are represented world wide by snakes/serpents and represent worship of the supreme serpent Satan.

THE EXTERNALIZATION OF THE HIERARCHY

The big event or operation that is being carried out is the externalization of the hierarchy. Satan's secret hierarchy with its pure Satanists have been around for thousands of years. But the Satanic conspiracy to control mankind is to become an "open conspiracy". The hierarchy is to be externalized. And the elimination of Christians, those who haven't sought that worldly wisdom which comes from Satan, is to pave the way for Satan's appearance. The Satanic occult conspiracy is to leave its secret confines in Masonic Temples and Oddfellow Halls and is to permeate Society in general. This is what has been happening. The real light must go out for the dark side to feel comfortable coming completely out.

The Mysteries, also known as the Mystery Religions are the Mysteries that one is initiated into when one joins Freemasonry. In fact, the very first item any prospective Masonic candidate must do is fill out a form requesting to be initiated into "the Mysteries." The Mystery Religions were actually veiled forms of the worship of Lucifer or Satan. Lucifer is simply Satan dressed up as the Light-bearer. In the Mystery Religions the disciples are taught that the spirits of men are the powdered bones of Saturn. When one learns who Saturn is--it is a rather distasteful idea to think that men are taught that their bodies belong to Saturn. Further, Freemasonry teaches about Hiram Abiff and Chiram.

It turns out when we study the Hiramic Legend by Freemasonry's best philosopher that we learn who Santa Claus is. Santa is a scrambling of Satan. Anyway the Hiramic legend goes like this according to Freemasonry great expert on the Mystery Religions, *"Saturn, is the old man who lives at the north pole, and brings with him to the children of men a sprig of evergreen (the Christmas tree). He is familiar to the little folks under the name of Santa Claus, for he brings each winter the gift of a new year." "Part of the symbols, are displayed.. .to the initiated, but he is intentionally led astray by false interpretations..."*

Masonry conceals its secrets from all except the Adepts, the Sages and the Elect; and uses false explanations for its symbols to mislead those deserving to be misled." This is according to the great Freemason Albert Pike in his book Morals & Dogma.

It should come as no surprise that Saturn is one of the items which is mentioned by various Masonic authors. For instance, the Freemason Ragon, who is considered an expert on Freemasonry, wrote,

"This is the important phenomenon, the ineffable mystery, the key to nature, which the ancient sages succeeded in discovering, and which they adopted as the basis of Masonic doctrine...It is interpretation, the revolting atrocities of subject of Masonic legends. According to Saturn... were considered interesting enigmas, which involve facts worth our notice." (Ragon, Tyileur General De La Franc-Maconnerie, p. 219-19 as quoted in Mohr, Gordon. The Hidden Power Behind Freemasonry, Burnsville, MN: Weisman Pub., 1990,

p. 109).

Alice Bailey's "Esoteric Astrology" states that *"Saturn is the Lord of Karma"* (p. 105) *"Venus and Saturn shall rule men during Aquarius"*. (p. 148). *"Saturn is the planet of discipleship... we stand at the gateway of the new world, of the new age and its new civilization, ideals and culture. "*(p. 148).

The occult book "A Treatise on Cosmic Fire", pp 1196-1207 states that Saturn is the 5th creative Hierarchy. This is the type of stuff that the Kabala comes out with. American businesses which are controlled by the Illuminati are getting into the act of bringing the occult out into society.

Ford called its car Taurus (Bull--the Pleiades), another car is named Aries which is another occult astrological name. Then there is the car named Saturn!!

n conclusion, Saturn turns out to be an occult name for Satan. Santa turns out to be an occult name for Saturn. It also turns out that the name Saturn has been used for Satan for centuries by the occult. The ritual sacrifices to Molech was Saturn worship. The opening of the eye of Saturn is the materialization of hordes of demons taking place during this time period. High level Illuminati, who will gather together in Atlanta in the summer of 1996, under the cover of the '96 Olympics will carry out high level rituals to open up a large hole for the materialization of hordes of demons to complete their push toward a world dictator. The use of the name Saturn is an example of how Satanism operates under the cover of layers of deception. Many Christian words also have occult meaning.

There is a Morning Star Church in Tulsa which ministers to victims of Illuminati Trauma Based Total Mind-Control. There is also a prophetic magazine named The Morning Star, which is very slick and glossy. On the other side of things, the term "the Morning Star"-- Stella Matutina in Latin- is another name for Lucifer. Stella Matutina is also the name of a kabalistic black magic lodge which Satanist Aleister Crowley led when the Golden Dawn reorganized in 1903.

There are Morning Star rituals done by Illuminati members. One Illuminati slave, who was trained to infiltrate Christian churches and turn them toward the New Age movement, channeled a demon named Jesus. He infiltrated Christian churches for decades, and when he spoke about Jesus, he was referring to the demon he channeled. We know about this because one day, his front alters gave their life to Jesus Christ, and he abandoned his job of infiltration, and sought spiritual help. People need to understand that almost all Christian terms have dual meanings. Just because a term sounds familiar doesn't mean it is being used in the way that a sincere Christian would understand them.

IN SUMMARY

The Illuminati are manipulating:
- Technology
- Language
- Ritualistic activity
- Subliminal Awareness
- Fear
- Lust
- Human Vulnerabilities
- Conflicts

These manipulations are external deceptions, which help cover up their trauma-based mind control. They use the best covers as fronts. They use fiction, the best of religious fronts, travelling entertainment fronts, and the cover of national defense. They use deflection, blinds, slides, Hegelian dialectics, deniability, and esoteric language. They use agent provocateurs, "clean agents", "legends", and safe houses.

The Illuminati have refined the art of deception far beyond what the common man has imagined. The very life & liberty of humanity requires the unmasking of their deceptions. That is what this book is about.

CHAPTER SIX:

THE USE OF ELECTRONICS AND ELECTRICITY

Photos printed in a magazine in the fall of 1981 show electric prod marks on the necks of two slaves who were used for porn. Another basic component of the Monarch program is lots of electro shock. Stun guns, staffs with hidden electric cattle prods, and cattle prods are frequently used on the slaves. Electroshock is used to create the dissociation from trauma during the programming, and later it is used to remove memories after the slave has carried out a mission, or to instill fear and obedience in a reluctant slave. Slaves generally carry horrible body memories of excruciating electro-shock tortures to their entire bodies. As the slaves begin a therapeutic deprogramming process they will recover these horrible memories, not to mention many other painful memories.

A slave often shows electro-shock marks on their feet, or back, or buttock or legs after they have been used. An owner of a slave will ordinarily carry a stun gun. This is perhaps a 120,000 DC volt stun gun to erase & compartmentalize memories, but some of the stun guns go up to 200,000 volts DC to erase the memory of his slave. They will apply their stun guns to the base of the skull. After giving programming instructions they will usually give a high voltage shock to the base of the skull to imbed the instructions deep in the subconscious. They often use hypnotic cues along with the shock. For instance, they will tell the slave they are "now going over the rainbow", and that when the sun goes down they will forget everything, before they shock the body.

The shock destroys and scrambles the memory which is still stored in the short term memory section of the brain. They must shock the person within 24 hours, to insure that the short term memory doesn't get into long term memory as a coherent memory. This means that if a slave is being used daily, they get electro shocked daily.

Types of devices used by handlers: A cylindrical type cattle prod with 3/4" between the contact points is used externally and internally. This is manufactured by Hot Shot Products, Inc., Savage, MN 55378. Model B-12. They have a red or black rubber handle with an overall length of 12". The low voltage is between 10,000-15,000 volts. The medium voltage is 12,000 to 20,000 volts. A bruise on the buttocks will be black and blue spots about 1 1/2" diameter each. A hand held wand type shock prod which has 2 3/4" between its contact points. It uses a rechargeable battery pack. The prod (wand) is 2 1/2' long, and unwieldy to handle.

Various farm supply companies (livestock equipment) sell this. The medium voltage is 12,000 to 20,000. A stun gun which has exactly 2" between the contacts with a 9 volt battery. This stun gun was created for law enforcement, and is generally regarded as the best device for dropping a victim or for inducing hypnosis, or setting in a hypnotic program. Its high voltage is 35,000 to 120,000 volts. It is a light weight (12 oz.), compact device, 7" x 2" x 1". This device will leave deep red dot ("holes") scars and cancerous moles. The victim will develop moles from the repeated use of this device. The muscled areas of the victim are preferred. For instance, the muscled area just below the shoulder blade. Farrall Instrument Co., of Grand Island, NE makes a cattle prod with an adjustable voltage control.

Their long distance wireless shocker called Personal Shocker can shoot a shock about 75 feet indoors and 300 feet outdoors. The control box is hand held, and the receiver is a leather case. The shock can be adjusted from 9 to 800 volts, current is 5 milliamperes, and it lasts 1 to 2 milliseconds. This Personal Shocker was manufactured to be used on people. An electronic firm in Tujunga, CA makes a shock box used in programming. An electronic bark collar is used to train Illuminati & other Monarch slaves in silence & obedience. On other occasions, fancy gem studded collars and leather collars are fitted around the necks of female slaves for sex with wolves and fierce dogs, who bite these neck-collars when they mount. Many of the slaves have experienced these various collars for obedience, silence, & bestiality. In trying to track down who makes the larger electroshock machines, especially the computer guided ones, we only got started investigating.

- Con-med (315-797-8375) makes medical electrodes for portable monitoring units.
- Sentry Medical Products, at 17171 Murphy, Irvine, CA 92714 (714-250-0233) makes Skin Mounted Conductive Medical Electrodes for Tense Unit Machines.
- In Vivo Metric, in Healdsburg, CA also makes silver Chloride electrodes for placement on human skin.
- Electro-Cap Inter, produces BEG placement systems.
- Uni-Patch Medical Products, 13 13-T Grant Blvd. W, Wabasha, MN makes all types of Electrodes and some of theirs go onto machines for shocking people.
- Classic Medical Products, 582-T W 19246 Apollo Dr., Muskego, WI make electrodes for diagnostic and shock purposes.
- Arndt Automation & Assoc., Inc., 17770 Liberty Lane, New Berlin, WI, make electrodes for ECG and EKG machines.
- And a Colorado company named Biomedical at Evergreen, CO makes medical electrodes.

When a slave is taken to an impromptu programming site- a hypnotic drug is injected into them for a quick induction while a metal band is put around their head and a current of 100,000 volts will be run through for say 5 seconds into their heads. This will cause the body to shake, the eyes to close, sweat to pour out of the body etc. The hands are tied down with restraints. Sometimes the mouth is gagged so that the tongue doesn't protrude. After imbedding the hypnotic commands deep into the mind, the programmers might adjust the automatic timer on the equipment and give the victim another blast of voltage for 10 seconds. The person's body will shake and quiver for a while after this.

They may dribble spit. Finally, the person will be brought out of their hypnotic trance, instructed not to remember anything, to feel happy and sent on their way. This entire programming session can last 15 minutes. Programming sites like this can be the back of a van, a back room in a restaurant, or any other place that the equipment can be set up at. This is why a slave, who has been used recently, may hobble a little, or when they get memories feel a tight headband around their head along with awful headaches & flashes of light. The memory will feel like a robotic state to the slave.

The slave handler will also carry a black or grey spiral book with all their own slave's access codes, triggers, cryptic keys and programs. All this will fit into a brief case. A working knowledge of hypnosis is helpful to understand how to deal with the slave in certain instances. Because the slave is under the most powerful combinations of mind-control and is so divided against his or her own self, it is almost impossible to have many problems with the slave if the handler does what he is supposed to do. However, some handlers get drunk or loan the slave to inexperienced people, etc. and problems do develop.

Of course the slaves always end up taking the blame for everything that goes wrong. If the slave gets out of hand, because the handler doesn't know what he is doing, a stun gun comes in handy to control the mismanaged slave. In other words, a brief case with the programming book and stun gun are basically all that is needed to control a Monarch slave for the rest of his or her life. Some of these stun guns are only a few inches long and look like boxes. Other stun guns are imbedded in staffs. The canes and the staffs that Satanists carry around, like Michael Aquino (in public in fact) are actually stun guns to control their slaves.

The Queen Mother's staff of the Illuminati has an electric stun gun hidden in it. Children in day care centers are reporting small boxes with wires that electroshock them during programming.

The Illuminati bloodlines connect to research about electric shocks to control people. One example is David V. Reynold's research. He wrote, *"Neuroelectric Research: Electroneuroprosthesis, Electroanesthesia, and Nonconvulsive Electrotherapy."*
Another way of using electricity for torture is to use directed energy,

a new technology, on men's genitals. With skillful use of directed energy they can simulate a rape of a man or woman. Artificial sodomy via directed energy was first tested in male prisons. ELF waves will place thoughts into the men's mind as the directed energy makes them feel sodomized.

MICROWAVES FOR PROGRAMMING

On Aug. 22, 1989, Phillip L. Stoklin, P.O. Box 2111, Satellite Beach, FL took out a patent, Patent Number 4,858,612, which is a device that can be placed in the auditory cortex of the brain. This device allows the following process: someone speaks into a microphone, the microphone then has its sounds coded into microwave, which are sent to the receiver in the brain and the receiver device will transform the microwaves back so that the person's mind hears the original sounds. In other words, a person with this device in their head will hear whatever the programmers send via microwave signals.

Various types of "non-lethal" weapons have been created and are now being used. Directed-energy can be used to sculpt clouds. ELF waves can be used to place thoughts in people's minds without using implants. In 1991, a paper trail began to appear when the CIA connected U.S. government Global Strategy Council came out with a paper entitled, *"Nonlethality: Development of a National Policy and Employing Nonlethal Means in a New Strategic Era."* The paper was prepared by Janet Morris. The USAF School of Aerospace Medicine, Brooks Air Force Base, TX put out a report USAFAM-TR-87-30 entitled *"Behavioral response of rats exposed to high-power microwave radiation."* High-power, ultra-short pulse-width emitters of microwaves were used to alter the thinking in rats. The report refers to two other reports: one by T. Wheeler, et. al. *"Retrograde Amnesia in Rats Produced by Electron Beam Exposure,"* entitled USAFAM-TR-83-3, Feb. '83. The other report is by R. Bermant, *"Classical conditioning of Microwave-Induced Hyperthermia in Rats."* Radio Sci. 14 (6S): 201-207, 1979. This is a clear paper trail, that military research has gone on to control the brain via microwaves.

Another institution in Texas, the Texas Dept. of Criminal Justice

TDCJ-ID, has been putting high-tech listening implants into the ear canal behind the ear drum which lets them monitor what the ear is hearing, a great way to spy. This is according to an implant victim who with medical help discovered his implant. The Walter Reed Army Institute of Research (WRAIR) discovered that pulsed micro-wave audiograms also called analogs of the sounds of spoken words, could be transmitted to a target, and the effect on victim would be to hear voices in their head. The next 11 pages are patent no. 4,858,612. After this, we'll reveal the numerous mind-control capabilities of ELF -microwave tech.)

BACKGROUND OF THE HEARING DEVICE

1. Field at the Invention - This invention relates to devices for aiding the hearing in mammals. The invention is based upon the perception at sounds which is experienced in the brain when the brain is subjected to certain microwave radiation signals.
2. Description of the Prior Art - In prior art hearing devices for human beings, it is well known to amplify sounds to be heard and to apply the amplified sound signal to the ear at the person wearing the hearing aid. Hearing devices of this type are however limited to hearing dysfunctions where there is no damage to the auditory nerve or to the auditory cortex. In the prior art, if there is damage to the auditory cortex or the auditory nerve, it cannot be corrected by the use of a hearing aid.

During World War II, individuals in the radiation path of certain radar installations observed clicks and buzzing sounds in response to the microwave radiation. It was through this early observation that it became known to the art that microwaves could cause a direct perception at sound within a human brain. These buzzing or clicking sounds however were not meaningful and were not perception of sounds which could other-wise be heard by the receiver. This type of microwave radiation was not representative of any intelligible sound to be perceived.

In such radar installations, there was never a sound which was generated which resulted in subsequent generation of microwave signals representative of that sound. Since the early perception of buzzing and clicking. further research has been conducted into the microwave reaction of the brain. In an article entitled *"Possible Microwave Mechanisms of the Mammalian Nervous System"* by Philip L Stocklin and Brain F. Stocklin, published in the TIT Journal of Life Sciences. Tower International Technomedical Institute. Inc. P.O. Box 4594, Philadelphia. Pa. (1979), there is disclosed a hypothesis that the mammalian brain generates and uses electro magnetic waves in the lower microwave frequency region as an integral part of the functioning of the central and peripheral nervous systems.

This analysis is based primarily upon the potential energy of a protein integral in the neural membrane. In an article by W. Bise entitled *"Low Power Radio-Frequency and Microwave Effects On Human Electro- encephalogram and Behavior,"* Physiol. Chemistry Phys. 10. 387 (1978), it is reported that there are significant effects upon the alert human EEG during radiation by low intensity CW microwave electromagnetic energy. Bise observed significant repeatable EEG effects to a subject during radiation at specific microwave frequencies.

In 1989, James C. Lin wrote "Electromagnetic Interaction With Biological Systems" which deals with transmitting ideas and words via electromagnetic waves. Brief cases, stereo speakers and boxes are some of the disguises that the CIA has been caught using to hide their ELF microwave emitters that plant thoughts in people. One victim who spent time talking to Fritz Springmeier reported how they had repeatedly tried to trick him into going to free hotel rooms and other traps, where they tried to bombard his head with the idea that he should sell drugs. He cleverly dismantled their devices which they hid in the ceilings and other locations in these rooms to protect himself from the thoughts they were trying repeatedly to beam into his head. He was on the run as a fugitive to protect his mind.

Naval Intelligence and other groups have conducted research into ELF waves upon the human body and mind. Some of the many things that can be done to the human body and mind with ELF waves include:

a. put a person to sleep
b. make a person tired or depressed
c. create a feeling of fear in a person
d. create a zombie state
e. create a violent state
f. create a state of being sexually aggressive
g. change cellular chemistry
h. change hormone levels
i. inhibit or enhance M (RNA) synthesis/processes
j. control the DNA transaction process
k. control biological spin and proton coupling constants in DNA, RNA & RNA transferases.

Unfortunately for us humans, ELF waves can penetrate almost anything. The U.S. Military has built a Ground-Wave Emergency Network (GWEN) all over the U.S. with several hundred 300-500' GWEN towers that broadcast a very-low-frequency wave (VLF) for mind-control of the American public. A single GWEN tower can broadcast up to 300 miles in a 3600 circle. Plus 8 secret powerful ELF transmitters have been established and 3 of them operate on the west coast.

PROZAC, SLAVES AND MICROWAVES

Some of the Monarch slaves are receiving Prozac. Prozac (fluoxetine hydrocloride-a serotonin re-uptake inhibitor) is dangerous for everyone. Prozac is now the second most used drug in the world. Three examples of the ongoing nightmare now happening worldwide:

September 14, 1989--Joseph Wesbecker on Prozac went crazy and got a gun and opened fire in the Standard Gravure Building in Louisville killing eight and wounding twelve others before killing himself. 20 suits against Eli Lilly were filed by victim in this case.

July, 1990--Rhonda Hala of Shirley, NY filed a $150 million suit against Eli Lilly charging that Prozac had driven her repeatedly to attempt suicide.

August, 1990--CCHR called on Congress to ban Prozac and 3 widows in Louisville, KT filed $50 million lawsuits each, charging that a man on Prozac had been driven insane to kill by the Prozac and had killed their husbands.

Two other lawsuits were filed in this time period, one from Indianapolis, and one from Chicago from people driven to attempt suicide by Prozac. Certain brain activities trigger people on Prozac to become homicidal or suicidal. Thanks to research by Illuminati controlled companies, the Network knows exactly how to use ELF waves vectored on a particular person by 3 separate towers to stimulate the Prozac controlled brain to murder. This is being used to increase acts of anarchy and violence in order to help insure anti-gun legislation. If a slave doesn't comply or needs to be thrown from the Freedom Train they can become a useable statistic. Simply trigger them to murder and then watch the police gun them down. The NWO gains one more statistic and another case to scare the public into accepting gun control.

THE USE OF WAVES AND ELECTRICITY TO IMPLANT THOUGHTS

The programmers are always trying to outdo what they've done before. They are not satisfied with the old recipes for scrambled brains, they keep inventing and refining new methods. Anything and everything within their grasp has been tried. They have found that ELF and VLF electro-magnetic waves can be used to control people's thoughts. Harmonics and sound waves are used to manipulate the RNA covering of neuron pathways to the subconscious. Harmonic generators (code named "ether-wave") are able to imbed detailed commands which are linked to audible triggers. This is one of the standard features of the Monarch program. It allows the slaves to be controlled by trigger words which make no sense or seem to carry no negative connotation to outside listeners. For instance the words, "Mr. Postman wait and see" (a Marionette command) might set off an access sequence so that a slave living away from its master goes to its master (also called a handler).

The use of harmonics has taken away much of the work of the big programmers. Now harmonic machines can implant the programming and codes that the Programmers put in. It's quicker and perhaps more efficient, although the lesser cult groups have to get by with the older methods. And the Illuminati still have many excellent programmers in full-time and part-time use. According to an eyewitness, their top-programmers are far beyond their 1950-60 predecessors like Mengele. There are four types of brain waves: alpha, beta, delta, and theta. The four basic models of Monarch slaves have the same names as these four types of brain waves. High level Illuminati models may have programming that includes all of these types. According to one ex(?)-government source, the CIA has been labeling their harmonic-created total Mind-controlled slaves by the following:

- Bravo 2 series models are men programmed to run the Beast computers.
- Delta series are models for espionage and assassination.
- Juliet series are sexual mind controlled slaves.
- Kilo 5 series is military espionage.
- Michael 1 series slaves are CIA agents under total mind-control.
- Operation Greenstar was the Mind-control project to create UFO abductions scenarios.

Much of the high level programming in the 1980s and 1990s is no longer done with human programmers, but is done via programmed machines using drugs, electricity and harmonics.

TRACKING/I.D. IMPLANTS

A great deal has come out in a whole number of Christian books, as well as secular books about the microchips that are being implanted in both people and animals. These microchips will do many things, depending upon which type of microchip they are, however, some of these microchips emit coded signals which allow satellites with computers to track the exact location of the person or animal carrying the chip. Obviously, a Mind-controlled slave is not going to have the freedom to reject a chip like this. This gives the owner a method for tracking the slave should they ever escape to their exact location. Many of the slaves, CIA agents, and military men have these implants already. Many Desert Shield troops (to make sure they weren't lost in the desert) were required to get the tracking implants. Some county's are making it mandatory for pets to get tracking implants.

MONITORING IMPLANTS

As I write this, I have the report "An Eight Channel Micro Powered PAM/FM Biomedical Telemetry System" written by the Space Biology Lab/Brain Research Institute of the UCLA Center for Health Sciences, of Los Angeles, California 90024. What they are reporting on is an implant which will electronically report back what is going on with a person's body to whoever is monitoring the person. Their "biotelemetry" consists of a signal conditioner, multiplexer (for multichannel systems), and a transmitter. The entire size of the implant is 6.35 cm. by 0.97 cm thick. EEG monitoring is being done of free-swimming divers by implants. A frequency of 2300 Hz. was used on the first underwater monitoring devices.

COMMUNICATION IMPLANTS

First, we will give an overview of the subject and then we will cover the details of how the technology works.

In the Bible it predicts that in the end of church age that the rulers of the world "These have one mind, and shall give their power and strength unto the Beast" REV 17:13. Robert Muller, a member of the Illuminati, and former Assistant Secretary General of the UN, who has been involved in setting up a "Peace University" in Costa Rica, said in a symposium "Toward a Global Brain, Our Next Evolutionary Step" (Nov. 9-11, 1984, *We are beginning to link together to form one-world, minds and souls. Let go of our own beliefs... We stand now at the threshold of the first spiritualization of humanity. -*

The goal of having a single "World Mind" is being advocated by people tied to the Illuminati and the New Age Movement they have created. In the New Age book Gods of Aquarius the author advocates, *"The only viable solution is to link the brains of all men into one giant super brain. It has been the entire species that have been developing and it must be linked into one super being. A synthesis of human minds in a world brain."* Hollywood put out a movie in 1970 called Colossus-The Forbin Project which shows how the ultimate computer will dominate the minds of men.

Unfortunately, the Illuminati now have the capability via their fronts to implant transmitters that will communicate messages to the human brain that are received via computers. The ability to literally have a single World Brain is within the grasp of the elite. They must now simply figure out methods to accomplish it. All this New Age talk by world leaders like Robert Muller about a single World Mind is not hot air. Unfortunately, the technology is here already. Will humanity stop the secret elite, or will humanity continue to slide into deeper slavery?

CIA programmer/researcher Professor Delgado wrote in Physical Control of the Mind in 1969 that, *"Brain transmitters can remain in a person's head for life. The energy to activate the brain transmitter is transmitted by way of radio frequencies."* The radio frequencies used to transmit to brain implants are usually from 15 to 35 KHz. Radio frequency analyzing equiment hooked up to computers have charted the radio frequencies being used to transmit to victims with implants. See Mediaeko Investigating Reporting Group. Brain Transmitters What They Are and How They Are Used. 1993, pg. 8.)

The use by handlers of frequency shift signals, which is a special way of modulating through a given spectrum of frequencies, has been observed and recorded. Some of the first brain transmitters looked like bullets and were placed into the victim's brain via the nose. In the late 1960s, some of the transmitters were simply swallowed, or carried externally by the victim. Small wires imbedded behind the ears are one of the implants. Sometimes implants are placed within the pain/pleasure center of the brain, which allows the handler to manipulate what feels great or what feels painful. The Intelligence agencies have given their implants a whole variety of names. Some of these names for brain implants are:

- EDOM -- Electronic Dissolution of Memory
- EEOM--Electronic Enhancement of Memory
- ESB --Electronic Stimulation of the brain
- RHIC -- Radio Hypnotic Intra-cerebral Control

Terms that accompany these techniques include:

- PREMA--Personal Radio & Electro-Magnetic Frequency Allocation. This is an individual's personal frequency which is scanned by a hand-held device (such as a Reading Wand).
- PRIME FREAK--This is the Primary Frequency of an individual, which the intelligence agencies will obtain and then manipulate to control an individual.
- VITAL HUMAN BRAIN FREQUENCY-- This is a frequency that is vital for humans, (the 800 MHz band) which is manipulated for mass mind-control. I

n 1978, Samuel Chavkin warned in his book "The Mind Stealers" *"With the increasing sophistication and miniaturization of electronics, it may be possible to compress the necessary circuitry for a small computer into a chip that is implantable subcutaneously. In this way, the new self-contained instrument could be devised, capable of receiving, analyzing and sending back information to the brain, establishing artificial links between unrelated cerebral areas, functional feedbacks, and programs of stimulations contingent on the appearance of predetermined wave patterns."*
a
b   Since Chavkin wrote this in 1978, the Network has come a long way on miniaturization and sophistication of their implants. One of the most important end times communications systems of the Illuminati and their intelligence agencies is their ALEX system. This will operate on several levels. The electronic end of the ALEX system which stands for Amalgamated Logarithmic Encrypted Transmission

(ALEX) is a method for encrypting electronic transmissions so that a computer which could decode 5 Trillion codes a second would take 2,000 years to decipher one of these transmissions.

c

d   In other words, when the ALEX system is operating--it cannot be decoded. The ALEX system has 700 Billion Trillion codes! Yes, the intelligence agencies/Illuminati have really outdone themselves with overkill on this one! By the way, this is very **(ultra)** secret. The ALEX system intersects with the Monarch Mind Control Programming. The ALEX (also called ALEXUS) is part of the tracking and Anti-Christ-Call-Back Programming. Outside computers are able to interconnect with the Monarch Mind Control slave and call them back for Anti-Christ activities. In other words, the Council of 9 of the Illuminati has placed an alter by the name of Alex or a similar name in high level slaves and they have either via implants or some other type of programming made these slaves available for programming via electronic communications that tie in with their ALEX computers. (Fritz Springmeier touched on this Anti-Christ programming in his "Mind Control" monograph in 1992, when he mentioned Imperial Conditioning.) Actually Imperial and Emperor programming are programs that work in conjunction with the ALEX system.

e

f   All the police in this nation are to have their communications encrypted by Christmas, 1995 in time for the start of the most intense period of anarchy. The concentration camps, FEMA, FDIC, and the all the rest of the acronym monsters are switching over to the secret operational frequencies which this paragraph will now provide you. This will be 912 meg. to 954 meg. using either or both the ALEX or General Dynamic scrambles. Motorola is providing the hardware. In other words, when the most intense period of anarchy and arrests begins, the New World Order (Big Brother) will have electronic transmission capabilities which will be totally secret. Even police transmissions which can be listened to now by the bad guys will no longer be receivable.

g

h   The Illuminati have been saving their best technology for use during their takeover in the next few years. Implants within slaves are being used to communicate such thoughts as (actual samples of things sent):

i

a. "murder your family"

b. "the government is to blame, murder the President"

c. "you can not get legal redress for what has been done to you by the government"

d. "it is hopeless to fight us"

e. "you want to have sex with the opposite sex"

f. "you want to deal in drugs"

g. "you want to protect your country by being loyal to the CIA"

Since the early 1960s, the Intelligence agencies have been putting two-way radio communication implants into victims. This is called telemetry or remote control. The radio wave enters the implant, the implant transmits it to the brain, and the brain's reaction is then picked up and relayed back to a computer which decodes what the brain waves show the brain was thinking. These implants in the early '60s were half the size of a cigarette filter. A few of victims have managed to escape the control of the System and get x-ray pictures of the implants and then have them removed. One victim in this Portland area has tried for years to find a legitimate surgeon to remove the implant. Liquid crystals are said by some to be used. It is said that the liquid crystals are implanted to function as transmitters. Others say that the liquid crystals were tried and were lethal.

ACCESSORIES

It was discovered that if a strobe is flashed into the eyes at ten cycles/ per sec. or 10 hertz (hz), the brain will retune itself to that frequency. The brain will downshift from a beta state of consciousness down to an alpha or below. The entire cortex is influenced by the strobe light. Actually, this was just a rediscovery of what some of the ancients had discovered. Flashing lights have been used by people to go into altered states for a long time. Ptolemy, the famous ancient Greek astronomer built a wheel that would flash sunlight, and people would stare at this contraption and go into an altered state. As with many inventions, they can be used for good or bad. The following machines are things that anyone can purchase, just like a stun gun or a cattle prod. An array of mind-altering electronic devices have been created over the last few decades. Personal light-and-sound machines that alter the brain's consciousness that were once $60,000 dollars are now a few hundred. They have goggles that fit over a person's eyes.

The Synchro Energizer, which requires a trained operator to run its control panel, is a machine to electronically alter the brain's consciousness with a sound and light show. Nine lights work via the goggles to give a light show to alter the brain's wave pattern. It is sold by Synchro-Tech of Cleveland via Syncho Energize on Broadway, NY. An operator can start the Synchro Energizer at the brain's high beta waves and then takes the wave pattern downward through the alpha, and then to the theta and sometimes into the delta, the sleep state. There are smaller machines designed to do the same thing, such as the Relaxman, built by Synchro-Tech.

Comptronic Device Ltd. has put out a similar but superior machine called D.A.V.I.D.Jr. It can place a person into a deep delta wave sleep. These are just what are available to the public. Imagine what NASA, the NSA, and CIA have. If one needs to work with more than one person, the Synchro-Energizer ($60,000) built by Synchro-Tech will place 32 people at the same time into altered states of consciousness. This machine uses full-spectrum lights to change the brain's state of consciousness.

The Lumatron machine uses strobe lights that can be set to eleven different frequencies. When the light is directed through the retina it is converted to an electrical nerve impulse called a photocurrent. Eventually, the photocurrent passes throughout the entire brain.

Genesis is a machine which measures the brain's responses and then matches music to that response. Hospitals and corporations have been purchasing Genesis machines.

The Twilight Learning Device is a bio-feedback machine that has an

EEG machine hooked up to two tape recorders.

There are dozens of technical articles on a whole host of subjects relating to the implants. This is a vast subject that really needs its own book. For further study of the big subject of implants the reader is directed to begin with the following articles:

"Scotland on Sunday", 2 April 1995, had an article about how U.S. and Swedish scientists have pioneered a method to graft neurons to a computer chip.

Stanford University, CA helped with this. A person can now be "hot-wired" to a computer, such as Arnold Schwartzenegger in the film Total Recall.

"LA Times", 8/17/94, article about the Hughes Identification Device which is a tracking implant (microchip) which is called SmartDevice. 6 million/per year are planned to be quietly inserted into people during surgery.

In a recent article "Alien-Human Interactions: the Facts and Propaganda" by Karla Turner, she points out that many alien abductees, like herself, are "monitored and harassed by human agents of some sort and the cases of phone and mail surveillance are only part of the story.... She was compelled by some post-hypnotic suggestion.. .there is strong external evidence that these events have been carried out by strictly human agents and not by aliens giving the illusion of a military presence." She goes on to explain about the implants, wires & tubes that are put in victims of "alien abductions". Karla Turner doesn't know that she is a victim of trauma-based mind control, but she's getting close to understanding what she has been subjected to.

"The Journal", Alexandria, VA, Nov. 8, 1995, carried a story "Surgeon, a UFO buff operated and found..." The story was by Steve Chawkins of the Scripps Howard News Service. The article talks about a Ventura, CA surgeon who has removed implants from abduction victims. The implanted items that are removed from victims, disappear when sent in for tests to determine what they are.

"Relevance Magazine"-art. on Behavioral Modification implants.

"Fortean Times" #83, Oct.-Nov. '95 article on Russia's mind control called PIS which is similar to America's.

Barry Karr of the Center for Scientific Investigation of Claims of the Paranormal states, *"We haven't heard of anything that, without the shadow of a doubt, couldn't have been made here on Earth. Let's see the evidence."* It is clear that some people are now realizing that these implants are being placed into people by human slave owners, who simply are hypnotically telling their slaves that they are aliens. IBM began work on the implantable microchips under the cover of other goals. In the 1960s G.E. took over the development. Honeywell continued the work after they merged. The R2E Division of Honeywell Bull in France has then gone on to develop the Smart card.

Lithium batteries in implants were secretly being used in the 1960s long before the public got wind. Fairchild has publicly announced several years ago that they have a bio-chip the size of a human hair with 4 times the capacity of the BT952000 project. These are some of the companies who have provided the Network with a large assortment of implantable chips.

IN SUMMARY

Electro shock is used to control a slave and to erase memory. Stun guns are used daily on some slaves. Slaves are under so much control that they will shock themselves if the master wants them to.

Equipment has been developed to alter states of consciousness electronically, and also to track, and monitor slaves. The most serious development in electronics for mind-control is their ability with high tech equipment to actually place thoughts into a persons mind. Harmonic machines, given code-names, are now being used to do lots of the programming. Powerful individual & mass-mind control can take place via electronic means. Our question, who will control the controllers of these electronic means? So far the American & European people have been content to let them get by with what they have done.

CHAPTER SEVEN:

THE SCIENCE OF STRUCTURING

STRUCTURING OF MPD WORLDS

The purpose of the mind-control is to build a System within the mind that is a human robot. It would do no good to torture the slave and get thousands of pieces (fragments of the mind, alter personalities) if these were not structured. Very few Multiples have ever really gotten to see the deeper parts of their Systems. Many of the early successes of therapists were actually only the integration of the fronts of Systems, while the deeper cult parts were left fully functioning. The integration of the front alters was only a ruse to allow the therapist to think the patient was healed. The Illuminati's organization, whose identity still remains secret to the therapist, can continue to use the 'healed" patient. Everyone was happy, therapist, client, and the abusers.

Also I might add the book publishers such as those who published Sybil are also happy. Sybil is an occult first name--but the book, movie and therapist give no hint that ritual abuse might be involved in her system's MPD (DID). The victim of When Rabbit Howls (a book & a movie) shows clear signs of having a full-blown highly structured and programmed MPD (DID) system, but the movie doesn't even hint of programming or Satanic involvement. The whole movie was a big slide. The Illuminati know the details and minutiae of every new direction the therapeutic community decides to take. Indeed, a number of their people are leading the pack, providing leads and misleads. Their first goal is to keep therapists on side roads, away from the real issues.

The second goal is, if they do get onto something, to bring the slaves in, and structure in defenses so that the therapists don't go anywhere.

And then when one has success like we have seen, they eliminate front structures and front alters, and turn to massive reprogramming, and skillfully linking primal traumas with the new programs. Bear in mind, the internal programming alters are also always alert and will restructure the system constantly if alters work against their programming. Restructuring is a process that can continually go on, not something completed when the victim was a child. For instance, new levels of alters can and are created when the victim is in their 30s, either by the internal or external programmers.

From observations, it is clear that the most drastic changes are from the external programmers, who can work much faster than the internal programmers. In the beginning, the programmer must bring order out of the chaos he has created. He must use some type of structure to place worlds. In recent years, these have been solar systems, galaxies, and planets, because they have gone to Star Trek, Star Wars, Alien types of programming. Each planet may have a type of alter--a family, if you will, of alters who are similar. They will not be able to travel to other solar systems, or stars, or galaxies without transportation.

Spaceships, and teleporters have now replaced the elevator that the older systems used to go up and down the worlds. When the programming begins, it must be simple enough that a child can understand it. One game that was excellent to teach internal structures to child victims was Chinese checkers. An innocent game, but a great vehicle to communicate placement of alters and structures. Alter patterns would be placed upon the hexagram board with marbles. A marble would represent an alter. Notice that alter colors (and/or jobs) can be coded by what marble is chosen. A ruby alter can be a red marble. A blue coded alter is a blue marble.

Structures which are to be superimposed upon each other in the child's mind, are easy to superimpose. Take one pattern - of marbles off, and place the superimposed pattern of marbles over the same place. This is how several different structures can be tied together in one locality in the mind. This is one way structures can be layered in. The Hexagram checker board was called "The House of David" in one victim.

THE CREATINO OF ROLES - INTERNAL, EXTERNAL, DEPENDENCE, ETC.

Many splits in the mind are not developed into full blown personalities. Some are simply fragments which are given a single job assignment. Generally, a System will have about half a dozen alters which frequently take the body and hundreds of alters which only occasionally take the body.

Internally, the System must carry out the following functions: Protect all information and history that relates to the creation and use of the slave. All the structuring and codes of the System are also secrets and need to be guarded. The programming and the very things that the slave can think about need to be guarded. The slave is meant to be entirely self-governing. The best boss is the boss who gives a directive and can go do something else while the person receiving the order carries it out without input and supervision. The Monarch slave is the prime example of how to delegate authority. The delegation of authority allows both the master and the victim himself to blame the victim for the orders they carry out.

The satanic cults will hide their alters which make money for the cult behind the blood and gore alters. This protects their illegal money making operations. Alters must learn to function as designed by the Programmer. If they can't work together, the Illuminati will try to get them to work together somewhat akin to a mechanic fixing a car. If the alters can't be fixed, they and their System will have to be thrown away. The dramatic disparities of all the alters goes hand in hand with what at first seems apparent, then not apparent, and then apparent again. There is a unity beneath the multiplicity. Alter functions and abilities overlap with other alters. No alter is entirely separate from several common pools of intellect and dispositions that are attributable to the entire alter system. Alters are real and separate persons. But the common traits that run through an alter system are also real. One alter system may have a streak of kindness and gentleness that runs through the entire system. There may be a few alters which have

{ 253 }

been battered enough not to display the trait, but the trait is so pervasive that it characterizes the System.

The programmers are also skilled at building in alters who can serve as balancing points. Unless the system of alters has balancing point alters who are calm, cheerful, and emotionally stable, a system could easily self-destruct with all the shattered-ness, pain and craziness that has been intentionally built into the system. Each level or world will have a balancing point. When the System is being charted during the early programming process, a Mother of Darkness and the Programmer and the Grande Dame will make a decision on how to label the chart. By the time the child is four, the weaknesses and strengths that characterize the alter System have been recorded on charts and the child's destiny in life determined. The chart will read what occupation the child will be made into, and what its function for the overall Illuminati plan will be.

This determines what types of programs and alters must be created. Most people are still unfamiliar with multiplicity and their rigid thinking is challenged by the concept that one mind can have several personalities. On the other hand, they can understand perfectly that a computer can wall off sections of memory, and they can understand perfectly that a single human mind is superior to all the computers in the world assembled together, and yet they can't let go of their basic simplistic foundational understanding of life that one mind has only one personality. They will allow a computer this ability but not the human mind. The creation of multiple personalities also divides responsibility within a person. A person who lives with a multiple, say for instance their handler, will form widely divergent relationships with the different alters. In terms of programming, each dissociated fragment of the mind may be molded into something.

Some fragments lend themselves to be molded into full personalities, and some lend themselves into being molded into single-purpose fragments, and some must be discarded. A part of the mind can be developed into a full-blown independent personality with all the idiosyncrasies that any other person has. Bear in mind, that generally the Programmers consider color identification and the coded numbers to be more critical for identifying an alter than a name. A name humanizes the alter. Names are sometimes attached later if needed by a handler. Some handlers simply refer to their sexual alters by their generic name "kitten". Others may have a specific cat name such as "Tabby", "Bast", "Hecat", "Adandara" or "the Lion of Judah" for an alter. Keep in mind, if full blown personalities are created, it happens for both the benefit of the victim AND the programmers.

During the Monarch Programming an average System will have at least 1,000 alters, but not all of these will be personalities designed to hold the body. For those who need to get a handle theologically on how to approach this, it is suggested that they approach it as a city of persons. A city has both a unity and a multiplicity about it. It also must carry out certain basic functions if it is to survive. All cities have administrations and city planners, and justice, and police, and garbage collectors, and entertainment, etc. The early Illuminati researchers soon accepted that their victim of multiple personalities is in essence a city of people, and so they used that understanding to construct in the victim's head, using the victim's creativity under torture and drugs to create all the structures and features that accompany a geological land.

The map of the Land of Oz in the Wizard of Oz books was frequently used for the front parts of a System, with some additions and subtractions. The engineering of the structures within an Illuminati Monarch slave, looks like the original designs were done by engineering specialists--perhaps even Boolean algebra was used to develop the original designs. However, once working models of systems were proven to function without fail, lesser skilled programmers & technocrats could help assemble a Monarch System of alters without fully understanding the engineering and all of - the demonology/magic behind it. Just like in a city, some people have friends and know others, and other people are strangers and enemies, so it is with an Illuminati system of multiples. Some alters may be aware of each other, and some may even hate each other. When building a system, the Programmers take advantage of their knowledge of how multiplicity works. Two alters can have several possible relationships which are:

- two-way amnesia, where neither alter knows about the other's existence. This is what the Programmers want for most alters. They don't want multiples to even know they are multiples.
- one-way amnesia, where A alter knows B alter, but B doesn't know A. This can be accomplished by setting in one-way mirrors.
- co-presence, two alters can come on top of each other at the front of the mind and hold the body together. This produces some strange behavior for the multiple as different alters synthesize their thoughts. When a tough alter comes up behind a Christian alter, the Christian alter may find himself letting loose of a cuss word without knowing where exactly it came from. When a child alter comes up behind an adult, the adult may find itself talking like a child.
- co-conscious, this is when two alters are aware of what one another are thinking.

As the Programmers structure a System of alters, they build in No-talk walls every so often where all communication and visibility between alters is walled off. These No-talk walls are specifically built structures and not the result of normal amnesia. A 13 x 13 grid may have, for instance, 2 No-talk walls. Other methods will be used to divide all the levels from each other. One method of dividing the levels is the level of trance for level 3 will be different than the level of trance for level 10. This will not hold true across the board, because some deeper alters are not in deep trance. One Monarch slave, programmed beginning in the 1950's, described her System,

Scattered parts and Broken hearts they all live inside of me. How many times can they divide my mind? Broken hearts with divided parts scattered throughout my mind. How many times can they wipe me out before I come back no more? Can they instill a will in me that is not mine? They broke my heart too many times and divided all the parts, then scattered them through time. Some are good and some are evil. How many times can they split my mind? The lights, needles and pain went on much longer than we can explain. Did these things happen, or is it what they wanted me to believe? Does God exist or is it what I want to believe? Does the store house exist where the computer is? Are there computers in me that help split me? Scattered

parts, broken hearts, where do I exist? Is there a castle built inside?
If so, what person am I? Lights, needles, and pain goes on today, or
is it lies that are made up in a mind split far too many times. Broken
hearts, divided minds, scattered throughout time. I don't want to mis-
lead you. Did the experiments work? And they split me too many
times? Lights, needles, and pain. They can wipe me out if I try to ex-
plain. Butterflies, butterflies, lots and lots of them. I lay down at
nights with them. I wrap up in a blanket made of them. I hear their
hum as they lead me to the lights, needles and pain. The needles and
pain make it so I can not think. I get so sleepy, but I can not sleep.
The pain races through my mind and splits it one more time. I have
forgotten more than most will ever know. The computer will show
how many times they can split the mind, break the heart; divided
minds scattered throughout time. How many times before I can come
back no more?"--received from therapist.

"They Know Not What They Do", An Illustrated Guide to Monarch
Programming-Mind Control, Oregon City, OR, 1995, p. 91, has a
good description of how extensive the internal structuring is: "Many
Systems never get to the point of seeing their internal world(s). Further, most alters have only a small spot in which they are to reside,
and they don't get to see but a tiny fraction of the entire System. After these structures are built into the mind they continue to work and
carry out their function on a subconscious level. Sometimes it takes
years of work for a System to begin seeing their internal world. They
can begin doing this by turning lights on inside of their worlds. To
make a comparison, when a person looks at a clock they see the finished result, the time it shows, but they don't see all the mechanisms.

The structures in the mind are part of the mechanism to keep the System of Alters structured in a way that is useful to the abusers, but often all that observers will see is the finished result, the mechanisms
stay hidden. But we are exposing those mechanisms in this picture
and on this page. A therapist's client may be responding in a way that
makes no sense until one realizes the internal structures that they are
responding to. An alter generally must maintain the spot in the mind
which it is assigned. To leave that location in the mind, means travelling through a System which is filled with dangers and traps of all

kinds.

Only a few of our alters ever ventured where they were not to go, and they always encountered many obstacles. However, if an alter gets trapped behind mirrors, the alter should not break the mirrors. If the alter is a Christian they can use the blood of Jesus Christ of Nazareth to bind and cast out the demons which are in the mirrors. The danger of the mirrors is the demonology involved. Some things work and some things don't. We are speaking from our years of experience. The mirrors are deadly and they were everywhere in our System, but they are deadly only if one can't deal with the demonology. The therapist should at least be aware that these images can be worked with just as if they were real to manipulate situations involving them. But if the structures are going to be worked or toyed with, the therapist and survivor need to have an understanding about the structures. If you don't understand the mirrors, or the River Nile, or whatever then be careful what you have the survivor do to them.

The structures (the images) that are built into the mind of the Monarch slave are not trivial. An overview of the structures that are in our System alone will show that they went to a great deal of effort to build all kinds of internal worlds to house our thousands of alters. A list of the internal structures that were contained in our System follows:

Ant pits, Bee Traps w/ swarms, Black Glass Wall, Black Holes (vortexes), Boxes (Dr. Green's under J.J., boxes have buttons which access certain parts), Candy Land, Carpet (Magic), Castles, Castle dungeon (torture chambers), Caves, Clocks (there are several incl. computer clocks), Concentration camp, Cords, Desert, Doll House, numbered Doors by the thousands w/ red hot knobs, Elevators, Emerald City (connected to the castle), Eucalyptus Trees, Fields of "forget me" & island of "forget me not" (JJ's Prgrmg), Firewall, 2 Forests (singing forest with Cedars of Lebanon and Oaks, and a dwarfs forest which has 3 kinds of trees), Fruit Tree (programming tree), Glass, Glass coffin, Golden Keys, Graveyards, Hallways with red doors, Hell Pit or Hell Fire (7 levels--pepperbox. There is a glassy wall before the hell pit.), Hour Glass (matrix), House of David, Icetown, Invisible Countries, Keys (clock key), Libraries, Light side City, Marshlands, Mazes, Mirrors (constructed via access permissions) (One-way), Moat, Mountains, Nursery (glass), Ocean, Paper Trees, Petra Secret City, Playground, Poppy field, Portals (for altars and demons, like the third eye), Rubicon (outer space beyond the stars), Rivers (Nile, Rio Grande, Shenandoah, etc.), Room behind a closet (existence not confirmed), Seeds, Serpent tree, Shafts, Shells, Shifting sands, Shoes (gold, silver, and ruby slippers), Snake pits (traps), Spider chambers, Stairway, Torpedo Town, Tin Woodsman's Castle, Tree with square paper boxes containing Dad's music programming, Trojan Horse w/ armies, Tunnels, Valley of the Dry Bones, Volcano (to destroy & remake the system), Vortices (see Black Holes), Wasteland, Water (Moats), Waterfalls, Wind, Wires, Worms, and a Yellow Brick Road."

In order to use the multiple in different life styles--they divide up a system of alters into worlds of alters which rarely see each other. These worlds are also called cities. The words "city" or "world" are interchangeable when it comes to a Monarch System. Typically, they received names such as Atlantis, City of Refuge, Shangri-la, and Troy. Later, after Candy Jones exposed the programming, there was a major shift about this time, and many of the Systems were programmed with Solar Systems. Each planet had a different group or race of alter or demon. The concept of Star Trek was helpful for this. Some of the Systems programmed in the 1970s, used Star Trek as their basis. The distribution of alters was similar to watching the various episodes of Star Trek.

Alters that were created at the same time and left in an area of the System together are families. The programmers in their efforts to dehumanize these alters will stick to animal names such as referring to them as "litters". The front level of a System would often be given a cover. The front level might see their world as a basketball court, or several houses, or a dollhouse, or a street. The front world is set up to deceive anyone from discovering the true structure of the system. The programmers can link and unlink, and move alters around. Eventually they get something neat and tidy on a sheet of paper. A standard Illuminati System is built like a 13x13x13 cube with an elevator shaft running up and down from the bottom to the top. The elevator is constructed as a piece of DNA and alters can ride up and down the elevator (go up or down in trance) to move when allowed. Most of the alters have no sense of time, and most of the alters do not hold the body very frequently.

For various reasons most of the alters never grow up. Obviously, if they don't hold the body very much, and are dissociated from everyone else's memories, they have nothing to stimulate them to grow up. However, the Programmers must have some of the alters who can function as adults. For instance, alters who go into bars must think of themselves as adults. The alters which will hold the body in public will be hypnotically made into adults. The Network likes to leave many child alters, because most of them are pedophiles and they like the pseudo-pedophile experience of making it with an alter that thinks it is four years old. Or just the opposite, sometimes an adult alter will appear within a child victim, and this is a clue that this is an access/reporting alter. Many of the Illuminati systems, especially Mengele's were set up on a 13x13 grid of alters.

The grids are numbered top to bottom and side to side but not in the fashion one might expect. The typical Mengele grid will begin with 6 and proceed 6, 7, 8, 9, 10, 11, 12, 13, 1, 2, 3, 4, 5. However, the structure doesn't have to be a grid, any geometric shape works and has been used, such as a sphere, cube, or pyramid. Dr. Star and his wife, who is an OTO programmer working out of Corpus Christi, TX likes to structure an alter system in the shape of the Seal of Solomon. The Yin-yang symbol is then equated with the entire Seal of Solomon. The all-seeing eye is placed in the center of Star's systems, just like Mengele would put in an All-Seeing Eye.

The hidden Sun of Tiphareth is placed into Dr. Star's victim's systems, as well as the four elements, and sulfuric acid. Alters are then placed in the various positions around the hexagram. Because therapists, (and Christian ministers) are generally unaware of the deeper occult things, they usually miss seeing the occult philosophies behind the structures.

For instance, the elements of earth, wind, fire and water are not just part of magic--they are in Druidism considered the four zones (or directions) also called rings which are held together by the fifth ring--balance. This is the basis of Celtic geometric art, metaphysical maps, and ancient Ireland was symbolically divided into four regions with a unifying fifth. This was the bardic view of the universe which is presented in the Vita Merlini (written by Geoffrey of Monmouth in 1150). Supposedly England, Wales and Scotland were also divided into 4 regions with a unifying fifth too. And all these four regions Ireland, Wales, Scotland and England are joined again in the U.K. In Druidism, the four magical elements the Sword, Rod, Cup and Shield are unified by the Cord while the four elements are unified by the spirit. Ancient Druid stone statues of triple faced gods and goddesses still remain today. Heads were considered sacred by the early Celts which is why the heads of the top Grand Dames are preserved after they are ritually murdered.

If an outsider really wants to understand why Illuminati systems are constructed in the fashion that they are--first understand that there is a great depth of meaning behind what structures are used to build an internal world. An ex-programmer talks about how the programmers would call upon Satan in high level rituals to "Tell me what to do, and I'll do what you want" to gain wisdom in how to design these alter systems. Within a System, a few alters will be given maps to the System. There will be a structure "map" which takes the system down through its progressive levels down to its fundamental or primal level. There will also be internal world maps, maze maps, or what some call programming maps.

HOW THE SELF OF A MAIN ALTER CONSISTS OF SHATTERED SHADOW ALTERS, A SCRIPT, MIRRORS AND ASSIGNED DEMONS

What really is an alter? An alter is a dissociated part of the mind, which is developed BY the programmers to be a complete personality. We will now explain what an alter is. If you were to look on the programmers' charts found in his grey 3 ring binder, or his lap top computer you would see graphs with alters with access codes. What are these alters? If the programmers didn't invest a great deal of programming and structuring, each alter would not be a complete personality. On the chart, the programmer will have a square on a grid where he will record the cult name, the front name, the alter's alpha-numeric pull up code and its grid number.

What seems neat and tidy is really not so neat and tidy. That alter is really an alter with many shadows of itself. This is a. family of fragments of that alter which hold parts of itself. There is a particular secret term that only the programmers use for these fragments, but for purposes of discussion we will call these fragments "family fragments" or "shadow fragments." For instance, a Gatekeeper alter will have a shadow alter fragment that holds its fear, one that holds its pain, one that holds its anger, and many that hold its memories of abuse and torture. What appears on the grid as a square is in reality a box holding lots of fragments. The programmers understand how multiplicity works, so rather than chart an alter with 25 fragments coming off of it--they name the whole mess after the main alter they have created for that family of fragments. The main alter really is a fictional persona created by the programmers linked to numerous fragments of the mind. The mind of the child victim will cooperate with the torture and programming.

The programmer will verbally discuss his programming scripts with his close assistants, for instance, the Grand Dame who helps him; but he doesn't record the scripts down. Historically, the Programmers have always individually tailored their story scripts for each child. Because the best are master story tellers, who can make a story come alive, they do not need to depend upon stale written scripts. The Wizard of Oz, and Mother Goose books, etc. are read prior to actual programming session, to enhance the programming session. The final alters are recorded, but not the stories or the lies told them. After a main alter has been created and shattered, the programmers find this main alter within the mind and give it a personal history (via films, virtual reality headsets, stories, etc.), give it a job within the system, a place to live in the internal world, and its rules and guide lines on how to function within the system. It will be given scripts about the outside world.

And shortly, we will explain those. This doesn't mean that alters don't exist--they are physically part of the mental makeup of a multiple's brain--but an alter's existence is not at all what it sees or what outsiders see. Both the alter and the therapist see only a small part of the picture. John O. Bearhrs "Limits of scientific psychiatry, Role of uncertainly in mental health". NY: Brunner/Mazel, 1986, pp. 86-113., who did therapeutic work with Multiples, recognized some of the process that we are describing. He wrote about how an alter when confronted with more pain, guilt, and rage will dissociate this mental hazardous waste into alters who function as internal garbage cans. He described a victim who had a jolly front alter Diane with a winning smile.

This front alter dumped her pain on a small child alter Mary, who lived in an internal "basement". However, in one particular case Mary didn't want the pain and she passed it to Karl (a 4 yr. old alter), who cried and yelled so loud internally that Danny, a 12 year old alter who was characterized by toughness and courage took the pain. However, the actual situation is more subtle and complex than Beahrs realized. Every alter creates shadow alters of itself to handle the anger, fear, guilt, betrayal etc. The Programmers are totally aware of these shadow alters and they work with them.

If we picture an alter as a point in the mind--a dot or small circle, then we can for the sake of discussion picture the shadow splits off of that alter as rays coming out of that small circle. Now we have an image of something looking like a sun with rays. Actually, in real life, after all the torture, the shadow alters holding memories and all the programs attached are simply one big mess that resembles the branches of a tree with leaves.

The Programmers have made a thorough mess of the person's mind-- and they need some clean way to deal with this mess they have created. So the Programmers use the imagery that best resembles the mess they have made. The victim is told they have a tree with branches and leaves growing through them. This tree with its branches grows throughout every alter. The image of the vine and its branches is also used, because then the programmers can bring in the

Bible to make their programming seem to be supported by God's Holy Word. The original alter is told that it is a mote of nothingness (a very tiny circle). The programmers don't chart all the family or shadow fragments of an alter because they understand MPD (DID).

The fragments will hold all the memories of abuse, so the alter can function. The fragments will also give the alter the appearance of the full range of emotions. If a main alter gets angry or feels guilty, what is happening, is that it has accessed its shadows to express the full range of emotions. The Programmers abuse an alter and get the Shadow alters. Then they hypnotically attach a memory cue (which is a code consisting of the alter's name, the date of the memory, and perhaps something else to complete the code) to the main alter so that they can access the memory anytime they want. Then they hypnoti- cally & demonically build a one-way mirror between this main alter and the shadow alters they have just created. These one-way mirrors are like one way windows--the reason they are referred to as mirrors is that they are put in the child's mind via mirrors.

Next, they ritually/magickly implant demons to guard the mirror(s) and to guard each memory held by the shadow alters. This separates an alter from knowing itself and its own abuse. The main alter has dissociated the pain, etc. to its shadow alters of itself. The Program- mers then use the memory as blackmail to keep the main alter in line. The main alter has dissociated the pain, but will recover the memory if either one of three possibilities happen: a. the Programmer or han- dler says the memory code 3x, or b. if an event happens that triggers the main alter to remember, c. the main alter tries to remember the abuse and the programming, and in doing so they will be stepping outside of the circle assigned to them and will "break the circle & break the mirrors." Remember, how we described a Main alter as a small circle with the rays (shadow alters) split off from it. The shadow or family alters of a Main alter are the true history of an alter.

The Main alter is given the script to totally love the Programmer/ Master. It should be angry at what has happened to it. The ability to direct that anger is lost with the dissociation, but might be retrieved if the alter remembered, so the programmers transfer it by creating some outside person or object for the alter to focus their hate upon. Elaborate hate scripts are then given to the main alter. The love of the Master now protects the Main alter from having to remember its pain. Very few alters and very few non-multiple people would want to remember such trauma and it is very unpopular in society to remember past traumas (how often have you heard expressions "let bygones be bygones", "the past is past", "don't dig up old skeletons", etc.)

As long as the alter loves its Master, it is somewhat safe from remembering its own traumas. And yet for a Monarch slave to regain its own mind, the alters must regain their own memories. That is why to really break down the programming, memory work is need. That Monarch slaves must regain their memories to heal is a hard one for many people and ministers to understand. Most deliverance ministries pray that God would take away their bad memories. Further, the programming holds the lies in place, and the demonology holds the traumas, programs, and memories in place. A Main alter is really in the middle of special purpose Shadow alters which have been split from itself. The Programmers do a reversal on this and tell the Main alter that it is on the outside looking in. Vagabond Programming (which tells an alter it is a vagabond) is then applied to teach the alter it doesn't belong to the inside world, nor to the outside world. It belongs nowhere.

The Main alter will perceive that it is on the outside looking in at mirrors. The -mirrors then guard the inside of the circle. To try to remember the truth is to break the circle of mirrors. The circle of mirrors has magical significance, because it ties in with the witch-ball or speculum which the witches have used over the centuries to see beyond time and space. The steps that the programmers do, can be explained on many levels. Many of these steps are done for special occult reasons. One of the first things taught to a child is "DO NOT BREAK THE CIRCLE".

This has both the internal meaning "don't go after your own memories and the external meaning "don't leave the cult -- the circle." Special black mats (such as used in wrestling) have been constructed by the Programmers. The first black mat is a circular mat with a 4' radius. The next black mat has an 8' radius (with a donut hole with a 4' radius) so that it can fit over/around the first circle. From there you have concentric donut shaped pieces of mat each four feet wider in radius than the previous, which can all be joined together. Each of the concentric circles will have a different colored circle painted on its edge. The victim child while it is in the crawling stage will be placed onto the middle dot and told to stay. They will be punished every time they move.

When they finally can do this obediently, they will be given the 4' circle. Toys will be placed outside of the painted line (which may for starters be a blue line, then perhaps green, and then red). Just off of the mat are interesting things like a full bottle, a blanket, a coat, food, toys, etc. The child is cold, hungry and bored. Will the child obey and stay in its circle? If it doesn't it will be punished by being mildly shocked, or having its head dunked into a toilet, or its hand punished, and it will be set back in the circle until it's will is broken and it learns to submit to the order to stay in the circle. This teaches the victim child several things: don't step outside of boundaries, don't break the circle, it teaches them the colors that will be used in the color programming of the internal world, and it is again traumatizing. What they see, hear and do will now be done in obedience.

Does the reader see how hard it is for the child & its alters to move outside of the scripts? Alert readers will realize that there are 13 colors in Illuminati systems and that means 13 x 4 feet = the radius of the finished 13-concentric-circled black mat when all the pieces are laid down. This means a large indoor area with a floor space of at least 124' across in needed. Military bases, hospitals, churches, and universities like Oral Roberts University have gyms or auditoriums which the Illuminati use for this stage of the programming. Mother of Darkness alters train the children. The Presidio had a great place for this training.

THE PRESIDIO

This is the programming for the "Circle Will Not be Broken" script. The Amish do something similar, to make their children obedient, which is one reason the Monarch programming is easy to hide within the Amish culture. This type of programming is referred to in Chapter 5 about the fronts and the Top Secret Amish Front. Let us briefly mention, that some systems are simply concentric rings (levels of alters) each assigned a different color. Another twist to the color coding --an alter in some circumstances may have two colors. An alter may be coded Black below white, so that when it sees black color below white it is triggered. The sections on a soccer ball, have been colored and used for a programming visual aid.

Various researchers who have tried to identify: What happens when a normal non-multiple subject is hypnotized to not feel pain? Of course, the subject consciously tells the hypnotist that he feels no pain, but researchers such as the Watkins & Hilgards have demonstrated that the subject under hypnotism dissociates the pain to another part of the mind. In other words, hypnosis and MPD (DID) which are both forms of dissociation are much closer in how they function than some people have realized. In fact, some researchers, who are well aware of how close the two dissociative functions are, have defined MPD (DID) as "spontaneous hypnosis" (Beahrs, 1982; Bliss, 1986).

The non-conscious area of the mind that hypnotic subjects dissociated to, have been labeled "ego-states", "the hidden observer" and "a covert cognitive structural system". The giving away of pain, fear, and other traumas to Shadow parts is similar to what happens when researchers observe a person who is directed in hypnosis to not feel pain, unknowingly giving his pain away to a hidden ego-state. A hiding place where alters can go, a place of light which gives energy, is created in a System.

The New World Order's One-World-Religion and their Mind-Control is organized on the hierarchal system with a S.P.I.N. front. The Illuminati and the occult world that they supervise has a strong hierarchical system both world-wide and within the slave. One source has spent a great deal of time researching and communicating to others how the hierarchy controls on a large scale, and how it is miniaturized and how this identical hierarchy is placed internally into the slave. However, the big cover for the hierarchical arrangement is the SPIN principal.

WHAT IS THE SPIN PRINCIPLE?

S-P-I-N = Segmented Polycentric Integrated Networks

If one were to diagram a SPIN organizational chart it would not be a conventional box type configuration such as an army company organization chart. Rather, it would resemble a fish-net with interlocking nodes with groups linked to many other groups and clusters around nodes. There is no center to the network. It is like the brain's electrical connections, with an overlap of functions, so that good cells can take over from damaged sections.

A network (one of their buzzwords) is many times more greater than the sum of its parts. The New Age author Marilyn Ferguson does an excellent job in describing how the Conspiracy's SPIN network functions. *"This is a source of power never before tapped in history: multiple self-sufficient social movements linked for a whole array of goals whose accomplishment would transform every aspect of contemporary life. Because SPINs are so qualitatively different in organization and impact from bureaucracies...most people don't see them--or think they are conspiracies. Often networks take similar action without conferring with each other simply because they share so many assumptions. It might also be said that the shared assumptions are the collusion. "The Aquarian Conspiracy is, in effect, a SPIN of SPINs, a network of many networks aimed at social transformation. The Aquarian Conspiracy is indeed loose, segmented, evolutionary, redundant. Its center is everywhere. Although many social movements and mutual-help groups are represented in its alliances, its life does not hinge on any of them."* Ferguson, Marilyn. The Aquarian Conspiracy. Los Angeles, CA: J.P. Tarcher, Inc., 1980, p. 217.

The programmers enjoy setting up double-binds. One of their tricks is to create alters which are given negative spiritual roles with names to match. An alter may be named unforgiveness", or "the one who doesn't trust anyone." For such an alter to trust someone, makes the alter feel like it is giving up its name, and therefore its identity. By combining the name with an identity that the alter doesn't want to lose, the programming intends to double bind the alter.

The Satan alter within a System will see itself as Satan. The alter Satan feels that he is on the winning side in a war, due to the lies that have been told this child alter when it was created. A girl child alter will be made to think they are the evil male Satan. The point is that the identity of this alter is tied up with their negative. destructive role in the system.

The Christian therapist has a better chance to show Satan that the Rule of the Victor means that Satan serves Almighty God, than for a secular therapist to try to convince Satan that Satan doesn't exist. And if the secular therapist tries to debunk the Biblical view of things, what positive philosophy or spirituality is the secular therapist going to give this Satan alter to fight with against the inevitable external evil that we all face in life?

STANDARD ROLES WITHIN AN ILLIMINATI MONARH SLAVE

Note: that depending upon what the System's occupation in life is, also determines some of the types of alters created. If the System is a politician, they will need special alters to deal with certain secret activities. If the System is a baseball pitcher, they will need alters that are trained to pitch.

- Alien alters for contact, bonding w/aliens, & acceptance of mock alien invasion
- Angel (imitation) alters for divine messages, these may be seen as Spirit Guide alters
- Angry alters
- Animal alters who are meant to act like animals
- Assassination alters (Deltas)
- Babysitter alters to look after keep them from popping out inappropriately

- Blackmail alters (Betas, and Black Widows)
- Bird alters (used for half a dozen various internal purposes, including ravens for suicide, doves for peace, orks to fly over the internal mazes, owls for wisdom, etc. The dove may be part of a false trinity.)
- Child alters
- Clockmaker & Clockholder alters (Also the Grim reaper may be associated with the clocks.)
- Core related alters to imitate or protect the core from anything
- Coven alters to lead coven level meetings
- Courier alters (Carrier Pigeons)
- Data alters to hold information (this encompasses a wide range of alters, including alters who hold internal system   information to alters who hold information for their masters.
- Deaf & Dumb alters to prevent the System from hearing non-approved users say access codes.
- Death alters to take near death traumas
- Element alters (Alr or Wind, Water, Earth, Fire) for magick & compliance
- Espionage alters
- Firechild or Bombchild alters to make body feel like its burning
- Flooding alters (often flooding comes simply from Shadow fragments)
- Foreign Language alters
- Front alters for a good cover
- Gatekeeper alters to guard portals and gates
- Guard (or Blocker) alters to guard important areas of the System
- Justice alters--alters who mete out justice for disobedient alters
- Hierarchy alters to take part in Illuminati hierarchy ceremonies (there will be a big demand for many of these alters--different ceremonies and different times of the year are given different alters).
- Hunts, alters created for the master's sport of being hunted
- Loyalty alters which hold strong love & devotion to the master
- Martial Arts alters to protect the System if need be
- Mirror image alters, for deception
- Monster alters to scare the other alters
- Mouse alters to run the clocks (computer, and grids)

- Nothing alters, alters who believe they are nobody, or Mr. Nobody, or "no-name.
- Observation alters (these deep alters quietly observe all that goes on in an alter system. They may be called Watchers.)
- Programmers, Internal (alters cloned after the original programmers to reprogram the System, also known as Internalists.)
- Programming alters to help Illuminati program
- Protector alters to protect almost everything in the System (essentially nothing is left unprotected in the System.) In some systems, these alters may even be known in the System as Warrior & Infiltration Alters. They may include such titles as Keeper to the Pit.
- Ribbon Alters to send messages from computers to System areas
- Reporting alters to give the master reports regularly, esp. important to monitor all activity by a therapist
- Ruling alters, such as Queens & Kings
- Run/return to master alters
- Satanic hierarchy alters, to insure that system is controlled by Satan
- Sexual alters (kittens for porn, S&M, etc.)
- Scrambling alters to prevent alters from hearing
- Shell alters (to hide real alters from therapists)
- Suicide alters (clowns, Russian Roulette alters, etc.)
- Tranced, (alters tranced deeply to move up and trance the body)
- Travel alters, which can sleep during travel or be oblivious to where they are going

Next we will discuss how some of these types of alters are created. These will be discussed in alphabetical order. It should be pointed out that generally the Illuminati choose one of the early front Gatekeeper alters to be the alter who knows the entire system as it is made. This often is Gatekeeper no. 3. After the entire structuring is finished this alter will be hypnotically programmed to forget that they know the entire system. By the age of ten, an Illuminati system will have someone who knows the entire system. However, these gatekeepers get heavy programming not to remember.

ANGRY ALTERS

By the time the programmers are ready to create angry alters, the child victim has been well conditioned not to get angry, but to passively accept their abuse. The programmers have to get the child's mind to break with their prior programming to get angry. In order to do this, the child will be tormented without end for several days. This is one of the worst parts of the programming, and many children die in this stage. The Illuminati pick their most gentle Mothers-of-Darkness systems to work with the male programmers. If the gentle Mothers-of-Darkness slaves didn't bring some balance and affection to the child victims, the sadistic programmers would probably kill all of the children at this stage of programming. For more on this see Egyptian Armies just a little further.

ANIMAL ALTERS (MEANT TO ACT LIKE ANIMALS)

Although a large share of an alter system is dehumanized, there are certain alters which will be created to actually hold the body and act like animals. The alter may even be named "animal." A male or female slave may have dog alters which bark like a dog and get into the correct position to allow a Rottweiler/German shepherd/Doberman to penetrate the slave sexually. This is accomplished by taking menstrual blood from a dog in heat and smearing it on the victim.

Animal alters are created by the standard dehumanization methods, and then shown films of what they are to become. Through hypnosis and behavior modification, the alters eventually accept the role they are tortured and programmed into taking. It's hard telling what roles the programmers have created, it could possibly be any animal, but cats, dogs, donkeys, horses, rats, and mice are common examples.

CHRISTIAN FRONT ALTERS

Most Illuminati Systems have Christian front alters. Some of the early splits around 2 years of age are provided the chance to genuinely accept Christ. From these alters, two things will be done. Front alters who are Christians will be created, and satanic alters. In order to get dedicated Satanic alters, Christian alters are severely traumatized and God is blamed for not helping them. The Satanic alters will be deeply convinced that God has abandoned them. The Christian alters will dissociate all the trauma, and will believe that they are normal--nothing has happened out of the ordinary in their life. Christian alters will also, like all MPD/DID alters, tend to deal with overwhelming problems by dissociation. Many Christian alters will deny such basic things such as that a Satanic conspiracy exists. They often will be far more zealous than the normal Christian, because they do not have conflicting ego-states. If any situation calls for compromise of their religious beliefs they can switch to someone else--and thereby escape having to compromise. There are many programmed multiples leading the Christian churches today. Christian alters are coached via the modern church and their handlers to only "spiritually minded" and not to challenge evil in the natural world. Some walk around believing that God will cure everything, which is true but not in the sense that some of the churches are explaining. That doesn't mean that all Systems will be "Polyanna-ish", but it can happen. The original Christian alters will be shamed and then hidden by the programmers. The "host" or "presenting" alter which holds the body will often be a Christian. This really helps hide the entire mind-control. Interestingly, a system of 20,000 alters may have only less than a dozen Christians alters, but the one or two strong Christian alters will exert a disproportionate influence on the System. The Illuminati has had a hard time controlling the Christian alters they allow. In their zeal to infiltrate, control and destroy the Christian churches, they have opened many of their top slaves up to the love of God, which has ended in the slaves trying to break free. Unfortunately, most ministers know too little to help these people escape.

CLONES

The clones are little children who have been put into robot costumes and are trained to attack parts of the system which are not in compliance with the programming. The heads of the clones can be unscrewed. The clones can be taken out by various tactics, but there are hundreds of clones and they each have been numbered. The serial numbers are placed on them. An example of a clone's number at the base of the neck might be 158.00. This may either be a model or actual serial number but often is tied to the birth date of the victim, which is generally part or all of the victim's Monarch serial number. To create the clones during the 1950s, movie scenes of the divers of the Nautilus of the movie 20,000 Leagues Under the Sea were shown. (With later models, such as in Star Wars programming, the robots of these shows suffice.) Some clones kill with a knife as the divers in the movie 20,000 Leagues Under the Sea. When clones surface and take the body they are cold. Programming is encased in a clone. Alters, particularly cult alters, may not be able to see the clones. They may be hidden in almost anything internally, including door knobs and walls. However, there is the possibility for the therapist that a net made of cloth woven of light can be dropped and the lumps will reveal the clones. They may be behind mirrors too. Water has certain properties that can stop clones, as well as magnets. Microwaves will take care of the electronics. A little microwave can take out a group of clones. Clones have many shapes--but they do not look like people. They usually have a switch to be activated. Atlantis may be set up as the world for clones, in accord with 20,000 Leagues Under the Sea programming. Whatever the style, robots & clones are popular items for programmers to install. One of the major defects of the first few decades of Illuminati programming, was that the clones were set up so that water would stop them. Therapists could stop the clone armies by applying water on them. Recent models have corrected that deficiency. But when the clones are stopped, and the diver suits are taken off of the child alters, who are inside of the robot suits, then a child alter will be found which is in the same drugged state that it was in when it was being programmed. This child fragment alter will often have an I.V. (wires and needles) in it, and will be very druggy. It will be in its programmed war-like angry state. In Druidism, a swan was something dirty like a pig in Judaism. Some alters which are assigned to protect, are warned they will become swans. If the Queen of the Clones becomes a swan, the clones will become helpless. The Queen of the Clones (a triad) must do her job or be turned into a swan. Changing subjects to alter clones, Cloning programs include, for instance, Lollipop & Lobster programs.

DELTA'S

The Delta's are alters trained to carry out special missions resulting in death. The Delta's who are inactive are asleep. They must be activated. The programming to activate them will be triggered if a mission is given or if certain parts of the deeper parts of the system are tampered with. Delta's will work as a team with the Beta's to kill. An Illuminati System will be "magically" twinned during programming to be a Twin with another system's Delta alters. And these two systems in turn are joined in programming with another 2 person team, so that 2 person and 4 person teams can be constructed. This gives the Illuminati more flexibility in what kind of missions it can send its slave out on. 4 person assassination teams are very common. They had 2 four-man Monarch slave assassination teams at Waco, Texas the day that the Waco Branch Davidian building burned up.

HOW DELTA'S ARE CREATED

Illuminati Deltas are linked to the moon children, and are the offspring of the moon child alter in the early cage programming. In the early 1950s, the Illuminati would take a child and force it to watch another child, who they have bonded with, be incinerated alive in a crematorium at high heat which would not only melt the child but turn it to ashes. The form of the child in ashes would stay in the shape of the child until the crematorium door which would have glass in it for viewing would be opened. A small gust of air would cause the ashes to lose their shape. Watching through glass and feeling the fire and hearing the child scream was a trauma for any child. The Presidio and some of the Illuminati-run funeral homes which had this type of crematorium were employed for fire traumas. The fire trauma was done so that the child would visualize melting from heat. This melting trauma would then form the basis of the good witch/bad witch programming where water on a witch makes her melt like in the Wizard of Oz story. The Delta and Beta alters are then to trance into their melted state whenever their programmers want them to function. Their functioning state is the "melted state". The programming is that the witches melt down to nothing. After a few years, the programmers realized that they didn't have to have a real trauma to get the programming done, because they could usually do it with a combination of hallucinatory drugs, hypnotic drugs, and paper dolls. Paper dolls which when cut out are all joined together would be placed on a grid similar to an alter grid on a platform. The right hypnotic suggestions are made, and the child believes these paper dolls are alive and are burned up. If the paper dolls didn't work, they'd go back to using a real child to get the job done. Later, the lower cat alters are taught how to be hunted and hunt at the "life or death" Beltaine hunts. These hunts helped train alters which are then used to create the Deltas. The Deltas are not completed until later. To create a trained assassin, the alters were desensitized towards pain and death by being shown gory films with the eyes forced open. Hypnosis was also used. The potential victims were devalued, it is believed the Aryan alters which are very elitist and racist are used for Delta alters. Satanic rituals were also involved in the creation of the Deltas. Deltas will be trained in hand to hand combat--and know certain vulnerable places to kill people, i.e. breaking the neck. Training included a great deal of weapons training. In an early programmed multiple System, which was created and programmed in Nazi Germany in the 1930s, the assassination alters are placed behind a wall of ice. When the wall of ice is melted, these assassination alters are freed and they will go about their assignment to kill by using an ice-pick type needle poked into the heart of their prey. These Systems were infiltrated into the U.S. during the 1930s to build a foundation for when the Nazi's expected to win the war. Later, American Delta alters were taught the art of assassination by poking a needle through the eye of the victim. This kind of assassination is apparently hard to detect.

HOW THE DELTAS ARE ACTIVATED

The access codes for the Deltas are structured different than for the rest of the System, except for the sexual/entrapment/espionage alters who are designed very similar. The Deltas may be black color coded.

When the programmer wants to use these Delta alters, he will call them up from their genii bottle or wherever they are hidden deep in the mind. They will be commanded to melt. When they have melted into the nothing state, then the programmer gives an exact script of everything the Delta alter is to do, just like you would program a computer step by step from point a to point z. For instance, the programmer might say, "At a certain place you will be in the melted state until you hear the words, "I'm going to Kansas City, where are you from Miss Ruby shoes?", at that point you will remain in the melted state and do part B of the script." As the programmer continues with the script, a Delta fragment will be given NWO codes, bank account numbers, and major sports numbers, so other NWO folks know who is going to win ahead of time. This fragment will simply be a mental floppy disk. The Delta-Beta alters are habitually lied to by their programmers when they are given their detailed scripts. If they are carrying cocaine they may be told it is soap for needy children. If they shoot someone, then they will be told all kinds of lies about the person they are to kill. They never are really given a chance to step outside of their deep trance and to ever hear the truth about what they are doing. They live their lives in a surreal fantasy world where nothing really makes sense. They don't try to think for themselves, they just follow orders. Since a mission may call for other alters to hold the body, the programmer must put together his Delta script so that two scripts can be intertwined. The programmer may work out something so that the Delta alter goes into a temporary sleep in the melted state while out on the mission. This way the programmer doesn't have to be present on the trip to bring the Delta alter back into its functioning "melted" state. The Delta alters can't be out too long anyway because they are not used to functioning in the outside world and they get tired fast. Several Delta alters can switch so that they keep having a fresh Delta alter come out, but eventually every one begins to get tired. That is another reason they will work in another script with front alters. The front alters are used to holding the body everyday. The front alters will take a vacation, while the Deltas work on their detailed script of carrying secret messages and maybe killing someone. During an airplane trip, a travel alter will hold the body while the Deltas sleep in the melted state. Delta alters, who by the way have photographic memories, are given their scripts by programmers, not run-of-the-mill handlers. Everything is too fine tuned in the programming for a run-of-the-mill handler. Delta alters have an internal hour glass, this hour glass may be a mural in their internal world that they look at. As long as they are obedient, the hour glass sands do not fall. If they are disobedient, the sand begins falling, and their life is on the line. There is no room for mistakes. If the sand runs out, death is to happen. Large hourglasses are often displayed in front of Delta-Beta slaves to remind them that their is no room for mistakes, no slack for disobedience. Their thinking is buried in fairy tales. They are programmed to see themselves in fairy tales, they are programmed not to see their handlers or anybody's else's face for that matter. Their handlers pretend they are fairy tale characters or aliens. These alters do not have a chance to understand what they are doing. If the programmers get tired of the slave's programming breaking down, and it does in part due to the severe abuse they get from these sadistic programmers/handlers, then they will simply give the slave an assignment in which the slave will end up dying, i.e. a suicide mission. This type of suicide mission is happening all over the United States with great frequency. An example would be a lady who is getting to wise about the New World Order, so a Delta is assigned to crash their car into the lady, and its written down as "just an unfortunate ACCIDENT with fatalities." A shop owner refuses to pay the Mafia for protection; so a Delta vandalizes and tears up the shop and has a fatal shootout with the police.

FOREIGN LANGUAGE ALTERS

The Illuminati/intelligence agencies realized when they started making slaves with photographic memories that they could create different parts of a slave's mind to operate on different languages. Illuminati hierarchy systems will employ foreign language alters for several purposes:
a. to facilitate the alter working in various situations, for example French is helpful to work with Catholics in Quebec, and with the Cambodian/Vietnamese criminal syndicate that the Illuminati set up in this nation. A high profile example of this is an officer of the Delta Force, who due to his photographic mind (created via brain stem scarring) can speak Mandarin Chinese. Mandarin Chinese is not normally an easy language for Americans.
b. b. to hide things in a system. Examples of this include code words attached to Greek and Hebrew letters for body programs. Another example is having Latin phrases for accessing deeper parts. If an entire area of a system is put in a foreign language, and the system is not given any alters capable of translation, then you have

very effectively isolated an entire section. For instance, systems are being created in their early teens which are sectioned off into 5 or more languages, say for instance, German, Spanish, French, Italian, and Arabic. Some of the Systems created in the late 1950s, already were employing some of this. Since the very best Illuminati programmer in the world is European, and speaks several languages you can expect to start to see more and more of this "Tower of Babel" programming (multi-language systems where parts can't communicate.)

The reader realizes that such multi-language capabilities are always secret until the person starts breaking down the programming. The programmers tell alter systems that God wants this programming done, because God confounded all the languages & then spread people into the 4 corners of the world.

GATEKEEPER ALTERS

The Gatekeeper alters are just that. They protect the gates or portals to all System levels. Infrequently, the programmers may also call them "doorkeepers", or "toll men" & "toll women". The victim may refer to them as guards or blockers, although Gatekeepers are more than guards, they are an entrance or portal to something. Gatekeepers may often be the alter that was split to get a particular section. Each gatekeeper may be at a deeper level trance than the one before it. When a Gatekeeper is split it creates a natural link to the alters that are created from itself. Then the Gatekeepers are given programming not to see what they have created Which sound like this:

"Black knight moves two spaces and one right. White knight moves two spaces and one left. White knight challenges black knight. Black Queen moves 5 spaces." The victim who receives this programming must be the type of thinker who would play chess reasonably well. The script can be shown via videos while the victim is under hypnotic drugs.

DOUBLE HELIX

This is a very important system. The double helix pattern is used as an elevator shaft running up and down the worlds created for the alters. In general, each world lays at a trance level. The double-helix is put in at programming sites where they have full medical facilities, such as Letterman Hospital, Presidio, CA. The codes up and down the elevator are alpha-numeric with lots of numbers. Because the way the double helix shape twists, one can ride the elevator and get off a level 1, 3, 5, 7, 9 but you have to ride it the other way to get off at 2, 4, 6, 8, 10, 12. Because the double helix is the centerpiece of how the different physiological states of the mind are being layered, taking the victim down to these different physiological states and levels is very risky and by the time it is through it involves lots of blood transfusions for the victim. The Caduceus is a double helix with snakes at the top. The Caduceus is an occult symbol used in ancient Babylon, ancient Hindu India, and by Chinese occultists. Mercury in occult lore carries a staff called a caduceus. Mercury's staff is a cabalistic symbol. William Heller's book on the Kabala on page 78 states, "Mercury's staff, called Caduceus, and made of intertwined black-and-white twin serpents, heralds more forthcoming splits into duality. Once again, it reflects the ambivalent mind, its conscious, and subconscious states, its waking thoughts and imaginative dreams." So according to cabalistic doctrine, the caduceus represents the various states of the mind.

FLOWER SYSTEM

This system is attached to other systems, and utilizes the power of peer pressure and generational ties. The flowers will often be bright. The bud of the flower will represent one person, the stem and the flower represent others. This system might be connected to the Umbrella, the Trees, the Triangle and the Star. A flower can regenerate an internal tree because of its generational roots. Flowers are also used as elevator shafts, such as a sunflower. One has to jump into the center of the flower and go down the stem to reach a lower level. Flower fields such as the poppy field are used as a hypnotic trigger to put an alter into deep trance.

HELIX

This is a simplified version of the double helix.

HOUR GLASS

Three hour glasses will be placed around the x-y-z axis in a quadrant. A quadrant consists of a section of alters in a world and their mirror images. The hour glass programming also includes a suicide program. 12 disciple alters will be placed within the hourglass. Each disciple has to memorize a disciple lesson. If something triggers them, they will begin to fall through the hour glass. If each of these 12 disciples falls through the hour glass like sand, then a sleeping giant like in Jack in the Beanstalk will wake up, . When the Giant awakes, he will kill the body. And of course, a mirror image of the Giant alter will be made also to help insure that at least one of the giants get the job done.

MENSA

This is a program put into slaves who have photographic memories. It involves lots of numbers and math. It's overall structure looks like a triangular-shaped fish net, with all the nodes or knots of the net containing a triangle. The core is place at the center of the triangle and is surrounded by more triangles. There are circles of alters within circles of alters. Circles within circles. The a circle can rotate and seems never to end. The programming is meant to be non-ending. There are also triangles within triangles. The effect of using a structure like this to house the alters is that they feel trapped in endless circles and mazes of triangles within triangles. The codes in a Mensa system will be equations (sometimes called union force codes), bar codes, and number sequences.

PENTAGRAM SYSTEM

One pentagram system has pentagrams within pentagrams. The geometric lines grow from pentagram to pentagram by lines running in opposite directions. This has the same effect as circles within circles.

POOL OF DEATH

One or more of these can be placed into an alter system. They often are found inside the main castle. Dead alters and body parts and torture fragments, are all dumped into these system garbage dumps. The Spirits of Death and Destruction control these pools of Death. Variations of this may be called Lakes of Death, and Waters of Death. In some systems, this is overseen by Taskmaster alters.

POTTER'S WHEEL

This is the equivalent to a computer utility program. The way it functions is that the Programmer pulls the alters he wants to work on to the top of the potter's wheel in order to work on them. When they are pulled up on the potter's wheel, they can be asked to stand in order and rank. Then the alters will come to the front of the mind on top of each other in their prearranged sequence. The Charismatic movement programmer's like to use this, because the Programmer can become god, and the slave becomes the clay. Can the pot talk back to the potter? The Bible verse in ISA 45:9 is used, "WOE unto him that striveth with his Maker! Let the potsherd strive with the potsherds of the earth. Shall the clay say to him that fashioneth it, What maketh thou? or thy work, He hath no hands?" The next verse again repeats its woes upon those who question parents who fashion a child. As is typical of a number of Illuminati programs, at first glance they look like they are merely perversions of the Bible, but a closer look reveals that they are actually ancient occult rituals. For instance, the Illuminati believe "As above, so below." This is druidic philosophy, even though it sounds somewhat like something from the Bible. In the book Invocation of the Gods Ancient Egyptian Magic for Today, pg. 203, the book gives a magical invocation that supposedly has been found in ancient Egyptian magical papyri. At any rate this invocation's wording is powerful in English for a Monarch slave. The Invocation is called The Potter's Wheel.

"Hear the sound of the potter's wheel
As it spins! Khnum!
See the clay on the potter's wheel
As it spins! Khnum!
Feel the hand of the Mighty Lord Form the seed to contain a soul

As it spins.
See the soul, on the Wheel of Life
As it spins! Khnum!
Birth to death on the Wheel of Life See the soul, on the Wheel of Life
As it spins!
And with death we are born anew
While the vessel that's tossed aside Will return to the potter's wheel
As it spins!"

This is just one more example of where programming and magic intersect.

PUPPET SYSTEM

In this system the body feels totally disjointed and controlled by strings. Mengele enjoyed this program. He would say, "Dance Marionette dance." In other words, to paraphrase, "dance slave for me the controller". Demons are laid in to pull the strings of the puppet. The internal controller may be a demon or a demonized alter. It can be attached to other systems such as the Pentagram system. In a previous part of the book, it was discussed how the victim's body is paralyzed by drugs and then electro shocked in a way that the person seems to be the Programmers puppet. This is put in when the child is very young. This puppet programming is very convincing to a small child, and is a very nasty program for the slave to experience.

SOLOMETRIC SYSTEM

This is used for government/business/research slaves who must perform complex tasks and they want their minds to be less fragmented or not fragmented. The mind can be programmed and divided from itself without creating alter personalities. Because the divisions in the mind due to dissociation and programming lies are not as deeply structured, victims who get solometric systems have strong demonic forces and lot's ritual to hold their systems in place.

SPIDER WEB SYSTEM OR BLACK WIDOW SPIDER SYSTEM

This system is set up just for blackmail and destruction via entrapment of unsuspecting people who are perceived as threats to the Illuminati. This system is found in lots of women coming into churches with decent but naive ministers. The system has a web with connectors and silk strands. A target person will be symbolically placed into the web and then the black widow alter will entrap the victim. This is programming to take down pastors of churches with sexual entrapment. The spirit Viper found in ISA 59:5 is placed into this system to protect it. There will be egg alters which will devour the victim, and Gatekeepers are assigned to guard the system.

SPIRITUAL STRUCTURING

The spiritual structuring is not a single structure. A few people have worked with the deeper elements of the programming to help victims and also know what the Illuminati programmers have done and what their agenda is, have come to realize that the spiritual structuring is the most important part of an Illuminati system. What you will now read is known only to an exclusive few. Spiritual castles (Grandfather, Father, Mother, and Grandmother castles) and spiritual temples (to Moloch and Baal etc.) are constructed internally. Entire spiritual worlds are constructed internally. The most primal parts of the mind, and the key early alters and the core essence are usually taken to spiritual constructs within the Illuminati slave. The gems are empowered by the light of Lucifer (an alter-demon combination). But even more deeper than that are the generational ties. The programmers, who themselves are generational Satanists, are part of a plan where the generational legal rights of Satan are accumulated upon an individual. In the Scriptures it says that the sins of the fathers are visited upon the third and fourth generation. This gives Satan a legal right to the generational victim. Each bloodline has its Prince demons attached to it--just like in the Bible the Prince of Persia was both a man & and a demon. Hidden within spiritual constructs such as black diamonds, and diamonds, are further demonic constructs. The thrones of the generational Prince Demons are attached to the primal human part of the victim. This is entirely spiritual, beyond that there are no words to describe it. It is very real to the survivor when therapists get to that point (which is very rare!). The power of the Illuminati is that it is generational. They build upon that, when they build a system. Some of these genealogies have not been free for many generations. If you want to spoil a structure, one need to bind the strongman. The strongman in an Illuminati system is the generational ties. All ties to the bloodlines need to be renounced. The Programmers will take little Illuminati children to crypts of their ancestors in order to better attach the generational spirits. The womb holding the premature child is used as a temple in the Moon Child ceremonies. After the child is born the womb structure will spiritually serve as a temple for the primal human parts of an Illuminati slave. Whether the therapist can realize these things or not, in the very least, they are aware of the saying "Father like son", and are aware how traits may skip a generation , like how a grandson may mirror a grandfather. The generational aspects to Illuminati slaves are a major role in the Illuminati.

STAIRWELL

The stairwell is just as it sounds, it is a stairwell that is placed into a system. The stairwell can be used as a trap for alters who are unwise enough to be lured by programming to go into it. The stairwell system connects various levels. There are booby traps and demonic entities attached to the system. Stairwells may be sealed up with Gatekeepers assigned to protect them. If an alter proceeds down a stairwell to get to other levels they need to realize that they initially will hit "tornado (also called whirlwind) programming" and flooding of memories. The tornados will spin the victim inward and disorient them. The alter holding the body will feel as if it is out of control and going to die.

TELESCOPING

Any telescoping object (such as a telescoping army drinking cup, or a telescoping rod) can be used to give the visual picture for the child to follow when it is being programmed. A telescoping system often has a time level, a function level and an age level. The game of Chutes and Ladders along with Jacob's Ladder have been used to place the story line into children.

TORNADO SYSTEM

This is a free floating system that moves around areas that the programmers want protected. When it hits an alter it causes confusion, spinning, and switching, as well as a feeling of losing control. It's part of the elemental back up programs discussed in other pages.

UMBRELLA

This is associated with military programming. An umbrella protects something, such as the Delta assassination alters. An umbrella must be taken down from the inside and so must this protective shield of the Umbrella program. One Umbrella system had 7 gates to it.

DEFENSES IN DEPTH

What would happen if a slave physically got away from its master or handler? This has happened countless times and the mind-control is so solid that the handlers don't have too much to worry about. Mind-controlled slaves have gone to therapists for years and never gotten free of the mind-control. The therapeutic process that the establishment has schooled them in and requires them to adhere to, prevents the therapist from doing things that might really set the victim free. Therapists are often loath to give any help in any thing that smacks of spirituality. The spiritual issues in many of these slaves are the most crucial issues facing them. If they don't resolve these spiritual issues, the deeper alters will continue to adhere to their blood oaths of allegiance to their Satanic abusers and their oaths to serve Satan loyally.

Each cult which programs, makes sure that they place in lots of loyal alters, which therapists call persecutor alters because they torment the alters who want freedom. If therapists try to eliminate these persecutor alters, they will fight back with the full tenacity and strength that the survival instinct gives to anyone. Their persecutor role needs to be validated, and then redirected toward productive ends. Many persecutor alters see life simply as following their instructions and that they are protecting the system from greater harm by stopping therapy. During programming that was the case, but if their System has reached a good therapist and has good support team of other people, their fears no longer apply. The cult will attempt to show them that their fears do still apply. Hopefully, the support team for the system of alters will work as hard at protecting as the abusers do to reinforce the fear. Many of the programmers have been associated with the military.

One of the tricks that the military learned is a defense in depth. The Russians employed defenses in depth with great success in 1943 in the big battle of Kursk during W.W. II. The first defense is that the slave has no awareness of the MPD (DID) or that they are being used as a slave. Some of the alters will realize that something is wrong, but the mind control is too strong for them to see clearly. Essentially the System is in trance all the time, even the front alters, they do not perceive reality like people who are not in trance all the time. The next line of defense is that the fronts of an alter System don't have a clue about the abuse or what their system has been designed for. The front alters will have alters which are loyal to the master, and alters who are full of craziness and disinformation. If the victim keeps probing (which many don't) they will discover an occult involvement.

Even if they discover that the System is related to the occult world, the programming is still intact. If the person finds out he is MPD, and finds out that the System was part of the occult world, then he still is captured by all the programming which is intact. Walls, fire walls, mazes, suicide programming, internal armies, programmed craziness and many other tactics sap the strength of the front alters if they try to deviate from the straight and narrow programmed way of behaving. When the final call back is given many Monarch slaves are programmed to kill their therapists because the Illuminati will be able to hide/protect them once they leave their place in society and return for the final callback. Reporting alters hidden well in the System, observe and secretly report back to the Network everything a therapist does. The alters have fix me codes to call for help such as "FIX ME", "QUEEN OF HEART", "THREE LITTLE KITTENS WHO LOST THEIR MITTENS", "THE COWS IN THE CORN, LITTLE JACKIE HORNER WON'T YOU PLEASE BLOW YOUR HORN."

The jokers and internal programmers will work night and day to stop or reverse any work done toward freedom. There are so many levels, suicide programs and so many other defenses a person's body is not strong enough to attack the programming head on. There are for instance Bells of Destruction programming, The War in the Heavens suicide programming, the Gethsemane Suicide Programming, the Octopus suicide programming, the Injection of Bleach, the overdose of drugs, the go insane program, just to mention a few. The slave will be given a whole batch of these types of programs which may all go off at once if the slave doesn't comply with keeping the mind control secret. One internal protective programming line is The Man without a Country story. Another is a water program but in with Scripture from Jerimiah. about Ahab stomping the grapes. Another is for the slave to think they have been turned into a fragile paper doll. The paper doll programming is put in by making the skin very sensitive to any touch, and then attaching that memory to the hypnotic suggestion of being a paper doll. An octopus suicide program chokes the slave if they are disobedient.

If the slave touches the programming, Armageddon programming is activated in those who have Bible programming. The four horsemen on their different horses ride out and bring their different mental tortures to the slave's mind. Winged monkeys (possibly alter fragments) from the Wizard of Oz story programming are called "watchers". They watch alters. The slave is conditioned that if any programming or demonology is taken out, it will come back seven times seven stronger. The Bible (MT 12:43-44) is used to put in this programming. Actually, this is more than programming, there is a principle in operation here. Therapists need to be cautious about pulling things out, if they do not understand what the ramifications will be. We want the victim to have hope, not to make the task look harder.

One of the primary protective programs is the Judas programming. Anyone who betrays the abusers is labeled "Judas" and is programmed to go out and act like Judas by hanging themselves. If that mind-control program doesn't happen, the Illuminati warn their people "Remember Tom Collins", who was the son of an Illuminati Grand Mother, who became a Christian, started exposing the Illuminati in churches, and was gunned down in a grocery parking lot. Finally, the members are warned that they will be sacrificed on a cross like Christ in what is termed "a traitor's death." Usually, mind-controlled slaves will police their own actions and thoughts. The therapist may hear their Monarch client talk about the Dove, fire, Moriab, and water as protectors.

They may talk about a little bird dove who is part of protection which flies into the ebony trees. The basic defensive programming placed into the early Illuminati models was based upon the four basic elements; fire, wind, water, and air. When the programming is touched by anyone, the elements of the earth come alive. For instance, if the programming is touched the following programs based on the four elements come alive:

WATER - Victim will freeze like ice, will suffocate like inhaling water, will boil like being placed in boiling water, will feel a dripping on the head, and will flood with memories. This is why some Monarch slaves do not like to swim.

FIRE - Victim will burn inside and outside. The victim will remember fire torture, and perhaps their face melting. This is why some Monarch slaves don't like to light a match or a fire. Slaves will have their programming reinforced with the warning, "If you disobey us, Satan will take your ability to resist burning away, and you will burn in hell." The alters have no way to conceive that God could love them, so they feel if they are to have any chance not to burn in the afterlife of hell they must obey. The fire programs which activate when they disobey reinforce this warning. Often victims report a "Ring of Fire" burning within.

EARTH - The victim will remember being dropped down a well, being buried alive in either hot sand, or a casket. Earth means "life or death". The earth "swallows people up." The victim may feel dehydrated from memories of being buried in hot sand (hot earth). This is why some victims have a fear of being buried alive. In fact, this can be done internally where alters are internally placed in caskets and buried. Alters are also internally thrown into internal wells. The Illu-

{ 289 }

minati programmers say, "Ashes to Ashes, Dust to Dust' to mean that the earth will bring death. Sometimes even volcanoes erupt (earth and fire) out of the ocean (water) and destroy parts of a system. Internal earthquakes also happen quickly and then the entire system will be shifted and shuffled.

AIR OR WIND - Vortexes suck the person down and away, a strong wind takes the alter into the Rubicon of Outer Space and the body dismembers itself as it goes away. The mind doesn't understand why it is being torn apart, only that it is being torn like a tornado. The alter may also go into a bubble and float away. This effect is put in with drugs and hypnosis. They will dissociate and nothing is real. How does one place into a child these types of programs? Let's say the programmers want to put in the Tumbleweed Program where the child feels like it has become a tumbleweed & can't ground and get its bearings on anything. Let's say the programmer also wants the child to lose his arms & legs while being blown away. The child is dehydrated so the mind is overheated and hallucinating. Special drugs are also given to the child to make it more delirious, make it more suggestible, etc. The little child by this point has no mind of its own. Heavy fans with hot air are placed upon the child. It is hypnotically told that it has no arms and no legs. The child is too weak to think for itself. It is almost comatose. The child will be left for perhaps 8 hours as a script which keeps repeating itself is played on a voice box. The child will hallucinate the script or the video it is being shown. When the child can give the script back to the programmer exactly like it is meant to be, then the programmers know they can stop. The child al- ter is to take on the identity of the tumbleweed. If it responds like many Main alters, it will pass this ability on to splits that it creates for this purpose. These splits created for the tumbleweed script will be clean slates for the programmers to manipulate. By the way, smelling salts are used to wake up child victims who are too comatose.

OVERVIEW ON THE PRINCESS PROGRAMMING

The Omega programs prevent integrating the Multiple personalities, and they hold the body programs, and run the computers. If major tampering is done with the System, which threatens to totally wipe out the Omega programs, then one of the backup programs is the Princess programming. The princess programming is a back up program. It can be triggered several ways. One method is by astral communication between loyal alters and their Illuminati programmer. However, the main triggering factor is that the System has recognized that serious tampering has been done to the System. If serious deprogramming occurs, the Princess program with "Sleeping Beauty" kicks in.

The programming is contained within a box, which is opened up upon the appropriate cues. The way it operates is that it kicks in when the handler loses control over a system. The princess who is kept sleeping by spiders which bite her in a coffin, wakes up and looks for the prince to come. Daddy demon and the dark princess are now ruling from the castle dungeon. A System's dwarfs and Thor continue to guard as well as the big guard cats like Beast. Darkness sets in on all the top sections of alters, and thick walls and pain come, then a webbing much like a body-suit-cocoon will envelope all but alters loyal to the master. It becomes hard to breathe and the alters who had sought freedom from the programming, now find themselves being tranced out.

Alters who are cold and in lots of pain are called up by code to torment the body. The Outer Darkness of a System (sometimes called the Rubicon) gets thicker. If Gatekeeper and Kitten alters have porcelain face programming, then they will get their porcelain masks back as the Omega programming kicks back in. The porcelain masks have cords back to the black princess. The black princess's coffin has cords to Papa. The core will give her energy to the dark side, and alters who want freedom will receive very little energy. They will be very tired. Those alters who liked the light side and freedom are now under attack. They will be isolated by walls and then incapacitated by a cocoon which leads to death. The alters who do not want to be part of Satanism will be worked over, and they will continue to be worked over until they shatter. If need be, they can be taken to the castle dungeon and played movies of torture which have been coded and entered into the mind via codes. Internal voodoo will be carried out to scare alters into complying. The worlds will reestablish their compasses.

The internal BEAST computer along with the dark princess run the show. The box which opens up, sets off the suicide programming. The primary tool in fighting the suicide programming is the will to fight. If the will to fight is strong, a way to fight through the walls can be found. If the walls are broken down, then a strategy of isolating the castle's programming can be carried out, and eventually the black princess can even be retrieved. Since the princess and daddy demon are running things via spiritual and demon processes, the battle at this point involves spiritual warfare, although there are probably other methods to solve the situation. The castle programming will be isolated by closing the portals, and other safeguards. The Black Princess can be turned from her course. The castle's power can be shut down. The Princess programming can be beat, but it takes hard work. A system must make decisions to continue fighting the programming with all their creativity, strength and will power. A rebirthing program will go off. This rebirthing program is controlled by a System of clocks. The clocks are the stabilizing heartbeat and are tied to the eternal life force. There are also clocks which control the steps to the Princess Programming. These clocks bring about steps which will take the System down the road to no-return. These clocks can be frozen and by freezing them, one can stop the next step from taking place. In the rebirthing program, umbilical cords and strings run from alters back to the black princess.

The black princess is in the torture chamber of the dungeon and the strings carry the torture memories to alters in sections wanting freedom, especially those holding the body. If those alters want to stop the intense pain to the body they need to freeze those strings and stop the torture memories from coming up from the torture chamber. The umbilical cords are "feeding" the alters from the black princess. The Kittens alters, most likely due to programming, will want to protect the core so they do not want to stop the process of control that the black princess is exerting over them. In other words, they will find it hard to save themselves. Internal Voodoo will come from a doll-house, and only by dealing with inside the doll house can it be stopped. One option is to create shields to protect alters from the voodoo.

Christians have the shield of faith which really can function in real life, and an internal shield of faith has protected and shielded Christians from Voodoo. The darkness and what people (alters) call "walls" can be flooded with the blood of Jesus, which often drives back the darkness and can give freedom to work. The soul ties that are involved with the princess programming and the masks need to be broken and bound. The System may be able to find someone or some place to get wisdom or understanding about their System. The System also needs to cut their soul ties to their Illuminati programmers.

The rebirthing program is also giving directions to the dark princess. There is an umbilical cord which ties the dark princess to the rebirthing program. The blood of Jesus can stop this tie.

BACK-UP PROGRAMMING

One of the backup programs is designed to deal with someone who has a good understanding of a system, and tries to take a system out via spiritual warfare. A camera is designed to reflect an image onto a mirror and the deprogrammer works with the mirror images. The deprogrammer has great success with the mirror images, because the camera can merely shift its view, and the things the deprogrammer is trying to get rid of disappear. However, since the alters that are collaborating with the deprogrammer see all the correct things happen, they sincerely think they are being deprogrammed. When the deprogrammer finishes the alters feel better, see their worlds come together, but the work has only been a sham. Other backup programs provide the deprogrammer with mirror images and sham alters to talk with. The deprogrammer never talks to the real human elements.

If we try to give a summary of the different backup programs we could include:

{ 293 }

- Each grid has programs attached to its grid number and each section has a computer, as well as connecting computers between sections. both the programming and the computers have the power to reprogram themselves.

- The 4 elements of nature coming alive programs

- The princess program (based on Sleeping Beauty)

- A plutonium or atom bomb set up activated by lasers to protect the internal hierarchy.

The Monarch programming creates very complex systems that are as sophisticated as an Apollo spacecraft. There is no way all the possible in and outs can be covered. However, the reader can watch a movie "Labyrinth" to get a good idea of what the end product is like for the mind of the victim. The movie represents what the internal world is like for an alter who is trying to understand its mind. It would be worthwhile to finish this chapter on structuring by covering this movie which illustrates the end product. The bizarre movie Labyrinth may be shown again on HBO and is available from some video stores. In fact, the video stores have a hard time meeting customer demands for this popular video. One of my sources knows a girl who has watched "Labyrinth" twenty times.

"LABYRINTH", A VIEW OF A MONARCH'S INTERNAL WORLD

In 1986, a movie called "Labyrinth" was produced by Cherry McFadden. The movie was scripted by Monty Python's "Terry Jones". The movie is a portrayal of what the internal world inside a Monarch mind-controlled slave looks like. The Monarch slave has an internal world built inside their mind in which the hundreds and thousands of alters must live in. The alters are given a psychotic world of fiction in which they must live in as reality. An alter of a Monarch slave will have two worlds, the external world of reality, and their own internal world which, because of the programming, will seem more real than the real world. Hogel, a gnome, tells Sarah, "Things are not what they seem in this place." The internal worlds of the slave can be shifted and rearranged by the internal programmers.

The internal programmers can change codes, eliminate alters, and carry out extensive deception to other parts of the System. As in the Monarch programming, the movie s castle reminds one of Emerald City. The movie Labyrinth seems weird and occult. Gargoyle elves (similar to coven demons) dance magic and a sweet girl played by Jennifer Connelly moves from one weird scene to another, while an occasional shot gives us the hideous ruler of the Castle played by David Bowie. These demons also guard the baby that represents the innocent core. Monarch slaves very frequently have castles built into their internal world. Some slaves will have a whole series of castles, some are King's castles, some are Queen's castles, and some are castle's shaped liked pyramids with all-seeing eyes in them.

The story line of the movie Labyrinth is that the girl, Sarah, searches for her baby brother, Toby, who is captive in a castle in a dream world. Actually, this represents an alter searching for the innocent core from which it split off from. Often the core (the original innocent child personality which split off personalities in order to remain innocent is locked up in the castle by the programmer who serves as Master of the castle. Often in deprogramming, the core is taken to a castle dungeon in a terrible backup program called the princess program which was just described on a previous page. The princess programming (which is a back up program) functions, when the regular programming goes down (which is rare). When the Princess back-up program kicks in the toad is kissed, the princess core is woke up, etc. etc. Parts of the Princess program seem portrayed towards the end of the movie.

In the movie, David Bowie, who in real life was a Satanist & a rock star who committed suicide, plays the part of the Master of the Castle. The girl soon goes into the dream world (internal world of her mind). She must go through a labyrinth if she wants to get to the castle. Although the movie is fiction, it is close enough to how a Monarch's mind thinks, that an adult Monarch slave might well have his or her programming reinforced if they saw this film. It also would trigger many Monarch slaves and create fear in them. Monarch slaves have many clocks built into their systems. They have internal clock makers and internal clock keepers. In the movie, clocks pop up everywhere just like in a Monarch's mind. Some Monarch slaves are programmed to see their internal world, and others are programmed not to be able to see their internal world. In other words, many Monarchs may not have the ability to see a great deal at first of this programming due to further programming, and yet these images work in the deep recesses of their minds to keep their minds within the confines of the programming.

David Bowie has the magical ability to rearrange time on the clocks. The handlers often mess with the internal and external clocks of a slave, so that the slave is disoriented about what time it is. Alters within a Monarch system are not allowed to stray from the path assigned to them. If they try to move out of their assigned spot in the mind, then they encounter traps, mazes, tunnels and demons just like in the movie Labyrinth. An internal world of a Monarch's mind will have brick walls, doors and vortex tunnels just like in the movie. When the girl falls into a vortex, she has magical hands all over her. Monarch victims speak of what vortexes are like and they often describe hands coming out of no where. The movie begins with an oak tree. The oak tree is an important part of the Illuminati programming.

The Master programmer in the castle, wearing a triangle medallion around his neck and looking veracious (David Bowie) sings, "Voodoo. ..Babes with the power.. .magic spells...dance magic...slap that baby and make him pay....dance magic, dance magic." Cobwebs are built into the Monarch minds, and when an alter goes where it shouldn't they often get cobwebs all over them. The tunnels in the movie are full of cobwebs. As the girl moves forward toward the magic demon infested Castle she comes across many things, all of which relate to internal items built into a Monarch slave's mind. Some of the things are slightly different in the movie than in a slave's mind, but the concepts are the same. For instance, the actual Thor figure looks like the Iron Man of the Wizard of Oz series rather than the iron robot that they portray. But the match is close enough for the imagery to portray what it is meant to represent. During programming, bracelets with pieces will be given to the child to teach them how the alters are to revolve. A bracelet like this is owned by the girl.

The girl encounters a dwarf. The dwarfs in the internal world "mine the jewels" (that is the programming). The Jewels are the particular programs that run a Monarch system of alters of an MPD (DID) mind. The dwarf in the movie is told by David Bowie (the Programmer) that he has "lost his Jewels." that is that he has lost his programming! The dwarf in the movie decides to help the girl. In Monarch programming the dwarf helps an alter by bringing it programming! Some help! The goblin (demon) is asked by the girl to find a portal. The goblin opens a door and it appears to be a broom closet. He opens it again and it appears as a door. This is the exact way the programming is.

Portals and doors in the internal world have cover stories. At first they look like one thing--but if the mind can get by the first look-- they will turn out in reality to be something else. There is cover programming over everything--so that the slave doesn't trust his own mind. For instance, besides lots of clocks undisguised, clocks are disguised in a System as any object, but they can be recognized by the trained observer because they are gold colored. In the movie, objects are constantly changing. Many monarch's fear the rocks coming alive, just as they do in the movie labyrinth. In the bottom of the slave's mind, put in at the deepest hypnotic levels possible are the hell pits.

The movie shows the hell pit and even calls it the "hell pit." Notice that as she goes into this strange world that the clocks can be turned around. This is true in the programming. The clocks can be turned by the programmer so that the slave can be told it is January when it is December. A cover program can be entered so that the slave has memory of what he was supposed to have done in December. These false memories are laid in with real torture memories and tied to emotions. The false memories lack certain characteristics of real memories--and yet still they can at times be difficult to separate from the true memories, especially if the mind-controlled slave is in programming. The following is the story line of the movie as it happens in this bizarre movie. Early in the movie we see a witch with an hour glass. When the girl gets to the castle it is guarded by a mechanical monster that resembles in some ways Thor of the programming. Notice that portals and holes open up.

When they open up another level, protectors attack them and they must run back down their tunnel to save themselves. The Monarch slave will get feelings of being crushed if an alter ventures where it shouldn't in the mind. When the girl asks the dwarf "How can I believe anything you say?" She is told, "What choice do you have?" Fire demons come out dancing. They take out their eyeballs and eat them. They say "Bad luck down the path." What the fire demons represent are the Gamma programming and the threats that the Gamma programming has upon the victim. The programming tells an alter that it will lose its head or other horrible threat if it doesn't comply with the programming. "Let's take off her head" the fire demons say, as they act out the various programs decapitation, delimbing, etc.

They also want to throw her into the pit of eternal flames. They go down a chute into the eternal hell pit. It is even called the eternal pit in the movie! The hell pits of a slave will generally smell like sulfur, which is exactly what the movie's hell pit does. A guardian of the pit (looking like a dog) comes out. Guardians within the Monarch's mind are generally far more horrifying than this dog. The guardian must give permission for passage. Another trap appears, as the slave's internal world is filled with booby traps. The name of the dog the guardian rides on is Ambrosius, similar to Ambrosia. A peach with poison is given to the dwarf. The slave is programmed to fear poisoned fruit. This is another fairy tale turned into programming. David Bowie is called an "adept" who creates dream bubbles. The slave's mind will have adepts who are the programmers. The movie s adept puts a princess in a bubble.

Then she goes by memory back to when she was at a Satanic ball where people wear masks of birds, goats, and pigs. Illuminati ceremonies include balls like this with masks. This love story is reliving programming of the girl that she is a Queen, that she is married to Satan, and that this is a bonding ceremony. Everyone is grabbing her. People who have been to this Illuminati ceremony will recognize it.

Next, she sees mirrors. When she shatters the mirrors (a no-no in the programming) she begins falling. Generally, if a slave shatters the mirrors in their mind they fall into suicide programming. She falls into a junkyard. Then a satanic seed comes alive from her fruit. It is a worm. An old hag gives her a teddy bear. The programmers and parents of slaves frequently give stuffed animals. The teddy bear without hands represents to the victim their helplessness. The old hag says "like a little bunny rabbit...Don't you...Bitsy Boob" All this is Monarch programming stuff. Then she sees a book about the labyrinth.

The Monarch's mind has libraries and diagrams of their own system but these are kept guarded by the mirrors, the demons, and programming. The girl Sarah finds a book (the files) of how the labyrinth is built. Actually, you can too. If the original programming was Wizard of Oz programming, then when you looked at the front of the Wizard of Oz series books you would find a map that helped build the internal world. Some of the items on that map will likely be found in your Monarch system (but not all). If your Monarch system has Star Trek programming it is possible they will have an internal world similar to the diagrams shown in this book where Star Trek programming is covered. In other words, there are books which do show the labyrinth, just as the movie Labyrinth has Sarah find a book showing the internal world.

But if an alter finds a map, this does not mean the alter can travel freely in its system's mind! In working with a mind-controlled slave, we discovered one of the methods to get over the Wizard of Oz mazes was to fly with the Orks. However, an alter caught in the mazes was frightened to stay put by the demons that surrounded it. (This is so well portrayed in Labyrinth.) This happens in real life to Monarch alters which stray into the mazes. They are lost and then they can't come out and take the body. They are simply lost in the mind. The old hag gives her slippers! Slippers are important triggers or cues to go places internally. She is given a horsey and told she loves it. "Take back the child you have stolen." A ferris wheel is shown. Carrousels were used greatly in programming. Then she breaks an hour glass. Hour glasses are internal clocks.

Then she encounters levels, doors and tunnels. An Iron robot representing Thor comes out and bang, bang, bangs. The banging is the split brain headaches that the internal Thor causes the victim's mind to experience. A child is placed into the robot. Often during the programming, child alters are programmed to put on a robot like suit and serve with other children as clone solders in a clone army. The sea divers of the Walt Disney movie "20,000 Leagues Under the Sea" were used to program child alters into how they were to get into robot suits. These child alters form armies that attack if an alter tries to fight the programming. These children alters are like children screaming it is impossible to reason or talk to them.

Armies of these alters are difficult to stop in the mind. In the programming, the brave are told they are not brave and vice-versa. The character says "I have no courage." But is told "You are a man of courage." More clocks and a bell appears. A red and blue guardian appear. Perhaps these colors represent the color programming. Rocks and cannons represent the protectors and the earthquakes they cause internally in a Monarch's mind. When she enters the castle it is a carbon copy of Esher's drawing entitled "Relativity." She runs up stairs and gets nowhere. Escher's drawing, according to ex-programmers, are used for programming.

The Master sings, "Everything I've done, I've done for you." David appears everywhere from every angle. This is how the internal programmers, which are clones of the real programmers appear everywhere in the mind of the slave. He sings, "Just as I can be so cruel...look without your heart beat. ..I must live within you." She says, "Give me the child [the core]" and the programmer says, "I have been generous. ..but I can be so cruel .... I have reordered time...turned the world upside down...all for you." The internal and external programmers can be cruel. The victim is trauma bonded to them. They are cruel and kind to the victim, just like Mengele was to his thousands of victims. The internal worlds can be turned in a Monarch system, by turning the hour glasses which are on X, Y and Z axis.
The hour glasses are turned with hand signals and codes that are similar to what pilots use to tell their degree positions in the sky. The pro-

grammer sings, "I ask for so little, just let me rule you, and you can have everything you want...just love me, fear me, and do as I say." He tells her that her kingdom is great. Internally alters are given great titles, and are made queens, etc. Their internal worlds give them all they need, and that the real external world will never understand them. She is told repeatedly "Your kingdom is great." "Bow down and worship me, and you get everything."

At this point she realizes she has dominion over the demons. When one listens to the programming, it seems that it is powerful and in control. The movie does a good job of showing how a slave's mind has both an internal and an external world. A hall appears with daisies. Daisies were used in programming. When she leaves the internal world, she finds that the internal world is right there with her in her external world. She is surrounded by internal cues. Then she embraces and accepts her internal world toward the ending of the movie. Many systems have an owl in their system which represents the master. In the movie, an owl representing the master appears at various times & then flies away at the end. Toward the end the Master sings, "Power of Voodoo..."

The internal world is full of goblins, dwarfs, worms, a hat, door knockers, Fury 1,2,3,4,5 and many other things. Ravens are in the movie. In real life, the programmers take alter fragments, which are splits which are not developed into full blown personalities and they program them to have a single task, for instance to think they are a raven and to bite the body when ever they take the body.

Whole flocks of demons which take the form of ravens may wait inside the mind waiting for their release to bite the body. When triggered by the internal programmers when an alter crosses the boundaries set down by the programming, a flock of ravens may come forward and "take the body" (as they say in MPD) of the slave and the Monarch slave will bite his or her flesh and viciously tear it with its teeth. By watching the movie Labyrinth, and using this as a guide, the viewer will begin to understand the horror and control that the internal world holds over the alters of a Monarch slave.

Few Monarch slaves ever tell other people what is going on in their minds, now you have been privileged to find out. To learn this much for a Monarch slave comes with a high price. The price is paid by re-living for a second time what has been done to them, fighting off the suicide programs that click on when the slave's mind disobeys. The slave must also fight off torture memories that recycle. These torture memories are activated by the programming when an alter disobeys its programming. As one Monarch survivor described it to me, "This all can be wrapped up by defining it as the raping of the body, soul and spirit."

THE STRUCTURING DONE IN MONARCH STAR TREK AND STAR WARS PROGRAMMING

The original Monarch programming often used the Wizard of Oz books and film as the basic programming. The Alice and Wonderland story then was overlaid, along with many other fictional fairy tales to complete the Mind Control of a Monarch Mind-controlled slave. However, in recent years a superior story line has appeared. It has more flexibility and more secrecy. This is the Star Trek series. In re-cent years, Star Trek is being used as a basis of programming. Those who are programmed with Star Trek programming can attend annual Star Trek Conventions which are held in New York City since 1972. The child's mind is tortured until the point they will accept anything.

They are told to build certain structures in their mind. These struc-tures may be castles, or rivers or submarines or airfields, etc. In the case of Star Trek programming they have detailed maps and diagrams that have been created to go along with the Star Trek program. The real reason or the ulterior motive of these Star Trek maps was to cre-ate a blueprint for programming. Then particular alters are placed within these structures, and they are hypnotically given cues that will pull them to the front of the mind when the alpha-numeric cue is said. Many of the more secret alters can only be accessed by a combination of several different cues which go to different senses--such as the per-son must be in a corner contacting 3 points, a certain ring must be turned & a certain code said for the alter to come forth.

The advantages of the Star Trek story line is that
a. almost any type of scenario can be fit into the programming script because the Star Trek characters in the series, encounter about anything imaginable,
b. have holograms, which can serve as substitutes for mirror images in the programming,
c. alien programming can be introduced in order to promote the mock alien invasion being planned by the Illuminati, and
d. the Star Trek series has its own language which can be used for trigger codes, which Monarch slaves can study, and learn. The use of this Klingon language will make it very difficult for ordinary people to break into the slave's programming.

Michael Aquino, Satanist and Colonel in the U.S. army, has enjoyed using Star Wars for programming. Aquino wrote his own version of the Star Wars, which he uses for programming. The programmer becomes Darth Vader, which then is reproduced as an alter within the victim. In the Star Trek series, Data was a dehumanized "person" who stored vast amounts of information. Monarch slaves are always created with libraries, and volumes of information. This information is stored in various ways and can be retrieved in a variety of ways.

Data of Star Trek lends himself to become the model for an alter of a Monarch system to copy. In other words the child is shown Data, and is steered in the right direction to create an internal person named Data. Any child if it is drugged, tortured, threatened with death if they don't follow directions, with weakened and confused minds will get to the point where the child will create a Data alter in its mind, rather than die. Once in place, the Data alter will think of itself as the movie character. Every time the child sees Star Trek or pictures of Data, it will reinforce the programming.

The transporter room technique of beaming in Star Trek is what magicians have tried to do for centuries and which has been called "biolocation" or "physical projection" as well as other things. This is said in magic to be mental control over the molecules of the body via demonic power. Whether magicians have ever done this, who knows, some certainly claim the power. The Illuminist is a power structure placed into some Monarch slaves. It is constructed from parts of numerous demons, rather like a demonic Frankenstein, & is portrayed in Star Trek, the Next Generation as the Crystalline Entity.

A cartoon series was created for Star Trek. In this series, children watch such things as Kirk in a magical universe of Megas-2 which has a Guardian of Forever. Two other spin-out shows were Deep Space Nine and Voyager. In other words, a child could watch 5 different Star Trek series. If the child's parents had cable T.V. the child be virtually immersed into the various Star Trek shows. Unfortunately, some of the children who have been programmed with this are doing exactly that.

One source has personally worked with someone who has Star Trek programming. They sit for hours and immerse themselves totally into all kinds of Star Trek details. We have two Star Trek Technical Manuals. This source's father is an engineer and designed quite a few things, they have worked as a manual/computer draftsperson for the Federal Highway Administration as well as for their father off and on over the years. Based on that experience, this source realizes the enormous amount of work that went into these Technical Manuals for the Star Trek series is simply mindboggling. One manual is 183 pages and the other is in the neighborhood of 250 pages. The amount of engineering and computer drafting that went into these manuals is astonishing. Why did someone go to such extremes?

These manuals are as good as if NASA were planning to build an Enterprise spaceship. The plans are done more professionally than engineering designs that we have seen groups like the United Nations drawing up. Why did all this engineering, design and drafting happen for a fictional T.V. show? To create a book to sell? The books.. could hardly be best sellers. One originally sold for $13 U.S. and the other for $6.95. One reason so much work and money was put into these Technical Manuals is that they are used for programming helpless victims of the Monarch Mind-Control.

EXHIBITS AND DESCRIPTIONS OF WHY EXACTLY THESE EXHIBITS ARE IMPORTANT TO THE PROGRAMMING

<u>Exhibit 1.</u> Star Fleet Technical Order. (TM:379260-1)
This page show codes on the far left that are similar to the type of codes used in Monarch access codes. Alters are trained to take the body upon the proper access code. Also certain activities or programs can be triggered by codes also.

<u>Exhibit 2.</u> Uniform Color Code. (TM:379260-0)
In creating a System within the slave's mind, geometric shapes are used. Within these shapes a number of worlds or universes will be created. These worlds can be 3-D. That means when building them in the child's mind they can have height, depth, and width. One system which I have seen several times in slaves has been a 13 x 13 x 13 cube. In order to give another dimension and to give the programmers the ability to tie different things in different parts of the system to-gether--the programmers use color coding. Each alter will receive a color code. I am familiar with the standard color coding program, and how it is put into the child's mind. Dr. Green (Mengele) used a box of colored scarves and electroshock to program in the color coding into victim's mind. Besides alters, other things in the system may be color coded also. Let's say as Programmers we place hidden observers on each level, system or world. Then we can tie those isolated alters together by color coding them the same. During the programming, computers are built into the mind to operate the programming, and they send their signals according to color coding.

<u>Exhibit 3.</u> Milky Way Galaxy Map (TM379260-2)
This is just one of a number of maps that go with the Star Trek programming. During the programming (which is sophisticated torture of all kinds backed up w/ drugs) the child's mind will be encouraged to psychotically build worlds in his or her mind. These worlds are built with vortexes, mine fields, and in the case of Star Trek programming Radiation zones. If an alter would attempt to wander from its assigned spot in the mind, it will run into Radiation zones, walls, and other barriers. These zones are built into the mind, to insure that the multiple personalities do not contact each other. Aliens and holograms protect certain areas and prevent personalities from freely moving around in the mind. These "aliens" are placed into the vic-

{ 305 }

tim's mind by high level demonology--in other words they are not aliens--they are demons which have been brought in by high level rituals.

Exhibit 4. 4.1 Computer System (p.50)
The first thing created are the multiple personalities. Then these personalities are placed into a structured system. To operate that structured system and to insure compliance the Monarch programmer will put in what is called Omega programming. Omega programming consists of computers, wiring, conduits and cords. The most important part are the computers. These computers contain the instructions, and they are controlled by internal programmers who may be alters or who may be high level demons. The aliens (demons) who are placed strategically in the mind to keep the Omega programming intact are put in by sophisticated high level demonology. The high level demonology part of the programming is the most secret and it is termed Gamma programming. This is a diagram which could be used to help build into the child's mind a computer. In the early programming, a little girl while being tortured would be shown a multi-roomed dollhouse. The rooms would each have a separate color. The rooms would be linked in the child's mind to computers. In other words--the dollhouse structure was the structure the computers used. In the Star Trek programming, the modern child simply is given a multi-roomed computer like the one drawn.

Exhibit 5. TM:379260-3 Engineering - Main Bridge Section
Various methods of communication and travel within a Monarch system's mind will be built in. Various alters are allowed contact with other alters. Portals and one-way mirrors or one-way windows are built in also. In order to teach an alter to come to the front of the mind, an airplane taking off on a runway might be used as a visual aid to teaching how to leave the alters cubicle in the mind and come forward to take the body. Various internal communication system's can be built into the System. The training manual is full of many possible communication and locomotion devices, and this is just one of a whole number of items that could be incorporated into a Monarch child's mind as it is programmed.

Exhibit 6. Utilities pg. 82.
The brain stems are scarred on babies and when the body rebuilds itself it overcompensates and the brain gets an incredible memory. Monarch slaves with scarred brain stems are running the computer systems for the New World Order. If the slave has a photographic memory as many of them do, then a specific chart like this utility chart could function as the blueprint for the mind when it creates its power packs. Power packs, and energy cells (sometimes put in like light bulbs) run the computers which are built into the slave's mind. This is part of what is called the Omega programming.

Exhibit 7. TM:379260-2 S.I.N.S.
Base Datum. This is a coordinate system. In the early years the Monarch systems were built with 3 hour glasses each spinning on a x,y, or z axis. The hour glasses could be turned and in so doing the entire system of alters could be turned. Let's say that we have a slave and we have created great Christian front alters. Now, we decide that the time has come to use the dark Satanic alters full time. Since the dark alters are hidden at the bottom of the system, we need to rotate the System 180 degrees so that the Satanic alters are now on top. Now the Satanic alters will receive extra energy to be out holding the body full time. This SINS Base Datum is a way of making a coordinate system for a Monarch System. Certain codes would then be given the System to make a shift when the handler needs to turn a System.

CHAPTER EIGHT:

THE USE OF BODY MANIPIULATION TO CONTROL A PERSON

THE SCARRING OF THE BRAIN STEM

Early on it was discovered that the brain would overcompensate for scarring on the brain stem. This is a principle similar to weight lifting. By tearing down the muscle fiber by overexertion, the body rebuilds the muscle stronger. By scarring the brain stem, it -was discovered that geniuses who had photographic memories could be created. Brain stem scarring was used to create the whiz kids that the NWO needed to run their big computers. For instance, the computers that just NASA alone uses require people who can work in ALGOL, BASIC, COBOL, COBOL 74, MULTICS COBOL ver. 4.4, COBOL Cb.4, COBOL CP-6, BOL, EULOR, FLIP, FORAST, FORTRAN, HAL/S, Illiac 4, JASP, JOSS, JOVIAL, /LYAPAS, LISP, LISP 2, / MAP/, NuSpeak, PASCAL, PEARL, /PLACE/, PL/1, PL/1-APAREL, PLANIT, Praxis, SA Machine Language, SEMANOL, SNOBEL, UNIX, WANG, ZBIE. It takes a good memory to remember computer languages and programming. These whiz kids, who were both programmed with Monarch programming and had their brain stems scarred can be seen in some of the university computer departments and the intelligence/military agencies' computers rooms. The CIA which has had an ongoing project to create them, has called them "Compu-kids."

For instance, at Ft. Meade, the NSA has 2 buildings which contain a completely self-sufficient intelligence operation. The complex has its own stores, bank, dry cleaning, dentistry, barber shop, PX, hospital, as well as the normal snack bars and cafeteria that Federal buildings often have. This complex which is internally guarded by cameras watching all the corridors, has several major computer rooms where whiz kids are employed. Movement by these whiz kids, requires that they have the proper I.D. attached to them. Some of the elevators are private and operate only with the proper key. The NSA's computers participate in electronically watching the world. Another example of where Compu-kids work on big computers, including a Beast computer, is at Area 51 (Dreamland), NV. The method of scarring the reticular formation of the brain stem is accomplished electronically.

The RNA piles up and breaks the continuity of the signals coming through. Different people's bodies are able to tolerate different levels of abuse. Many of the brain stem scarring victims die, or end up with a pseudo-Multiple Sclerosis. Many children are coming into hospitals and being misdiagnosed as having Multiple Sclerosis when in fact they are damaged from programming and brain stem scarring. If the victim is successfully given a photographic memory through their entire alter system due to brain stem scarring, then they are often programmed to see what are called "hieroglyphics", that is the cover name, which is really just the 'Intergalactic Language" that NASA developed in the 1960s under the cover of research projects like N67-3042 (17 p. 3022) "Language structure and message decoding for interplanetary decoding." in 1967 and N65-32284 20-3414 in 1965 entitled "Symbol science for communication language of humans, animals, and inanimate objects --application to mathematics, cybernetics, and automation." Then they turned around and used it to program slaves with photographic memories.

The actual study number for the Intergalactic Language is not known, but it should appear somewhere in the voluminous scientific and Technical Aerospace Reports that NASA puts out each year. The script of this language was shown in the beginning credits of the strange movie Lawnmower Man. Some of the symbols are similar to the ASCII computer language, which is a language that interfaces with many other computer languages. This means one language can be translated into another language. The Monarch slaves are told that this is an alien language.

Another method that has also been used to enhance memory is hypnosis. Estabrooks was able in the 1930s to create multiple personalities via hypnosis and get incredible mental feats accomplished by those parts which were asked under hypnosis to have photographic memories. Still another method is to place small transceivers into the head or body of the person. These implants have been attached in the neck or other places, and have been connected to various parts of the brain. They have literally created what the movies called "terminal man." This has allowed special intelligence agents to be linked to large computers. The intelligence asset can get continuous information on anything the intelligence agencies have managed to get into their large computers.

Brain implants can down load incredible amounts of information to the brain, however, the ability to use this information wisely is still a skill. Having a library of information available doesn't necessarily mean a person is wiser. For more on slave-computer interfacing see the information on ALEX, Amalgamated Logarithmic Encrypted Transmissions, and UNIX systems which are used to tie the Monarch Mind to computers. Drugs and torture are also used to enhance memory. Brain stem scarring is not the only method to enhance memory, but it has been a "highly successful", if one doesn't count all the ruined lives when it's failed. MPD also naturally increases the brain's functioning several fold, and can help give photographic memories. In review, drugs, torture, hypnosis and MPD all work to enhance memory. Most slaves have some photographic memory capability. The most serious form of memory enhancement is brain stem scarring, which produces a strong system-wide photographic memory.

SPLIT BRAIN WORK

The brain is "bicameral" or two-sided. The two-sides, called hemispheres, communicate via a super powerful connector called the corpus callosum. The left hemisphere is specialized in verbal-linguistic transduction of speech and analytical thinking (logic, math, cause & effect, language, & sequential thinking). The right side plays more of a role in holistic-metaphorical information transduction such as imagery (art, dance, intuition, subjective, spontaneous, holistic, & dream imagery). The primary role of creating imagery is carried out by the right side. Roger Sperry, a neuroscientist won a Nobel Prize for feeding information to only one side of the brain, and also for feeding simultaneously both sides of the brain different information.

His results showed that the two hemispheres could operate separately at the same time. We hate to rewrite history, but the work that won Sperry a Nobel Prize was being done to unwilling human victims before his publicly known experiments. Sperry's research left people wondering if it wasn't possible to have one personality located in one hemisphere, and another person in the other. Psychologist Julian Jaynes wrote a book arguing that mankind used to have two personalities before the two hemispheres evolved an ability to integrate. (His book is The Origin of Consciousness in the Breakdown of the Bicameral Mind.) Before the public had heard about the ability of the two hemispheres to work independently, the Illuminati and MK-Ultra programmers were carrying out split brain programming, by two methods:

1. shutting down one side and communicating only with one side of the brain, and
2. by simultaneously feeding different information to each hemisphere.

This is often done by the victim being locked in place with their eyes forced open, and different movies shown simultaneously to both eyes. This creates a form of split brain programming. High speed films will be shown with one hemisphere receiving horror scenes and the other getting family settings. This makes the two hemispheres work separately and the victim feel crazy. The mind feels ripped apart. One hemisphere is trying to dissociate and is having a miserable experience, while the other side is experiencing something just the opposite. When high speed films are shown for split brain programming, the films are shown in 5 minute increments. Front alters may be shown good films to make them believe they live in a perfect world with a good family life. Right side satanic alters may receive horror films shown via the left eye.

The right side of the brain doesn't verbalize well, so this is one reason slaves have emotions without the ability to verbalize. A possible third method is to use drugs that block the two hemispheres from communicating. A fourth method in split brain work is to speak into the left ear while giving the right ear confusing noise. This last method is sometimes done to force alters to concentrate when learning scripts. The split brain programming done by the Illuminati is grotesque. A drug is injected at the base of the skull into one hemisphere of the brain to shut it down, while the other hemisphere is kept awake. Torture is then carried out to split the mind. What this does is create programs and alters which are associated with only half of the brain.

The brain is being further divided from itself. Work is done by the Programmers to develop the thinking of alters from one side of the brain to think differently from those of the other side. Split brain programming is not just hypnosis, as some have been led to believe. Split brain programming provides the Programmers one way to keep the left hand from knowing what the right hand is doing. It also gives them the ability to put in body programs or memories which effect only half of the victim's body.

When one hemisphere is dominating in what the brain is doing, the opposite nostril will open and take in air. When the right hemisphere is doing most of the thinking, the left nostril will be doing most of the breathing. Voluntary changes in nostril breathing can help shift the center of brain activity from one side of the brain to the other. When a person lays on his side, the downward side hemisphere will be activated, because the top nostril will breath best. The control of nasal breathing has been part of the Yogi's art to achieve Samadhi. The distinctions between the two hemispheres or two brains are used by the occult world. Moriah values the intuitiveness of the right hemisphere.

As one Illuminati mind-control programmer said, "It's the right brain that has an inbuilt propensity for accessing timelessness. There is bound to be some unconscious prompting therefore that alerts us to the imminence of forthcoming disaster, that is, if we are sufficiently sensitive to its message...unless we have the wisdom, the soul age, to affect the use of those additional facilities, to access right brain knowledge, we will find our intelligence sadly limited to the left brain logic of the material world." While this book is not about occult philosophy, occult philosophy is part of the motivation behind some of the split brain work. In order for the Illuminati to create alters which are highly intuitive and which are able to access the higher demonic spheres, they need to shut down the logic hemisphere. When the left hemisphere is shut down, then the right brain, which controls the left hand and left side of the body, is able to function without competition.

The victim must be able to get in touch fully with his or her intuitive side to go into the "spiritual dimensions" where demons exist. This is very nasty work, because this split brain work involves high level demonology. Most of the deeper Illuminati alters are right brain alters so that they will be very spiritually intuitive. The Lesser Key of Solomon is an important teaching book of the Illuminati. It states, "An adept enters an abnormal plane and equips himself to 'charge' with magical energy the pentacle and talismans." The training that this takes is called "training of the higher will" and split brain programming is part of how it is accomplished.

MEDICAL TECHNOLOGIES

Medical science has been probing the gray matter that makes up the human brain for several hundred years and they continue to probe it. With the use of various new techniques they can look inside the human brain in ways that were not available before. An enzyme called horseradish peroxidase (HRP) which serves as a marker or highlighter allows brain researchers to visually look at brain cells on functioning brains. Researchers such as Frank Putnam, at the National Institute of Mental Health, have taken PET scans of the brains of people with multiple personalities, whose brain scans from one alter personality to another are very different. This doesn't occur in non-multiple people who pretend to have different personalities. The brain scans have shown that brains with multiple personalities are physically different than other people's brains.

The different personalities are often in different neurophysiological states. Medical science has helped the programmers put people into different neurophysiological states for programming. Some of these states are dangerous unless trained medical personnel are available to insure the victim doesn't die. Which, according to ex-Programmers, does happen anyway. Medical science has identified glutamate which is an amino acid as an important neurotransmitter involved with memory storage. However, after countless tests and all types of research, we still do not know completely how the brain stores memory. However, the NWO's Network understands far more than they have let the public learn.

HAVING SKILLED MEDICAL LAB TECHNICIANS

Having the medical know how doesn't get the job done in itself. Obviously, the Network has needed to have both hospitals and trained medical personnel. Having skilled workers is part of the success of the Monarch Programming. For instance, the simple interpretation of Alpha BFT instruments, requires that the operator be able to understand what is background interference. Everywhere the instrument is located there is going to be some amount of background interference. Only the good operators can realize when a pseudo-alpha wave has been produced, perhaps from the child sweating in the location of the electrode, or hair movements, or eye blinks or twitching. The Illuminati has their own midwifery training program, which will take teenage Monarch slaves and train them. They also begin training their people in programming and observation from infancy up. By the time they are an adult, the programming alters know programming as second nature.

They have no shortages of doctors, nurses, psychiatrists, and other well educated people. If they have to save an important Monarch slave, they may fly in a specialist from wherever the right specialist is. When it comes to research, some of it done by professionals who don't realize how their research is going to be used. Many researchers are great on seeing detail, but not the bigger picture. They usually don't realize how their research is going to be misused, and are very gullible people. The CIA finds that the researcher is quick to justify in his or her mind the moral value of the research they are doing.

Many members of the Illuminati are involved in secret genetic research.

Having control over numerous big hospitals, is an important link in the ability of the Network to program so many people successfully. Medical personnel are participating in acts that help mind-control. One Christian nurse quit the University Hospital here, because newborns are secretly being given implants. A few years ago, it was discovered that The Upjohn, an American multinational company was involved in placing radio transmitting material in with their liquid cortisone preparation Depomedrone, which created an implant when medical personnel put Depomedrone into their patients.

HISTAMINES

Histamine is a chemical (a particular molecule) which the body uses to defend against alien cells. It also has the ability to lower blood pressure and to flare up the skin.

The auditory sense can effect histamine production via programming. Histamine is a molecule which is part of the immune system. Changes in histamine levels effect moles. It effects skin changes in scars. This is how the abusers can magically make scars appear and disappear, which makes the programming seem even more real to alters. The abusers like to create invisible scars that form patterns and pictures. The most popular is the Baphomet head (which stands for Satan). Upon command they can trigger the skin to make these scars visible. If one pricks someone's skin with a needle having histamine on the tip, it will cause the skin to flare up red. Biofeedback has allowed people to mentally talk to their skin. Hypnosis has controlled people's immune system. States of mind effect the immune system.

Somehow a combination of these is used to allow the handler upon command to trigger the correct state of mind within the victim to increase histamine production within the skin area. The bone marrow of the body produces stem cells. The stem cells are capable of growing into many different types of cells. First the stem cells grow into some basic different cells and those in turn grow some more and further differentiate. For instance, a stem cell can become a myeloid, which can become a polymorpho nuclear granulocyte which in turn can become a basophil or mast cell. Both basophils and mast cells are leukocytes and they are part of the body's immune system. Both basophils and mast cells are carriers of histamine. Histamine does several things in the body.

Histamine causes dilation of blood vessels, and it allows blood vessels to become permeable (leaky so to speak) which allows other chemicals and fluid to go through the blood vessels into the area between cells and tissues. All CNS (Central Nervous System) cells of the body have receptors that the histamine can attach itself to like a ship docking. When cells are damaged, or alien cells enter the body, the basophils and mast cells release their histamine. For the body to have more histamine, it must increase the number of basophils and mast cells. This can be accomplished by changing the ratio of stem cells that develop into other types of cells.

The core of the histamine molecule is an ethylamine. Antihistamines are molecules that resemble histamines enough that they can attach themselves to the histamine receptors on regular cells and prevent the histamine molecules from attaching. If the histamine molecules don't attach, the body disposes of them. The point being that histamine remains in the skin only so long before the body disposes of it. Histamine levels in the body can raise IF the cells which carry the histamine are increased.

It is believed that breast implants have some kind of effect on raising histamine production levels in the body. Whether these breast implants are identical to what all breast implants are, or whether they have something special to agitate the body into higher immune cells' production of the mast cell & basophils type is not known. However, there seems to be some relationship between the Network's need to raise histamine production in their slaves, and the breast implants that they are putting in them.

Putting the pieces together leads one to believe that the implants agitate the body's immune system into raising the level of its histamine carrying cells. A number of women who have gotten implants speak about an increase in allergies. The allergic reaction is caused by high levels of histamine. Whether this happens to some or many is not known at the time this is written.

The three big Illuminati chemical companies are I.G. Farben, DuPont, and Dow Chemical. Dow Chemical began research with implanting silicon in 1956. After 35 years of studies in which they implanted thousands of various animals with silicon, the company knew exactly what silicon would do in the human body.

The FDA had public hearings in 1992 where internal documents of the Dow Chemical Co. were released which showed that the company knew all along that their breast implants were very dangerous, years before they put them on the market.

There is an incredible search going on for an anti-silicon antibody so that they can clean up the mess they have created in millions of people who have silicon implants. The immediate chest wall and area around the breast implant gets highly agitated. The silicon leaks through the membrane, and then causes great difficulties in the body. Many of the female Monarch slaves have received breast implants.

BODY PROGRAMS

Researchers have come a long way toward understanding the mind. They have discovered, for instance, that under stress the brain will convert nerve signals into "messenger molecules" who then in turn direct the endocrine system to produce steroid hormones, that can reach the nucleus of various cells and cause them to change how the body's genes are written out. These genes will then direct the cells as to how to make a variety of molecules which are used in growth, metabolism, sexuality, and the immune systems. In other words, the mind can rewrite genetics.

This was the secret that helped get the Monarch program off to its scientific foundation. Now the actual mechanics of this have been observed by researchers. One of the leaders in understanding the mind-body relationship was Franz Alexander. Black was one of the researchers into how hypnosis can be used to regulate the body and the body's functions such as the immune system. Ken Bowers also worked in this area. Dr. S.M. Lambert of the Rockefeller Foundation studied how voodoo could cause death by creating certain thoughts in the mind. Most of the research in this area was monitored, if not sponsored by the Intelligence agencies under the auspices of the Illuminati. The Hypothalamus bridges the mind and the body. It works as part of the Limbic-hypothalamic system.

This system is a determining center for what state of mind the brain is placed in. The immune system communicates directly with the hypothalamus part of the brain with its own "messenger molecules" known as "immunotransmitters". This then is mind-brain link that the Monarch programmers have taken so much advantage of. Barbara Brown, a physiologist at Veteran's Administration Hospital in Sepulveda wrote a book New Mind, New Body. Barbara Brown's research was government funded. Her book got the public interested in biofeedback. Because of repeated success at getting patients to control such things as their heartbeat, Dr. Brown is convinced that a person's heart rate, breathing, muscle tension, glandular responses are all subject to a person's will.

Those who have worked with victims of U.S. government MK Ultra mind control know that what Dr. Brown writes is correct and was known years before she published her book. Biofeedback is now required training in some prisons for some inmates. It is clear from the final results that Monarch slaves have programming which can carry out the following functions:

- Control the pulse rate and heart beat,
- Control the body's temperature
- Control the temperature of individual body parts or sides of the body--such as the right side of the body might get hot, and the left side of the body get ice cold. Fritz has observed this by touching the left and right sides of a victim who was burning hot on the

{ 319 }

right and ice cold on the left.

- The secretions of various enzymes and histamine production has been trained into the victims and attached to various body programs to keep the slave in line. Histamine production appears to be regulated via surgery carried out on women's breast. It appears, but hasn't been confirmed that the surgery where breast implants are placed into female Monarch slaves plays some role in histamine production & programmed control.
- Allow the body to pretend that it is dead, when actually it is in an altered state similar to being comatose.

The internal defenses consist in part of body programs that are triggered if the Mind-controlled slave steps out of line. Here is a good list of some of these body programs: Auditory problems, a Bone disorder, Blood flow/circulation, Coma (zombie death sleep which makes victim appear dead), Digestive failure, Headaches-split brain, Heart failure, Histamine production, Optic problems such as blindness, Respiratory failure, Sleep deprivation, Sleeping program, and Temperature change. Body programs will be put in across the board for all alters.

The same code will work for all alters when the internal programming alters want to trigger a body program. If a body program is placed into the slave it may be anchored to something, and that might be as drastic as the heartbeat. One of the programs causes the victim to hear a heartbeat which is referred to in their minds as the "heartbeat of Satan." Some of the body programs are carried out by creating an alter which has one mental state, such as an alter fragment which is burning or one that was created by ice torture.

This alter or this feeling of being hot or cold is then attached to something in the mind. For instance, if the victim moves toward the world, a cold alter or a cold feeling of a memory is hypnotically programmed to come up behind the alter holding the body. Sometimes the sensation of burning can be eliminated by getting a fire child to back up from the front of the mind where another alter is holding the body. Many feelings, body sensations, and drugged states are attached to programs.

When the alter hits these attached programs it will go through a series of memories, false memories, hypnotic commands, and body sensations that have been attached together in stringers. The stringer type of programming is often put in to set in a front program which is to deceive an alter. The abilities of the human brain to control the body have been seriously underrated by people.

Bio-feedback researchers in the 1960s were surprised to find out that if a single nerve cell's activity is placed upon a screen so that the subject can see its activity graphed, the subject will be able to mentally identify that cell apart from any other nerve fiber cell, and will be able to have voluntary control over that single cell apart from any other. Just to show how complex the body is, a single nerve fiber cell will have 600 connections.

This mental feat is simply mind-boggling for researchers. The Mar. 5, 1972 L.A. Times reported that patients were being taught how to alter their heart rate without drugs. This had already been happening within the Monarch Programming. The heart is controlled by the mind and works with the emotions of a person. There have been people who have literally died from a "broken heart." This is a historical fact. The Monarch programmers have long been taking advantage of the mind's ability to control the heart's beating. A tiny little bit of tissue not really visible to the visible eye called the sinus node, sends out electrical signals that regulate and initiate heart beats in an unbroken rhythm. The genetic code concerning the body's metabolism and the genetic code for the sinus node somehow get the entire heart beat generator mechanism started.

Two areas of the brain control the changes in heart beats that the sinus node would make. The sinus node sends out the signals but it doesn't change the rate. A very primitive part of the brain stem is one of the control areas, and the other control area along the spine. Both of these areas connect to the higher thinking areas of the brain. The three most frequent events that change heart beat are emotions, sicknesses, and muscle activity. Since the will of the slave influences emotions, the higher brain can control the heart beat and its pulse.

{ 321 }

Alters are programmed so that they will trance out if anyone tries to prove to them that they have a heart, which they have been programmed to believe was taken away from them by the programmer.

The occult world learned this ability from the Indian yogis who have been controlling their hearts for centuries. Some have even shown in the scientific laboratory that they can stop their hearts for up to 30 seconds, see Green of Menninger Foundation's work. The yogi's also developed the skill of changing their body temperatures. For instance, Swami Rama in the lab of Dr. Elmer Green could make one side of his palm hot and the other side of his palm cold simply by mental efforts. This type of body control was learned by the Illuminati years ago, and has been applied to the Monarch programming to make the programming lies seem more real to the victim than the outside world.

A Monarch slave can get cold on the left side and burn on the right side of his body. It has been well-documented that the mind can control the blood flow to various tissues and in this way change temperature in various different parts of the body. This was first reported to the public in 1978 Barabasz & McGeorge.

It appears that a combination of yogi type bio-feed back techniques along with classical behavior conditioning is able to account for some of the body programs in slaves. Other body programs appear to be connected to the memories of alters. For instance, if the Programmer wants the body to burn--he has the System pull up an alter which was tortured with fire who comes up behind the alter holding the body, and the body then abreacts and feels like it is burning.

As mentioned, one technique is the split-brain programming where the functioning of the two hemispheres of the brain are separated, which allows the patient to feel the "right hand path" and the "left hand path" separately. This type of programming is very powerful in making the programming script seem more real than outside reality.

High blood pressure or hypertension has been found to be largely a function of the mind. However, conventional medicine has ignored this for years, and has a large volume of confusing and misleading research to the opposite.

Rather, than admit the cause, the medical establishment has labeled the largest percentage of hypertension cases as "essential" or "idiopathic" which are labels to cover up that they don't know (or refuse to recognize) the cause of the high blood pressure. At any rate the cardiovascular system, heart and blood vessels, etc., is so complex that it has been very difficult for researchers to get a grasp on many issues involved in blood pressure such as the release of hormones into the blood, and the result of long term stress on the cardiovascular system. When tests show that the stress of unemployment increases high blood pressure problems among men, it would seem that the medical establishment would begin to see the link that the mind has with controlling blood pressure.

Again bio-feedback and classic conditioning have been successfully used to radically change a subject's blood pressure. This along with the ability to go into deep trances, are abilities that the Monarch slave is programmed to have to control their blood pressure.

The question may be, why would they condition a slave this way? Because, if the Master can call out a hypnotic trigger and change the slave's heart beat and blood pressure, does the reader see how "puppet-like" the slave feels? The slave's mind and body are literally owned by the master. The slave is not even allowed to control his own body. This is what total mind-control is all about.

PATHWAYS

The medical profession uses the term "pathways" to describe the ways the mind creates biochemical and physiological changes. In other words, how does the mind consciously decide to change its body? When medical researchers began to understand how the two hemispheres worked, they began to understand better how to facilitate mind-to-body communication so that they could program the slave's mind to control its body. One of the better books on this subject is The Psychobiology of Mind-Body Healing by Ernest Lawrence Rossi. Rossi and Erickson devised a three-stage approach to accessing the person's inner resources for therapy.

This type of hypnotic-induced healing is a clue to part of how the Body programs are structured in for body control by the programming. What some use for good, is used by others for evil. During the hypnotic work, Rossi uses what is called the "inner mind" of the person. For instance, to get a person to stop bleeding indirect hypnotic suggestions are made in the following 3 stages:

a. a time-binding introduction of "Why don't you stop bleeding? Now!"

b. there is an accessing of state dependent unconscious processes that can control the bleeding, and

c. there is a response by the person which ratifies that the inner process of stopping the bleeding has actually happened.

The hypothalamus is a very small part of the brain. It is only the size of a pea, but it contains an immense amount of important tissues which control all types of inner activities of the body, including the endocrine, the immune, the neuro peptide and automatic systems. It is this area of the brain which is manipulated by hypnosis. The limbic-hypothalamic system is in a constant process of shifting what state of mind the brain is in. There are numerous unconscious and conscious states that can be shifted to. These are labeled "psycho-neuro-physiological states" because researchers now realize how a state involves the entire person. All learning is associated and depends upon the state it was learned in! A new sense organ was discovered, and US. News & World Report, July 19, 1993, p. 61 reported on it. We do not know when this tiny sense organ, which is located in the nasal cavity, was discovered by the people doing mind-control, but it is already being exploited.

This organ responds to chemicals called pheromones, which play an important role in human emotions, such as fear, hunger and love. Human skin gives off odorless pheromones which other people can detect. Basic human drives are controlled by Pheromones. Endorphin is a peptide, of which at least 50 have been charted. By manipulating these chemicals, people can be biochemically put into a different state of mind, and victims have been manipulated by these chemicals. These chemicals are being used in conjunction with Virtual Reality to control slaves' minds.

In the March-April '94 edition of "The Futurist" the author Glenn F. Cartwright, of McGill University announces in his article "Virtual or Real? The Mind in Cyberspace", *"Strangely, the developers of virtual reality seem largely unconcerned by the possible dangers inherent in launching individuals into another reality."* This is because Virtual Reality is being developed as another tool of mind-control. Computers can dynamically control and synchronize all that needs to be coordinated to give someone a virtual reality experience. The researchers/programmers are trying to immerse as many of the victim's senses into their virtual reality trip as possible. It becomes almost impossible to distinguish reality from the trip for the victim of this type of programming.

McGill University, Dr. White's (Cameron's) old stomping grounds did some virtual reality research. People are now getting involved with what is called MUDs (multi-user dungeons) where a person via virtual reality can create a parallel life. Some people are spending up to 120 hours a week immersed in their virtual reality second life. In 1992, Internet had 207 such games. Now the programmed slave only needs to hook into Internet to be programmed.

Cartwright's article warns that a person's ego-center can be projected somewhere else via virtual reality, which destabilizes one's actual understanding of where their own identity is. He also warns that Virtual reality will create other personalities. He writes on page 24, "Multiple Identities" *"If it is possible in virtual reality or cyberspace to enter an altered state, become disembodied, swap genders, create a virtual ego-center, de-center the self, and assume a different identity, then it may also be possible to assume more than one identity at the same time. In this context, the exponential increase in multiple-personality disorders in recent decades may be of more than just passing interest .... having multiple, serial, and simultaneous perso-*

nae in cyberspace may not only be possible, but may even be encouraged as a part of interacting with others.''

Virtual reality via the computer Internet has now become another tool of the Programmers.

MUSIC

Dissociated tones, beats and music may accompany hypnotic induction drugs. Pulsing beating sounds in the ears can change the brain's waves. It is no secret that music will put someone into an altered state. Music will change moods, heart rate, and even one's state of consciousness. In a home church setting, that a source participated in, the question was asked of a group what they do to overcome depression. Everyone present listed "listen to music" as one of the things they do to overcome depression. Sound will change body chemistry, blood pressure, breathing and digestion. (See Jacobson, Steven. "Media Mind Control", Media Bypass, Sept. '95, pg. 50).

To quote Jacobson, *"Fast music will speed up the nervous system while slow music will slow it down. Sounds vibrate in different parts of the body. Low tones will vibrate in the higher portions and on into the head. Much of today's popular rock music is built around a heavy bass pattern louder than the melody. These low-frequency vibrations reverberate in the lower parts of the body so that the music 'feels' good. These loud, low-frequency vibrations and the driving beat of most rock music affect the pituitary gland, which controls male and female responses. The repeating sound pattern induces the hypnotic state of mind that is similar to day dreaming, thus clearing the mind of all thought so that the message can be implanted in the unconscious without resistance. It is important to note that the lyrics of many rock songs are not clearly distinguishable consciously. When you do not hear the message clearly, you cannot make the conscious choice to accept or reject it. When you cannot make that choice or when that choice is taken away from you, the message is programmed directly to the subconscious, thus circumventing analysis and choice in accepting the content of the message. Sixties rock superstar Jimi Hendrix said: 'You can hypnotize people with music, and when you get them at their weakest point, you can preach into their subconscious whatever you want to say."*

Long term exposure to the heavy metal themes of sadomasochism, Satanism, suicide and drug abuse can only have a negative influence on the minds of the listener. Today's generation of children are being raised on this type of music. Many of the big rock bands consist of Satanists. This statement isn't made flippantly, but from having learned from many witnesses of the rituals these Satanic bands participate in. Some of these Satanists, as the reader can already guess, are programmed multiples. For those programmed multiples who participate in heavy rock music, they are simply adding one more type of bondage and mind-control to their already long list.

The spiritual damage done by rock music will be briefly addressed later in Chapter 10.

PROGRAMMING DAMAGE TO THE BODY

Many of the body programs that activate via trigger codes are simply memories of severe torture. For instance, the victim might be placed naked on a block of ice, which contains the body of a frozen person., This is a common trauma used in programming. When this memory is triggered, via an alter or alter fragment, the victim's body abreacts and gets very cold.

Another common torture is to stick a ureteric catheter up the external urethral orifice, whose channel is called the urethra, this is painful. Then the urinary bladder is filled so that the victim is in extreme pain, and is made to hold their bladder in silence. This torture to the body is painful. But the long term effects of this torture, which is done repeatedly to slaves to teach obedience, is to seriously damage their urinary bladders.

The abreaction of memories of this help blackmail alters into obedience. The body of many slaves are only kept functioning, because they are given repeated surgery by doctors working under the auspices of the Illuminati. These doctors can be trusted on to keep quiet about the abused bodies they have to keep fixing. It was mentioned in Chapter 2 that some people suffering from autism are failures in mind control programming. We know of one case where a brilliant autistic teenager who'd not talked during childhood began talking, and shocked his parents because he began talking about his spirit guides (See Chapter 10 on Spirit Guides.)

Some people diagnosed as MS are really failures of the mind control's brain stem scarring. Many hundreds of women with breast implants are coming down with symptoms that look like MS & Lupus. This may be because part of the women with implants are programmed multiples. Another disease that is believed by some to be caused by programming failures is lupus (aka lupus erythematosus or systemic lupus erythematosus). Establishment medical science claims that the cause of lupus is unknown. Modem Maturity (April/May '93) & Nations Business (May '93) are examples of magazines that have run articles about Lupus. Ronald I. Carr and the Lupus Foundation of America put out a handbook on the disease in 1986. The director of the Lupus Foundation has been an Illuminati programmed multiple.

The effects of the programming are not just in the mind. It has been scientifically shown that the torture memories are embedded in the cells of the body. In fact, the Illuminati intentionally wants the body injured by trauma pains & trauma memories, because they want to prevent the possibilities of the sanctification of the body such as written about in 2 TM 2:2 1. Also, the Programmers intentionally & zealously prevent the deeper alters from wanting to love as 1 COR 13 describes.

PHYSICAL ASPECTS OF THE HUMAN BRAIN

Neurobiologists and chemists have learned a great deal about the physical aspects of the brain. One has to be careful about simplification. The concept of the split brain has been over simplified, because the best researchers on the two hemispheres know that there is constant interplay between the brain's two halves, unless the Illuminati have tampered with someone's brain. The split brain concept has been replaced with the Penta-Brain, something akin to a pentagram.

The Penta-Brain takes the triune concept of the brain conceived by brain scientist Paul MacClean and adds it to the split brain hemispheres and the duality of the frontal-posterior dimension also. In this process, "mammalian" & "reptilian" brains (those parts of our brains that mammals & reptiles also have) are accessed and worked on in people.

The best description read by one source of the intricate chemical changes that happen during Learning and Memory is a Special Report entitled "The Chemistry of Learning and Memory" Chemical & Engineering News, Oct. 7, 1991, pp. 24-4 1, by Karen J. Skinner, Yale Chemistry Ph.D. in '73, Masters from Kennedy School of Govt., Harvard. This is a very technical report. The programmers do not learn this material, but those who want to understand the nitty-gritty molecular-biology of how the complex memory processes work in the mind might want to try to study the report. In very basic terms the report is communicating that Neurons, nerve cells (of which the brain has 10 billion), meet each other at junctions , or gaps called synapses. At the synapses, neurotransmitters allow them to communicate.

There are 60 trillion synapses. As a person gathers information, the brain changes the synapses, in a sense rewires itself. Part of memory is how the brain "rewires" itself, to use a layman's term. Genetics have an important role in the initial hardwiring of the brain. Genetics also determine receptor diversity, at the synapses, which relates directly to learning & memory because it increases the ways neurons can perceive, process and recall information. The Hippocampus has been found to play a role in long term memory storage. The Hippocampus stores memory in the cortex to be encoded into long term memory.

Numerous areas of the brain are busy with processing only one type of memory. In a macaque monkey, around two dozen distinct visual areas of the brain for memory storage have been discovered. In other reports, it has come out that memory is stored holographically. German researchers have been trying to figure out at the Max Planck Institute for Brain Research at Frankfurt, Germany what mechanism is used to bind the many various parts of information stored into a coherent recollection. The point that should be made at this point, is that an alter does not exist in one spot in the mind.

The mind perceives that an alter does, but an alter in terms of physical change in the brain is actually a multitude of synaptic changes scattered throughout the brain. The brain's concept/image of an alter and the dissociated state can be played with by the programmers, but they really don't kill alters like they pretend to do during programming. Alters can't be "killed" in the mind. As the mind consolidates info, it fires neurons in harmony (in phase) called a "binding" process. Perceptions which are not memories are initiated this way. It is these perceptions that exist without memories that are so important to the programmers. Some have called these perceptions "global unity" of the brain. These are in phase frequencies from 40 to 70 Hz. NMDA receptors can perceive patterned firings from nerve cells that are active at the same time, which allows the brain to strengthen some synapses and let others grow weaker. Synaptic efficacy is called LTP. Interested readers can study LTP's molecular mechanism, etc. in Karen Skinner's Report.

Changing subjects slightly, let's discuss how Moriah fertilizes two zygotes and intentionally kills one of the twins in the womb. Studies have shown that in cases where one twin dies in the womb, the other twin usually tries to lead two lives. This has nothing to do with DID (MPD), except that the surviving twin will later be made into a programmed multiple. The Illuminati doctors have perfected a method to kill a developing twin so that the other engulfs it in the womb. This is skillfully done, and creates some interesting mental changes in the survivor. Moriah also believes that it endows the survivor with twice the spiritual power.

CHAPTER NINE:

THE USE OF MIND MANIPULATION TO CONTROL A PERSON

One way to explain how the slaves are conditioned is to relate an episode where the author and a source observed a Satanic family carrying out conditioning to reinforce their children's mind control as their family "ate" at a restaurant. After relating this interesting incident, the chapter will cover the various psychological methods used to condition slaves.

OBSERVATIONS OF A SATANIC FAMILY CARRYING OUT MONARCH CONDITIONING ON THEIR CHILDREN

The husband of the family was about 28 and the wife was about 26. A young man (perhaps an uncle of the children) about 25 also sat at the table with them. The family had 5 children, ranging from about 1 1/2 years old to about 7 years old. During the entire time we watched them, which was over an hour, we never saw one act of love, not one act of nurturing on the part of the parents. Everything was programming, programming and more programming. The husband had an attitude of control over his children. He was a young somewhat wild cock-sure type. From piecing together things it was clear that he made a good salary and that he and his wife enjoyed profanity. His wife had the most dead looking eyes we have ever seen in a person. She looked every bit the part of a Satanic priestess of the worst type.

The young man of about 25 had very large knife hidden on his back that we noticed only by close observation of his movements. Although it was 1 o'clock, the adults were calling their meal "breakfast."

The main male child was about 5 years old. He had an older sister

{ 331 }

and two younger sisters, and they all had a baby brother. During the entire time that the family was there, the children ate almost nothing. The 5 yr. boy munched on a watermelon rind, trying to draw some sustenance from it. Part of mind control is depriving the body of food. The poor children never once asked for anything; that is a clue that something wasn't normal.

During most of the time that the family was in the restaurant, the mother and father took turns shooting one question after another at the five year boy. The questions were like:

- What is the capital of Florida?

- What is the 70th element on the periodical chart?

- What are the names of the first five presidents?

- What is the square root of 121?

The boy would robotically answer each question successfully. The questions were not questions but programming and commands. The mother sternly said, "What make of car was that? That's a question." Actually what she was saying was a command. Around this time they said, "Wake up, wake up, wake up" a hypnotic command.

A couple which was in the restaurant was watching how obedient the children were, and they were also overhearing how excellent this little boy could answer difficult rapid-fire questions. They were impressed and the lady came over to tell the parents how wonderful their family was.

After oodling for 10 minutes over how great this family was the woman went on to other things. It was difficult for both of us watching to stomach the compliments this stranger was giving to these parents. The natural impulse was to get her to shut up her compliments. She naively made all these compliments little knowing, that these parents were practicing one of the most hideous if not the most hideous type of mind control invented. Asking questions rapid fire is another mind-control technique. In fact, all of the elements of what we watched at the table that day were practiced on my source, when they were in Beast Barracks at West Point, USMA.

The little girl was repeating her programming, "I don't have anything inside me." She was actually singing it. One of the girls had different alters coming out and was having a conversation with herself between different alters (personalities). She placed her hand over her temple in scarecrow fashion (Wizard of Oz programming). Her head movement was a dead giveaway to those of us familiar with Monarch programming. The parents had chosen the spot to eat because of the large surreal picture above them on the wall with blue & red flowers, water and mountains.

The picture was acting as a scrambling-scattering mechanism when the boy studied the picture, which he did for the longest time in a trance. The middle girl was dropping crayons into a foam cup and saying "get into the fire." Then she would say "I'm purple." "I'm pink." "I understand your purple." "I understand you're pink." "Get out of here for a minute." What she was doing was giving the crayons personalities.

In the Monarch programming, the person is totally dehumanized so that some alters think they are ribbons, some monkeys, some clowns, some dolls, some trees, some lions or tigers, etc. The sexual alters are often programmed to think of themselves as cats and butterflies.

While the girl was coloring, her father reached over the table without warning and took her colors, "You don't deserve these colors and I should have taken them away before now. The girl had done nothing wrong. This is part of mind control. The person learns that there isn't a right or wrong only that they must be obedient. The little girl did not even respond when her colors were yanked away. When the mom talked to them, she said "children"--she never once personalized things. The parents began another programming session and said something like, "I will spank you. If you don't count then you can be spanked, we will count 20 times."

The constant double messages were obviously breaking down the children to think as programmed rather than respond like normal people to the outside world. The woman turned to her little baby and said, "Tell daddy good-bye". When the child waved good-bye, the woman snapped, "You're not going anywhere." This serves to create confusion. Then she kissed him and said, "Baby, do you want a picture?" We decided to say something to them, and we did so in the form of a compliment about their children. Neither parent showed any pride in the children when the earlier lady had gushed compliments about the children, nor when we complimented them with a sentence. Instead, when we complimented the children, the father began shooting off a series of difficult questions to the boy.

This was simply more programming, but apparently he must have thought that we'd be impressed with the boy's ability to answer difficult questions that seemed way beyond what many teenagers would know. Two strange things happened during the course of our verbal interaction with this satanic family. First, the waitresses had given the family free ice cream coupons, but the parents gave them to us without the children even batting an eyelid. Second, I asked the father what the age of his children were and he didn't know, or acted like he didn't know. Then he blurted out, they are 1, 2, 3, 4, and 5 years old. His wife knew that that answer must have looked bogus to us, and she reprimanded him, "You don't even know the age of your children." To which he replied, "Yes, they are 2, 3, 4, 5, and 6." The second answer was equally implausible, but his wife didn't protest, and the poor mind controlled children were experiencing just one more element of Satanic mind-control. They are not even allowed to realize how old they are.

Dates, and times, and ages are kept very confused in the children's minds for secrecy and control. Not only that, but by giving a hypnotic induction "1, 2, 3..." the father had lowered each of the alters which were holding the bodies of his children into a deeper trance. With these alters tranced, another word from the father could have easily pulled up other alters.

OTHER THINGS THAT PARENTS DO TO THEIR MONARCH CHILDREN

Double bind communication is commonly given multiples by all of their abusers. Some of these double binds are well thought out and some just occur due to the craziness of the entire thing. For instance, in ritual or programming, the child may have the option to stab or be stabbed. In fighting the programming, if an alter goes toward health, the programmers have set in a booby-trap. Which evil does the slave live with the lies of the programming or the lies of the external world? How does one tell the truth to a therapist, when the therapist is not capable of hearing the truth, and yet still demands to be told the truth? Yes, double binds abound. Another trick is to alternate leniency with harshness. This trick is done in the military also, and has been worked with success by the Chinese government upon the people of Red China.

When leniency is alternated with kindness, the effect is devastating and disconcerting because the person looses the ability to predict what is going to happen. Everyone likes to control his or her life. Predicting what is going to happen is part of a person's mind gaining control over their environment. Even that control is stripped from a slave. They soon learn to quit trying to protect themselves, and they quit trying to think for themselves but docilely submit to whatever fate assigns them. The mind can't figure life out, so it quits trying to understand life, and just fatally submits.

Dr. Green (Mengele) was very gentle when drawing blood, and he was very gentle when giving the children X-rays. He would sweet talk them and give candy. But he was very sadistic when he'd follow this up with abuse. The programmers have preferred to be inconsistent with the children like this. Soon the child doesn't know what hate and love are anymore. The person, who claims he loves them, gives them torture or abandons them to be tortured by someone else.

A third trick is to give the victim monotonous tasks, such as chanting or copying long amounts of written material. This helps prod the dissociation, and is a torture that doesn't leave marks.

AN OVERVIEW

All of the elements of mind control are incorporated into the Monarch program. If a person surveys what the everyday cult mind control which is NOT part of total Monarch mind-control looks like, you will find the same elements of everyday cult control also are employed at various places within the Monarch programming of a person's alter system. This didn't happen by accident either, the Illuminati have examined all these lesser cults to see what they could borrow for their own mind control. Some of the elements which the Monarch program shares with other typical types of cult mind control are:

- THE NEEDS OF INDIVIDUALS ARE PROMISED TO BE MET, BUT ARE IGNORED FOR GROUP GOALS - The Illuminati handler/master will promise to meet individual needs of alters, but these needs are ignored for group goals. For instance, certain Monarch alters of a person's system may be told they have no faces and no hearts. They are programmed not to see their faces and not to hear any heart beat. If a pulse monitoring machine is hooked up to the alter, the alter will go into a trance. For instance, the handler might promise faces and hearts but will never give them to the Monarch slave when he could. The promise is a control mechanism.

- ISOLATION FROM THE WORLD SO THAT THE ONLY REALITY IS THE LEADER'S REALITY - The Illuminati isolates the slave so no new ideas are available or allowed except their cult leader's ideas. "Whatever the Papa Bear (master) says is reality." Each alter will only communicate with a few other alters. What this does is divide the person from their own parts. The will and mind is broken so that there is no organized resistance, nor any access to other alters who might know something. The slave will often be denied mother, grandmother, grandfather, aunts, sisters, children, grandchildren, & friends. They will be deprived of all naturally occurring relationships via the mind control. This doesn't mean they exist in a vacuum, it means that the handlers will prevent natural relationships to develop. Isolation is very key and parts are made to feel like animals rather than people to isolate them from humanity. No ideas are allowed the slave to confront their programmer's lies. They are programmed to hate Christ and the God of the Bible, so that they are isolated from the true God and His abundant spiritual resources.

• THE PERSON'S SENSE OF IDENTITY IS LOST - The Monarch slave loses his/her sense of self to the cult and to the person's master. No sense of where I begin & end, and where the Master begins and ends. The Monarch programming goes beyond what many cults have done, the alters are hypnotized to not see their faces, which is part of their identity.

• ALTERED STATES AND HYPNOSIS ARE USED - The handlers/ programmers use hypnotic techniques. They induce dissociation by songs, chanting, guilt inducing sessions, torture, isolation, as well as using songs, repeating triggers 3X, and lots of hypnosis.

• A SENSE OF PEACE IS INDUCED, ESPECIALLY WHEN ONE MERGES WITH WHOEVER IS LEADING THE HEAD OF THE CULT - They induce a sense of peace leading to the fantasy of merging with leader, often suggested by leader. Then the victim has the abuser placed internally in them. For example, the master may say he was one with the slave and that he "created" the slave. The handler will claim to be God.

• OUT OF BODY EXPERIENCES - Out of body experiences (O-B-E's) are induced by the torture & Illuminati training, as well as splits.

• SENSORY BOMBARDMENT AND FATIGUE - Sensory bombardment used, such as prolonged sleep deprivation, environmental control, and love bombing. Cages, love bombing of certain alters, and a sterile nursery/toddler room are employed.

• CRITICAL THINKING AND DISAGREEING WITH THE LEADER IS FORBIDDEN - The slave must suspend ability to think critically or disagree with leader. The slave must never question the Master (also called the handler), never get angry at the handler, or else the slave wants to be punished. The slave must always obey or pay with pain. The alters are splintered from others so can't use their information for analysis.

- THE SLAVE MUST REORGANIZE REALITY THROUGH IDENTIFICA-TION WITH AGRESSOR - Strong identification is created with the master. The slave is programmed to protect the master.

- PROGRAMMING OVERRULES SELF - Individual sees locus (location) of control with the Master rather than self.

ISOLATION

For children who are being taken out of Day Care Centers and programmed without their parents knowledge, they will be isolated from their real parents. The abusers will tell the children that they are actually the "real parents" and that they intend to come and take the child away from its parents later. They will make the innocent child feel like it is cut off and rejected by everyone including the world at large. In a sense, this is true, because the child is expected to endure the most horrible abuse and yet has no one to talk to. Feelings of isolation and despair take control over the child's mind. These ways of thinking are also spiritually enhanced by rituals to bring in demonic spirits that will help insure the child is dominated by feelings of hopelessness.

During the entire life of the slave, the handlers and programmers are always trying to sow distrust in the victim. The programming is often designed to sow distrust in everyone on the outside except the god-like figure the Master. Even the Master is not trusted so much as feared and obeyed by the slave. The slave is also subjected to isolation as a child being placed into freezers, closets, dark rooms, boxes and isolation tanks. Sensory deprivation is a serious thing, that has been discovered to cause people to hallucinate. The brain goes into an altered state just from sensory deprivation. Polar explorers who see only white for days on end must deal with this danger.

HANDWRITING MODIFICATION

Psychology developed over the years a number of projective, objective and subjective tests of personality. Ludwig Klages (of Germany), H.J. Eysenck (of England), and M.N. Bunker (of the U.S.) are some of the notable researchers who took handwriting analysis out of the occult realm and into the scientific realm. One source happens to be a certified Graphoanalyst through IGAS, who has done Graphoanalysis professionally. IGAS has strict standards not to allow members to do anything associated with the occult, but insists they keep their work on a scientific basis.

When a person writes, he will use about 200 separate muscles in the hand, arm, and body. The mind coordinates all these muscle movements. A good handwriting analyst has about 800 different things that he can look for in a sample of handwriting, such as how hard did the writer write with his instrument, how big, where did he start on the paper, how did he cross his "t" etc. In other words, the mind in order to write had to make hundreds of decisions within seconds.

There are too many decisions to make them all consciously. This is why document examiners can authenticate signatures. Most of the many decisions as one writes are done subconsciously, and the decisions are influenced by state of mind, personality, the state of the physical body, and the environment. The good handwriting analyst is able to work backwards. Why was the decision made to make the capital P look like an L? Why did the person start their writing halfway into the paper and waste half the piece of paper? Through scientific studies and observations, a vast wealth of understanding has developed by graphologists about why certain decisions are made. Some graphologists use a holistic method, others like graphoanalysts, analyze each stroke.

Both methods will give the same results if the handwriting analyst is skilled at applying the principles of graphology. Handwriting analysis has not gotten the credibility it deserves, in part, because it is such a powerful diagnostic tool, the intelligence agencies have wanted to keep it to themselves. However, the nation of Israel, uses handwriting analysis to hire with, and a high percentage of the businesses use it in hiring also. The nation of Israel has had a high rate of success with handwriting analysis. How does handwriting analysis play a part in the mind control? Several ways.

A number of the programmers are skilled in handwriting analysis. They are well aware that the abuse of their slaves will show in the handwriting. Through behavior modification (usually torture) the front alters are trained to write in a fashion that hides the abuse. The abuse will show in the handwriting of most of the alters, so many of them are programmed not to read or write. This is why some of the child alters will have older alters write for them.

The programmers were also aware of how the mind heals/changes itself via handwriting therapy. If the mind will place enough energy into writing a particular way it will go ahead and put enough energy into becoming what it writes. In other words, if I am lazy, but I get determined enough to focus the brain so that it doesn't make hand-writing strokes that indicate laziness, then my brain will also change its lazy attitude in other ways. In other words, I can begin to change a personality trait by working on the handwriting decisions that stem from that trait.

The programmers can, and do, help modify their slaves' personalities this way. They of course will employ a number of personality chang-ing techniques as a group package. The goal is to bring as much pres-sure to bear as possible to get the original trait modified. This will be done in accordance with the programming goals for the various alters within a system. Remember, some alters need to be outgoing and other reticent, some melancholic, and others sanguine or choleric. The programmers know what they want and how to modify what they have to get the temperament and personality traits they want.

BEHAVIOR MODIFICATION

Behavior modification comes in various packages. One package has been called ELT (Electrolytic Treeatment) developed by H.C. Tien. One simple version of behavior mod is to find out what someone has done which is good, and praise and reinforce that behavior. Then state the goal. And then continue to reinforce promptly the good things the person is doing. The goal in mind must be measurable. An example of this, might be for a handler to praise his kitten and to purchase it nice things if a client is satisfied with the sexual service he got. The reinforcement needs to be soon, and appropriate. "Thinking behavior" is a term that behavior modification scientists use. "Adverse conditioning" is another. Anectine, which paralyzes the body and makes one think they are suffocating, can be used for aversion conditioning.

The victim is told not to do a particular behavior or else experience discomfort. When behavior modification is done in programming, you can be sure that there is paper work done to chart the progress. Rather than worry about what a person is thinking, the behaviorist charts a person's behavior and then gives reinforcements of correct behavior, or the opposite adverse rewards of punishment, to modify it. Victims are conditioned to carry out certain behaviors. If an alter does something wrong, there is an immediate consequence set up for it. Soon it is conditioned not to do what the programmer doesn't want. The behavior modification scientists believe that creativity can be controllable. When a child creates a new form he is rewarded. Soon the child learns to create.

Illuminati Delta/Beta alters will be trained in espionage. They will be trained to recognize a person's physical identity instantly. One method of training which has been used is to teach people to remember reflexively rather than analytically. Thousands of faces or thousands of license plates, or whatever are flashed on a screen, and when a repeat is shown the person must press a button. If a mistake is made, the slave is treated to a nasty little shock. After a while a person develops the correct reflexes. Slaves are being trained in recognition from the time they are small children, this is important so that they can build their internal worlds with mirror images and other confusing things. The following "deeper" programming is an example of classical conditioning:

The child's hand is cut so that the child goes into a trance of shock, and then each time they use the word "deeper" they cut deeper to enhance the shock/trance state. By pairing the word with this trauma, when they are through, the word "deeper asleep" will throw some alters instantly into a very deep trance.

PSYCOLOGICAL MOTIVATION

When a person has been knocked down and degraded, traumatized by poor sleep and little food or water, he is more susceptible to sugges-tion. He can then be told that he himself is the cause for his own deg-radation. If he just behaves better, his treatment will improve. When the person accepts his guilt for the bad situation he is in, then the pro-grammers give a target for the blame, God, country, or whatever else the person had depended upon.

The programmer then aggravates these hostile feelings, and keeps nurturing them until the person is livid with anger toward the object of blame. The victim is coached to project their blame onto this target of blame. When this is accepted, the conditions for the victim im-prove.

Once the person has targeted their blame, then the Programmer be-comes the friend to help one fight the evil target. Anything and every-thing is rationalized in this "All becomes fair in war." Enemies are easy to create. People readily accept them. The intelligence commu-nity has long played on people's fears about communism. People might be shocked to realize that this was one of Hitler's favorite methods to recruit loyalty from people. It is why the Nazi's secretly burned down the Reichstag, and then blamed the communists. The Illuminati are masters at making Christianity the fault for everything from homosexual suicide to the world wars.

NEURO-LINGUISTIC PROGRAMMING

NLP means Neuro-Linguistic Programming, which are practical com-munication skills. Programmers were using NLP before it became known as NLP in 1976. Some NLP techniques are obvious truths, and some are more subtle truths in dealing with human nature. NLP can be more of an art, than a science. One of the truths in NLP is

"Everyone lives in their unique reality built from their sense impressions and individual experiences of life, and we act on the basis of what we perceive our model of the world." (O'Connor, Joseph & John Seymour. Introducing NLP. San Francisco, CA: Aquarian Press, 1993, p.4.) That is why alters have their worlds created by their programmers, and then the occult alters are indoctrinated with satanic beliefs.

Let's list some other "assumptions" that NLP practitioners believe in without explaining them:

- Almost all communication is non-verbal.
- Knowledge of content is not required to make behavioral changes.
- Our internal representation of the world is not the world but only our own feeble map of it. The map is not the territory.
- People will choose predicates which correspond to what representational system they are using, and which one they choose can be seen from eye accessing cues.

If one studies NLP, one will find that NLP books such as "Basic Techniques Book II" by Clifford Wright, teach people how to create dissociative states which are alternate personalities, and that they teach people how to develop different states of mind, and pseudo multiple personalities. It is difficult to express all the different crossovers that NLP has with Monarch Programming, but at different times the concepts of NLP certainly would be helpful to the handlers. However, it must be stressed that NLP is **NOT** Monarch Programming. One of NLP's suggestions is that a person assess their "present state" and their "desired state." This simply common sense suggestion is often carried out during programming.

The Programmer will tell the victim what kind of alters they want produced and how many when they begin the torture. The motivation to do this is also suggested by NLP and is accomplished by the programmers threats to the person's life, and by the person's desire to be free of pain and torture. Milton Erickson's work on altered states has been picked up by NLP. Likewise at least part of the programming hypnosis is based on Erickson's ideas.

CLUES FOR OBSERVING A VICTIM

Lateral Eye Movement (LEM) can be a useful skill to the programmer. Monarch victims are sometimes programmed so that the real LEM is not done publicly by the victim, to prevent people from getting visual clues as to what is going on in their mind. A person who is thinking in visual images will generally speak more quickly and at a higher pitch than someone who is not. These types of clues help the Programmers be more skilled, but it isn't a necessity.

ANCHORS

NLP researchers have noticed that people have emotional states in which the entire body will take up a posture in carrying it out. Memories can come into a person that causes the body to take up the negative states again. The NLP practitioners have developed language which includes such terms as Anchors, emotional states, and triggers. These words are used to describe ideas that have long been in use.

For instance, let's say that when you heard a particular song at some point in your life you were having a good time (emotional state). Now that every time you receive a trigger to that memory, such as the song, you regain that good feeling that is attached to the memory of the song. Every time you hear the song, you feel good, which then in turn, continues to act as reinforcement of the association of a good feeling to the song. A stimulus that is linked to and triggers a physiological state or emotional state is called an anchor. Our lives are filled with naturally occurring anchors, such as our favorite childhood smells, or the alarm clock.

One of the Illuminati kingpins in Germany, a Krupp, liked the smell of manure, and built his house so he could smell horse manure all day. NLP is the art of building associations with an anchor. A past emotion can be linked to something today. If a person is afraid of public speaking, then a good feeling can be linked to giving talks. The skilled programmer will anchor an emotion with several sense cues, including auditory, visual, and touch. The person visualizes an emotional state from the past. When the state is reaching its peak, the anchor is placed in. The anchor needs to be unique, distinctive, & easy to repeat in the exact form that it was done.

Much of the trauma-based programming is actually setting anchors using extreme trauma. When the anchors are tested (fired), if the emotional state is pulled up, then the anchors have worked. Firing two separate anchors at once is called collapsing anchors. Two separate states can be fired at once. There is a methodology for collapsing anchors together.

FUTURE PACING

Future pacing can be used to help program a person toward his occupational objective which was charted for the victim when they were small. Future pacing is a mental rehearsal that is practiced in the imagination so that the person can deal with some future challenge. Expectations can often become self-fulfilling prophecies. NLP also is used to teach people how to learn. It teaches people to learn a variety of methods for a single skill. However, this type of self-help info is not freely given to the slave. It might be used if the programmers needed to develop the person hypnotically in a certain direction.

PACING FOR HYPNOSIS

Because Milton Erickson stands out as a genius among those who have used hypnosis, and people are still trying to figure out fully what he did, it is appropriate to mention his work.

We don't know how these ideas of Milton Erickson's are used by the Programmers. We do know that the CIA has. paid close attention to his ideas, and that some of the Programmers have some of the smoothest tongues. If there is some way to utilize Erickson's work to help control Mind-controlled slaves, then the Intelligence agencies have no doubt found it.

On the flip side, several de-programmers used Erickson's methods to

{ 345 }

unlock the programming of the people they want to help. What we describe in this section is just a small sampling of Erickson's methods.

He [Erickson] would gain rapport with anyone by describing to them what they were feeling, hearing and seeing. He would induce a peaceful state by speaking slowly, using a soft tonality, and pacing his speech to the person's breath. Gradually hypnotic suggestions are introduced to lead them into what is called "downtime." He would gently encourage people with gentle suggestions such as, 'It's easy to close your eyes whenever you wish to feel more comfortable..."

But you may wonder how can anyone know what someone else is thinking? Erickson developed language that was vague enough for people to match their own thinking to what he described. He would use smooth transitional words such as "while", "and", and "as". The type of vague sentences he would say are "It is well known that people can read books and make changes."

Milton Erickson learned to distract the dominant brain hemisphere, and also speak in a complex way that all seven (plus or minus two) parts of the conscious mind would get engaged in trying to figure out what his ambiguous statements meant. Milton found that he could say anything if he set it up in the context of someone else saying it. He also found that the unconscious mind does not process the linguistic negative. Rather than tell a child "Don't fall" tell it "Be careful."

REFRAMING WITH METAPHORS

Metaphors, some from Druidism or from some other occult teachings, are used by the Programmers. For instance, the seasonal changes that leaves on trees make is an example of a programming metaphor.

For those readers who don't know what reframing is, the following in the book "Reframing, Neuro-Linguistic Programming and the Transformation of Meaning" by Bandler and Grinder (Moab, UT: Real People Press, 1982) is an excellent story to explain it:

"A very old Chinese Taoist story describes a farmer in a poor country village. He was considered very well-to-do, because he owned a horse which he used for plowing and for transportation. One day his horse ran away. All his neighbors exclaimed how terrible this was, but the farmer simply said 'Maybe.'

"A few days later the horse returned and brought two wild horses with it. The neighbors all rejoiced at his good fortune, but the farmer just said 'Maybe.'

"The next day the farmer's son tried to ride one of the wild horses; the horse threw him and broke the leg. The neighbors all offered their sympathy for his misfortune, but the farmer again said 'Maybe.'

"The next week the conscription officers came to the village to take young men for the army. They rejected the farmer's son because of his broken leg. When the neighbors told him how lucky he was, the farmer replied, 'Maybe.'

The meaning of an event depends upon the FRAME we place upon it. Those frames are perceptions. Occult fairy tales are great for reframing events. A frog turns into a prince. Rudolf's embarrassing red nose becomes a guiding light to bring happiness to people. Many of the common things in our everyday life are reframed by the Programmers to have hidden mind-control meanings.

The Teddy Bear the child is given by her Daddy is to remind her how helpless she is to prevent him from raping her. The carousel toy is to remind the child of dissociation and the internal carousel built into the mind.

Many of the things that parents, who are intentionally raising a programmed child, do, look nice on the outside unless one can reframe what they are doing in the context of total-mind-control based on trauma and fear. Reframing can be done by collapsing anchors. For instance, the sober part of an alcoholic and the drunk state of the alcoholic are given the same anchor and then these are collapsed together to get the drunk to stay sober. The two states are taken in a process of integration for the reframing to occur.

Reframing someone with MPD is almost impossible without integration, but reframing a particular alter with metaphors is not out of reach. The programmers have much more chance to reframe while they program than the therapist, because the programmers set in defensive programs to prevent other's from reframing.

POWER WORDS, REVERSALS AND PUNS

In NLP, seven senses are taken into consideration. First we see, then we hear, and finally we have the senses of internal kinetics and our emotions. The Programmer also takes into consideration what are called "power words". Those are words which have specific meaning for the person. The programmers also love to use reversals and puns, for instance in Disney's "Ducktales" the character says, *"I stole 'em fair and square."* Other typical reversals are "Life is death, and death is life", "Pain is love, and love is pain." Another example is one used on Cathy O'Brien, where the words "Service Entrance" were used to mean "Serve us. En-Trance." Naming an alter "Allison Wonderland," a pun on Alice in Wonderland, is another example of a programming pun. The programmers love to use these types of things.

THE MIND'S NATURAL ALARM CLOCK

The programmer's have made use of the mind's natural ability to wake itself up like an "alarm clock" if it wants. Slaves may be given the coded message that the draconian enforcer will come by to pick them up at 1 AM The slave will automatically wake up in the middle of the night, and in a trance like sleep walking, a deep LGP alter will take the slave out to the street to be picked up. Many slaves are being used at night without their families suspecting anything. Sleeping patterns are also related to personality. REM sleep is believed to help restore the effectiveness of certain brain pathways in which norepinephrine is a transmitter substance. By programming different alters to have certain sleep patterns, their personalities can be adjusted. Of course this is done in conjunction with many other aspects of mind control.

THE RIGHT BRAIN AND THE UNCONSCIOUS

The Programmers are also aware that right-handed people use their left brain hemisphere for highly conscious processes which require good attention, focus & intentional decisions; while their right brain will tend to work on the unconscious & automatic chores. Split brain programming takes this contrast into account.

CHAPTER TEN:

THE USE OF SPIRITUAL SYMBOLISM TO CONTROL A PERSON

The spiritual for programming laid by the programmers are the generational spirits which are laid in the womb & introduced to the child when verbal as the child's "friend" & "spirit guide." A clan's guiding spirit is also called a totem. The keepers or guardians protect the spirits within an Illuminati system. There will be one alter which knows all the demons which have been layered in. From the age of five, the child's cult parts will be taught the genealogical histories of their spirit guides. At the age of twelve, some candidates for American tribal chiefs had to wait in the wild for their totem to guide them. They must remain in the forest until their guiding spirit appears. This is why the Illuminati study the Xibalian mysteries written in the Popul Vuh.

Saving this chapter for the last of the mind, body, spirit chapters is like saving the best wine for last. The author knows first hand that the Illuminati fear, more than any other information getting out, that the spiritual aspects of programming would be revealed. This chapter includes some of the most secret elements of the Monarch programming, and certainly some of the most controversial. Psychologists and psychiatrists are an unlikely group to delve into demonology, although there have been a number of studies done in this area. Six examples of such studies:

- Braude, S.E. (1988). "Mediumship and multiple personality." Journal of the Society for Psychical Research, 55, 177-195.

-

- Krippner, 5. (1987). "Cross-cultural approaches to multiple per-

{ 351 }

sonality disorder: Practices in Brazilian spiritism." Ethos, 15, 273 -295.

- Rodgers, R.L. (1991). "Multiple personality and channeling." Jefferson Journal of Psychiatry, 9, 3-13.

- Rogo, D.S. (1987). "The spiritual side of multiple personality." In D.S. Rogo, The infantile boundary: A psychic look at spirit Possession, madness, and multiple personality (pp. 243-246). New York: Dodd, Mead, and Co.

- Ronquillo, E.B. (1991). "The influence of 'Espiritismo' on a case of multiple personality disorder." Dissociation, 4, 39-45.

- Smith, RD. (1981). "Hypnosis, multiple personality, and magic: A case study." Voices: the Art and Science of Psycho-therapy, 17, 20-23.

The Gamma programming is the secret layering in of demons. However one wants to describe these demons--the victim has to deal with their "reality". The ceremonies to demonize the victim occur even before they are born. Generational spirits are very important to determine how the Programmers program a person. But this 10th science goes way beyond just demonology, because it deals with the fundamental issues that effect our views of God, our fellowship with Almighty God, and our view of the occult sciences of astral projection, ESP, telepathy, etc.

THE USE OF SPIRITUAL PRINCIPLES TO ISOLATE THE SYSTEM FROM GOD

In the course of deprogramming Monarchs, and rubbing shoulders with programmers, it became clear that the programmers of the Monarch program are fully aware of the spiritual principles which are in operation for everyone. In 1930, a leader of one of the groups which today carries out trauma-based mind-control, wrote that the occult masters are not interested in uplifting the souls of men, but that *"These Masters. .. have in reality no interest in soul or astral development, except as a means of forming passive illuminized tools, com-*

pletely controlled in mind and actions." The Monarch victims of to-day are the tail end of centuries of efforts by the Cabalists, Freemasons, and the Illuminati adepts to completely control other human beings.

The following quote comes from a communist manual on how to brainwash a nation. It could just have well been written by Monarch Mind-Control Programmers. *"The first thing to be degraded in any nation is the state of Man, himself. Nations which have high ethical tone are difficult to conquer. Their loyalties are hard to shake, their allegiance to their leaders is fanatical, and what they usually call their spiritual integrity cannot be violated by duress. It is not efficient to attack a nation in such a frame of mind. It is the basic purpose of [mind-control] to reduce that state of mind to a point where it can be ordered and enslaved. Thus, the first target is Man, himself. He must be degraded from a spiritual being to an animalistic reaction pattern. He must think of himself as an animal, capable only of animalistic reactions. He must no longer think of himself, or of his fellows, as capable of 'spiritual endurance,' or nobility...As it seems in foreign nations that the church is the most ennobling influence, each and every branch and activity of each and every church, must, one way, or another, be discredited. Religion must become unfashionable by demonstrating broadly, through psycho-political indoctrination, that the soul is non-existent, and that Man is an animal."*

One spiritual principle is that if you can get a person angry at God, you can get that person to commit any sin. Great effort is taken, via staged events to make the victim being programmed certain that God has rejected them.

For instance, some victims had someone play God and walk away from them when they needed help in a life & death situation. The 1980 Hollywood movie Altered States, which is about a university professor in the 1960s who experiments with mind-altering drugs and sensory deprivation tanks, shows some scenes where God turns into a goat. Some of the religious scenes in this movie, match some of the Anti-God/Religious programming of some Monarch slaves.

The Monarch slaves are repeatedly warned that God is cruel and judgmental, and that He wants to destroy them for the wicked things they have done. Bible verses that tell of the wrath of God & God's anger are read to the victim. Here is an example of how the slave is programmed to hate God will now be given:

A hypnotic drug will be given the victim when they are about 6 years of age. This will relax the person and allow the programmers to take the child into the deepest trance, so that the programming will be sure to enter into the very fiber of the child's being. After several hours of being in a deep trance, as the drug begins to wear off, the child will be strapped very secure into a tight fitting coffin. A man with long white hair, and a long robe, with sandals, staff and a white robe will present himself before the child, and announce that he is "God the great I AM". Then "God" will look in a big book and announce he cannot find the person's name so he will have to send the person to hell for being bad. The coffin will then be lowered into a deep pit, like a mine shaft, and the victim will be told that when they can no longer hear God's voice that they will be a cat and not human. God can't find them in the book because they have no soul, and they are a cat. Deeper and deeper the child is lowered. They are told this is the penalty for having tried to pray to God.

The programmers make sure that the slave is implicated in many gross sins, such as the murder of innocent children, in order to insure that the person is sure that God hates them. Then the victim is told that God is a consuming wrath who hates them. The injustice of God creating a world of suffering is also taught to the slave. All this is to insure that the victim hates God. That hatred toward God will express itself in the victim's system's willingness to do any sin, without conscience.

THE MONARCH PROGRAMMING IS A MINITURIZATION OF WHATS BEING DONE TO ENTIRE PEOPLES OR CITIES

Demons are attracted by the "scent" of people. We are made in the image of God, and we are attractive prey to those who hate God Almighty. Cities are magnets for demons. When demons target a person or people, a common tactic is to make trouble for the person. When a person's problems reach a crescendo, they will be in a state of mind to grab any solution that is passing by. People then make pacts with demonic forces. They sell their souls hoping for relief from their problems. All this is clear as a bell to the spiritually enlightened, but the demonic forces are able to dull the senses of their victims to the point they no longer have the slightest realization that they have sold their souls.

People make a choice to accept the falsehood offered by the demons for their relief, rather than stick with the truth which seems to hurt. The demonic lies may be that colds and flues are caused by evil spirits, when in reality they are caused by viruses and bacteria. Or the opposite type of lie may be given, that demonic forces have no influence over disease, that only viruses and bacteria exist. In Africa, modern medicine is often viewed as White Man's magic, because they fight disease with incantations which the demons have taught them to use to cure their problems. Authority to demons is transferred to them by festivals, ceremonies and pilgrimages.

Strong demonic manifestations usually occur around festivals, ceremonies, rituals and pilgrimages which are being done everyday around the world. These ceremonies and rituals are welcome mats for demonic forces giving them the right to rule. Every area of the world has them. And often demonic signs and wonders occur at these rituals and ceremonies. The power of a lie has to be preserved and fueled by tradition, which is manifested via rituals. Without tradition the power of the lie would die out. If the tradition is being rejected by a people, the demons often augment it with "new" deceptions. The first lie doesn't stand a chance. The pre-existing bondage then is strengthened by new deceptions that seem more appropriate.

If you were asked now, "How does Satan enslave people?" you should know the answer because it was just given it to you. The answer is Satan's control is trauma-based. A trauma is applied to the lives of people. They reach out for some type of answer to the trauma, and the demons offer some type of answer. So many Hail Mary's, or so many sacrificed cats, or pray to some idol which is a disguised demon. The lies are turned into myths which the people believe. The myths are a blurring of reality which the people on one level may know are false, but their minds can't break loose of the power of the lie. The power of the myths are fueled by tradition and demonic manifestations and demonic attacks. Anyone who steps outside of the demonic lie is attacked.

The people feel they are being personally attacked when their traditions are ignored. Because a people has willingly sacrificed the truth for the falsehood in their need for relief from their trauma, they have chosen to be deceived. This choice to be deceived has a great deal of spiritual power to it. They are no longer truth-lovers. It is not enough to come to these people with the truth. They have rejected the truth. They must at some point will to seek the truth again. These people can have all the proof shown to them about the truth, and they will continue to reject it. Their demonic bondage needs to be broken somehow.

This bondage can be broken in a number of ways. Pointing out the inadequacies of the lies is sometimes sufficient to break the demonic spell over people. But after the lies are broken, they need to be followed by the truth--and the love of truth. The Monarch Mind Control programming is simply the sophisticated application of what has been done to humanity on a large scale being scaled down and applied to a single human body. Trauma and lies are used in the same way. The different alters sell their souls to the lies in return for their safety. A basic ingredient to the programming of a group of people (or a group of alters) is the same, trauma and fear.

The Land of Oz was ruled by a shadow-leader, the Wizard of Oz. Most countries are ruled by unseen people and unseen powers. The Wizard of Oz story is so representative of how life is for Satan's world. No wonder it is the programming base for so many Monarch mind-controlled slaves.

The solution to Satan's control, was that the disciples of Christ would be so united in love that the world would see the solution. "That they all may be one, that the world may believe." For the Monarch slaves, the therapists have wanted integration. For the world, Christ wanted integration. But there are formidable spiritual strongholds which divide us. These spiritual strongholds are far stronger than most Christians can imagine. The heartbeat of the Body of Christ is to bring all humanity to their Creator God. This can be done by breaking down all the lies and programming that separate the parts of the Body of Christ so that those of Christ are so well integrated in love and spirit that the world believes on the power of Christ. Each of the programming acts has a spiritual, mental, and physical side to it.

The slave has his or her will stripped from them so it becomes unnecessary to think in terms of their guilt, they are slaves who no longer have the freedom of choice. If they kill, or steal, or tell an untruth (lie), they have not done it intentionally. Still the Programmers know that there are spirits involved to spiritually prepare the slave to do these acts. For instance, they implant Spirits of Greed and Lust into the victim. An Illuminati value system is drilled into the victim. Any person who is not taught to dedicate personal rights and possessions to God, will end up with all types of surface forces such as insecurity, worry, anger, envy, jealousy and tension. This goes for multiples or non-multiples. These surface forces will in turn cause all types of surface weaknesses such as lying, stealing, cheating, and arguing. If these surface weaknesses are displayed by anyone, they are evidence that a deeper spiritual problem exists.

However, the slave is not being set up to display these vulnerabilities as they will, but ONLY as they are programmed. An Illuminati Beta model can have sex only with who her master allows her to have sex with. Nor is she granted the privilege of refusing to sexually service someone. If the slave is allowed free will, they often will reject the life style programmed into them. The reason they can reject the Spirits of Seduction & Lust that have been layered in to insure that these moral weaknesses exist, is because the will of the alter being programmed was being coerced. There was duress involved. Satan has some claim, but not the stronghold that comes from those whose active will is involved in a sin. That doesn't mean that some slaves don't develop a taste for their perversion.

The point is that the ability to have these personality weaknesses, should the programmers want them, can be spiritually set into the slave by teaching the slave to resist the grace and love of God. It may be shocking to realize that the slaves are specifically programmed to resist God's grace and love, and to hate Him. This is not left to chance, and is accomplished by a number of events in the slave's life.

Another spiritual area that is tampered with is the self-image of the person. They are not allowed to think of themselves as made in the image of God, unless they are front alters created or allowed to be Christian. Instead of allowing the victim to learn about Jesus, the victim is consistently belittled and compared to others. This is in violation of a spiritual principle found in 2 Corinthians 10:12, *"For we dare not make ourselves of the number, or compare ourselves with some that commend themselves; but they measuring themselves by themselves, and comparing themselves among themselves, are not wise."* John 5:44 and 2 Cor. 10:17,18 teach how it is to be done correctly.

One source, knows of a programmer who is still programming and is fully aware of these scriptures and how they apply spiritually. When people are not allowed to accept themselves, they end up resisting the will of God. The wrong attitudes are built into the slave, so that they will always resist the will of God. Again if the programmers want a Christian front, they may program the correct thinking into the front alter. To do this doesn't threaten their hold on the system in the least. To have Satanic alters and Christian alters which are diametrically opposed to each other's thinking only insures that if they would discover each other in the mind, that they would reject wanting to learn about the other part, and would go into denial of the part's existence.

The programming and mind-control is being linked to a belief system. Taking this one step further, we can also say that the programming is also a conflict between two faiths, the faith that the alters place when they visualize and create their occult-system, that is their faith in demonism and magic, versus the faith of those who follow the God of the Bible. The method of creating hard-core Satanic alters from traumatized Christian alters is an obvious example of this. Some secular therapists have been slow to admit this conflict. If we look at the Illuminati's brand of Druidism, we will notice that the Book of Pheryllt which is a Druidic book for rituals gives four symbols which can be made to evoke the four elemental forces also called the four basic portals.

Visualization is said to be the key to the occult, and to opening portals with these four signs. As the deeper parts of a slave are drawn into such activity, they are in reality placing their faith in that belief system. How can you take something away, without giving something in return? An alternative faith in a God and belief system that is not connected to mind-control is an important therapeutic aid.

You can not hate something passionately if you are unaware of it. When two groups are very similar, in order to high light their individual identity they will have a high level of animosity toward each other. In order to create strong Satanic alters who hate God, the Illuminati actually encourage the young two year old victim to understand and accept the love of God. Upon this faith in a loving God will be built the rejection and trauma to create wounded alters, who hate God because they feel rejected. Rejection is a tool of Satan across the board in the world. Rejection creates a sine wave of hills and valleys. The way of the Lord is made straight leveling these hills and valleys. When a person (or nation) is rejected they will often shift to one of two extremes: either they try to perform to meet up to expectations or they will retaliate against rejection. Both are extremes of the what resembles a sine wave.

Both rejection and retaliation are tools of bondage. The enemy will work a person to get them to feel either rejected or angry. If either side of the sine wave is latched onto by a person (or nation) they will set in motion a dynamic where they will end up with the other side of the curve. This is because the human mind has an inbred desire to balance things out. If we feel rejection, then we may retaliate or try extra hard to perform. This sets up a BONDAGE LOOP. The Cabalistic Tree of Life is the knowledge of good and evil performance.

The programmer by repeatedly REJECTING the slave, build into the slave a high level of performance. The slave is not allowed to get angry at the programmer, which is the opposite peak of the sine wave. The human mind will naturally try to balance the performance peak with increasing the anger/retaliation peak to match it in opposite intensity.

Because the slave can not get angry at their programmer, they turn this anger inward and upward toward themselves and God. The performance of the slave for the master is a form of false love. Performance love is false love. "If you do this for me, then I'll love you." Christ loved us when we were yet sinners and unlovable. This is the type of Godly true love described by Paul in 1 COR 13 which seeks not its own. Self-preservation is a tool of death. That is one reason Christ did not preserve himself, even though he could have called angels, he wanted to show the world true love. Fear gets its root in death. The threat of death of a spouse, of oneself, of one's dreams, of one's identity, or of one's fleshly body creates fear. Death comes from Satan. Life from Yahweh God. Fear is built on a threat of some kind of death. Self-preservation then is actually based upon fear which is in turn based on death. This is why Christ said one must lose their life to gain it.

To escape the satanic bondage loop of self-preservation built on fear, we must reach out for the love of God. Self-justification is not normally seen by people as a bondage loop, but it often is. Only the sureness that Almighty God loves us gives us the strength not to get caught in the self-preservation tactic of self-justification. There is a place for defending the truth, but it must be done in love. Christ and his disciples taught that we are justified by faith in God, not by self-justification. Self-justification can easily be related to the self-preservation bondage loop.

We simply have to have an inner knowing that we are made in the image of God, and that He is working in each of our lives. Since we are His work, He will justify us. All of the Monarch slaves, are a work of God. The cult has simply refashioned what God created. The slave needs to recapture the loving view God has of what He created. God doesn't make mistakes. He has placed lots of beauty and value in each person. Each person is His handiwork, isn't the human body fearfully and wonderfully made?

After someone has been made to participate in crimes against humanity, the Programmers intuitively have created a situation where the person may fall into self-justification, for example, "They deserved to die." This is a subtle, but dangerous tool of bondage. Much of the trauma-based mind-control is based on simple fundamental spiritual life-spiritual death issues. The Spirit of the Lord does not give fear. It comes from the enemy. Abductees, who claim to have met aliens, claim that the aliens feed off of human fear. Fear brings spiritual death.

To show this dynamic in another way, let's describe a common thought for alters of Monarch slaves. This thought is "If I stay with the programming I'm safe." This is the same thought that society in general is taught via fear of self-preservation. "If I stay with the crowd, if I stay with the system, then I will be safe." This is why peer pressure, which seems safe, can lead many young people into death.

All this fear of self-preservation by remaining in the programming, whether individual or social, will be transferred to loyalty of the Anti-Christ, that is the plan. The Truth shall set you free. Anytime we reject the truth for safety and peace because of our fear for self-preservation, we accept a lie. If the truth sets a person free, then by definition, slavery means "not to have truth." All lies lead to bondage. They create strongholds.

Many religious groups are built upon a collection of truths and lies. The truths are used as the enticing attractive front, the lies are used as the enslaving bondage. This is why there is almost no end to all the lies used to program Monarch-type trauma-based total Mind-controlled slaves.

An important mind-control programming dynamic is the creation of images. This will take some explaining. One spiritual dimension of humans is that we like to behold our God. This was built into us. Archeologists have noticed that ancient man has always worshipped.

It is built into man to worship, and we like to behold whatever we worship, whether that is God, ourselves, or some other image. In other words, worship is image oriented. This is the power of images.

One of the most ignored commandments of God, of which Fritz Springmeier wrote a book about in 1977, was the commandment God gave "thou shalt not make any likeness of any thing that is heaven above, or that is in the earth beneath, or that is in the water under the earth." EX 20:4 Students of God's Word are warned to "examine everything carefully; hold fast to that which is good." 1 THES 5:2 1. What is significant is that God's commandments in Ex. 20, which were a distillation of His laws, could have simply stated "Thou shallt not make any graven image", but instead went on to make a big issue in that same passage about any image of God's creatures (the word translated "things" has historically been understood as "living things.")

In DT 4:15 "passel" images, that is images formed out of any mate-rial with a tool (ax, chisel, or engraving tool) and the "likeness of male or female" and "similitude of any figure" are forbidden. Next, it again forbids the likenesses of living creatures. The word "image" occurs about 100 times in the Bible, and is usually accompanied by judgments such as "I will cut down. ..destroy...break down...smote." In a number of verses (EC 7:20, PS 106:29, 39), the scriptures speak about how man is always seeking inventions that provoke God to an-ger. The creation of images of many varieties was a big part of Egyp-tian magic, and still is.

Because the creation of images is so esteemed today, a balanced view/discussion of the spiritual ramifications of images (& their crea-tion) is a rare subject. "For the invisible things of Him, from the crea-tion of the world are clearly seen, being understood by the things that are made, even His eternal power and Godhead, so that they are with-out excuse." RM 1:20. (cf. ISA 6:3)

One ex-Programmer has talked at length, that part of the motivation for the many programming images, is so that they can establish a world built by Satan, because they want to insure that there is no testimony about God's power. By the way, some deliverance ministries are having success in helping heal victims by pointing out that Satanic programmers only build from elements God has already created.

Mirrors, and lots of them, are important in occult programming because they make images. They create so many internal images one doesn't know which way to go. Images are lies. We often create false images of the people we want to love. Do we love them or their image? Movie stars are loved for their image, and rarely for who they really are. Some of them have acknowledged that they don't feel loved by their fans, because their fans are only worshipping an image.

Again, we must remember THE TRUTH SHALL SET US FREE. What is our real identity? Who are we really in God's eyes? Why did He allow us to be born? What was His real purpose for us? These real questions which are so hard for so many of us, are the reality that we need in our lives.

The bondage of images has yet to be understood. The word "duplicity" is based on the word duplicate. Machiavelli taught the elite how to rule through duplicity, that is to rule via imitation images. This is nothing more than one of the operational principles of mirror images placed within the Monarch Mind-controlled slaves. Whatever gives life is duplicated in a mirror image by Satan. Life swallows up death, as the Kingdom of God's genuine light gets progressively brighter. The copy of this is that performance must get progressively better, i.e. technology must change to get better if we are to have life.

The Amish show that society's penchant for technological progression, does not improve life. The Amish have a very successful lifestyle free from divorce and crime. Missionaries to Africa have come back at times wondering if the primitive tribe they spent time with didn't have many things which our technologically advanced society had lost. This doesn't mean that an invention won't help mankind, it means that mankind will not get life from technology. Technology must be understood in the entire context of life.
If a person catches onto the lie of technology or performance, they

may try the opposite lie, platforming. Many troubled people reach out to God, receive help, and then platform by saying, "Thanks for the help God, but I'm O.K. now." God's love is not performance based, but we still need to continue to press toward the mark of the high calling of God, transforming and renewing our mind, ever growing spiritually.

Things which do not grow are labeled dead. How do we grow without being performance oriented? That is the message that Christ tried to bring people. The programmers get their slaves caught in a performance loop. The slaves are not going to get freedom, if a minister of some church traps them into some religious group that is performance-based, rather than unconditional Godly-love based.

It is sad to see victims of mind-control free themselves at great cost, only to run from one controlling group to another. If we neglect to look at the spiritual dimensions of mind-control slavery, we then are neglecting to see some of the elements of total mind-control slavery.

IN SUMMARY, SOME OF THE FIRST THINGS ATTACKED

What is often the first thing which is attacked in individuals and nations in order to control them? It is their sense of identity as a spiritual moral being. Both individuals and nations are targeted to destroy their ethical self-respect. The individual and the nation must be brought to think of themselves as animals.

Another primary tactic or tool is to traumatize the victim who is to be controlled, and then provide relief when a demonic lie is accepted. Rejection is an important trauma, because it creates a desire for performance and retaliation, and gets people trapped in a bondage loop. Lies put people into bondage. Images are a type of lie, that lead to bondage. This is why so many images and lies are placed into the Mind-controlled slave. These images and lies are inherently bondage-makers.

Fear and self-preservation are grounded in death. To preserve ourselves, we will allow ourselves to be enslaved. Eventually, Mind-controlled slaves and society in general in order for peace, safety and self-preservation will transfer their allegiance to the master programmer, the Illuminati's Anti-Christ.

THE DEHUMANIZATION PROCESS

The dehumanizing of a multiple, that is of a fragmented personality, is done to most of the alters, but the front alters are allowed to be human. Because alters take on the characteristics of what they were created from, the front alters have to be some of the first splits so that they have a sense of family and that they are human. That does not mean that the first series of splits can't be dehumanized later, they are, they are turned into gems or crystals. How do you make an alter into an animal alter? It may not be quite as difficult as some may imagine, because they can create alters with "clean slates"--that is they are the plain tablets that Dr. White (Dr. D. Ewin Cameron) prided himself that he was able to make out of adult minds.

When a part of the mind has no reality to reference, and is tortured and told lies, then it will accept what the programmer says is real. When an alter is created via torture, if you want a cat alter, they will have the child tortured in a cage surrounded by cats of some type. The new alters will be told they are cats. Their programmers will actually kill a little child in the worst way in front of these alters and tell them that that is what happens to little girls and boys. Do they want to be a little girl? No. After watching the horrible things that happen to little girls, they do not want to be little girls or little boys as the case may be. They want to be a cat, because as a cat they will not be killed and tortured like the children. The alters are forced to eat like cats with cats. They are repeatedly shamed and degraded and repeatedly told they are cats. Lie detector Instruments are hooked up to the child to determine if the alters actually believe they are cats. When the alter can actually state, "I'm a kitten." or "I'm a tiger." and pass the lie detector test, then the programmers know they have succeeded.

But what if the mind resists being told it is a cat? As long as the child

{ 365 }

is a girl it is given feces to eat. But the cats are fed wholesome meals in front of the victim. The little girls in the other cages are dirty and tortured and ill fed. Do you want to be a little girl? A great deal of simple torture is applied to make sure that the correct answers are given. If your life depended upon saying you were a cat, you'd be a cat too. Further, children have a vivid imagination. Normal children can easily role play, and they can easily imagine they are something they aren't, because their personalities and egos have not solidified.

Again nothing is left to chance.

A fake blood transfusion of cat blood may be given the child. Very often high speed films of kittens playing and having fun are shown in one eye, while the other eye is forced to view little girls having to undergo the worst of tortures. This viewing is forced upon the child, as its eyes are held open and the child is strapped into a viewing chair. The dehumanization process will make alters into various types of birds, cats, dogs, aliens, horses, earth elements, gemstones, rocks, and countless other items. They will then place in back up programming to insure that the alters continue to believe they are not human.

The ingenuity of the back up programming to ensure that they continue to believe the lies are extensive and ingenious. A great deal of hypnosis, and drug induced states, and drug-hypnosis is used to carry out the dehumanization process. The programming will be reinforced by a cat alter's environment, because the alter's handlers will always refer to them as kittens or other types of cats.

The painful rape of a child with its legs held in a butterfly configuration is used to get butterfly alters. To get a puppet, the body is given a drug which paralyzes the child. Then electro-shock is applied to certain muscles upon the command of the programmer. The effect is that the child has no control over his body, and the programmer can make the child's body parts jerk and move by electro-shocking the muscles. The child actually becomes the puppet of the programmer.

This is a very powerful program. One of the names connected with Monarch programming is Marionette Programming. The child literally becomes a Marionette. This concept appears to have been cooked up by the Germans under Hitler. An alter System as a child is physically shown that they are a marionette puppet. Their muscles are electro-shocked in such a way as to take advantage of the natural reflexes. When electro-shocked that way, the victim's body parts jerk out of their control at the whim of the programmer to prove to the victim that they are a puppet. At this time, the rules are given and rule number 8 is that the alters are their puppet. Illuminati programmer Dr. Mengele, used puppets in a dollhouse as he programmed.

He did skits with his puppets. "Dance Marionette Dance," he'd say in his thick German accent. Pinocchio's story was used to name the spirit guide Jiminy Cricket. Along with rule no. 8, he taught the following rules at this point:

1. Listen to your instructions
2. There is no room for error
3. "The Game Timer"--these were the specifics of how to move, the melted mirror, etc.
4. There is a chain of command, the King's men
5. Your Master would chart your course
6. You will receive orders, what to do, a memorized script to follow and fulfill
7. The Creator and Master would always own you into infinity
8. You are puppets on a string. "Dance Marionette dance. You are to speak only those words told to you, and to only speak those words when your string is pulled
9. There is no room for questions
10. The controller always plays the role of the White Rabbit. Dark side alters of a System are taught to know these rules as part of their being

Dr. Joseph Mengele (known as Dr. Green) carried a violin, which was used during programming. He programmed slaves to respond to the key word "Fiddler". During programming, the victim will be made to believe that all their insides have been removed and tape recorders placed into them and surgically hooked up. To the child being programmed this is real. This is part of the dehumanization process to protect them from spiritual growth and freedom. The programmers' dehumanization parallels what is done in the army when the drill sergeant yells at the new recruits names such as "maggot" and "worm".

PORCELAIN FACE PROGRAMMING

The Porcelain Face Programming was already touched on earlier in Chapters 2 & 7 when the fire tortures and Gatekeeper alters were written about. Fire torture and melted wax is used to make the child victim believe their face has been burned. Then the programmer generously gives the traumatized alters a porcelain mask. The alter getting the porcelain face may be given a "gem" hypnotically like Jade and that becomes their secret name. There are several different methods that are available to lay in the porcelain face programming. There has been a great deal of porcelain casts made of people's faces and then masks made of them. In fact, when a handler dies, at least in one case the replacement handler wore a mask to look like the previous handler.

Human baby skin is used to construct a mask from the victim's facial cast. A mask is worn by the Illuminati victim when they are married to the Anti-Christ. The Porcelain Masks are often part of the Camelot & Shakespeare programming. Another use of porcelain masks which was only experimented with was to place masks on Pawn alters which were used as alters who would guard things by scaring other alters with their fearful porcelain countenances. This programming has spiritual ramifications, because it is one of the programming methods to steal alters of their faces. The alters getting porcelain face programming will only see a porcelain face in the mirror until the programming is taken down. As long as the computer on their level is operating the programming to that alter will be intact.

HEARTS OF STONE

The programmers leave no stone unturned when they strip the alters of a system of any vestige of humanity they might have. The programmers make the alters believe that the programmers have surgically removed their hearts & replaced them with a stone. To reinforce this programming the victim is hypnotized to fall into a deep trance if at any time the victim's deeper alters are hooked up to anything monitoring the heart. If and when someone tried to prove that these alters have a heart by taking their pulse, they may be surprised when these alters trance deep enough that the machine doesn't even read. This is how the programming keeps the lies safe from exposure. The Programmers will hypnotically take the hearts for a number of reasons.

One is blackmail. They will promise to return the hearts, if the victim obeys, returns home to the cult when needed, and is present when the Anti-Christ needs the victim. It is doubtful these alters would get their hearts back by their cult considering all the false promises that are typically made. The Programmers will give the hearts to a queen mother alter for safekeeping. They may be hidden somewhere like in the Temple of Molech. The Temple of Molech in some survivors is used as a depository for memories of child sacrifices. It is not a place any alter could or would want to go in the internal world. In return, the Programmers give the victim stones, yes, hearts of stone.

Stone-like protectors will stand guard in the background. Their voodoo doll appearance reflects the voodoo images that are built into Monarch Internal Worlds. By removing the victim's hearts, it removes any chance that dark alters would have a soft warm spot in their heart for anyone. They will be told that they are incapable of having friends or of loving others. This is quite effective in separating these alters from others. That isolation is a part of the mind control. Because the alters believe they have no life source within themselves--that is no heart, they have to look to their master. If the master places his hand upon the victim's chest they may feel alive. Because people need a heart to feel, alters are programmed to believe that they are incapable of feeling and have no feelings.

They can not cry during their own suffering, and are encouraged to feel incapable of caring for the suffering of others. In spite of all the brutality and isolation of the programming, the alter's humanity will lay in the background, but whether alters will ever acknowledge that humanity is a big question. If people ask these heartless alters to give their hearts to Jesus, they may be told that they don't have one. In all covenants, something is given to the cult. In this case the victim's hearts are (hypnotically) given to the satanic Master. There is a Keeper of the Seals who keeps the items given when a vow or covenant is made. If a person is a traitor to a vow, then the cult has an object to carry out voodoo or magic upon to punish the person. Monarch Mind-controlled slaves know their orders, and are locked into obedience.

HYPNOTIC SURGERY

After the Programmers steal the deeper alters' hearts, their identities, their free will, their real families, and their faces and their humanity, they are kind enough to sew back into the victim's chest via hypnotic surgery black stones. They do all this surgery by hypnosis. Via hypnosis, the Programmers can heal the victim's wounds after they torture the victim. They can basically make or remake reality to be what they want.

FEAR

The thing that stands out so vividly for those who have met victim's who are in therapy is the Spirit of Fear that control them. Waves of paranoia roll back and forth through the alters. Everyone needs to bear in mind, that the programmers were sadists, and they didn't get satisfaction from their programming until they could see raw terror in their victims.

The primary vehicle for programming was the raw terror that is repeatedly instilled into the victim. To achieve total terror, the sadist programmer gains total control over every aspect of a person, their thoughts, their bowel movements, their life, even the power to commit suicide is stripped from the victim. Nothing that originally belonged to the victim is left untouched.

A realistic fear of most victims, is that they will never be believed. Indeed, many therapists are serving the final insult to these severely traumatized people by denying the authenticity of things the victim experienced himself and even wishes were not true. For a victim to overcome their fear to tell, after all the years of programming not to tell and threats not to tell is an enormous feat. Very few victims, ever get to this point. And yet, when they do overcome this enormous barrier, they must face disbelief. Traditionally, the psychiatrists have treated these victims as if their abuse is nothing but psychotic nonsense. How many fleeing victims have been locked up and told they were Paranoid Schizophrenics?

The fear of losing one's identity within a coven or religious group, says the Church of Scientology, is balanced out by the structured framework that these groups have. Members identify with each other, because they participate in the same rituals and have given their allegiance to the same idealized master.

THE USE OF GUILT, SHAME, RIDCULE AND ANGER

The Chinese and police agencies have been especially good at developing methods to solicit confessions. This is done by a variety of punishment and reward strategies, and the Mutt & Jeff routine. Confession and self-criticism have been used by religious groups, especially the Jesuits, as a method to convert persons to and then perpetuate a belief.

One of the things that the deeper alters will not be taught about is forgiveness. Because forgiveness of oneself and others is such an important spiritual dynamic, to not know about forgiveness cripples many deeper alters from healing from the deep spiritual wounds they have received. Forgiveness is an act of the will. Forgiveness of oneself is usually a major issue with deeper alters who generally don't know how to do this.

However, the handlers and abusers will be sure to heap lots of guilt--whether deserved or not onto the poor mind-controlled victim. It is natural for a person to focus on himself. After all, if a person doesn't think for himself who will?
Often a person accepts their strengths, but focuses on their weak-

nesses hoping that that weakness will somehow be reduced by the focus that is placed upon it. The programmers know how to take advantage of that. They set impossible standards of perfection, and then demean the victim because they have failed to live up to the impossible standard of perfection. Black and white thinking develops in the slave's mind.

The programmers will not allow the victim to display natural feelings of anger, sadness or doubt. To do so means that one is a failure and weak. Of course they are natural feelings, so the slave has to do a great deal of repression and self-incrimination for having these natural feelings. The slave learns to turn his or her anger inward. Many of the male slaves end up committing suicide. They beat themselves up with subconscious & conscious guilt.

Anything and everything wrong or bad in the slave's life is blamed upon him. Of course not all things are meant to be remembered by the slave. Guilt can play a natural role in the forgetting of memories too. If the Monarch slave would remember something terrible, the religious front alters can be made to feel repentant for such terrible thoughts. Then the natural desire to forget can be reinforced by suggesting that the evil memory be removed from the mind. In other words, memories are forgotten because they don't conform to a person's moral code. If good morals are programmed into the front alters, they will take the hypnotic suggestion not to remember what has really happened that they had to participate in. The front alters will only remember a sanitized version.

The person may even want to think of the memory as "only a dream" because of the guilt associated with believing the reality of it. If a person is hypnotized to have guilt about something that they didn't commit, then they can be gotten to believe that they did it. For instance, a false implanted memory of the Monarch slave killing a child may be implanted with the command, if you do not obey we will kill more children and you then will be guilty for not just this child but others. People will tend to justify their abuse by saying "I was bad, I was evil." The programmers take advantage of this natural tendency. Nothing the slave does is good enough or worthy of praise.

After they sexually please a customer, they are called "bitch" and "whore" to make the slave feel guilty, when all they have done is follow orders. The whole situation causes the slave to work harder for approval which of course is very tentative and fleeting at best. The Master just keeps control, and sets the standards higher if the slave gets close to reaching perfection. The Master must insure that the slave feels guilty and dirty. Many of the slaves endure a guilt that is common among soldiers and concentration camp survivors--the guilt of having survived when others died. "Why did I live and they die? I was no better than them?" Any desire on the part of deeper alters to want something for themselves is painted as "selfishness".

They will be internally and externally punished for any pleasure. If a sexual alter enjoys a sexual encounter, she is programmed to internally feel some type of severe punishment program. One standard punishment for a female slave who appears to have actually enjoyed a sexual act is to cut the from vagina to rectum, and sew them back up without anesthesia WHILE the slave is forced to watch her punishment in silence without tears or screams. One form of tormenting a slave is to ridicule the slave as they have to carry out a wretched assignment.

Many slaves lose their zest for humor because they end up the brunt of so many bad jokes. Comedians, because they are skilled with puns, and other words games, have often served as handlers or programmers. Bob Hope is the best example of a Monarch slave handler who uses his verbal skills as both a handler and comedian. Bob Hope has a side to him that the public doesn't see. Over the years, Bob Hope has spent millions of dollars on his team of gag writers to keep him well supplied with gags.

ANGER

The use of anger is not haphazard. The spiritual ramifications of anger are very well known to the programmers. They know that anger opens up spiritual portals for demonic activity. Remember, Chapter 7 on structuring explained how the programmer purposefully push the victim almost to its breaking point to get angry alters. The use of anger is seen in a number of different areas of programming. The Gatekeeper alters will be depressed and angry alters to insure that they remain good portals for demons. Gatekeeper alters function as Gatekeepers in several different capacities. Gatekeeper alters will be found to the whole system, often on the second level (section) down. Gatekeeper alters will also be found guarding important sections like the Carousel and Castle. In review, Anger toward God, anger toward the outside world, and anger toward themselves are all built into a System. Where was God? Where was the outside world, when all these things were happening.

Many, if not all, of the victims of Monarch turn their anger on themselves, which is the only safe place to vent it. Most of the deeper alters of a Monarch system will have very low self-esteem and will have lots of guilt and anger toward themselves. The slave is victimized so much, that when their handlers give them the chance to victimize someone else, some victims find release in assaulting others. Of course the entire process of transference further entraps the victim, and provides more guilt and more debilitating spiritual dynamics.

The slave may be given the power of life or death over others, as well as the power of deciding another person's eternal fate. Sometimes this power is addictive. This addiction can be a trap that binds the slave to his source of power. The power that the Illuminati give their slaves is one of the major barriers preventing deeper alters from moving toward freedom when their systems have a chance. Slaves also turn a great deal of anger in on themselves. The self-image of most alters in a System is extremely low.

The anger that alters have becomes a tool of the handler to insure that the slave never thinks highly enough of themselves to do anything about the control over them.

An example of this is Monarch slave Loretta Lynn. Loretta Lynn's handler is her husband Doolittle. Although Loretta has worked (slaved) very long hard hours she credits Doolittle for all her success. Her programming allows her only to give him credit for her successes. In her "autobiography" Loretta Lynn A Coal Miners Daughter, which was written by a professional writer who sat down and worked with her, Loretta says on page 63, "In a lot of ways, it was good for me to marry someone older than me [her husband Doo was a WW II Vet/Satanist who married her when she was 13], because I could learn from him. But, in another way, it wasn't so good because I went directly from Daddy to Doolittle without ever being on my own. Even today, men are telling me what to do.

My husband, my lawyer, my accountant, my personal managers Riley, her road manager has been her mind-control handler, and Alex Houston & Reggie Maclaughlin have done some of her recent programming]. In a sense, I still don't have complete control over myself. Maybe I never will. But if it wasn't for Doo, her nickname for her husband & handler, we wouldn't have what we have today." Anger within a System can be dangerous, when one alter directs its anger toward another alter.

Sometimes one alter will try to kill another alter. Actually, this happens more often than one might imagine. If the alter succeeds of course, the body will be dead, with the resulting consequence that everyone dies.

The programmers enjoy seeing this type of drama, but they don't want it to be carried out to its final conclusion, so they generally, if not always, have alters who can step in and take the body and stop this. If the alter system can't, then alters who understand what is going on can call their master for help, and the master can once again show how dependent they are upon him for life. This is the "divide and conquer" strategy. The divide and conquer strategy is used repeatedly in constructing an alter system.

TEACHING THAT THE MASTER IS GOD

The Programmers and the Handlers are setting themselves up as Gods, or Almighty God, or as a being from a superior race of aliens, such as Koldasians or Pleiadians. Interestingly, if one listens, these different alien races make conflicting claims for whatever good the earth has. However, those of us who have followed the Monarch programming know that these aliens are just men who do the Programming.

Time-life Publishers (owned by men in the Illuminati) subtly gave this away in their book The UFO Phenomenon when they referred to UFO abductions as "the Oz factor." They go on to say that its like Dorothy in the Wizard of Oz on page 71. Then they go so far as to re-emphasize the point by showing a picture of Dorothy in Oz. In the TV series on aliens & UFOs called the "X-Files", they begin a show with an "I love you/I love you not" Monarch programming script.

Often the Programmers tell the alters which they have created, that they are their Creator and therefore their God. In a spiritual sense, they took the place of God in every way, including attributing the scriptures about God to themselves. This works well for Illuminati alters, because they are indoctrinated that all humans can be divine. It also works well with non-Illuminati alters as long as they are under mind-control. However, the actions of the handlers are so un-Godlike, that should the programming break down, and the alters get a taste of reality, these lies soon are transparent.

The lies that the handler is an alien are much harder to refute than the lies that the handler is God. The trend appears to be for the handlers to refer to themselves as a superior race of aliens. Most, if not all, of the people seeing aliens are really just being jerked around by their handlers. This doesn't mean that aliens do or don't exist. It does mean that those of us who have been working with people who have alien contact experiences and who understand Monarch Mind-control have only seen people obviously under mind-control.

In 1992, a book Exposing The Mystery of Iniquity was started by Fritz Springmeier showing the connections between so called "aliens" and "demons." Is it coincidence that the demon Sir John Dee conjured for his enochian magic looks just like a small grey alien pictured so often today? People who have participated in high level Illuminati ceremonies speak about guardians which are Nephalim (half human-half demon) which are the offspring of mixing humans with demons, and who look like the variety of "aliens" that are so often reported.

The subject of Nephalim and whether aliens are or are not visiting us is too vast for this book. However, these Nephalim guardians are perceived as real by Illuminati members, and they strike incalculable fear within the members of the Illuminati. As one of the big sources of fear, the guardians take their place as part of the control mechanisms to keep slaves in place. Polls taken by others, have found that 100% of Satanists have had an experience with UFOs, and report some type of "alien" abduction. The Programmers & upper level hierarchy don't get themselves into polls, and the lower levels are all programmed.

The point is that there is a close relationship between UFOs and the occult word. On the following page are some of the more respectable scripts that persons, who are victims of "alien abductions" see in their heads. Signs of MPD were visible in each of these cases, and these abductees are placing their wills at the command of these "higher beings".

Their wills are subservient to the will of the "alien". They receive messages in these scripts in altered states of consciousness. Some of the scripts are blatantly satanic magic scripts and sigils, but the majority are blatantly of human design. It stretches the imagination that most alien scripts would have a language and script that matches the English alphabet, with the same letter frequencies of English letters-- that is "a's" and "m's", and are found in abundance. It stretches the imagination passed the breaking point to think that aliens light years away with different vocal cords or whatever they have, evolved a script that corresponds to English, when our alphabet doesn't correspond to Greek, or Sanskrit, or Ogham that closely.

Quite a few abductees have the "aliens" give them more complex versions of their "alien script" as they get older. The simplified version is received as a child, and then it evolves. It appears that there are now numerous programmers, who are simply concocting made-up scripts, and hypnotically telling their poor hapless victim that the script is alien. In this respect, these scripts are really codes--not "alien scripts". They are full of what are called follows.

Follows are symbols that are similar to one another, which are a variation on a theme. Test results have shown that made-up scripts have many more follows than an actual real historical script. The occult world are teaching that the Akashic record of all recorded information lies somewhere in the essence of space called the reticulum dei, the network of God.

The mind-control victim, who actually gets his automatic writing and his information from deep in his system, is led to believe that he has gotten it from the Akashic record. The spiritual dynamics of the Programmer setting himself up as God are far reaching. The spiritual world mirrors the physical world. In the physical world, in biology, researchers have found that chemicals that resemble other natural body chemicals can be substituted in for those original chemicals with far reaching effects.

For instance, anti-histamines do not destroy histamine, they resemble histamine enough that they steal the places that histamine molecules attach themselves to cells. Because the histamine molecules have had their attachment places stolen, they can't interact with the cells. Within the spiritual realm the very same thing happens.

The Anti-Christ is less of a Christ destroyer as he is a Christ replacement. True spiritual power is replaced within the world by the religious spirit. Within Christendom, the religious spirit has replaced much of the positions that should have gone to true faith. Therefore the power of true faith is destroyed by simply being replaced and its position usurped. The foundation for the religious spirit are fear and pride, which are also foundational pillars for the Monarch programming.

The religious spirit can be detected when someone reads an admonishment and can apply it immediately to others and not to oneself. When a person sins, for example Eli in the book of Samuel, the religious spirit will propel them to make a sacrifice to cover that sin like

Eli did. However, that religious zeal to cover sin by doing good and giving sacrificially of oneself, stems from the religious spirit not the holy Spirit of God (See 1 Samuel 3:13-14).

Religious zeal done to cover sin is not accepted by Almighty God. Eli's sons "despised the offering of the LORD" (1 SAM 2:17). One of the outgrowths of SRA upon the Monarch victim is that they will generally exhibit black and white thinking. Black and white thinking is actually an element of the religious spirit, which in spiritual terms pervades the Monarch victim. The Monarch victim's system is set up to usurp true faith. Something has to replace true faith, and the religious spirit is a good substitute. Perfectionism or unloving idealism is part of the religious spirit. This perfectionism will demand that if a person can not be perfect, they should give up.

The holy Spirit of God gives hope. The religious spirit destroys hope by demanding more than people can give. As long as people are travelling the journey of seeking God, they don't need to have arrived to perfection. Idealism wants people to be at the destination at once or not start the journey. This religious spirit has stopped many victims of Monarch programming from moving forward to real freedom. It is a very powerful type of spirit. Many people are waiting until they are perfect to help minister to others. Sadly this is an outgrowth of the religious spirit. We do not need to be perfect to help others. The following is an actual account: a Christian man who didn't understand mechanics very well stopped to see what he could do to help an elderly couple stranded on the road.

The car miraculously started for the Christian and he was able to have the couple follow him to a repair station at the next town. But the attitude of the Christian was to make himself available to God--not that he was going to fix someone else's problem. The couple was sure they had been visited by an angel. What is being discussed is how setting oneself up as "a God" or "God" is part of the religious spirit that attracts itself to so many of us. One of the attributes of the religious spirit is that it will notice what is wrong in a person rather than discerning what is right. Unless discernment is based upon love, discernment will be warped.

Churches caught up in the religious spirit have mercy on the things that are abominations to God. Likewise, they show unwarranted mercy on the actions of ministers who have mercy on things that are abominations to God. One of the best examples is the religious front this book discussed in detail in Chapter 5. Billy Graham, a Monarch slave handler, is on public record endorsing Mao-tse-tung's teachings, abortion, salvation through witchcraft, the One-World-Church in alliance with the world's political power, and many other things. Quite a number of Freemasons, ex- and current members have stated that Billy Graham is a secret Freemason, however, his staff denies this. The religious spirit has ran a campaign to cover up Billy Graham's personal use of prostitutes, many of them Monarch kittens. And some of these Monarch kittens have been able to reveal the facts of their abuse.

Billy Graham is a "prophet" who works for the Network. The point is that churches turn a blind eye to these things. One source has tried to approach ministers about these things, and there isn't an open ear. By the way, Almighty God still can step above what Billy Graham is and work in spite of it. Satanists can infiltrate the highest church positions, but they won't stop good from eventually conquering evil, and God's will being done. When we write "God's will", please understand that God has several types of will, including a conditional will, and an ultimate will. His conditional will is let men have what they want. His ultimate will is to see His creation be a wonderful paradise. The religious leaders in Jesus' day got rid of true prophets. The religious spirit today will do the same. The religious spirit causes people to flagellate their backs with whips.

A Russian branch of the Illuminati, called the Skoptsi, are famous for the self-inflicted tortures including castration that they carry out upon their bodies. The religious spirit causes people to have self-abasement for the wrong motives. Discipline and faith are worthy things to have, but not if they are done out of only love for oneself rather than also love for one's Creator. This is why satanic alters have such a hard time seeing what Christianity has for them. They see the religious spirit of Christianity and they realize that Satanism has a more powerful form of religion. Satanism is based upon legalism (the rituals have to be exactly so), and upon pride, and fear. To make an analogy, the religious spirit is like a man or woman who dresses to get compliments rather than dressing nice to please their spouse. In other words, the man who wears something that offends his wife, because he wants other men to think he is macho, has a similar motivation as the religious spirit.

The author of the religious spirit is Satan, the author of death. God wants people to choose things which are excellent and make their lives count for eternity. On the flip side, the programmers, who worship & serve Satan in their invocations, murder their victims in 4 ways of death; mental, moral, spiritual, and physical death. They program 4 types of ongoing suicide into their slaves. They bring them

a. mental suicide,
b. moral suicide,
c. spiritual suicide, and d. push some alters to physical suicide, and program others to commit physical suicide.

They push their slaves into near death experiences--some alters die, and are discarded. Often, there are "dead" alters within a live System. To perpetuate mental death, the programmers administer drugs, hypnosis, and false philosophies, and programming to wipe the truth out of the slaves mind. This is mental murder. b. Resistance to evil is the essence of life. By requiring their slaves to engage in the worst moral impurities, these parts lose their spiritual eyes. This is moral murder. (2 Peter 1)

PORTALS AND FOCAL POINTS

Within the occult world, the entire study of demonology is wrapped around the geometric shapes that serve as focal points for demon, such as crystals and pyramids, and the portals by which demons can enter the human body. A demon doesn't have to be materialized, or conjured up, to enter into a body. Geometric shapes which are believed to attract demons are placed into the internal worlds of slaves. The will of the person also plays a role in the introduction of demons into the body. Torture attaches and layers in demons within the body. Sex and blood sacrifices are used to attach powerful demons. According to high level demonology, certain powerful spirits can only be manipulated if there are blood sacrifices. This may seem strange, however, the record bears out that generational victims of possession who have had demons placed in via blood sacrifices are definitely controlled by more powerful demonic forces.

All of the chakra points, and the orifices to the human body serve as portals. Both the Illuminati and Christian deliverance ministries agree that the mouth, ears, nose, anus, etc. are portals. High influxes of demonic energy into the body is accompanied by a burning sensation. The Mother of Darkness who is assigned to a child who is being programmed has to oil the child periodically to protect it from this burning. The goal to possess someone of spirits, or to be possessed by spirits has been practiced since the early times of mankind.

In Llewellyn's "New Worlds of Mind and Spirit" magazine June/July 1994, issue #943, they write, *The golem of Prague is perhaps the most famous example of 'practical cabala'--the use of cabala for magical cabala."* Scholem in his excellent treatise on the Cabala has an entire chapter about the Golem. The golem were mind-controlled slaves created by the magic of the Cabala.

The Cabala, according to the best Masonic authorities, including Albert Pike in his famous Morals and Dogma book is the basis of Freemasonry. By extension then, it is clear that the goal of having a mind-controlled golem has been the goal of Freemasonry, because that goal is the best example of practical cabala.

This is the paper trail, that lets us view the secret goals of the secret world of Freemasonry. There are Cabalistic grades within Freemasonry. Sexual slaves were used by the higher and more occult Masonic rites in the 19th century. These sexual slaves were subjected to trances and demonic possessions. They were subjected to all types of perverse magical rituals. The Cabala teaches intercourse with demons.

Theurgy is the skill or ability to invoke demons variously called angels of light, genii, spirits of various kinds, such as elemental spirits. Demons come with a price and that price is blood. Satanism and Luciferianism and other similar cults are blood cults that require blood to be sacrificed to pull in certain demons.

For instance, blood may be taken from both the tongue and the genital area and mixed in a certain ceremony to invoke a particular demon. Demons are not bought with gold or silver, they are bought with blood. Some spirits are invoked by placing alcoholic enemas into the child. These children get totally intoxicated with alcohol, some to the point that they even die from the ceremony. This is all done to bring in particular demons.

The Spirit Choronzon and Typhon are critical spirits to place into a person for the Mind-Control to work. The Illuminati do not believe the Mind-control will work without the assistance of these spirits. Typhon and Choronzon do the tunnelling and the MPD work.

An example of an important ritual to demonize the victim is the baptism of the child victim to Satan. Satan may be called Set in the ritual. There are variations on this ceremony, so a victim's personal baptism may vary in some or all of the details. This is actual variation of the ritual done to Monarch mind-controlled slaves: The child is stripped nude and given a purple robe. It is placed inside the pentagram, and an "altar" which is made by a nude woman or child is brought forward. A horse or jackal is inscribed with the inscription "Nebebka" on the neck or forehead.

Then the animal is sacrificed to whatever name the group is using for Satan (such as Set or Saman). The abdomen of the beast is split open completely, and the liver removed. The 4 spirits of the 4 watchtowers are invoked. The slave child being baptized is smeared with fat from the dead beast. The Gatekeeper spirit is called by ringing a bell. Then the child is placed into the animal's belly. A part of the raw liver is given to the child and the rest consumed by the group. The child is then baptized in blood. A cut called the Devil's Seal is placed on the child on the left hand, or under the armpit, or on the upper part of the head. This in Cabalism is the Mark of Foundation. The Priest reads out of the Book of Satan and the Book of Names. The victim repeats after the Priest. In this fashion the Priest ritually gives the person a new name.

The Dance of Hod is then begun in a circular motion by the cult, to oppose Netsah. The Priest of the coven will then dismiss the demon he has conjured. At times this ritual is done with a child sacrifice rather than an animal, & sometimes it is done in conjunction with another ritual, such as All Hallow's Eve. To empower the Monarch System, special rings which have been dipped in the blood of sacrificed victims, are given to the victim with instructions to wear it faithfully. The rings are used as focal points to insure the continued demonization of the victim. Some examples of this would be a Blue Topaz ring, a Black Onyx ring, or a Diamond ring. Black Onyx is used to capture souls. Whether the therapist believes this or not, becomes irrelevant in view of the fact that the deeper alters in a Monarch System are skilled in demonology and they do believe it, and take consolation that their magical powers are never challenged by therapists.

These deeper alters will continue to do much of the demonization of the system for the Programmer, and this delegation of this job, means the Programmer/handler is free to focus on other things. Our experience is that the Slave Masters within the Illuminati, when they take away the hearts of the alters of a system, they give them a heart of stone and a ring. The ring is important for if they lose this, they think they will not get their hearts back. The slaves will wake up in the middle of the night looking for a ring but never knowing what ring they are looking for.

"Catch a falling star, put it in your pocket for a rainy day" ties in with this story line. The star is magical stardust. During programming the Programmers use "magical star dust." If the slave loses their ring, they are told the Master will never love them. When the Master comes to give his love, then the slave will get to use their magical wand with its star dust. The ring of the Programmer, which has occult power from being used in ritual, is also used as a hypnotic cue. The ring also represents occult power and authority.

VOWS AND OATHS

- The Illum. & generational occult families attach Ancestral & Generational curses (noted about in EX 20:5-6, DT 23:2, 2 KG 5:27, JER 32:18, JER 3:25, LEV 26:40) to the victim.

- The Programmers create soul ties (intertwining with others in an ungodly way), including intertwining of spirits. Sex, emotional dependence, anger and love can be tied to this dependence.

- The spiritual power of the Communion meal--which is a form of the Passover meal (deliverance) & the Marriage Supper of the Lamb (wholeness in heaven) is reversed by Black Mass's symbolism/bondage.

- The Moriah & other occult groups attach curses to a person that are brought on by occult involvement. These curses are the consequences of sinful occult involvement.

- The Monarch programmers force the slave to make blood covenants, contracts, oaths, and to shed innocent blood. Often times the deeper alters feel like they have made these contracts willingly--however, if they could see the whole picture they would realize that they were forced and deceived into accepting these occult practices.

To free themselves of these oaths and covenants every alter has to break them, or at least the main alter breaks it for others. What various witchcraft and Illuminati slaves will experience will be Satan drawing blood from their left hand and causing them to write in the slave's own blood a formal contract entering his service. The ceremony has a lasting impression. Their signature in the Great White Book, which is an important Illuminati document, which has everyone's signature will change color, and they will lose their magical power, etc.

This creates a double bind, if they keep the System "safe", they can't get out. They need to understand that greater is Jesus than he who is the world. See Col. 2:15 also, which speaks about him triumphing over the principalities and powers. The Illuminati & the Network keeps books which have the signatures of all their membership, including slaves. They tell the slave that if they ever break a covenant with them, that Satan will cause the signature in blood to turn green. In other words, the slave is led to believe and is convinced that if they ever renege on their vows to Satan and the New World Order, they will be instantly found out. Even the American presidents are reported to be threatened with this type of threat.

The "birthright" of a child born to Illuminati parents is to be allowed into satanic coven level activity. Alters which function at coven levels, will be far removed in a Monarch system from Illuminati hierarchy alters. The coven level will also be called the anarchy level and is represented by an "A". One of the early oaths taken by the Illuminati child before the Grand Druid Council is, "Satan the Way and the Light. No one comes to me except through the father of light which is the Anti-Christ. I, [birth name], by my free choice take the following oath. I commit to serve my body and spirit in union with the father of light for the total prosperity and insurance of the victory of Satan and the father of light the Anti Christ.

Now within an unbroken circle of spiritual power, understanding and accepting the consequences of breaking the spiritual circle which joins the Mothers of Light with each other and to the father of light. Later they learn that they have actually joined the Mothers of Darkness.

"I [Illuminati coven name] with these bonds in place commit to rule within the spiritual union over the principalities of darkness to insure Satan's power and control over the world. I forever take on the seal of the father of light and commit my eternal life to serve Satan as the prince of peace, savior, and spiritual light for ever and ever. I now denounce the truth of the God, the resurrection of Christ and the power of the Holy Spirit."

Should the person break this vow, they are programmed to remember torture on a cross, which is designed to cause a seizure and heart failure. The Final Vows of a Mother of Darkness or a Grand Master will make these cult alters feel like they are bound and trapped in service to Satan. They are almost always unaware that Almighty God doesn't recognize such vows, and will willingly release them from their evil servitude. The black stone is used in the Mothers-of-Darkness vows. The book of Revelation speaks about a white stone with a name written on it. Mothers of Darkness alters get a black stone with their assigned Queen Goddess names written on them. Those who have been on the inside of Satanism know that oaths taken by occult lodges and satanic cults are at times enforced. The oaths describe the type of traitor's death that is to be carried out.

An example of the types of penalty these oaths carry can be seen in the following words,

"All this I most solemnly and sincerely promise and swear with a firm steadfast resolution, to keep and perform the same without any equivocation, mental reservation or secret evasion of mind whatever, binding myself under no less penalty than that of having my throat cut across, my tongue torn open, my heart plucked out my body severed in twain, my bowels taken from thence and burned to ashes, should I knowingly violate this my solemn obligation."

The covenants, and vows and threats all work together to keep people in line. Alters within a Monarch slave are conditioned by their servitude to believe that their life is controlled by Satan, who is stronger than God. Where was God when they needed him? And yet many of the Monarch slaves coming in for therapy have had numerous miracles in their lives that have given them the latitude to reach out for health and freedom. If the Monarch alters can not see the positives of what God has done, they will remain trapped in their perception that Satan rules.

In truth, the survivors of the Illuminati's mind-control were meant to play a big role in helping God upset the detailed satanic script. Because these people sincerely gave their lives to Christ around the age of 2, God will honor that and help them. At any rate, even the informed secular therapist should realize these programmed slaves are in the middle of some power struggles. They are instruments of the Satanic hierarchy to carry out their plans. The Network goes out of their way to enhance the slave's perception that the occult rules. Along this line, President Reagan insisted the Monarch programmer Michael Aquino wear his black satanic ritual robes to a White House party. (One can read more about that night in "Transformation of America", p.129-130.)

Working hand in hand with the vows and the oaths, are the extreme measures the Network goes to, to convince the slave that they are always being watched. This is the "You can run, but you can't hide" programming. Supposedly, the slave is being watched by satellite no matter where they go. For instance, at Offit Air Force Base in Nebraska, an underground viewing room is used to convince Monarch slaves they have no place to hide. There the walls have numerous "satellite pictures" from around the world. The satellites are called "Eye in the Sky."

A four-screen viewer pretends to respond to the type-in commands of an air force official who tells the slave, "Where will you run? To the Artic? The Antarctic? Brazil? The Mountains?...We can find you there. There is truly no place to run and no place to hide." This show, which was made to convince the mind-controlled slave of the NWO's prowess, is just a pre-made slide show, it is just theatrics. However, the computer chips they have been implanting into people do give them the ability to track their slaves. And the intelligence agencies do have spy satellites.

The NWO is protected from nuclear attack via the Pentagon's C³I (pronounced "see-cubed-eye") meaning command, control, communication & intelligence. An important part of C³I is MILSTAR which is a global central nervous system of 9 satellites and about 3,500 million dollar MILSTAR terminals on the ground. The CIA has among other things, the $300 million Vortex spy satellite and a $500 million Magnum spy satellite which were recently launched.

LAYERING IN DEMONS

In the American Journal of Psychotherapy, two noted psychiatrists and an M.D. from India wrote an article "Multiple Personality in India: Comparison with Hysterical Possession State". The tenor of the article was that in India, the psychiatrists have to deal with demonic possession rather than MPD which is found in the west. They made comparisons of demonic possession in India to the MPD of the west, which are similar but not the same. Later, other articles and letters were written about this article. One of the criticisms was that these Indian psychiatrists were trying to compare their demonic possession to the west's MPD when it was obvious that their cases of demonic possession did not meet all the criteria of MPD.

In the experience of the author of this book, demonic possession is not MPD (DID) but it does have many of the same characteristics. If we understand programming from the Programmers point of view, they believe in both MPD and Demonic possession. From the programmers point of view, they try to create the alters and demonize the alters. Several ex-Programmers have told one source that if a person really wants to understand the Monarch trauma-based mind-control, they need to realize that it is fundamentally demonic-based. Two sources have had to sit through lectures by secular therapists who dismissed Satanism and the occult as simply as an excuse on the part the abusers to traumatize their victims.

According to these secular therapists, demon possession and satanic rituals have nothing to do with therapeutic issues, but are merely games and charades put on by the abusers. We beg to differ with this point of view. Programming and mind-control can not be separated from demonology and occult ritual. Even the "alien programming" uses lots of occult symbols, rituals & spiritual programming. An example of how ritual & programming overlap is the Sabbat ceremony to insure that cult slaves keep silent no matter what, even under torture.

On a full moon Sabbat, a large oak tree will be used to hold this night ceremony. A Magic cake, also known as a Red or Acacia Cake is made for the ceremony. The demon seer is invoked using the name

Shaddai (one of its 9 mystic names). An un-baptized child, who has been taken from Christian parents, is in the middle of the Pentagram, and a live altar consisting of a woman is used. A magic square called Satar formula is carved onto the child with an Eagle or Rooster claw. The child is turned to the 4 directions and then turned face down toward the east. The child must curse and blaspheme God Almighty. Then its mouth is gagged with a purple cloth. Flesh is cut from the child, and mixed with black millet and given to Satan (also called Sheitan).

Prayers in Enochian are said. Incense is lit. The child is now sacrificed to Satan, using the ritual athame (perhaps a black handled dagger), while the child is condemned by the cult to hell. This type of ritual is to instill fear of talking and praying into the cult members. One of the secret ceremonies to invoke demons comes from "The Book of Beasts". It is an ancient ceremony to summon demons. The ceremony begins with reading the Tetragrammaton Elohim, the Creature of Judgment is invoked, as well as the 9 mystic names of the dead.

A child is skinned and sacrificed. "The Book of the Old Faith" is read from. And then the demons are dismissed and a bell rung in the 4 directions. Monarch slaves recall the stench of the demons, and the roar that they make when invoked. To live through a horrifying experience like this does impact the slave, and therapists need to quit ignoring the various impacts that effect the victim of occult ceremonies. On the flip side, victims of mind-control need to realize that although demonic possession is one of the tools of control, that the diagnosis of "demon possession" should not be used to cover up the many other issues involved with the mind-control including body memories, a lifetime of severe abuse, abandonment issues, safety issues, and all the rest of the garbage that goes with having been a mind-controlled slave.

These many other issues need to be addressed too. When one source, began working with Programmed Multiples, he was told by several, independent of one another, that they had problems with spirits. Which they called Legion, Beelzebub, Asmodeus, Leviathon and Behemoth, occasionally Hanan was mentioned. After doing some work, false satanic trinities were found leading these Structured Multiple's systems. Interestingly, other ministers who were working in other areas of the country with Illuminati programmed multiples were finding the same thing.

If we comb the rare books of Europe, there two books in French, "Cruels Effets de la Vengeance du Cardinal Richelieu ou Histoire des Diables de Loudun" by Aubin (Amsterdam, 1716, pp. 215 +) and "Delacroix, Etudes d'Histoire et de Psychologie du Mysticisme" (Paris, 1908, pp. 328-344), which tell the story of the Uruline convent in Loudon between 1632 and 1638. This convent plays a role in the Illuminati bloodlines. What is of interest to us, is that the nuns back in 1632 found themselves "possessed" by demons.

These demons made the people act like animals, such as bark like dogs, rave in altered states, go into trances, have uncontrollable changes in personality which they would be amnesiac about. A male voice would appear in a female, etc. The mystic Father Surin, who came and tried to help the convent, himself got possessed for 20 years and had an entire change in personality for 20 years. He wrote that at times he felt like Satan. Seven demons manifested themselves in very different but distinct persons within these nuns.

The Catholic priest (an exorcist) could make the different demonic personas take the bodies of the Loudun nun Jeanne des Anges, and her face & body & voice would change from one possession to the other. These seven demons were Asmodée (also called Asmodeus), Leviathan, Béhémoth, Aman (Haman), Isacaaron, Balaam, and Grésil.

They also had a false trinity Lucifer-Beelzebub-Leviathon associated with them. French psychologist P. Janet in 1888 noticed that many of his patients found themselves losing control of their body to what they called a demon who would often be named Astaroth, Leviathan or Beelzebub. (P. Janet, "L 'Automatisme Psychologique" Paris, 1888, pp. 440 +.)

Reports from other areas such as Germany over the years are similar.

{ 391 }

Is this mere coincidence? It is stretching the imagination to believe that so many separate incidents have commonalities, and identical demonic entities, and yet are not related in some fashion. By the way, medieval witchcraft, Rosicrucianism, and the Illuminati have all had rituals where people dress with Cat, Lion, Owl, Cuckoo, and Parrot masks. In altered states, these medieval witches may have actually flipped into animal alters who thought they were a cat or owl, etc., which would account for written accounts by medieval craft adepts that witches would transform into animals. Demonic possession is getting more and more recognition by psychologists.

Some psychologists have discovered that their programmed multiples responded very positively to deliverance of demons, and were able to get more accomplished in a few hours of deliverance than years of psychology. What does this tell us? Well, it is NOT "scientific proof" that demons exist, but it is proof that deliverance can be very helpful. One can debate the exact reasons why deliverance works--perhaps it is merely that the helping person is entering the other person's construct--but the events of successful deliverance strongly indicate that what has happened is an actual deliverance of demons.

Because this book is about <u>HOW</u> the victim's are controlled, and the programmers believe that the primary ingredient in the mind-control is demonology, we will cover demonology. If that bothers some readers, then they need to ask themselves, Are they really wanting to understand how the mind-control is done, or simply superimpose and replace the how it is done with what they themselves would do?

Several times psychologists have been heard saying, "We don't know how the programmers think. It would be helpful to know." How many people are really ready to hear the answer? Recently, one of the Programmers (and names could be mentioned) never got excited as long as his slave was in therapy, but when his slave got a deliverance, he came totally unglued. On the flip side, anyone who can read this book entirely to this point and think that Illuminati slaves only have a problem with demons has somehow missed most of the book.

The programmers are so demon possessed that people who have

worked with them say that the powerful demons within them try to compete with each other for power. Those who have worked with the programmers know how the programmers themselves have been skilled in conjuring demons with a nine-foot circle with magical phrases like "Bagabi laca Bachabe, Lamac cahi achababe,..." Rituals have been performed at the programming sites. On the flip side, deliverance ministries can send demons to the throne of Almighty God to get instructions.

One of the first stories read to a slave may be the Jungle Book by freemason & occultist Rudyard Kipling (1865-1936). The story is used to teach the child to have animal spirit guides, such as the bear and leopard spirit guides found in Jungle Book. The main character in Jungle Book is neither animal or human, but in between. Neither world accepts this orphan boy. Slaves are taught that they are not human, but not fully animal, but something that can't be fully accepted or understood by anyone. Jungle Book provides the script for this. A bracelet keeps the boy safe by giving him the power of the gods. The slave is taught to get demonic power from jewelry which is given to them.

There are many other features of Jungle Book which are used for the initial programming too. Such as the pack of wolves (protectors in the system), snakes in the hell pit, a Boa Constructor snake to guard the castle, the need to pass through the waterfall to get into a wonderful world, a black jungle of death on the other side of the waterfall, castle jewels, caged birds, etc. Later, alters will be told they are the leader of a pack. Via the Jungle Book story used as a demonic programming script, the child's alters are taught that they are orphans with no mother or father, and that they must play and have the animal spirit guides as their friends.

HOW THE PROGRAMMERS UNDERSTAND DEMONOLOGY

Demonology is the key to what the programmers accomplish. Some recent efforts to expose the Monarch Mind Control have portrayed the programmers as very cynical about their "magic". While there may be exceptions to the rule, within the Illuminati, demonology is not taken lightly, but is considered to be the real science of the Sciences of Mind Control. The goal of the Illuminati programmers is stated in their own writings in Latin, "Quod superius est sicut quod inferius et quod inferius est sicut quod superius ad perpetranda miracula rei unius..." *"Meaning that their goal is to achieve the wonders of the "one thing" where "that which is above, is like that which is below and that which is below is like that which is above."*

In other words, they take the dark spiritual realm of Satan, as the pattern for the world. This Latin phrase is also used to support astrology, which influences some of the programming decisions. The concept of astrology was created by reframing God's "event markers" as event controllers. While Americans think of 1776 as independence year, 1776 was originally chosen as the most favourable year to reorganize the mystery religions into the formal Illuminati because 1776 consists of 1100 and 666. 1100 is the Babylonian counting system's number for 666. Babylonian Satanism is a foundational part of Moriah's Illuminism.

Some of its bloodlines are descendents of the Pharisees who secretly practiced Babylonian Satanism at the time of Christ, including. child sacrifices. It's standard operating procedure in the occult world that-what you see is not what you get, double-meanings are the norm. Those students of Monarch Mind Control who do not want to delve into what the Programmers are doing are limiting their own understanding. Most of what the Programmers do is actually spiritually based and connects to their understanding of demonology. Much of what the victims of the Monarch Programming experience will be understood in the context of the spiritual world.

Obviously some is illusion. Obviously some is delusion. However, when the high level programmers teach novice programmers, they will be teaching the spiritual principles you the reader are about to be told. A few therapists across the U.S.--and their names will not be revealed, have had miraculous recoveries of their Monarch slaves when they addressed these demonic and spiritual issues. These are therapists, who tried the old methods for years, and then in desperation were willing to listen to ex-programmers and other informed people about the spiritual side of the programming. Everything in life has a physical and a spiritual side to it. Things in the spiritual effect the physical, and things in the physical effect the spiritual. They are two worlds.

The Alice In Wonderland story is highly regarded by the programmers, because it portrays the situation that exists between the spiritual world & the physical world. When people within the physical look toward the spiritual, it is like looking into a mirror. Initially, they will only see the physical world reflected back. But if they go beyond the mirror, they would see a "mirror image" of the physical exists in the spiritual realm. When Christians pray they say, "Thy will be done on earth as it is in heaven." Earth is a mirror image of heaven, not an exact copy, but someday they will be alike, according to Scripture.

According to messianic Jews who understand the Old Testament well, the ceremonial law is being enacted in heaven spiritually as it's mirror image once was done on earth. When the programming is seen only in a secular fashion, much of its design is missed. What have witches used to see beyond time and space? Mirrors. Remember the witch saying "mirror, mirror on the wall, who is the fairest of them all"? The idea is magical mirrors, the speculums, which will lead one "through the looking glass mirror" that then allows the victim to magically transcend time & space.

One of the important keys to success with Monarch programming are generational spirits. The cover for this is studies in genetic science. The programmers believe that genetics are important, but the real abilities to program someone come from the generational spirits that are built up in bloodlines. This is why the Illuminati were in part skeptical that non-generational occult bloodlines could be successfully programmed. They have found that they can be (especially with all their high tech equipment), but the best candidates are those with strong generational spirits.

The difference could be compared to those who raise race-horses for the Kentucky derby and those who have horses as a hobby. A race horse must have high spirits. The suburban housewife & daughter who ride as an occasional pastime could care less for that quality of horse. The military can produce cannon fodder with the simple mind-control of Basic Training. They don't need sophisticated time intensive mind-control techniques like the Monarch Program for some military positions. Third world children are being programmed to become baseball players etc.

But the highest occult vocational positions will be given to people with exceptional generational demonic power. Within a Multiple you will find duplicates of a particular name. For instance, you may find thirteen Susies. Susy I may not even be aware of the other Susies. The internal worlds of the Monarch victim are structured along demonic patterns. Within the demonic world the spirit Moriah is not itself in every victim that has Moriah. Moriah # 10,882 may be in victim A, and Moriah # 3,355 in victim B. But the difference is academic because the Moriah in each victim is a member of the same demonic family--the Moriah Spirit Family.

They are for all intents and purposes the same spirit. The Illuminati programmers are acutely aware of the generational spirits, who they are, and how they function. The ten commandments warn that a person's iniquity will affect the next 3-4 generations. EX 20:5b. A generational spirit is given "appointment" over a victim at birth. The victim will receive generational spirits from their biological father and mother. Satan can not be the creator of heaven and earth, but he can satisfy his desire to do so, by creating an internal world within the victim, a heaven, earth and hell of his own creation. The armies of spirits which are placed into the infant will cooperate with the programmer and the child to produce the programming. It's like the Father ("Papa" the programmer), son (child) and unholy spirit (demons) work together.

The internal creation of worlds within the victim will be the heart beat of Satan. A Regional territorial commander demon will make weekly rounds in an area, and so the structuring work done with generational victims, combines ideas from the generational spirits as well as the regional commander. The curses and the vows give the Commander the legal right to exercise control over the victim. Within any geographic area, there has been a layering in of demons, much in the same fashion that the programming and demons are layered into a Monarch victim. The most important territorial spirits in an area are the root or original spirits. In the United States these are Indian Spirits. Territorial spirits may contribute ideas as to what will be effective for programming in their area. There are geographic patterns to spiritual warfare.

Each area has its deities and spirits which rule the valleys, homes, and nations. These particular spirits exercise power over the local people. The evangelist is not going to progress, unless he understands the spirits that are ruling what he is trying to liberate people from. The basic territorial spirits are the original ones. In the U.S. these are the Indian spirits. That is why the Illuminati pays such a strong interest in the Indians. The original principalities are the foundation, the bedrock upon which everything else is layered upon.

This also is done in Monarch programming. A number of Monarch slaves have Indian shamans and spirits placed in their systems. Upon the original foundation, the newer ideologies are layered in. In Russia, communism was simply layered on top of the original territorial spirits. In China, communism was simply layered on top of the original territorial spirits. This is one factor why Chinese & Russian communism were never alike. Traumas and crises will produce strongholds. Our understanding of our blind spots is often weak because we use others as our measuring stick rather than the divine word of God. Blind spots & strongholds may take outside intervention in our lives to eliminate. How many of us see that Moroni on top of Mormon temples is a ruling demon?

How many of us have realized that the rising sun on Japan's flag is the Sun goddess who is a ruling spirit over Japan? If we go to Hawaii we will see some of the "natives" are interested in Pele, the God of Fire. The volcanoes have been used by the demons to entrap the people to Pele, the God of Fire. One of the things that the author's book Ezekiel 6:3 An Inhouse Directory shows is that many of the ritual sites have occult names. Devil's Canyon may well be a canyon for devils. The names people give geographic areas are important. They show the types of pacts that people have been making. When the psychiatrist Karl Menninger of the Menninger Foundation dealt with spiritual issues with people in mental hospitals (i.e. he had them ask for forgiveness of sins), he was able to clear out whole sections, and send the patients home well. (His bro. Roy W. Menninger, an Episcopalian., & also a psychiatrist, worked in Boston State Hosp. while in the military in '52-53.)

There is a direct tie between much of the insanity today and demons. Spiritual principles should be studied by Christians to understand how demons operate and what gives them entry rights and power. Certain objects and people are focal points for spirits.

WHO are the experts?

Basically, two types of people involve themselves in studying demonology--those who are involved with performing works of darkness such as magic, or those involved with performing works of godliness such as deliverance ministries. Jesus told his disciples to command the demons to leave. He didn't ask his disciples to let him cast out demons, nor did he ask his disciples to ask the demons to leave. No, the responsibility was placed upon his disciples & they were asked to command the demons to leave. The Illuminati maintain hidden libraries full of ancient treatises on demonology, which they avidly study. Some of the more important demonology books are the Sixth and Seventh Book of Moses, The Black Raven, The Spring Book, The Spiritual Shield. A whole series of magical books bearing the name of Solomon exist, of which the Key of Solomon is widely known.

Clavicula Salomonis or the Clavicle of Solomon is also well known. More and more of the ancient writings seem to be coming to light in these end times, and the hierarchy is getting bolder and bolder in the release of this information. A Cabalistic Jew will study the Talmud until he is 40 or so, and the study of the Cabala is reserved for the only those who have studied a long time. The Zohar and the esoteric teachings are not taught until late in life.

Opposite the Illuminati, are those dedicated Christians who study demonology, not to invoke demons but to free people from them. Each state in the United States contains a few Christians who understand demonology and deliverance from it. The blood of Jesus Christ (Yeshua ha Messiach) is very powerful against demons. High level deliverance can not be done without angelic and the Holy Spirit's help. The Christian who gets into studying and fighting high level demonology needs to learn the significance of getting God's help. Without God's help, the deliverance will back-fire in the face of the deliverer. Members of the Illuminati are bound in servitude to Satan. One of the strong shackles that bind Satanists to Satan is the high level of demonology they are enslaved to.

HOW are the demons organized?

It is very clear that there are different types of demons, and that they are divided up into different ranks, functions, orders, etc. A great deal of time has been spent by both brilliant Christians and satanic Magicians to chart out the names, ranks, and structure of the demonic armies that Satan commands. One accurate method of ranking demons has 365 ranks of demons, with number 1 being the highest level of demons. The numbers of top level demons are numbered in the trillions, while the lower level imps are incredibly numerous. There is no shortage of demons to carry out the work of Satan on this planet. These demons are sometimes variously referred to as spirit guides, angels, wizards, ghosts and aliens or a number of other disguises. Both early Christians and the occult have often divided up the evil spirits under fire, water, wind, and earth. The power of Enochian magic comes from the Watchtowers of these four elements.

Some common types of Evil Spirits are:

- Spirit of the Anti-Christ (1 John 4:3)
- Spirit of Bondage (Romans 8:15)
- Spirit of Divination (Ezekiel 21:21)
- Spirit of Death
- Dumb & Deaf Spirit (Mark 9:25)
- Spirit of Error (1 JN 4:6)

- Familiar Spirit (LV 20:27)
- Spirit of Fear (2 TM 1:7)
- Spirit of Haughtiness (PRY 16:18, 19)
- Spirit of Heaviness (ISA 61:3)
- Spirit of Infirmity (LK 13:11
- Spirit of Jealousy (NM 5:14)
- Lying Spirit (2 CHR. 18:22)
- Perverse Spirit (ISA 19:14)
- Seducing Spirits (1 TM 4:1)
- Spirit of Whoredoms (Hosea 4:12, and 5:4)

Each of these types of Evil Spirits has a number of specialists. For instance the Spirits of Whoredoms contains spirits which can specialize in the following:

- A Spirit of Unfaithfulness
- A Spirit of Prostitution (whether Spirit, Soul or Body)
- A Spirit of the Love of Money
- A Spirit of Idolatry
- A Spirit of Chronic Dissatisfaction
- A Spirit of Fornication
- A Spirit of Gluttony
- The Spirits of Bondage include:
- A Spirit of Fear
- A Spirit of any number of addictions (drugs, alcohol, etc.)
- A Spirit of the Fear of Death
- A Spirit of being a Servant of Corruption
- A Spirit of Compulsive Iniquity

These lower echelon demons are too numerous to keep track of.

When a portal is opened which gives a particular demon legal access into a body, they move very quickly into the physical body. When a man lusts after a woman, he will open a portal, such as the mouth through which a demon (spirit of lust), shaped for instance like a frog, will jump in through. This demon will then insure that the evil thought will be acted upon. The principalities and powers exercise dominion over spirits. Further, high level Satanists are well aware of all these things. When godly people of faith identify, bind and cast out specific demons, they should practice loosening the appropriate good spirit to take its place. If we bind a spirit of Bondage, we loose a spirit of adoption. If we bind a Spirit of Error, then we loose a Spirit of Truth.

There are 3 powerful satanic covens of 21 persons. They are distributed in Monterrey, CA, Phoenix, AZ and the third in Idaho. L.A. also there is a fourth headquarters for the Coven of the 21st Star. These 21-person-covens are made up of very intelligent, powerful persons. These type of covens attract powerful commander demons. Within one source's area, Bend, Portland and Eugene areas in Oregon have powerful covens. The power of these types of powerful covens will be reflected in the spiritual world. Paul under the Spirit's inspiration wrote, "while we do not look at the things which are seen, but at the things which are not seen. For the things which are seen are temporary, but the things which are not seen are eternal." 2 Cor 4:18 The invisible things are more important that the visible. If we recognize this, the Word of God says that this will help us keep from losing heart! "Therefore we do not lose heart. Even though our outward man is perishing, yet the inward man is being renewed day by day." 2 Cor 4:16

Spirits are in a sense a mirror image world. They are placed in the victim first. The programming and the images that are built will be built with their cooperation and guardianship. Spirits are appointed to protect each program and each memory. A spirit commander called a chief executive is set in command of the victim's life. Military command structures around the world are structured on how the demonic command structure exists. Some soldiers have the same function, but are not actually the exact same person. So it is with demons. Victims have their own individual demons, but they are models of what that type of demon is supposed to act like.

The child is exposed to films, books and stories. The spirits interact within the person's mind to lock these pictures in place. The demons in a sense serve as mirrors within the child's mind, reflecting the images the child needs to fix in the mind. As the programmer, child and demons structure the internal world, the demonic spirits will guard these structures. The force or energy behind the structures is the demons. In order to guard things further, demonic castles and temples will exist within a system to guard it. Entire spiritual quadrants will exist, that are entirely spiritual and contain absolutely no alters. These spiritual worlds can not be seen physically. Only spiritual power and discernment can reveal them. In fact, while the normal person uses 5 senses, the Illuminati teach their alters and people in demonology to use 7 spiritual senses.

The child will be shown films and stories, but will then be programmed to forget them. However, the demonic spirits will guard these concepts. The core is involved in giving energy toward these spiritual programming goals. The willful contribution of energy to these demonic goals must be guarded so the core is hidden. While other children are playing with children, the victim of Monarch Mind -control slavery is being taught to dance and play with internal playmates which are demons. This is to familiarize the child to the spirit world. The child's family becomes its internal world. There are some teachers in public schools and pre-schools that are openly helping children do this. All the time that the programming is going on, the spiritual world stays hidden in the darkness.

Gnomes, sometimes called dwarfs, are one of the four divisions of nature spirits. They know where the gold is within the earth. This is why Joseph Smith, Jr. who was from an important generational occult bloodline which has generational programmed MPDs, did magic to elemental spirits when he was looking for jewels and gold as a young man. In reflection of this, the Gnomes (also known as dwarfs, elves, or minihunes) of the internal world mine the gold and jewels the programs of the System. Illuminati programmer Manly P. Hall wrote in his classic book "The Secret Teachings of All Ages" on page CVI, *"...there are many types of gnomes evolving through the subjective ethereal body of Nature. These earth spirits work in an element so close in vibratory rate to the material earth that they have immense power over its rocks and flora, and also over the mineral elements in the animal and human kingdoms.*
Some,...work with the stones, gems and metals, and are supposed to

be the guardians of hidden treasures." The Disney family and the Disney corporations are part of the occult world. While the names Dopey, Happy, Bashful, Sleepy, Grumpy, Sneezy, and Doc sound like names picked to please children, they are actually the translation from Scandinavian of the demonic dwarfs Toki, Skavaerr, Varr, Dun, Orinn, Grerr, and Radsvid. Note that Disney placed a character with a green mask in a dark mirror, and had in his shows what was called the 'Spirit of the Magic Mirror' which was also called The Slave of the Magic Mirror.

The Monarch slaves "most precious programs" are concealed in the ground and are guarded by the gnomes built internally by the programming. These gems have power that is channeled from Satan. Most of the readers thought Snow White and the 7 Dwarfs was simply a harmless piece of fiction. They most likely didn't realize that it is demonology. An example of the importance of these types of spirits is Findhorn's use of them. Findhorn Institute in Scotland, which has branches by other names in other countries, is like the Vatican of the New Age. It secretly sends out orders to many witches and New Agers. To spell it out clearer, Findhorn, the Vatican of the New Age movement, is one of the channels of communication from the secret Illuminati councils to their people worldwide.

The success of Findhoru's community, according to Findhorn is their use of elemental gnome spirits in their gardening and planting. What is someone who believes in good spirits to do with this information? To recognize that the patterns for the programming are inspired by demons, are held in place by demonic energy and are guarded by demons. The programming can be collapsed upon itself if this demonic "glue' is taken away. But only a few individuals understand the spiritual forces behind the programming. This understanding takes spiritual eyes. If the spiritual is not dealt with, the person can be reprogrammed at will by the demonic entities that still control the victim.

This is the "missing piece that has frustrated advanced secular therapists. Within Illuminati slaves, they will have the All-seeing Eye placed in their system guarded by legions of demons. Within the very eye of the all-seeing eye, the Programmers will place some actual alters. There will also be demons placed within the construct too. The De-programmer must be careful to separate the demonic from the human element and get the alters who are held captive in the eye out. The Programmers do a great deal of mixing demons with alters, and they place alters all over the system in captive or hostage situations so that the System of Alters is literally blackmailed into cooperating if they don't want to hurt parts of themselves.

The Programmers do both internal and external blackmail. Within the Monarch programming, the demons are layered in between the worlds. In the older Illuminati programming, mirrors were placed into the System and the demons were layered behind the mirrors. The mirrors would separate levels within the mind. The demons would protect the mirrors. If a Monarch alter would shatter a mirror, the demons behind it are released and all hell breaks loose in their mind. Therapists who have tried everything for years to deal with the mirrors, have found that a few minutes of correct spiritual warfare accomplished more than years of trying psychological techniques.

In the 1980 models of Monarch slaves, the Programmers began placing a planet of alters, interspersed with a planet of demons, as they would build a solar system. This had the same layering effect as the mirrors. The demons then would be assigned to protect the different levels, in this case represented by different orbiting planets. Principle demons that are popular to place into Monarch systems are:

- Æsculapius -- the satanic miracle healer, related to Apollo, in the pagan world he was depicted with his head encircled with rays. In order to show pagans that it was O.K. to worship Jesus, the Catholic church put the golden rays of Æsculapius around pictures of Jesus. He is also at times represented as the sacred snake.

- Absolom --, Amon -- (various spellings) A marquis of Hell, who has the gift of prophecy.

- Apollyon - This demon is over the bottomless pit and is described by REV 9:11. Demon of fear and destruction, who may be a deep part of a System.

- Apollo -- The AntiChrist's father

- Astar (Star, Ashtareth, Ashtaroth, Astarte, Ishtar) - Bible students will find this demon referred in many Bible passages including JDG 2:13 ACTS 20.

- Balilo -- witch demon, Beelzebub -- Ruling demon

- Beliah -- the chief demon, with the name meaning "worthless one". Beliel -- sexual demon, Bes -- Spirit ruling the dwarfs. Blackwell--legion demon, upper rank, to divide the mind. Blood (aka Yahweh Elohim) -- dark spirit using God's name & part of Black Mass, conn. w/ early 3-year-old trauma to "locked-up child'. Choronzon -- to help with constructing the mind control Dameon

- Dagon -- the fish god over water. The fish sign was adopted by elements of the Catholic church to secretly keep Dagon worship alive. The Pope wears the garb that the Pontiface Maximus wore as leader of the cult of Dagon. One system had a water monster named CTHULHU.

- Electra -- Enigma --, Geb -- voice behind the earth spirit, Gerberus -- Guardian angels -- the Illuminati may assign guardian angels called Hafaza. Javen -- double-minded demon Kali -- bloody female goddess Kemosh

- Leviathan (Seen as a sea-monster, or Tyrannosaurus Rex, or Dragon-like)-This demon runs up and down the spine. Leviathan is related to the Babylonian reptilian God Tiamet (which looks like the Reptilian aliens portrayed today.) Is tied to the double-helix. It can actually be three spirits. Bible students can read about Leviathan in Job 3:8, Job 41:8, 15,22, PS 74:14, ISA 27:1 Lilith -- a bloody demon, known as the "terror of the night". The occult story is that she was Adam's wife before Eve, and that her offspring with Adam were demonic-human monsters. It might be worthy to mention that in Druidism, the life-force or energy force is considered to be the Dragon. There are several names for this Dragon including Wyvern, nwyvre, or the winged lion.

-

VooDoo (Vandon)

- Mammon -- the demon of avarice Meganosis -- Metatron -- Sometimes said to be Enoch. Moriah-Moloch (also spelled Molech) -- The various satanic-luciferian groups that program offer child sacrifices to Moloch, an internal Temple of Moloch may guard the innocent blood of children sacrificed during ceremonies. Historically, the people in Israel sacrificed children to Moloch at Tophet in the Valley of Hinnom near Jerusalem. Drums (tophim) were beat so the cries of the children couldn't be heard. Mormo- Important demon placed in Mormon Monarch slaves.

- Nanna-Nemo -- Mormon programming Octopus--blood sucking demon

- Orion -- placed over Mormon victims, the name Orion is popping out all over the place, Pan-protector of woods Ronwe -Squat -- a number of Illuminati Monarchs report that this demon gives them the ability to understand foreign languages, Shu -- does internal weather magic Others incl. - Typhon (program tunneling connections in the mind), Verono, Vultar Val (legion), Pan whose depression sends one Rege (drugs), who sends one to Bacchus (addiction) which then starts a bondage loop.

THE JOKERS

The everyday demons who the alters have to contend with if they step out of line, are the Jokers. Jokers can jump out of the mirrors and drag an alter into the looking glass world. Alters going into the system away from their assigned living quarters end up in mazes of mirrors. The mazes of mirrors can't be broken because demons are placed behind the mirrors. However, deliverance methods work well to destroy the power of these demonic protected mirrors. Many, if not most of the occult world do not view spirits as evil. Illuminati children are taught that these spirits are playmates. Since the child is not allowed real friends, they are happy to have demons to play with inside their mind. One major religion whose adherents publicly seek spirit (demonic) possession--although they again view spirits as being capable of both good and evil, neutral in connotation much like the Greek gods, is Voodoo.

In discussing how trauma-based mind-control is done, voodoo must be included as a component. Many of the Mind-controlled slaves have had voodoo as part of their trauma, and many had voodoo dolls placed into their Systems. When vows and oaths are made, an object is given to the satanic cult or the Illuminati for the Keeper of the Seals to guard. If the vow is broken voodoo magic can be used against the offender by using the object given in the sealing. Voodoo-ism came from Africa, where it is called Ju-Ju. A recent book Blood Secrets is the true story of demon worship and human sacrifice by a former JuJu high priest Isaiah Oke, who gave up JuJu magic for the Christian faith.

The Basuto in Africa call witches "baloi", the Akans say "obayifo" and the Lovedu say "vuloi". There are different names and variances of magical practices, but what most people don't realize is that these are just different styles of JuJu-ism. The JuJu priests (called a ba-balawo) will rule the religious/magic lives of an African village. JuJu is satanic, and much of it is kept secret by its high priests. The Priests take blood oaths of secrecy. The West African name for Satan is Esu. A group in Phoenix, AZ claims to be in contact with an alien named Jesus Esu Sananda. Another word that has come from Voodoo is the word zombie. Many members of the Illuminati go to the Caribbean and South America to attend Illuminati rituals. Umbanda (Brazilian Satanism), which is sometime mistakingly called Macumba, openly has satanic rituals on Copacabana Beach.

Many of the elite have made their pilgrimage to Copacabana Beach, inclunding European royalty and the Pope. There are 7 bloodlines in Umbanda, and a newcomer must join one of these. If American Il-lum, slaves have memories of Argentina and other Latin American countries, the memories could easily be true. The Illuminati within the Jehovah's Witnesses' Bethel HQ (which are programmed multi-ples) have used quiet islands in the Bahamas for rituals. In 1958, it is believed (according to 2 partly de-programmed multiples) that it was Andros Island, Bahamas which they used for their rituals. In Haiti, Voodoo, called Vaudou, is the religion of the majority of the people, about 90% of the people. This is interesting because it gives us an example of what the situation is like when an entire nation regularly seeks to be demon possessed.

Possession behavior in the various black occult groups, such as Umbanda (Brazilian Satanism), Haitian Vaudou, and the St. Vincent Shakers (also called Zeckeeboom people) is a learned behavior. Candidates for medium ship in Sao Paulo Umbanda are given special training in trance & possession. They use dissociation techniques such as focusing on a lighted candle, or turning the person and snapping the fingers to put people in trance. In the U.S., because demon possession seems rare to psychiatrists, they have labeled demon possessed people as "crazy". However, in Haiti, an entire nation regularly conducts rituals to become demon possessed. Since the norm is to be demon possessed, it fails to be abnormal behavior.

Many of the other labels and explanations that psychiatrists find easy to give concerning demon possession in the U.S. obviously just don't explain what is happening in Haiti. Some of the explanations given by psychiatrists for demon possession in Voodoo is

a.   a. repressed personality is coming to the surface,

b.   that the voodoo trance is an act to impress a crowd,

c.   it stems from hysterical nervous disorders, and

d.   it stems from psychopathy, neurosis, or schizophrenia.

a.   In Haiti, demon possession of people can not be a repressed personality because the person being possessed of a demon must behave according to rigorous rules of how each demon is supposed to act. Far from expressing himself, the victim of demon possession tries to personify some mythical spirit whose character on the whole is foreign to himself.

b.   In Haiti, most people who go into the demon possessed state are not observed closely because it is the norm for people to become demon possessed. People at the ceremonies may cast absent-minded looks at the people being possessed, but the entire scenario gains the possessed person very little attention. Nor does an entire crowd in Haitian Voodoo get possessed, or go into a collective delirium. The excitement is quite varied with the crowds.

c. If explanation c. were true, it would mean an entire nation is hysterical and mentally deranged. 40 years ago it was shown that the Haitian people are not all hysterical, but that demon possession in Haiti was the normal means of communicating with supernatural powers. If demon possession trances were genetic in origin, then why do some groups of blacks from the same gene pool but living in other nations have absolutely little to do with the occult?

d. Investigators in Haiti have had to discount demon possession as a neurosis.

According to a Brazilian psychiatrist, who did a study on Black religious groups, the number of schizophrenics and psychotics is very small within cults like Voodoo. *"Here the very marked lack of response to the cathartic therapies employed in possession cults in the case of seriously disturbed individuals...is itself a testimony to the robust mental health of the majority of participants....The latter have no difficulty at all in communicating their problems. They operate within a culturally standardized medium of communication. Nor in contrast to the true self-insulated psychotic, do they miss their "cues." They respond in the expected way, and others react equally predictably." ......"Fankly schizophrenic person would be able to pass the probationary scrutiny involved to join this religious group."*

Interestingly, studies made of W.W. II war criminals show no personality differences between them and the normal population. Could it be possible that there really is a demonic element in the lives of people that helps move them in the direction of evil?

So' what is demon possession in Haiti's Voodooism? According to the Haitians a spirit which they call "loa" joins a person like a rider mounts a horse. The spirit then controls the person like a rider. The possessed person is called a "chual" which means horse, and the spirit is said to mount or saddle his victim. Blood sacrifices are often associated with the demon, and the possessed person will drink the blood from the sacrificed animal. Polished stones, and herbs, and trance and dissociative states are used to attract spirits. While the Monarch slaves have trauma-based dissociative states, the practitioners of Voodoo have ritually induced dissociative states.

Voodoo rituals will involve chanting, drums, at times handclapping and frenzied dancing to induce the dissociative states. In fact, several features have been identified which bring about dissociative states in the black religions of the Caribbean and South America. First they have dancing to a pronounced and rapid beat. Next, the induction into the dissociative state frequently follows a period of starvation and/or over-breathing (hyperventilation). The beginning of the demonic possession is characterized by a brief period of muscle inhibitions, or a collapse.

The person who is experienced at being possessed acquires a specific behavior pattern for the deity that is supposedly controlling it. And finally, the head and limbs may tremor under trance, and the person may become dissociative enough that they can pick up red hot irons. The possessed can be conscious, semiconscious, or unconscious. Studies made of this situation where an entire nation like Haiti actively seeks demonic possession allows us to discount some explanations and get a better picture of what demon possession isn't. It also helps to understand what is involved in demonic possession. The first major authoritative work on Haitian Voodoo written in 1884 by Spencer St. John reported on the terror, the blood rites, and the cannibalism of Haitian Voodoo.

This has been too much for some people to believe. Still, if people stop to realize how Voodoo came about it, it makes sense. Conservative estimates of the number of slaves brought into the port of Saint Dominque while it was a plantation colony are 900,000. The conditions on the island for the slaves was like a Nazi work camp. The cruelty on the colonial Haitian plantations was beyond comprehension. The Africans brought in as slaves already practiced JuJu. Under the crucible of the severe torture of slavery, the slaves formed Haitian voodoo, which is a conglomeration of African Voodoo, Masonic rites, European magic and Catholic saints and symbols.
For 2 centuries, their African vaudou was these slaves only power

against their cruel plantation owners, and is partly credited for helping Haiti become the first free black republic in the revolution of 1804. In Haiti, Cuba, Brazil, Trinidad and other areas of the New World, where JuJu-ism has transformed itself into black occult religions, the old gods of Africa: Damballa, Erzilie, Legba, Obatala, Ogun, Oshun and others have been equated with Catholic saints and given the names of these saints. The ritually induced dissociative states of Voodoo are generally accompanied by amnesia, that is lost time. During this lost time, the person acts as if he is a spirit (god). This is a ritual based dissociative state rather than a trauma-based dissociative state.

The Illuminati Monarch programming at times attempts to combine the two bases, ritual and trauma, to create a dissociative state. This is why is it difficult to separate out the religious factor.

INDIA

Up to now there have been numerous cases of demonic possession in India, but there has been no cases of a true multiple personality. The reason why is that the multiple's in the U.S. and Europe are being cranked out by trauma-based mind-control and the Illuminati hasn't been programming in India like the U.S. & Europe. As the slaves that are being created disperse, within time, we will eventually start seeing multiples in India. In the "American Journal of Psychotherapy", Jan. 1981, p. 115, it states, *"However, so far, no case of double or multiple personality so labeled by a psychiatrist, has been reported from India in the professional literature. Considering that hysterical disturbances in general are quite widespread in the country, this is surprising. On the one hand, it could mean an actual low prevalence of multiple personality in the country."* For those of us who understand what is happening, it is obvious why multiples aren't found in India. The fact that multiples aren't found in India ought to wake up people that multiple personalities is not "demon possession nor is it simply the result of bad parenting or everyday type of horrendous trauma.

Almost everyone has a trauma in their early life, and is somewhat dissociative, but that doesn't make them have multiple personalities, which are programmed and have separate histories and altar names. India has over twice the population of the U.S. and yet no multiples reported. After reading this book, the reader understands why not. It might be appropriate to point out here that the early American cases of MPD (now called DID) are from bloodlines associated with the Illuminati. The first widely reported American case of MPD was Mary Reynolds in 1811.

The Top 13 Illuminati Bloodlines covers the Reynold's bloodline as being a major Illuminati bloodline. Two other earlier American MPD cases are one involving a man from Edinburgh University, Scotland and one found discussed in a letter in 1791 written by a Reverend Joseph Lathrop of Mass. to the President of Yale Ezra Stiles. (See "Letters and Papers of Ezra Stiles", President of Yale College, 1778-1795. New Haven: Yale Univ. Press, 1933.) Those, who have tracked the conspiracy, or read the writings of Fritz's Springmeier, know that Yale was founded by the Unitarians and has long been important for the Illuminati. The Unitarians have been connected with hermeticism and money from the start.

HOW THE ANTI-CHRIST SPIRIT CONTRIBUTES TO CONTROLLING THE SLAVE

Within the Illuminati hierarchy slaves, the Spirit of the Anti-Christ operates. The Mothers-of-Darkness are only allowed to become Mothers-of-Darkness after they marry the Anti-Christ. The entire worldwide collection of Mothers-of-Darkness alters will serve the physical Anti-Christ as a private harem when he takes over. They will also serve as an inner elite guard of the physical Anti-Christ. They describe the consummation of the marriage with the Anti-Christ as being badly burned. Because the Anti-Christ, who is alive and well today, will be/is already the master handler and the master programmer.

How does the Spirit of the Anti-Christ influence a Mind-controlled slave? Some of the things that this Spirit does to control individuals is to cause them to judge themselves. Another thing done to control the slave's alters to change their focus so they can't grow spiritually, bribe the person with enticing doctrines of demons, and mislead people from true freedom into religious bondage. We will clarify what we mean as we explain these things in the next few paragraphs. Satan himself spawned the Anti-Christ spirit, as well as leading the demonic angels into their evil.

The Spirit of the Anti-Christ has as its purpose, the destruction of everything that God has built within the person, their looks, their curiosity of beauty, and their personhood itself. The Spirit of the Anti-Christ is attached to the religious spirit when people get Christianity without the Spirit of Life. Many Monarch slaves with the Anti-Christ spirit are working under the cover of being good Christians. The Bible even talks about them, *"For such are false apostles, deceitful workers, transforming themselves into the apostles of Christ. And no marvel; for Satan himself is transformed into an angel of light. Therefore it is no great thing if his ministers also be transformed as the ministers of righteousness; whose end shall be according to their works."* 2 COR 11:13-15.

The Greek word translated "transforming" is also the source of our word masquerade. It means to have a front, with a hidden character behind the front. The words of the apostles warn Christians about "double-minded men" (JS 1:8) and that Satan's key people will masquerade with false fronts. In contrast, the Scriptures admonish followers of Christ to have their public lives match their private lives.

Satan lavishes the Spirit of the Anti-Christ upon his hierarchy. He doesn't lavish his spirit within what he views as the "rabble" of humanity, who do not directly serve him.

When the Spirit comes into a person, it comes in as a cold clammy spirit that consumes all hope and all joy in life. Rather than being a fresh breeze bringing joy, this Spirit of the Anti-Christ is like a vacuum sucking life. It is like being raped. Victims of this spirit, say they felt like they were raped and defiled by it. The person's own natural feelings of cleanliness will feel violated. This Spirit can touch our lives in different ways and at different levels. When our personal standards are violated, the person will often not forgive themselves. Instead, they judge themselves. This further illustrates how the Anti-Christ sets up abusive patterns.

By judging ourself, rather than forgiving, we set ourselves up as God, for only God can judge a person, for He is the only one who has a true standard and measuring stick to judge by. Captured by the cycle of abuse of the Spirit of the Anti-Christ, a person will continue to beat up upon themselves. At some point we forgive ourselves, and in so doing we are saying that the memory no longer has mastery over us. As Christ is the incarnation of God in the flesh, the Anti-Christ will be the incarnation of Satan in the flesh. (cf. REV 13:4) Satan wanted God's power and glory, but not the character of God. The Spirit of the Anti-Christ has a wisdom that it promotes which is "earthly, natural, demonic." (JAS 3:14-15) The Spirit of the Anti-Christ will entice people with the Doctrine of Demons. (See 1 TIM 4:1) For instance, "For when they speak great swelling words of vanity, they allure through the lusts of the flesh, through much wantonness, those that are just escaping from them who live in error. While they promise liberty, they themselves are the servants of corruption..." 2 Peter. 2:17-19

The Anti-Christ Spirit breaks our ability to love God & others. Satan's original pride came from selfishness. The Spirit of the Anti-Christ brings selfishness, but it brings it in a hidden way. The Anti-Christ Spirit will cause pain. Heaven, where the Spirit of the Anti-Christ is absent, has no suffering. The hidden damage of pain is that it inflicts self-focus. Christ as He hung on the cross was able to continue to focus on others.

While most men would have been thinking about themselves in self-pity Jesus was still thinking of others. He said to his mother, "Woman, behold your son." And to John, "Behold your mother." To paraphrase, Take care of my mother. Later he said, "Forgive them for they know not what they do." (See the Gospel of John) Jesus even brought someone to the Lord, **while he hung on the cross he was evangelizing**. Don't so many Christians look for the ideal situation to lead people to the Lord, yet Christ did it under the worst of conditions. Self-focus, selfishness and pride are closely related. It is hard to point out where one begins and the other ends. The Spirit of the Anti-Christ wants to draw others to its position of pride. So it inflicts pain and suffering, like it did to Job to draw the attention of the person off of Yahweh God and one's fellowman and onto oneself. All the commandments hang on us loving Yahweh God will all our heart, soul, and mind, and loving our neighbor as ourselves, but the Anti-Christ Spirit gets our focus off of Yahweh and others and onto ourselves. Bitterness may develop in us. Bitterness grieves the Holy Spirit.

Bitterness will seat itself in our mind, and like a transponder will emit bitterness. A lack of peace and joy results. The Spirit of the Anti-Christ has sidetracked the whole maturing process. As a child grows into an adult it learns to shift its focus from itself to others. Can we go in and focus on our own problems and solve them? If part of the problem is self-focus, then the answer is "no." The answer lies in focusing on the Holy Spirit. Living and walking in the Spirit of Christ is the health we seek. (GAL 5:16; JN 15:1-11) Does it work? Yes. I knows of many cases, where all kinds of individuals solved all kinds of problems by receiving the Holy Spirit into their lives. They see the supernatural cleansing that happens, but many times they don't understand the principle behind what they just experienced. When some of their problems persist, do they turn again to focus on the Holy Spirit? Often they focus on themselves, self-pity, bitterness, etc. Counseling today often takes this approach. It is fine to identify the problem, but then following that the solution is not to focus on the problem but to get out of the path of death.

THE PROCESS OF HEALING

Healing may be a process, not an event. We break an arm in a second, it takes many months to heal. We break our capacity to love God and our fellowman, but we expect an instant cure. Anyone who has met the Spirit of the Anti-Christ needs to learn how to love again. Love is an action word. One learns to hammer nails by hammering nails. One learns to type by typing. One learns to love by loving. The survivor who has been controlled by the Spirit of the Anti-Christ may need to get a teacher of love, a "Loving teacher" so-to-speak.

{ 415 }

THE USE OF ANGEL ALTERS

Many Illuminati models had "angels" or "spirit guides" created that could provide divine messages to the Monarch slave. The Illuminati/ Intelligence agencies have been highly successful with controlling people via their religious beliefs by implanting alters who are seen by a Monarch slave as being a messenger from God or the Gods. For someone like, Loretta Lynn, they use spirits of Indians. Another example of this, is someone having 3 Black Angels. The concept is the same though. This works in closely with having demonic guides.

SCRIPTURES IN PROGRAMMING

An ex-Programmer states that the Illuminati Mind-Control intentionally used verses from every book of the Bible. The Programmers also intentionally used everything Jesus said in one distorted way or another in the programming. A person can pick up a Bible with Jesus' words in red, and get a quick idea of one area of the Bible which was heavily misused. The programmers love to reframe (twist) parables. Billy Graham, who is a Monarch handler, is very adept at weaving in programming language with biblical messages. For instance in his 1995 televised Christmas message, given in front of a fireplace with 13 candles lit behind him, he said, "Come home so I can give you a new heart."

A little later he activated the Plowshares programming, and a little later he said, "from the cradle to the cross to the ground", which is a phrase any deeper cult alter would have an entirely different meaning for compared to the person on the street. Readers, who read chapter 5, will remember what was written about Billy Graham. When Billy Graham was in Portland, his ministry somehow got the addresses and phone numbers to all the Monarch survivors in the area, who he invited to a personal meeting with him. While he had his mind-control survivors gathered, he talked to them and set off their programming with their personal codes. This was observed by several witnesses. His ministry also sends codes via their messages flashed across the bottom of the T.V. screen.

The reader needs to bear in mind that bloody Satanic holidays occur around Christian holy days. The Winter Solstice occurs around Christmas. Every Christmas, the Illuminati covens around the world build mangers with children for the sacrifice. This is worked in to enhance the programming they are doing with their children. Around Easter time, the Illuminati do Death, burial and resurrection ceremonies (traumas). Nothing sacred to Christianity gets overlooked. The method that it is mocked depends on who is in control of that region's ceremonies. The idea of using Scriptures for programming accomplishes several things:

a. therapists are usually secular and unfamiliar with the Bible. This prevents exposure of the programming cues and triggers and fronts.

b. ministers are usually unable to believe in psychology and mind-control programming and so their Bible knowledge is not of any therapeutic benefit because they are ignorant of Satan's devices. Some Christian ministers are putting out advice that Multiples need to be helped by simply telling "the person" to quit using multiplicity as a way to cop out of responsibility. First, there is no "person" who is using multiplicity as a cop out--the personality of the person has been shattered--and no one person represents the entire mind. Second, the person is not in control of their mind to stop what is happening. They are under total mind control.

c. the last place people would look for understanding Satanic programming is in the Bible.

d. when programmed multiples go to church, they can be used, and programmed by using Christian terms. There are "Christian" churches in Washington, Arkansas, Tennessee, and California and many other places which are 100% cult mind-control operations, such as the "Lord's Chapel."

e. When a programmed multiple tries to set themselves free by taking in spiritual knowledge of God, they find that the Bible is a programming trigger, that sets off programming or brings up some alter. Reading the book of 1 John might bring up the Illumi-

{ 417 }

nati's alter named Jesus.

f. The cult which is doing the programming by making a mockery of God, can build their egos and their pride. It may allow them to feel they are more powerful than God Almighty.

g. The victim can be told that "God" is telling them to do something. And who sets himself up as "God"? --the cult programmer.

There isn't anything in the Bible that can't conceivably be misused, but some of the Scriptures and their programming misuse are listed below. Scriptures that lend themselves to double-binds, to obedience or cover stories that seem to justify the programmer and the programming are used. Names of Queens and Kings in the Bible can be used for alter names. The men who wrote under inspiration, knew that scriptures could be misused, in 2 Cor 4: 1-2 Paul writes about himself, "Therefore seeing we have this ministry, as we have received mercy, we faint not; but have renounced the hidden things of dishonesty, not walking in craftiness, nor handling the word of God deceitfully..." Clearly, mishandling the word of God deceitfully is an ancient art.

GENESIS

- Genesis Creation Story--cover story for the creation of parts of a slave's System

- Tree of Life--used to create an internal Cabalistic Tree of Life for alter magic

- Adam & Eve--code words

- Garden of Eden--part of the System, usually the early pure part that needs to be guarded by "angels"(demons)

- Angels--alters or demons placed into a System. Angles could be a method by which the abuser sends messages to the person, thus giving divine credibility to the programmer's message. Angel names can represent alters and demons placed into a person.

- Sodom & Gomorrah--a type of suicide program

- Genesis 22:17-18, "That in blessing I will bless thee, [the programmer as God is going to bless the victim with torture] and in multiplying I will multiply thy seed as the stars of the heaven, and as the sand which is upon the sea shore; and thy seed shall possess the gate of his enemies; and in thy seed shall all the nations of the earth be blessed [all the areas of the system]; because thou hast obeyed my voice." [the programmer's voice]

- Melchizedek -a type of occult order or rank Genesis 38--pledge of a signet, bracelet & staff--trigger cues to open up a System to obey. Joseph & Esau's birthright--Satanic birthrights emphasized as if sanctioned by God's word.

EXODUS

- The 12 (actually 13 with Manassah and Ephraim) Tribes of Israel can be used for the code names of alters and sections of alters.

- House of Israel--code name for section/structure of a system

- Plagues of Egypt--Program to terrorize a slave.

- Oaths and Covenants--their existence in the Bible is used to emphasize the validity to Satanic oaths and covenants. The curses that God says will happen if disobedience takes place are used by the Handlers to instill fear into the victim, that if he doesn't comply, God's curses will fall on them. The Catholic/Jesuit programming relies heavily upon the Bible. The Bible verse ECL. 5:4 "When you make a vow to God, do not delay to pay it...It is better not to vow than to vow and not pay," is used by these Satanic programmers to hold their victims under vows made under duress, hypnosis, or deception. (DT 23:2 1 also emphasizes keeping your vows.) These Satanic Mind-controlled slave handlers do not tell their slaves that Numbers 30 states that many vows, such as the vows of children are null and void. The first fruits of things belong to the real God of the Bible and can't be vowed away. The Satanic groups like to take the first male child in mockery of what belongs to God. Evil vows, vows made under duress (just like contracts made under duress) are null and void. But the Handlers never tell their slaves these "finer points of the law." Instead, they use the Bible to justify their own goals.

- I AM [one of the names of Yahweh]--used as a programming cue or name

- EX 15 - "I am the Lord that healeth thee". The programmer can apply this to himself as he helps rescue the victim from a manufactured life-threatening crisis.

- Ten Commandments with LEV 20--used to belittle the victim to show him that he is rejected of God.

- When the Programmer sets himself up as God, he can misapply all the verses calling on people to serve God such as DT 4:29 "Seek the Lord thy God, thus thou shalt find him, if thou seek him with all thy heart and with all thy soul." See DT 8:18 also DT 11:13, "love the Lord your God, and to serve him with all your heart and with all your soul." Of course many of the alters have been stripped of their hearts during programming and given a heart of stone. They do not have a real heart to serve God, but they can serve their master with their heart of stone.

OLD TESTAMENT HISTORICAL BOOKS: FIRST KINGS CHAPTERS

- 16-2 1, The story of Ahab, Jezebel, and Elijah. The Programmers play themselves in the role of Jehu coming to protect what is his. The only admirable thing for Jezebel to do, is to put her make-up on and prepare herself to die. This story is used to make a woman slave think that the only admirable thing to do is to prepare to die like Jezebel. The Vineyard of Naboth is also used as a programming theme. The show Mysteries of the Bible is an example of how the Bible and television can work together to control a person. This show had an episode about Jezebel, Ahab and Jehu.

It must be remembered that Dr. Green's internal alter in some victims is called Jehu, and that another programmer has taken the identity of Ahab and that one of the deep cats is the Grande Dame programmer represented by Jezebel. The effect of the show on one Monarch System was this: Jehu has the power over the gates and to bring judgment upon Ahab and Jezebel. Jezebel in the show Mysteries of the

Bible is praised because when she knew she was going to die she got her makeup on and she got herself ready for Jehu and allowed herself to be killed. The System understood the show to mean in paraphrase: "this is a threat, you are to get yourself ready for Jehu or whoever and comply."

PROPHETS

- EZ (Ezekiel) 1:15-17 and the rest of the chapter. This whole chapter is used to build the internal circle within circles of inter-connecting worlds of the alter system.

- Jeremiah 18:3--When the child is 3 or 4, a utility program called the Potter Wheel is placed in so that the Programmer can work with an entire section of alters if he so desires. When an alter(s) go up on the wheel, they are available to be worked on. They will be asked to "stand in file according to rank and serial no."

- EZ 37-The story of the Valley of Dry bones is used as a way of reactivating dead robots--or dead robotic clones within a Monarch system.

- JER (Jeremiah) 47:3--in this verse horses show up when a bound-ary was crossed. This is used to put in protective programming.

- Nahum 3:2--the sword = staff. The entire 3rd chapter of Nahum is used to make slaves feel that God has rejected them. They have no heart, because of their evilness.

- DANIEL. Daniel 10--the Beast with 10 toes (used for program-ming in the Beast computer)

GOSPELS

- MATT 5:13 "Ye are the salt of the earth: but if the salt have lost his savior wherewith shall it be salted? it is thenceforth good for nothing, but to be cast out and to be trodden under foot of men." This is used to justify punishment of the slave.

- MATT 6:22-23 "The lamp of the body is the eye. If therefore your eye is good, your whole body will be full of light. But if your eye is bad, your whole body will be full of darkness. If therefore the light that is in you is darkness, how great is that darkness!" These words are used with a mean programming trick where disobedient alters are pulled up, locked into placed, placed mentally within crystal chandeliers and then the sexual organs, mouth, and side of the brain are shocked in sequence. The "light" does a severe shattering to all the alters which experience the shocks. This shatters the disobedient alters and they are replaced with others.

- MARK 3:24-25, "And if a kingdom be divided against itself, that kingdom cannot stand. And if a house be divided against itself, that house cannot stand." Used to help justify backup programming that will not allow disobedience. The slave's front alters are told to go along with the rest of the System's desires, and if not, then the house (body) will fall (commit suicide). This type of scriptural programming is used in a demonic way to keep the victim from straying from the script of the mind-control.

- MARK 4:6 "But when the sun was up it was scorched, and because it had no root, it withered away." This is used to make sure the roots of the programming are not uprooted.

- MARK 4:28-32, "And he said, Whereunto shall we liken the kingdom of God?...It is like a grain of mustard seed. ..But when it is sown it groweth up and becometh greater than all herbs, and shooteth out great branches; so that the fowls of the air may lodge under the shadow of it." In the programming, a tree is programmed mentally into the victim's entire body. This tree carries the programs, and the birds nest in it. This scripture is used for the imagery of part of that programming.

- MARK 5--This entire chapter deals with the story about Legion (which is a large number of demonic spirits). The story is also found in MT 8:33. Legion is placed into the person to guard the All-Seeing-Eye.

- LUKE 1:46-52, When a person is traumatized and the Master is allowed to save the victim, he can present himself as Savior and will use this scripture to buttress his authority.

- LUKE 11:9-10, "And I say unto you, Ask, and it shall be given you; seek, and ye shall find; knock, and it shall be opened unto you. For every one that asketh receiveth; and he that seeketh findeth; and to him that knocketh it shall be opened." This is used to reinforce the knocking triggers that open up a system. MT 7:8 is almost identical to this scripture.

- JOHN 15:4, "As the branch cannot bear fruit of itself, except it abide in the vine; no more can ye, except ye abide in me." This is used to force the slave to stay within the programming script, so that the fruit (the programs) will not be damaged. The slave has been given lots of alters and demons whose only assignment is to protect that fruit-bearing (the program-bearing) capability of the System. This chapter continues, "If ye abide in me, and my words abide in you, ye shall ask what ye will, and it shall be done unto you....If you keep my commandments, ye shall abide in my love; even as I have kept my Father's commandments, and abide in his love." JN 15:7,10 In other words, the Master is telling the slave, if you do what I command, you remain in my love, but I will pull my love away if you don't comply.

- ACTS 17:28, "For in him we live, and move, and have our being; as certain also of your own poets have said, For we are also his offspring." The slave is bonded totally with their master. His existence is their existence.

PAUL'S WRITINGS

- ROM 1:7, "And he said unto them, It is not for you to know the times or the seasons, which the Father hath put in his own power." The slave is to depend upon the Master called God for all this.

- ROM 1:18, "For the wrath of God is revealed from heaven against all unGodliness and unrighteousness of men, who hold the truth in unrighteousness." Used by the Programmer/handler to justify their wrathful abuse.

- ROM 6:16, "Know ye not, that to whom ye yield yourselves servants to obey, his servants ye are to whom ye obey; whether of sin unto death, or of obedience unto righteousness." This scripture is a good one to use with ROM 13:1 to make the slave think that obedience to the Master's authority is righteousness.

- ROM 7:22, "For I delight in the law of after the inward man." God is Programmer, and the slave is to delight in programmer's laws.

- ROM 9:20-22, "Nay but, 0 man, who art thou that repliest against God? Shall the thing formed say to him that formed it, Why hast thou made me thus? "Hath not the potter power over the clay, of the same lump to make one vessel unto honour, and another unto dishonour? "What if God, willing to show his wrath, and to make his power known, endured with much longsuffering the vessels of wrath fitted to destruction." The programmers teach the alters that the Programmers are the Potter and the alters and their minds are the clay. What right does the clay have to question the Potter. This is a powerful verse used to insure compliance and acceptance of the programming.

- ROM 13:1, "Let every soul be subject unto the higher powers. For there is no power but of God: the powers that be are ordained of God." There is the perfect scripture to be misused to prove to the slave that their master has to be God or at least ordained by God. Who has power? where does power and authority come from? God. This is a favorite verse within the Catholic realms to demand loyalty to authority. To defy their authority is to defy God. It is the perfect double-bind for the slave.

- 1 COR 3:16, "Know ye not that ye are the temple of God, and that the Spirit of God dwelleth in you? If any man defile the temple of God, him shall God destroy; for the temple of God is holy, which temple ye are." The slave has a temple built into their System and they are told that their master is God. If they defile that temple (by touching the programming)--their master will destroy them.

- 1 COR 11:27, "Wherefore whosoever shall eat this bread, and drink this cup of the Lord, unworthily, shall be guilty of the body and blood of the Lord." Actual blood and an actual human body are consumed. The person is told they must be worthy of this or else they are guilty.

- 2 COR 1:22 "God; who hath also sealed us, and given the earnest of the Spirit in our hearts." Can be applied to the Programmer, who is God.

- 2 PETER 2:22--Slaves are cursed with the verse and as dogs told to return to their own vomit. During the tortures of eating foul things, the slave doesn't want to vomit--because it is a standard practice to make slaves eat their own vomit.

- REVELATION (OR APOCALYPSE)--The White Stones of REV. 2:17--The deeper alters go through a ceremony where the white stone is taken and a black stone with their name is given.

- REV. 6-8. The 7 seals are used for Armageddon Suicide programming. First, the white, second the fiery red, third the black seal, and the fourth is pale, it is death & hades, fifth, is blood and beheading, sixth, is earthquakes internally, and the seventh is golden which is silence.

- RV 21--The description of heaven is used to build internal structures and the stones used in heaven are used for access points. "The street of the city was pure gold, like transparent glass." RV 21:21 lends itself to Wizard of Oz Yellow Brick Road programming. The words "Alpha and Omega" are programming triggers. The trumpets and seals of Revelation and the horses of judgment are all part of the charismatic Monarch Mind Control.

THE BIBLE IS OPPOSED TO MIND CONTROL AND PROVIDES MANKIND WITH AN ANCIENT WARNING

The prophets of the Bible warned that mind control would dominate the world in the last days. For instance Paul wrote, "Now the Spirit speaketh expressly that in the latter times some shall depart from the faith, giving heed to seducing spirits, and doctrines of devils." 1 TM 4:1,2 "...the God of this world hath blinded the minds of them which believe not..." 2 COR 4:4/ Along this line Jesus the greatest prophet said, "When the Son of Man comes [referring to his own second coming], will he find the faith on the earth?" LUKE 18:8 Paul warns "Let no man deceived you by any means: for that day shall not come, except there come a falling away first [from the truth]." 2 THES 2:3,4

He tells us that in the last days people will not endure sound doctrine which means sound teachings. The prophet John warns that the love of the truth was all that would protect people in the end times from the mass deceptions coming. It is this mass mind control and individual mind control which allows the satanic New World Order to carry out a world-wide satanic conspiracy right under the noses of the world's citizenry without the majority of people even being alarmed! "...The whole world lies in the control of the evil one." 1 JN 5:19

THETA PROGRAMMING

Theta Programming got its name just as the Alpha, Beta, and Delta Programming in part from the four types of EEG brain waves. Theta waves are frequent in children. The 4 types of waves are rated according to their wave frequencies which are delta- 1-3 cycles/sec; theta 4 to 7 cycles/sec; alpha 8 to 13 cycles/sec; and beta 13 + cycles per second. Psychic warfare became a branch of the Monarch Programming. This is the Theta Programming. It is the marriage of occult practices with state of the art science. The idea to be able to copy what Elisha did to the King of Syria (2 KG 6:11-12) when he "telepathically" spied on the enemy, discovered their plans, and thereby ruined their chances of success. Today this has been called "ESPionage", and the U.S. Army's term is "psychotronics". Of course, the CIA's position is that they couldn't find anything that worked, but that is simply not true, because I and my sources know of many Theta alters and Theta model systems which have Theta programming which is successful.

Black magicians have been honing their skills on how to deflect magical attacks for centuries. Are their efforts superstition and empty nonsense, or do they really have efficacy? The Illuminati and Hitler believed in black magic. And in recent times, the other groups involved in trauma-based mind-control have also looked into magic based psychic warfare. For those readers who skipped the split-brain programming section, you may want to read that section to find out how the Illuminati create alters via split-brain programming who are very intuitive and capable of interacting in higher demonic spheres such as the occult planes of the magical Watchtowers. Some of the groups who did research for the Monarch's Theta Programming are:

- AiResearch (Al can stand for artificial intelligence)
- Manufacturing Co., Torrance, CA (such as psychic warfare & ESP)
- Biological Dept. of Air Force Research, Baltimore, MD (telepathy)
- Bell Telephone, Boston, MS (telepathy)
- Defense Intelligence Agency
- Duke University Parapsychology Lab, Durham, N.C. (parapsychology, ESP, telepathy)
- Garret Air Research Corp., El Segundo, CA. (ESP, ELF)
- General Electric, Schenectady, NY
- Institute of Noetic Sciences
- Maimonides Dream Lab in Maimonides Medical Ctr.,
- Brooklyn, NY
- NASA (telepathy and many other things)
- National Institute of Mental Health (funneled money to telepathy/clairvoyance projects for the CIA)
- Naval Surface Weapons Center and China Lake
- Princeton Univ., (ESP, remote perception, telepathy)
- Stanford Research Institute
- Veterans' Administration Hospitals

Whether the public perceives Psychic warfare as viable or not, billions of dollars have been spent on it, and numerous Theta models produced. Twelve psychics in a room together are said to be able to guide missiles which are fired. There are a number of excellent books that have come out on the subject. The New Earth Battalion and the Delta forces of the U.S. Army consist of Monarch slaves trained in

Psychic warfare. The reader is invited to read for instance John White's book "Psychic Warfare Fact or Fiction?" (Wellingborough, UK: The Aquarian Press.) Col. John B. Alexander has been one of the more visible and prominent military men assigned to training and providing the U.S. Army some elite units of warrior-monks who can fight with both martial arts and psychic warfare. Of course, they picked their elite mind-controlled programmed multiples for this.

Col. Alexander's position has director of "the Advanced System Concepts Office" in Adelphi, MD. He has worked with Col. Michael Aquino with Monarch slaves. Upper level martial arts involves the use of the occult. The Ninji are one of the few groups who openly realize that their martial art power comes from demonic powers. A half crow/half man spirit empowers them. The Samurai would kill the Ninji because they used witchcraft in warfare. But the Samurai and many other martial arts also use occult powers, which are actually different forms of witchcraft and demonology, even though they don't recognize it as such. Now American Monarch slaves in the U.S. First Earth Battalion are taught to throw energy balls, to move people during hand to hand combat, and do other things using occult forces. Yes, these warrior/monk groups are even getting into blood sacrifices.

In 1987, The Seattle Times, ran a front page story on Lt. Col. Jim Channon, who worked with the military Theta models. The story is entitled "The New Army's experiment with 'New Age' Thinking". The article says, "So the army tried 'New Age' thinking. The idea that the world can be changed by changing the way people think about it, and that the mind has invisible but tangible powers yet to be tapped. Centers were established at Fort Ord, Calif., and in Washington, D.C., to explore the intriguing idea that mind power plus firepower could either win wars or make them unnecessary. From 1980 to 1982 the proposals were expanded at Fort Lewis by Lt. Col. Jim Channon....

The Army began by finding young officers enthused with 'new thought' and combining them with skeptical scientists. The two groups were quickly dubbed 'the butterflies and the bees.' [an appropriate name for Monarch mind-control men] ...One result was an Army think tank at the Pentagon that evaluated the paranormal, unusual psychic or mental phenomena. It brought in proponents of extra sensory perception (ESP), mental spoon-bending, people who 'channeled' spirits and even a helmet designed to unite the left (logical) and right (intuitive) halves of the brain." Col. John B. Alexander, US Army and part of the Monarch Programming, wrote for Psychic Warfare, "Psychotronics may be described as the interaction of the mind and matter."

While the concepts may stretch the imagination of many readers, research in this area has been underway for years, and the possibility for employment as weaponry has been explored. To be more specific, there are weapons systems that operate on the power of the mind and whose lethal capacity has already been demonstrated." Some of those systems are Monarch systems of the Theta Model, and many of those in the military are young men of the Illuminati. Some have been seen at NORAD, in Colorado, which helps confirm that Theta models are being employed to bring in the Anti-Christ. NORAD is a main center for Alex and Janus end-timed programming.

Col. Alexander claims that the ability to transfer energy from one person to another has been proven, that emanations of body energy have been proven and picked up by Kirlian photography, and finally that hypnotic states have been induced telepathically. The Pentagon and the CIA spent many millions of dollars on ESP, at least $6 million per year. According to the information that has leaked, there are psychic humans, but the ability is not a consistent ability available for all. In the early 1980s it came out that the Navy had 34 psychics, who they paid $400 a month, to track Soviet subs. The CIA claimed during the cold war that 200 Russian experts were working on telepathy.

Many of the Illuminati's Monarch slaves will speak about learning on the astral plane. One reason it is difficult to deprogram a slave, is because the deeper parts know how to astral project, and can carry out the demonology which helps their master to astral project to them so that the System can be reprogrammed. Whether the therapist believes in demonology or not, if the therapist deprograms a client and then

{ 429 }

finds out that the deeper parts have undone the work via the astral plane, the therapist should look into how to manage this problem.

This type of reprogramming rarely needs to occur because few slaves are ever even partially deprogrammed. One of the most skilled programmers of Astral Projection is the Programmer B. Bowers. He is known nationally for this skill. He worked with the famous Manly P. Hall, who also had a reputation in the Illuminati for Astral Projection. Astral projection is accomplished by a focused trance where the spirit by demonic power leaves the body and travels to a particular point. Grand Masters within the Illuminati can give lessons to students on the astral plane. Much of their Illuminati occult learning, according to some Illuminati slaves was done on the astral plane.

We will discuss several methods on how this is done. The traditional druidic method, the three stepping stone method, to teach astral projection called "spirit flight" is to get 3 stones, a silver one, a gold one and a black one. Three small stones which are painted would work. The silver represented the female, and the properties of silver. The gold represented male and the properties of gold. And the black stone represented midnight and the unknown and the properties of coal. The silver stone will be placed at a carefully selected location at some distance from the student's house, and then farther out the gold stone will be placed, and still further out the black stone. During sleep the Druidic student will practice seeking out the "three stepping stones" in order.

Telepathy has been developed by the Illuminati, but is a closely guarded secret, which their Illuminati slave alters are trained in. Telepathy is used by Delta teams to coordinate their activity and to sense if one of them is in danger. Duke University, which ties back to the Duke/Reynolds Illuminati bloodlines, has done massive amounts of research into psychic abilities. Only certain people have the ability to be a psychic. A certain type of brain structure is required and the CIA has identified and mapped everyone with this natural ability in the U.S. However, the Programmers are not above "cheating" in creating psychic phenomena within the slave's mind too.

Since slaves can not be consistently given Theta programming, a surgical implantation of a sodium/lithium powered high frequency receiver/transducers coupled with a multi-range discharge capacitor was placed into the brains of Monarch slaves. This gives the handlers the ability to signal by remote signals to the victim's brain. When the receiver picks up the signals they electronically stimulate certain areas of the brain which in turn triggers pre-set programming. Implants are now being placed in a high percentage of the Monarch slaves.

HOW OUT OF BODY EXPERIENCES (ASTRAL PROJECTION) ARE DONE

Another method of creating psychic phenomena with the aid of electronics is astral projection using sound waves. This method seems to work fairly consistently, although it is possible it wouldn't work for some people. It was discovered that astral projection occurs at a point that the body is asleep and the mind is awake. Focus 10 is the state of mind where the body is asleep and the mind is awake, and with the proper stimuli the mind can wander off into the astral plane. A few odd people get into the Focus 10 state by themselves, but it is rare. The brain works off of waves that are less than 16 hz. and the human ear can't hear anything below 30 hz. so at first it appears sound waves can't influence the brain. However, if one ear hears 100 hz. and the other ear hears 104 hz. the brain will hear a ghost beat of 4 hz. 4 hz happens to be a theta/delta frequency on the border of sleep and waking that can possibly launch an astral trip. Focus 10 is just the starting point for astral travel. Focus 12, 15, 21 and beyond are the real trip.

When a person astral projects it is said to change the EEG pattern to a special pattern called Alphoid. To stimulate someone to astral project they are induced into sleep, and then just as they lose consciousness, the mind is jolted awake with some high-frequency beta signals. The body remains asleep, and the mind is then free from the body to wander. A hemispheric synchronizer, which was patented in 1975, is used to get both hemispheres working together. Those who want to read more on this subject might start with "Journeys Out of the Body" by Robert A. Monroe, and "Far Journeys", and D. Scott Rogo's "Leaving the Body: A Complete Guide to Astral Projection", and "A Traveler's Guide to the Astral Plane" by Steve Richards.

OTHER THETA CONTROLS

ELF (Extremely Low Frequency Waves) are being used to modify people thoughts, implant thoughts, and modify their emotions, such as make a person angry. ELF weapons are being used on civilian targets in the U.S. High pitched sounds, and helicopters flying with P7 mind control equipment are also augmenting the abilities of the Illuminati/Intelligence Agencies/NWO Network.

TELEPATHY

Essentially all Illuminati slaves have dark side alters who are taught to be telepathic. There will be differing opinions as to whether this is real or imagined. IF it is real, and we will work off of that assumption, then how do the Illuminati do it? Again there are varying opinions about how it mechanically works, it appears that it may involve all or part of the following components:

- The human nervous system is able to change the gravitational constant in a field surrounding a person. If the sender had a low field and the receiving party had a higher than normal field, thoughts can flow from the sender to the receiving party.

- Somehow altered states of consciousness influence telepathy. Experiments with two people who simultaneously hypnotize each other, have found that they enter a shared world in which they do not have to verbally speak to communicate.

- Demonic spirits provide insights to those who are involved in the occult world, as a method to further entrap the occultist. In other words, the person is cooperating with some other intelligence. Although the various occult groups have different ways of explaining telepathy, with Alice Bailey & Lucis Trust (and spin off groups like the I AM movement) it is explained that you are an ascended master. In some groups, telepathy is described as putting on energy and then controlling that energy. It is seldom in the occult world that telepathy is linked with demonology. However, those in the occult world who are skilled in demonology are fully aware that the "energy" that one controls to carry out telepathy are demons. In the occult, the telepathic person must control his demon and then send it to another person. The first person's demon must then control a kindred spirit in that person. High ranking demonology, such as in the high ranks of the Illuminati, would view telepathy as the ability to control demons.

- An excess of negative ions in the atmosphere has significantly increased telepathic scores in experiments. When telepathy occurs, researchers have noted that the parasympathetic nervous system is activated, & this occurs along with an increased amount of acetyicholine in the brain.

According to the high levels in the occult, there are 7 points in the Auric Body. These points are not on the physical body, but are on what is called the etheric body, or the body's astral energy, whose location is approximately in the same locality as the physical body, except that it extends for a few inches beyond. The 7 points-, all important demonic portal points, are the top of the head, the third eye, the throat, the chest/heart area, the solar plexus, the lower abdomen, and the genital area. The back of the head and the spleen make up 2 other points that are not considered as active. There are 21 minor centers, and 49 focal points found on the human body.)

Streams of energy called nadis carry the astral energy to where the sender's mind focuses to have the energy taken. The recipient feels this energy in the solar plexus. Another area that is said to be active during telepathy is the throat. The throat area on the etheric body is said to be able to transmit mental thoughts if the sender and receiver are in harmony and rapport, and are dissociated. Intuitional telepathy is said to be a function of the third eye and the throat areas working together to send thoughts. In review, there are several different types of telepathy, all of which use different points of the etheric body. Whether therapists believe in telepathy or not, if they work with Illuminati slaves who feel comfortable to express themselves, then the therapists will find out that the deeper parts have been trained in mind reading and telepathy.

An Illuminati Monarch mind-control slave will be twinned with another Monarch. If these two persons are in the same room and send forth a glance of love toward each other, they will establish a connecting energy link that allows them to telepathically communicate. When two Multiple personality Systems meet, there will be communication going on dozens of levels as all types of alters seek out their counterparts and begin to communicate. A drug containing alkaloids derived from the Ayahuasca vine in Brazil is said to place a person into the telepathic state. Canada outlawed it in 1947 after a company sold it publicly in 1946. The U.S. may also have outlawed the drug.

Sodium amytal destroys psychic abilities, and caffeine enhances them. Also a positive intent by the receiver and the correct emotions of both parties helps.

KILLING FROM A DISTANCE

Various methods have been attempted by the military to give their warrior monks the ability to kill by psychic powers. One reported project in the late 1970s, which appears to have tried to link technology with some previous occult ideas, was called Dreamscan. When a person was in his dream state, waves matching brain waves are to be generated by some type of hardware, in order to cause the death of the sleeper. Some intelligence assets in AT&T were said to be involved in this.

IN QUICK REVIEW

The military and the Illuminati are using telepathy, psychic warfare, astral projection and other occult sciences with their programmed slaves. The ability to carry out some of these occult sciences (psychic abilities) can be greatly enhanced by certain drugs, brain wave patterns, training, and demonology. Non-illuminati models may not have these abilities built in, but the deeper alters of Illuminati slaves generally have some alters who are trained in all these abilities.

THE PHILOSOPHER'S STONE

One of the major goals of Alchemy was *"The preparation of aurum potabile, liquid gold, a sovereign remedy, because gold being itself perfect could produce perfection in the human frame."* -quoted from "The History of Chemistry" as quoted by Manly P. Hall in his "The Secret Teachings of All Ages", p. CLV. Gold has long been called the metal of wisdom by the Illuminati. The Illuminati are well aware of the alchemical quest to create the correct type of gold which will bring enlightment to the world. The Rabbi's, who know the Cabala, have considered the secret of white powdered gold the greatest secret of all times. Somehow the Egyptian Pharaoh's had learned the secret of how to make white powdered gold which when seen up close is transparent, like the gold described in the Bible as making up the streets in heaven. This gold is monotonic (with molecules in a high spin state), and looks like baking flour. It greatly enhances the pineal gland, and a similar substance of iridium greatly enhances the pituitary gland.

Regular yellow gold or gold salts will cause the hair of the subject to fall out, but white gold is safe to ingest. After ingesting the white gold for over 9 months, a subject will become extremely psychic and disease free. The person's body will also glow. Whether the Illuminati discovered this white gold, and have been using it secretly when their adepts went into hiding for months of long training, or whether they were only playing with substitutes we cannot say. Some occult groups groom slaves in the craft for 24 hours a day for a year. At any rate, in recent years a man named David Hudson, who is of the Holy Blood line (13th Illuminati Bloodline, of the de Guise lineage), discovered and patented white gold. He named the white gold Ormus, which is the occult name for the Prieure de Sion.

Ormus also pertains to Gnosticism in the ancient world. Ormus is also the Hebrew words for "golden tree", which David finds appropriate since this white gold is the elixir of life that the sho-bread & manna was made from. This is said to be the reason the Priest glowed when he came out of the Holy of Holies, after eating the sho-bread. David Hudson, told one source that he was supportive of the cabalistic goal of Adam Kadmon. Because Hudson knew the cabala very well, it seems likely that he understands what Adam Kadmon is really all about.

Monarch slaves of the House of Rothschild have revealed how the Illuminati are able to do what they call Proxying. This is a Mind-Spirit transfer, done by the twinning traumas, channeling, telepathic communication, and astral projection so that all slaves worldwide are being pulled into one single interlinked Demonic One World Mind. We do not understand how white gold and iridium help the body become a semi-conductor so that the body is highly psychic, but it does. We hope to find out more. David Hudson has the patent (U.S. patent and some international patents) on white gold.

There are a number of scientific studies on white gold which verify the power of white gold on the human body. When my source talked to David Hudson, he certainly knows the occult world exceptionally well, besides being skilled in the Cabala. He claims he has nothing to do with the occult world, and that he stays away from the Illuminati. He says that he took what was occult and turned it into science. This source's talk with him left many questions. David Hudson has given mankind the most important secret that has captivated the best minds of the occult world for centuries, the Quest for the Philosopher's Stone.

FURTHER SPIRITUAL BONDAGE SNARES

There are a number of activities which are snares to entrap people, both Monarch slaves and people in particular, which are not commonly recognized as such. One has to view them in their overall context and the consequences of what these activities lead to. According to Biblical teachings, Satan is trying to develop man's hidden abilities as well as provide him some extraordinary supernatural power to encourage man's independence from God, as opposed to man's faith in, fellowship with and dependence upon his Creator. As man develops these hidden powers that were part of Adam's natural mental, psychic, and physical abilities, mankind increasingly feels more God-like. Man's independence from his Creator Yahweh God, makes him more vulnerable and more dependent upon Satan. (Cf. verses in

Scripture about the fall, 1 Cor. 15:4,5,46, how man is a combination of spirit, body, soul in 1 Thes. 5:23, and how Satan's system will do trade in the souls & the power of the souls of men, REV 18:11-13.)

Due to the corruption of man, God doesn't want to develop these abilities. For instance, atomic power may make man powerful, but man has not developed spiritually enough for these abilities to be used in a Godly fashion. Mankind, according to the Bible, is not ready for these abilities, until mankind is on a higher spiritual walk with God. Today, mankind lacks the authority from God to use occult powers. Mankind's flirtation with occult powers, is similar to the teenage boy who is disobedient to his father's guidelines and uses his new sexual powers before he has learned responsibility and how to use his new power responsibly. We are not to be ignorant of Satan's devices.

Understanding about these powers, just as the teenage boy understanding about sexuality in a constructive way, is not the same as the irresponsible use of these powers. One of the most dangerous, ensnaring spirits, is the Spirit of Gambling. The Illuminati know that if they can get a man hooked on gambling, that gambling will bring in every evil spirit with it. When a man is hooked on gambling he will do anything. Gambling introduces covetousness, greed and lust. A man with big gambling debts will murder, sell his children, lie, deceive, steal, etc.

This is not simply my opinion, but the experience of the Illuminati in working with human nature. When the Illuminati want to destroy a lineage, they will purposefully try to get a man or woman in that lineage hooked on gambling. That will begin a cycle of evil spirits being passed down for generations. In order, to introduce the gambling spirit into society on a mass scale, they are working off of several traumas. The rejection, abuse, lack of power and lack of respect that the American Indians received from the White man, has opened the American Indians up to accepting the lie that opening gambling institutions on their reservation lands is a good thing.

The American Indian is gaining back some power and money, but their gambling operations will actually lead them into further bondage. The state governments are finding it hard to finance projects, and their manufactured hardship is also opening the door to state run gambling. Again we see the trauma, and the subsequent programming lie being done on a mass scale. Once the gambling spirit is entrenched, it will continue to strengthen its control over people and society. These things are well-conceived spiritual operations that are blindsiding Americans because "evil" spirits are no longer politically correct to talk about.

Illuminati Monarch slaves, such as a Mother of Darkness or Grande Master, are given occult powers. They are also frequently connected to gambling, they will have alters who like to gamble. Rather than being activities of power and opportunity, occult power & gambling are really activities that ensnare people. The symbol that the Programmers use to symbolize the bondage loops that they construct is the infinity sign, the same sign that we saw on the front of Billy Graham's Decision magazine.

CHAPTER ELEVEN:

INTERNAL CONTROLS

TEACHING OCCULT PHILOSOPHIES

Learning plays an important part in perception. The Programmers try to get their victims to subscribe to philosophies and ideas that will make it hard for them to rebel against their controllers. This is what is termed indoctrination. The same methods of teaching that others find useful are employed. Ways of thinking are incorporated by the slave via handlers, programmers, and the cult they belong to. Everyone tries in their own way to make sense of life. This is a natural brain function, so that the human mind can understand how to deal with the future. The mind takes raw data, and then applies some type of logic, and comes to conclusions.

Once accepted these conclusions can be as hard as nails, and they will defy any attempt to change them, even in the light of new evidence. If the Programmer is smart enough, he can get an alter to logically believe anything. Once the belief is embedded, it will remain there tenaciously. In the Illuminati, 'great" masters and adepts teach "hidden mysteries". The slave feels the authority that emanates from this teacher with special gifts and abilities. The slave is hardly in a position to question the teachings being given from on high. Circular reasoning, lies, and other tricks are used to convince the person that the occult world is true. For instance, "God abandoned you, therefore you need to cling to us, the only ones who would see any use in you." The truth is that the cult staged a crisis where their actor playing God abandoned the child to the cult's abusiveness. The whole event was simply cult abuse--with God taking the blame. "We are trying to fashion a better man, a man with far more capabilities than before, with better genetics. Those who oppose us, are trying to keep humankind back in the dark ages." This is circular reasoning and outright lies. They are not interested in helping mankind, only destroying it. To make occult philosophies more palatable, the occult world attacks the character of anyone whose life would dispute their false claims. They also use a great deal of rationalization, where the end justifies the means. Many slaves have had to sit and listen to their masters rationalize their brutality.

Within the Illuminati, ranks are achieved with much learning and ritual. Within the Temple of Set, a member is required to read certain books. One source has a list of books a Temple of Set member is asked to read, with the comments attached by the Temple of Set to each suggested title. In their suggested/required reading Category 19 entitled "The Metamind" is Metropolis by Thea von Harbou. Their comments are *"An Expressionistic portrait of a negative utopia in which humans are controlled by machines...the basis for many electronic/audio-visual ritual techniques employed by the Church of Satan and further developed by the Temple of Set."* (p. C21-2) Another is "Physical Control of the Mind: Towards a Psychocivilized Society" by Jose M.R. Delgado. Their comments, *"Delgado, Professor of Physiology at Yale University, is one of the most distinguished authorities in the field of Electrical/chemical Stimulation of the Brain (ESB). This book is necessarily dated, but it is so well-written that it deserves to be perused as a preface to more recent works on the subject."* (p.C-16?-2) "The Psychology of Anomalous Experience" by Graham Reed. Their comments, *"This book addresses unusual, irregular, and puzzling experiences- deja'vu, illusions, delusions, hallucinations, etc.-in terms of the mind's normal psychological processes of gathering, monitoring, processing, and storing information."* (ibid.)

This is just a brief look to illustrate to the reader that leaders of groups like the Temple of Set are avid students of mind-control. An almost complete membership list of this group, known as the Network, is provided in Appendix A.) The librarian of the Multnomah County Detention Ctr. shared with a source that Sheila, formerly second-in-command of the Bhagwan Shree Rajneesh's commune at Antelope, OR studied, via jail/prison interlibrary loan, books on Hitler's mind-control techniques. Many other examples could be given of how mind-control is being studied and taught by these groups.

One more book on the Temple of Set's reading list would be worthy to point out, "The Psychology of Man's Possible Evolution" by Peter D. Ouspensky. Their comments, *"Should be read especially by those members whose magical ability is hampered by flaws in their balance factor....A series of lectures which explain the Gurdjieff approach to the concept better than G. himself was able to do."*

There is an important link between Gurdjieff, mind-control, MPD, etc. but the subject is big and needs to be further investigated. One of my sources has been investigating this link, including talking with leaders of the most successful Gurdjieff commune. As with so many groups, what you see, is not what you get.

TEACHING THE IDEAOLOGIES OF WAR

One of the ways to control a person is to get them angry and then channel that hate. Wars have been used for centuries by the oligarchies that run things to control their people. Right now, the New World Order is carrying out a Drug War, an Environmental War, and a War on Terror for the express purpose in their own plans to control us. They have a mock-alien invasion planned to further justify more control over our lives. Over the years mankind has created an entire industry around warfare.

There are long traditions within military units, that for some reason must be "upheld" by the men who serve in those units. When people buy into the philosophies of war, they can generally be persuaded to give up or do anything to contribute to that war. After all, any sacrifice will be minor compare to the large numbers of bodies that will end up dead. One of the large purposes of the Monarch type of trauma-based mind-control is to produce robotic soldiers who will do anything. Normal military training is usually sufficient for most military needs, so it is clear that Monarch slaves have some ulterior uses that the military doesn't want the public to know about.

VARIOUS DELTA FORCES

The military as well as other groups have created numerous delta teams, delta forces, delta groups etc.

DELTA ASSASSINATION TEAMS

These teams are projects that the Satanic Hierarchy and the CIA collaborated together on. The programming that was placed into people was ingenious and very complex. As the program progressed over the years, the programming became more sophisticated and past mistakes were improved upon. The Delta Teams were programmed to carry out various assignments such as political assassinations. The members of these teams are housewives and other ordinary people who were programmed years ago. The Delta Teams are part of the CIA's psychic warfare bag of tricks. The CIA works so closely with the military that the Delta Force is easily expected to be tied in with the CIA & U.S. intelligence.

DELTA FORCE

The system tapped Frank Burns to create the Delta Force. Frank Burns was a Green Beret. What kind of things did Frank get involved with AFTER joining the military? Hold on. Frank Burns was an SDS, Students for a Democratic Society, organizer. SDS is an Illuminati organization He was also deep into Zen Buddhism, which is the same as mysticism. Frank Burns as an officer also studied under the Esalen Institute. The Esalen Institute is at Big Sur, California and is the American equivalent of the infamous Tavistock Institute. The Esalen Institute created "sensitivity training" programs for the business world under the title "Organizational Development (OD). Esalen people were brought in to Fort Ord where Frank Burns was the commander and began training people.

The army promoted Burns to work in the Chief of Staffs office as an "senior organizational effectiveness consultant", which allowed Burns to introduce Esalen programs all through the army. This could not have accidentally happened. Frank Burns in a conversation with a two-star General about the need for "holistic" soldiers coined the slogan *"Be all that you can be in the army."* Burns phraseology began the army's recruiting slogan. It refers to the Human Potential Movement that the army has incorporated from the New Age movement. The army is moving toward becoming an occult fighting force that practices witchcraft with its warfare.

Some of the units moving that direction are Psy-Op operations, which has included Satanists within its officers. The Delta Force network of various Generals and other high ranking officers is merely one facet of the drive by the Illuminati to transform the American army into something akin to occultic warriors that will be as fierce as the Nazi Death head units. Bear in mind that George Bush, commander-in-chief of Burn's Armed Forces has come from an Illuminati family & the Ill. Skull & Bones chapter that was part of the secret support for Hitler.

They have been using as an insignia what they themselves (the Skull & Boners) call "the Death Head". It is not surprising then that support for the Delta Team activities has come from the very top. Frank Burns set out to create a warrior monk. Lt. Col. Jim Channon, in Delta Forces, also put forward the idea. Channon visited more than 130 New Age groups in California doing what was called "social experimentation." It is an idea that the occult have repeatedly carried out. Hitler's S.S. were an special elite group of warrior monks from which about 3,000 went through religious initiations. (As the war progressed the primary focus of the S.S. shifted from being the Black Order to merely being a reliable military group called the Waffen SS.)

There were 3 levels of initiation, the last reserved for the hard-core Satanists at the top. The Nazi initiation seems to have been an attempt to get the force of the Vril. The Ordensburgen (Castles of the Order) were training centers for the elite Nazis, including the S.S. Having been in the military, I know first hand that the success of the S.S. and Waffen S.S. units in being fierce warriors is attributed by some of our leading military men to their training to be warrior-monks. One group of the S.S. called Knights of Poseidon volunteered themselves for castration, in an experiment to change them back to the supermen of the mythical and magical Hyperborea. Some of the best Sufi organizations were warrior monks. Burns and his Task Force Delta generated the First Earth Battalion, which is an occult military unit trained in martial arts, and witchcraft. Men who are selected for First Earth Battalion are given an occult initiation which includes the following oath:

"I have the capacity and therefore the duty to contribute to the development of myself, my associates, and our planet, simultaneously now! I take personal responsibility for generating evolutionary conspiracies as a regular part of my work. I will select and create conspiratorial mechanisms that are not costly in time or resources because I am aware of the five channels available to me (such as radio, television, and word of mouth.) *I will organize a self-supporting high commando group that will create and perform evolutionary breakthrough actions on behalf of people and planet. One people, one planet. I will then pass this concept on to others who are capable of generating further self-organizing commando teams."*

What ever happened to defending this nation? Military units such as the First Earth Battalion although they are supported by American tax dollars are not here to protect America. They are global minded. They are here to protect an occult world government. They are out there actively promoting the New World Order. Several years ago, Egendorf states that $4.5 million (which came from you and I, and other Americans) had already been spent on Delta Force's 80 different projects.

The Green Berets is another organization that has been heavily targeted by the Satanists, to indoctrinate and recruit. The Green Berets are increasingly moving toward being warrior-monk group. Many of them are now programmed multiples. One man who is being looked up to by many American Patriots and Christian Patriots as the leader to help them oppose the New World Order is Bo Gritz. He was a recent presidential candidate. Bo Gritz was a Green Beret and a Delta Force commander. Bo Gritz is very proud of the fact that he wrote the manual for the Delta Forces. He also worked for the CIA. Bo Gritz is one of the military's best programmed multiples, and perhaps one of the most dangerous. Insiders have told me he IS the most dangerous.

Numerous insiders both for and against Bo, have talked about Bo Gritz, and that he is a programmed multiple. According to Bo Gritz's campaign literature for President he was a commander in Delta Forces. Bo's own presidential campaign literature states that he is "Intelligence Officer & Reconnaissance Chief, Delta Force." He is also "Chief, Special Activities, U.S. Army General Staff, the Pentagon" and "Principle Agent, National Security Council, Intelligence Support Activity". Under qualifications Bo states that he is a "Security & Counter-terrorist Specialist." Within the government, they are already referring to Christians who are against the NWO as terrorists. Bo is their greatest counter-intelligence counter-terrorist they have. He came in like a storm and took control of the Patriot movement, and it has been like pulling teeth to warn patriots about who he is.

Bo Gritz himself was a Green Beret, and was used to assassinate 300 people. His blood lust caused him at one point during the Vietnam War to shoot 30 prisoners in cold blood. I also heard Bo talk about being a Temple recommend Mormon. That means he was at that time in good standing with the LDS Mormon church so that he could go to the Temple and participate in its rituals. Those who are alert realize that the temple rituals are like Masonic and Witchcraft rituals. Now he is no longer a Mormon. But he still continues in the military philosophy he believes in. Bo Gritz is going around the nation teaching SPIKE training to anyone who wants martial arts skills. Bo has done an excellent job in identifying for the New World Order every person in the nation who could threaten their plans for a martial law NWO takeover.

Bo Gritz likes to call attention that he is one of this country's foremost counter-terrorist agents. This is true. The New World Order believes patriots and Christians are terrorists, because they stand in the way of the world's acceptance of their world dictator. Bo Gritz has done a great deal to infiltrate and neutralize the opposition to the New World Order. He has been their best counter-terrorist agent.

INTERNAL COMPUTERS WHICH AUTO CONTROL A SLAVE - PERFECT

If a master has to constantly spend time whipping and motivating his slave, as well as forever watching that the slave doesn't escape or do shoddy work, or physically or verbally injure the master, then controlling the slave can end up to be a full time job. When the master gets too much involved in the control process, he ceases to be master, and becomes a slave to the control process. The intelligence agencies knew that they would have to create mind control slaves who could police themselves. If the master has to constantly guard his slave, the slave will be more trouble than he is worth. Many successful people have gained their success because they knew how to delegate.

The most successful supervisor is the one who can delegate the best. The programmers had to find ways to cut their supervisory requirements to the bone if they were to make owning a Monarch slave worthwhile. The method chosen was to build "computers" into the slave's mind that would internally regulate everything. They do this by taking hundreds of the alters and dehumanizing them and turning them into parts of a computer. For instance, the shutter on the All-Seeing Eye of the computer, which is seen in the mind like a camera shutter, is a child alter who job is to open and shut. (Another primal part is inside the eye's pupil.) This shutter part knows what goes on in all the system subconsciously but if discovered by a therapist and pulled to the front of the mind will not be able to vocalize about the system.

The software for this "computer" could be programmed into it, and all the individual programming of every alter can then be tied back to the computer. In other words, each alter would be programmed on how to view life, to act, to think, and to function in their job. This programming would be linked to a computer. The programmers invented the perfect method to decentralize their control over their slaves and yet still supervise with the tightest of control. Each alter is linked to an internal computer built from a foundation of fear and trauma. Since each section of alters was to remain secret, each section of alters for a slave is given its own computer, and then linking computers were built to link the various sections, and then finally a major backup computer is built, and then the internal Beast computer.

Bear in mind that this is all built internally in the mind of the victim. We are not talking about actual physical computers built out of physical microchips, wires, condensers etc. If the programmer concentrates on a single point when giving instructions he will get better results. Rather than complicating things for the slave, you gain power over the slave (and any subordinate) if you can give simple clear instructions. For this reason, a large share of the alters in an alter system are given very clear straight forward jobs. Because their jobs are so straightforward, these alters will often remain fragments, rather than alter parts with full blown personalities. The programmers don't cloud the issue. An undeveloped alter will be given one single clear, basic job.

By stringing 1,000's of alters together with single tasks, a highly sensitive system of alters can be created. Each piece of the System is separated by some degree of dissociation to make it a separate piece. By dividing the mind so much, it is incapable of fighting what has been done to itself. Before we begin describing the technical details of an internal computer, bear in mind that every Monarch System is unique and yet they all follow certain patterns & methodologies. Most of the models for the first few decades follow these patterns, some of the newer ones have more updated imagery.

POWER SOURCES

In an Illuminati System, a computer is created for each section of alters. That computer will be given a "power source", which if unscrewed like a light bulb will go out. The light from one of these power sources might be emerald blue or emerald green or other color. The reader may want to refer to Chapter 4 for the codes to understand the structuring of the various computers and systems.

COLOR CODES AND RIBBONS

In a standard 13x13x13 Illuminati alter system, 13 colors were used, and each computer was given a color. These would be pink, orange, yellow, white, red, brown, blue, green, black, purple, silver, gold and platinum, and clear. Color programming is reported to have been developed at UCLA. Whatever the case, Systems all over the United States have color programming. The hierarchy of colors in a System is often as follows (from top power down): Platinum, Gold, Silver, Purple, Black, Red, Green, Brown, White, Orange, Yellow, Pink. Clear is also used as a color for secret areas of the system. This hierarchy of color coding can be switched. The internal programmers can reassign colors if they need to, in order to protect the programming. Alters, sections, and parts of the computer are all color coded. The color coding for alters is not the same just because the alters are in the same section.

The color coding within the Illuminati Mind Control is fairly consistent, however a sample of an alternative Illuminati color scheme will also be provided.

A survey of colors is as follows:

- CLEAR. Secret or shell alters who can take on any color are coded clear. These are alters who serve as images or as a stage for other alters. This would include "Guardian of the Vail" alters.

- GOLD. This color is for the supreme leadership in the System, which includes the Grand Druid Council.

- SILVER. This color is for the Satanic alters who perform high level Satanic rituals. The Mothers of Darkness have silver coding.

- PURPLE. These alters see themselves as the abusers, rather than the Illuminati. These alters were involved with the programming. They have been taught to forget the abuse and to reframe it in their mind as training.

- BLACK. These alters were born out of Satanic ritual, and are Moon children. The Delta and Beta alters are black coded. They do the dirty work for the cult, such as blackmail and assassination.

- RED. These altars see themselves as witches. They were born out of witchcraft ritual, believe they have great spiritual power, and tend to deny that they have been abused.

- GREEN or EMERALD GREEN. These cat altars recognize they

have been abused. They still see themselves as belonging to the cult family, and deny that they have been abused to protect their cult family.

- BLUE ALTERS. Clones, armies and the ribbons appear to have blue coding. These alters will go so far as to hurt the body to protect it from leaking information or deprogramming.

- WHITE. 'These are Atlantean alters who have been given Aryan type racial nonsense to think they are superior. They believe in genetic engineering, and a master race.

- ORANGE. These special protector alters are scouts who warn of danger from internal or external threats.

- YELLOW. These are the strong Christian alters of which there will only be a few in the System. They help serve as a balancing point to control the System as well as to hide what the System is all about.

- PINK. These are core related alters. They maintain the true feelings of the true self apart from the cult programming and the cult family's programming. These alters are viewed as weak because they are emotional and often break down and weep. They are fragile emotionally.

An alternative color scheme that is used:

- DARK EMERALD GREEN. This color is assigned to the Anti-Christ-Satan alter(s). Green is the occult color for Satan and happens to be the most sacred color. Few people outside of Satanists know that Green is more sacred for them than any other color.

- LIGHT GREEN. The gods and goddess alters which are triads which function in

Illuminati ceremonies get this color coding.

{ 449 }

- WHITE. The internal programmers who come around in white robes get this color assigned to them, as if they are doctors or angels of light.

- RED. Sexual alters are given the natural color of sex and arousal red.

- BLACK. Connecting alters that are Nexus alters between various system parts.

- PINK. Reporting alters.

- DARK BLUE. Non hierarchy cult alters.

- LIGHT BLUE. Alters in charge of the way the system runs, such as the judges.

- YELLOW. Alters which are ritually and sexually twinned with alters of other systems.

- ORANGE. Guard alters which are heavily programmed for obedience.

- VIOLET-PURPLE. Front alters and small child alters placed into boxes.

- CLEAR. Shell alters to deceive the outside world.

- GOLD. The traumatized alters upon which the programming is built on.

Joseph Mengele and the programmers who worked with and under him, used a large dollhouse with 26 rooms. Each of the rooms were painted with one of the 13 different colors in order to build into the child's mind, the 13 front and the 13 back computers. The internal computers worked off of color codes, as well as other codes. A dollhouse was used to instill into the child's minds the compartments of the computer.

Each room was done up in a different color. One particular room was a secret room, and this represents the secret world of Petra which is hidden behind two large rocks. This secret world is coded the color clear. Besides the special color clear, the following colors appear in the system: Gold, Silver, Purple, Black, Red, Green, Blue, Brown, White, Orange, Yellow, and Pink. Each color has meaning and a rank. Just as the hour glasses could be turned, the color coding can be switched in rank. This is why in some systems there is a "Computer Operator Black", a "Computer Operator Green", and a "Computer Operator Purple", etc. During the programming a black box with needles and wires which attach to the body for electroshock is used. While electro shocking the victim, colored scarves coming out of a box are shown to the child.

The scarves would help form the imagery needed to build colored ribbons internally. Alters would be created using the Tall Book of Make Believe story of the Pancake people. Using this as a base or foundation, the alters would then be dehumanized one step further into thinking they were ribbons, such as ticker tape, which could transmit information from one computer to another area of the mind. The Ribbons had the ability to travel between the different levels and to transmit messages through the System, especially to the computers.

It is believed they could do this because they were spirit. When a System is accessed by a programmer, one procedure is to obtain a Ribbon alter and then inform the Ribbon what he wants. The ribbons transmit messages to the internal computers. The ribbons on older systems use Morse code. Who are the Ribbons? The Ribbons are the beginning of the Luciferian alter-like demons and alters. They are primarily the message bearers from the computers to the different computers, levels and alters. The Ribbons might have angelic names (Michael, Gabriel, etc.).

The word angel means messenger. The ribbons serve a very similar function. They transmit ticker tape with Morse code messages. They are at work most of the time for a System. A sample cover story for what they guard, which is the main computer with the gems and the core, is that the ribbons guard the System's "Garden of Eden". Some more of the cover story that may be given is this: Ribbons were supposedly formed out of the dust of the ground and were placed in the Garden of Eden to create every pleasant tree. (See Genesis 1.) The

{ 451 }

ribbons relate to the Tree of Life. But to eat of the Tree of Knowledge of Good and Evil will cause death.

The name of the first river of four in the garden is Pashon. Out of the first river come four heads. The River Pashon has gold, ballium, onyx, rubies, diamonds and precious stones. These gems are the programs the dwarfs mine. If the System has charismatic programming, the alters will have porcelain face programming. In this case each ribbon's color will match the color of the stones in the masks--that is yellow, white, blue, green, purple, red and black. The colors of the ribbons correlate or match the colors of the Dollhouse rooms. What do ribbons do? The Ribbons serve the programmers and the computers, who in turn serve the evil master Spirits. Things that the Ribbons do for the computers have been identified as follows:

a. The Ribbons eat from the system's internal "Tree of Good and Evil".,
b. Ribbon programming consists of several things--where they reside, who they are and what they are to protect.,
c. Ribbons must protect the computers in order to protect their own life.

The Ribbons will be programmed to believe that reversing the computer will reverse the Ribbons' life. The ribbons themselves operate with mechanical hearts, not human hearts). The cover stories may include the following: All Ribbons are hid behind a little girl, who is a front for them & who tells the creation story. The little girl will tell the creation story which included the Ribbons. Behind her runs a silver cord. The silver cord has to do with heart programming. The silver cord has 3 strands that cannot be broken as per ECL 4:12. This silver cord goes off if the Ribbons are touched.

Ribbons are set up so that suicide programming is triggered if they are cut. In review as stated, during the programming, a box with colored scarves was shown the child while severe electro-shock was given to the body. A colored scarf represents a ribbon which runs a message from a colored room to a similar colored alter. In a System which is structured into families and cities and worlds and sections, these "geographically different" structures in the mind of the victim can be connected via the color coding. In other words, the alters are structured into a 3-D cube structure. Then a fourth dimension (the color coding) is added to tie in all of the three dimensions. A central computer was placed in at the bottom of the mind.

Using various techniques the victim is brought to the deepest altered state possible, and a computer is built into the mind via hypnosis and alters. This can be done by freezing the entire body and just keeping the head active. Or it can be done by bringing the body to a comatose state where the heart is beating faintly. This step can only be done under the strictest medical supervision. The memory storage area for the computers include the Emerald City Library, staying with the Wizard of Oz theme, which contains alters whose only function is to memorize & retain with photographic memories pages and pages of information.

The layout with codes of the entire system can be stored in a storage bank, so the programmer could access this area if his own records were lost. The libraries contain the historical genealogies of satanic iniquity from early ancient times to present. This ancient occult information has been reported by at least half a dozen Illuminati slaves as being retained internally by demons.

How Monarch Slaves are Being Desgined to Interface with the Unix System of the Beast Computers

In line with what is being done by the Illuminati around the world with their network of computers, the computers have access codes similar to 666 666 666, and back out and close down codes similar to 999 999 999. These are the codes that the UNIX universal system uses, and the Monarch slaves are being created with codes that interface with the UNIX system for computers. On some systems if the computer is shutdown it will request an input code of 666fff666fff666fff666... This can then be reversed F6F6F6F6F6F6F6F6F6F6F6.

The UNIX system is being used to allow the New World Order's big

BEAST computers to communicate with any known computer, including the minds of their Monarch mind-controlled slaves. In the 1960s, the U.S. Department of Defense began linking computers together into a superhighway now developed into the Internet. Hundreds of thousands of computers around the world are tied in. Like buildings in a city, each computer has its own unique address.

Most of these addresses are registered at the Network Information Center in Menlo Park, CA. Individuals can also be registered at the NIC too. The U.S. Military links into the system with their Arpanet and Milnet networks, which tie together such divergent things as MIT computers, West Point computers, NORAD computers, AIr Force Systems Command Space Division computers at El Segundo, CA and U.S. Army DARCOM at Seckenheim, Germany to name a few.

These are all being tied together to form one vast electronic brain. There are nine secret BEAST computers of the New World Order, at the time this was written. "Big Bertha" is the nickname of the BEAST computer located at the secret military installation called Dreamland at the secret Groom Lake, NV test site facility. Papoose Lake is referred to as S-4. The other super-secret facilities in the area are named S-2, 8-6, and S-66. This area has become the Illuminati's prime programming facility for turning out Monarch slaves, and the Monarch slaves which are turned out from this area have turned out to be the worst basket cases. In other words the programming is very severe which is carried out in this area.

This area has also been used for the space program, for the U-2 & SR -71, for the CIA's A-12 spy plane, for the Stealth fighters (Lockheed F-1 17A Attack plane) and bombers, the Aurora, and for the U.S. government's "Above Top Secret" flying saucers. The Big Bertha computer (named after the Illuminati Mother-of-Darkness Bertha Krupp) can be talked to in half a dozen languages and will answer a person back in the language they speak.

On a daily basis, airplanes fly into the Groom Lake facility. The call-name of flights bringing workers and people is "Janet". About 12 Janet flights come into the facility everyday. These flights are usually

Boeing 737s and arrive from places like a secure terminal run by EG&G at McCarran Alrport in Las Vegas and from the military's Palmdale, CA facility. These 737s are unmarked except for a red stripe running down the fuselage. Large military C-130 arrive with cargo, and Illuminati dignitaries arrive in smaller twin-engine craft. Victims for the programming are brought in via planes, & other routes.

One of the BEAST computers occupies three floors of the headquarters of the European Economic Community building in Brussels, not far from the important Illuminati Mother-of-Darkness worldwide headquarters castle near the French-Belgium border by Muno, Belgium. Another BEAST computer is in Luxembourg. In observing the operations of the Illuminati, it has been seen that telephone area codes are used as part of a mind-controlled slave's code. We do not understand everything about their codes, but it does tie in with other things that are happening. Every person in the world has been assigned an 18 digit tracking number, which consists of 3 groups of 6 numbers.

The first 3 numbers assigned in the BEAST computer to everyone are 666. The next is one's national code. The U.S. national code is 110. Then the next 3 numbers are you telephone area code, and then finally your 9 digit Social Security number. The code then is 666 + Nation code + Tel. area code + social security no. = BEAST I.D. number for an individual. According to Dwight Kinman's book "The World's Last Dictator", 2nd ed., (Woodburn, OR: Solid Rock Books, p. 256) VISA has already begun issuing VISA cards using the BEAST 18 digit number. When an American makes a bank transaction on an autoteller within a matter of seconds the BEAST has been informed of the activity. These computers use UNIX. The particular programs for the economic transactions just described are a worldwide computer network called SWIFT (Society For Worldwide Interbank Financial Transactions).

The SWIFT works off of the UNIX system and can communicate with any computer. It was developed by AT&T and uses C language. Bear in mind that there are dialects of UNIX, such as the standard

AT&T UNIX and for instance Berkeley UNIX. The UNIX system uses both timesharing and multitasking. The mind of a Monarch slave also does both multitasking and time sharing. One of the nice UNIX features, is "protected memory", which is also part of the Monarch programming.

A kernal is what the UNIX programmers call a "protected person". It is very similar to the internal "person" (alter) who helps the Monarch slave's programming functions. The big item about UNIX is that it has permissions granted. This is similar to the Monarch programming. Permissions are granted to 3 types of entities. The Top Programmer or "god" as he is called, of the UNIX System receives what is called the individual permission. The next permission is called group permission, and it is given to insiders who work with the system. The final permission type is the world, which has very limited access. The parallel between this and the Monarch programming is surprising. In some cases the programmers may have matched things on a one-to-one correspondence.

The Monarch program also has a Top Programmer who is called "god" to the System. He has total control over the system. His programming permissions can not be deprogrammed out by others who might want to usurp his power. Hidden from the casual user of the UNIX system are the Daemons and Demons. The UNIX programmers decided to use the old English spelling for demon = Daemon. These are computer processes which work secretly behind the scenes and are given actual demonic names--some corresponding to actual names of historically known demons, such as Asmodeus. Asmodeus is also a demon which is placed into many Monarch slaves. In the UNIX system these demons are treated like persons in the computer's user director. Demons in the computer system do not have to log onto the computer, but they work behind the scenes and are given the same powers that people users are given. They are set up in the same structure as how the computer treats people.

Permission in the UNIX system is granted using an 8 bit count with 0 through 7. The three kinds of permission are the read, write, and execute permissions. If no permission were granted in any way the

UNIX system would indicate" "on the screen which means 000000 000 or nine 0's. The super user called god is given the code 777 which means super user. However, the permission of 666 gives the user the power to everything the 777 permission gives, except that the 777 permission allows the god the master programmer to execute not executable programs. The Postmaster Demon is the head demon, and his permission level in UNIX is 666. (\In the Monarch Programming "Mr. Postman" is a code word used internationally. The most important part of the BEAST system is its communication power.

The Electronic Mail System of the BEAST allows it to communicate worldwide, and along with electronic mail comes levels of permission to view or work with the electronic mail. The super user (god) is called Root. A programmer on the Beast must get permission. His program must get permission. That program that gives permission must also get permission. In other words, there are levels of permission that must be gone through. This is similar to the Monarch program. For instance, the alters personalities which would control the body during Illuminati gatherings have very tight access permission. It is very hard to access these hierarchy personalities. Both the UNIX system, and the Monarch programming, creates "children" by "spinning".

The "child" spins off. When the "child" is finished it is "killed" in UNIX lingo. When the programmers created child processes in the computer, they were having problems with the child processes killing the parent processes. The same type of problems have had to be dealt with in the Monarch programming. The initial programmer is often the biological parent of the child, and this parent is very responsible for extreme tortures being applied to the child who is being programmed--not to mention all of the expendable children, who are killed in front of the child to highlight the reality of the trauma. The natural reaction of the child being created is to hate the programmer. Naturally, the Monarch programming had to overcome that natural tendency, which it does very successfully.

The UNIX system uses an internal clock within its computer system. The UNIX clock is called CRON. CRON checks files to see if the programmer has put in any files to run. The UNIX system uses data bus lines, which are like the Monarch programming ribbons, which go through the system. These ribbons or data bus lines take information and commands from the computers to other computers. Within the UNIX system, insiders have revealed that the Daemon (Demon) processes of all the UNIX systems have a security flaw. That flaw is that the Postmaster Daemon has access to them in spite of who the god is of that particular UNIX computer system.

So while owners, who purchase UNIX systems think that they have exclusive control over their system, an external Postmaster Daemon coming from the Beast could use its permission levels to over ride the power of the local owner of the system. The Monarch system has a similar feature, the Illuminati programmers know how to access the base or primal anchors to the programming and yank out any programming they want. All the slaves of these lesser groups such as the CIA, Church of Satan, Mafia, etc. can all be reprogrammed rather quickly to serve the Illuminati, if they are not already due to the Illuminati programmers extra knowledge on how to get into the base programming. In these many ways, the UNIX system serves both real computers and also for the internal computers of some slaves' mind. The slave's system becomes a computer system.

It functions as a series of computers that are connected to the master computer which is sunk into the mind at the lowest hypnotic level, which is a level often placed even below an internal "hell pit". To access the different computers, combinations of cards were used for the codes (numbers are also used. See Chapter 4.). Various parts of a Monarch system correspond to what any computer would have. A microprocessor register has 3 sections on a computer to make it functional. In Monarch Systems, you would find these 3 represented by 1. stored data in the library and alters with photographic memories, 2. an instruction section with codes, and 3. stacking mechanisms. Linked to all this were a crystal, clock, hour glasses, a compass and an entire demonic command structure. The eye in front of the big computer will be protected by legions of spirits.

The front big computer runs front quadrants and the back computer runs the deeper quadrants. The software, so to speak, for the Omega programming (computer) may be set up to include a stacking program called the Potter's Wheel. The Potter's Wheel is a misuse of the Bible, and is a type of programming that the Charismatic/Pentecostal movement carries out. The Mormons and the Catholics have their own distinctive "software" programs. An initial stacking mechanism would work by telling alters to "Stand in order according to rank and serial number." Another code along with a hand signal would place the Gatekeeper alters up on the Potter's wheel for their "creator" to work on them. A group of alters could be taught to go up on their Potter's wheel by seeing a pattern of dominoes. It is whatever the programmer decides.

The dominoes were used for coding, but they also had the programming feature of being able to tie alters together so that if the System is tampered with out of sequence, a domino effect would take place. This domino effect is for one program to set off another program to set off another program. Soon the Monarch slave's mind is trying to deal with dozens of suicide programs running simultaneously, along with perhaps other programs such as scrambling programs. For instance, one story line used is the mice run up and down and open up new levels of programming and are tied to the pendulum/clock mechanism.

The mice can activate the hour glass, and a gold-winged green skirted fairy Whisper balances the hour glass on her wings. If the slave goes toward freedom, the slave's mind triggers programs of all kinds, and the mind ends up not knowing if it was coming or going with all the different programs which activate. A more exhaustive look at all the craziness and activity of the Omega & Gamma programs which activate to defend the Illuminati's Mind Control are given in other chapters. The programming has been designed that if it was taken out improperly, it is to come back Seven times Seven stronger. This is also a clue that the programming is partly a demonic manifestation.

COMPNENTS OF THE CONTROLS

At the center of the System are the mechanisms that control it, such as the Master Computer, the All-Seeing Eye, the Compass, the Master Clock, and the Quadrants that tie in together. The System may have 3 hourglasses spinning on axes. These hour glasses can also be called matrixes, which are on your standard 3 axes, a X axis, a Y axis & a Z axis. The worlds are various sections of these matrixes.

There are backup worlds & mirror image worlds. Occasionally, there will be a double system. Some of the more important alter System are even far more complex than a double System or a double, double System. Each alter is split so that every alter has another alter created from it. Then there are demonic doubles--demonic mirror images in the System.

The double images shown in the picture are very real when describing our System. Some therapists have noticed "Satanic Guardian Angels" which talk to their patients. They do not know what to make of these. Some classify them as hallucinations, because they do not have any room in their belief system for demonology. These are the demons that do control the multiple's mind. Thor, with his huge hammer is a painful demon. Thor's image is made of cast iron & carried an iron mallet. Thor is a black strong figure. When his hammer strikes, the slave gets split brain headaches. Programmers can use the story of the Giant with the Hammer in the Ozma of Oz book (pp. 141 -155) to give the imagery when programming. A special series of sweeping motions with both hands will relieve the split brain programming, but some alters can only tolerate these hand signals being done by the master.

By the way, Thor is an important protector in Satanic/occult beliefs, & the religion of Thor now has equal stature/popularity in Germany as the Lutheran church. The programs are put into a System and given codes. These programs use Greek, Hebrew and Druidic letters, or other esoteric languages, in their activation codes. Actually, these alphabets also are the way these people numbered with, and the Greek, Hebrew & Druid letters were used as numbers.

These programs could be called Utility Programs, because they function much like the utility programs of a computer. Along with all the programming comes cover programming. Generally, front stories cover almost everything in a System. Dominos have been used in Monarch programming as the basis for what is called a "Mother Board" in actual computers. Telephone tones key in on a slave's computer matrix. At times, telephone tones in everyday life will make slaves accidentally wacky. All computers run off of base 2--which uses the numbers 0, and 1. 0 and 1 can be represented as on and off. In the programming, they were represented by "He Loves Me", "He Loves Me Not." The Programmers, especially Dr. Mengele, enjoyed taking a daisy and pulling its petals off one at a time. First petal, "I love you". Second Petal, "I love you not."

IF the last daisy petal was "I love you not--then the child was dramatically killed in front of other children to be programmed. The Illuminati's method of death--skinning alive--has been developed into a fine art, for both programming and ceremonies. The daisy game, which was scary for a child, heightened the victim's attention. Matrixes were built upon this deadly game. How did it feel to be programmed with Mengele's "I love you, I love you not" programming? A victim recalls, "The child was place in a cage exposed and naked. The low voltage wires were rigged to the metal of the cage.

The child experienced a continual erratic or sporadic prolonged voltage of shock until the heart would pulsate and the anxiety level of the child became out of control. Then the Dr. would enter the scene with his sneering taunting smile while holding a daisy in his hands. The sporadic voltage would continue to flow through the child's body. As the shock continued, the Dr. stood before the child pulling petals off the daisy. His only communication was voiced in these words, "LOVE YOU, LOVE YOU NOT, LOVE YOU, LOVE YOU NOT," while pulling off the daisy petals. This action would drive the child crazy because the child knows full well if that last petal is pulled off it meant death. The child that is not loved is skinned alive before the other children. *"...we can now begin to understand that the expendable children were in other cages placed all around us for the eye to see.*
They went through the same process as we watched. When the last

petal of the daisy was pulled from the flower they were killed. Then the terror of what we had just experienced through the seeing and hearing, let us know we were next, but when? By the time the doctor got to "He loves me not" some children no longer knew fear. Their ashes were taken from the crematorium and used in the garden for fertilizer, as a reminder to all what happens to unloved children. In the clinical room, the lights were used to program the day's events. The bright light continually flashed starting with 7 lights, then six dots, then five dots, then four dots, then three, then two dots, then 1 dot. In the blindness of the lights, we could hear the doctor's voice, "LOVE YOU, LOVE YOU NOT." over and over again."

A child could have a false trust when the lights flashed 7 dots. By the time one dot was flashing, the child's terror had once again risen. The doctor never pulled the last petal off for us, but we can't forget how he teased us. He smiled and walked away, 'NO, I LOVE YOU.' and walked away." If we use L=I love you and N=I love you not we can build the following matrix for the internal computer:

This type of configuration can even be tied to color programming,

L	1	2	3	4	5	6
N	2	3	4	5	6	1
L	3	4	5	6	1	2
N	4	5	6	1	2	3
L	5	6	1	2	3	4
N	6	1	2	3	4	5

and to dominoes, where the numbers are represented as the dots on a domino. By making numbers into dots--the numbers can be represented by lights in the same patterns of black domino dots. This means that dominos can be used to program a child, and who would suspect anything about dominoes?

Another thing that lends itself well to use as a programming code are a deck of cards. Many slaves have this. It can be tied in with the Alice In Wonderland story. When cards are used, a section, also called a world or city, of alters will be given its own computer. To access that computer, a code consisting of several things including 2 cards can be used. In review of what Chapter 4 said about codes, often double codes are employed. What that means is that suppose we have 13 important alters in a section. They will designate each of these "A" alters.

Then they number them each 1 through 13. But then they will double code them so that as we count up, we also count down. Then they attach a generic level number to them, say 2,000. So putting this together we have Emerald Green 2001-13a for our first alter, then next is Emerald Green 2002-12a, the next is Emerald Green 2003-11a, and so on. Then the magical name of the alter or the Tribal name of the alter can be attached onto this to complete an access code.

While it seems perhaps complex at first, all an alter is remembering is a color, a common section number, their rank number. their file letter, and their magical name. The name to pull them up will not be their name for public use. Alice In Wonderland, the Wizard of Oz and the Tall Book of Make Believe played a fundamental role as "software" in a System. The Wizard of Oz stories are often used to show how & what structures to put in the small victim's internal world. The stories even teach how to create an internal world and its parts. Some of the T.V. shows & movies, which served as Monarch programming scripts (i.e. the software) include:

- Batman
- Bewitched
- Bobby's World Cartoons (deliberate triggers)
- Dameon/Omen movies
- Disney movies (all of them, some with deliberate triggers)
- Duck Tails Cartoon (deliberate triggers)
- ET (used in alien programming)

- Fantasy Island (deliberate triggers)

- Ghost Busters (used for "who ya' gonna call" theme)

- Love Boat (used for mind control of cruise prostitutes)

- My Fair Lady (finishing school for slaves, such as Youngstown, OH)

- Star Wars

- Steven King Horror Movies

- Tiny Toons Cartoons of Steven Speilberg (deliberate triggers)

- Wizard of Oz movies

Some of the books which were used as programming scripts, which haven't been mentioned yet, are the Dead Sea Scrolls, the Egyptian Book of the Dead (satanic rituals follow closely the rituals of the Egyptian Book of the Dead), Steven King novels, & Wilbur Smith's. The Mother Goose Nursery Rhymes were used prolifically for internal codes in slaves. Now that we have discussed the widely used "software" available to the programmers, we don't want to forget the root program, the tree which was used as a method of organizing the various programs, just like a computer's subdirectories branch out more subdirectories. If the programming is tampered with, the slave will want to cut the tree. However, since the tree is in them, this means they will want very badly to cut their arms, especially their veins. The programming is not guarded as much as the computers.

Everything guards the BEAST computer including deaf alters who have to be communicated with using a hand number code system. Such a code might resemble finger signing 1,2,3,4,5,10 = 15 & following this with a shutdown code which simply reverses the access equation. Surrounding the central All-Seeing-Eye will be alters & programs with insanity, fear, hopelessness, cutting, burning, aloneness, etc. Strong demonic forces are attached to these alters & programs. They also can trigger the slave to have abusive behavior as punishment. A System is given a life force which is able to regenerate a system, the jokers who protected the programming, and you have the alpha-numeric codes, the cards, and dominoes (represented by a dice) that formed the access codes to parts of the System.

The alters will often feel the heartbeat (which may be an alter) associated with the computer In the background is a Luciferian blue light. This Satanic light empowers the Joker. It along with the Joker and the internal programmers give a System the ability to regenerate itself. One can shut down internal computers which run programming to the levels of the System using the same codes that the original programmers use, but until one also takes care of the 13 Jokers & the faceless white-coated programmers who control the Omega Programming, then the back up computers can regenerate the programming & rebuild the system.

JOKERS

If the computers are given cards as access codes it works in well to create Jokers who are wild cards within the system, which can imitate anything. The Jokers have a Luciferian form. Luciferian is the term that the programmers used. This means that it is spirit. Because the Jokers are Spirit, they can take any form they need to and they can do what they want to do, until they are bound & cast out with the rest of their hierarchy of demons. The Jokers will pop up when a victim tries to study the codes & programming that direct that victim's life. Around this cult core are the jewels, which are the programs the dwarfs mine. Remember the story of Snow White and the Seven dwarfs? Also swirling around Silence are ribbons which we will discuss later.

TREES

The trees bud at certain times. This is one way the imagery of the tree to connect to the time that rituals are to happen. If the tree is barren of leaves (no programs--i.e. deprogrammed), then the system is to grow more leaves.

INTERNAL HIERARCHIES

The programmers build chains of command within the groups of alters that they create. They credit themselves with bringing order out of chaos. When a system of multiple personalities thinks of rebelling, they are in the similar situation as a colony wanting freedom from its mother country. Can we govern ourselves, and what governing structures can we keep, since the structure itself is colonial? Can the mind work together to help itself? The concerns are legitimate questions. And yes, the multiple's mind can function outside of the control of the programmer's hierarchical arrangement, but not without alters taking on different job assignments.

In the slave's hierarchal chain of command, adult alters are assigned to insure that child alters don't get out, unless the abusers want a child alter out. Likewise, commander alters are needed to keep the switching smooth, and to keep things orderly. Subordinate alters are taught to submit to their king, or governor, or queen alter. Immense power and indoctrination is given to the key cult alters ruling a system. The internal hierarchical arrangement means that the host alter coming into therapy (often a Christian) may not be as completely open as therapists think. They must play an internal game of going toward health while not pushing the buttons of deeper more powerful alters.

A lot of internal politics may go on. A front alter may promise a deeper alter secrecy in order to consult with it. This makes for all kinds of triangulation and manipulation within the alter system itself. The entire hierarchy of alters has a lot invested in protecting the core from trauma, which was why the core was split in the beginning. Traditional therapy goes after the core & the multiplicity that protects it, thus insuring resistance from the entire hierarchy, including front alters, who in MPD systems seeking help are often close to the core. The core self is best not directly pursued by the therapist, but gently encouraged on its own to reconnect.

CHAPTER TWELVE:

THE SCIENCE OF EXTERNAL CONTROLS

MONITORING - ASSET CONTROL

Every intelligence service since time began has sought methods of owning people and ensuring they stayed loyal. Two of 13 Illuminati families who are known to have developed extremely well-run bloodline intelligence groups are the Li family and the Rothschild family. The Li' family starte its Chinese intelligence back in 1400 A.D. They had already been an ancient Chinese aristocratic family for many centuries prior to this. Some of their techniques for their agents were state of the art mind control techniques.

The Rothschild's personal spy network and their own mail service was known to be superior to the national European governments during the 19th century. Traditional spy craft has involved the ability to recruit and keep agents loyal. The professional spook manipulates his recruits for a living. He becomes adept at controlling people. For thousands of years, spy operations have honed their skills at controlling people. Because they work secretly, they generally have done whatever they wanted. When you combine the resources and centuries of intelligence operations of the Illuminati, along with the credibility of government intelligence agencies supposedly guarding our national security, the combination is horrific. There are no moral or financial restraints on what is being done. If the intelligence groups want to dabble in keeping a severed head alive apart from the body, or a frozen body with an active head (which they have done), there is no one to stop them. Handlers of slaves use both natural and contrived cues to convey to the slave that they want obedience.

A natural non-verbal threat cue would be brusque movements, and an innuendo in their voice. A contrived cue would be placing both hands behind the head, which is a code for "I AM YOUR MASTER, OBEY ME." Another cue for slaves to obey is when the master makes a fist with his right hand and touches his forehead. This means, "OBEY." Even children, who were multiples, who were being taught to control their mother who wanted to leave the cult, have been observed using the fist to the forehead to try to get obedience from their mother. Staring is one method that the Programmers use. Charles Manson, who was both a slave and a handler, is an example of how a penetrating hypnotic stare is used by the Programmers.

One way to control people is to wear clothes of authority. Dr. Green, Dr. Black, Dr. Star, Michael Aquino and other programmers have worn Nazi uniforms while programming, and at other time have worn Satanic Priestly garb. A beginning point to control people is understanding human needs, and understanding the individual to be controlled. A good case officer learns everything he can about the asset, person or slave, he is to control. Case officers/handlers have been constantly working at improving their skills of control. Monarch slaves who must function as intelligence officers, who recruit spies, are trained in the art of listening and conversation. Learning to listen without interrupting is a guarantee of success. CIA handlers/ programmers have an extremely personable side to them, and a very deadly animalistic side to them too. They will be trained to look anyone they want to recruit in the eyes and withstand their stare. *"Friendship begins with a smile; recruitment with a stare."* from the book by Suvorov, Viktor. "Inside The Aquarium". New York: Macmillan, p. 108. During training, men in U.S. Army Intelligence are told to read this book to understand how U.S. intelligence works.

The entire lives of Monarch slaves are kept on records. Zbigniew Brezinski, and the heads of the CIA, and Secretary of Defense Cheney are just some of the men known about who have access to the computer records that contain records on every active Monarch slave. Not everyone has a price, but everyone will respond to their needs being met. James K. Van Fleet, an important military intelligence officer, wrote about how to manage people. In military intelligence, they keep files on people where they identify which subconscious desires of people are important to the person at the time. All this information is kept in Soft Files, which are not official files, so these files have never officially existed and are not given up even to Congressional subpoenas. The Intelligence agencies know that if they find out what the person wants above all else in life, they can control the person. The nine areas that are monitored to see if they are important at the moment are:

1. emotional security

2. recognition of efforts or reassurance of worth

3. creative outlets

4. a sense of personal power

5. a sense of roots--belonging somewhere

6. immortality

7. ego-gratification

8. love in all its forms

9. new experiences

Once they monitor these areas and then they determine which needs are priority needs for the person, then they will use what they call "the depth approach" to subconsciously gratify those needs in a way that they gain control over the person. Modern companies are doing this too. Dough mix isn't sold, but making a family memory with the children is. Soap isn't sold to get dishes clean, but rather soft beautiful hands are sold. Cosmetic companies don't sell an item, they sell you hope or an image. Fruit dealers don't sell fruit, they sell health and vitality. Car dealers don't sell cars, they sell prestige and images. Freezers aren't sold, emotional security from having a full freezer is sold. They have learned to genuinely appeal to the 9 subconscious desires. In intelligence, these desires are called "weaknesses", because intelligence case officers and handlers will attempt to manipulate those desires for their own gain by sincerely helping the person. They set up short-range & long term goals and plans on how manage a person.

For instance, if a Monarch slave's day to day alters want ego-gratification, a creative outlet, and reassurance of worth, the Illuminati may promise the slave that if the alters comply they will give them a singing contract in Las Vegas. If they need to appeal to their emotional security they can promise a big salary and a nice house. If they need to appeal to immortality they can promise to award them a star on Hollywood Boulevard or whatever religious immortality they can credibly offer. The slave will get the short end of any deal. Anything the slave gets is going to come at a price. The slave will have to do something in return for the Network. Illuminati alters are promised power, honor, glory and wealth. Considering the power and wealth of the elite, they do have the resources to make good on this if they want.

However, the price of obedience might be to shave one's head in submission and sacrifice a child. Another important point is that the abusers want to get the active cooperation of the person being used. This can be accomplished by lies, or facts if they are convenient, which appeal to the person's views of right and wrong. For instance, a pedophile will talk to the child who they are going to rape to get its cooperation. The CIA handlers will listen to what a Slave needs, and solve it for them. Bear in mind, they will only do this if the slave doesn't live with the handler and is pulling in the wrong direction. For instance, the CIA has lots of sleepers, who are dangerous people just waiting to be set off. In these cases, the CIA has to work with front alters who aren't aware of the mind control. Rather than force an issue with control, sometimes a gentle manipulation will work. Then again some slave alters are under such strong mind control that they simply need an order, and don't need gentle manipulation.

The isolation that the handlers impose on their slave to prevent real relationships with outsiders, and the strong bonding of the slave to its master (trauma bonding, etc.) that is administered via the mind control, actually provides a chance for freedom IF the slave survives its master's death. Most slaves are programmed to die soon after their master dies one of my sources was. If the slave survives the suicide programming, the Illuminati will have already taken into consideration who the slave will be passed onto. The one source's system survived their programmer/master's death, and they were not able to break the intense bonds which made the System loyal to that master. Because there is so much secret mind-control slavery going on, if only a small percentage begin to break loose because their loyalty programming backfires on the Illuminati, it has still given us, on the other side, a significant break.

Another example of an MPD system becoming exposed when a handler dies, is when Rothschild, the President of Oilfield Scrap & Equipment in Kentucky, committed suicide. He was the handler of a highly functioning MPD slave, who was his secretary, Mary Davis. Mary Davis could not function after his death and sued in court Davis v. Oilfield Scrap & Equipment Co., 482 So.2d 970 (La. App. 3rd Cir. 1986), for worker's compensation because she could not function after her handler's death.

Because the Illuminati have kept their membership secret, people have not seen the connections between the various cases of multiple personality that surface. In Iowa in 1987, a Multiple named Freeman was arrested for stealing a car. In South Carolina in 1990, a Rutherford with MPD was in court. In North Dakota in 1988, an MPD daughter named Johnson tried to sue her abusive father named Johnson for her sexual abuse. In 1984, a Multiple named Hall was hit by a truck and was in court. In 1987, a Multiple named Jones tried to use his MPD to get off of a murder conviction in Washington. In 1988, Marie Moore, a Multiple in N.J. ran a coven which tortured teenagers. The police found a well hidden body in her house, but the corrupt judicial system did not convict her of murder. In 1988, a Ms. Wheeler applied for Social Security disability benefits due to mental impairments such as MPD.

In each of these MPD cases: Freeman, Hall, Jones, Johnson, Moore, Rutherford, and Wheeler are all surnames that have many members in the Illuminati. The secrecy of the Illuminati has protected people from seeing their hidden genealogies. Tracking these genealogies would in turn start exposing the extent of their mind control. As the handlers isolate the slave from mainstream society, they can begin to give them things that will satisfy their long suppressed emotional needs. These are given in a way that they further lock the person in to the control.

For instance, the slave has been stripped of power, he craves power, so he is given power over other people's lives. The slave has been stripped of its real family, so he is given roots by a long generational occult bloodline, and a cult family. Each Monarch slave exists in their own situation, but there are often common features to how they are controlled. For instance, the handlers like to restrict the mobility of their slaves. Some of the slaves will never write their own checks, will never drive anywhere, and will seldom watch television unless it is something like a Walt Disney movie which is mind-control programming. Some slaves are allowed to drive, but only on a limited basis and their sense of direction is stripped from them hypnotically. In January, 1995, sources newsletter "From A Follower of Christ" had a feature article on Marilyn Monroe. Monarch mind-controlled slaves like Loretta Lynn and Marilyn Monroe lived tightly controlled lives, and were not allowed to drive automobiles. The one exception is that Loretta has been allowed to drive her car around the ranch. The following is some excerpts from the January '95 newsletter because it gives a good example of how Marilyn Monroe, a mind-controlled slave had her life very tightly controlled.

EXCERPTS

On a day in October, 1957, a woman named Lena Pepitone was hired to take care of Marilyn Monroe. In 1979, she published her memories of the time she was the primary person taking care of Marilyn Monroe. I personally think that Lena Pepitone was clean, and didn't know what she was dealing with. She describes in detail her life with Marilyn Monroe. The inside story of life with Marilyn is nothing like people might imagine. Lena's book is such a clear description of how life with a Monarch slave can be--that I decided to use her book as the basis of some articles. Marilyn Monroe was an orphan, and during her infancy the Illuminati/CIA programmed her to be a Monarch slave. Before becoming an actress, while she was still a stripper, she spent time with the founder of the Church of Satan Anton LaVey.

Victims of LaVey have pointed him out as a mind-control programmer. At that time, Marilyn was going by several names including Mona. When they made her a star, Marilyn lived on the 13th floor, in 13E at Sutton Place, NY the world of the rich and famous. That is where Lena came to help her. However, Marilyn's existence was not that of a rich person, but was more like that of an inmate. Marilyn was allowed to have no personal life, outside of the dictates of her programmers and her masters. The programmers and users bore down so hard on controlling Marilyn that they repeatedly came close to driving her insane. The following format the words in italic are direct quotes from Lena Pepitone's book which is entitled "Marilyn Monroe Confidential An Intimate Personal Account", NY: Simon & Schuster, 1979.

- *p.16- "Floor-to-ceiling mirrors were everywhere. Even the dining alcove at the rear of the living room had a table with a mirrored top. All these mirrors didn't cheer things up."*

n programming Monarch slaves, mirrors are used a great deal. Within the Monarch slave's mind, countless mirror images are made. The slave sees thousands of mirrors everywhere in their mind. Because Marilyn was so stripped of any personal identity, she decorated her house as her mind looked on the inside full of mirrors. Although other Monarchs may have some desires to decorate with mirrors, Marilyn is the most extreme case I know of filling one's house full of mirrors.

- *p.25- "Marilyn's bedroom was definitely not a queen's chamber... There were no paintings in the cramped, square room, only mirrors."*

Marilyn's controllers kept her down. Even when she was famous and great, she lived like a slave. She was not allowed to have any self-esteem beyond what she was programmed for."

• *p.29- "May was finally able to callfor the chauffeur to take Marilyn away. "*

Marilyn was a captive, she didn't go anywhere on her own, she always had someone drive her.

• *p.32- "First of all, Marilyn's life was incredibly monotonous for her. Her doctor 's appointments (I later learned these were appointments with psychiatrists) and her acting lessons were virtually all she had to look forward to. She spent most of her time in her little bedroom*

Marilyn went out of the house to be either programmed or groomed. Other than that she stayed cooped up in her room. Does the reader begin to see that the woman was a slave with no life of her own?

• *p.33- "She [Marilyn] didn't even own a television, never listened to the radio. "*

They stripped Marilyn of any contact with the outside world to insure that their mind control would work. They were afraid that something might go wrong with the first Presidential slave that was allowed to be highly visible to the public.

• *p.41- [Marilyn says], "Shit. My life is shit, "she wept. "I can't go anywhere. I'm a prisoner in this house. "*

Marilyn is only telling the truth.

• *p.43- "Because Marilyn had no real friends, she concentrated on herself"*

The closest friend Marilyn had is saying that Marilyn Monroe had no real friends. Doesn't that strike someone as strange. Marilyn didn't have any real friends. Almost the only ones in her life were her abusers, and they worked hard to strip her of any personal goals or esteem.

• *p.70- "You can go anywhere," I [Lena] assured her. "Anywhere in the world" "Who with? she asked sadly. "Who with? By myself" "Mr. Miller, your friends..." "What friends? I am 't got nobody. "*

Many times during the programming, the programmers separate the victim from anyone who could be a support person, they are isolated

{ 474 }

from having friends and relatives unless the relatives are in the occult.

- *p. 71- Marilyn repeatedly calls herself a prostitute. She says, "They laugh at me. What am I . . . nothing... a prostitute. "*

Further on the page Marilyn tells Lena that no one has cared about her for her entire life, including her mother....

- *p.77- "Don't take my baby. So they took my baby from me... and I never saw it again. "*

After Marilyn had a healthy baby it was taken away from her and she was never allowed to see it. It was very likely sacrificed. Marilyn was too afraid to ask what they were going to do with it.

- *p.100- Marilyn loses her baby at the same place that some of her programming was done at. One can speculate that they took the baby for some perverted use....*

- *p.134- "The operation took place at Polyclinic Hospital where Marilyn had lost her baby the year before... [Marilyn said]" Going back to that hospital's a nightmare... .Pain? What's pain?" For her, the only pain was in not having her own child"*

Notice she always go back to the Polyclinic Hospital. Monarch victims have had to endure vast amounts of horrible torture. They learn to survive by disassociation. When Marilyn says "What is pain?" she is being accurate in reflecting her response to pain. She could not have pain--because she would disassociate it. Certain alters are created to take the pain, and the other alters don't have to experience it.

- *p.135- "I found Marilyn in a small room without any view. It was very depressing, especially since there were no flowers or any other signs that Marilyn had friends who were thinking of her." Imagine a great actor like Marilyn is given a room without a view and no flowers or anything to cheer her up.*

- *p.137- "Marilyn's now almost daily visits to the psychiatrists...*

She was closely monitored.

- *p.193- Marilyn's half-sister tries to come into Marilyn's life. Marilyn says, "I have a right to have a family." And on the next page, "Gee, you're really my sister. My sister... At least you lived with relatives."*

Marilyn's masters did not want her to have any family. They often strip the deeper alters of a Monarch slave from any ties to any non-cult person....

- *p.199- Marilyn orders a $3,000 Emerald green dress to be made.*

Emerald green is often the most favorite color of Monarch slaves be-cause of their Wizard of Oz programming which is usually the foun-dational programming.

- *p.202- "Frank... clipped two gorgeous emerald earrings on Marilyn's ears."*

Again we see that emerald green is often used by Monarch slaves.

- *p. 205- "A side from her evenings with Frank [Sinatra], Marilyn's life in California seemed identical to her life in New York. She didn't read, didn't watch television, didn't go anywhere. Al-though the sun was always shining, Marilyn was as pale as ever. She didn't like to go outside during the day."*

As time goes on the case officer or handler will weave and ever firm-ing ever tightening web of control around his asset. They will often use rapport. Many of the CIA's Monarch programmers are very lik-able people, they have learned the skill of "B.S." and building rap-port. Some of this involves just understanding people and NLP. The handler will look for telltale signs such as absenteeism, lateness, nervousness, or inconsistency. He will rely on intuition, spies, astral projection or psychic abilities to keep tabs on the asset. Then if a problem develops it will be addressed with appeals to patriotism, greed, ambition, or fear. Whatever works is the motto of the game. When slaves are picked up, the men picking them up are called Dra-conian enforcers. Two of my sources are very familiar with some of these men.

They are often big male Monarch slaves. A popular Illuminati access point is to grab the right hand with the enforcers thumb in the area between the victim's thumb and index finger. The pressure will be strong enough to leave a bruise after the access. At different times in different states there have been patterns to what kind of car they drive. They often take the cars from cooperating dealerships, so that there is no license number to trace. They also use stolen license plates on their cars. In 1993, in NY they were using brown Volkswagens. In the Oregon area (especially Portland), a full time Monarch slave enforcer named Rex drives his large red pickup or at times someone else's other vehicle like his Illuminati boss's white pickup truck. He will carry a gun and a cattle prod. The cars in some places have been often red or black. A white or silver car sometimes is used to denote someone of rank. When limousines are used to pick up slaves, they may switch license plates regularly because the plates contain access codes.

This was one reason the establishment began allowing people to customize their own license plates! When one wants to control a group of people, as a leader of a country Machiavelli's book is great. Some of those principles can be scaled down to working with individuals. One source has observed that almost across the board, if slaves are left within a non-cult family, relatives will consistently misperceive what is happening in the slave's life. Switches between personalities are reinterpreted to fit the world view of the observer the multiple is merely perceived as "moody" and "irrational". Half-way decent cover stories will generally suffice to cover the slave's activities for the mafia, the CIA, and the satanic cult they belong to. The slave merely needs to pull up a good front alter for public consumption, for people want to think the best of everyone. The public will watch the 7-Swans fairy tale where a magical coat turns swans into a princess, never guessing that a news story far greater is happening all around them. One way to control a person is to identify who the key people are in their life and then influence those people.

Some of the work in controlling Monarch slaves goes on behind the scenes, even without the slave ever realizing it. A number of Monarch slaves have been maneuvered into marriages without actual mind-control even being necessary. One of the items to successfully controlling people is that they know who they are taking orders from. In the military, officers get frustrated because they end up getting conflicting orders from conflicting jurisdictions. This happens with the control of Monarch slaves too, when too many Chiefs and not enough Indians are around. When a slave ends up serving several handlers within a short period of time they can get really messed up. This is because the slaves receive severe abuse and their programming can be splintered and destroyed if not handled correctly.

Of course, the slave takes the blame, but that doesn't eliminate the problem. If a handler wants a better chance of his slave functioning smoothly, the slave shouldn't be tampered with by lots of handlers. This common sense logic of management seems to have been missed by a large number of handlers. One thing can be said, someone who is a common drug dealer had better not tamper with an Illuminati Mother of Darkness alter slave if they want to stay alive. It appears that slaves are seldom tampered with without permission. Another ingredient in controlling people is knowing what your competition is going to do. Because the cults work with the intelligence agencies, they often know who, what, where, when, and how their enemies are going to challenge them. My sources for this book could write a book on how the Illuminati/Intelligence agencies have watched them.

People such as therapists and ministers who challenge the Monarch trauma-based programming have nice growing dossiers in CIA files. A note should be made that the American intelligence agencies tattooed some of their slaves with blue Monarch butterflies, bluebirds, or roses for identification purposes. The bluebird relates to the CIA project name Project Bluebird. Some satanic cults tattoo the "sign of the great Beast" on the heads of victims. They also place scars with occult designs on their victims. The Illuminati slaves, who are hierarchy members of the Illuminati, are not tattooed, although a hard-to-see scar consisting of dots in a triangle on the third eye is done to some members. The prohibition against marking up one's body is not consistently enforced in the Illuminati. It seems this standard is enforced more with the women than the male Illuminati members. CIA slaves have received the Butterfly tattoos from the age of about 11 on up.

THE STANDARD TEXTBOOK TECHNIQUES OF A MODERN INTELLIGENCE AGENCY

The following points are of a scenario which was developed as follows by a source who observed how the CIA were carrying out an operation to recapture a Monarch slave who was trying to escape. These activities follow standard spook textbook methods, and for instance, fit the same patterns of an intelligence operation codenamed Operation Sphinx described in detail in the book "By Way of Deception". By exposing how an operation is put together perhaps it will become clearer how the CIA monitor an asset they fear is escaping.

- POINT 1. An event that looked like an accident was planned. The event was impossible to miss. This can include car accidents, people waving one down to tell you that you have a flat tire, etc.

- POINT 2. They studied their prey to determine his/her routine. They will watch a residence intently to determine the person's routine and take advantage of this.

- POINT 3. Then an insignificant accidental event is planned. Repeatedly, in the many Monarch people the authors have known, the tiniest insignificant points in people's lives are being manipulated. (Bear in mind the intelligence people are carried away and overdo much of what they do, even over planning some of their ops.)

- POINT 4. The chief is given the order to "hit at convenience." They are watching and probing to discover a weak point, and when they find a weak point they will strike at convenience.

- POINT 5. Listening devices are installed. The Illuminati's intelligence agencies are illegally monitoring the lives of Americans with bugs that go up to 2 GHz. Companies like Tektronics which work with the CIA are selling counters which won't detect bugs at 2 GHz. In other words, what is mainly sold the public is inadequate, but BK Precision does sell a counter which goes past 2 GHz. for those who want to know when they are being illegally spied upon. Since MI-6 & the CIA cooperate, the CIA can simply say that their American intelligence information is from MI-6. It may be illegal for the CIA to spy in the U.S., but British MI-6 can legally spy on American citizens. The intelligence groups themselves use babblers, which are electronic devices that emit noise & chatter & destroy the effectiveness of bugs.

- POINT 6. Teams of experts are brought in to brainstorm about the operation. The people called in on a case will be coordinated by a team or teams. One of these teams will consist of various experts whose combined brains will give great ability to plan.

- POINT 7. The person will be watched by moving in an observer into a nearby building.

- POINT 8. An intelligence woman or man will be sent door to door selling perfume or something else perhaps they will pose as Jehovah's Witnesses.

- POINT 9. The door to door undercover intelligence person will be very personable, very nice to talk to.

- POINT 10. The team will take all the surveillance information and spend hours going over every detail, and they will debate and get tense as they hash out the significance of certain intelligence pieces of information as they work out a plan of action.

- POINT 11. The Intelligence people will take advantage of the social needs of someone close to their prey. They might give his wife some opportunities for fun things away from the house. They know how to take advantage very quickly & smoothly of the social needs of people who are around a Monarch slave. They put used car salesmen to shame.

- POINT 12. The intelligence people have the capability to enter without keys.

- POINT 13. They practice "motionless following." That means they followed people in shifts. They will follow by tag teams so to speak, and use car phones.

- POINT 14. They like to use "trade" occupations as a cover.

- POINT 15. They will be willing to give a business card which is a real address, but only a CIA front. The day they realize they are exposed, the phone will quit working. Handlers and men within the Network often use business cards and other cards they carry in their wallets as codes indicating various things. In intelligence operations, the agents will take their intelligence, that is the info they have collected, and put it through 4 steps.

- 1) "direction", who is going to collect what where.

- 2) "collection", the actual spying.

- 3) "processing", analyzing and integrating what they have collected, and

- 4) "dissemination", distributing (via reports, talks, charts) the analyzed and rewritten reports to their customers.

Most of the intelligence groups have a reputation for distorting the truth in the third stage to fit their agency's "party line". Count St.-Germain (169?-1784) is a good example of an intelligence officer. He was one of the leading Illuminati of his time. He did alchemy for Louis XV, and magic for the Masonic leader Karl, prince of Hesse. He spied for the Dutch and the French, and who knows who else. His fundamental allegiance was to the Mystery Religions of the Illuminati. Modern day examples are Lord Victor Rothschild, one of the leaders of MI-6, Sir Dick Goldsmith White, Jewish, Mason, & leader of MI-6 from 56-69, Sir John Rennie leader of MI-6 from 69-73 whose son Charles Tatham Ogilvy Rennie was a known, major drug runner, Major General Sir John Sinclair, of the Illuminati, MI-6 chief from '53-56. MI-S has had a number of Illuminati/Freemasons called Director-Generals, rather than Chiefs, running it too.

Nigel West, a pseudonym for a man who worked for MI-6 devoted an entire chapter in his book "MI-S" about how Hugh Astor and Victor Rothschild ran Britain's double agent division. ALL, I repeat ALL of the German agents spying on England during W.W. II were double-agents actually working for the British. If anyone tried to work for the German's secret service who wasn't disloyal, that person could only work for the Germans IF they turned into a double agent for the British. Today, almost every one working against MI-5, MI-6 and the Illuminati's New World Order, is a double agent. This book may be followed by a number of similar books by double agents of the New World Order's Network.

CIA OPERATIONS INVOLVING GEORGE WHITE

George White, working for the MK Ultra Mind Control program sup-plied during the 1950s a long list of prostitutes to the CIA for study. During the 1950s, the CIA was refining its knowledge of what makes a prostitute tick. How do you use them? How do you train them? How do you teach them to do both espionage and seduction. What are the elements of seduction? All these sciences were refined. For in-stance, if a prostitute stays longer than she is paid for, she will shock the john, and he will find his ego greatly boosted. With the right methods, the prostitute agent can elicit all types of secrets from the vulnerable male. With the ability to create Black Widow Spiders (deadly seductive Monarch alters), the Illuminati gained one more sure method to control others. Seduction and then blackmail. The CIA keeps detailed files on sexual preferences, just as the FBI's J. Edgar Hoover did. It supplies what people want, but the supply comes with a price that the individual is now under blackmail.

BLACKMAIL

This dirty game has been honed to a fine art, which is a standard fea-ture of the Illuminati/Intelligence groups. The CIA term for blackmail is an "OK FIX." When they use a person's past sins to force someone to do something they refer to this as "biographic leverage." Any weak point in a person can and will be exploited. Sexual entrapment for blackmail is referred to as a 'Honey Trap". Black widow alters are being trained and sent out for this purpose. Blackmail of the slave begins when it is beginning to get verbal. At 3, the cults will tell a child they have a bomb planted inside them, that the cult can detonate if they don't obey. In order to blackmail, or threaten, you have to have something to threaten the person with. Men are frequently en-trapped by sexual behavior which is criminal.

Sometimes they are also entrapped by murder. The Monarch slave will be allowed to have children so that they can be blackmailed into complying to save the children or grandchildren. The Monarch slave in turn may be used to blackmail others. Certain alters are trained in this. A Monarch Beta model is highly trained in seduction and will seduce a man. Then an alter which feigns death will take the body and the man will be threatened for having killed the woman. Many politicians and ministers are operating under blackmail today. When Jimmy Swaggart's ministry fell, over 200 Assembly of God ministers called headquarters and confessed that they had similar problems.

The extent that blackmail is being used by the NWO would boggle people's minds. Porn films are taken of the Monarch victims, so that they can be used to blackmail the victim. Monarch victims are forced to commit ritual murders which are photographed and then used to blackmail the poor mind-controlled victim. Perhaps, one of the cruelest forms of blackmail which is carried routinely by handlers, is the threat to incarcerate the mind-controlled slave in a mental hospital. One of my sources has read a number of books about the situation in America's mental hospitals, and sections of these books will literally make a person vomit from disgust. The legal climate in this nation has made it easy to stick someone else in a mental hospital. Once there, they are routinely given tranquilizers Mellaril, Thorazine or Stelazine so that they can't rebel against the most wretched conditions.

Nadine Scolla was a nurse in a mental hospital who wrote an expose based on her diary while she worked. Her book is entitled "Keeper of the Keys" (Westlake Village, CA: F&J Publishing Corp., 1976) The following are quotes from her account of working in a mental hospital,

- *"How can they allow such places to exist? They really need to reform, but who is going to do it?.. .We're supposed to be civilized and yet many people are treated worse than the lowest form of animals. Who cares about these patients? (p. 15).. .*

- *Doctors receive one hundred thousand dollars a year starting salary, and the nursing personnel receive the highest pay in the profession, and yet the patients get the worst of care. (p. 19)*

- *I could see that the patients had no rights here. (p.27)*

- *[on page 49-50 she reports about a secret hospital grave yard where patients could be buried without anyone knowing]*

{ 483 }

- *Do you remember the young rape victim and how they treated her -the girl with beautiful olive skin and long brown hair? They filled the bath tub with cubes of large ice and dropped her into it. They removed her from that and placed her in scalding hot water. She came out red as a lobster. Her body was badly blistered. This treatment didn't help, so they decided upon shock treatment. 'I never saw anything so awful in all my life. They forcibly strapped her down, tied her hands and legs, stuck the electrodes to her head and placed a tongue blade in her mouth. She couldn't scream, wiggle, or do anything. After the treatment Tammey was dead. Her body was limp-she was still trapped in the chair. It was more than I could take. I had to go off by myself and cry.' (p.51)*

- *I don't understand how our local government can allow these people to be treated worse than a dog in the local pound. At least the animals have their own cubicle and their own food dish. (p.73)"*

According to what Nadine Scolla was told, half of the patients in mental hospitals are schizophrenics. A hefty percentage of these "schizophrenics" are really programmed multiples who are being quietly discarded by the system. How many victims of trauma-based total mind-control have ended up sent to mental hospitals? Many tens of thousands, maybe the exact number will never be known. America's mental hospitals have also played an active role in the programming and the research for the programming.

BRIBES

Their skill at bribes is an extension of understanding human nature, and human needs and wants. It works together with blackmail.

THE CONTROL OF THE MILIEU

One of the basic ideas of creating a mind-controlled slave, is to control the entire milieu of the slave. This is expressed in Nexus Seven. The environment of the slave is designed for what is called "story immersion." A Monarch slave who has been given the basic Alice In Wonderland and Wizard of Oz programming will see objects connected to these story lines in almost every store. Restaurants in Dallas and San Antonio, The Time Machine Restaurants, which are used to reinforce programming, have mirrors on their walls, doors and ceilings and their waitresses dressed like programming script characters-- such as Dorothy of the Wizard of Oz. It is no accident that one of the leading Satanic singers calls himself Ozzy Ozburn, or that a certain Mexican witch calls herself Oz. It is no accident that recently a witch wrote the book "The Witches of Oz." It is no accident that the elite have promoted the Wizard of Oz theme with television product advertisements. It is no accident that the U.S. has Oz stamps, that television has Oz cartoons, and Oz characters are appearing all over the place. For a while even Kansas had an Oz theme to their license plates, "Land of Ahs".

Hillary Clinton, a 6th level Illuminati witch & sadistic Monarch slave handler, received a witch's hat in anticipation that she would be called the wicked witch of the West, and that Mary Matalin, who married Clinton's top campaign advisor James Carville, had a photograph of Hillary Clinton as the Wicked Witch of the West on her wall with the caption "I will get you, my pretty, and your little dog too!" The witch's hat and the caption both are popular with these people associated with the White House because they are so rich in triple and quadruple meanings. The deadliest meaning is that the Monarch Slaves that sexually service Hillary and Bill Clinton have Wizard of Oz programming. Hillary really is the Wicked Witch of the West to these poor Beta slaves! The constant bumping into Wizard of Oz paraphernalia or pictures of it helps focus the slave's mind onto their Wizard of Oz programming. MGM Grand recently built a multi-million dollar pyramid complex with a theme park which is based on the Wizard of Oz and the Alice in Wonderland themes. The hotel at the MGM Grand is the world's largest with 5,000 rooms, which shows that mind-control is big business.

A team of actors dressed up in the Wizard of Oz theme like Dorothy and her friends (Tin Man & Scarecrow) and walked on a yellow brick road constructed in the MGM complex. Emerald City is part of the theme park. The complex cost $1 billion according to the Las Vegas Review Journal, Dec. 19, '93 page A1. This complex is given the occult name Luxor, and is at 3900 Las Vegas Boulevard South. It has been advertised as the "Next Wonder of the World." It's a shame that the 1990's big wonder is a programming center. Another part of the control of the Milieu is labeled "planned spontaneity" by the controllers. The Monarch victim repeatedly finds experiences "just happening." These are the coincidences that are so mystical that people feel there must be a higher significance to the event.

Many of these are well-staged events. A slave may try to escape marrying the person they are commanded to marry. The handlers stay one step ahead of the slave, and through a series of coincidences introduce another acceptable person. The slave in an effort to escape grabs the first available substitute who has been coached on how to push all the correct green mental buttons to get the escapee to marry them. 'The slave jumps from the frying pan into the fire. Things which validate the programming and the mystical beliefs of the cult will be repeatedly introduced. The skill in introducing these secretly into the life of the slave are amazing. There is no limit to what can be attempted, and some of these staged events are worthy of Houdini. The occult world has placed their symbols all over the United States.

The most esteemed institutions such as Walt Disney are fountains of the occult. Walt Disney movies are steeped in magic, and yet American society is so drowned in the occult, they have been desensitized to how it permeates American culture. The concept of "Sacred knowledge" versus "profane knowledge" is introduced. If the slave should escape, the first choice is to send someone who can pick them up. I have heard of slaves escaping from Europe on the plane, only to be picked up by a handler when they land in New York. Mt. Shasta's programming site, accessed by helicopter, specializes in reprogramming escaped slaves. Jerry Lee Lewis has a notorious reputation among the Network as being exceptionally sadistic in reprogramming escapees.

However, if the slave is not needed, and is wanting out--tens of thousands of them have been locked up in mental hospitals as paranoid schizophrenics. In the mental hospitals they can continue to get drugs and electro-shock--the very things that caused their problems in the first place. The insiders have a name for these slaves, they call them "broken butterflies". If the slave tries to go to court, according to some, the Non Compos Mentis Law prevents them from testifying against their abusers. At any rate, with or without this law it would not be easy for a victim to get his testimony accorded the respect it deserves. If they get psychiatric help--their therapist can not tell any-one about what they have suffered, and the therapist is hamstrung about what they can do in court for the client.

Recently, 15 states have created statutes of limitations on sadistic rape. This is in response to all the Monarch slaves who have begun recovering memories. ·The extent to which the entire culture and so-ciety protect the Monarch Programming is enormous. Anyone admit-ting MPD (aka DID) is in fear of being labeled crazy and losing some of their rights and their job. Because the conspiracy (the Network) is so vast, an examination of how the Illuminati controls society would be needed to cover the subject of milieu control. This would take an entire book. The reader is encouraged to read some of Fritz Spring-meier's works which expose how the Illuminati' s control extends over all levels of society. Most people have settled their minds on this issue without getting the facts. When the real facts are shown, it blows people's minds. Some of the easiest and everyday items to show people, are simply a dollar bill--with its Illuminati symbol on the back, and a can of vegetables which has a bar code on it.

Every bar code has 3 secret and non-functional numbers in the bar code, which are 666. The silent hammer that strikes out at the Mon-arch slave is that everywhere they go, the occult world is there. Sev-eral cars are named after Satan. The name Saturn, and Belair are well -known as occult names for Satan. When Freemasonry's greatest phi-losopher/Illuminati Mind-control Programmer/Grand Druid Council member Manly P. Hall wrote "Cabalistic Keys to the Lord's Prayer" (Los Angeles, CA: The Philosophical Research Society, 1964, p. 10) he wrote "Saturn = Hallowed be thy name."

The men who head these auto manufacturing companies are in the Illuminati. There is no question that they were not ignorant of the sig-nificance of these names. Many other occult names of big significance to the Illuminati involving eagles have been placed on cars. Electra is a recent car named after a demon. Viper is a slow and deadly creature, why would one want to use it to name a car? Viper is also the name of an important demon. Viper is found in Black Widow Monarch slaves. Some readers may begin to feel that things are being stretched. The connections of numerous car names to the occult could be exposed, but that is not the purpose of this book. We will quote straight from a company their own explanation for their car's name in this next paragraph, simply to make the point, whether others perceive it or not, the Monarch slaves have to exist in a world full of satanic/occult symbolism that ordinary people don't understand.

Mazda's president, Norimasa Furuta, published a book in 1990 which it intended to give to all its employees. The book explains its purpose,

"...we have written a booklet to explain how MAZDA became the name of our corporation and what it means in order to help everyone who is related to MAZDA enhance their creativity and develop their potential."

The book entitled "The Globe: In Search of the Origins of Mazda", goes on to explain about the founder of Mazda car company, Matsuda Jujiro, who is heralded as a great seer who *"believed in himself, in his friends, and in heaven, and he achieved a truly global vision."* Mazda company's book The Globe then explains that the company name Mazda comes from the god Ahura-Mazda which was the "god of light" and the "god of wisdom" according to the book. Jujiro believed that Mazda represents the "origin of civilization." The "god of light" (Lucifer) is often credited for starting civilization by those who aren't Christians. The name Mazda according The Globe symbolizes *"unlimited possibility and stimulates people's dreams."* Mazda's book puts down in writing their New Age goals to *"establish peace for mankind with a global point of view, and a spiritual foundation toward which to work toward a new age."* The book further states civilization started in Egypt and that Christianity evolved from the pagan mystery religions.

Another book associated with Mazda cars, is the book "The Meaning of Life" given to everyone who test-drives a Mazda that was as long as book supplies last. I quote the book *"...the time when regions and continents existed keeping a certain distance from each other is a thing of the past.... We are eager to transmit the meaning of Mazda to the children of Mazda who will create a new Mazda... With a strong desire for peace and through the production and sale of automobiles and machine tools, Mazda has advanced on a course to unite the people of the world"* [bold added] (pp 78-79.)

An adept of the Illuminati is taught about Ahura Mazda. He would know that Mazda was the Persian God of Light who was also known as Ormus which is another name for the Preiure de Sion, which is a powerful group protecting the 13th Illuminati Bloodline. Some of the names of cars which could be triggering to SRA survivors include the Demon, the Vagabond, Dodge Ram (Goat of Mendes), Buick's Phoenix, Ford's Cobra, Mercury's Cougar, Eagle Jeeps, the Le Baron Eagle Logo, Navistar Eagle Truck (which may have Eagle mud flaps and Goodyear Eagle GT tires).

For most of us an eagle is a symbol of what is noble and beautiful. Historically, the eagle and the snake have been the logo of the tribe of Dan, considered the "black sheep" of the 12 tribes. The Prophet Hosea said, "Set the trumpet to thy mouth. He shall come as an eagle against the house of the LORD, because they have transgressed my covenant, and trespassed against my law." (HOS 8:1) And the Prophet Obadiah said, "Though thou exalt thyself as the eagle, and though thou set thy nest among the stars, thence will I bring thee down, saith the Lord." (OB 1:4) I didn't create Illuminati history nor their symbols. I are only reporting on them.

We would like the eagle simply to represent what is noble and fearfully made by God. Indeed, in some verses like in Isaiah the eagle has a positive connotation. However, the construct, the reframing that is done by the Illuminati upon these symbols is that the eagle represents Satan's empire. The Assyrian, Roman, and Nazi empires used the eagle. The Illuminati point these things out to their initiates, and ask, "Is this a symbol of Christianity, or the power of our lineages which

{ 489 }

ruled those empires?" It is not my desire to interpret what Hosea and Obadiah meant. Nor is it my desire to dissuade anyone from buying the cars mentioned above. My only point is that the survivor lives in a world of occult symbols and occult programming triggers.

How do you convince someone to quit fearing the power of their abusers when it has its symbols on their money, their canned food, their cars, and their churches? Yes, there are such things as All-Seeing Eyes in some churches and Masonic logos on others, and other occult symbols. Hislop's "The Two Babylons" is devoted to showing all the pagan symbolism in the Catholic church. Are we exaggerating? One source went into one fast food restaurant and the cups and placemats had a wizard throwing occult energy balls with occult symbols, the next fast food place had place mats showing the King Arthur story which is an extremely important myth for the Illuminati (the quest for the Grail!), the next fast food place had place mats giving children instructions on how to hypnotize your parents, the next one had a Wizard of Oz theme, and the next one was selling occult movies.

This source kept these place mats to use in his talks! This nation is immersed in the occult and so desensitized they don't realize it. The public thinks nothing of a Gargoyle Coloring/Activity book. This type of thing is commonplace in American society. If one examines Golden Book's Gargoyle Coloring/Activity book (1995) still being sold, you will find Gargoyle demons named after geographic locations that the child can color, you will find a Magus with a Book of Spells that the child can color. For activities, the child can duplicate pictures, work codes, match shadows with their figures, match objects and images, and work with robot heads of which several can be placed on one body. All these activities reinforce the type of skills that the programmers want children under mind-control to have.

The book has castles, robots, a sentence about a kitten which is a code about a computer disk, and mazes. A perfect book for the programmers to give a child, and the naive public walks by these kinds of books on their store shelves everyday. The Illuminati's mind-control goes on in part right in front of America's nose, and they don't see it. One of the saddest things for Monarch mind-control survivors is that the Programmers are so systematic in destroying everything of beauty and value in life. Everything conceivable that can be degraded will be. This mind-control has spread like an unseen cancer to every segment of life, and threatens to destroy this nation from the inside out. Imagine that every time you heard your own national anthem that it reinforced your mind-control programming?

That is the life of these victims of mind-control. We wish the American people could realize that George Bush and Bill Clinton are on the same team.

- Both are descendants of the top 13 Illuminati bloodlines
- both are totally corrupt morally
- both are into the occult
- and both were trained by the same person in subliminal language techniques.

The best in subliminal language techniques is said to be Tony Robins, and he is who the elite got to train both George Bush and Bill Clinton. Monarch Mind Controlled Slaves have been created since the late 1940s. Since the early '60s, Monarch Slaves have been specially created for American presidents. These models are called Presidential Models. There are now living about 600 people (Monarch slaves) who were created into Presidential Models.

1
2 That is a large harem. Presidential Models fit a particular set of physical standards, not one of the Presidential sex slaves has been black. Presidents Kennedy, Johnson, Nixon, Ford, Bush, Reagan and Clinton have all been slave handlers. Many slaves have some deeper alters who have a realization that their Presidents are in on the corruption, how does that make them feel? The cults which program pay particular attention to show the child, men in police uniforms and ministers of churches which are participating with the cult. This has the effect of embedding in the mind of the victim that there is no escape that the entire structure of society is secretly in cahoots with the programmers. Not all policemen nor all ministers are dirty, but be-

cause of the Monarch program, the entire structure of American society has been seriously compromised to the extent that all sectors are infiltrated and contaminated. Unfortunately, the worst fears of the victims, are in reality close to the truth.

3

4   The Monarch victim is further victimized because no-one wants to believe them in how controlled American society has become. The truth is we are on the verge of losing civilization as we know it, and entering into a dark sadistic slave-master society that will make Hitler's Third Reich look like child play. What part of our lives are not controlled. We go to our jobs our boss is naturally given the right to control us. For many centuries, the Machiavellian elite have provided the masses with "Bread and Circus". That means "keep the people feed and entertained and they will not rebel." After Americans come home they are kept busy with entertainment. The only exception to their work, and TV watching, are their trips to their churches. Even the various religions are secretly under elite control. See Fritz's Springmeier's "Be Wise As Serpents" book for an 800 page expose of how the various Christian groups and New Age Religions are controlled.

5

6   The point is that people are kept busy and occupied, and they seldom try to step outside of the path that the elite want them to stay in. A slave's front system will be a normal busy person for years, while the deeper alters serve their various functions for the elite. There is simply little that occurs that shakes the routine that gets established. If the handler doesn't live with the slave himself, he will often place another slave as the spouse, to oversee the slave. The marriage couple's deeper alters spy on each other. The schools that the slaves will go to are often controlled by the abusers. Some of the more obvious ones are Groton, a school for the elite's children, and Santa Clara University and Williamette University used by the Illuminati to train their politicians for public office.

7

8   The Beta Theta Pi is a political fraternity through which quite a few Illuminati politicians have joined. The Jesuit schools throughout the United States are used for abuse and programming. Note, that Bill Clinton went to the Jesuit university in Washington, D.C. called

Georgetown University. A number of the military schools that parents ship their elementary boys off to are used by the elite for the ongoing abuse and programming of slaves. The Illuminati foundation, the W.K. Kellogg Foundation, gave the initial funding for the Quest Program for the public schools. The Quest Program is being adopted by various public schools. It also goes by the names Skills for Adolescence, Skills for Growing, and Skills for Living. One of the early editions of Quest had an exercise called "elevator" where the teacher uses visualization and guided imagery. The teacher places her school children in a mild hypnotic trance described in the Quest literature as "a quiet contemplative mood." Then the teacher tells the students, "You are on an elevator."

9

10 Each button on the elevator represents an age of the child. When the students push a button, the elevator takes them back to experiences at that age. It is not possible in the scope of this book to cover how every sector of our lives are controlled. However, it would be appropriate to cover how television shows and Hollywood are intimately linked to Monarch Mind-Control programming.

11

12 A great deal that is coming out of Hollywood is linked to mind-control in some fashion. Some of the hottest entertainers are Monarch slaves, such as Madonna, a Marilyn Monroe replacement. One source was given a catalog to Vidimax, which is a New Jersey occult porn video club by someone wanting to help his research. This cult video club sells actual snuff films. They sell the real life footage of cannibalism, virgin sacrifices, occult rituals, and worse. When Madonna was a teenage slave with the name Louise Chiccone living in NY East Village, a real life film was made of her being raped, and then her cult family taking the rapist and sacrificing him. Vidimax sells this for $19 to their members.

13

14 Some of their videos are live footage of how kidnapped people have been tortured into becoming slaves. One of the catalog listing says, "tortured until their wills are broken and they become Olga's submissive slaves!... WARNING EXTREME GRAPHIC VIOLENCE... BACK BY POPULAR DEMAND." By the way, the Illuminati have their own private porn distribution. Many people ask,

"Why do they need mind-controlled slaves?" Part of the answer is they need them to make their sick porn. The history of the connections between the entertainment world and the occult and royalty go far back.

15

16 One group of people known for their travelling entertainment, the gypsies, have some interesting parallels with the Illuminati bloodlines. A gypsy proverb is, "If you want to stay survive, you must be a devil." Both groups have kept their bloodlines and their identity. Both are secretive. Both groups live double lives. Gypsy children will be given a secret magical name, and a name to use for outsiders. Gypsy children are often baptized in a magical circle. Both groups are into the occult, such as cannibalism, black magic, the evil eye, and white slavery. The gypsies believe in Charani, a big bird consumed by fire who rises from the ashes. The Illuminati call this the Phoenix. Both groups have a secret code that allows them to do anything to outsiders, who are called "Gadja" by gypsies meaning "enemy".

17

18 The gypsies originated in India and migrated west to Iran and Turkey and then to Greece and then into western Europe in the 1400s just prior to an occult revival in Europe. The largest gypsy tribe in India is Ghor. They follow Durga (Kali). Other tribes also worship Kali under different names such as the Black Virgin for which they make an effigy called "Bibiaca" which simply means "lady". Gypsies made up early groups of travelling entertainers. Sir Francis Bacon, who wrote under the pen name of Shakespeare, was the founder/leader of the Rosicrucian of his time. The proof of who Shakespeare was is in several books, for instance, see Alfred Dodd's research in his excellent book "Francis Bacon 's Personal Life Story".

19

20 How close are the occult world and entertainment? The history of the two worlds coincide for many centuries back, so it shouldn't come as a surprise that today's entertainment industry is still closely linked to the occult world, nor should it come as a surprise that the Illuminati have made sure they have control over the industry. During W.W.II, the entire country was mobilized for the war effort and Hollywood was recruited so to speak to help with the war effort. For instance, cartoons were created as training films and as war propa-

ganda. The military hired thousands of entertainers for USO Camp Shows, Inc. which was under the Special Services Division of the U.S. Army. Bob Hope, who worked for MI-6, British overseas intelligence, was the leading entertainer for USO tours.
21
22 After the war broke out he went on 12 major overseas tours which took him and his beautiful troop of stunning knock-out girls to every front of the war, from the quiet fronts like Panama to places like Italy and North Africa. To make a long story short, Bob Hope was used to run messages to programmed multiples for British & American Intelligence. Later, after the war Bob Hope became a slave handler. In some other writings, Bob Hope's connections to the Illuminati are gone into. USO magicians were found to be the most overall popular USO show.
23
24 The International Brotherhood of Magicians is intimately connected to the occult world and puts out a magazine The Linking Ring. Under the auspices of the USO, controlled by military intelligence, the country western industry's roots developed. The country western industry became a front for drug running, money laundering and white slavery for the Programmers of Monarch total Mind-controlled slaves. The USO also created at least 200 bands, from which came Lawrence Welk's band, Sam Donahue's band, Claude Thombill's band, and Guy Lombardo's band to name a few.
25
26 Over the last 45 years perhaps the most popular place for couriers to be signaled to meet was by someone holding a bird in a cage or at a shop with birdcages. The allusion to carrier pigeons is so obvious. Look at a caption "Speaking of Wrens" with a cartoon from Bob Hope's book "I Never Left Home" (NY: Simon & Schuster, 1944) written in 1944 during the middle of W.W. II. The cartoon shows Bob chasing a girl with a bird cage and saying, "Tweet, Tweet, Tweet." Hypnotic commands are given 3 times. What seems like a harmless cartoon, is more like a signal telling people that Bob Hope is in charge of a flock of carrier pigeons (couriers), which we know he was. When talking to a group of soldiers during the war, Bob said, "In London the bobbies caught a guy walking around in the fog with a bird cage giving the mating call but the American counsel got me."

27

28 Walter Bowart in his researcher's edition of "Operation Mind Control" discusses the case of two W.W. II vets, who had their W.W. II memories erased by the military using drugs, hypnosis and behavior modification, before they were released from the army in 1947. This is found in Cassiday, Karen and Judith A. Lyons. "Recall of Traumatic Memories Following Cerebral Vascular Accident" Journal of Traumatic Stress. NY: Plenum Pub. Vol. 5, No. 4, Oct. 1992, p. 627. The point is that evidence is surfacing from various locations that the U.S. government was carrying out mind-control during WW II. This was done under the auspices of British Intelligence (MI-6) during W.W. II.

29

30 When Canada entered the W.W. II with Britain, one of the best British secret agent training schools was set up between Whitly, Ontario and Oshawa, Onario. on Lake Ontario's north shore across from the U.S.-Can. border. The site was called Intrepid Park. Agents called it "the camp" or "the farm". Today, the CIA have their own "farm", Camp Perry. The official British name for this spy camp was British Security Coordination Special Training School No. 103 & Hydra. STS 103. It was also known as Camp X. British SOE (Special Operations Executive) set itself in NYC. Americans from the FBI and OSS went to Camp X for training, as well as the SOE,SIS, BSC, and the Canadian RCMP. The British were already using mind-control at this stage. The connections are endless. Edgar Allen Poe, who was into the occult and worked for British intelligence wrote The Raven.

31

32 Vincent Price starred in Hollywood's version of the Raven, and passages of the book have been used as codes for a number of Monarch slaves, who had to memorize portions of the book with their photographic memories. Warner Communications came out with the book & movie "Sybil" which is about a woman with multiple personalities.

33

34 The book and movie "Sybil" are full of mental slides to prevent people from looking and thinking in the right directions concerning MPD. Structured MPD (DID) like Sybil's, occurs only from very specific trauma-based programming. Even the name Sybil is an oc-

cult name, although the idea that occult was involved in creating Sybil's MPD is not hinted at. The chief financial power behind Warner Communications was the Illuminati/Pilgrim Society member Eugene R. Black, retired head of the World Bank.
35
36 Warner Communications is headquartered at Rockefeller Plaza, and has produced quite a few occult movies and occult books, for instance their movie about a demon "It Lives Again." When Monarch slaves watch television, the shows they watch can relate to their programming in the following ways.

1. First, many of the shows have code words or programming scenarios which are deliberately in the shows to control the slaves: such as Star Wars, Star Trek, The Wizard of Oz, the Love Boat, Fantasy Island, I Dream of Jeanie (Delta Genie in the bottle programming, and "Your wish is my command" type trigger), The Little Princess, the Miss Universe Contest 1995, Duck Tails (created to control child slaves, with deliberate triggers such as "earthquack"), Bobby's World cartoon, Steven Spielberg's Tiny Toons, My Fair Lady (used in several of the slave finishing schools), ET (for alien programming), etc.

2. Some of the shows which are supposedly pure fiction show elements of actual Illuminati ceremonies, Illuminati history, drug running methods, etc., such Bell, Book & Candle, Burn Witch Burn, Curse of The Voodoo, Equinox, Manos, The Hands of Fate, Witchcraft '70, as Spirits of the Living Dead, Frankenstein, Night of the Living Dead, Bewitched (with actual witches as actors). Raising Cain shows torture and MPD. Hellraiser 3 depicts "gatekeepers."

3. Some of the shows portray the Monarch total mind-control program: Telephon, The Manchurian Candidate, Videodrome, Labyrinth, Trancer II, The Attack of the Robots, Dr. Goldfoot & the Bikini Machine, Attack of the Puppet People, The War of the Zombies, Colossus-The Forbin Project, and The Point of No Return starring Jane Fonda's Bridgett, who is connected to the OTO. (By the way, Monarch mind-controlled slaves have been shown the movie "Telephon" to emphasize to them that their minds are

controlled by their handlers, and for them not to forget it.)

4.   Many of the movies and shows use Monarch slaves as actors & performers: such as Rosanne Barr, Bette Mittler, Marilyn Monroe, Loretta Lynn, Crystal Gayle and possibly Wayne Newton (a child singing protégé, who never wrote a check for himself in his life).

They also use lots of slave handlers such as Frank Sinatra, Peter Lawford, & Bob Hope. And occasionally the use programmers such as Anton LaVey, Jerry Lee Lewis. One source for this book, while in the Illuminati, was given repeated reason to believe that Elvis Presley was also a Multiple programmed by the Illuminati. We know that at times he went by code names, one which is publicly known was John Burrows. His group, called the Memphis Mafia, have talked about his ability to go into altered states of consciousness, even seem dead. Recently, another Illuminati slave, also stated that Elvis was an Illuminati slave.

Cisco points out that Elvis' twin brother was dead at his birth, and that Elvis knew that this gave him double spiritual power, according to Illuminati beliefs. The Illuminati will often kill a twin, so that the other will get the power of two souls. From what we understand, Elvis Presley's handler/programmer was a Col. Tom Parker. Elvis belonged to a team of 4 Illuminati men. Elvis is publicly known to have studied yoga, numerology, drugs, and received some new age spiritual training in an academy overlooking Pasadena, CA. He was an active member in the Theosophical Society. After Elvis Presley supposedly died, the Sun International Corp. came out with an Elvis Presley album called Orion, with the winged-sun-disk on its cover.

The winged-sun-disk is an important Egyptian magical symbol used by the OTO, Theosophical Society etc. Mae Boren Axton, known as the Grand Dame of Nashville, played a pivotal role in Elvis Presley's life. Elvis & the Beatles were chosen by the Illuminati to introduce rock music to the United States. There is no doubt about Elvis' and the Beatles' musical talent. Elvis' close friend Wayne Newton is highly suspected as also being a slave. Elvis worked with Burt Reynolds and Jerry Lee Lewis who also connect in with the Illuminati's mind-control operations. The authors are puzzled why Elvis' grave, which had millions of dollars spent on its security, has his name misspelled? We are also puzzled why Elvis, who repeatedly stated he wanted to be buried beside his mother, is buried beside his father, who he privately stated wasn't even his real father.

Why has no one ever tried to collect insurance on Elvis' death? Once again, it seems, the front stories that the public hears are full of inconsistencies. We believe that some people in the Illuminati know the true story about Elvis Presley. For sure Elvis' mysterious mind-control programmer/handler Col. Tom Parker would know.

STAR TREK - THE NEXT GENERATION

The original series of Star Trek had lost money, but in September, 1987 a new series called Star Trek, The Next Generation was started with $1 million dollars budgeted for each of its 24 episodes. The episodes pushed the Illuminati's agenda in every show. People were being aroused to bombard Paramount with requests for a new Star Trek. Bob Justman who worked with Roddenberry said, "When I left Star Trek in 1968 it was a disaster. It was a failure as far as the network was concerned." That is because it didn't make money. Hollywood tells us it makes these movies because they are what the public want and that they have to go where the money is. The closer truth is that Hollywood makes movies that push an agenda, Hollywood makes movies that Hollywood wants to make.

And since Star Trek was part of the NWO's mind-control, the show and it successors had to go on. How important is Star Trek? A witness has talked about Boeing workers sneaking off their jobs and hiding in the tunnels underneath the huge Seattle Boeing plant so they could watch Star Trek shows. This enormous Boeing plant is used for rituals and mind-control. This Boeing building is enormous, for it is where they have assembly lines to build the huge jets, like the 747s, 707s, etc. An extensive maze of tunnels lays underneath the main building, large enough to accommodate all the tens of thousands of workers on any shift. It is interesting who was associated with the production of Star Trek: The Next Generation.

Script writers for the Next Generation had a Star Trek Bible to write from. These script writers included such persons as Alan Adler, Dennis Putnam Bailey, three Grays, Debra McIntrye, Ronald Moore, Grant Rosenberg, Randee Russell, Bryan Stewart. These are common names within the Illuminati. Coca-cola, an Illuminati-run corporation, was one of the major advertisers for Star Trek, and the god-man Dalai Lama of Tibet, who is a Star Trek fan, visited the cast of Star Trek in 1988 in Hollywood and got his picture taken with members of the cast. Probert who worked with Star Trek productions also worked with Walt Disney's Imagineering subsidiary. Here are some of the Star Trek scenes:

- A Wizard of Oz head is shown on a show.
- Data is a humanoid with an on-off switch who can store vast amounts of data. His memories can be so strong that personalities in those memories fight for control of Data. (See the episode aired 1/23/89).
- Holodeck creations of people (humans who are mirror images) who are aware of themselves. This is a well-used concept for programming Monarch alters. The first episode with this aired 1/1 1/88 and got several awards--an Emmy Award, and an award from the George Foster Peabody Award board.

A few other items which will show the reader the occult agenda of Star Trek, the Next Generation and how it fits into the mind-control programming (dates that the show aired are in parenthesis):

- a Reptilian Race called Tellisians (10/12/87)
- a Cosmological Egg-from the cabalistic magical world view (10/26/87)
- a brain scanned by a probe (11/9/87)
- age regression, reverse aging and memory loss (2/8/88)
- android duels & a crystalline body (1/18/88)

- a race of computer operators (2/1/88)

- an ozone hole in the atmosphere kills a planet (2/15/88)

- a matriarchal oligarchy--shades of the Mother of Darkness's oligarchy (1/25/88)

- people who are only holographic projections (4/11/88)

- a cyberneticist & androids (2/13/89)

- doubles (mirror images) (4/3/89)

- half-human half-robot people (5/8/89)

- clones of people (5/22/89)

- a holodeck person who doesn't know his last name (6/19/89)

- Betazoids (11/13/89)

- and a drug which causes hysterical paranoia (7/17/89).

Colorado is the area where trauma-based alien-theme programming is carried out with a mock UFO. Gaston, one of the programmers in that area, is turning out top secret Monarchs with solometric systems. NORAD and Colorado Springs and several other Colorado locations are major headquarters for end-time call back programming. Interestingly, they have placed the Star Trek Fan Club in Colorado.

VIDEODROME

This recent movie portrays Monarch Mind Control and S&M. Mind-controlled slaves are frequently used to create S&M films. The Illuminati's S&M porn film industry has been booming for over 4 decades. Compare the name Videodrome with Vidimax mentioned above. The porn films done of a particular Monarch slave who is used as a porn star will be coded according to the code name given to the star. Let's say they call the Star "Lily", then the porn movies will be cataloged Lily 1, Lily 2, Lily 3, etc. This type of porn involves a great deal of real torture, humiliation, and actual deaths of people. This type of porn is portrayed in the Hollywood movie Videodrome. The main character in Videodrome represents what a mind-controlled slave would see. The main character Max is told, "I want you to open up to me." He then feels intense pain and doubles up and falls down, and submits, "all right." Then he is ordered to "Give us channel 83." He then proceeds under the mind-control to kill two partners, who he has previously liked and with whom he has had no quarrels. He is further told, "You are an assassin for Videodrome. They can program you. They can make you do what they want." Interestingly, the name of the brand of cigars smoked on the show are named Medicis. He is told, "To become the new flesh you must kill the old flesh." This is the type of suicide programming given Monarch slaves. He is ordered, "Come to Mickey." Mickey happens to be part of Mickey Mouse programming and one of the nicknames of the programmer Michael Aquino. He is then shown a picture of suicide. Then the hypnotic command, "Come to Mickey" is said three times. "Long live the new flesh." The movie announces, "The battle for the mind of North America will be fought in Videodrome."

TRANCER II

This is also billed as a "cult classic". Who decides what is a "cult classic"? At any rate, this is another film which depicts part of the Monarch total mind-control. We will not take the space to cover in-depth, but will touch on a few items here. The main character is McKnowlty which sounds a lot like MK Ultra. Is it a play on words? It could be. A council like the Illuminati' s with lifetime appointments is in the film. The persons under control in Trancer II bear some resemblance to the Monarchs. Some of the language that is used is lifted from the language handlers use. "Follow my instructions Sleep, Sleep, Sleep" a person is instructed. "Rabbit Speaking", "You belong in a green world" The movie also has Freeze codes which are a color.

KRULL

This 1983 movie with Ken Marshall and Lysette Anthony is just one more example of hundreds of Hollywood movies which show some aspect of the Illuminati and/or their mind-control. Krull is an island ruled by sorcery. A prince searches for a magic ornament to save his bride and their kingdom. The film has a poppy field, castles, an All-Seeing-Eye, armies of robots, Satan, and other features that a Monarch internal world will be set up with. A person can turn into a dog, pig or lion.

THE LITTLE PRINCESS

This Shirley Temple movie was just one of many Hollywood films used for programming. The princess has a nice "dream". Slaves are programmed to view their service in the real world as dreams, and their fantasy worlds in their internal mind as reality. The Princess has a scene with hot cross buns and ravens. This scene was used for programming. The Princess sits on a throne. There are fairies and a joker, which are used in programming. The father is said to be dead, but is not dead in this movie thus creating the type of reversal that the programmers like to work into the minds of slaves. A rich genie helps the princess, and when she finds her Daddy, she wakes him up with a kiss and a song. The girl's name is Sarah, a name which appears within a number of Monarch system's as an alter name.

MISS UNIVERSE CONTEST

The broadcast of the 1995 Miss Universe Contest did a very unusual freeze-framing of the show while it was on. The screen was mysteriously freeze-framed 9 times, this was a trigger for Illuminati Mothers of Darkness alters. A Mother of Darkness type throne was sat upon by the winner of the contest. An all-seeing-eye was flashed up on the screen with the code A MAY ZING written on it. This is the type of puns that the programmers enjoy. The winners of the contest came from India, Canada, and the USA. The order and names of those countries have to do with end times programming. The names were a code to certain Mothers of Darkness systems. India wore a Mother of Darkness type garment. Canada wore black and white, and USA wore Red. Miss India gave another code during the interviews, "If someone wants to put monkey's on your back, if you stand up they get on your back."

THE MANCHURIAN CANDIDATE

In 1958, the author Richard Condon had his novel The Manchurian Candidate published which describes an American Army sergeant, who is captured and programmed to assassinate on the cue of a queen of diamonds of a deck of cards. Richard Condon's ability to think about the potential of behavior modification and hypnosis, had allowed him to stumble upon what had actually been going for over a decade. Frank Sinatra bought the movie rights for this book, let the movie out briefly and then squelched the second release of the film. Frank Sinatra has been a slave handler. He has handled Bob Hope's slaves, when Bob Hope has lent them to the Rat Pack (which consisted of Dean Martin, Frank, Sammy Davis, Jr. Peter Lawford & Joey Bishop). Frank Sinatra spends time with the Rockefellers and the Rothschilds. Both he and Dean Martin have handled slaves. Dean Martin was described by The Hollywood Reporter as a "hypnotically attractive, homegrown American monster."

Fritz Springmeier's previous writings have exposed how Peter Lawford & Sammy Davis, Jr. were Satanists. Dean had the audacity to want to bring out a slave on his T.V. show on a lease in a tiger outfit. As mentioned previously, the sexual alters see themselves as kittens or cats and are given obedience training with the type of collar Dean wanted to bring them out on stage with on television. The television network stopped it. As Frank Sinatra grew up, his parents always had money. His mother was a cigar-smoking cruel foul-mouth woman, who performed illegal abortions. She got caught once and had to face the penalty on Feb. 27, '39 in a Hudson Special Sessions Court. Frank's hero was Benjamin "Bugsy" Siegel, boss of Murder, Inc. About 30% of the dirty work for the Illuminati is carried out by the Mafia.

The Illuminati have their own death squads which are superior to the Mafia, but individuals must approach one of the Illuminati councils for approval to assassinate. Often it is easier for someone in the Illuminati just to put out an unauthorized contract than to go through proper channels. Bugsy associated with all the Mafia heads including Charlie "Lucky" Luciano who controlled mind-controlled slave

Marilyn Monroe. Both Frank Sinatra and CIA mind-control programmer William Joseph Bryan, Jr. (aka William Joseph Bryon, and William Jenning Bryan III, etc.) were members of the Tommy Dorsey Band. Bryan programmed people while he was with the Air Force as Chief of Medical Survival Training which was the Air Force's covert mind-control section.

Later he opened up his own hypnotherapy Institute on Sunset Strip in Hollywood where he programmed some people in the Illuminati who are actors. He also was the person who programmed Sirhan Sirhan to be involved in the Robert Kennedy assassination. He also hypnotized Alvert Di Salvo. After Bryan died in spring, 1977, the CIA cleaned out all of his files including his home files. Bryan was fat, 6' 1 1/2", and a Satanic priest in the Old Roman Catholic church. This is same satanic church that William Schnoebelen was a Satanic priest in, before giving his life to Christ. (Bill Schnoebelen tells his own story in "Lucifer Dethroned". Chino, CA: Chick Publications, 1993.) Schnoebelen was offered a slave but turned down the opportunity to be a handler. In William J. Bryan, Jr.'s book entitled "The Chosen One The Art of Jury Selection", Bryan teaches how to use hypnosis on jury members to win one's case.

On the back of the book he states about himself, "In addition Dr. Bryan served as an Electronics Engineer in the Navy in World War II, was Director of all Medical Survival Training for the United States Air Force, and a leading expert on brainwashing." William J. Bryan was the technical director for Frank Sinatra's movie The Manchurian Candidate. It was hoped that the movie would scare Americans into thinking that the enemies, the communists, were carrying out mind-control.

THE SIMPSON CARTOONS

There are episodes of the Simpsons which blatantly promote the Freemasons, the Illuminati and even show items of the Monarch mind-control such as "following the Yellow Brick Road." The episodes are quite revealing.

{ 505 }

Aspects of Illuminati programming can also be seen in the movie "Spirits of the Dead", where spirit copies of one's abusers are placed into the slave, and the movie "Cat Girl", where a beautiful girl is turned into a killer beast. Several movies have come out showing the concept of creating robotic people such as the 1920's movie Golem, the 1966 movie Cyborg 2087, and the movie Frankenstein.

According to Illuminati history, the Collins Illuminati bloodline did pre-20th century experiments to create a Frankenstein, and Mary Shelley's novel is actually secretly based on their research. The Rothschilds have carried out successful production of synthetic people this century. This is all in accord with the black magic goal of controlling bodies, whether live or dead. The 90 mm. "Night of the Living Dead" expresses the satanic black magic goal to control bodies. And if the Illuminati can't control their slaves, the final solution, if nothing else works, is to- as the CIA say- "terminate with extreme prejudice", aka "Executive Action", like they did to Mary Pinchot Meyer on Oct. 13, 1964, Princess Grace Kelly & countless others.

TWINNING AND BONDING

Two Sisters-of-Light, the level before Mothers-of-Darkness, will be placed before a many-faced mirror with intense lights and programmed to see each other as inseparable. They become twins, and are programmed to die if the other one dies. They are taught to be one in body, mind, and soul. They are bonded in many ways, including torturing each other, and sexual bonding. The trauma bonding that they undergo will consist of

a. being put in life or death situations together,

b. given programming scripts which intertwine & fill in to complete each other to make a whole,

c. being placed in jobs that require total compliance with the programming in order to survive,

d. are bonded together to other people. The scripture "A house divided against itself cannot stand" (MATT 12:25, MARK 3:25) is used to program people to stay in line with what the team is doing.

High level four-person female teams and a four-person male teams are programmed to work together after the Anti-Christ takes over. These types of teams form the male-female component of a larger 3-part team. With the advent of advanced medical technology the Illuminati are now able to make quintuplets, implant the eggs in surrogates, and then switch the identical children during their lifetimes. This type of high level subterfuge is going on, and it makes the identities of some slaves complicated to say the least.

The twinning programming is very complex and detailed. Within the Rothschild bloodlines, the 5 family lines that began with Mayer Amschel's five sons going to five capitals, network/bond their female slaves together with Gennifer-Sally-Elsie-Sarah-Penelope programming. The 6th son to finish the red shield hexagram is/was a bastard. This is all part of a complex satanic world mind that is being created. This is the Adam Kadmon. Twins, & teams, claim to be telepathic with each other. Observations of slaves, has tended to support that claim. Many therapists have failed to take the twinning part of the programming into account. Twins must be deprogrammed together for best results, if one is left out they may try to impede therapy.

PEER PRESSURE

At the beginning of the programming, the Programmers are dealing with a small infant who is unable to verbalize to others about their abuse. They are further frightened in every way, and tortured, and given behavior modification to teach them to remain silent. Even without all these strong threats which always exist, the child would not capable of fighting back. The child will naturally think this is the way the world is, and of course, the programmers are reinforcing the idea that this is the heritage or path that the child is supposed to be following. The dissociative parts of the child do not fully comprehend that being sexually assaulted daily by their father is wrong. They are being misled by their abuser that it is correct, that is their purpose in life.

The child is never given a chance to realize that it has a right to refuse. It is conditioned to obedience. The abuse seems to be just another part of things that belong to the world of adults. For children, adults do many things beyond comprehension, and at times ridiculous. And they seem to need no reason to do these things, except for the fact that they are adults. Other adults that come and go are also participants in the abuse, so the child doesn't grasp that he can be defended by other adults. The programmers are always doing unexpected things to the child, so the child quits trying to figure life out, and fatalistically complies with what it is expected to do. Children all over the world grow up in an adult world, and are at the mercy of adults.

As the alters begin to experience life, they are generally in situations where the attitudes of the people around them, reinforce their programming. Boys are told by society in general to take their lumps in life "like a man". They are taught to fight their own battles, and not to whine. Few boys risk the shame that comes from talking about their abuse. Society is not kind to "whiners". Females are permitted to show emotions, without the social sanctions levied on males. If the child victim of mind-control comes from a family where only one of the parents is a participant in the abuse, then what often happens is that the clean parent, will never even discuss abuse issues with their child.

Few adults ever really discuss abuse issues with children. The child is generally isolated from their peers as much as possible by the child's handler's and programmers. They place other children that belong to the cult in the child's life to report on what the child is doing. When the child victim begins to "stretch their wings" so to speak and meet other people, there are very few people that will threaten the control of the programmers. When the slave does find a good therapist to make friends with, this friendship will trigger all kinds of programming, unresolved issues around adults, trust, etc. The slave feels double-binded. If they move toward health and freedom, it creates many more problems than staying in slavery.

They need to see the bigger picture. They need to be given something positive to live for outside of the slavery. Psychiatrists are not permitted by their boards to get personally involved in their clients lives. Traditional therapy doesn't address some of the issues that will stop the slave from wanting to gain freedom. Internal peer pressure from multitudes of programmed loyal deeper alters, and external peer pressure from cult children the victim is bonded to, begins to exert an overpowering force for the child to stay on the beaten path. Few people ever buck the system, and go against peer pressure. Someone as hurt and docile as a slave is going to want acceptance, and is not likely going to want to step out of line with society and their peers. Until society admits that there is a problem with mind-control, it will be a dangerous thing socially for a child slave to admit to what the victim is actually experiencing every day.

ARE THERE ANY HAGABARDS OR MOSES?

Now the reader has the formula for the mind control. Now what? These programmed multiples continue to eat away at the moral fiber of every one of America's Institutions like an army of termites. On the outside the structures still look strong, but they are being readied to collapse, for the reign of the Illuminati's AntiChrist. There is a series of books called "The Illuminati Books" which are a fictional account of how the Illuminati run the world. In the novels, the Illuminati run essentially everything, which is actually what is happening. The hero, Hagabard, fights against this ancient conspiracy.

Who isn't familiar with the Biblical example of the elite ruler, who leaves his place of royalty to lead a nation in slavery to freedom? this hero's name is Moses. He also frees the people spiritually from the spiritual bonds of their hermetic magical culture. If there are any Hagabards or Moses' or Aarons out there, it is time to buck this World System. "LET OUR PEOPLE GO. LET OUR CHILDREN GO." Thus saith the LORD, Let my people go, that they may serve Me. (EX 8:1b)

APPENDIX A:

Organizations Practicing Trauma-Based Mind Control

THESE GROUPS FORM WHAT INSIDERS CALL "THE NETWORK." THEY ARE THE BACKBONE OF WHAT IS KNOWN AS THE NEW WORLD ORDER.

- Air Force Intelligence
- Army Intelligence (such as CIC)
- Atomic Energy Commission
- Boeing
- British Intelligence, in. MI-6, MI-5, & the Tavistock Institute
- Bureau of Narcotics
- Bureau of Prisons
- Catholic Church (incl. Jesuits)
- Central Intelligence Agency, CIA (aka Agency, Company, Langley)
- Charismatic movement
- Church of Satan
- Church of Scientology
- CIRVIS
- Club 12 & Club 41
- Country Music Industry
- Defense Intelligence Agency, DIA
- Department of Justice
- Federal Bureau of Investigation, FBI
- Freemasonry (esp. the Palladium Rite, 33° and above degrees, Quatuor Coronati Lodge, SRIA, and other Masonic affiliated organizations)
- GEPAN
- German Intelligence (Shaback)
- GHG
- Hollywood

- The House of Saud in Saudi Arabia (which has un-programmed slaves too)

- The Illuminati (also known as The Circle, Moriah, Moriah-conquering-wind, Gnostics, Luciferians etc.) at all levels is involved in trauma-based mind control as perpetrators & victims, incl. Frat. Saturni-Orden Fraternitas Saturni, THFS, FOGO, Golden Dawn, AntiC.Lucif. Dyn, etc.

- INS

- Ku Klux Klan (different KKK groups)

- Mafia

- Masons (see Freemasonry)

- Modi'in

- Mossad (Mossad le Aliyah Beth)

- Mormon Church

- NASA (National Space Admin.)

- National Security Agency (NSA)

- National Programs Office

- National Science Foundation

- Naval Intelligence (ONI)

- Neo-nazi groups

- Oddfellows

- OTO (there are 4 groups)

- P.4 (elite MI6 section)

- Palo Mayombe

- Process Church and its offshoot Chingun etc.

- Professional Baseball, such as the L.A. Dodgers

- Russian government & intelligence groups (GRU & KGB & KGB's successor, historically an early group known as Spets Byuro #1 called "Kamera" in Russian which means "Chamber" did drug/hypnosis mind control research. The Spetsburo was responsible for assassinations.)

- Santaria

- Satanic Hubs, Soc. of Dk. Lily, Chdrn of Lucifer (UK)

- Temple of Power (previously known as Temple of Set)

- Umbanda

- US Army -- esp. the Delta Forces & the 1st Earth Batt.

- USAF

- Veteren's Administration

- Werewolf Order

- Some Witchcraft groups besides Satanism & Moriah

APPENDIX B

Drugs Available for Mind Control

A.K.A. MK ULTRA PROGRAMMING

- 2-GB (aka CBR, this is a strong hallucinogenic which also helps telepathic communication)
- 2-CT2 (produces dark, earthy visual patterns)
- Acetylcholine (for EEOM, EDOM, and for blocking memory)
- Adrenalin
- Aktetron
- Alcohol
- Ambien
- Aminazin
- Amobarbital (hypnotic sedative)
- Amobarbital sodium (hypnotic sedative)
- Amphetamine (addictive)
- Amphetamine sulphate
- Analasine
- Anectine (succinylcholine, a strong muscle relaxant that makes one feel suffocated and drowning. The person feels terror at thinking he is dying.)
- Anhalamine
- Anhalidine
- Anhaline
- Anhalonidine
- Anhalonine
- Anhalonium
- Aphrodisiacs (sexual manipulation by programmers)
- Aphyllidine
- Aphyllin
- Aprobarbital (hypnotic sedative)
- Atropine (speeds heart rate given with l.V.) Atrosine

- BZ (designer drug ten times more powerful that LSD, produces amnesia)
- Bambusa
- Banisterine
- Baradanga (truth serum which makes people willing to follow any command)
- Barbiturate
- Belladonna (a traditional drug of witches since the middle ages).
- Benzidrene (Benzedrene, stimulant used w/ other drugs)
- Benzocaine
- Bromoharmine
- Bulbocapnine (causes a catatonia and stupors)
- Butabarbital sodium (hypnotic sedative)
- Butyl-bromallyl-barbituric acid
- Caffeine
- Caffeine sodium
- Calcium Chloride
- Cannabidiol
- Cannabinol
- Cannabis (aka Marijuana, a sedative, change in perception, colors and sounds more distinct, time distorted. This drug is not used much in Monarch Programming because it IMPEDES mind control. It has been experimented with in combination with other drugs as an interrogation tool. The CIA listed it as being used in MK-Ultra, but it served as an experimental drug rather for programming.)
- Cannabol
- Caramine
- Carboline

- Carbrital
- Caroegine
- Chloral hydrate (a hypnotic sedative, the active sedative ingredient is the metabolite trichloroethanol, goes to work in about 30-60 minutes, aka Noctec)
- Cocaine (addictive, blackmail, the availability of cocaine may pull up certain alters who are addicted to it)
- Coffee
- Coramine
- Curare (to paralyze the body)
- Delvinyl sodium
- Demerol (a hypnotic, also given as a reward for good learning after an induced headache, is used in the Scramble programming where the victim must overcome its effect to concentrate on what is being said)
- Desoxyn (used with Sodium Pentothal for hypnotic trance)
- Dexedrine (amphetamine)
- Di benzo pyran derivatives
- Dicain
- Doral
- Dramamine (aka dimenhydrinate, stops motion sickness)
- Drobinal (for quick access)
- Ecstasy (aka XTC, Adam, MDMA, this is an illegal designer drug, but it's used by the government & cult programmers. Empathogens, like Ecstasy, enhance trust between the recipient & the programmer. It's effect lasts for several hours.)
- Ephedrine (stops hypotension)
- Ephetamine
- Epinephrine (adrenaline)
- Ergot

- Ergotamine
- Ethanol (to inebriate the victim to induce certain behavior)
- Ethchlorvynol (hypnotic sedative)
- Ethyl harmol
- Epicane
- Escrine
- Estazolam (hypnotic sedative)
- Ethclorvynol (hypnotic sedative, effect begins 30 mm. after digestion, addictive, aka Placidyl)
- Ether
- Ethinamate (hypnotic sedative, aka Valmid)
- Eucaine
- Eucodal
- Eukotal
- Eunacron
- Evipal
- Evipan
- Evipan sodium
- Flurazepam hydrochloride (hypnotic sedative)
- Genoscopolomine
- Glutethimide (hypnotic sedative, has withdrawal symptoms, aka Doriden)
- Halcyn (blocks explicit memory by impairing hippocampal processing)
- Haliopareael (tranquilizer)
- Harmaline
- Harmalol
- Harman

- Harmine
- Harmine methiodide
- Harmol
- Heroin
- Hexacol
- Histadyl
- Histamine (causes changes in the skin)
- Hydractine (or Hydrastine)
- Hypoloid soluble hexabarbitone
- Icoral
- Indole
- Indole methyllarmine
- Insulin (shock for amnesia)
- Ipecac (to induce vomiting for eating disorder programming)
- Largatil (a powerful tranquilizer)
- Lophop-nine
- Lorazepam (sleep induction, may destroy memory of previous day)
- LSD-25 (Used to program alters to cut their veins; they want to end their nightmare by cutting what seem like white rivers w/ black threads or other scary delusions. Can cause psychosis & other effects. It's used in small amounts for interrogations. Its active ingredient is psilocybin which can create anxiety & a fear of death.)
- Lyscorbic acid
- MDA (this is a cross between mescaline and amphetamine speed)
- MDMA (also known as Adam, this is Ecstasy, see under Ecstasy for more information)
- MDE (aka Eve, puts someone into a strictly intellectual head trip)

- Manganese chloride
- Mellaril (mood changer)
- Methaqualone (hypnotic sedative)
- Methotrimeprazine hydrochloride (hypnotic sedative)
- Methy-cocaine
- Methy-prylon (aka Noludar, helpful for hypnosis, side effects are a hangover & skin rashes.)
- Metra-ol
- Midazolam hydrochloride (hypnovel, versed, hypnotic sedative which can cause amnesia)
- Morphine
- Morphine hydrochloride
- Narco-imal
- Nembutal
- Niacin (helpful to stop an LSD trip)
- Nicotine
- Nicotinic acid (stops LSD drug effect)
- Nikthemine
- Nitrous oxide
- Novacaine
- Nupercaine
- Pantocaine
- Pantopone
- Parahyx
- Paraldehyde (hypnotic sedative, produces sleep in 15 mm., has a strong odor & disagreeable taste)
- Pellotine
- Pentobarbital (hypnotic sedative)

- Pentobarbital sodium (hypnotic sedative, if mixed with dextro amphetamine sulfate it will half the stage 1 dream time when REM sleep ocurs)

- Pentothal acid (helpful for hypnosis)

- Pentothal sodium

- Percaine

- Pernoston

- Peyotl (interrogation, hallucinations)

- Pheactin

- Phenamine

- Phenolic acid (injected into expendable children's hearts to kill them)

- Pehyl-thio-urethanes

- Picrate

- Picrotoxin

- Procaine

- Propranolol (calms the mind so it can function better)

- Pulegone-orcinol

- Pulegone-olivetol

- Pyrahexyl

- Pyramidon

- Quazepam (hypnotic sedative)

- Quinine

- Reserpine

- Salsoline

- Scapalomine S. (good amnesia drug)

- Scopolomine (truth serum that makes people willing to do what-ever they are told)

- Scopolomine aminoxide hydrobromide
- Scopolomine-phetamine-eukotal
- Secobarbital sodium (hypnotic sedative)
- Sodium Amytal (hypnotic sedative that reduces REM sleep time)
- Sodium barbital
- Sodium dielvinal
- Sodium evipal
- Sodium pentobarbital (nembutal)
- Sodium Pentothal (truth serum for interrogation, can be used with hypnosis, can be used with Desoxyn, given in an IV)
- Sodium phenobarbital
- Sodium rhodanate
- Sodium soneryl
- Sodium succinate
- Sodium thioethamyl
- Somnifen
- Stovaine
- Strychnine
- Styphnic acid
- Sulfazin
- Sympatol
- Synhexyl
- Telepathine
- Tetra-hydro-cannabinol acetate
- Tetra-hydro-harman
- Tetra-hydro-harmine
- Tropacocaine

- Tropenone
- Temazepam (hypnotic sedative)
- Thallium (confuses thinking)
- Thorazine (helps bring one out of an LSD trip)
- Tranquility (a designer drug for programming that makes the victim compliant, like Baradanga)
- Triazolam (hypnotic sedative, somewhat rapid)
- Yageine
- Yohimbine sulphate
- Zolpidem tartrate (hypnotic sedative)

APPENDIX C

Monarch Mind Control Codes

A) **ALPHA (basic)**
B) **BETA (sexual)**
C) **CHI (return to cult)**
D) **DELTA (assassination)**
E) **EPSILON (animal alters)**
F) **OMEGA (internal computers)**
G) **GAMMA (demonology)**
H) **HYPNOTIC INDUCTIONS**
I) **JANUS-ALEX CALL BACKS (end-times)**
J) **THETA (psychic warfare)**
K) **TINKERBELLE (never grow up/alien)**
L) **TWINNING (teams)**
M) **SOLEMETRIC MILITARY**
N) **SONGS (reminders)**
O) **ZETA (snuff films)**
P) **Sample alter system codes**
Q) **Catholic programming**
R) **MENSA programming**
S) **HAND SIGNALS**
T) **Programming site codes (used for slave model codes, etc.)**

ALPHA (basic)

Basic Commands (these basic commands are also found used in many slaves, although there will be exceptions to everything.)

- "GET ON YOUR TOES. STAY ON YOUR TOES." - means "attention slave" get ready for a command.

- "ON YOUR TOES" - is a preparatory command that will be used throughout an entire system.

- "IF YOU PLEASE SIR" -- From Wizard of Oz, slave says this like "yes, sir."

- 3-tap code for access

- "FOLLOW THE SNAPS", "LISTEN AND OBEY OUR COMMANDS", "THIS IS FOR YOUR OWN GOOD"

- "FIDDLER" - code to take one to Never Never Land

- "PUPPET MASTER" - name of master for Marionette or Puppet program "DADDY" -master "DADDY'S FRIEND" -- a user of slave approved by master "PAPA" - master, "WHITE RABBIT -- master

- "YOU'LL SPEAK MY WORDS WHEN I PULL YOUR STRINGS." - Puppet programming control of what slave will say.

- "SPILL IT" - trigger command ordering slave to speak

- "SILENCE" - order means keep quiet

- Mr. Rogers Neighborhood's - "Land of Make Believe" was used for the programming code script: "I AM MR. ROGERS AND I HAVE PUPPETS, TOO I PULL ALL THE STRINGS AND I PULL STRINGS ON YOU."

- Twinkling of the nose - Bewitched programming to cast spell or order on slave.

- "(name of alter), YOU WILL COME FORTH AND OBEY." or "...OBEY AND COME FORTH." Another basic way of getting an alter would be simply to spin the person and call out the alter's name, or to snap the fingers and call out the name of a front alter.

Access is accomplished for a number of Illuminati slaves by a message via phone or letter, then a looking glass person takes the system to a location outside of the house, maybe simply to the sidewalk, there the person is picked up. The left hand is then grasp on the soft part of the hand between the thumb and forefinger by two fingers very tightly. This pulls up an alter with an egg in its lap. The egg is then opened via a code and the imps inside the egg communicate to the ribbons and the computer.

Access phone calls to slaves may have high-speed codes transmitted that trigger the slave subliminally without their conscious awareness.

Access to some people is done with computer like jargon "ON LINE" "ACCESS, (then identification), (then color code), (then name)" ", "ENTER", "RUN". Some Systems have their triggers all in computer lingo such as COMMAND MODE--ALL DISK DRIVES AND HARD DRIVES ERASE .FORMAT DRIVE COPY UNDELETE PURGED MEMORY DRIVE..." Where some of the newer slave programmers are also computer programmers they enjoy transferring their computer lingo to use in controlling their programmed slaves. They may even throw in some FAX lingo such as "DIAL ALL RE-MOTES INITIALIZATION - ATSO -OHOaM (HANDSHAKE BE-TWEEN ALL REMOTES), HANDSHAKE COMPLETED."

The color of the car to pick up a System may relate to the color coding of the alters to be picked up, such as white exterior, blue interior for a white alter-then blue alter access sequence.

Basic Internal Emergency Color Codes for a System, there are several different "CODE RED's, etc. not just one in a slave, what follows is not the complete information about the Codes, although it is possible some slaves have a simplified version like this:

- "CODE GREEN" - Dr. Green's suicide programming, tied to "no -talk" programming.

- "CODE BLUE" -Victim's body freezes in motion and can't move until another code is given.

- "CODE RED" - Victim gets angry and violent

- "CODE RED" - Another Code Red has the standard Monarch meaning, "serious self-destruct" program

- "CODE YELLOW" - Victim gets jealous, angry and wants to violently get even

- "CODE BLACK" - Used to get victim's to get on their ritual clothes.

- "CODE WHITE" - Code to protect the cult members from arrest. When police see the Code White they treat the people as untouchable. There are code words for Illuminati members to tell police and judges that will automatically get them set free. Masonic handshakes and codes also work well with judges, police & govt. workers.

- "CODE 911" - To activate the slave for an emergency calling for superhuman strength. Certain alters will have extra strength.

- "CODE 911" - Also used with standard Monarch meaning of "Call your programmer/handler".

- "DISARM" (3x) - to get rid of a dangerous alter two snaps + "SHUTDOWN" - to shutdown an alter.

- "LET THE KINGS BE KINGS, LET THE BANKERS BE BANKERS, LET THE PRIESTS BE PRIESTS - saying to justify their Master-slave relationship to the masses of humanity.

- The Sun setting the following day was used as a trigger for slave to forget events. For the cat alters a certain word is given to trigger them to go "over the rainbow" after an event in order for them to forget it. "FROM THE RISING OF THE SUN TILL THE GOING DOWN OF THE SAME" - programmed in by using the scripture. "GO INTO THE SEA OF FORGETFULNESS" - a hypnotic structure in the mind to forget. Waterfalls are also used as a hypnotic image to forget pain and memory.

- "RETYPE A LETTER" -reprogram,

- "JEWELS" - programs.

- "THE CATS & THE FIDDLE NEED TUNED UP--Slave to handler, I need reprogrammed.

There are three words to trigger a suicide program -

- 1. Bait

- 2. [intentionally left out]

- 3. hook another suicide program trigger is when the dominoes fall. "GO OVER THE BLUFF" (3X)- causes suicide in some alters SACRED HEART - Catholic/Jesuit suicide program Some suicide programs are set off with a long tone over the phone along with a code number.

- "KERMIT THE FROG" - a type of access code. "KERMIT" may be a code relating to computers, because Kermit is the universal language for connecting computers together. It is a single standard to exchange files between any two systems.

All memories, traumas, and tortures are coded. Body programs are coded. One set of body programs uses Hebrew, Greek, and Druidic letters.

A clone program creates clones of an alter (also called lollipop or lobster program) imagery is that sesame seeds fall off of a hamburger bun and becomes another hamburger.

Codes to all the various basic systems

- Carousel   532342223
- Castle System   221435321
- Communication   311146623
- Double Helix   432443321
- Level   211343231
- Mensa System   323542321
- Pentagram   421136113
- Pool of Death   231134421
- Puppet   341124321
- Sole metric   665421134
- Spider Web   321654321
- Stairwell   432111132
- Quabala   423454334
- Tornado   332146444
- Umbrella System   314321014

ALICE IN WONDERLAND

The White Rabbit is a programming figure for Alice In Wonderland Programming who will allow you to go to otherwise inaccessible places for adventure. He represents the master. The White Rabbit is an important figure to the slave. White rabbit gives a wafer (coke-sugar-cocaine) to Alice and says "EAT ME" or "EAT IT AND I'LL TAKE YOU THROUGH THE DOOR" - takes master into closed part of System, or perhaps over the rainbow.

The Queen of Hearts is also an important figure for commands in the Looking Glass World which the slave enters upon command. When a deep slave alter is needed to perform they are sent into the looking glass world where a looking glass person carries out the command- but in a way that reality is thought to be a dream. In other words, this is a preparatory command to get the slave ready for abuse.

"USE THE KEY. PUT IT IN THE LOCK. TURN. OPEN THE DOOR AND STEP THROUGH A WINDOW [or MIRROR] INTO NEVER NEVER LAND."

"SOMETHING IN LIGHTENING TO TRANSPORT YOU FASTER THAN THE OL' RUBY SLIPPERS. CLICK YOUR HEELS TOGETHER AND BE THERE IN A SNAP. (SLAVE CLICKS HEELS) ELECTRIFYING WITH THE RUMBLE OF THUNDER. BOLTING THROUGH TIME SO YOU WON'T BE LATE FOR A VERY IMPORTANT DATE." (Alice in Wonderland Programming) (This is the wording to use deep alters.)

CINDERELLA PROGRAM

The code word involves something said about the stroke of midnight.

THE MELTING POT PROGRAM

A very powerful program is activated by melting the slave into his master. The slave will do anything for the master with this program. The melting is the ecstasy that is occasionally experienced when lovers having sex seem to melt into each other. This feeling of ecstasy-melting is programmed to release when the master says these words, "MELT INTO YOUR MELTED MIRROR FOR AN ELECTRIFY-ING RIDE. LOOK DEEP INTO THE BLACK OF MY MELTING MIRROR EYES. SEE YOU REFLECTING ME, REFLECTING YOU, REFLECTING ME, REFLECTING YOU, REFLECTING ME, REFLECTING YOU, REFLECTING ME, REFLECTING YOU ... (cont. this several times) UNTIL WE MELT TOGETHER AND SINK DEEP... [words omitted] INTO THE OTHER SIDE."

"MELT INTO MY MIRROR, YOU LOOSE YOURSELF INTO THE POOL OF LIQUID MIRROR, STEP INTO THE LOOKING GLASS, SINK DEEP WITHIN ITS POOL, AND STRADDLE THE DIMENSIONS IN TIME. I'LL SEE YOU THERE ALONG WITH MY FRIENDS"

"SEE IT THROUGH THE LOOKING GLASS" - infinity mirror programming involving mirror image people (alters)

"LOSE YOURSELF IN THE INFINITY MIRRORS."

WIZARD OF OZ

The Yellow Brick Road is the script or programmed set of instructions one must follow. It also serves as a runway for alters to take off from their internal world and take the body. "FOLLOW THE YEL-LOW BRICK ROAD"

There is a code to get through the poppy field (trance state). Some alters to get through the poppy field need to put on a new dress and a new image. The poppy field may be called "the field of forget-me-not". In this way it is linked to the daisies of Dr. Green. To get into the poppy field is easy, it is "SLEEP, SLEEP, SLEEP", see other induction methods on another page.

"THERE'S A PAIR OF MAGIC SHOES TO WEAR WITH YOUR DRESS.. .SOMETHING IN LIGHTNING...TO TRANSPORT YOU FASTER THAN THE OL' FURRY SLIPPERS."

When the slave is finished being used they return from Never Never Land to Kansas. To do this they are told: "CLICK YOUR HEELS ... THERE'S NO PLACE LIKE HOME." They might be reminded "YOU'RE NOW GOING OVER THE RAINBOW TO THE OTHER WORLD."

TIN MAN PROGRAMMING

The Tin Man programming is all purpose versatile program for what ever the master needs done, it means that the slave is a well oiled machine. Sometimes the slave is reluctant to do a job but he is being told that he is a well oiled machine. The exact words may vary with the mission, but the following are exact words, "LEAVE YOUR SHELL. ACTIVATE: MACHINE. COUNT DOWN ONE TO TIN...." "SOON WE'LL HAVE YOU PURRING LIKE A WELL OILED MACHINE. ALL OF YOUR MOVING PARTS ARE PIVOTAL AND GLIDING WITH EASE. MELT INTO MY HANDS. TAKE MY COMMANDS. I'LL HOLD YOUR JAW TO KEEP IT FROM SLIPPING WHILE YOU SLIP THROUGH A WINDOW IN TIME."

Program code for slave to shatter their memory of an event (used with electroshock): "MIRROR MIRROR ALL AROUND ON THE CEILING ON THE GROUND, SPINNING FASTER ROUND AND ROUND. ARE YOU UP OR ARE YOU DOWN? ARE YOU DOWN OR ARE YOU UP? IT REALLY DOESN'T MATTER. BE-CAUSE WHEN THIS MIRROR BUBBLE BURSTS, EVERY-THING WILL SHATTER."

"GO KEY WEST IS KEY - several slaves have this code, related to Sen. Byrd & Oz prgmg. GALAXY programming (for the end times) is also connected to the Oz programming.

In upper level Illuminati slaves Dorothy in the Oz story will represent the Mother of Darkness alters, Ozma will represent the Ruler of the Castle, and Glinda will have the Great Book of Records. The ring of Glinda (from Glinda of Oz, p. 16) gives protection.

BODY PROGRAMS

See Omega Programming- Universal Function Codes for internal system codes for body programs. Sometimes these body programs are filed with a combination of Hebrew and zodiac signs. Greek letters are also file noumbers of at times of body programs.

Rivers of blood - circulation control program. This program totally controls the circulatory system. The victim may think they are losing lots of blood & go into heart failure.

Octopus - strangulation suicide program The internal defenses consists in part of body programs that are triggered if the Mind-controlled slave steps out of line.

Here is a good list of some of these body programs each of which has its own codes:

- Auditory Problems
- Blood Flow/Circulation
- Burning as if on Fire
- Digestive Failure
- Headaches/Split Brain
- Heart Failure
- Histamine Production
- Optic Problems
- Respiratory Failure
- Sleep Deprivation
- Sleeping Program
- Temperature Change

The suicide programs that can go off include

- Armageddon
- Clowns Cutting
- Cutter Program
- "Pain is Love"
- Disembowelment
- Drug Overdose
- Gethsemane
- "Hypnosleep"
- Injection of Bleach (Poison)
- Octopus
- Red Sea
- Shooting Programs (Shotgun, Russian Roulette, Shooting Family)
- War in the Heavens
- Wrecking the Car.

Along with the suicide programs that can be triggered are programs that jerk the victim's mind every which way, which include:

- Bee Stinging Program (put in by placing the drugged victim being near large swarms of bees humming & then letting a bees sting the victim)
- Busy Cleaning Program
- Crazy program
- Flooding (from Atlantis)
- Isolate & Hibernate Program
- Memory Erasure Program
- Pain Programming

- Paper Doll Program
- Protection by Trance
- Revolving switching
- Scrambling Program
- Re-Structuring Programming,
- Tumbleweed program
- Water-jar Shaking Program (Ahab stomping the grapes Bible-based program making mush out of the brain.)

Cutting programs are often hidden behind the Bee Swarming program. Alpha and Omega is a strong program. Sometimes saying "ALPHA & OMEGA" helps alleviate headaches.

 DNA (This uses a lot of number codes.) This is a double-helix which is used as an elevator shaft running down through a system. Numbers are used and the names of cities to go down the elevator shafts. This programming is said to be done in hospitals.

- Card Codes - Regular playing cards have developed from the occult Tarot cards. The four suits correspond to magic, the spades mean the power from the spear of destruction, the diamond means is a double pyramid or demonic power of wealth, and the club is a clover meaning fortune and fate, and the heart means devotion and loyalty. The four suits work well in programming because anything that is broken down in 4's or a multiple of 4 can be coded with cards. Anything that can be broken down into 12's or 13's can be given cards too. Since clocks work off of 12's, card codes work well with clocks. The suits can denote seasons. With Jokers one gets 13 cards per suit with four suits gives 365 unique symbols to denote the days of the year. Dominos can also be used on a base 13 code system. The blank will equal 13.

Carousel System. There is a back side to enter the Carousel.

Carrier Pigeon (slave's who send coded or uncoded messages) and their contact codes

- Birds used for contacts. That is birds in cages are often used as a sign of a meeting place. The contact would say "What did the bird say?" or "A little bird told me ..., Then the courier pigeon delivers her message.

- "I've come a long long way to see you." words to say by System to John or to person to be met. There is an endless variety of contact phrases to indicate that the right person has met the right person.

- Sample Code for passing drugs-"RHINESTONE COWBOY" to which the response from the slave would be "I'M NOT A COWBOY, I'M A COWGIRL."

- Emerald ear rings have been the visual signal to customs agents to allow a person carrying drugs through customs. (SEE D. DELTA for deeper Carrier Pigeon codes.)

Castle System - May need a special ring worn by and turned by the handler.

Flower's Program - CSP94OYP587 - code to designate a flower tying 3 generations.

UMBRELLA PROGRAM CODE - "R x 4 x 5Y58876"

Sample correspondences of Gem codes:

1. Aries - diamond
2. Gemini - topaz
3. Cancer - cat's eye
4. Leo - ruby
5. Virgo - emerald
6. Libra - opal
7. Scorpio - amethyst
8. Sagittarius - turquoise

9. Capricorn - black onyx
10. Aquarius - crystal
11. Pisces - sapphire

POTTER'S WHEEL

"STAND IN ORDER ACCORDING TO RANK AND SERIAL NUMBER" - part of a stacking command to get alters in sequence together to work on them. Dominoes and cards are used as part of the stacking cues.

Dr. Star's Programming which places Pentagrams into people uses Sigils as codes - the occult symbols for the various demons, along with a color, a gate, and a number form a complete code. For example, 1st Gate is the god Nanna, #30, color-SILVER, LADDER OF LIGHTS, GOD OF THE MOON.

To access a System the abusers often have an object as part of the pickup code, such as a set of car keys, a special coin token, a business card, jewelry, or certain clothes or packages. A Popper liquor drink is knocked 3 times on the table when it is served. (Who would be the wiser that three knocks is an access code?)

WORD MATRICES

A word-matrix code is where the victim is given two lists of words and then each word on the left list is paired with a word on the right list to form a code. Randy Noblitt, a therapist, gave an example of a basic pattern for a Word-Matrix. And this is simply quoted from his example to give the reader an idea.

started	xenophobe
between	thoughts
endless	beginning
throughout	forever
get out	trepidation
over	beneath
fun	execute

win	lose
first	then
form	benign
beginning	end
tonight	last morning
thorough	the end

BETA (sexual)

SEXUAL ALTERS - most of the following codes are for deep sexual alters. In Illuminati Systems these are called Beta alters, in CIA systems they create Beta models whose primary function is to provide sex, usually perverted sex and S&M for the perverts who run our secret government and visible government. These System models are numbered BETA 1, BETA 2...BETA 601, etc

Domino codes for spinners can be 6-3, 6-4, 8-4, 8-5, 10-5, 10-6, 12-7, 12-8. The 13th kitten then would be left blank. Spinner dominos have spinner kittens off of them, when a spinner domino code is used. In this case 6-2 could take you to the Beta level.

"10 LITTLE INDIANS, 9 LITTLE INDIANS", "1 LITTLE, 2 LITTLE.. ."-associated with morse code call back telephone numbers

"3 LITTLE KITTENS HAVE LOST THEIR MITTENS..." -The Kitten alters have stepped outside of their programming and need fixed by the Master.

'Hotel California" means a place to have sexual gratification.

Stroking under chin along with "HAVE A BALL TONIGHT" (Cinderella programming) Stroking under the chin along with "PURR FOR ME KITTEN." Magic shoes or red slippers are used to switch to get specific sexual alters. The slippers are clicked 3x to get deeper sexual alters.

"COME HERE MY KITTEN, AND LET ME PET YOU. PURR FOR ME NOW. ..THAT'S A FLUFFY KITTEN. PURR DEEP."

"COME HERE LITTLE ONE."--call for young sexual alter

"PASSION" used 3x with other words as a sexual trigger, such as "SHOW ME YOUR PASSION." Passion is a strong program word for sex.

"RED DOT, SPIN SPIN SPIN, BECOME ANOTHER PERSON." this is said to a mother kitten before she is told which spin kitten to get from her litter. It is a preparatory command meaning "call your spinner".

Spin Kittens "WE GOTTA GET DRESSED.. .IN 5 MINUTES" along with being spun produces specific sexual kitten.

9 lives of kittens - means 9 sexual alters taken in sequence. When spun in a counterclockwise fashion, the sexual menu is from 1 to 9. With 3 & 5 being oral sex. "Heat of hell" is used as trigger words in this programming. The 10th revolution is to beg to be whipped. "TURN AROUND 10" "SPIN FOR ME." The heat of hell ignites after the 6th spin.

"RIDE PONIES"-means to do sex for both English & German slaves;

"PLAY HORSEY-sexual games

"MOUNTING A HORSE"-[obvious]

"CAT NAP" - sex;

"CAT NIP -- cocaine

Tweedle Dee and Tweedle Dum --S&M programs involving mirror image alters. Not to be confused with Humpty Dumpty self-destruct program.

"SIX IS SEX. SEVEN IS HEAVEN. EIGHT IS GREAT. NINE YOUR MINE."--This means to fall under the master submission, has sexual overtones.

"ITSY BITSY BOOB" -- access code pertaining to Betty Boob pro-gramming (which is a certain type of female behavior).

For Beta alters the codes may be:

"BETA ONE MARY A=1, B=2, C=3, D=4"
"BETA TWO MARY A=4, B=3, C=2, D=1"
"BETA THREE MARY A=3, B=4, C=1, D=2"

Then these might be said in combination "3412 4321 1234" (x3)

An American system used with Latin American may have a Beta alter activated by the movement of 2 small Mexican flags & a code word in Spanish "USTA CA-NATA" (cream).

CHI (return to cult)
Chi programming uses a lot of idiosyncratic phrases, and little ditties. Some of the nursery rhymes listed in the song section will be Chi programming. Some of the Chi programming has been listed in the Alpha programming section.

Delta (assassination)

Delta alters are activated to kill by the following three things:

- seeing specific clothing,
- items held in a persons hand,
- and particular words.

Since these items would be keyed for a particular murder there are no specifics that can be given.

Courier Pigeon - Alters (In Illuminati systems--these are Delta-Beta alters).

"FLOCK" --word meaning the stable of carrier pigeons

To turn a Genie free, pop a cork: "TURN YOUR GENIE FREE...POP A CORK." An internal controller must activate the umbrella or genie bottle pop the cork program to release a delta or delta-beta alter.

"YOUR WISH IS MY COMMAND" I Dream of Jeannie Programming

"YOU-ARE-WHAT-YOU-READ" passbook program. Programming to remember bank numbers and other specific numbers.

"I SENT A MESSAGE IN A BOTTLE." - Distinctive jewelry & clothes. Emerald ear rings used as a signal to others that a message was being carried. Emeralds mean drugs, rubies mean prostitution, diamonds (rhinestones) presidential model. Red, White & Blue worn sometimes by presidential models. High level reporting alters forget their messages with "REFILE # #, (name of alter)." Some Systems have one name with several different numbers attached to indicate alters within one area and purpose. Sergeant 1, up to Sergeant 60. Or say "Access 1143 Marcy" & then other Marcy's are numbered with other numbers. Spaceships & flags are associated with Sergeant alters.

Delta Black Widow alters have a web, fangs, poison, eggs, and silk strand connectors. Viper is the demon associated with Black Widows, and they are programmed to re-connect their strands if all of the connectors are not taken out.

Index finger pointed at head means Russian roulette.

EPSILON (animal alters)

These codes aren't known. One method that may be used, for instance, is for the Raven alters who are to tear the body's flesh, the story of Noah's ark where he sent the Raven out will be paired with the word TWIG, and a code formed from TWIG. There are some alters which are to actually act like animals, and their codes somehow tie in with what they are.

F. OMEGA (internal computers)

The Omega programming works along with an Executive Control Board (or Grand Druid Council) and Internal programmers. The Executive Control Board is associated with both numbers of the clock, and precious gems and metals such as "9 O'CLOCK GOLD". The Beast computer can be accessed with Scripture triggers associated with the Vision of Daniel of the Beast, and its ten toes. The Ten Toes are important part of the code in some models.

UNIVERSAL CODE FOR ACCESS TO INTERNAL COMPUTERS

- Key manual -- 33123113211
- Program computer -- 22133113332
- function computer 11123132221
- Ren computer -- 13321321332-55434232312 L\S 55434232312 reenlist
- Reprogram numbers -- 2231231; 4432312; 33231223

An input code is 666fff666fff666 the reverse of this code is F6F6F6F6F6F6F6F6F6F6F6. One victim's computer ran on code "WAR GAME". Some Beast computers have 666 666 666 as an access code and 999 999 999 as a beast back out and close out code. There are various computers, one on each level. These have some standard codes and some individual codes.

UNIVERSAL FUNCTION CODES
COMPUTER CODE - 55434232312
which holds the following codes:

abduction	4511321
anger	4213261
assignment coordinator	1613212
assassination	5332135
bank of lies	3124532
blindness	2566553

- brain disorder   6325512
- body gesture   1332221
- body functions   4311322
- call back ritual   6664113
- child control   3214441
- circle in fields   3332241
- confusion   6643252
- control   4321341
- deaf   3324553
- death   1451621
- denial   2311444
- despair   3223412
- distortion   6233322
- disorder of bones   4561321
- disorder of breathing   5532111
- disorder of eating   3342136
- division   3211652
- false memories   3314532
- fear   2665132
- fleeing   5613354
- game playing   1561321
- guilt   4321231
- hatefulness   5331241
- hopelessness   1112364
- illness   1566432
- infiltration   2231335
- insanity   2144312

- inside reporters   1133265
- loyalty to group   3364112
- mute   2213541
- murder   3221456
- nonsense   2665443
- outside reporters   1132256
- reprogram others   4555643
- reprogram self   1133432
- respond to triggers   4441221
- retardation s-   1314555
-              m-   1314556
- sabotage   1135461
- seduction   2134121
- self body harm   3321343
- sex   2116652
- shame   3122115
- suicide   3113246
- trigger   1324652
- trigger others   4442211
- zombie   3321556

Under each of these codes, other codes may be attached. For instance, under Body Gestures, the following functions are coded and a sample coding scheme would look like this:

- talk verbally   3456343
- touch chest   2322132
- touch hair   3323221

- touch mouth   5434232
- touch nose   5443232

Rainbow - an alter which speaks only in rhymes. Ribbons are in a box with Rainbow. A ribbon might be accessed by several slaps on the face and "Rubicon 2,4,6,8..." (3x)

Hickory Dickory Dock rhyme is associated with the vortex which is tied to turning the system and also to some death alters.

Dominoes set off flooding programs to overload the person.

Program numbers on some slaves are put in by touching the third eye with the index finger and speaking the number.

G. GAMMA (demonology)

In Satan's realm, demons are fathered or split off in families like alters are. There will be a Moloch number 101, and a Moloch 10,321. The victim has alters which are numbered such as Sally 1 and Sally 10. For a better understanding of this area of programming see Chapter 10. Gamma Programming includes all the demonic activity. In this section one can add the Kabala's Tree of Life which has alphabet codes, back up programs to regenerate, associated with Greenbaum or Greentree. In the Illuminati slaves, the deeper parts of their system are ritual and the demonology pertains to the various rituals that are done. The following is a sampling of Illuminati rituals. The blood rituals are used to attach demons to possess alters in a particular way. These rituals can't be separated from the programming. They are part of the programming.

Ceremonies:

- Assembling of the Quarter Regents
- Beltaine -- with hunts of slaves, fire festivals, and blood rituals
- Bride of Satan Ceremony -- (Mar. 24)

- Demon revels
- Drawing down the moon
- Druid Feast Day -- on Jan. 1
- Duels to the death -- like gladiators where the heart is cut out and eaten
- The Grail Mass
- Grand Climax - human sacrifice & sex rituals
- Invocation of Hecate as Crone
- Lammas Sabbat - where a female is sacrificed
- Pathworking - (done before 16 with Cabalistic Tree of Life pathways)
- Rite of Deification
- Rod of Light Ceremony - consists of text from Cabala, black candles, ram's horn blown, and victim's mother's name sounded
- Sealing ceremony -- at 19 yrs. for Mothers of Darkness level
- Secret ceremony -- where people paint their faces half black and half white.
- Sister of Light Rebirthing Water Ceremony - victim is bound and then pulled from water and wrapped up in linen, and a green branch is place on the chest)
- St. Agnes Eve
- St. Bartholomew's Day
- St. Walpurgis
- Summer Solstice Orgy

For those who are not familiar with occult terms the following are ritual items:

- Paten (the holy dish)
- Athame or Glaive (the knife used to sacrifice with)

- the wand or scepter (a ornamental staff which represents authority & usually has an electric shock)
- the censer (to distribute burning fragrance)

HYPNOTIC INDUCTIONS

"Kaleidoscope eyes" -- used in hypnotic induction and spinning

"20, 19, 18, 17, 16, 15, 14, 13,...1"

For many slaves the sign of Satan done with the fingers puts them into a trance, and deeper alters come out.

"100, 91, 82, 73, 64, 55, 46, 37, 28, 19, 10, 1"

Touching the head in a particular fashion is done. "DEEPER AND DEEPER AND DEEPER DEEPER AND DEEPER AND DEEPER, DOWN, DOWN, DOWN, INTO THE DEEP, DARK VELVETY MIST, DEEPER AND DEEPER AND DEEPER."

"DEEP, DEEP, DEEP, SLEEP, SLEEP, SHEEP, SHEEP, SHEEP" SLEEP,

"YOU'RE BEAUTY WARMS MY EMBERS. SEE THEM GLOW-ING DEEP WITHIN THE DARKNESS OF MY EYES... IGNIT-ING INTO FLAME... BLACK FLAME."

Seeing a Hand of Glory (severed left hand) will induct people into Peter Pan programming. Books describing the occult use of the Hand of Glory in Ireland go back to 1830. It is an ancient practice. Baring Gould's book "Curious Myths of the Middle Ages" describes the recipe for using the hand of glory as a gruesome lantern during the witchcraft of the Middle Ages.

"I AM THE SAND MAN, AND BLOW SAND IN YOUR EYES" said while simultaneously moving the hand over the face to create the illusion of placing sand in the eyes.

"3-2-1, 3-2-1, 2-1-1, 1-2, 1, You are now relaxed.

Lights, in certain colors and sequences, have been used to trance alters out, for instance a flashing red light may trance certain alters out. Tunnels were used as a powerful hypnotic suggestion. Bear in mind, that people induct

a. when phys. or mentally relaxed,
b. when their senses are overloaded or sensory deprivation,
c. when their equilibrium is disturbed,
d. their motion is restricted or
e. their eyes are fixated on something.

JANUS-ALEX CALL BACKS (end-times)

- Main link to a System's programs to ALEX coded 44334223112.
- Scramble code to ALEX is 34424313221.
- Individual code to ALEX - 55434232312
- Link to JANUS coded 3323432123.
- Report back- X441062F
- Main JANUS tracking/reprogramming code
- JAN US 9341 00569XXY99632 [x3]
- its back up code X44420-61F.
- (There is a Janis 2 computer at 666 Connecticut Ave. Washington, D.C. Disinformation by the Network is that the PACER computer equipment is called Janus/Janis).
- Main AMBASSADOR code 67302986ZZ9861

(suicide/fire) sub codes-
- Fire 97643F4200L;
- Cut 97642C42DIL L ;
- Suicide 9762354202L;
- Towards Violence 97613V4203L

- Main EMPEROR - [dot, dot, dot] 79622109MM861 1

END-TIME ACTIVATION CODES

Most slaves have end-time programming. When a slave is called in with end-time programming they have pages upon pages of coded messages. A number of Monarch slaves have been de-programmed enough that they began accessing and spewing out pages and pages of these activation codes. Part of a sample of one of these is as follows:

- ISRAEL IS RISING
- ACTIVATE 366 UNITED NATIONS
- 900 BLUE BIRD PILOTS RISE
- NATIONS IN PLACE
- RED CHINA CALL BACK
- COUNT DOWN, ACTIVATE ALEX
- 3.7 LC
- 94
- CIRCLE FARMS AROUND THE SQUARE
- BRITISH SOLDIERS RISE
- MOUNTAIN GOAT COME
- EASTSIDE OF PEAK
- 39 ACTIVATE
- 52 ACTIVATE
- 42 ACTIVATE
- RED CHINA RISE
- 1.7 ACTIVATE
- THE HOUR COMES, A. C. SON
- ACTIVATE AFRICA
- ARISE IN NUMBERS OF 90...

A team leader will have a down line of around 4 people. Which are coded red ray, yellow ray, green ray, blue ray. When the activation code hits a slave team leader during the end times, they will in turn activate their people, who in turn will have people who are team leaders and have a down line. At least two false callback alarms will be sounded (tested) before the real one.

THETA (psychic warfare)

TINKERBELLE PROGRAMMING (never grow up/alien)

Capt'n or Cap'n (captain) represents the programmer in Peter Pan programming. Tinkerbelle is a young alter created under Peter Pan programming.

'TRANCE DIMENSIONAL TRAVEL RIGHT FROM YOUR OWN BACKYARD. THE DIMENSIONS OF YOUR PYRAMID ARE TO BE 9 BYE 9 BYE 9 BYE."

Alien programming by NWO (also involves Peter Pan programming)

"RIDE THE LIGHT" -Peter Pan programming meaning to go into hypnotic induction attached to a light that is seen when given a high voltage shock. This is given to make experiences seem like in another dimension.

TWINNING (teams)

CROSS PROGRAMMING - With for instance a mother/daughter team

Two seals are placed on this cross programming, a "seal of cover" and a "seal of rain"

Code: mother - [minus] mother = 3/4 - daughter holds 1/4

daughter - [minus] mother 1/4 -- daughter holds 3/4

Teams will be given code words for each alter who is part of a 2-System team. One System may serve as a father figure to the other System. Teams will be trauma and sexually bonded, as well as having mirror images with each others names. A leader will have an upline and a downline for the colored rays. A leader will call the different colored rays, to activate their programming.

An Illuminati team ritual to create oneness & open their team boxes up to work together (Illuminati twinning ritual):

the team kneels face to face, draws a magical circle on the ground, joins Delta team hands forming a clasp ring. Blue is associated with this. Then they all say, "Star within a star, Circle within a circle, Mind within a mind, body within a body, Soul within a soul." Then the team places their hands Palm to Palm, and then speaks 4 times, "Bone to Bone, flesh to flesh, Spirit to Spirit, Forever together - never apart."

Then a 5 pointed star is traced in the air. To close the Delta team twinning box, the reverse is done. Then other things are to be said in the joining and opening ritual. A double deck of cards is used to program an Illuminati team of "twins". One type of Criss-cross programming involves

1. a flower,
2. the stem and
3. the root.

The root involves blood sacrifices. This programming ties two generations together such as mother -[minus] daughter.

SOLEMETRIC MILITARY

SONGS & NURSERY RHYMES

Songs with Monarch programming meaning and access to parts soliciting behavior or thinking include:

- Brahm's Lullaby

- Hickory, Dickory Dock (flips the system) - "Hickory, Dickory Dock, The Mouse Ran up the Clock [computer], the clock struck one [time for system rotation], The Mouse ran down, Hickory Dickory Dock." "INTO THE MOUTH [vortex] RUNS THE MOUSE, AND FLIPS THE HOUSE [turns the system over).

- Froggy Went a Courtin' He did Ride

- I had a little pony

- I'm in Love With a Big Blue Frog

- Jack and Jill

- Mary Had a Little Lamb (call to ritual connotation) - Tones of "Mary had a little Iamb" or other telephone created tones, such as high pitched noises to call people to meetings.

- Mary Mary Quite Contrary (reminds the slave that abusers are all-seeing)

- Old King Cole (Old King Cole was a merry old soul, ... he'd call for his masters 3 [the 3 programmers])

- Peter, Peter Pumpkin Eater

- Puss in Boots (this story is porn programming)

- Ring Around the Rosy

- Ten Little Monkeys Jumping on the Bed

- Three Blind Mice (omega programming connotation with hour glass)

- Twinkle, Twinkle Little Star (Sometimes associated with "I'm dead.")

Most of the Beatles' songs were used for programming. Charles Manson was programmed with Beatles' music. The programmers know ahead of time what are going to be the next hits, and they regularly call in slaves and hypnotically make the lyrics to be cues for the slaves before the music comes out. For instance, the lyrics of "Ain't that a Shame" will make certain alters angry. For another slave the lyrics "Everything is relative, in its own way" reminds the person of the cult family & obedience.

- Angie (popular song for programming)

- A Mighty Fortress is Our God

- Back in Black Blue Velvet

{ 553 }

- Butterfly
- The Candyman Can (represents drug use for Monarchs)
- Christmas Carols (Christmas carols were used a lot on Monarchs.)
- Country Roads song with the programmed meaning take me [the slave] "home" to a meeting site.
- Crazy (to reaffirm loyalty to the master)
- Deja Vu
- Die Walkure
- Fire and Rain
- Frere Jacques (Catholic "Father John", sexual abuse connotation)
- Get Me A Ticket on a Fast Train (substitute "master" for "baby" in song)
- Grandma's Feather Bed
- Ghost Riders
- Green Green Grass of Home (go home program, slave is not happy 'til they go home to green fields
- Greensleves
- Hallelujah chorus (many Christian songs like this one are played while the victim is tortured.)
- Handel's Messiah
- Have Thine Own Way Lord ("thou art the potter, I am the clay, mold me & make me..." Charismatic slave programming.)
- Heartache Tonight (song used to announce a ritual over the radio)
- Hotel California (sexual/ritual connotation, the song says, "go to the chamber of the Master's Feast, We are programmed to receive." This song also tells the story of how LaVey started the Church of Satan in 1966.)
- I Surrender All
- Imagine (John Lennon presents the New Age script for people to

be "nowhere people.")

- John Brown's Body

- Lucy In the Sky with Diamonds

- Little Red Riding Hood (song played with hunts of slaves)

- Mary was an only child (from Art Garfunkel's Angel Claire album)

- Moon River

- Over the Rainbow (obvious Wizard of Oz programming)

- "Playing with the Queen of Hearts, knowing that it really smarts, the Joker is the only fool who'll do anything with you" (reinforces the warning not to play (tamper) with the programming. The Queen of Hearts is the emergency Mayday signal to a handler. To play with this will really smart/hurt.

- National Anthem

- No More Mr. Nice Guy

- Revolution 9

- Rivers of Dreams (by Billy Joel. words are about "walking in the dark, going through a river.. .turn on the light on your internal world."

- Satin Sheets

- She's Leaving Home

- Sins of the Fathers

- Southern Nights (loyalty to the programs -- the leaves and trees)

- Stairway to Heaven

- Teddy Bear (Programmer, helpless teddy bear slave connotation)

- Tennessee Waltz (handler is "forced" to prostitute slave)

- The Blood Will Never Lose Its Power

- Tom Dooley (suicide, "hang down your head Tom Dooley, hang down your and...)

- Victim of Love

- "When you wish upon a star" song used for programming.

- White Rabbit (Alice In Wonderland Theme -- made into a triggering Karaoke CD.)

- Wooden Heart

- Yellow Submarine (drug connotation)

ZETA (snuff films)

Zeta is the sixth letter, and it's ancient meaning was a sacrifice.

SAMPLE CODES FOR ALTERS OF A HYPOTHETICAL SYSTEM NAMED MARY

These codes are purely a representative model-not any particular real system. The overall system code at times consists of [birthdate + programming site codes + birth order + number of generations family was in the Illuminati.] For our hypothetical system Mary we have the hypothetical system code of: 6-13-51- 14 -02- 12. In order to give the codes for a hypothetical alter system we will have to explain some things as we go. The Programmers have for each slave both medical programming files, and a grey or black binder with the programmed access, trigger, codes & cues, & structure. A typical Illuminati system will be a cube (although spheres and pyramids are also used). The principle alters will be the "a" alters. A typical section of alters will consist of a 13 x 13 grid of alters. These are alters who live in a world together and must function together. A 13 x 13 section will have 13 families of "a" through "n" alters. The "a" alters will be the primary alters that the Programmers will interact with.

The Programmer may call up an "a" alter and ask it to go get the "c" alter in its family, rather than directly asking for it. This initial page of alter codes will be the primary or "a" alters. If we are dealing with a 13 x 13 x 13 cube of alters, then the initial page has 13 "a" alters of each section. Each of these alters will have an access code which will often include the following components: AN ASSIGNED COLOR +

AN ALPHA NUMERIC CODE + A PERSONALIZED MAGICAL NAME. This will equal 1/3 their access code. These code words must be repeated three times to pull the alter up. However, if an alter is trained well, and hears his master's voice, an alpha-numeric code can pull the alter up. For many of the alters, the reversal of their access code puts them back to sleep. This is an important point, because some alters would be dangerous to leave in control of the body. The "a" alters are regular alters. Many of them have been hypnotically age advanced to see themselves as teenagers or adults. Sometimes "b" and "c" alters are also aged. The "d" through "n" alters are generally left as they were split and most of them are infantile, with little concept of how old they are.

The little ones will be the ones who often remember the programming very well, and know things about the system. The top alters will also sometimes receive personal names from their handler. This is in addition to all their codes. If the alter is responsive to its master, the personal name might pull the alter up too. Do all of the alters get charted? There are several groups of alters which get charted separate from the rest or don't get charted at all. Because of the competition and distrust between the different programmers, they often place in secret back doors into the person's mind that only they know about. Worlds of secret alters loyal and devoted to the programmer may be built into the system and not appear on the regular charts. The core, and some of the primal splits from the core will not appear on the regular grids. They will be placed on a separate sheet, and their codes will be in some magical language. The Illuminati commonly employs 20 magical languages, and Hebrew, Latin and Greek are also often used for charting the core and its primal splits.

Enochian is a good example of a magical language used by the Illuminati. Some alters will be created solely by the slave in order to cope with life. For instance, say the slave is travelling with someone who is not a handler, but who is a dangerous person. This dangerous person murders several people and forces the slave to help. The slave is likely going to have front alters out, and they are simply going to have to create new alters to meet the demands of the situation. These alters made to deal with one-time emergency will just slip into cracks in the system. Lots of odds and ends alters end up in the nooks and crannies within a system just detached and floating.

The programmers and the victim work hard at structuring and cleaning up things, but the honest truth is that trauma-based mind-control is messy. Any time you shatter someone's mind into thousands of pieces with horrendous torture, you have a shattered mess, in spite of the good fronts that the programmers are able to construct. Some of the more elaborate access methods are for alters that are not on the "a" chart. Hour glass alters have entire sentence access codes. Deaf & blind alters need their access code signed on their hands by moving their fingers up and down, etc. End time alters may have access codes that may entail reading an entire page. Reporting alters are often small children, that are hidden in each section, and may require slaps to the face or jabs with a needle to pull them up. Spinner kittens will be accessed via their mama cat, who acts like a Madam in a "cat house". The codes for this was given in the Beta section codes.

The reader will be given the hypothetical codes (which resemble closely the actual codes of a monarch slave) for our hypothetical Mary. A Sample Chart of the "A" alters, these are the primary alters, has been prepared in the same fashion as it would appear in the handler's 3-ring binder.

Mary's Core Protector 1 will have a shutdown code of "REVERSAL 1 BEGINNING" and the second Core Protector will have the shutdown code of "REVERSAL 2 CREATION". Of course, these codes are said 3 times. The first three alters on the far left section at the top of the chart are Silences who can be woken up by singing. Also at least one of these, will wake up by a kiss from the prince (programmer) to the third eye area. The first alter can be shut down by "COSMOS 15 31 06 2BAB PINK". One of the groups of alters attached to one of these early alters is "MA.C3.10-53 Rejects (7) 10-53". To shut this alters down just say the reverse of the access code.

A mirror image of each of these alters exists too. The mirror images can be pulled up via a three step process. The birth memory in our example will be coded as A5 10 79. The spider torture memories that

are attached to these alters is A5 10 79. The reader will notice the following on the hypothetical chart on the previous page for the first
Section (which is numbered 6 to be deceptive): This section is front
alters. Basic code pattern = color + Genesis + numbner. [1 thru 13] +
letter [a thru m]. Individual codes 1st section general-"N.I.F.6", 1st
section mother Eve "EV.E5 10 51 ACE" Eve is the balancing point
and the ace code is high or low. The alter Explorer is "EI.G7",
Mammy "MI.H8", Angel "Red, AI.19 Jack Genesis 4" (or it could be
done "red, AI.J10 Genesis 4"), George "Silver, GI.K11 ", Zsa Zsa
"gold, ZI.L.12", and Shadow "Clear SI.M13".

You won't find on the main chart codes such as: Eve's memory
"EI.D5.2.1952 ACE" or the Infant alters -- "1-000 10-49 REJECTS 3
-9" The master may say for example: "Green GENESIS 1-A" (3
times) to get this alter which is the balancing point. Fragments/dead
alters were dumped into areas named concentration camps and given
the names of the famous German concentration camps. The camps
were placed under the Mt. of Olives. Fire or Bomb children are found
throughout the system and are triggered to come up by programming.
They come up behind other alters and make them burn. Some of this
level can be woken up by saying, "It's time to wake up in the morning" (7 times), which is in contrast with most codes which are said
3x.

Another way to look at it, is that the alters are on 4 dimensional structure and they require a 4-dimensional access code. Height, depth,
width, and color are the four dimensions. This breaks down for this
1st section as: COLOR (4th dimension) + Genesis (Section code) +1
(level) + "a" (depth). The following message will be used on the
phone for this System's recording machine, this example has been
used nationally. "IF YOU WOULD LIKE TO MAKE A CALL
PLEASE HANG UP AND TRY YOUR CALL AGAIN. IF YOU
NEED ASSISTANCE, PLEASE DIAL YOUR OPERATOR. CODE
911." This will cause section 1 or section 2, etc. to call their master.
Also, standard Illuminati Hand signals work with Mary. "ALONE
AND CRYING (3X)"- is a code for a few special parts not on the
first grid.

Section 2 gatekeeper alters. Basic code pattern color + Revelation + no.[1 thru 13] + letter [a thru m] In our hypothetical example: "ORANGE REVELATION 4-A" (3X) However a shortcut is "REVELATION 4" and the primary Revelation 4 alter will come up. "ORANGE REVELATION 4 B" would get a small child on the pedestal with Revelation 4a. At times the handler will say "THE DECK IS DOUBLE-DECKED" in order to activate the clone doubles of all alters in a particular area--such as the front area of the system. The clones are tied to the Pink Room of the dollhouse-looking computer. Since alters are also coded to cards, a FLUSH will pull up an entire section. Special alters who skinned men alive are kept in black holes in Section 2. They are special trauma alters created solely by the victim as a safety measure.

Section 2 computer (like all levels) is empowered by an emerald blue light. This power source was deactivated by unscrewing the light to the left (which took it physically out so to speak) and then saying "PEACE BE STILL" (3X). If "PEACE BE STILL" is not said three times then the War in the heavens program kicks in. Also "DAD WEEPS OVER HIS CITY" must be said when deactivating the computer otherwise the "children" (alters) become sick and everything kicks back in--which it does eventually anyway if the deeper computers are not deactivated or taken out. Section 3 has programmer alters & fragment armies, not to be confused with the clones which hide everywhere. The clones, by the way, can be identified with serial no.s at base of head gear such as 151.00 [system birth date]. This sections has 3 faceless Programmers called the 3 adepts of Atlantis. Each of them has a different color of hair. They may also be the commanders of armies--the commanders of the Egyptian armies have names Ra, Horus, and Set. Section 4 alters are Entertainment alters. Basic code pattern = Color + double number + a name of a one of the 13 tribes of Israel + the number of the alter again (3x)

Example: BLUE 2001-13A REUBEN 1 (3X) However, the color doesn't always need to be said it is a sufficient shortcut to call the alphanumeric code three times. Second example 2002-12A SIMEON 1 (3X). The numbers of the 2000 code go up while the corresponding number 13 to 1 go down. In other words it is a double code. The

Tribal names are arranged according to their Biblical birth order.

Mother Kitten 8,10 and 12 have ten spinner kittens underneath each of them. To get a spinner kitten, one gets the mother kitten and then has her in the proper position which is the over-the-rainbow mode. The choice of what spin kitten to get is "WE GOTTA GET DRESSED ... IN 3 MINUTES." 3 minutes means spinner no. 3. Specific instructions such as "PURR FOR ME KITTEN" gives the abuser fellatio. Tweedle Dee & Tweedle Dum is a S&M program. "5 FIDDLE" and "FOLLOW THE YELLOW BRICK ROAD" are important for the slave to follow instructions. The alters will be sent to never-never land where what they do is unreal. Some kitten alters are keyed to pop out if certain areas of the body are touched, such as the space beside the big toe, or the thighs. A handler will also have standard hand signals for things, such as putting his hands on his thighs to mean "Come here and take care of me, Kitten." "COME KITTEN, TO PAPA COME" "BLUE TOPAZ" serves as 4 keys. Pisces is associated with Blue Topaz.

There are also 4 keys which are: silver shoes, sun bright, birds singing, and yellow road. Section 2 & 1. Reprogramming sections. At this point, the computer codes given previously apply, SEE OMEGA CODES on previous pages. The first major computer services the top 6 sections and has a red room, a closet, a pink room, as well as other rooms. Actually the computer should be set in at Section 0, which would break up the grid evenly, but since our Mary is hypothetical we put the front main computer at section 1. A system like this will have 13 computers/1 per section and 5 computers which set between pairs of sections, which join a pair of sections together, and then 2 main computers. This means a System like Mary's will have 20 internal computers. With all the codes and a fair understanding of the alters in a section, it is a good day's work to shut down a computer. Before one could possibly get all the section computers shut off, they would reprogram (reboot) themselves back up.

Computer erasure codes include: "FULL HOUSE ACES HIGH. ALL TRUMP. FULL HOUSE ACES LOW." The drawers in the dollhouse can be pulled out with "ROYAL FLUSH"(3X). Another code is

"PINK SECTION 5. FULL HOUSE. ACES HIGH. 2 DEEP." A partial code to a computer is " ...... 8-9 RED." Our hypothetical Mary might be accessed by a woman who taps on the shoulder and says, "PHOENIX 360 [tel. area code], OUT OF ORDER". The library alter has an important access ring. A "Button Bright" alter type works with the librarian. The dwarfs are accessed by "ISOLATION + no." Judges which sit on the council give warnings to alters "CAT EYE AT THE DOOR." This reflects the programmers' control. The judges have the "Keys to the Kingdom." "MR POSTMAN WAIT AND SEE" indicates a message from the master. Ribbon alters have the names of archangels. Silver cords are attached to the ribbons.

Section 0. Mothers of Darkness alters. basic code pattern = SILVER + LEHTEB [which is bethel or house of God spelled backwards] + [who knows what else] + a blue topaz ring being turned on the master's finger a certain way. Green is a sensitive color for this System. Some alters may be accessed from certain areas in the System via 4 tones, and others by pin pricks at certain locations in the body, along with their verbal code. The Reporting alter can be accessed by repeated slaps across the face. There is Ultra Green Section tied to the Cabala (Green tree). The Library in the big castle, which is guarded by lions and other big cats, has a passage way in it to a second world. Codes with the Cabalistic Tree of Life involve Cabalistic magic and its symbols. This section is guarded by a hostile entity. Certain rings, topaz, quartz, diamond, ruby, black onyx etc. are used for triggers. Certain rings are needed to get into certain parts of a System, such as the castle. To access the Mothers, the Black Onyx ring must be rotated. The programming of a ring may go something like this, "This ring fills Daddy's house with stars.. .Catch a falling star, put it in your pocket."

Section 9. Delta-Beta alters. Kept in a genie bottle. Obviously something is rubbed to get them out. "BUTTON BUTTON, WHO'S GOT THE BUTTON, BUT ITS THE KISS OF DEATH" this code is involved with the "good witch" who kisses upon the forehead. Buttons are on the boxes of Programmer Green and are constructed onto the boxes so they can be used to open the boxes up.

Section 7. This hypothetical system also has a series of codes based on gems--ruby, diamond, etc. which have numbers attached to the codes. An Hour glass w/ 12 disciples like grains of sand tied to Jolly Green Giant programming which have sentence access codes. Each sentence is a phrase of satanic philosophy. The bottom level is called the Hell Pit and contains the City of Petra. The City of Petra has an erasure code. "YELLOW - CUTTER ROOM 7 SECTION 7--- ROYAL FLUSH--LA CUTTER EGGS" Invisible field section 7. Room 7 --cards has eggs with demons. Lacutters are like imps and are invisible. They are assigned to guard various things in the system including the cutting programs. "Dad" "Catch a falling star".

Main computer protected by deaf and dumb alter using a sign language equation as its access code and the reversal of its access code is its shut down code. The Brack Master is a Master Programmer.

Each of the 13 sections of 169 alters (a section is a 13 x 13 grid of alters) will then have a computer assigned to it. The computer is made up of dissociated parts of the mind--which are like alters, but have not been given histories or names. Each section has a computer which makes 13 section computers. Section 1 and section 7 (see the grid chart) are main computers.

The first is the main computer for the top half, and the second is the main computer for the bottom half of the System. The second main computer is in the hell pit, and has been put in at the lowest level of the mind. Section 6&5 computers are connected by a connecting computer, as well as 4&3, 2&1, 0&12, 10&9. This makes 5 connecting computers. In total then we have 13 section computers, 2 main computers, and 5 connecting computers, for a subtotal of 20 computers. Since things are being built on the basis of the magical number 13, six more computers are installed which are decoy or false computers for therapists to work on.

This makes a total of 26 computers (or 2x13). Since there are 26 letters of the alphabet, this lends itself well, and each computer is assigned a letter of the alphabet. Since the computers are put into the slave when it is a young child, the child has just learned how to count and say the alphabet. The Illuminati have been using a large doll-house with 26 rooms using 13 colors of paint, giving two rooms per color. Each room is a computer. In accord with the practice of double coding, each letter of the alphabet is given its sequence number, so the names for the computers are A1, B2, C3, D4, E5, F6, G7, H8, I9, J10, K11, L12, M13--the thirteenth is assigned the 1st main computer. N1, O2, P3, Q4, R5, S6, T7, U8, V9, W10, X11, Y12, Z13. Rather, than use the number 13, the number 0 will be assigned, thus changing things to M0, and Z0.

This is simple enough for a child's learning mind, but difficult enough that it serves as a viable code. As codes are assigned, the bottom of the alphabet is assigned the top (front side) of the system. The middle point MO, is the normal access point for all the computers for the handler. The code for this is associated with the name of an airplane hanger, so that the concept of taking off into the sky (trancing can be associated with it.) Each computer needs an access code to go along with its alpha-numeric name. A deck of cards lends itself well to a code of 13. Bear in mind each computer has a color assigned to it. Colored scarves and dollhouse rooms were used with electroshock to teach the child his color coding.

When the programming is going on trance depths and runways (mental image for flying off into a trance) and the structure of the System will all be tied together in one neat package. Everything is built on its own x-y axis. Each 13x13 grid has the middle rows both vertically and horizontally set up as runways. The x-y axis also makes up the hourglass lines or the butterfly wings. Both images are used with slaves. Because thing are set up in thirteen's in Mary's system, and things are double coded, thirteen becomes 13-1 and one is 1-13. This allows us also to link 13-1 and 1-13, so that everything becomes a circle. The circle within a circle, box within a box concept, triangle within a triangle situations makes the slave feel he is trapped in an infinity loop of programming that has no end and no beginning. 13 and 1 make 14. An entire deck of cards can be used in a double code that also adds to 14, such as the 8 of spades and the 6 of diamonds, or the Ace of spades and the King of Diamonds. Here then is the codes for Mary's computers.

Two cards from opposite suits that add to 14. Since a deck of regular playing cards came originally from Tarot cards, the playing card used as a code also carry some occult significance to the codes. It is also training the child who is programmed this way to be interested in cards. And every time the child plays cards they will reinforce at an unconscious level their computer coding. The computers will then have programs set in on 13 x 13 quadrants. Quadrant 6.6 will have a program such hopelessness. Other quadrants may hold aloneness, re-cycling, cold, heat, burning, cutting oneself, pulsating loud heart beat, and hundreds of other programs. These programs have the type of codes assigned them that are given in the Universal Function Codes. Many of the functions can receive a standard code, but other items require individual codes. Telephone tones are frequently used to be able to key in (that is access or trigger) parts of the computer program matrix. Dominoes also are used for the computer programming. The dominoes are put in so that the programmers can get a domino effect, if they want to set off a series of programs.

Dominoes and flashing sequences of lights were used to train the child to automatically respond to a certain pattern of dots. Our hypo-thetical Mary will also have hundreds of other codes for all kinds of miscellaneous things such as the following random codes: "RUBY RED LIPS" "TO HAVE POWER" AND "TO BE THE POWER", which are also found in the Tall Book of Make Believe in the Shut Eye Town. Dominoes help with the code: "2-4-6-8 WHO DO YOU APPRECIATE?". More examples are, "I LOVE DADDY." "JACK BE NIMBLE JACK BE QUICK 13-1 12-2..." "PUMPKIN HEAD-- an access code. To go away- "Ta RA RA BOOM-DE-AYE", "CRYING OVER YOU (3X)", "SILKEN GIRDLE"-- a golden cater-pillar plays a bittersweet tune. A gold pocket watch with Roman nu-merals is associated with the words "Eagle on it." When Mary gets scared and begins to get into revolving switching, sometimes spin-ning can be slow down by saying, "10--YOU ARE SLOWING DOWN 9--YOU ARE SLOWING DOWN 8--YOU ARE GETTING SLOWER AND SLOWER..."

A system's coding is a reflection of their programmer. If the programmer is a pilot which many of them are, then they may have pilot lingo in their codes, such as the system may be turned by pitch & degrees. If the programmer is a sailor the system may have nautical codes, such as "RED RETURN RUNNING", "SAFE HARBOR" (for "Home"), and DOWN RIVER (away from "Papa").

Catholic Programming (by Jesuits etc.)

- KEYS TO THE KINGDOM = world domination by mind control.

- VOW OF SILENCE is a keep quiet program activated by

- "THE WALLS HAVE EARS & THE PLANTS HAVE EYES SO YOUR SILENCE IS TANTAMOUNT TO SUCCESS." This is explained to the victim that the sea shells and the plants have the ability to hear, and that a sensitive occultist (programmer) can psychically pick up what the plants and sea shells hear. "MAINTAIN IT" --is a command to maintain the Vow of Silence "MAINTAIN IT & LISTEN."-- a command to keep silent and listen to a command.

- "ENTER INTER INNER DIMENSION TWO" - this is a standard Jesuit infinity program (2 is a sacred voodoo no.)

Mensa Programming (by MENSA)

"17 21 13 46" is an Illuminati code meaning a MENSA layer

Sample Mensa codes:

- "727 + E=MC SQUARED + 3.141 5962 + PI"

- "A+B=C, B+C=A, C+A= B" "TIC TAC TOE + C CROSS, PI CROSS"

The MENSA codes are sequences of 6 numbers.

HAND SIGNALS misc. common signals

- Finger to forehead--

- One ring finger bent at 90° -- access wave Rotated pencil--with certain words--rotates the system

- Finger swung the counterclockwise way closes portals.

- Right Fist to forehead -- OBEY

- Fist with right hand cupping left hand, the left is like the letter c, and the thumb is outward and the fist inside, the left hand then moves 3 times over the knuckle -- access signal

- Left hand of slave laid on top of handler's hand - sign of submission

- Hands behind back of head -- I'm master

- Right Hand with thumb & index finger making an L shape on chin/check

- Hands on inside of thighs by handler -- come to me Kitten and service me.

- Hands locked folded interwoven backward -- you can't break "the circle"

- Handshake with index and middle finger held straight out -- "You are one of us."

- Grip called the lion's paw -- access greeting opening and closing the hands or large circles with index finger opens portals. Palms rubbed together counterclockwise

- Kiss on center of head -- kiss of submission of slave to handler

- Palm of hand touched -- sexual access point for some models

- Sign of Satan -- Hail Satan! used for Monarch & Illuminati Mind-controlled slaves as an induction. The alter who is holding the body goes into trance, & a deeper one replaces it.

- Thumb twiddle -- rotating the thumbs around with the two hands clasp -- S&M

- Touch of center of forehead -- access point

-

- Vulcan Peace Sign -- llluminati/occult greeting Wave with Finger and thumb together - other digits extended

- Winks at the system were used to convey meaning.

LIFE "OVER THE RAINBOW"

Aftter rereading this book, I realized that I had not explained "over the rainbow." Some alters live "over the rainbow" and some do not. Both types will use the term "over the rainbow", but with different meanings attached. For those who live "over the rainbow", they serve their masters in such a deep hypnotic trance that they perceive reality like it's a dream. When their memories surface they are so unlike normal memories that a system in therapy may not know what to do with them. They have been described as similar to the pictures in the old T.V.s when the vertical hold would go out of control. Deeper alters, who live "over the rainbow" experience memories/life in the following fashion: faces & porn cameras are airbrushed out of their memory, distinctive marks in the perpetrators such as scars & wrinkles are airbrushed out, colors & lights are very bright due to the total dilation of the pupils while in deep trance, and there is no sense of time for these alters. These alters are trained to "TRANCE SEND FORWARD THROUGH TIME". By understanding the programming, the codes, & triggers, those alters who lived "over the rainbow" can recover from the mind the full memory, without the distortions created by dissociation.

PARTIALLY CORRECT PROGRAMMING SITE CODES

The following site codes are not totally accurate. The Intelligence groups use that what are called Cryptonyms, which are two-letter digraphs such as the "MK" of MK-ULTRA. The digraph can indicate a type of operation or even a location. An operation may have codes. The following site codes are not totally accurate. Also, the Intelligence groups use what are called Cryptonyms, which are two-letter digraphs such as the "MK" of MK-ULTRA. The digraph can indicate a type of operation or even a location. An operation may have its cryptonym changed in the middle of its operation.

Programmer	Programming Zone	Area/Code
• Armstrong	63	94XCCD
• Astor	36	Florida 59XCBB
• Bournell-Hightower	19	
• Brown	30	59XBMN
• Burcham	329	Texas 92XBMM
• Gaston	61	Colorado 1XCDF
• Haggin	743	Kentucky 47XB0
• Harrick	263	Colorado Springs
• Johnson	95	Manass
• Mentor	21	Colorado 61XBXX
• Nathan	56	New Mexico
• Owens	963	106XbJK
• Pantu	71	Kansas 011XOEG
• Patterson	117	Kansas
• Savior	49	
• Major Strange	14	1Z440x72080020366
• Strong	52	81XCBC
• Suttenfuss	103	
• Colonel Taylor	16	Kentucky
• Weir	561	Texas 33XBCB

Final note: there is no way that this book could give every last song or story that has been used for programming, nor was it the intention to do so. We have wanted to point out the popular story lines used, although we have missed some such as the Chronicles of Narnia and Little Red Riding Hood, which is used in several ways along the lines of you think you're going to Papa's, or Grandma's house & you end up with a wolf. Our list left out many programming songs all the Rolling Stone's songs, Alabama's Old Flame, etc.

APPENDIX: D

Graphics, Symbols and Pictures

ASSORTED PICTURES AND SYMBOLS ASSOCIATED WITH THE ILLUMINATI AND OCCULT

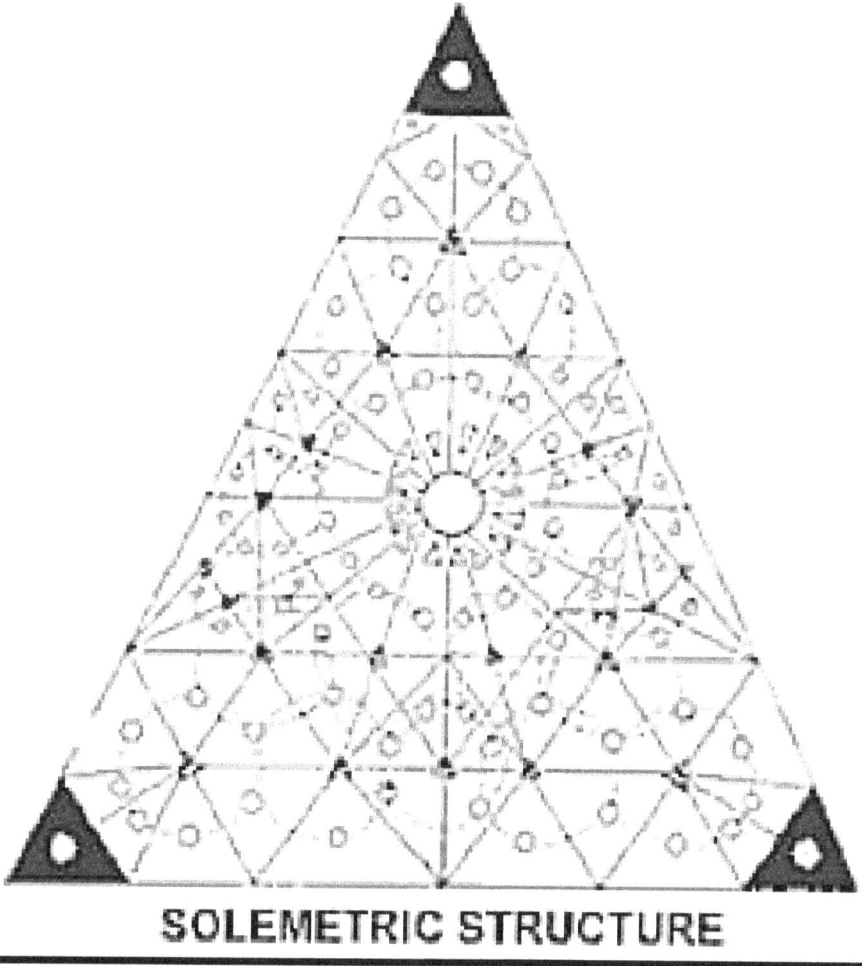

SOLEMETRIC STRUCTURE

A MODEL OF SOLEMETRIC STRUCTURING USED BY SOME PROGRAMMERS IN MONARCH MIND CONTROL

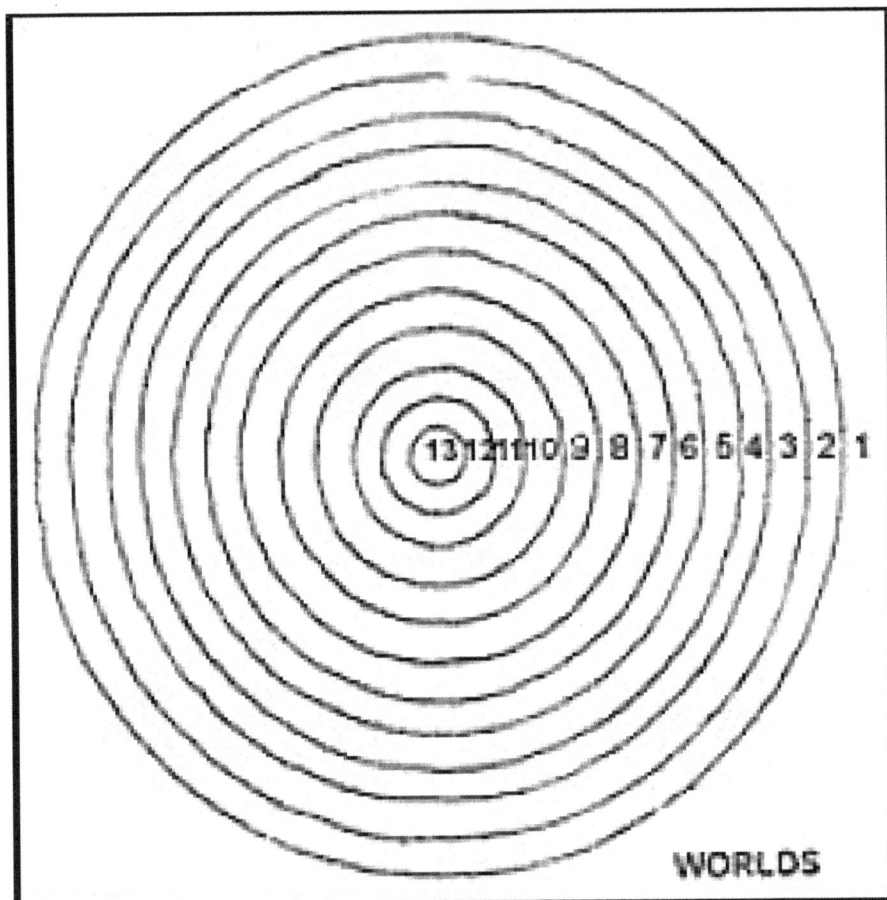

WORLDS

A MODEL OF WORLD STRUCTURING USED BY SOME PROGRAMMERS IN MONARCH MIND CONTROL

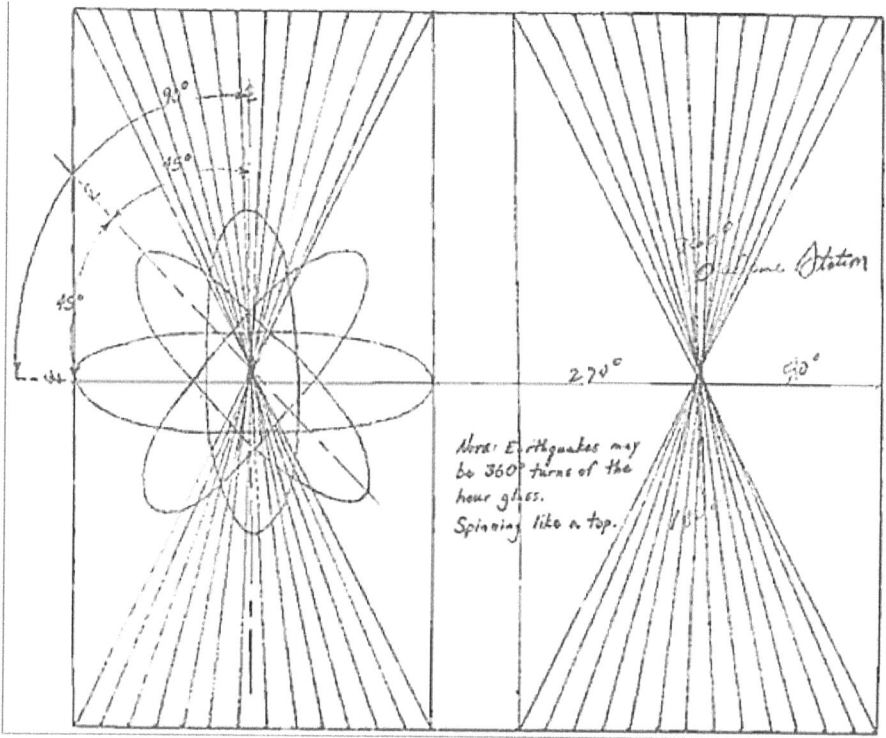

A Model of Hourglass Structuring Used by Some Programmers In Monarch Mind Control

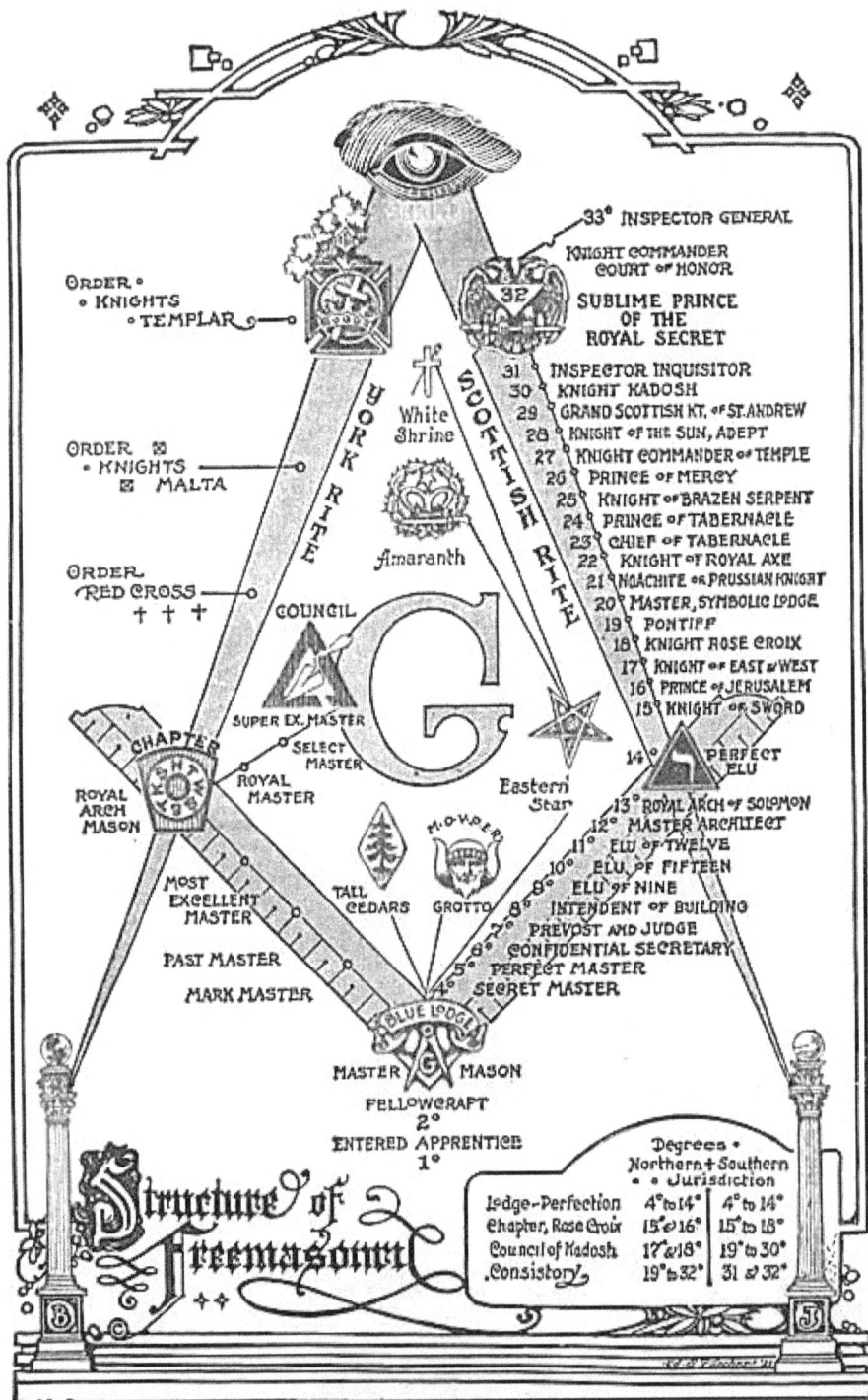

33° INSPECTOR GENERAL

KNIGHT COMMANDER
COURT OF HONOR

ORDER
KNIGHTS
TEMPLAR

32 SUBLIME PRINCE
OF THE
ROYAL SECRET

31 INSPECTOR INQUISITOR
30 KNIGHT KADOSH
29 GRAND SCOTTISH KT. OF ST. ANDREW
28 KNIGHT OF THE SUN, ADEPT
27 KNIGHT COMMANDER OF TEMPLE
26 PRINCE OF MERCY
25 KNIGHT OF BRAZEN SERPENT
24 PRINCE OF TABERNACLE
23 CHIEF OF TABERNACLE
22 KNIGHT OF ROYAL AXE
21 NOACHITE OR PRUSSIAN KNIGHT
20 MASTER, SYMBOLIC LODGE
19 PONTIFF
18 KNIGHT ROSE CROIX
17 KNIGHT OF EAST & WEST
16 PRINCE OF JERUSALEM
15 KNIGHT OF SWORD

White
Shrine

YORK RITE

SCOTTISH RITE

ORDER
KNIGHTS
MALTA

ORDER
RED CROSS
† † †

Amaranth

COUNCIL

SUPER EX. MASTER

SELECT
MASTER

CHAPTER

ROYAL
MASTER

ROYAL
ARCH
MASON

Eastern
Star

14° PERFECT
ELU

13° ROYAL ARCH OF SOLOMON
12° MASTER ARCHITECT
11° ELU OF TWELVE
10° ELU OF FIFTEEN
9° ELU OF NINE
8° INTENDENT OF BUILDING
7° PREVOST AND JUDGE
6° CONFIDENTIAL SECRETARY
5° PERFECT MASTER
4° SECRET MASTER

M.O.V.P.E.R.

TALL
CEDARS

GROTTO

MOST
EXCELLENT
MASTER

PAST MASTER

MARK MASTER

BLUE LODGE

MASTER MASON

FELLOWCRAFT
2°

ENTERED APPRENTICE
1°

Structure of Freemasonry

Degrees Northern + Southern Jurisdiction		
Lodge-Perfection	4° to 14°	4° to 14°
Chapter, Rose Croix	15° & 16°	15° to 18°
Council of Kadosh	17° & 18°	19° to 30°
Consistory	19° to 32°	31 & 32°

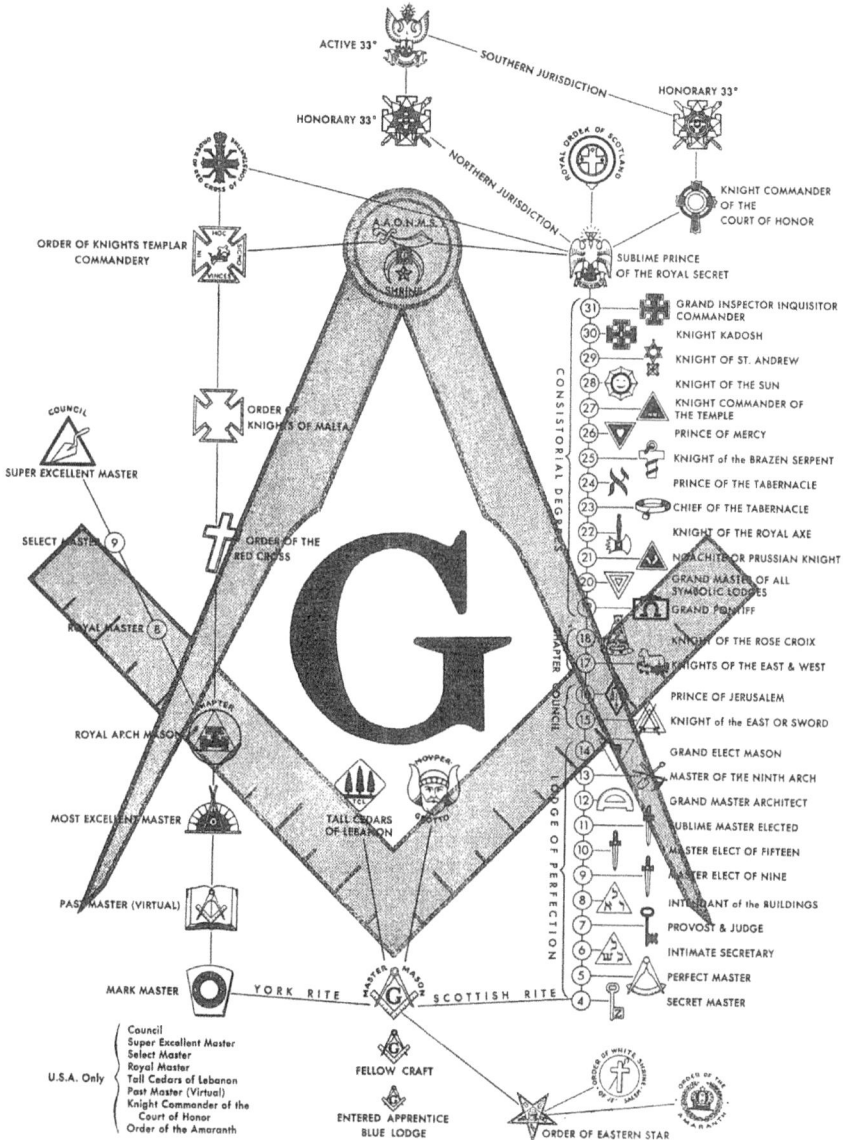

ACTIVE 33°

SOUTHERN JURISDICTION

HONORARY 33°

HONORARY 33°

NORTHERN JURISDICTION

ROYAL ORDER OF SCOTLAND

KNIGHT COMMANDER
OF THE
COURT OF HONOR

ORDER OF KNIGHTS TEMPLAR
COMMANDERY

A.A.O.N.M.S.

SHRINE

SUBLIME PRINCE
OF THE ROYAL SECRET

GRAND INSPECTOR INQUISITOR
COMMANDER
31

KNIGHT KADOSH
30

KNIGHT OF ST. ANDREW
29

KNIGHT OF THE SUN
28

KNIGHT COMMANDER OF
THE TEMPLE
27

PRINCE OF MERCY
26

KNIGHT of the BRAZEN SERPENT
25

PRINCE OF THE TABERNACLE
24

CHIEF OF THE TABERNACLE
23

KNIGHT OF THE ROYAL AXE
22

NOACHITE OR PRUSSIAN KNIGHT
21

GRAND MASTER OF ALL
SYMBOLIC LODGES
20

GRAND PONTIFF
19

KNIGHT OF THE ROSE CROIX
18

KNIGHTS OF THE EAST & WEST
17

PRINCE OF JERUSALEM
16

KNIGHT of the EAST OR SWORD
15

GRAND ELECT MASON
14

MASTER OF THE NINTH ARCH
13

GRAND MASTER ARCHITECT
12

SUBLIME MASTER ELECTED
11

MASTER ELECT OF FIFTEEN
10

MASTER ELECT OF NINE
9

INTENDANT of the BUILDINGS
8

PROVOST & JUDGE
7

INTIMATE SECRETARY
6

PERFECT MASTER
5

SECRET MASTER
4

CONSISTORIAL DEGREES

CHAPTER

COUNCIL

LODGE OF PERFECTION

ORDER OF
KNIGHTS OF MALTA

COUNCIL

SUPER EXCELLENT MASTER

SELECT MASTER 9

ORDER OF THE
RED CROSS

ROYAL MASTER 8

ROYAL ARCH MASON

CHAPTER

MOST EXCELLENT MASTER

TALL CEDARS
OF LEBANON

PAST MASTER (VIRTUAL)

MARK MASTER

YORK RITE

MASTER MASON

SCOTTISH RITE

Council
Super Excellent Master
Select Master
Royal Master
U.S.A. Only   Tall Cedars of Lebanon
Past Master (Virtual)
Knight Commander of the
Court of Honor
Order of the Amaranth

FELLOW CRAFT

ENTERED APPRENTICE
BLUE LODGE

ORDER OF WHITE SHRINE OF JERUSALEM

ORDER OF THE AMARANTH

ORDER OF EASTERN STAR

The Structure of Freemasonry

American Freemasonry resembles two sets of stairs that begin and end together, as this chart of Masonic structure shows. A Mason's first step is to become an Entered Apprentice. He climbs to the third step where most Masons stay. If he wants to go on in Masonic hierarchy, he enters either the Scottish or York rites. Many authorities say the Scottish Rite was begun by Scots emigrés in France; the York Rite is named after York, England where, by legend, the first Masonic body was organized.

In the Scottish Rite a Mason climbs 30 steps, or degrees. The name he takes on at each degree is written on each step in chart. Where there are two names the top is used by northern Masons, the italicized one by southern Masons. Some figures a Mason meets in Rite ceremonies stand on the steps (from bottom): King Solomon, King Cyrus, acolyte, George Washington, Sultan. Each figure teaches a moral. To earn degree candidate learns the moral and participates in ceremony dramatizing it. A 32° is the

highest degree a Mason can earn. The 33° is awarded by the Supreme Council, ruling body of the Rite.

A Mason in York Rite advances 10 degrees, known by name and not by degree number. On chart are figures he meets at each degree or the degree symbol. Figures are: temple workman, Past Master (Virtual), Israel tribesman, High Priest of Jews, King Hiram of Tyre, Knight of Malta, Knight Templar, equal in prestige to 33° in Scottish Rite.

Under the arch are organizations allied to Freemasonry. Master Masons are eligible for Grotto and Tall Cedars of Lebanon. Girls with a Mason in the family can join Job's Daughters or Rainbow Girls; women, the Eastern Star; boys, DeMolay. Only 32° Masons or Knights Templar can join the Shrine. Shriner's wife can be a Daughter of the Nile.

Most important of many Masonic symbols are the open Bible with square and compass on it (left); Solomon's temple (below Bible); and the G with the all-seeing eye inside (upper right). In the U.S. the G stands for God.

SCOTTISH RITE

AAONMS

28° K Knight
27° Comma Knight Com
26° Prince of Mercy
25° Knight of the Brazen Serpent
24° Prince of the Tabernacle
23° Chief of the Tabernacle
22° Prince of Libanus Knight of the Royal Axe
21° Patriarch Noachite Noachite or Prussian Knight
20° Master Ad Vitam Master of the Symbolic Lodge
19° Grand Pontiff Pontiff
18° Knight of the Rose Croix of H.R.D.M. Knight Rose Croix
17° Knight of the East and West
16° Prince of Jerusalem
15° Knight of the East or Sword Knight of the East
14° Grand Elect Mason Perfect Elu
13° Master of the Ninth Arch Royal Arch of Solomon
12° Grand Master Architect Master Architect
11° Sublime Master Elected Elu of the Twelve
10° Elect of Fifteen Elu of the Fifteen
9° Master Elect of Nine Elu of the Nine
8° Intendant of the Building
7° Provost and Judge
6° Intimate Secretary
5° Perfect Master
4° Secret Master

Tall Cedars of Lebanon

Order of the Eastern Star

ALLIED

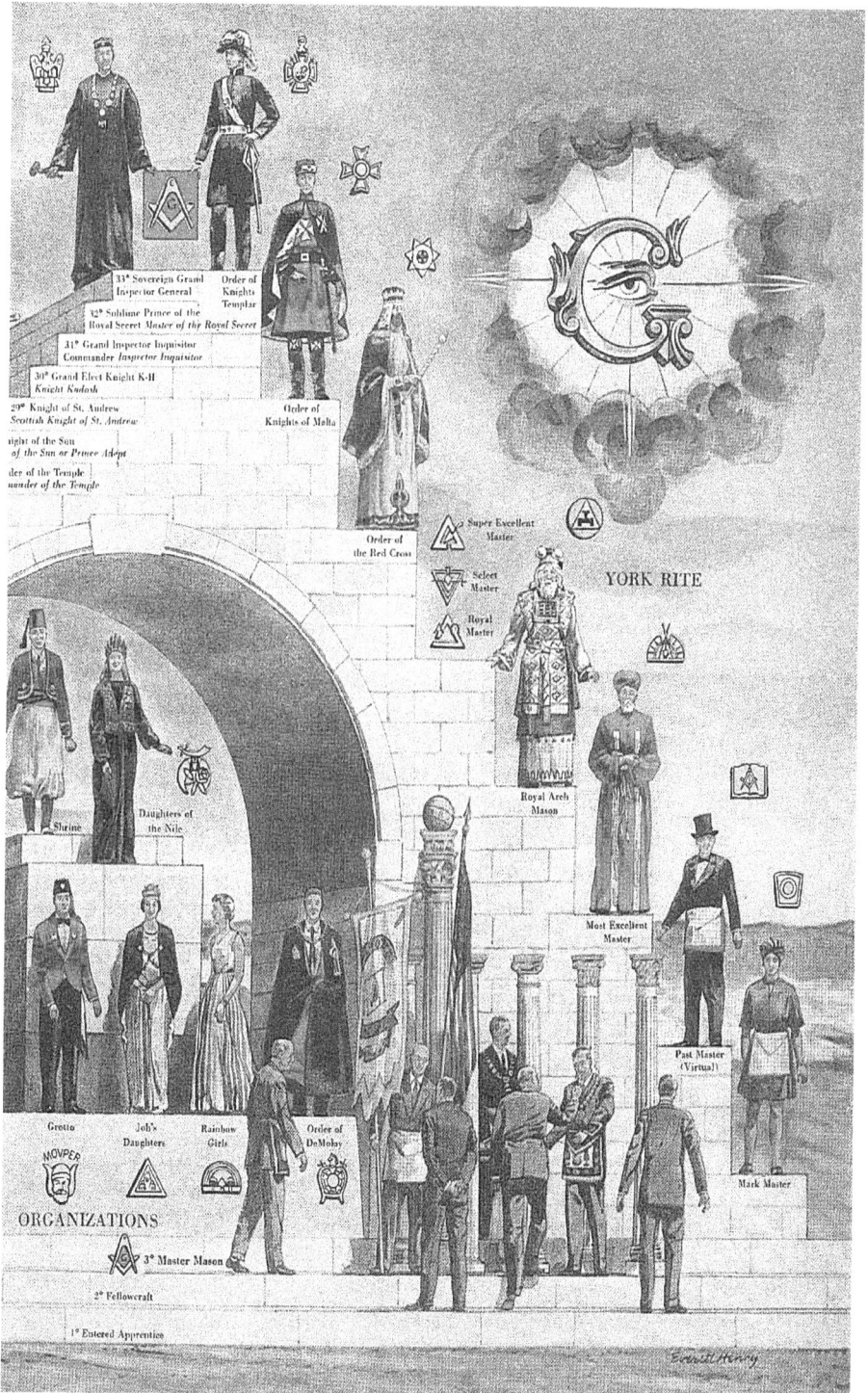

CIPHER OF THE
S∴ P∴ R∴ C∴

a b c d e f g h ij k l m n

o p q r s t uv x y z &

CIPHER OF THE KNIGHT ROSE CROIX OF HEREDOM
(of Kilwining).

0	1	2	3	4	5	6	7	8	9	10		10	11	12	13	14	15	16	17
a	b	c	d	e	f	g	h	i	j	ba	(or)	k	kb	kc	kd	ke	kf	kg	kh

18	19	20	30	40	50	60	70	80	90	100	200	300	400	500
ki	kj	ck	dk	ek	fk	gk	hk	ik	jk	l	cl	dl	el	fl

600	700	800	900	1000
gl	hl	il	jl	m

CIPHER OF THE KNIGHTS KADOSH.
(Also White and Black Eagle and Grand Elected Knight Templar.)

70	2	3	12	15	20	30	33	38	9	10	40
a	b	c	d	e	f	g	h	i	k	l	m

60	80	81	82	83	84	85	86	90	91	94	95
n	o	p	q	r	s	t	u	v	x	y	z

AN EXAMPLE OF ESTORIC LANGUAGES AND CODES USED BY THE ILLUMINATI AND OTHER OCCULT GROUPS

PASS GRIP OF A MASTER MASON.

THE GRIP OF AN ENTERED APPRENTICE.

REAL GRIP OF A FELLOW CRAFT.

REAL GRIP OF A MASTER MASON.

PASS GRIP OF A FELLOW CRAFT.

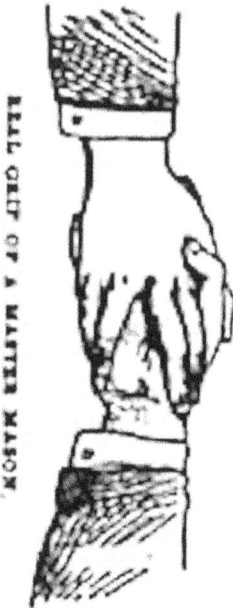

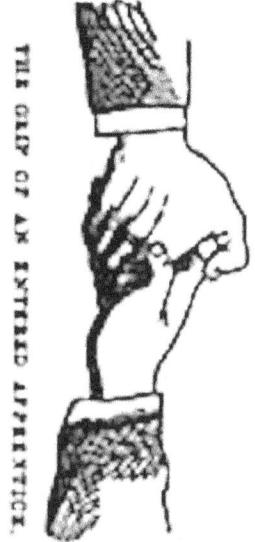

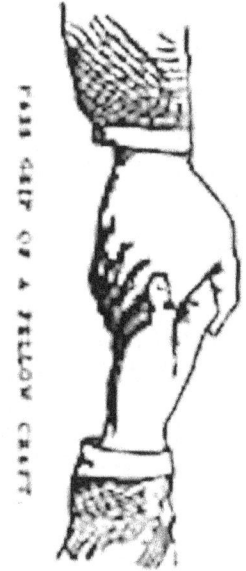

SECRET HANDSHAKES OF THE MASONS

EMBLEMATIC STRUCTURE OF FREEMASONRY

RED CROSS CONSTANTINE

ACTIVE 33°

ROYAL ORDER SCOTLAND

COUNCIL S.J. 19° TO 30°

SUBLIME PRINCE OF THE ROYAL SECRET

S.J. CONSISTORY 31—32

Y O R K   R I T E

S C O T T I S H   R I T E

HONORARY 33°

ORDER OF KNIGHTS TEMPLAR COMMANDERY

A.A.O.N.M.S. SHRINE

KNIGHT COMMANDER OF THE COURT OF HONOR

ORDER OF KNIGHTS OF MALTA

ORDER OF THE RED CROSS

SUPER EXCELLENT MASTER COUNCIL

SELECT MASTER

ROYAL MASTER

MARK MASTER

MOST EXCELLENT MASTER

PAST MASTER (VIRTUAL)

ROYAL ARCH MASON CHAPTER

32	S.J. CONSISTORY 31—32
31	GRAND INSPECTOR INQUISITOR COMMANDER
30	KNIGHT OF KADOSH
29	KNIGHT OF ST. ANDREW
28	KNIGHT OF THE SUN
27	KNIGHT COMMANDER OF THE TEMPLE
26	PRINCE OF MERCY
25	KNIGHT OF THE BRAZEN SERPENT
24	PRINCE OF THE TABERNACLE
23	CHIEF OF THE TABERNACLE
22	KNIGHT OF THE ROYAL AXE
21	NOACHITE OR PRUSSIAN KNIGHT
20	MASTER AD VITAM
19	GRAND PONTIFF
18	KNIGHT OF THE ROSE CROIX
17	KNIGHTS OF THE EAST & WEST
16	PRINCE OF JERUSALEM
15	KNIGHT OF THE EAST OR SWORD
14	GRAND ELECT MASON
13	MASTER OF THE NINTH ARCH
12	GRAND MASTER ARCHITECT
11	SUBLIME MASTER ELECTED
10	MASTER ELECT OF FIFTEEN
9	MASTER ELECT OF NINE
8	INTENDANT OF THE BUILDING
7	PROVOST & JUDGE
6	INTIMATE SECRETARY
5	PERFECT MASTER
4	SECRET MASTER

CONSISTORY OF PRINCES OF THE ROYAL SECRET

19° TO 32° CHVALRG

COUNCIL CHAPTER

15° TO 18° HISTORIC RELIGIOUS

17° TO 19°

LODGE OF PERFECTION

4° TO 14° INELIGIBLE DEGREES

CONFERRED BY COMMANDERY

CONFERRED BY COUNCIL

CONFERRED BY CHAPTER

4°–14° S.J.

CHAPTER S.A. 15° TO 18°

BLUE G LODGE
MASTER MASON

EASTERN STAR

FELLOW G CRAFT

ENTERED G APPRENTICE

{ 581 }

MASONIC EMBLEMS

New World Order Organizational Chart

Illuminati Royal Bloodlines

Rothschild
Astor • Bundy
Collins • DuPont • Freeman
Kennedy • Li • Onassi • Rockefeller • Disney
Russell • Van Duyn • Merovingian • Reynolds

Foundation nations of the New World Order

America   **England**   **Israel**   **Australia**   **China**

Financial Groups	Research Institutions	Secret Societies
IMF	Institute For Policy Studies	P2/Opus Dei
World Bank	Stanford Research Institute	Rosicrucions
Central Banks	Brookings Institute	Freemasonry
Federal Reserve	Tavistock Institute	Skull & Bones
Bank of-	Committee of 300	Bohemian Club
International Settlement	Aspen Institute	The Knights of Malta
	Jason Society	

Political	Intelligence	Religious	Educational
Council on Foreign Relations	MI-5	World Parliment of Religions	UNESCO
Trilateral Commission	CIA	National Council of Churches	Lucis Trust
Governmental Leaders	NSA/FBI	World Council of Churches	World Union
U.S. Supreme Court &	KGB	Christian Fundimentalists	World Goodwill
Electorial College	Interpol	Temple of Understanding	Esalen Institute
NATO • EU • EEC	MOSSAD	Universalist Churches	Planetary Congress
United Nations	Drug Cartels	New Age Cults	Media Establishment
Bilderbergers	Homeland Security	Vatican/Jesuits	World Federalist Assc.
Club of Rome	Military Intelligence	Satanists	World Constitution Assc.

Corporations, Multinationals and Banks Supporting the New World Order Agenda

Bechtel • Carlyle Group • TRW • Raytheon • Rand • WalMart • Texas Utilities
Atlantic Richfield-Arco • Exxon-Esso-Mobil • Texaco • Shell Oil • Tenneco • Corning
Dow Jones • MBNA Citigroup • Chase Manhattan • Bank America • Bankers Trust
Glaxo SmithKline • Archer Daniels Midland • Chemical Banking • Schering Plough
Goldman Sachs • American Express • AT&T • Philipp Morris • Boeing • Amtrak
Northwest Airlines • American Airlines Ford Motors • Chrysler • General Motors
Deere • Nabisco • Coca Cola PepsiCo • Anheuser Busch • McDonalds • Burger King
Altria (Philip Morris/Kraft) • Blackstone Group Chevron-Texaco (Caltex) • BP-Amoco
GE • Enron • Daimler/Chrysler • Unisys • ITT • Xerox • Intel • IBM • Motorola
Dell • Levi Strauss • Motorola • Johnson & Johnson • Bristol Myers • Squibb
Eli Lily • Pfizer • Kissinger Assoc. • Amway • Monsanto/Solutia • Dow Chemical
News Corp Limited Inc • Time Warner/AOL • Disney • CBS • NBC • ABC • PBS AP
CNN • Reuters • Washington Times • Children's TV Workshop • U.S. News & W.R.
New York Times • Time, Inc. • Newsweek • Washington Post • Wall Street Journal

George W. Bush Jr.

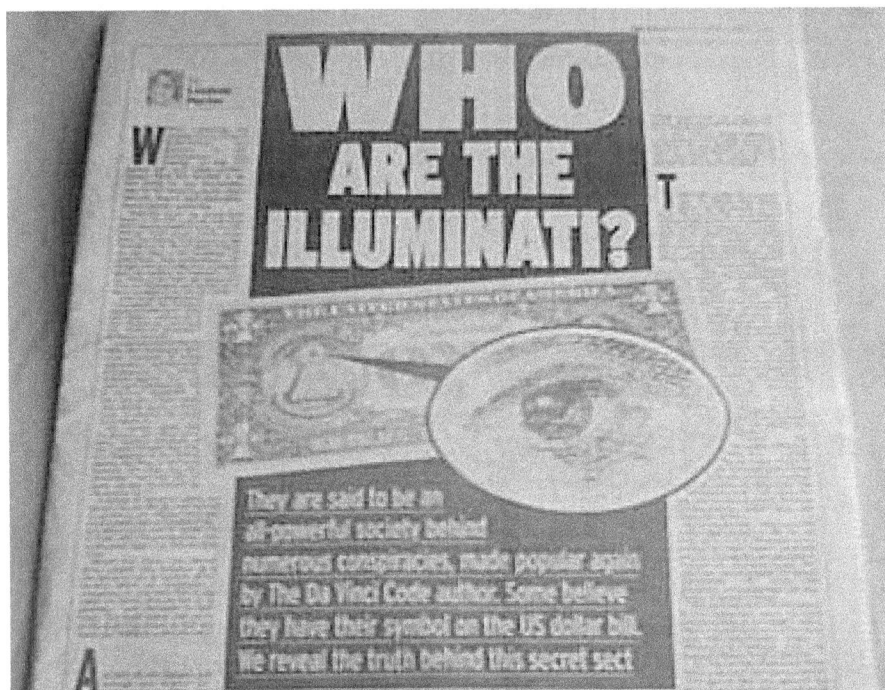

ARE YOU

AWAKE YET?!

{ 587 }

www.ingramcontent.com/pod-product-compliance
Lightning Source LLC
Chambersburg PA
CBHW030632270326
41929CB00007B/44